STANDARD

ENGLISH POEMS

Spenser to Tennyson

SELECTED AND EDITED

BY

HENRY S. PANCOAST

NEW YORK

HENRY HOLT AND COMPANY

1906

Miss Marjorie Wait

g

10-10-49 hm
11-1-49 vc

TO THE

Rev. John Kemper Murphy, D.D.,

WHO TAUGHT ME LONG AGO TO DELIGHT IN THE MASTER POET OF
ENGLAND, AND WHO HAS SINCE HELPED ME IN MORE WAYS THAN
MAY BE HERE SET DOWN,

THIS BOOK OF ENGLISH POETRY

IS

REVERENTLY AND AFFECTIONATELY DEDICATED.

PREFACE.

NOT only is poetry one of the noblest and most uplifting of the arts; it is peculiarly fitted, from one aspect at least, to be the art most universally enjoyed. Few can hope to own—even to see—the greatest pictures or statues; their beauty must of necessity be monopolized by a country, or a class, while the elaborate requirements of performance keep much of the greatest music from the multitude; but the beauty of the greatest poems is spread for men's delight almost as liberally as the wonders of dawn and sunset; it is almost as free as sunlight or the stars.

Yet it is not unlikely that many of us are deceived by the very ease with which the greatest poetry can be obtained; it is not unlikely that many of us who would cross the Atlantic to see the master-works of Raphael, and approach them in reverence and awe, would leave the master-works of Milton neglected on our shelves or glance over them with an easy self-assurance. It is easy to confuse the physical ownership of a book with the actual or spiritual possession of it; it is easy to forget that, obtainable as poetry may seem to be, it is often made inaccessible to us by our own limitations, and that in our reading of it "we receive but what we give." The truth is that an appreciation of poetry at once fine and liberal, capable of delighting in widely different kinds of excellence, and combining a delicate susceptibility to beauty with a vigorous intellectual grasp;—the truth is that such a high appreciation is rarely attained even among what are called the educated classes. The first step is to recognize the difficulty of gaining this power. We shall then cease to regard great poetry as a means of casual amusement, and learn to approach it reverently, as one of the loftiest of the arts; we shall come to realize the presumption and absurdity of facile and ignorant judgments, knowing that good taste in poetry is not merely a matter of nature but of nurture. I know of nothing, at least among the arts, that is fairly comparable to poetry as a means to general culture, but I am convinced that, available as it seems, this means is far too little used. In a vast number of cases poetry fails to exert its full influence, because so many never perceive that it is a serious and even exacting subject of study. There is a prevalent impression that if we do not "like poetry," nothing can be done; and that, on the other hand, if we do "like" it, nothing further is required. Others again have a vague feeling that the pure enjoyment of a poem is marred by an endeavor to analyze and understand it; that, because it is possible to enjoy some poems without knowing what they mean, enjoyment and understanding are in some way antagonistic. These fal-

lacies or half-truths all tend to retard the true
appreciation of poetry, and keep it out of the place
it ought to hold. The power to take the greatest
poems into our lives is almost invariably dependent
upon a strenuous effort of mind and will, as well as upon
the sympathetic response of our spirits. Poetry may
speak from the heart and to the heart; it may be the
apparently spontaneous expression of irrepressible feeling; but we must remember that it is also a difficult
and highly technical art; that it is often the pro-
foundest thought touched by emotion; and that it
frequently demands for its interpretation both a substantial basis of learning and an unusual penetration
of mind. In a word, it is by the systematic and
strenuous study of poetry, by sedulously training ourselves to view it in all its historic and human relations, by broadening and deepening our appreciation
until we learn to delight in all its rich variety, its
wit, satire, cleverness, and depth of thought, as well
as in its beauty, color, or haunting musical cadences,
—it is only by this that we can hope to win from it
those great benefits that it is so peculiarly fitted to
bestow.

I have tried to make a collection of English verse,
which should serve as an introduction to such a
serious and systematic study of one of the richest and
noblest poetic literatures the world has produced. I
have hoped to make a book which should promote
the genuine love and appreciation of English poetry
by promoting a fuller understanding of it; a book
which should furnish a convenient avenue of approach

to poetry of many different styles and of many times. In this attempt I have kept before me a few simple and, as it seems to me, obvious principles.

With a few exceptions, I have given only complete poems; believing that the practice of misrepresenting an author by extracts or fragments of poems is unjust both to the poet and his reader; a bar to the fullest enjoyment, and a discouragement to any rational method of study. In the few cases in which I have departed from this rule, I have broken it in the letter rather than in the spirit. For instance, although selections are given from the *Faerie Queene*, *The Seasons*, *The Task*, and *Childe Harold*, each of these poems has a looseness of structure which permits it to be fairly represented in this manner, if the selections are reasonably full and are carefully chosen and arranged. Three of these poems consist of a series of descriptive and meditative passages, each of which is practically complete in itself. In the *Faerie Queene*, the only one of these poems in which there is any approach to a continous narrative, I have connected the selections by a brief prose argument and arranged them so as to preserve the continuity of the story; I have also given in the notes the general scheme and purpose of the poem. At best the *Faerie Queene* is itself a gigantic fragment, marvellous in parts, but lacking in symmetrical proportion as a whole; this seems to justify the belief that Spenser can be more adequately represented by selections from his masterpiece than by some of his minor poems. On the other hand, poems of closer narrative structure which were too long to be given complete, such as *Paradise Lost* or *Marmion*, had to be reluctantly omitted.

Our literature is so rich in poetry that the chief perplexity which confronts the compiler of an English anthology is not what to put in, but what to leave out. In the present instance my task has been greatly simplified by the distinct object I had in view. That object was to provide a general introduction to the study of English poetry, and I felt that this end could be gained only by complying as far as possible with two distinct and sometimes conflicting requirements—that of individual excellence and of historic importance. The poems selected must have an intrinsic interest or beauty, and they must have also an independent value as illustrations of the history of English poetry, or as examples of the various poetic forms. As my primary object was not simply to bring together the poems that I personally admired, I have invariably preferred to follow the settled judgment of time rather than my individual preference. As a rule, however, my personal liking has been in accord with this general judgment, and I have been persuaded that the opinion which has been held by successive generations of critics and readers is, in a large majority of cases, the right one. Certain poems (such as "Go, Lovely Rose" or "Shall I wasting in despair") have come to be generally accepted as representative, and the probabilities are that in such cases we may look in vain through the works of their authors for anything that will represent them better. But even if this were not the case, the taste of an individual ought not to take precedence of the general verdict in a selection of this character; such poems should still be included, because by common consent they are poems with which every fairly cultivated person is expected to be familiar. So far, therefore, from hesitating to include a poem because it was famous and popular, its assured place in the literature has been a powerful argument for its admission. I could not, of course, give all the poems which a person of average cultivation should know, but I have at least tried to give nothing but those poems which are, or ought to be, indispensable.

The first requirement—that each poem should have an independent, intrinsic value—had to be reconciled with the second—that the poems should have a value as a whole by virtue of their historic continuity or their representative character. In some cases choice became a compromise between the conflicting claims of these two requirements, and a work of superior intrinsic merit had to be excluded, because it threw the book out of proportion, or because it had to make way for some work inferior in purely poetic value, but indispensable from the historic point of view. On the same principle the best example of an inferior class of verse might present claims for admission that could not be safely ignored.

My endeavor has been to make the book useful to the student of poetry not only by a chronological arrangement, but also by an intelligent division and grouping of the poems. The strongly marked historic periods are indicated by the main divisions of the book: within these divisions the selections have been grouped under the various authors of the period or under an especial poetic form, as the case seemed to require. So far as this arrangement allowed, the selections are given in their chronological order as nearly as it could be ascertained. The historical side has also been emphasized by giving with the text of each poem the name and dates of its author, and the date, or approximate date, of its composition or first publication, with the name, in the latter case, of the book in which it first appeared. This has been supplemented by briefly indicating in the notes the general relation which the poem and its auther hold to literary history. Formal biography has been kept within the briefest limits or dispensed with altogether, as the outward events of an author's life can be readily found elsewhere, and as there was no space for anything beyond the driest summary. In a few cases, where I had treated the matter in my *Introduction to English Literature*, I have referred to what I had already said rather than repeat it in an abbreviated form.

In the annotations I have tried to give such help as an average reader would be likely to require. The ideal note-maker—if there be any such—avoids no difficulty on the one hand, and intrudes nothing irrelevant or superfluous on the other, but I am fully sensible that to do this is to steer an almost impossible course. Frankly, while I regard notes as a necessity in a book of this character, I regret the conditions that make them indispensable. When chapels are churches, and poor men's cottages princes' palaces, every school and every household will be furnished with an adequate library ; every teacher of English will train his pupils in the scholarly use of books ; and every pupil will have enough leisure and enough love of learning to be his own commentator. Until then, I fear that readers must be told many things which they could with great pleasure and profit find out for themselves.

I have endeavored to give an accurate and reliable text in conformity with that of the best editions. In a very few instances I have ventured to depart from the punctuation of a standard edition, or to adopt the reading of one that seemed to me better in that particular instance, although less authoritative on the whole. The spelling of the old ballads has been left untouched, but in some of the comparatively modern poems where the differences were trifling, the spelling and capitalization have been made to conform more nearly to the present usage.

My obligations to others are so great and various that specific acknowledgment has not always been practicable or possible. The material for the notes has been drawn from many sources, and I have freely availed myself of the mass of comment that has grown up about our great classics. In many cases, where the notes dealt with matters so familiar that they may be considered common property, it seemed unnecessary to refer to the long line of editors who had furnished the same obvious information, but wherever I could trace my indebtedness to any particular source, especially if it were a matter of opinion or interpretation, it has been duly noted.

Beyond this, I am glad to take this opportunity of acknowledging the help I have received from many quarters in the difficult duty of selection. The number of those who have shown a kindly and practical interest in the work is so great that I must content myself with this general expression of appreciation.

For obvious reasons I have thought it desirable to exclude poems by living authors. I have done this, in spite of many temptations, except in a single instance. I trust that this one lapse will need no justification, and that the impulse which led me to conclude this collection of the glories of English poetry with Kipling's *Recessional* will be understood and pardoned.

GERMANTOWN, July 5, 1899.

CONTENTS

Preface .... i–xi

BALLADS.

Chevy Chase.. 1
Sir Patrick Spens..................... 11
Waly, Waly, love be bonny........ 13
The Twa Sisters o' Binnorie 14
Bonnie George Campbell................... 18
Helen of Kirconnel.................................. 19

SPENSER TO DRYDEN.

SPENSER.

The Faerie Queene (Selections) 21
The Courtier (from *Mother Hubberd's Tale*)............ 53
Sonnet XL (from *Amoretti*)........................... 54

ELIZABETHAN SONGS AND LYRICS.

LYLY.

Apelles' Song....................................... 56

GREENE.

Content... 56

MARLOWE.

The Passionate Shepherd to his Love.................... 57

DEKKER.

O Sweet Content...................................... 58

T. HEYWOOD.

PAGE

Good Morrow.................................... 59

CAMPION.

To Lesbia...................................... 59
The Armour of Innocence....................... 60
Fortunati Nimium.............................. 61

J. FLETCHER.

Song of the Priest of Pan...................... 63
Song to Pan................................... 64

BEAUMONT.

On the Life of Man............................ 65
On the Tombs in Westminster Abbey............. 65

WOTTON.

The Character of a Happy Life.................. 66

RALEIGH (?).

The Nymph's Reply to the Passionate Shepherd......... 67

JONSON.

To the Memory of Shakspeare................... 68
Simplex Munditiis............................. 70
The Triumph of Charis......................... 71
Song, To Cynthia............................. 72

SHAKESPEARE.

Silvia.. 73
Under the Greenwood Tree..................... 73
O mistress mine, where are you roaming?........ 74
Take, oh take, those lips away.. 74
Hark, Hark the Lark 75
Dirge 75
A Sea Dirge 76
Ariel's Song.................................. 76

ELIZABETHAN SONNETS.

SIDNEY.

Sonnet XXXI.................................. 77
Sonnet XXXIX, On Sleep....................... 77

DANIEL.

                                                    PAGE
Sonnet LI, To Delia............................... 78

DRAYTON.

Sonnet LXI.. 79

DRUMMOND.

On Sleep.. 79

SHAKESPEARE.

Sonnet XXIX (" When, in disgrace," etc.)............ 80
Sonnet XXX (" When to the sessions," etc.). 80
Sonnet XXXIII (" Full many a glorious morning," etc.). 81
Sonnet LX (" Like as the waves," etc.)................ 81
Sonnet LXXIII (' That time of year," etc.). 82
Sonnet CXVI (" Let me not to the marriage," etc.)...... 82

DONNE.

Sonnet X, On Death................................ 83

DRAYTON.

Agincourt... 83

SEVENTEENTH-CENTURY SONGS.

DONNE.

An Elegy upon the Death of the Lady Markham........ 88
A Valediction Forbidding Mourning.................. 90
Song 91
A Hymn to God the Father.......................... 93

HERBERT.

Vertue... 93
The Pulley.. 94
The Elixir.. 95
The Collar.. 96

VAUGHAN.

The Retreate...................................... 97
Departed Friends.................................. 98

WITHER.

The Author's Resolution in a Sonnet................ 99

COWLEY.

PAGE

A Vote.. 101
The Grasshopper....................................... 102

SHIRLEY.

A Dirge.. 103

CAREW.

Disdain Returned...................................... 104

SUCKLING.

Orsames' Song... 104

LOVELACE.

To Lucasta on Going to the Wars....................... 105
To Althea from Prison................................. 106

HERRICK.

Argument to Hesperides................................ 107
Corinna's Going A-Maying.............................. 107
To Primroses Filled with Morning Dew.................. 110
To the Virgins, to make much of Time.................. 111
To Daffodils.. 111
The Hag... 112

WALLER.

On a Girdle... 113
Song 113
On the Foregoing Divine Poems......................... 114

MILTON.

L'Allegro... 115
Il Penseroso.. 119
Song. Sweet Echo (from *Comus*)....................... 124
Song, Sabrina Fair (from *Comus*).................... 125
Lycidas... 126
Sonnet, On his having arrived at the age of twenty-three. 131
Sonnet, On the Late Massacre in Piedmont.............. 132
Sonnet, On His Blindness.............................. 132
Sonnet, To Cyriack Skinner............................ 133

MARVELL.

The Garden.. 134

DRYDEN TO THOMSON.

DRYDEN.

PAGE

Mac-Flecknoe.................................... 137
Achitophel (from *Absalom and Achitophel*)............... 143
A Song for St. Cecilia's Day............................ 145
Alexander's Feast ; or, The Power of Music............ 147
Under Mr. Milton's Picture............................ 190

PRIOR.

To a Child of Quality Five Years Old.................. 154
A Better Answer....................................... 155

ADDISON.

The Spacious Firmament................................ 156

GAY.

Fable XVIII, The Painter who Pleased Nobody and
    Everybody... 157
On a Lap-dog.. 159

POPE.

The Rape of the Lock.................................. 160
Elegy to the Memory of an Unfortunate Lady.......... 184
Universal Prayer...................................... 187
Epistle to Dr. Arbuthnot (Selection).................. 188

THOMSON TO TENNYSON.

THOMSON.

Spring (from *The Seasons*) 195
Summer (from *The Seasons*)........................... 198
Autumn (from *The Seasons*)........................... 200
Winter (from *The Seasons*)........................... 202
Rule Britannia.. 206

COLLINS.

Ode to Evening.. 207
The Passions.. 209
Ode written in the beginning of the year 1746......... 213
Dirge in Cymbeline.................................... 213

GRAY.

PAGE

Ode on a Distant Prospect of Eton College............ 214
Elegy written in a Country Churchyard............... 217
The Bard................................... 222

GOLDSMITH.

The Deserted Village.............................. 227

CHATTERTON.

The Minstrel's Roundelay........................ 240
The Ballade of Charitie.......................... 242

COWPER.

The Task (Selections)............................ 245
On the Receipt of my Mother's Picture out of Norfolk... 257
On the Loss of the Royal George.................. 261
The Castaway................................ 262

BLAKE.

To the Muses................................ 264
To the Evening Star........................... 265
Introduction (from *Songs of Innocence*)............. 265
The Lamb................................... 266
Night..................................... 267
To the Divine Image.......................... 268
On Another's Sorrow.......................... 269
The Tiger.................................. 270
Ah ! Sunflower.............................. 271

BURNS.

The Cotter's Saturday Night...................... 272
To a Mouse................................ 279
To a Mountain Daisy......................... 280
Tam O'Shanter............................. 282
Bruce's Address to his Army at Bannockburn......... 289
The Banks of Doon.......................... 290
A Red, Red Rose........................... 291
Is there for Honest Poverty.................... 291
O wert thou in the cauld blast.................. 293

WORDSWORTH

Lines composed a few miles above Tintern Abbey........ 293
Expostulation and Reply........................ 298
The Tables Turned............................ 299

PAGE

Three years she grew.. 300
She dwelt among the untrodden ways.................... 302
Michael : a pastoral poem................................. 302
My heart leaps up.. 317
The Solitary Reaper.. 317
Ode, Intimations of Immortality.......................... 318
I wandered lonely as a cloud 324
She was a phantom of delight.............................. 325
Ode to Duty.. 326

SONNETS.

Written in London, September, 1802...................... 328
London, 1802.. 328
When I have borne in memory.............................. 329
Composed upon Westminster Bridge, 1802. 329
Composed upon the Beach near Calais, 1802............ 330
"The world is too much with us"........................ 330

COLERIDGE.

The Rime of the Ancient Mariner.......................... 331
The Good Great Man.. 353
Youth and Age 354
Work without Hope... 355

SOUTHEY.

The Battle of Blenheim 356
My days among the dead are past......................... 358

JOSEPH BLANCO WHITE.

Sonnet To Night... 360

SCOTT.

Harold's Song to Rosabelle (from *Lay of the Last Min-
strel* 360
Ballad, Alice Brand (from *Lady of the Lake*)........... 362
Edmund's Song (from *Rokeby* 366
Song, A Weary Lot is Thine (from *Rokeby*).............. 368
Song, Allan-A-Dale (from *Rokeby*)...................... 369
Song, The Cavalier (from *Rokeby*)...................... 370
Hunting Song 372
Jock of Hazeldean 373
Madge Wildfire's Song..................................... 374
Border Ballad... 375
County Guy.. 376

CAMPBELL.

PAGE

Ye Mariners of England........................... 376
Hohenlinden...................................... 378
Battle of the Baltic.............................. 379
Song, Men of England............................ 381
Song, To the Evening Star....................... 382

MOORE.

As slow our ship................................. 383
The Harp that once through Tara's Halls............ 384

BYRON.

Stanzas for Music................................ 385
She walks in beauty.............................. 386
Sonnet On Chillon (Introduction to *The Prisoner of Chillon*) 387
Childe Harold's Pilgrimage (Selections)............ 388
Don Juan (Selections)............................ 403

SHELLEY.

Ode to the West Wind............................ 406
To a Skylark..................................... 409
The Cloud.. 413
Adonais.. 416
Time... 437
To ——... 437
To Night... 437
A Lament... 439
To ——... 439

KEATS.

The Eve of St. Agnes............................. 440
Ode to a Nightingale............................. 455
Ode on a Grecian Urn............................. 458
To Autumn.. 460
La Belle Dame Sans Merci. 461

SONNETS.

On First Looking into Chapman's Homer............. 463
Sonnet ("To one who has been long," etc.).......... 464
On the Grasshopper and Cricket................... 464
Last Sonnet...................................... 465

HUNT.

To the Grasshopper and the Cricket................ 465

LANDOR.

PAGE

Mild is the parting year, and sweet...................... 466
Ah, what avails the sceptered race...................... 466
Yes: I write verses..................................... 467
To Robert Browning 468
Introduction to the Last Fruit Off an Old Tree.......... 468

PROCTER.

A Petition to Time..................................... 468

H. COLERIDGE.

Song.. 469

LAMB.

To Hester.. 470

HOOD.

The Death Bed 471
The Bridge of Sighs.................................. 472

VICTORIAN VERSE.

MACAULAY.

Battle of Ivry... **477**

TENNYSON.

Locksley Hall... 481
Ulysses 493
The Epic.. 495
Morte d'Arthur....................................... 497
Sir Galahad.. 506
Break, Break, Break.................................. 509
Tears, Idle Tears (from *The Princess*)............... 509
Bugle Song (from *The Princess*)..................... 510
In Memoriam (Selection). 511
Maud (Selection)..................................... 512
Crossing the Bar..................................... 515

BROWNING.

My Last Duchess...................................... 516
Song (from *Pippa Passes*)........................... 518
Home Thoughts, from Abroad.......................... 518
The Guardian Angel.................................. 519

                                                          PAGE
Andrea Del Sarto.. 521
Prospice..... 529
Rabbi Ben Ezra... 530
Epilogue (from *Asolando*).............................. 538

E. B. BROWNING.

A Musical Instrument................................... 539

SONNETS.

Cheerfulness Taught by Reason.......................... 541
The Prospect... 541
Work... 542
Sonnet I (from *Sonnets from the Portuguese*).......... 542
Sonnet VI (from *Sonnets from the Portuguese*)......... 543
Sonnet XXXV (from *Sonnets from the Portuguese*)....... 543
Sonnet XLIII (from *Sonnets from the Portuguese*)...... 544

KINGSLEY.

Song (from *The Saints' Tragedy*)...................... 544
The Three Fishers...................................... 545
The Sands of Dee 546
Clear and Cool... 547

CLOUGH.

Qua cursum ventus 548
With whom is no variableness neither shadow of turning. 549
Say not, the struggle naught availeth................. 549
The Stream of Life..................................... 550

M. ARNOLD.

Stanzas from the Grande Chartreuse.................... 551
Geist's Grave... 558
Dover Beach... 560
Lines written in Kensington Gardens.................. 562
Self Dependence 563
Shakspeare.. 564

ROSSETTI.

The Blessed Damosel................................... 565
The Sea Limits.. 570

SONNETS.

Sybilla Palmifera..................................... 571
Sonnet XIX, Silent Noon............................... 571

PAGE

Sonnet LXIII, Inclusiveness.......................... 572
Sonnet XCVII, A Superscription...................... 573

W. MORRIS.

An Apology (from *The Earthly Paradise*)............. 573
The Day of Days...................................... 575
Drawing Near the Light............................... 576

KIPLING.

Recessional.. 576

Notes.. 579
Index of Titles...................................... 743

STANDARD ENGLISH POEMS

PART FIRST

BALLADS

(OF VARIOUS AND UNCERTAIN DATES)

CHEVY CHASE

(Sometimes called *The Hunting of the Cheviot*)

THE Persë owt off Northombarlonde,
  and a vowe to God mayd he
That he wold hunte in the mowntayns
  off Chyviat within days thre,
5 In the magger of doughtë Dogles,
  and all that ever with him be.

The fattiste hartes in all Cheviat
  he sayd he wold kyll, and carry them away:
'Be my feth,' sayd the dougheti Doglas agayn,
10 'I wyll let that hontyng yf that I may.'

Then the Persë owt off Banborowe cam,
  with him a myghtee meany,
With fifteen hondrith archares bold off blood and
    bone,
  the wear chosen owt of shyars thre.

15 This begane on a Monday at morn,
 in Cheviat the hillys so he;
The chylde may rue that ys unborn,
 it wos the more pittë.

The dryvars thorowe the woodës went,
20 for to reas the dear;
Bomen byckarte uppone the bent
 with ther browd aros cleare.

Then the wyld thorowe the woodës went,
 on every sydë shear;
25 Greahondës thorowe the grevis glent,
 for to kyll thear dear.

This begane in Chyviat the hyls abone,
 yerly on a Monnyn-day;
Be that it drewe to the oware off none,
30 a hondrith fat hartës ded ther lay.

The blewe a mort uppone the bent,
 the semblyde on sydis shear;
To the quyrry then the Persë went,
 to se the bryttlynge off the deare.

35 He sayd, 'It was the Duglas promys
 this day to met me hear;
But I wyste he wolde faylle, verament;'
 a great oth the Persë swear.

At laste a squyar off Northamberlonde
40 lokyde at his hand full ny;
He was war a the doughctie Doglas commynge,
 with him a myghttë meany.

Both with spear, bylle, and brande,
   yt was a myghtti sight to se;
45 Hardyar men, both off hart nor hande,
   wear not in Cristiantë.

The wear twenti hondrith spear-men good,
   withoute any feale;
The wear borne along be the watter a Twyde,
50   yth bowndës of Tividale.

'Leave of the brytlyng of the dear,' he sayd,
   'and to your boÿs loek ye tayk good hede;
For never sithe ye wear on your mothars borne
   had ye never so mickle nede.'

55 The dougheti Dogglas on a stede,
   he rode alle his men beforne;
His armor glytteryde as dyd a glede;
   a boldar barne was never born.

'Tell me whos men ye ar', he says,
60   'or whos men that ye be:
Who gave youe leave to hunte in this Chyviat
   chays,
   in the spyt of myn and of me.'

The first mane that ever him an answear mayd,
   yt was the good lord Persë:
'We wyll not tell the whoys men we ar,' he says,
66   'nor whose men that we be;
But we wyll hounte hear in this chays,
   in the spyt of thyne and of the.

'The fattiste hartes in all Chyviat
70   we have kyld, and cast to carry them away:'
'Be my troth,' sayd the doughetë Dogglas agayn,
   'therfor the ton of us shall de this day.'

Then sayd the doughtë Doglas
 unto the lord Persë:
75 'To kyll alle thes giltles men,
 alas, it wear great pittë!

'But, Persë, thowe art a lord of lande,
 I am a yerle callyd within my contre;
Let all our men uppone a parti stande,
80 and do the battell off the and of me.'

'Nowe Cristes cors on his crowne,' sayd the lord
  Persë,
 'who-so-ever ther-to says nay;
Be my troth, doughttë Doglas,' he says,
 'thow shalt never se that day.

85 'Nethar in Ynglonde, Skottlonde, nar France,
 nor for no man of a woman born,
But, and fortune be my chance,
 I dar met him, on man for on.'

Then bespayke a squyar off Northombarlonde,
90 Richard Wytharyngton was his nam;
 'It shall never be told in Sothe-Ynglonde,' he
  says,
 'to Kyng Herry the Fourth for sham.

'I wat youe byn great lordes twaw,
 I am a poor squyar of lande:
95 I wylle never se my captayne fyght on a fylde,
 and stande my selffe and loocke on,
But whylle I may my weppone welde,
 I wylle not fayle both hart and hande.'

That day, that day, that dreadfull day!
100   the first fit here I fynde;
And youe wyll here any mor a the hountyng a the
      Chyviat,
    yet ys ther mor behynde.

The Yngglyshe men hade ther bowys yebent,
    ther hartes wer good yenoughe;
105 The first off arros that the shote off,
    seven skore spear-men the sloughe.

Yet byddys the yerle Doglas uppon the bent,
    a captayne good yenoughe,
And that was sene verament,
110   for he wrought hom both woo and wouche.

The Dogglas partyd his ost in thre,
    lyk a cheffe cheften off pryde;
With suar spears off myghtte tre,
    the cum in on every syde:

115 Thrughe our Yngglyshe archery
    gave many a wounde fulle wyde;
Many a doughetě the garde to dy,
    which ganyde them no pryde.

The Ynglyshe men let ther boÿs be,
120   and pulde owt brandes thet wer brighte;
It was a hevy syght to se
    bryght swordes on basnites lyght.

Thorowe ryche male and myneyeple,
    many sterne the strocke done streght;
125 Many a freyke that was fulle fre,
    ther undar foot dyd lyght.

At last the Duglas and the Persë met,
　　lyk to captayns of myght and of mayne;
The swapte together tylle the both swat,
130　with swordes that wear of fyn myllan.

Thes worthë freckys for to fyght,
　　ther-to the wear fulle fayne,
Tylle the bloode owte off thear basnetes sprente,
　　as ever dyd heal or rayn.

135 'Yelde the, Persë,' sayde the Doglas,
　　　'and i feth I shalle the brynge
Wher thowe shalte have a yerls wagis
　　of Jamy our Skottish kynge.

'Thou shalte have thy ransom fre,
140　I hight the hear this thinge;
For the manfullyste man yet art thowe
　　that ever I conqueryd in filde fighttynge.'

'Nay,' sayd the lord Persë,
　　'I told it the beforne,
145 That I wolde never yeldyde be
　　to no man of a woman born.'

With that ther cam an arrowe hastely,
　　forthe off a myghttë wane;
Hit hathe strekene the yerle Duglas
150　in at the brest-bane.

Thorowe lyvar and longës bathe
　　the sharpe arrowe ys gane,
That never after in all his lyffe-days
　　he spake mo wordës but ane:
That was, 'Fyghte ye, my myrry men, whyllys
　　　ye may,
156　for my lyff-days ben gan.'

The Persë leanyde on his brande,
   and sawe the Duglas de;
He tooke the dede mane by the hande,
160   and sayd, 'Wo ys me for the!

'To have savyde thy lyffe, I wolde have partyde
     with
   my landes for years thre,
For a better man, of hart nare of hande,
   was nat in all the north contrë.'

165 Off all that se a Skottishe knyght,
   was callyd Ser Hewe the Monggombyrry;
He sawe the Duglas to the deth was dyght,
   he spendyd a spear, a trusti tre.

He rod uppone a corsiare
170   throughe a hondrith archery;
He never stynttyde, nar never blane,
   tylle he cam to the good lord Persë.

He set uppone the lorde Persë
   a dynte that was full soare;
175 With a suar spear of a myghttë tre
   clean thorow the body he the Persë ber,

A the tothar syde that a man myght se
   a large cloth-yard and mare:
Towe bettar captayns wear nat in Cristiantë
180   then that day slan wear ther.

An archar off Northomberlonde
   say slean was the lorde Persë;
He bar a bende bowe in his hand,
   was made off trusti tre.

185 An arow, that a cloth-yarde was lang,
  to the harde stele halyde he;
 A dynt that was both sad and soar
  he sat on Ser Hewe the Monggombyrry.

 The dynt yt was both sad and sar,
190 that he of Monggomberry sete;
 The swane-fethars that his arrowe bar
  with his hart-blood the wear wete.

 Ther was never a freake wone foot wolde fle,
  but still in stour dyd stand,
 Heawyng on yche othar, whylle the myghte dre,
196 with many a balfull brande.

 This battell begane in Chyviat
  an owar befor the none,
 And when even-songe bell was rang,
200 the battell was nat half done.

 The tocke . . . on ethar hande
  be the lyght of the mone;
 Many hade no strenght for to stande,
  in Chyviat the hillys abon.

205 Of fifteen hondrith archars of Ynglonde
  went away but seventi and thre;
 Of twenti hondrith spear-men of Skotlonde,
  but even five and fifti.

 But all wear slayne Cheviat within;
210 the hade no strengthe to stand on hy;
 The chylde may rue that ys unborne,
  it was the mor pittë.

Thear was slayne, withe the lord Persë,
   Sir Johan of Agerstone,
215 Ser Rogar, the hinde Hartly,
   Ser Wyllyam, the bolde Hearone.

Ser Jorg, the worthë Loumle,
   a knyghte of great renowen,
Ser Raff, the ryche Rugbe,
220 with dyntes wear beaten dowene.

For Wetharryngton my harte was wo,
   that ever he slayne shulde be;
For when both his leggis wear hewyne in to,
   yet he knyled and fought on hys kny.

225 Ther was slayne, with the dougeti Duglas,
   Ser Hewe the Monggombyrry,
Ser Davy Lydale, that worthë was,
   his sistar's son was he.

Ser Charls a Murrë in that place,
230 that never a foot wolde fle;
Ser Hewe Maxwelle, a lorde he was,
   with the Doglas dyd he dey.

So on the morrowe the mayde them byears
   off birch and hassell so gray;
235 Many wedous, with wepyng tears,
   cam to fache ther makys away.

Tivydale may carpe off care,
   Northomberlond may mayk great mon,
For towe such captayns as slayne wear thear,
240 on the March-parti shall never be non.

Word ys commen to Eddenburrowe,
   to Jamy the Skottische kynge,
That dougheti Duglas, lyff-tenant of the Marches,
   he lay slean Chyviot within.

245 His handdës dyd he weal and wryng,
     he sayd, 'Alas, and woe ys me!
Such an othar captayn Skotland within,'
   he sayd, 'ye-feth shuld never be.'

Worde ys commyn to lovly Londone,
250   till the fourth Harry our kynge,
That lord Persë, lyff-tenante of the Marchis,
   he lay slayne Chyviat within.

'God have merci on his solle,' sayde Kyng Harry,
   'good lord, yf thy will it be!
I have a hondrith captayns in Ynglonde,' he
     sayd,
256   'as good as ever was he:
But, Persë, and I brook my lyffe,
   thy deth well quyte shall be.'

As our noble kynge mayd his avowe,
260   lyke a noble prince of renowen,
For the deth of the lord Persë
   he dyde the battell of Hombyll-down;

Wher syx and thrittë Skottishe knyghtes
   on a day wear beaten down:
265 Glendale glyterryde on ther armor bryght,
   over castille, towar, and town.

This was the hontynge off the Cheviat,
   that tear begane this spurn;
Old men that knowen the grounde well yenoughe
270   call it the battell of Otterburn.

At Otterburn begane this spurne
uppone a Monnynday;
Ther was the doughtë Doglas slean,
the Persë never went away.

275 Ther was never a tym on the Marche-partes
sen the Doglas and the Persë met,
But yt ys mervele and the rede blude ronne not
as the reane doys in the stret.

Jhesue Crist our balys bete,
280 and to the blys us brynge!
Thus was the hountynge of the Chivyat:
God send us alle good endyng!

SIR PATRICK SPENS

(From *Percy's Reliques*, pub. 1765. Date uncertain, but a
popular ballad in 1580)

The King sits in Dumferling toune,
Drinking the blude-reid wine;
'O whar will I get guid sailor,
To sail this schip of mine?'

5 Up and spak an eldern knicht,
Sat at the king's richt kne:
'Sir Patrick Spence is the best sailor,
That sails upon the se.'

The king has written a braid letter,
10 And signed it wi his hand,
And sent it to Sir Patrick Spence,
Was walking on the sand.

The first line that Sir Patrick red,
 A loud lauch lauched he;
15 The next line that Sir Patrick red
 The teir blinded his ee.

'O wha is this has don this deid,
 This ill deid don to me,
To send me out this time o' the yeir,
20 To sail upon the se!

'Mak hast, mak haste, my mirry men all,
 Our guid schip sails the morne:'
'O say na sae, my master deir,
 For I feir a deadlie storme.

25 'Late late yestreen I saw the new moone,
 Wi the auld moone in hir arme,
And I feir, I feir, my deir master,
 That we will cum to harme.'

O our Scots nobles wer richt laith
30 To wut their cork-heild schoone;
Bot lang owre a' the play wer playd,
 Thair hats they swam aboone.

O lang, lang may their ladies sit,
 Wi thair fans into their hand,
35 Or eir they se Sir Patrick Spence
 Cum sailing to the land.

O lang, lang may the ladies stand,
 Wi thair gold kems in their hair,
Waiting for thair ain deir lords,
40 For they 'll se thame na mair.

Haf owre, haf owre to Aberdour,
  It's fiftie fadom deip,
And thair lies guid Sir Patrick Spence,
  Wi the Scots lords at his feit.

WALY, WALY, LOVE BE BONNIE

(From Allingham's *Ballad Book*, 1864)

O Waly, waly, up the bank,
  O waly, waly, doun the brae,
And waly, waly, yon burn-side,
  Where I and my love wer wont to gae!
5 I lean'd my back unto an aik,
  I thocht it was a trustie tree,
But first it bow'd and syne it brak',—
  Sae my true love did lichtlie me.

O waly, waly, but love be bonnie
10 A little time while it is new!
But when its auld it waxeth cauld,
  And fadeth awa' like the morning dew.
O wherefore should I busk my heid,
  Or wherefore should I kame my hair?
15 For my true love has me forsook,
  And says he 'll never lo'e me mair.

Noo Arthur's seat sall be my bed,
  The sheets sall neir be press'd by me;
Saint Anton's well sall be my drink;
20 Since my true love's forsaken me.
Martinmas wind, when wilt thou blaw,
  And shake the green leaves off the tree?
O gentle death, whan wilt thou come?
  For of my life I am wearie.

25 'Tis not the frost that freezes fell,
    Nor blawing snaw's inclemencie,
'Tis not sic cauld that makes me cry;
    But my love's heart grown cauld to me.
Whan we cam' in by Glasgow toun,
30   We were a comely sicht to see;
My love was clad in the black velvet,
    An' I mysel' in cramasie.

But had I wist before I kiss'd
    That love had been so ill to win,
35 I'd lock'd my heart in a case o' goud,
    And pinn'd it wi' a siller pin.
Oh, oh! if my young babe were born,
    And set upon the nurse's knee;
And I mysel' were dead and gane,
40   And the green grass growing over me!

THE TWA SISTERS O' BINNORIE

(From the same)

There were twa sisters sat in a bow'r;
    (Binnorie, O Binnorie!)
A knight cam' there, a noble wooer,
    By the bonny mill-dams o' Binnorie.

5 He courted the eldest wi' glove and ring,
    (Binnorie, O Binnorie!)
But he lo'ed the youngest aboon a' thing,
    By the bonny mill-dams o' Binnorie.

The eldest she was vexed sair,
10   (Binnorie, O Binnorie!)
And sair envied her sister fair,
    By the bonny mill-dams o' Binnorie.

Upon a morning fair and clear,
   (Binnorie, O Binnorie!)
15 She cried upon her sister dear,
   By the bonny mill-dams o' Binnorie.

'O sister, sister, tak' my hand,'
   (Binnorie, O Binnorie!)
'And let's go down to the river-strand,'
20   By the bonny mill-dams o' Binnorie.

She's ta'en her by the lily hand,
   (Binnorie, O Binnorie!)
And down they went to the river-strand
   By the bonny mill-dams o' Binnorie.

25 The youngest stood upon a stane,
   (Binnorie, O Binnorie!)
The eldest cam' and pushed her in,
   By the bonny mill-dams o' Binnorie.

'O sister, sister, reach your hand!'
30   (Binnorie, O Binnorie!)
'And ye sall be heir o' half my land'—
   By the bonny mill-dams o' Binnorie.

'O sister, reach me but your glove!'
   (Binnorie, O Binnorie!)
35 'And sweet William sall be your love'—
   By the bonny mill-dams o' Binnorie.

Sometimes she sank, sometimes she swam,
   (Binnorie, O Binnorie!)
Till she cam' to the mouth o' yon mill-dam,
40   By the bonny mill-dams o' Binnorie.

Out then cam' the miller's son
　　(Binnorie, O Binnorie!)
And saw the fair maid swimmin' in,
　　By the bonny mill-dams o' Binnorie.

45 'O father, father, draw your dam!'
　　(Binnorie, O Binnorie!)
'There's either a mermaid or a swan,'
　　By the bonny mill-dams o' Binnorie.

The miller quickly drew the dam,
50　　(Binnorie, O Binnorie!)
And there he found a drown'd womàn,
　　By the bonny mill-dams o' Binnorie.

Round about her middle sma'
　　(Binnorie, O Binnorie!)
55 There went a gouden girdle bra'
　　By the bonny mill-dams o' Binnorie.

All amang her yellow hair
　　(Binnorie, O Binnorie!)
A string o' pearls was twisted rare,
60　　By the bonny mill-dams o' Binnorie.

On her fingers lily-white,
　　(Binnorie, O Binnorie!)
The jewel-rings were shining bright,
　　By the bonny mill-dams o' Binnorie.

65 And by there cam' a harper fine,
　　(Binnorie, O Binnorie!)
Harpèd to nobles when they dine,
　　By the bonny mill-dams o' Binnorie.

And when he looked that lady on,
70   (Binnorie, O Binnorie!)
He sigh'd and made a heavy moan,
   By the bonny mill-dams o' Binnorie.

He's ta'en three locks o' her yellow hair,
   (Binnorie, O Binnorie!)
75 And wi' them strung his harp sae rare,
   By the bonny mill-dams o' Binnorie.

He went into her father's hall,
   (Binnorie, O Binnorie!)
And played his harp before them all,
80   By the bonny mill-dams o' Binnorie.

And sune the harp sang loud and clear,
   (Binnorie, O Binnorie!)
'Fareweel, my father and mither dear!'
   By the bonny mill-dams o' Binnorie.

85 And neist when the harp began to sing,
   (Binnorie, O Binnorie!)
'Twas 'Fareweel, sweetheart!' said the string,
   By the bonny mill-dams o' Binnorie.

And then as plain as plain could be,
90   (Binnorie, O Binnorie!)
'There sits my sister wha drownèd me!
   By the bonny mill-dams o' Binnorie.'

BONNIE GEORGE CAMPBELL

(From Motherwell's *Minstrelsy*, 1827.   Date of ballad
uncertain)

Hie upon Hielands,
   And low upon Tay,
Bonnie George Campbell
   Rade out on a day.
5 Saddled and bridled
   And gallant rade he;
Hame cam his gude horse,
   But never cam he!

Out cam his auld mither
10   Greeting fu' sair,
And out cam his bonnie bride
   Rivin' her hair.
Saddled and bridled
   And booted rade he;
15 Toom hame cam the saddle
   But never cam he!

"My meadow hes green,
   And my corn is unshorn;
My barn is to big,
20   And my babie's unborn."
Saddled and bridled
   And booted rade he;
Toom hame cam the saddle,
   But never cam he.

HELEN OF KIRCONNELL

PART SECOND

(From Scott's *Border Minstrelsy*, 1802–3)

I wish I were where Helen lies!
Night and day on me she cries;
O that I were where Helen lies,
   On fair Kirconnell Lee!

5 Curst be the heart that thought the thought,
And curst the hand that fired the shot,
When in my arms burd Helen dropt,
   And died to succour me!

O think na ye my heart was sair,
10 When my love dropt down and spak nae mair!
There did she swoon wi' mickle care
   On fair Kirconnell Lee.

As I went down the water-side,
None but my foe to be my guide,
15 None but my foe to be my guide,
   On fair Kirconnell Lee!

I lighted down, my sword did draw,
I hackèd him in pieces sma',
I hackèd him in pieces sma',
20   For her sake that died for me.

O, Helen fair, beyond compare!
I'll make a garland of thy hair,
Shall bind my heart for evermair,
   Until the day I die.

25 O that I were where Helen lies!
   Night and day on me she cries;
   Out of my bed she bids me rise,
     Says, "Haste, and come to me!"

   O Helen fair! O Helen chaste!
30 If I were with thee, I were blest,
   Where thou lies low, and takes thy rest,
     On fair Kirconnell Lee.

   I wish my grave were growing green,
   A winding-sheet drawn ower my een,
35 And I in Helen's arms lying,
     On fair Kirconnell Lee.

   I wish I were where Helen lies!
   Night and day on me she cries;
   And I am weary of the skies,
40   For her sake that died for me.

SPENSER TO DRYDEN.

EDMUND SPENSER

Cir. 1552–1599

THE FAERIE QUEENE

(From the First Book, which contains *The Legend of the Knight of the Red Crosse, or of Holinesse*, published with Bks. II. and III., 1590)

I.

Lo! I, the man whose Muse whylome did maske,
As time her taught, in lowly Shephards weeds,
Am now enforst, a farre unfitter taske,
For trumpets sterne to chaunge mine oaten reeds,
And sing of knights and ladies gentle deeds;   5
Whose praises having slept in silence long,
Me, all too meane, the sacred Muse areeds
To blazon broade emongst her learned throng:
Fierce warres and faithfull loves shall moralize my
      song.

II.

Helpe then, O holy virgin, chiefe of nyne,   10
Thy weaker novice to performe thy will;
Lay forth out of thine everlasting scryne
The ántique rolles, which there lye hidden still,
Of Faerie knights, and fayrest Tanaquill,
Whom that most noble Briton Prince so long   15
Sought through the world, and suffered so much ill,
That I must rue his undeserved wrong:
O, helpe thou my weake wit, and sharpen my dull tong!

III.

And thou, most dreaded impe of highest Jove,
Faire Venus sonne, that with thy cruell dart   20
At that good knight so cunningly didst rove,
That glorious fire it kindled in his hart;
Lay now thy deadly heben bowe apart,
And with thy mother mylde come to mine ayde;
Come, both; and with you bring triumphant Mart,
In loves and gentle jollities arraid,   26
After his murderous spoyles and bloudie rage allayd.

IV.

And with them eke, O Goddesse heavenly bright,
Mirrour of grace, and maiestie divine,
Great ladie of the greatest Isle, whose light   30
Like Phoebus lampe throughout the world doth
     shine,
Shed thy faire beames into my feeble eyne,
And raise my thoughtes, too humble and too vile,
To thinke of that true glorious type of thine,
The argument of mine afflicted stile: 35
The which to heare vouchsafe, O dearest Dread, a
     while.

CANTO I.

The patron of true Holinesse,
   Foule Errour doth defeate;
Hypocrisie, him to entrappe,
   Doth to his home entreate.

I.

A gentle Knight was pricking on the plaine,
Ycladd in mightie armes and silver shielde,
Wherein old dints of deepe woundes did remaine,
The cruell markes of many a bloody fielde;   40

Yet armes till that time did he never wield:
His angry steede did chide his foming bitt,
As much disdayning to the curbe to yield:
Full iolly knight he seemd, and faire did sitt,   44
As one for knightly giusts and fierce encounters fitt.

II.

And on his brest a bloodie crosse he bore,
The deare remembrance of his dying Lord,
For whose sweete sake that glorious badge he wore,
And dead, as living ever, him ador'd:
Upon his shield the like was also scor'd,   50
For soveraine hope, which in his helpe he had,
Right, faithfull, true he was in deede and word;
But of his cheere did seeme too solemne sad;
Yet nothing did he dread, but ever was ydrad.

III.

Upon a great adventure he was bond,   55
That greatest Gloriana to him gave,
That greatest glorious Queene of Faery lond,
To winne him worshippe, and her grace to have,
Which of all earthly thinges, he most did crave:
And ever as he rode, his hart did earne,   60
To prove his puissance in battell brave
Upon his foe, and his new force to learne;
Upon his foe, a Dragon horrible and stearne.

IV.

A lovely Ladie rode him faire beside,
Upon a lowly asse more white then snow;   65
Yet she much whiter; but the same did hide
Under a vele, that wimpled was full low;
And over all a blacke stole shee did throw:

As one that inly mournd, so was she sad,
  And heavie sate upon her palfry slow;   70
  Seemed in heart some hidden care she had;
And by her in a line a milke-white lambe she lad.

V.

So pure and innocent, as that same lambe,
  She was in life and every vertuous lore;
  And by descent from royall lynage came   75
Of ancient kinges and queenes, that had of yore
Their scepters stretcht from east to westerne shore,
  And all the world in their subiection held;
  Till that infernall feend with foule uprore
Forwasted all their land, and them expeld;   80
Whom to avenge she had this Knight from far
    compeld.

VI.

Behind her farre away a Dwarfe did lag,
  That lazie seemd, in being ever last,
  Or wearied with bearing of her bag
Of needments at his backe.   Thus as they past,   85
The day with cloudes was suddeine overcast,
  And angry Iove an hideous storme of raine
  Did poure into his lemans lap so fast,
That everie wight to shrowd it did constrain;
And this faire couple eke to shroud themselves were
    fain.   90

VII.

Enforst to seeke some covert nigh at hand,
  A shadie grove not farr away they spide,
  That promist ayde the tempest to withstand;
Whose loftie trees, yclad with sommers pride,
Did spred so broad, that heavens light did hide.   95

Not perceable with power of any starr:
And all within were pathes and alleies wide,
With footing worne, and leading inward farr:
Faire harbour that them seemes; so in they entred ar.

VIII.

And foorth they passe, with pleasure forward led,
Ioying to heare the birdes sweete harmony,   101
Which, therein shrouded from the tempest dred,
Seemd in their song to scorne the cruell sky.
Much can they praise the trees so straight and hy,
The sayling pine; the cedar proud and tall;   105
The vine-propp elme; the poplar never dry;
The builder oake, sole king of forrests all;
The aspine good for staves; the cypresse funerall;

IX.

The laurell, meed of mightie conquerours
And poets sage; the firre that weepeth still;   110
The willow, worne of forlorne paramours;
The eugh, obedient to the benders will;
The birch for shaftes; the sallow for the mill;
The mirrhe sweete-bleeding in the bitter wound;
The warlike beech; the ash for nothing ill;   115
The fruitfull olive; and the platane round;
The carver holme; the maple seeldom inward sound.

X.

Led with delight, they thus beguile the way,
Untill the blustring storme is overblowne;   119
When, weening to returne whence they did stray,
They cannot finde that path, which first was showne
But wander too and fro in waies unknowne,

Furthest from end then, when they neerest weene,
That makes them doubt their wits be not their owne:
So many pathes, so many turnings seene,   125
That which of them to take, in diverse doubt they
  been.

XI.

At last resolving forward still to fare,
Till that some end they finde, or in or out,
That path they take, that beaten seemd most bare,
And like to lead the labyrinth about;   130
Which when by tract they hunted had throughout,
At length it brought them to a hollowe cave,
Amid the thickest woods. The Champion stout
Eftsoones dismounted from his courser brave,   134
And to the Dwarfe a while his needlesse spere he gave.

XII.

" Be well aware," quoth then that Ladie milde,
" Least suddaine mischiefe ye too rash provoke:
The danger hid, the place unknowne and wilde,
Breedes dreadfull doubts: oft fire is without smoke,
And perill without show: therefore your stroke, 140
Sir Knight, withhold, till further tryall made."
" Ah Ladie," sayd he, " shame were to revoke
The forward footing for an hidden shade:
Vertue gives her selfe light through darknesse for to
  wade."

XIII.

" Yea, but," quoth she, " the perill of this place   145
I better wot then you: though nowe too late
To wish you backe returne with foule disgrace,
Yet wisedome warnes, whilst foot is in the gate,

To stay the steppe, ere forced to retrate.
This is the wandring wood, this Errours den,   150
A monster vile, whom God and man does hate:
Therefore I read beware." "Fly, fly," quoth then
The fearful Dwarfe; "This is no place for living
    men."

XIV.

But, full of fire and greedy hardiment,   154
The youthfull Knight could not for ought be staide;
But forth unto the darksom hole he went,
And looked in: his glistring armor made
A litle glooming light, much like a shade;
By which he saw the ugly monster plaine,
Halfe like a serpent horribly displaide,   160
But th'other halfe did womans shape retaine,
Most lothsom, filthie, foule, and full of vile disdaine.

[The Red Cross Knight, assisted by Una, does battle
with the dragon, Error. As the combat progresses, the
hideous serpent-brood of Error, "deformed monsters,
foul and black as ink," swarming about the Knight
sorely encumber him. The poet thus compares them
to a cloud of gnats.]

XXIII.

As gentle shepheard in sweete eventide,
When ruddy Phebus gins to welke in west,   245
High on an hill, his flocke to vewen wide,
Markes which doe byte their hasty supper best;
A cloud of cumbrous gnattes doe him molest,
All striving to infixe their feeble stinges,
That from their noyance he no where can rest;   250
But with his clownish hands their tender wings
He brusheth oft, and oft doth mar their murmurings.

XXIV.

Thus ill bestedd, and fearefull more of shame
Then of the certeine perill he stood in,
Halfe furious unto his foe he came, 255
Resolved in minde all suddenly to win,
Or soone to lose, before he once would lin;
And stroke at her with more then manly force,
That from her body, full of filthie sin,
He raft her hatefull heade without remorse: 260
A streame of cole-black blood forth gushed from her
corse.

. . . .

XXVII.

His Lady seeing all that chaunst, from farre,
Approcht in hast to greet his victorie; 290
And saide, "Faire Knight, borne under happie
starre,
Who see your vanquisht foes before you lye;
Well worthie be you of that armory,
Wherein ye have great glory wonne this day,
And proov'd your strength on a strong enimie; 295
Your first adventure: Many such I pray,
And henceforth ever wish that like succeed it may!"

[Having re-mounted his steed, the Red-Cross Knight
and Una at length meet in the forest an "aged sire"
clad in black, having a gray beard and a sober aspect.
The Knight, having saluted him, is conducted to a
hermitage on the skirts of the forest, where the old
man tells him in pleasing words about Saints and
popes: so they pass the evening in discourse.]

XXXVI.

The drouping night thus creepeth on them fast;
And the sad humor loading their eyeliddes,   380
As messenger of Morpheus, on them cast
Sweet slombring deaw, the which to sleep them
    biddes.
Unto their lodgings then his guestes he riddes:
Where when all drownd in deadly sleepe he findes,
He to his studie goes; and there amiddes   385
His magick bookes, and artes of sundrie kindes,
He seekes out mighty charmes to trouble sleepy minds.

XXXVII.

Then choosing out few words most horrible,
(Let none them read!) thereof did verses frame;
With which, and other spelles like terrible,   390
He bad awake blacke Plutoes griesly dame;
And cursed heven; and spake reprochful shame
Of highest God, the Lord of life and light.
A bold bad man! that dar'd to call by name   394
Great Gorgon, prince of darknes and dead night;
At which Cocytus quakes, and Styx is put to flight.

XXXVIII.

And forth he cald out of deepe darknes dredd
Legions of sprights, the which, like litle flyes,
Fluttring about his ever-damned hedd,
Awaite whereto their service he applyes,   400
To aide his friendes, or fray his enimies:
Of those he chose out two, the falsest twoo,
And fittest for to forge true-seeming lyes;
The one of them he gave a message too,
The other by him selfe staide other worke to doo.   405

XXXIX.

He, making speedy way through spersed ayre,
And through the world of waters wide and deepe,
To Morpheus house doth hastily repaire.
Amid the bowels of the earth full steepe,   409
And low, where dawning day doth never peepe,
His dwelling is; there Tethys his wet bed
Doth ever wash, and Cynthia still doth steepe
In silver deaw his ever-drouping hed,
Whiles sad Night over him her mantle black doth
          spred.

XL.

Whose double gates he findeth locked fast;   415
The one faire fram'd of burnisht yvory,
The other all with silver overcast;
And wakeful dogges before them farre doe lye,
Watching to banish Care their enimy,
Who oft is wont to trouble gentle Sleepe.   420
By them the Sprite doth passe in quietly,
And unto Morpheus comes, whom drowned deepe
In drowsie fit he findes; of nothing he takes keepe.

XLI.

And, more to lulle him in his slumber soft,   424
A trickling streame from high rock tumbling downe,
And ever-drizling raine upon the loft,
Mixt with a murmuring winde, much like the sowne
Of swarming bees, did caste him in a swowne.
No other noyse, nor peoples troublous cryes,
As still are wont t' annoy the walled towne,   430
Might there be heard; but carelesse Quiet lyes,
Wrapt in eternall silence farre from enimyes.

XLII.

The messenger approching to **him** spake;
But his waste words retournd to him in vaine.   434
So sound he slept, that nought mought him awake.
Then rudely he him thrust, and pusht with paine,
Whereat he gan to stretch: but he againe
Shooke him so hard, that forced him to speake.
As one then in a dreame, whose dryer braine
Is tost with troubled sights and fancies weake,   440
He mumbled soft, but would not all his silence **breake**.

XLIII.

The Sprite then gan more boldly him to wake,
And threatned unto him the dreaded name
Of Hecate: whereat he gan to quake,
And, lifting up his lompish head, with blame   445
Halfe angrie asked him, for what he came.
"Hether," quoth he, "me Archimago sent,
He that the stubborne sprites can wisely tame;
He bids thee to him send for his intent   449
A fit false dreame, that can delude the sleepers sent."

XLIV.

The god obayde; and, calling forth straight way
A diverse dreame out of his prison darke,
Delivered it to him, and downe did lay
His heavie head, devoide of careful carke;   454
Whose sences all were straight benumbd and starke.
He, backe returning by the yvorie dore,
Remounted up as light as chearefull larke;
And on his litle winges the dreame he **bore**
In hast unto his lord, where he him left afore.

XLV.

Who all this while, with charmes and hidden artes,
Had made a lady of that other spright,   460
And fram'd of liquid ayre her tender partes,
So lively, and so like in all mens sight,
That weaker sence it could have ravisht quight:
The maker selfe, for all his wondrous witt,   465
Was nigh beguiled with so goodly sight.
Her all in white he clad, and over it
Cast a black stole, most like to seeme for Una fit.

XLVI.

Now when that ydle Dreame was to him brought,
Unto that Elfin Knight he bad him fly,   470
Where he slept soundly, void of evil thought,
And with false shewes abuse his fantasy,
In sort as he him schooled privily.
And that new creature, borne without her dew,
Full of the makers guyle, with usage sly,   475
He taught to imitate that Lady trew,
Whose semblance she did carrie under feigned hew.

[This phantom, in the outward semblance of Una,
conducts herself with such lightness that the Knight is
perplexed with doubts of her goodness and truthful-
ness. At last, restless and tormented by evil delusions
conjured up by Archimago, the Knight mounts his
steed and flies with the dwarf. Thus parted from Una,
or Truth, by the wiles of the Enchanter, the deluded
Knight falls into peril in a meeting with Duessa, or
Falsehood.

Meanwhile the heavenly Una, his true bride, missing
her Knight, sets out in search of him, alone and sorrowful. The poet then tells how the lion comes to
guard her in her need.]

CANTO III.

Forsaken Truth long seeks her love,
*   and makes the Lyon mylde;*
Marres blind Devotions mart, and fals
*   in hand of treachour vylde.*

I.

Nought is there under heav'ns wide hollownesse,
That moves more cleare compassion of mind,
Then beautie brought t' unworthie wretchednesse
Through envies snares, or fortunes freakes unkind.
I, whether lately through her brightnes blynd,   5
Or through alleageance and fast fealty,
Which I do owe unto all woman kynd,
Feele my hart perst with so great agony,
When such I see, that all for pitty I could dy.

II.

And now it is empassioned so deepe,   10
For fairest Unaes sake, of whom I sing,
That my fraile eyes these lines with teares do steepe,
To thinke how she through guileful handeling,
Though true as touch, though daughter of a king,
Though faire as ever living wight was fayre,   15
Though nor in word nor deede ill meriting,
Is from her Knight devorced in despayre,
And her dew loves deryv'd to that vile witches shayre.

III.

Yet she, most faithfull ladie, all this while
Forsaken, wofull, solitairie mayd,   20
Far from all peoples preace, as in exile,
In wildernesse and wastfull deserts strayd,

To seeke her Knight; who subtily betrayd
Through that late vision, which th' enchanter wrought,
Had her abandoned. She of naught affrayd,   25
Through woods and wastness wide him daily sought;
Yet wished tydinges none of him unto her brought.

IV.

One day, nigh wearie of the yrksome way,
From her unhastie beast she did alight;
And on the grasse her dainty limbs did lay   30
In secrete shadow, far from all mens sight;
From her fayre head her fillet she undight;
And layd her stole aside. Her angels face,
As the great eye of heaven, shyned bright,
And made a sunshine in the shady place;   35
Did never mortall eye behold such heavenly grace.

V.

It fortuned, out of the thickest wood
A ramping lyon rushed suddeinly,
Hunting full greedy after salvage blood;
Soone as the royall Virgin he did spy,   40
With gaping mouth at her ran greedily,
To have attonce devoured her tender corse.
But to the pray when as he drew more ny,
His bloody rage aswaged with remorse,   44
And, with the sight amazd, forgat his furious forse.

VI.

Instead thereof he kist her wearie feet,
And lickt her lilly hands with fawning tong;
As he her wronged innocence did weet.
O how can beautie maister the most strong,

And simple truth subdue avenging wrong!   50
Whose yielded pryde and proud submission,
Still dreading death, when she had marked long,
Her hart gan melt in great compassion;
And drizling teares did shed for pure affection.

VII.

"The lyon, lord of everie beast in field,"   55
Quoth she, "his princely puissance doth abate,
And mightie proud to humble weake does yield,
Forgetfull of the hungry rage, which late
Him prickt, in pittie of my sad estate:—
But he, my lyon, and my noble lord,   60
How does he find in cruell hart to hate
Her that him lov'd, and ever most adord,
As the God of my life? why hath he me abhord?"

VIII.

Redounding teares did choke th' end of her plaint,
Which softly ecchoed from the neighbour wood;   65
And, sad to see her sorrowful constraint,
The kingly beast upon her gazing stood;
With pittie calmd, downe fell his angry mood.
At last, in close hart shutting up her payne,
Arose the Virgin borne of heavenly brood,   70
And to her snowy palfrey got agayne
To seeke her strayed champion, if she might attayne.

IX.

The lyon would not leave her desolate,
But with her went along, as a strong gard
Of her chast person, and a faythfull mate   75
Of her sad troubles and misfortunes hard:

Still, when she slept, he kept both watch and ward;
And, when she wakt, he wayted diligent,
With humble service to her will prepard:
From her fayre eyes he took commandëment,   80
And ever by her lookes conceived her intent.

[Archimago, learning of the whereabouts of Una,
assumes the arms and appearance of the Red Cross
Knight, and,—being too fearful of the lion to join her,
—approaches near enough to her to be seen. Una seeing, as she supposes, him whom she has sought through
wide deserts, and with great toil and peril, goes up to
him in joy and humbleness, while Archimago, feigning
to be her Knight, greets her with words of welcome
and vows of faithful service.]

XXX.

His lovely words her seemd due recompence
Of all her passed paines; one loving howre
For many yeares of sorrow can dispence;
A dram of sweete is worth a pound of sowre.
Shee has forgott how many woful stowre   275
For him she late endurd; she speakes no more
Of past: true is, that true love hath no powre
To looken backe; his eies be fixt before.
Before her stands her Knight, for whom she toyld so
     sore.

XXXI.

Much like, as when the beaten marinere,   280
That long hath wandred in the ocean wide,
Ofte soust in swelling Tethys saltish teare;
And long time having tand his tawney hide
With blustring breath of heaven, that none can bide,

And scorching flames of fierce Orions hound;   285
Soone as the port from far he has espide,
His chearfull whistle merily doth sound,
And Nereus crownes with cups; his mates him pledge
    around.

XXXII.

Such ioy made Una, when her Knight she found;
And eke th' Enchanter ioyous seemde no lesse   290
Then the glad marchant, that does vew from ground
His ship far come from watrie wildernesse;
He hurles out vowes, and Neptune oft doth blesse.
So forth they past; and all the way they spent
Discoursing of her dreadful late distresse,   295
In which he askt her, what the lyon ment;
Who told her all that fell, in iourney as she went.

XXXIII.

They had not ridden far, when they might see
One pricking towards them with hastie heat,
Full strongly armd, and on a courser free   300
That through his fiersenesse fomed all with sweat,
And the sharpe yron did for anger eat,
When his hot ryder spurd his chauffed side;
His looke was sterne, and seemed still to threat
Cruell revenge, which he in hart did hyde;   305
And on his shield *Sans loy* in bloody lines was dyde.

[Archimago, in the guise of the Red Cross Knight,
thus journeying with Una meets a Paynim, or Saracen,
named *Sansloy*. *Sansloy* attacks Archimago, who is
overthrown. When he is unhelmed, Una sees to her
surprise the face of Archimago instead of that of the
Red Cross Knight. The Paynim, leaving Archimago
dying, rudely approaches Una and drags her from her

palfrey.　The poet then describes the combat of the
Paynim with the lion.]

XLI.

But her fiers servant, full of kingly aw
And high disdaine, whenas his soveraine Dame　380
So rudely handled by her foe he saw,
With gaping iawes full greedy at him came,
And, ramping in his shield, did weene the same
Have reft away with his sharp rending clawes:
But he was stout, and lust did now inflame　385
His corage more, that from his griping pawes
He hath his shield redeemd; and forth his sword he
　　drawes.

XLII.

O then, too weake and feeble was the forse
Of salvage beast, his puissance to withstand!
For he was strong, and of so mightie corse,　390
As ever wielded speare in warlike hand;
And feates of armes did wisely understand.
Eftsoones he perced through his chaufed chest
With thrilling point of deadly yron brand,
And launcht his lordly hart: with death opprest　395
He ror'd aloud, whiles life forsooke his stubborne
　　brest.

XLIII.

Who now is left to keepe the forlorne Maid
From raging spoile of lawlesse victors will?
Her faithful gard remov'd; her hope dismaid;
Her selfe a yielded pray to save or spill!　400
He now, lord of the field, his pride to fill,
With foule reproches and disdaineful spright
Her vildly entertaines; and, will or nill
Beares her away upon his courser light
Her prayers naught prevaile; his rage is more of
　　might.　　　　　　　　　　　　　　405

XLIV.

And all the way, with great lamenting paine,
And piteous plaintes she filleth his dull eares,
That stony hart could riven have in twaine;
And all the way she wetts with flowing teares;
But he, enrag'd with rancor, nothing heares.   410
Her servile beast yet would not leave her so,
But followes her far of, ne ought he feares
To be partaker of her wandring woe,
More mild in beastly kind, then that her beastly foe.

[After many mishaps and adventures the Book ends
with the happy union of the Red Cross Knight and
Una;—the marriage of Holiness and Truth.]

BOOK II.

CANTO VI.

THE STORY OF SIR GUYON, OR THE KNIGHT OF TEMPERANCE

Guyon is of immodest Merth
  Led into loose desyre;
Fights with Chymochles, whiles his bro-
  ther burnes in furious fyre.

I.

A harder lesson to learne Continence
In ioyous pleasure then in grievous paine;
For sweetnesse doth allure the weaker sence
So strongly, that uneathes it can refraine
From that which feeble nature covets faine;   5
But griefe and wrath, that be her enemies,
And foes of life, she better can abstaine:
Yet Vertue vauntes in both her victories;
And Guyon in them all shewes goodly mysteries.

[Sir Guyon having met a damsel who represents intemperate pleasure, is tempted by her to neglect duty in inglorious idleness and self-indulgence. He falls under the spell of her blandishments and his coming under her allurements to the Idle Lake, the home of pleasure, is thus described:]

XI.

Whiles thus she talked, and whiles thus she toyd,
They were far past the passage which he spake, 101
And come unto an island waste and voyd,
That floted in the midst of that great lake;
There her small gondelay her port did make,
And that gay payre, issewing on the shore, 105
Disburdened her. Their way they forward take
Into the land that lay them faire before,
Whose pleasaunce she him shewde, and plentifull
    great store.

XII.

It was a chosen plott of fertile land,
Emongst wide waves sett, like a little nest, 110
As if it had by Nature's cunning hand
Bene choycely picked out from all the rest,
And laid forth for ensample of the best:
No daintie flowre or herbe that growes on grownd,
No arborett with painted blossomes drest 115
And smelling sweete, but there it might be fownd
To bud out faire, and throwe her sweete smels al
    around.

XIII.

No tree whose braunches did not bravely spring;
No braunch, whereon a fine bird did not sitt;
No bird, but did her shrill notes sweetly sing; 120
No song but did containe a lovely ditt.

Trees, braunches, birds, and songs, were framed fitt
For to allure fraile mind to careless ease:
Carelesse the man soone woxe, and his weake witt
Was overcome of thing that did him please;   125
So pleased did his wrathfull purpose faire appease.

XIV.

Thus when shee had his eyes and sences fed
With false delights, and fild with pleasures vayn,
Into a shady dale she soft him led,
And layd him downe upon a grassy playn;   130
And her sweete selfe without dread or disdayn
She sett beside, laying his head disarmd
In her loose lap, it softly to sustayn,
Where soone he slumbred fearing not be harm'd.
The whiles with a love lay she thus him sweetly
    charmd: 135

XV.

"Behold, O man! that toilsome paines doest take,
The flowrs, the fields, and all that pleasaunt growes,
How they themselves doe thine ensample make,
Whiles nothing envious nature them forth throwes
Out of her fruitfull lap; how, no man knowes,   140
They spring, they bud, they blossome fresh and faire,
And decke the world with their rich pompous
    showes;
Yet no man for them taketh paines or care,
Yet no man to them can his carefull paines compare.

XVI.

"The lilly, lady of the flowring field,   145
The flowre-de-luce, her lovely paramoure,
Bid thee to them thy fruitlesse labors yield,
And soone leave off this toylsome weary stoure:

Loe! loe; how brave she decks her bounteous boure,
With silkin curtens, and gold coverletts,   150
Therein to shrowd her sumptuous belamoure!
Yet neither spinnes nor cards, ne cares nor fretts,
But to her mother Nature all her care she letts.

XVII.

" Why then doest thou, O man, that of them all
Art lord, and eke of nature soveraine,   155
Wilfully make thyselfe a wretched thrall,
And waste thy ioyous howres in needelesse paine,
Seeking for daunger and adventures vaine?
What bootes it al to have, and nothing use?
Who shall him rew that swimming in the maine 160
Will die for thrist, and water doth refuse?
Refuse such fruitlesse toile, and present pleasures
     chuse."

XVIII.

By this she had him lulled fast asleepe,
That of no worldly thing he care did take:
Then she with liquors strong his eies did steepe, 165
That nothing should him hastily awake.
So she him lefte, and did herselfe betake
Unto her boat again, with which she clefte
The slouthfull wave of that great griesy lake:
Soone shee that Island far behind her lefte,   170
And now is come to that same place where first she
     wefte.

[Sir Guyon, having escaped from the temptations
of Idle Pleasure, next encounters Mammon, or the
temptations of Avarice.]

BOOK II

CANTO VII.

Guyon findes Mamon in a delve
*   sunning his threasure hore ;*
Is by him tempted, and led downe
*   To see his secret store.*

II.

So Guyon, having lost his trustie guyde,   10
Late left beyond that Ydle Lake, proceedes
Yet on his way, of none accompanyde;
And evermore himselfe with comfort feedes
Of his own vertues and praise-worthie deedes.
So, long he yode, yet no adventure found,   15
Which Fame of her shrill trompet worthy reedes:
For still he traveild through wide wastfull ground,
That nought but desert wildernesse shewed all around.

III.

At last he came unto a gloomy glade,   19
Cover'd with boughes and shrubs from heavens light,
Whereas he sitting found in secret shade
An uncouth, salvage, and uncivile wight,
Of griesly hew and fowle ill-favour'd sight;
His face with smoke was tand, and eies were bleard,
His head and beard with sout were ill bedight,   25
His cole-blacke hands did seeme to have ben seard
In smythes fire-spitting forge, and nayles like clawes
          appeard.

IV.

His yron cote, all overgrowne with rust,
Was underneath enveloped with gold;
Whose glistering glosse darkened with filthy dust, 30
Well yet appeared to have beene of old

A worke of rich entayle and curious mould,
Woven with antickes and wyld ymagery;
And in his lap a masse of coyne he told,
And turned upside downe, to feede his eye　　35
And covetous desire with his huge threasury.

V.

And round about him lay on every side
Great heapes of gold that never could be spent;
Of which some were rude owre, not purifide
Of Mulcibers devouring element;　　40
Some others were new driven, and distent
Into great Ingowes and to wedges square;
Some in round plates withouten moniment;
But most were stampt, and in their metal bare
The ántique shapes of kings and kesars stroung and
　　rare.　　45

VI.

Soone as he Guyon saw, in great affright
And haste he rose for to remove aside
Those pretious hils from straungers envious sight,
And downe them poured through an hole full wide
Into the hollow earth, them there to hide;　　50
But Guyon, lightly to him leaping, stayd
His hand that trembled as one terrifyde;
And though himselfe were at the sight dismayd,
Yet him perforce restraynd, and to him doubtfull
　　sayd:

VII.

"What art thou, Man, (if man at all thou art,)　　55
That here in desert hast thine habitaunce,
And these rich hils of welth doest hide apart
From the worldes eye, and from her right usaunce?"

Thereat, with staring eyes fixed askaunce,
In great disdaine he answerd: "Hardy Elfe,   60
That darest vew my direfull countenaunce!
I read thee rash and heedlesse of thy selfe,
To trouble my still seate, and heapes of pretious pelfe.

VIII.

"God of the world and worldlings I me call,
Great Mammon, greatest god below the skye,   65
That of my plenty poure out unto all,
And unto none my graces do envýe:
Riches, renowme, and principality,
Honour, estate, and all this worldës good,
For which men swinck and sweat incessantly,   70
Fro me do flow into an ample flood,
And in the hollow earth have their eternall brood.

IX.

"Wherefore, if me thou deigne to serve and sew,
At thy commaund lo! all these mountaines bee;
Or if to thy great mind, or greedy vew,   75
All these may not suffise, there shall to thee
Ten times so much be nombred francke and free."
"Mammon," said he, "thy godheads vaunt is vaine,
And idle offers of thy golden fee;
To them that covet such eye-glutting gaine   80
Proffer thy giftes, and fitter servaunte entertaine.

X.

"Me ill besits, that in derdoing armes
And honours suit my vowed daies do spend,
Unto thy bounteous baytes, and pleasing charmes,
With which weake men thou witchest, to attend;   85

Regard of worldly mucke doth fowly blend,
And low abase the high heroicke spright,
That ioyes for crownes and kingdomes to contend;
Faire shields, gay steedes, bright armes, be my
delight;
Those be the riches fit for an advent'rous knight." 90

XI.

" Vaine glorious Elfe," saide he, " doest not thou
weet,
That money can thy wantes at will supply?
Shields, steeds, and armes, and all things for thee
meet,
It can purvay in twinckling of an eye;
And crownes and kingdomes to thee multiply. 95
Doe not I kings create, and throw the crowne
Sometimes to him that low in dust doth ly,
And him that raignd into his rowme thrust downe,
And whom I lust do heape with glory and renowne?"

XII.

" All otherwise," saide he, " I riches read, 100
And deeme them roote of all disquietnesse;
First got with guile, and then preserv'd with dread,
And after spent with pride and lavishnesse,
Leaving behind them griefe and heavinesse:
Infinite mischiefes of them doe arize; 105
Strife and debate, bloodshed and bitternesse,
Outrageous wrong and hellish covetize,
That noble heart, in great dishonour, doth despize.

XIII.

" Ne thine be Kingdomes, ne the scepters thine;
But realmes and rules thou doest both confound, 110
And loyall truth to treason doest incline:
Witnesse the guiltlesse blood pourd oft on ground;

The crowned often slaine; the slayer cround;
The sacred diademe in peeces rent,
And purple robe gored with many a wound,   115
Castles surprizd, great cities sackt and brent:
So mak'st thou kings, and gaynest wrongfull govern-
      ment!

XIV.

"Long were to tell the troublous stormes that tosse
The private state, and make the life unsweet:
Who swelling sayles in Caspian sea doth crosse,   120
And in frayle wood on Adrian gulf doth fleet,
Doth not, I weene, so many evils meet."
Then Mammon wexing wroth: "And why then,"
      sayd,
"Are mortall men so fond and undiscreet
So evill thing to seeke unto their ayd;   125
And having not, complaine, and having it, upbrayd?"

.   .   .   .

XIX.

"Me list not," said the Elfin Knight, "receave
Thing offred, till I know it well be gott;
Ne wote I but thou didst these goods bereave
From rightfull owner by unrighteous lott,   175
Or that blood-guiltinesse or guile them blott."
"Perdy," quoth he, "yet never eie did vew,
Ne tong did tell, ne hand these handled not;
But safe I have them kept in secret mew
From hevens sight and powre of al which them pour-
      sew."
                                    180

XX.

"What secret place," quoth he, "can safely hold
So huge a masse, and hide from heavens eie?
Or where hast thou thy wonne, that so much gold
Thou canst preserve from wrong and robbery?"   184

"Come thou," quoth he, "and see." So by and by
Through that thick covert he him led, and fownd
A darksome way, which no man could descry,
That deep descended through the hollow grownd,
And was with dread and horror compassed arownd.

XXI.

At length they came into a larger space, 190
That strecht itselfe into an ample playne;
Through which a beaten broad high way did trace
That streight did lead to Plutoes griesly rayne:
By that wayes side there sate infernall Payne,
And fast beside him sat tumultuous Strife; 195
The one in hand an yron whip did strayne,
The other brandished a bloody knife;
And both did gnash their teeth, and both did threten
    Life.

XXII.

On th'other side in one consórt there sate
Cruell Revenge, and rancorous Despight, 200
Disloyall Treason, and hart-burning Hate;
But gnawing Gealosy, out of their sight
Sitting alone, his bitter lips did bight;
And trembling Feare still to and fro did fly, 204
And found no place wher safe he shroud him might:
Lamenting Sorrow did in darknes lye;
And Shame his ugly face did hide from living eye.

XXIII.

And over them sad Horror with grim hew
Did alwaies sore, beating his yron wings;
And after him owles and night-ravens flew, 210
The hatefull messengers of heavy things,

Of death and dolor telling sad tidings;
Whiles sad Celeno, sitting on a clifte,
A song of bale and bitter sorrow sings,
That hart of flint a sonder could have rifte; 215
Which having ended, after him she flyeth swifte.

XXIV.

All these before the gates of Pluto lay;
By whom they passing spake unto them nought;
But th' Elfin Knight with wonder all the way
Did feed his eyes, and fild his inner thought. 220
At last him to a litle dore he brought,
That to the gate of hell, which gaped wide,
Was next a liogning, ne them parted ought:
Betwixt them both was but a litle stride, 224
That did the house of Richesse from hell-mouth divide.

XXV.

Before the dore sat selfe-consuming Care,
Day and night keeping wary watch and ward,
For feare least Force or Fraud should unaware
Breake in, and spoile the treasure there in gard:
Ne would he suffer Sleepe once thether-ward 230
Approch, albe his drowsy den were next;
For next to Death is Sleepe to be compard;
Therefore his house is unto his annext:
Here Sleepe, there Richesse, and Hel-gate them both
      betwext.

XXVI.

So soone as Mammon there arrivd, the dore 235
To him did open, and affoorded way:
Him followed eke Sir Guyon evermore;
Ne darknesse him, ne daunger might dismay.

Soone as he entred was, the dore streight way
Did shutt, and from behind it forth there lept   240
An ugly feend, more fowle than dismall day;
The which with monstrous stalke behind him stept,
And ever as he went dew watch upon him kept.

.   .   .   .

XXVIII.

That houses forme within was rude and strong,
Lyke an huge cave hewne out of rocky clifte,
From whose rough vaut the ragged breaches hong
Embost with massy gold of glorious guifte,   265
And with rich metall loaded every rifte,
That heavy ruine they did seeme to threatt;
And over them Arachne high did lifte
Her cunning web, and spred her subtile nett,
Enwrapped in fowle smoke and clouds more black then
        iett.   270

XXIX.

Both roofe, and floore, and walls, were all of gold,
But overgrown with dust and old decay,
And hid in darknes, that none could behold
The hew thereof: for vew of cherefull day
Did never in that house it selfe display,   275
But a faint shadow of uncertein light;
Such as a lamp, whose life does fade away;
Or as the moone, cloathed with clowdy night,
Does shew to him that walks in feare, and sad affright.

XXX.

In all that rowme was nothing to be seene   280
But huge great yron chests, and coffers strong,
All bard with double bends, that none could weene
Them to efforce by violence or wrong;

On every side they placed were along.
But all the grownd with sculs was scattered   285
And dead mens bones, which round about were flong;
Whose lives, it seemed, whilome there were shed,
And their vile carcases left unburied.

XXXI.

They forward passe; ne Guyon yet spoke word,
Till that they came unto an yron dore,   290
Which to them opened of his owne accord,
And shewd of richesse such exceeding store,
As eie of man did never see before,
Ne ever could within one place be fownd,   294
Though all the wealth which is, or was of yore,
Could gathered be through all the world arownd,
And that above were added to that under grownd.

XXXII.

The charge thereof unto a covetous spright
Commaunded was, who thereby did attend,
And warily awaited day and night,   300
From other covetous feends it to defend,
Who it to rob and ransacke did intend.
Then Mammon, turning to that warriour, said:
"Loe, here the worldës blis! loe, here the end,
To which al men doe ayme, rich to be made!   305
Such grace now to be happy is before thee laid."

XXXIII.

"Certes," said he, "I n' ill thine offred grace,
Ne to be made so happy doe intend!
Another blis before mine eyes I place,
Another happincs, another end.   310

To them that list, these base regardes I lend:
But I in armes, and in atchievements brave,
Do rather choose my flitting houres to spend,
And to be lord of those that riches have,
Then them to have myselfe, and be their servile
     sclave."   315

XXXIV.

Thereat the Feend his gnashing teeth did grate,
And griev'd, so long to lacke his greedie pray;
For well he weened that so glorious bayte
Would tempt his guest to take thereof assay:
Had he so doen, he had him snatcht away   320
More light then culver in the faulcons fist:
Eternall God thee save from such decay!
But, whenas Mammon saw his purpose mist,
Him to entrap unwares another way he wist.

[The poet then goes on to tell of the further temptations to which Guyon is subjected, and of how the
Knight withstands them. At length, after three days
have passed, according to men's reckoning, Guyon
begs to be taken back into the world, and Mammon,
though loth, is constrained to comply with the request.
But as soon as Guyon reaches the vital air he swoons,
and lies as one dead. The next *Canto* (which ends
with the Knight's recovery and re-union with the
Palmer, his appointed guide,) begins with the following stanzas on the care of God for man, thus leading
us to anticipate the happy ending.]

(From *Canto* VIII.)

I.

And is there care in heaven? And is there love
In heavenly spirits to these creatures bace,
That may compassion of their evils move?
There is: else much more wretched were the cace

Of men then beasts. But O! th' exceeding grace
Of highest God that loves his creatures so,   6
And all his workes with mercy doth embrace,
That blessed Angels he sends to and fro,
To serve to wicked man, to serve his wicked foe.

II.

How oft do they their silver bowers leave,   10
To come to succour us that **succour** want!
How oft do they with golden pineons cleave
The flitting skyes, like flying Pursuivant,
Against fowle feendes to ayd us militant!
They for us fight, they watch and dewly ward,   15
And their bright sqadrons round about us plant;
And all for love, and nothing for reward.
O! why should hevenly God to men have such regard?

THE COURTIER

(From *Mother Hubberd's Tale*, 1591)

Most miserable man, whom wicked fate
Hath brought to court, to sue for had ywist,
That few have found, and manie one hath mist!
Full little knowest thou that hast not tride,   895
What hell it is in suing long to bide:
To loose good dayes, that might be better spent;
To wast long nights in pensive discontent;
To speed to day, to be put back tomorrow;   899
To feed on hope, to pine with feare and sorrow;
To have thy Princes grace, yet want her Peeres;
To have thy asking, yet waite manie yeeres;
To fret thy soule with crosses and with cares;
To eate thy heart through comfortlesse dispaires;

To fawne, to crowche, to waite, to ride, to ronne,
To spend, to give, to want, to be undonne.   906
Unhappie wight, borne to desastrous end,
That doth his life in so long tendance spend!
Who ever leaves sweete home, where meane estate
In safe assurance, without strife or hate,   910
Findes all things needfull for contentment meeke,
And will to court for shadowes vaine to seeke,
Or hope to gaine, himselfe will one daie crie,
That curse God send unto mine enemie!

SONNET XL.

(From *Amoretti*, 1595)

Mark when she smiles with amiable cheare,
And tell me whereto can ye lyken it;
When on each eyelid sweetly doe appeare
An hundred Graces as in shade to sit.
Lykest it seemeth, in my simple wit,   5
Unto the fayre sunshine in somers day;
That, when a dreadfull storm away is flit,
Thrugh the broad world doth spred his goodly ray:
At sight whereof, each bird that sits on spray,
And every beast that to his den was fled,   10
Comes forth afresh out of their late dismay,
And to thy light lift up their drouping hed.
    So my storme-beaten hart likewise is cheared
    With that sunshine, when cloudy looks are cleared.

SONNET LXXV.

(From the same)

One day I wrote her name upon the strand;
But came the waves and washed it away:
Agayne, I wrote it with a second hand;
And came the tyde, and made my paynes his pray.

" Vayne man," sayd she, " that doest in vayne assay
  A mortall thing so to immortalize;   6
For I myselve shall lyke to this decay,
And eek my name bee wyped out lykewize."
" Not so " (quod I); " let baser things devize
To dy in dust, but you shall live by fame: 10
My verse your vertues rare shall eternize,
And in the hevens wryte your glorious name;
    Where, when as death shall all the world subdew,
    Our love shall live, and later life renew."

ELIZABETHAN SONGS AND LYRICS

John Lyly

1553–1606

APELLES' SONG

(From *Alexander and Campaspe*, 1584 ; acted 1581)

Cupid and my Campaspe played
At cards for kisses,—Cupid paid ;
He stakes his quiver, bow and arrows,
His mother's doves, and team of sparrows :
Loses them too ; then down he throws   5
The coral of his lip, the rose
Growing on 's cheek (but none knows how) ;
With these the crystal of his brow,
And then the dimple of his chin :
All these did my Campaspe win.   10
At last he set her both his eyes ;
She won, and Cupid blind did rise.
O Love, has she done this to thee ?
What shall, alas ! become of me ?

Robert Greene

1560–1592

CONTENT

(From *Farewell to Folly*, 1591)

Sweet are the thoughts that savour of content,
    The quiet mind is richer than a crown,

Sweet are the nights in careless slumber spent,
  The poor estate scorns fortune's angry frown:
Such sweet content, such minds, such sleep, such bliss,
Beggars enjoy, when princes oft do miss,   6

The homely house that harbours quiet rest,
  The cottage that affords no pride nor care,
The mean that grees with country music best,
  The sweet consort of mirth and modest fare,   10
Obscurèd life sets down a type of bliss:
A mind content both crown and kingdom is.

Christopher Marlowe

1564–1593

THE PASSIONATE SHEPHERD TO HIS LOVE

(In *The Passionate Pilgrim*, 1599, enlarged form in *England's Helicon*, 1600)

Come live with me, and be my love,
And we will all the pleasures prove,
That valleys, groves, hills and fields,
Woods or steepy mountains yields.

And we will sit upon the rocks,   5
Seeing the shepherds feed their flocks
By shallow rivers, to whose falls
Melodious birds sing madrigals.

And I will make thee beds of roses,
And a thousand fragrant posies,   10
A cap of flowers and a kirtle
Embroidered all with leaves of myrtle;

A gown made of the finest wool
Which from our pretty lambs we pull;

Fair-lined slippers for the cold, 15
With buckles of the purest gold;

A belt of straw and ivy-buds,
With coral clasps and amber studs:
An if these pictures may thee move,
Come live with me and be my love. 20

The shepherd swains shall dance and sing
For thy delight each May morning:
If these delights thy mind may move,
Then live with me and be my love.

Thomas Dekker

Cir. 1570—*cir.* 1637

O SWEET CONTENT

(From *The Patient Grissell*, acted 1599)

Art thou poor, yet hast thou golden slumbers?
      O sweet content!
Art thou rich, yet is thy mind perplexèd?
      O punishment!
Dost thou laugh to see how fools are vexèd 5
To add to golden numbers, golden numbers?
O sweet content! O sweet O sweet content!
  Work apace, apace, apace, apace;
Honest labor bears a lovely face;
Then hey nonny nonny, hey nonny nonny! 10

Canst drink the waters of the crispèd spring?
      O sweet content!
Swim'st thou in wealth, yet sink'st in thine own tears?
      O punishment!
Then he that patiently want's burden bears 15

No burden bears, but is a king, a king!
O sweet content! O sweet O sweet content!
  Work apace, apace, apace, apace;
Honest labor bears a lovely face;
Then hey nonny nonny, hey nonny nonny!   20

Thomas Heywood

1581 (?)–1640 (?)

GOOD MORROW

(From *The Rape of Lucrece*, 1608 (printed), acted *cir.* 1605)

Pack, clouds, away, and welcome day,
  With night we banish sorrow;
Sweet air blow soft, mount lark aloft,
  To give my love good-morrow.
Wings from the wind to please her mind,   5
  Notes from the lark I'll borrow;
Bird prune thy wing, nightingale sing,
    To give my love good-morrow,
      To give my love good-morrow,
      Notes from them both I'll borrow.   10

Wake from thy rest, robin-redbreast,
  Sing birds in every furrow;
And from each bill let music shrill
  Give my fair love good-morrow.
Blackbird and thrush in every bush,   15
  Stare, linnet, and cock-sparrow,
You pretty elves, amongst yourselves
  Sing my fair love good-morrow;
    To give my love good-morrow
    Sing birds in every furrow.   20

Thomas Campion

D. 1619 (?)

TO LESBIA

(In Rosseter's *Book of Airs*, 1601)

My sweetest Lesbia, let us live and love,
And though the sager sort our deeds reprove
Let us not weigh them. Heaven's great lamps
 do dive
Into their west, and straight again revive;
5 But soon as once set is our litle light,
Then must we sleep one ever-during night.

If all would lead their lives in love like me,
Then bloody swords and armour should not be;
No drum nor trumpet peaceful sleeps should
 move,
10 Unless alarm came from the Camp of Love:
But fools do live and waste their little light,
And seek with pain their ever-during night.

When timely death my life and fortunes ends,
Let not my hearse be vext with mourning
 friends;
15 But let all lovers, rich in triumph, come
And with sweet pastimes grace my happy tomb;
And, Lesbia, close up thou my little light
And crown with love my ever-during night.

THE ARMOUR OF INNOCENCE

(From the same)

The man of life upright,
 Whose guiltless heart is free

From all dishonest deeds,
  Or thought of vanity;

5 The man whose silent days
   In harmless joys are spent,
Whom hopes cannot delude
  Nor sorrow discontent:

That man needs neither towers
10   Nor armour for defence,
Nor secret vaults to fly
  From thunder's violence:

He only can behold
  With unaffrighted eyes
15 The horrors of the deep
  And terrors of the skies.

Thus scorning all the cares
  That fate or fortune brings,
He makes the heaven his book;
20   His wisdom heavenly things;

Good thoughts his only friends,
  His wealth a well-spent age,
The earth his sober inn
  And quiet pilgrimage.

FORTUNATI NIMIUM

Jack and Joan, they think no ill,
But loving live, and merry still;
Do their week-day's work, and pray
Devoutly on the holy-day:

5 Skip and trip it on the green,
And help to choose the Summer Queen;
Lash out at a country feast
Their silver penny with the best.

Well can they judge of nappy ale,
10 And tell at large a winter tale;
Climb up to the apple loft,
And turn the crabs till they be soft.
Tib is all the father's joy,
And little Tom the mother's boy:—
15 All their pleasure is, Content,
And care, to pay their yearly rent.

Joan can call by name her cows
And deck her windows with green boughs;
She can wreaths and tutties make,
20 And trim with plums a bridal cake.
Jack knows what brings gain or loss,
And his long flail can stoutly toss:
Makes the hedge which others break,
And ever thinks what he doth speak.

25 Now, you courtly dames and knights,
That study only strange delights,
Though you scorn the homespun gray,
And revel in your rich array;
Though your tongues dissemble deep
30 And can your heads from danger keep;
Yet, for all your pomp and train,
Securer lives the silly swain!

John Fletcher

1579-1625

SONG OF THE PRIEST OF PAN

(From *The Faithful Shepherdess*, Act II. sc. 1, acted 1610)

Shepherds all, and maidens fair
Fold your flocks up, for the air
'Gins to thicken, and the sun
Already his great course hath run.
5 See the dew-drops how they kiss
Every little flower that is;
Hanging on their velvet heads,
Like a rope of crystal beads;
See the heavy clouds low falling,
10 And bright Hesperus down calling
The dead night from under ground;
At whose rising mists unsound,
Damps and vapours fly apace,
Hovering o'er the wanton face
15 Of these pastures, where they come
Striking dead both bud and bloom:
Therefore from such danger lock
Every one his lovèd flock;
And let your dogs lie loose without,
20 Lest the wolf come as a scout
From the mountain, and, ere day,
Bear a lamb or kid away;
Or the crafty thievish fox
Break upon your simple flocks.
25 To secure yourselves from these
Be not too secure in ease;
Let one eye his watches peep
While the other eye doth sleep;
So you shall good shepherds prove,

30 And for ever hold the love
   Of our great god. Sweetest slumbers,
   And soft silence, fall in numbers
   On your eyelids! So, farewell!
   Thus I end my evening's knell.

SONG TO PAN

(From the same, Act. V. sc. 5.)

   All ye woods, and trees, and bowers,
   All ye virtues and ye powers
   That inhabit in the lakes,
   In the pleasant springs or brakes,
5   Move your feet
        To our sound,
     Whilst we greet
        All this ground
   With his honour and his name
10 That defends our flocks from blame.

   He is great, and he is just,
   He is ever good, and must
   Thus be honoured. Daffodillies,
   Roses, pinks, and lovèd lilies,
15   Let us fling
     Whilst we sing
     Ever holy,
     Ever holy,
   Ever honoured, ever young!
20 Thus great Pan is ever sung!

Francis Beaumont
1586 (?)–1616

ON THE LIFE OF MAN

(From *Poems*, 1640)

Like to the falling of a star,
Or as the flights of eagles are,
Or like the fresh spring's gaudy hue,
Or silver drops of morning dew,
5 Or like the wind that chafes the flood,
Or bubbles which on water stood;
Even such is man, whose borrowed light
Is straight called in and paid to-night.
The wind blows out, the bubble dies,
10 The spring entombed in autumn lies,
The dew's dried up, the star is shot,
The flight is past, and man forgot.

ON THE TOMBS IN WESTMINSTER ABBEY

(From *Poems*, 1653)

Mortality, behold and fear!
What a change of flesh is here!
Think how many royal bones
Sleep within this heap of stones;
5 Here they lie, had realms and lands,
Who now want strength to stir their hands;
Where from their pulpits sealed with dust
They preach, " In greatness is no trust."
Here's an acre sown indeed
10 With the richest, royall'st seed
That the earth did e'er suck in
Since the first man died for sin:
Here the bones of birth have cried,
" Though gods they were, as men they died!"

15 Here are sands, ignoble things,
    Dropt from the ruined sides of kings:
    Here's a world of pomp and state,
    Buried in dust, once dead by fate.

Sir Henry Wotton

1568–1639

THE CHARACTER OF A HAPPY LIFE

(Written *cir.* 1614)

How happy is he born and taught
    That serveth not another's will;
Whose armour is his honest thought,
    And simple truth his utmost skill;

5 Whose passions not his masters are;
    Whose soul is still prepared for death,
Untied unto the world by care
    Of public fame or private breath;

Who envies none that chance doth raise,
10   Nor vice; who never understood
How deepest wounds are given by praise;
    Nor rules of state, but rules of good;

Who hath his life from rumours freed;
    Whose conscience is his strong retreat;
15 Whose state can neither flatterers feed,
    Nor ruin make oppressors great;

Who God doth late and early pray
    More of his grace than gifts to lend;
And entertains the harmless day
20   With a religious book or friend.

This man is freed from servile bands
　Of hope to rise or fear to fall;
Lord of himself, though not of lands,
　And having nothing, yet hath all.

Sir Walter Raleigh (?)

1552–1618

THE NYMPH'S REPLY TO THE PASSIONATE SHEPHERD

(From *England's Helicon*, 1600)

If all the world and Love were young,
And truth in every shepherd's tongue,
These pleasures might my passion move,
To live with thee, and be thy love.

5 But time drives flocks from field to fold,
When rivers rage and rocks grow cold;
And Philomel becometh dumb,
The rest complains of cares to come.

The flowers do fade, and wanton fields
10 To wayward winter reckoning yields;
A honey tongue, a heart of gall,
Is fancies spring but sorrows fall.

Thy gowns, thy shoes, thy beds of roses,
Thy cap, thy kirtle, and thy posies,
15 Soon break, soon wither, soon forgotten,
In folly ripe, in reason rotten.

Thy belt of straw and ivy-buds,
Thy coral clasps and amber studs,
All these in me no means can move,
20 To come to thee, and be thy love.

> But could youth last, could love still breed,
> Had joys no date, had age no need;
> Then those delights my mind might move
> To live with thee and be thy love.

Ben Jonson

1573–1637

TO THE MEMORY OF MY BELOVED MASTER WILLIAM SHAKS-PEARE, AND WHAT HE HATH LEFT US

(From First Folio edition of Shakespeare, 1623)

> To draw no envy, Shakspeare, on thy name,
> Am I thus ample to thy book and fame;
> While I confess thy writings to be such,
> As neither Man nor Muse can praise too much.
> 5 'Tis true, and all men's suffrage. But these ways
> Were not the paths I meant unto thy praise;
> For silliest ignorance on these may light,
> Which, when it sounds at best, but echoes right;
> Or blind affection, which doth ne'er advance
> 10 The truth, but gropes, and urgeth all by chance;
> Or crafty malice might pretend this praise,
> And think to ruin where it seemed to raise.
>
> .   .   .   .
>
> .   .   .   .
>
> 15 But thou art proof against them and, indeed,
> Above the ill fortune of them, or the need.
> I therefore will begin: Soul of the age!
> The applause, delight, the wonder of our stage!
> My SHAKSPEARE, rise! I will not lodge thee by
> 20 Chaucer, or Spenser, or bid Beaumont lie
> A little further, to make thee a room:
> Thou art a monument without a tomb,

Thou art alive still while thy book doth live,
And we have wits to read, and praise to give.
25 That I not mix thee so my brain excuses,—
I mean with great but disproportioned Muses;
For if I thought my judgment were of years,
I should commit thee surely with thy peers,
And tell how far thou didst our Lyly outshine,
30 Or sporting Kyd, or Marlowe's mighty line.
And though thou hadst small Latin and less
    Greek,
From thence to honour thee I would not seek
For names, but call forth thund'ring Æschylus,
Euripides, and Sophocles to us,
35 Pacuvius, Accius, him of Cordova dead,
To life again, to hear thy buskin tread,
And shake a stage; or when thy socks were on,
Leave thee alone for a comparison
Of all that insolent Greece or haughty Rome
40 Sent forth, or since did from their ashes come.
Triumph, my Britain, thou hast one to show,
To whom all scenes of Europe homage owe.
He was not of an age, but for all time!
And all the Muses still were in their prime,
45 When, like Apollo, he came forth to warm
Our ears, or like a Mercury to charm!
Nature herself was proud of his designs,
And joyed to wear the dressing of his lines,
Which were so richly spun, and woven so fit,
50 As, since, she will vouchsafe no other wit.
The merry Greek, tart Aristophanes,
Neat Terence, witty Plautus, now not please;
But antiquated and deserted lie,
As they were not of Nature's family.
55 Yet must I not give Nature all; thy Art,
My gentle Shakspeare, must enjoy a part.
For though the poet's matter nature be,
His art doth give the fashion; and that he

Who casts to write a living line, must sweat
60 (Such as thine are) and strike the second heat
Upon the Muses' anvil, turn the same,
And himself with it, that he thinks to frame;
Or for the laurel he may gain to scorn;
For a good poet's made, as well as born.
65 And such wert thou! Look, how the father's
          face
Lives in his issue, even so the race
Of Shakspeare's mind and manners brightly
          shines
In his well turnèd and true filèd lines,
In each of which he seems to shake a lance,
70 As brandished at the eyes of ignorance.
Sweet Swan of Avon! what a sight it were
To see thee in our waters yet appear,
And make those flights upon the banks of
          Thames,
That so did take Eliza and our James!
75 But stay, I see thee in the hemisphere
Advanced, and made a constellation there!
Shine forth, thou Star of Poets, and with rage
Or influence chide or cheer the drooping stage,
Which, since thy flight from hence, hath mourned
          like night,
80 And despairs day but for thy volume's light.

SIMPLEX MUNDITIIS

(From *Epicœne ; or, The Silent Woman*, Act I. sc. 1.,
1609–10)

Still to be neat, still to be drest,
As you were going to a feast;
Still to be powdered, still perfumed:
Lady, it is to be presumed,
5 Though art's hid causes are not found,
All is not sweet, all is not sound.

Give me a look, give me a face,
That makes simplicity a grace;
Robes loosely flowing, hair as free:
10 Such sweet neglect more taketh me
Than all the adulteries of art;
They strike mine eyes, but not my heart.

THE TRIUMPH OF CHARIS

(From "A Celebration of Charis" in *Underwoods*, 1616)

See the chariot at hand here of Love,
  Wherein my Lady rideth!
Each that draws is a swan or a dove,
  And well the car Love guideth.
5 As she goes, all hearts do duty
    Unto her beauty;
And enamoured do wish, so they might
    But enjoy such a sight,
That they still were to run by her side,
10 Through swords, through seas, wither she would
          ride.

Do but look on her eyes, they do light
  All that Love's world compriseth!
Do but look on her hair, it is bright
  As Love's star when it riseth!
15 Do but mark, her forehead's smoother
    Than words that soothe her;
And from her arched brows, such a grace
    Sheds itself through the face,
As alone there triumphs to the life
20   All the gain, all the good of the elements' strife.

Have you seen but a bright lily grow
  Before rude hands have touched it?
Have you marked but the fall o' the snow
  Before the soil hath smutched it?

25 Have you felt the wool of beaver?
　　Or swan's down ever?
　Or have smelt o' the bud o' the briar?
　　Or the nard in the fire?
　Or have tasted the bag of the bee?
30 　.O so white,—O so soft,—O so sweet is she!

SONG.—TO CYNTHIA

(From *Cynthia's Revels*, Act V. sc. 3, 1600)

Queen and huntress, chaste and fair,
Now the sun is laid to sleep;
Seated in thy silver chair,
State in wonted manner keep:
5 　Hesperus entreats thy light,
　Goddess. excellently bright.

Earth, let not thy envious shade
Dare itself to interpose;
Cynthia's shining orb was made
10 Heaven to clear, when day did close;
　Bless us then with wished sight,
　Goddess excellently bright.

Lay thy bow of pearl apart,
And thy crystal-shining quiver;
15 Give unto the flying hart
Space to breathe, how short soever:
　Thou that makest a day of night,
　Goddess excellently bright.

William Shakespeare

1564–1616

SILVIA

(From *The Two Gentlemen of Verona*, IV. 2, 1598; acted about 1592–93)

Who is Silvia? what is she,
    That all our swains commend her?
Holy, fair, and wise is she,
    The heaven such grace did lend her,
5 That she might admired be.

Is she kind as she is fair?
    For beauty lives with kindness:
Love doth to her eyes repair,
    To help him of his blindness;
10 And, being help'd, inhabits there.

Then to Silvia let us sing,
    That Silvia is excelling:
She excels each mortal thing,
    Upon the dull earth dwelling:
15 To her let us garlands bring.

UNDER THE GREENWOOD TREE

(From *As You Like It*, II. 5, acted 1599)

Under the greenwood tree
Who loves to lie with me,
And turn his merry note
Unto the sweet bird's throat,
5   Come hither, come hither, come hither:
    Here shall he see
    No enemy
But winter and rough weather.

Who doth ambition shun
10   And love to live i' the sun,
Seeking the food he eats
And pleas'd with what he gets,
Come hither, come hither, come hither:
Here shall he see
15   No enemy
But winter and rough weather.

O MISTRESS MINE, WHERE ARE YOU ROAMING

(From Twelfth Night, II. 3, about 1601)

O mistress mine, where are you roaming?
O, stay and hear; your true love's coming,
That can sing both high and low:
Trip no further, pretty sweeting;
5 Journeys end in lovers' meeting,
Every wise man's son doth know.

What is love? 'Tis not hereafter:
Present mirth hath present laughter;
What's to come is still unsure:
10 In delay there lies no plenty;
Then come kiss me, sweet and twenty,
Youth's a stuff will not endure.

TAKE, OH, TAKE THOSE LIPS AWAY

(From Measure for Measure, IV. 1, 1603)

Take, oh take those lips away,
That so sweetly were forsworn;
And those eyes, the break of day,
Lights that do mislead the morn;
5 But my kisses bring again,
bring again.
Seals of love, but seal'd in vain,
seal'd in vain.

HARK, HARK, THE LARK

(From *Cymbeline*, II. 3, 1609)

Hark! hark! the lark at heaven's gate sings,
    And Phœbus 'gins arise,
His steeds to water at those springs
    On chalic'd flowers that lies;
And winking Mary-buds begin to ope their golden eyes;
With everything that pretty is—My lady sweet, arise:
    Arise, arise.

DIRGE

(From the same, IV. 2)

Fear no more the heat of the sun
    Nor the furious winter's rages;
Thou thy worldly task hast done,
    Home art gone, and ta'en thy wages:
Golden lads and girls all must,   5
As chimney-sweepers, come to dust.

Fear no more the frown o' the great,
    Thou art past the tyrants' stroke;
Care no more to clothe, and eat;
    To thee the reed is as the oak: 10
The sceptre, learning, physic, must
All follow this, and come to dust.

Fear no more the light'ning flash;
    Nor the all-dreaded thunder-stone;
Fear not slander, censure rash;   15
    Thou hast finished joy and moan:
All lovers young, all lovers must
Consign to thee, and come to dust.

No exorciser harm thee!
Nor no witchcraft charm thee!   20
Ghost unlaid forbear thee!
Nothing ill come near thee!
Quiet consummation have;
And renowned be thy grave!

A SEA DIRGE

(From The Tempest, I. 2, 1610)

Full fathom five thy father lies;
 Of his bones are coral made;
Those are pearls that were his eyes:
 Nothing of him that doth fade,
 But doth suffer a sea-change   5
 Into something rich and strange.
Sea-nymphs hourly ring his knell:
      Ding-dong.
Hark! now I hear them—Ding-dong bell.

ARIEL'S SONG

(From the same, Act V. sc. 1)

Where the bee sucks, there suck I:
In a cowslip's bell I lie;
There I couch when owls do cry.
On the bat's back I do fly
After summer merrily.   5
Merrily, merrily shall I live now
Under the blossom that hangs on the bough.

ELIZABETHAN SONNETS

Sir Philip Sidney

1554–1586

SONNET XXXI

(From *Astrophel and Stella, cir.* 1591)

With how sad steps, O Moon, thou climb'st the skies!
How silently, and with how wan a face!
What, may it be that even in heavenly place
That busy archer his sharp arrows tries?
Sure, if that long-with-love-acquainted eye   5
Can judge of love, thou feel'st a lover's case;
I read it in thy looks, thy languished grace,
To me, that feel the like, thy state descries.
Then ev'n of fellowship, O Moon, tell me,
Is constant love deemed there but want of wit?   10
Are beauties there as proud as here they be?
Do they above love to be loved, and yet
Those lovers scorn whom that love doth possess?
Do they call virtue there ungratefulness?

SONNET XXXIX—ON SLEEP

(From the same)

Come, Sleep! O Sleep, the certain knot of peace,
The baiting-place of wit, the balm of woe,
The poor man's wealth, the prisoner's release,
The indifferent judge between the high and low;

With shield of proof, shield me from out the prease 5
Of those fierce darts Despair at me doth throw:
O make in me those civil wars to cease;
I will good tribute pay, if thou do so.
Take thou of me smooth pillows, sweetest bed;
A chamber deaf of noise, and blind of light; 10
A rosy garland and a weary head:
And if these things, as being thine in right,
Move not thy heavy grace, thou shalt in me,
Livelier than elsewhere, Stella's image see.

Samuel Daniel

1562–1619

SONNET LI

(From *Delia, Containing certain Sonnets*, 1592)

Care-charmer Sleep, son of the sable Night,
Brother to Death, in silent darkness born:
Relieve my languish and restore the light;
With dark forgetting of my care, return,
And let the day be time enough to mourn 5
The shipwreck of my ill-adventured youth:
Let waking eyes suffice to wail their scorn
Without the torment of the night's untruth.
Cease dreams, the images of day desires,
To model forth the passions of the morrow; 10
Never let rising sun approve you liars,
To add more grief to aggravate my sorrow.
   Still let me sleep, embracing clouds in vain,
   And never wake to feel the day's disdain.

Michael Drayton

1563–1631

SONNET LXI

(From *Idea's Mirror*, 1594)

Since there's no help, come let us kiss and part,
Nay I have done, you get no more of me;
And I am glad, yea glad with all my heart,
That thus so cleanly I myself can free;
Shake hands forever, cancel all our vows,   5
And when we meet at any time again,
Be it not seen in either of our brows
That we one jot of former love retain.
Now at the last gasp of Love's latest breath,
When his pulse failing, Passion speechless lies,   10
When Faith is kneeling by his bed of death,
And Innocence is closing up his eyes:
  Now if thou would'st, when all have given him over,
  From death to life thou might'st him yet recover.

William Drummond

1585–1649

ON SLEEP

(From *Poems, Amorous, Funeral*, etc., 1616)

Sleep, Silence' child, sweet father of soft rest,
Prince whose approach peace to all mortals brings,
Indifferent host to shepherds and to kings,
Sole comforter of minds which are oppress'd;
Lo, by thy charming rod, all breathing things   5
Lie slumb'ring, with forgetfulness possess'd,
And yet o'er me to spread thy drowsy wings
Thou spar'st, alas! who cannot be thy guest.

Since I am thine, O come, but with that face
To inward light, which thou are wont to shew,   10
With feigned solace ease a true-felt woe;
Or if, deaf god, thou do deny that grace,
   Come as thou wilt, and what thou wilt bequeath,
   I long to kiss the image of my death.

William Shakespeare

SONNET XXIX

(From *Sonnets*, 1595–1605)

When, in disgrace with fortune and men's eyes,
I all alone beweep my outcast state,
And trouble deaf heaven with my bootless cries,
And look upon myself, and curse my fate,
Wishing me like to one more rich in hope,   5
Featured like him, like him with friends possess'd,
Desiring this man's art, and that man's scope,
With what I most enjoy contented least;
Yet in these thoughts myself almost despising,
Haply I think on thee, and then my state,   10
Like to the lark at break of day arising
From sullen earth, sings hymns at heaven's gate:
   For thy sweet love rememb'red such wealth brings
   That then I scorn to change my state with kings.

SONNET XXX

When to the sessions of sweet silent thought
I summon up remembrance of things past,
I sigh the lack of many a thing I sought,
And with old woes new wail my dear time's waste:
Then can I drown an eye, unused to flow,   5
For precious friends hid in death's dateless night,
And weep afresh love's long since cancell'd woe,
And moan the expense of many a vanish'd sight:

Then can I grieve at grievances foregone,
And heavily from woe to woe tell o'er   10
The sad account of fore-bemoaned moan,
Which I new pay as if not paid before.
   But if the while I think on thee, dear friend,
   All losses are restored and sorrows end.

SONNET XXXIII

Full many a glorious morning have I seen
Flatter the mountain tops with sovereign eye,
Kissing with golden face the meadows green,
Gilding pale streams with heavenly alchemy;
Anon permit the basest clouds to ride   5
With ugly rack on his celestial face,
And from the forlorn world his visage hide,
Stealing unseen to west with this disgrace:
Even so my sun one early morn did shine
With all-triumphant splendour on my brow;   10
But, out, alack! he was but one hour mine,
The region cloud hath mask'd him from me now.
   Yet him for this my love no whit disdaineth;
   Suns of the world may stain when heaven's sun
     staineth.

SONNET LX

Like as the waves make towards the pebbled shore,
So do our minutes hasten to their end;
Each changing place with that which goes before,
In sequent toil all forwards do contend.
Nativity, once in the main of light,   5
Crawls to maturity, wherewith being crown'd,
Crooked eclipses 'gainst his glory fight,
And Time that gave doth now his gift confound.
Time doth transfix the flourish set on youth
And delves the parallels in beauty's brow,   10

Feeds on the rarities of nature's truth,
And nothing stands but for his scythe to mow:
    And yet to times in hope my verse shall stand,
    Praising thy worth, despite his cruel hand.

SONNET LXXIII

That time of year thou may'st in me behold
When yellow leaves, or none, or few, do hang
Upon those boughs which shake against the cold,
Bare ruin'd choirs, where late the sweet birds sang.
In me thou see'st the twilight of such day   5
As after sunset fadeth in the west;
Which by and by black night doth take away,
Death's second self, that seals up all in rest.
In me thou see'st the glowing of such fire,
That on the ashes of his youth doth lie,   10
As the death-bed whereon it must expire,
Consumed with that which it was nourish'd by.
    This thou perceivest, which makes thy love more strong,
    To love that well which thou must leave ere long.

SONNET CXVI

Let me not to the marriage of true minds
Admit impediments. Love is not love
Which alters when it alteration finds,
Or bends with the remover to remove:
O, no! It is an ever-fixed mark,   5
That looks on tempests and is never shaken;
It is the star to every wandering bark,
Whose worth's unknown, although his height be taken.
Love's not Time's fool, though rosy lips and cheeks
Within his bending sickle's compass come;   10
Love alters not with his brief hours and weeks,
But bears it out even to the edge of doom.
If this be error and upon me proved,
I never writ, nor no man ever loved.

John Donne

1573–1631

SONNET X.—ON DEATH

(From *Holy Sonnets*, written before 1607)

Death, be not proud, though some have called thee
Mighty and dreadful, for thou art not so;
For those whom thou think'st thou dost overthrow
Die not, poor Death; nor yet cans't thou kill me.
From rest and sleep, which but thy picture be,   5
Much pleasure, then from thee much more must flow:
And soonest our best men with thee do go,
Rest of their bones, and souls' delivery.
Thou art slave to Fate, chance, kings, and desperate
    men,
And dost with poison, war, and sickness dwell,   10
And poppy or charms can make us sleep as well,
And better than thy stroke; why swell'st thou, then?
One short sleep pass, we wake eternally,
And Death shall be no more; Death, thou shalt die.

MICHAEL DRAYTON

Michael Drayton

1563–1631

AGINCOURT

TO MY FRIENDS THE CAMBER-BRITONS AND THEIR HARP

(From *Poems, Lyrics and Pastorals*, 1605 ?)

Fair stood the wind for France,
When we our sails advance,
And now to prove our chance
  Longer not tarry,
5 But put unto the main,
At Caux, the mouth of Seine,
With all his warlike train,
  Landed King Harry.

And taking many a fort,
10 Furnished in warlike sort,
Coming toward Agincourt
  In happy hour,
Skirmishing day by day
With those oppose his way,
15 Where as the gen'ral lay
  With all his power:

Which in his height of pride,
As Henry to deride,
His ransom to provide
20 Unto him sending;

Which he neglects the while,
As from a nation vile,
Yet with an angry smile,
    Their fall portending;

25 And, turning to his men,
Quoth famous Henry then,
'Though they to one be ten,
    Be not amazèd;
Yet have we well begun,
30 Battles so bravely won
Ever more to the sun
    By fame are raisèd.

'And for myself,' quoth he,
'This my full rest shall be,
35 England ne'er mourn for me,
    Nor more esteem me.
Victor I will remain,
Or on this earth be slain,
Never shall she sustain
40   Loss to redeem me.

'Poyters and Cressy tell,
When most their pride did swell,
Under our swords they fell,
    No less our skill is
45 Than when our grandsire great,
Claiming the regal seat,
In many a warlike feat
    Lopp'd the French lilies.'

The Duke of York so dread,
50 The eager vaward led;
With the main Henry sped,
    Amongst his henchmen.

Excester had the rear,
A braver man not there,
55 And now preparing were
    For the false Frenchman,

And ready to be gone,
Armor on armor shone,
Drum unto drum did groan,
60   To hear was wonder;
That with the cries they make
The very earth did shake,
Trumpet to trumpet spake,
    Thunder to thunder.

65 Well it thine age became,
O noble Erpingham,
Thou did'st the signal frame
    Unto the forces;
When from a meadow by,
70 Like a storm suddenly,
The English archery
    Stuck the French horses.

The Spanish yew so strong,
Arrows a cloth-yard long,
75 That like to serpents stong,
    Piercing the wether;
None from his death now starts,
But playing manly parts,
And like true English hearts
80   Stuck close together.

When down their bows they threw,
And forth their bilbows drew,
And on the French they flew:
    No man was tardy;

85 Arms from the shoulders sent,
   Scalps to the teeth were rent,
   Down the French peasants went,
     These were men hardy.

   When now that noble king,
90 His broad sword brandishing,
   Into the host did fling,
     As to o'erwhelm it;
   Who many a deep wound lent,
   His arms with blood besprent,
95 And many a cruel dent
     Bruisèd his helmet.

   Gloster, that duke so good,
   Next of the royal blood,
   For famous England stood,
100   With his brave brother,
   Clarence, in steel most bright,
   That yet a maiden knight,
   Yet in this furious fight
     Scarce such another.

105 Warwick in blood did wade,
   Oxford the foes invade,
   And cruel slaughter made,
     Still as they ran up;
   Suffolk his axe did ply,
110 Beaumont and Willoughby
   Bear them right doughtily,
     Ferrers and Fanhope.

   On happy Crispin day
   Fought was this noble fray,
115 Which fame did not delay
     To England to carry;
   O when shall Englishmen,
   With such acts fill a pen?
   Or England breed again
120   Such a King Harry?

SEVENTEENTH CENTURY SONGS

John Donne

1573–1631

AN ELEGY UPON THE DEATH OF THE LADY MARKHAM

(First published 1633)

Man is the world, and death the ocean
To which God gives the lower parts of man.
This sea environs all, and though as yet
God hath set marks and bounds 'twixt us and it,
5 Yet doth it roar and gnaw, and still pretend
To break our bank, whene'er it takes a friend:
Then our land-waters (tears of passion) vent;
Our waters then above our firmament—
Tears, which our soul doth for her sin let fall,—
10 Take all a brackish taste, and funeral.
And even those tears, which should wash sin, are
    sin.
We, after God, new drown our world again.
Nothing but man of all envenom'd things,
Doth work upon itself with inborn stings.
15 Tears are false spectacles; we cannot see
Through passion's mist, what we are, or what she.
In her this sea of death hath made no breach;
But as the tide doth wash the shining beach,
And leaves embroider'd works upon the sand,
20 So is her flesh refin'd by Death's cold hand.

As men of China, after an age's stay,
Do take up porcelain, where they buried clay,
So at this grave, her limbec (which refines
The diamonds, rubies, sapphires, pearls and
    mines,
25 Of which this flesh was) her soul shall inspire
Flesh of such stuff, as God, when His last fire
Annuls this world, to recompense it, shall
Make and name them th' elixir of this all.
They say the sea, when th' earth it gains, loseth
    too;
30 If carnal Death, the younger brother, do
Usurp the body; our soul, which subject is
To th' elder Death by sin, is free by this;
They perish both, when they attempt the just;
For graves our trophies are, and both Death's
    dust.
35 So, unobnoxious now, she hath buried both;
For none to death sins, that to sin is loath,
Nor do they die, which are not loath to die;
So she hath this and that virginity.
Grace was in her extremely diligent,
40 That kept her from sin, yet made her repent.
Of what small spots pure white complains!
    Alas!
How little poison cracks a crystal glass!
She sinn'd, but just enough to let us see
That God's word must be true,—*all sinners be.*
45 So much did zeal her conscience rarify,
That extreme truth lack'd little of a lie,
Making omissions acts; laying the touch
Of sin on things, that sometimes may be such.
As Moses' cherubims, whose natures do
50 Surpass all speed, by him are wingèd too,
So would her soul, already in heaven, seem then
To climb by tears the common stairs of men.
How fit she was for God, I am content

To speak, that Death his vain haste may repent;
55 How fit for us, how even and how sweet,
How good in all her titles, and how meet
To have reform'd this forward heresy,
That women can no parts of friendship be;
How moral, how divine, shall not be told,
60 Lest they, that hear her virtues, think her old:
And lest we take Death's part, and make him glad
Of such a prey, and to his triumphs add.

A VALEDICTION FORBIDDING MOURNING

(Sometimes called " *Upon Parting from his Mistris*,"
written, 1612?)

As virtuous men pass mildly away,
    And whisper to their souls to go,
Whilst some of their sad friends do say,
    'Now his breath goes,' and some say, 'No;'

5 So let us melt, and make no noise,
    No tear-floods, nor sigh-tempests move;
'Twere profanation of our joys,
    To tell the laity our love.

Moving of th' earth brings harm and fears,
10   Men reckon what it did, and meant;
But trepidations of the spheres,
    Though greater far, are innocent.

Dull sublunary Lovers' love,
    (Whose soul is sense) cannot admit
15 Absence; for that it doth remove
    Those things which elemented it.

But we, by a love so far refin'd
    That ourselves know not what it is,
Inter-assurèd of the mind
20   Careless eyes, lips, and hands, to miss.

Our two souls therefore, which are one,
　　Though I must go, endure not yet
A breach, but an expansion,
　　Like gold to airy thinness beat.

25 If they be two, they are two so
　　As stiff twin compasses are two;
Thy soul, the fixt foot, makes no show,
　　To move, but doth if th' other do.

And though it in the centre sit,
30　　Yet when the other far doth roam,
It leans and harkens after it,
　　And grows erect, as that comes home.

Such wilt thou be to me, who must
　　Like th' other foot, obliquely run;
35 Thy firmness makes my circle just,
　　And makes me end where I begun.

SONG

(From *Poems, with Elegies on the Author's Death*, 1633)

Sweetest Love, I do not go
　　For weariness of thee,
Nor in hope the world can show
　　A fitter Love for me;
5　　But since that I
Must die at last, 'tis best
Thus to use myself in jest,
　　Thus by feignèd death to die.

Yesternight the sun went hence,
10　　And yet is here to-day;
He hath no desire nor sense,
　　Nor half so short a way.

Then fear not me;
But believe that I shall make
15 Hastier journeys, since I take
More wings and spurs than he.

O how feeble is man's power,
That, if good fortune fall,
Cannot add another hour,
20   Nor a lost hour recall.
But come bad chance,
And we join to it our strength,
And we teach it art and length,
Itself o'er us t' advance.

25 When thou sigh'st, thou sigh'st no wind,
But sigh'st my soul away;
When thou weep'st, unkindly kind,
My life's-blood doth decay.
It cannot be
30 That thou lov'st me as thou say'st,
If in thine my life thou waste
That art the best of me.

Let not thy divining heart
Forethink me any ill;
35 Destiny may take thy part
And may thy fears fulfil;
But think that we
Are but turned aside to sleep:
They, who one another keep
40   Alive, ne'er parted be.

A HYMN TO GOD THE FATHER

(First published 1631)

Wilt Thou forgive that sin where I begun,
  Which was my sin, though it were done before?
Wilt Thou forgive that sin, through which I run
  And do run still, though still I do deplore?
When Thou hast done, Thou hast not done;   5
    For I have more.

Wilt Thou forgive that sin which I have won
  Others to sin, and made my sins their door?
Wilt Thou forgive that sin which I did shun
  A year or two, but wallow'd in, a score?   10
When Thou hast done, Thou hast not done;
    For I have more.

I have a sin of fear, that when I have spun
  My last thread, I shall perish on the shore;
But swear by Thyself, that at my death Thy Son   15
  Shall shine, as He shines now and heretofore:
And having done that, Thou hast done;
    I fear no more.

George Herbert

1593–1633

VERTUE

(From *The Temple*, 1631)

Sweet day, so cool, so calm, so bright,
The bridall of the earth and skie:
The dew shall weep thy fall to-night;
    For thou must die.

5 Sweet rose, whose hue angrie and brave
Bids the rash gazer wipe his eye,
Thy root is ever in its grave,
    And thou must die.

Sweet spring, full of sweet days and roses,
10 A box where sweets compacted lie,
My musick shows ye have your closes,
    And all must die.

Only a sweet and vertuous soul,
Like season'd timber, never gives;
15 But though the whole world turn to coal,
    Then chiefly lives.

THE PULLEY

(From the same)

When God at first made man,
Having a glasse of blessings standing by,
'Let us,' said He, 'poure on him all we can;
Let the world's riches, which dispersed lie,
5   Contract into a span.'

So strength first made a way;
Then beautie flow'd, then wisdome, honour,
    pleasure;
When almost all was out, God made a stay,
Perceiving that, alone of all His treasure,
10   Rest in the bottome lay.

'For if I should,' said He,
'Bestow this jewell also on My creature,
He would adore My gifts in stead of Me,
And rest in Nature, not the God of Nature:
15   So both should losers be.

Yet let him keep the rest,
But keep them with repining restlessnesse:
Let him be rich and wearie, that at least,
If goodnesse leade him not, yet wearinesse
20   May tosse him to my breast.'

THE ELIXIR

(From the same)

Teach me, my God and King,
    In all things Thee to see,
And what I do in anything
    To do it as for Thee:

5   Not rudely, as a beast,
        To runne into an action;
    But still to make Thee prepossest,
        And give it his perfection.

    A man that looks on glasse,
10   On it may stay his eye;
    Or if he pleaseth, through it passe,
        And then the heav'n espie.

    All may of Thee partake:
        Nothing can be so mean,
15 Which with his tincture 'for Thy sake,'
        Will not grow bright and clean.

    A servant with this clause
        Makes drudgerie divine;
    Who sweeps a room as for Thy laws,
20   Makes that and th' action fine.

    This is the famous stone
        That turneth all to gold;
    For that which God doth touch and own
        Cannot for lesse be told.

THE COLLAR

(From the same)

I struck the board, and cry'd, ' No more;
        I will abroad.'
What, shall I ever sigh and pine?
My lines and life are free; free as the road,
  Loose as the winde, as large as store. 5
        Shall I be still in suit?
Have I no harvest but a thorn
To let me bloud and not restore
What I have lost with cordiall fruit?
        Sure there was wine, 10
Before my sighs did drie it; there was corn
  Before my tears did drown it;
  Is the yeare onely lost to me?
  Have I no bayes to crown it,
No flowers, no garlands gay? all blasted, 15
        All wasted?
  Not so, my heart; but there is fruit,
        And thou hast hands.
    Recover all thy sigh-blown age
On double pleasures; leave thy cold dispute 20
Of what is fit and not; forsake thy cage,
        Thy rope of sands
Which pettie thoughts have made; and made to thee
  Good cable, to enforce and draw,
        And be thy law, 25
  While thou didst wink and wouldst not see.
        Away! take heed;
        I will abroad.
Call in thy death's-head there, tie up thy fears;
        He that forbears 30
  To suit and serve his need
        Deserves his load.

But as I raved and grew more fierce and wilde
    At every word,
35 Methought I heard one calling, 'Childe';
    And I reply'd, 'My Lord.'

Henry Vaughan

1621-1695

THE RETREATE

(From *Silex Scintillans*, Part I., 1650)

Happy those early dayes, when I
Shin'd in my Angell-infancy!
Before I understood this place
Appointed for my second race,
5 Or taught my soul to fancy ought
But a white, celestiall thought;
When yet I had not walkt above
A mile or two from my first Love,
And looking back, at that short space,
10 Could see a glimpse of his bright face;
When on some *gilded Cloud* or *Flowre*
My gazing soul would dwell an houre,
And in those weaker glories spy
Some shadows of eternity;
15 Before I taught my tongue to wound
My conscience with a sinfull sound,
Or had the black art to dispence
A sev'rall sinne to ev'ry sense,
But felt through all this fleshly dresse
20 Bright *shootes* of everlastingnesse.
  O how I long to travell back,
And tread again that ancient track!
That I might once more reach that plaine,
Where first I left my glorious traine;

25 From whence th' inlightened spirit sees
    That shady City of Palme trees.
    But ah! my soul with too much stay
    Is drunk, and staggers in the way!
    Some men a forward motion love,
30 But I by backward steps would move;
    And, when this dust falls to the urn,
    In that state I came, return.

DEPARTED FRIENDS

(From *Silex Scintillans*, Part II., 1655)

They are all gone into the world of light!
    And I alone sit ling'ring here!
Their very memory is fair and bright,
    And my sad thoughts doth clear.

5 It glows and glitters in my cloudy brest
    Like stars upon some gloomy grove,
Or those faint beams in which this hill is drest
    After the Sun's remove.

I see them walking in an air of glory
10   Whose light doth trample on my days;
My days, which are at best but dull and hoary,
    Meer glimmerings and decays.

O holy Hope! and high Humility!
    High as the Heavens above;
15 These are your walks, and you have shew'd them
        me
    To kindle my cold love.

Dear, beauteous Death; the Jewel of the Just!
    Shining nowhere but in the dark;
What mysteries do lie beyond thy dust,
20   Could man outlook that mark!

He that hath found some fledg'd bird's nest may
    know
  At first sight if the bird be flown;
But what fair dell or grove he sings in now,
  That is to him unknown.

25 And yet, as Angels in some brighter dreams
    Call to the soul when man doth sleep,
So some strange thoughts transcend our wonted
    theams
    And into glory peep.

If a star were confin'd into a tomb,
30 Her captive flames must needs burn there;
But when the hand that lockt her up gives room,
  She'll shine through all the sphere.

O Father of eternal life, and all
  Created glories under thee!
35 Resume thy spirit from this world of thrall
  Into true liberty!

Either disperse these mists, which blot and fill
  My perspective still as they pass;
Or else remove me hence unto that hill
40 Where I shall need no glass.

George Wither

1588–1667

THE AUTHOR'S RESOLUTION IN A SONNET

(From *Fidelia*, 1615)

Shall I, wasting in despaire
Dye, because a woman's fair?
Or make pale my cheeks with care
Cause anothers Rosie are?

5   Be she fairer than the Day
       Or the flowry Meads in May,
       If she thinke not well of me,
       What care I *how* faire she be?

       Shall my seely heart be pin'd
10 Cause I see a woman kind?
       Or a well disposed Nature
       Joyned with a lovely feature?
           Be she Meeker, Kinder than
           Turtle-dove or *Pellican:*
15   If she be not so to me,
           What care I how kind she be?

       Shall a woman's Vertues move
       Me to perish for her Love?
       Or her wel deservings knowne
20 Make me quite forget mine own?
           Be she with that Goodness blest
           Which may merit name of best:
           If she be not such to me,
           What care I how Good she be?

25 Cause her *Fortune* seems too high
       Shall I play the fool and die?
       She that beares a Noble mind,
       If not outward helpes she find,
           Thinks what with them he wold do,
30   That without them dares her woe.
           And unlesse that *Minde* I see
           What care I how great she be?

       Great, or Good, or Kind, or Faire
       I will ne're the more despaire:
35 If she love me (this beleeve)
       I will Die ere she shall grieve.

If she slight me when I woe,
I can scorne and let her goe,
For if she be not for me
40   What care I for whom she be?

Abraham Cowley
1618–1667

A VOTE

(From *Poetical Blossoms*, second ed., 1636)

65 This only grant me, that my means may lie
  Too low for envy, for contempt too high.
    Some honour I would have,
  Not from great deeds, but good alone;
  The unknown are better than ill known:
70   Rumour can ope the grave.
  Acquaintance I would have, but when 't depends
  Not on the number, but the choice of friends.

  Books should, not business, entertain the light,
  And sleep, as undisturb'd as death, the night.
75   My house a cottage more
  Than palace, and should fitting be
  For all my use, no luxury.
    My garden painted o'er
  With nature's hand, not art's; and pleasures yield,
80 Horace might envy in his Sabine field.

  Thus would I double my life's fading space,
  For he that runs it well, twice runs his race.
    And in this true delight,
  These unbought sports, this happy state,
85 I would nor fear, nor wish my fate,
    But boldly say each night,
  To-morrow let my sun his beams display,
  Or in clouds hide them, I have liv'd to-day.

THE GRASSHOPPER
(From *Miscellanies*, 1650)

Happy Insect what can be
In happiness compar'd to thee?
Fed with nourishment divine,
The dewy morning's gentle wine!
5 Nature waits upon thee still,
And thy verdant cup does fill.
'Tis fill'd where ever thou dost tread,
Nature selfe's thy Ganimed.
Thou dost drink, and dance, and sing;
10 Happier than the happiest King!
All the fields which thou dost see,
All the plants belong to thee,
All that summer hours produce,
Fertile made with early juice.
15 Man for thee does sow and plow;
Farmer he and land-lord thou!
Thou doest innocently joy;
Nor does thy luxury destroy;
The shepherd gladly heareth thee,
20 More harmonious than he.
Thee country hindes with gladness hear,
Prophet of the ripened year!
Thee Phœbus loves, and does inspire;
Phœbus is himself thy sire.
25 To thee of all things upon earth,
Life is no longer than thy mirth,
Happy insect, happy thou,
Dost neither age, nor winter know,
But when thou'st drunk, and danced, and sung,
30 Thy fill, the flowery leaves among
(Voluptuous, and wise with all,
Epicurean animal!)
Sated with thy summer feast,
Thou retir'st to endless rest.

James Shirley

1596–1667

A DIRGE

(From *The Contention of Ajax and Ulysses*, 1659)

The glories of our blood and state
  Are shadows, not substantial things;
There is no armour against fate;
  Death lays his icy hand on kings:
5   Sceptre and crown
      Must tumble down,
And in the dust be equal made
With the poor crooked scythe and spade.

Some men with swords may reap the field,
10 And plant fresh laurels where they kill;
But their strong nerves at last must yield;
  They tame but one another still:
      Early or late
      They stoop to fate,
15 And must give up their murmuring breath,
When they, poor captives, creep to death.

The garlands wither on your brow,
  Then boast no more your mighty deeds;
Upon Death's purple altar now
20 See, where the victor-victim bleeds:
      Your heads must come
      To the cold tomb,
Only the actions of the just
Smell sweet and blossom in their dust.

Thomas Carew
1589–1639

DISDAIN RETURNED

(Printed, without concluding stanza, in Porter's *Madrigalles and Ayres*, 1632)

He that loves a rosy cheek,
  Or a coral lip admires;
Or from star-like eyes doth seek
  Fuel to maintain his fires,
5 As old Time makes these decay,
So his flames must waste away.

But a smooth and steadfast mind,
  Gentle thoughts and calm desires,
Hearts, with equal love combined,
10   Kindle never-dying fires;
Where these art not, I despise
Lovely cheeks or lips or eyes.

No tears, Celia, now shall win,
  My resolved heart to return;
15 I have searched thy soul within
  And find nought but pride and scorn;
I have learned thy arts, and now
Can disdain as much as thou!

Sir John Suckling
1609–1641

ORSAMES' SONG.

(From *Aglaura*, acted 1637)

Why so pale and wan, fond lover?
  Prithee, why so pale?
Will, when looking well can't move **her**,
  Looking ill prevail?
5   Prithee, why so pale?

Why so dull and mute, young sinner?
    Prithee, why so mute?
Will, when speaking well can't win her,
    Saying nothing do't?
10   Prithee, why so mute?

Quit, quit, for shame, this will not move:
    This cannot take her.
If of herself she will not love,
    Nothing can make her:
15   The devil take her!

Richard Lovelace

1618–1658

TO LUCASTA, ON GOING TO THE WARS

(From *Lucasta*, 1649)

Tell me not, sweet, I am unkind,
    That from the nunnery
Of thy chaste breast and quiet mind
    To war and arms I fly.

5 True, a new mistress now I chase,
    The first foe in the field,
And with a stronger faith embrace
    A sword, a horse, a shield.

Yet this inconstancy is such
10   As you, **too**, shall adore,—
I could not love thee, dear, so much,
    Loved I not honour more.

TO ALTHEA FROM PRISON

(From the same)

When Love with unconfined wings
   Hovers within my gates,
And my divine Althea brings
   To whisper at the grates;
5 When I lie tangled in her hair,
   And fettered to her eye,
The birds that wanton in the air
   Know no such liberty.

When flowing cups run swiftly round
10   With no allaying Thames,
Our careless heads with roses bound,
   Our hearts with loyal flames;
When thirsty grief in wine we steep
   When healths and draughts go free,
15 Fishes that tipple in the deep
   Know no such liberty.

When, like committed linnets, I
   With shriller throat shall sing
The sweetness, mercy, majesty,
20   And glories of my King;
When I shall voice aloud, how good
   He is, how great should be,
Enlarged winds that curl the flood
   Know no such liberty.

25 Stone walls do not a prison make,
   Nor iron bars a cage;
Minds innocent and quiet take
   That for an hermitage;

It *I* have freedom in my love,
30   and in my soul am free,
Angels alone, that soar above,
     Enjoy such liberty.

Robert Herrick

1591–1674

ARGUMENT TO HESPERIDES

(From *Hesperides*, 1648)

I sing of brooks, of blossoms, birds, and bowers,
Of April, May, of June and July-flowers;
I sing of May-poles, hock-carts, wassails, wakes,
Of bride-grooms, brides, and of their bridal-cakes;
5 I write of youth, of love, and have access
By these to sing of cleanly wantonness;
I sing of dews, of rains, and, piece by piece
Of balm, of oil, of spice and ambergris;
I sing of times trans-shifting, and I write
10 How roses first came red and lilies white;
I write of groves, of twilights, and I sing
The Court of Mab, and of the fairy king;
I write of hell; I sing, (and ever shall)
Of heaven, and hope to have it after all.

CORINNA'S GOING A-MAYING

(From the same)

Get up, get up for shame, the blooming morn
Upon her wings presents the god unshorn.
     See how Aurora throws her fair
     Fresh-quilted colours through the air:
5   Get up, sweet slug-a-bed, and see
     The dew bespangling herb and tree.

Each flower has wept and bow'd toward the east
Above an hour since: yet you not dress'd;
   Nay! not so much as out of bed?
10   When all the birds have matins said
And sung their thankful hymns, 'tis sin,
   Nay, profanation to keep in,
Whenas a thousand virgins on this day
Spring, sooner than the lark, to fetch in May.

15 Rise and put on your foliage, and be seen
To come forth, like the spring-time, fresh and
     green,
   And sweet as Flora. Take no care
   For jewels for your gown or hair;
   Fear not; the leaves will strew
20   Gems in abundance upon you:
Besides, the childhood of the day has kept,
Against you come, some orient pearls unwept;
   Come and receive them while the light
   Hangs on the dew-locks of the night:
25   And Titan on the eastern hill
   Retires himself, or else stands still
Till you come forth. Wash, dress, be brief in
     praying:
Few beads are best when once we go a-Maying.

Come, my Corinna, come; and, coming, mark
30 How each field turns a street, each street a park
   Made green and trimm'd with trees; see how
   Devotion gives each house a bough
   Or branch: each porch, each door ere this
   An ark, a tabernacle is,
35 Made up of white-thorn neatly interwove;
As if here were those cooler shades of love.
   Can such delights be in the street
   And open fields and we not see 't?

Come, we'll abroad; and let's obey
40 The proclamation made for May;
And sin no more, as we have done, by staying;
But, my Corinna, come, let's go a-Maying.

There's not a budding boy or girl this day
But is got up, and gone to bring in May.
45 A deal of youth, ere this, is come
    Back, and with white-thorn laden home.
    Some have dispatched their cakes and cream,
    Before that we have left to dream:
And some have wept, and woo'd, and plighted
    troth,
50 And chose their priest, ere we can cast off sloth:
    Many a green-gown has been given;
    Many a kiss, both odd and even;
    Many a glance, too, has been sent
    From out the eye, love's firmament;
55 Many a jest told of the keys betraying
    This night, and locks pick'd, yet we're not
      a-Maying.

Come, let us go while we are in our prime;
And take the harmless folly of the time.
    We shall grow old apace, and die
60 Before we know our liberty.
    Our life is short, and our days run
    As far away as does the sun:
And, as a vapour or a drop of rain
Once lost, can ne'er be found again,
65 So when you or I are made
    A fable, song, or fleeting shade,
    All love, all liking, all delight
    Lies drowned with us in endless night.
Then while time serves, and we are but decaying,
70 Come, my Corinna, come, let's go a-Maying.

TO PRIMROSES FILLED WITH MORNING DEW

(From the same)

Why do ye weep, sweet babes? can tears
　　　　Speak grief in you,
　　　　Who were but born
Just as the modest morn
Teem'd her refreshing dew?　　　　　　　5
Alas! you have not known that shower
　　　　That mars a flower,
　　　　Nor felt th' unkind
　Breath of a blasting wind,
　Nor are ye worn with years,　　　　　　10
　　　　Or warp'd as we,
　Who think it strange to see
Such pretty flowers, like to orphans young,
To speak by tears, before ye have a tongue.

Speak, whimp'ring younglings, and make known　15
　　　　The reason why
　　　　Ye droop and weep;
　Is it for want of sleep?
　Or childish lullaby?
Or that ye have not seen as yet　　　　　20
　　　　The violet?
　　　　Or brought a kiss
　From that sweetheart to this?
No, no, this sorrow shown
　　　　By your tears shed　　　　　25
　Would have this lecture read:
That things of greatest, so of meanest worth,
Conceiv'd with grief are, and with tears brought forth.

TO THE VIRGINS, TO MAKE MUCH OF TIME

(From the same)

Gather ye rosebuds while ye may,
   Old time is still a-flying:
And this same flower that smiles to-day
   To-morrow will be dying.

5 The glorious lamp of heaven, the Sun,
   The higher he's a-getting,
The sooner will his race be run,
   And nearer he's to setting.

That age is best which is the first,
10   When youth and blood are warmer;
But being spent, the worse, and worst
   Times still succeed the former.

Then be not coy, but use your time,
   And while ye may go marry:
15 For having lost but once your prime
   You may forever tarry.

TO DAFFODILS

(From the same)

Fair daffodils, we weep to see
   You haste away so soon;
As yet the early-rising sun
   Has not attain'd his noon.
5   Stay, stay,
   Until the hasting day
      Has run
   But to the evensong;
And, having prayed together, we
10   Will go with you along.

We have short time to stay, as you,
    We have as short a spring;
As quick a growth to meet decay,
    As you, or anything.
15   We die,
    As your hours do, and dry
         Away,
    Like to the summer's rain;
Or as the pearls of morning's dew,
20   Ne'er to be found again.

THE HAG

(From the same)

    The hag is astride
    This night for to ride,
The devil and she together;
    Through thick and through thin,
5   Now out and then in,
Though ne'er so foul be the weather.

    A thorn or a burr
    She takes for a spur,
With a lash of a bramble she rides now;
10   Through brakes and through briars,
    O'er ditches and mires,
She follows the spirit that guides now.

    No beast for his food
    Dare now range the wood,
15 But hush'd in his lair he lies lurking;
    While mischiefs, by these,
    On land and on seas,
At noon of night are a-working.

    The storm will arise
20   And trouble the skies;

This night, and more for the wonder,
   The ghost from the tomb
   Affrighted shall come,
Call'd out by the clap of the thunder.

Edmund Waller

1605–1687

ON A GIRDLE

(From *Poems,* 1645)

That which her slender waist confin'd,
Shall now my joyful temples bind;
No monarch but would give his crown,
His arms might do what this has done.

5   It was my heaven's extremest sphere,
The pale which held that lovely deer,
My joy, my grief, my hope, my love,
Did all within this circle move.

A narrow compass, and yet there
10 Dwelt all that's good, and all that's fair:
Give me but what this riband bound,
Take all the rest the sun goes round.

SONG

(From the same)

Go, lovely Rose,
   Tell her that wastes her time and me,
That now she knows
   When I resemble her to thee,
5 How sweet and fair she seems to be.

Tell her that's young,
   And shuns to have her graces spied,
That had'st thou sprung
   In deserts where no men abide,
10 Thou must have uncommended died.

Small is the worth
Of beauty from the light retired;
Bid her come forth,
Suffer herself to be desired,
15 And not blush so to be admired.

Then die, that she
The common fate of all things rare
May read in thee;
How small a part of time they share,
20 That are so wondrous sweet and fair.

ON THE FOREGOING DIVINE POEMS

(1686 ?)

When we for age could neither read nor write,
The subject made us able to indite.
The soul, with nobler resolutions deckt,
The body stooping, does herself erect:
5 No mortal parts are requisite to raise
Her, that unbody'd can her Maker praise.
The seas are quiet when the winds give o'er:
So, calm are we, when passions are no more:
For, then we know how vain it was to boast
10 Of fleeting things, so certain to be lost.
Clouds of affection from our younger eyes
Conceal that emptiness, which age descries,
    The soul's dark cottage, batter'd and decay'd,
Lets in new light, thro' chinks that time has
    made:
15 Stronger by weakness, wiser, men become,
As they draw near to their eternal home.
Leaving the old, both worlds at once they view,
That stand upon the threshold of the new.

JOHN MILTON

John Milton

1608–1674

L'ALLEGRO

(1634)

Hence, loathèd Melancholy,
Of Cerberus and blackest Midnight born
In Stygian cave forlorn,
'Mongst horrid shapes, and shrieks, and sights
    unholy!
5 Find out some uncouth cell,
    Where brooding Darkness spreads his jealous
      wings,
And the night-raven sings;
    There, under ebon shades and low-browed rocks,
As ragged as thy locks,
10   In dark Cimmerian desert ever dwell.
    But come, thou Goddess fair and free,
In heaven ycleped Euphrosyne,
And by men heart-easing Mirth;
Whom lovely Venus, at a birth,
15 With two sister Graces more,
To ivy-crownèd Bacchus bore:
Or whether (as some sager sing)
The frolic wind that breathes the spring,
Zephyr, with Aurora playing,
20 As he met her once a-Maying,
There, on beds of violets blue,
And fresh-blown roses washed in dew,

Filled her with thee, a daughter fair,
So buxom, blithe, and debonair.
25   Haste thee, Nymph, and bring with thee
Jest, and youthful Jollity,
Quips and cranks and wanton wiles,
Nods and becks and wreathèd smiles,
Such as hang on Hebe's cheek,
30 And love to live in dimple sleek;
Sport that wrinkled Care derides,
And Laughter holding both his sides.
Come, and trip it, as you go,
On the light fantastic toe;
35 And in thy right hand lead with thee
The mountain-nymph, sweet Liberty;
And, if I give thee honour due,
Mirth, admit me of thy crew,
To live with her, and live with thee,
40 In unreprovèd pleasures free;
   To hear the lark begin his flight,
And, singing, startle the dull night,
From his watch-tower in the skies,
Till the dappled dawn doth rise;
45 Then to come in spite of sorrow,
And at my window bid good-morrow,
Through the sweet-briar, or the vine,
Or the twisted eglantine;
While the cock, with lively din,
50 Scatters the rear of darkness thin;
And to the stack, or the barn-door,
Stoutly struts his dames before:
Oft listening how the hounds and horn
Cheerly rouse the slumbering morn,
55 From the side of some hoar hill,
Through the high wood echoing shrill:
Some time walking, not unseen,
By hedgerow elms, on hillocks green,
Right against the eastern gate

60 Where the great Sun begins his state
   Robed in flames and amber light,
   The clouds in thousand liveries dight;
   While the ploughman, near at hand,
   Whistles o'er the furrowed land,
65 And the milkmaid singeth blithe,
   And the mower whets his scythe,
   And every shepherd tells his tale
   Under the hawthorn in the dale.
     Straight mine eye hath caught new pleasures,
70 Whilst the landskip round it measures:
   Russet lawns, and fallows gray,
   Where the nibbling flocks do stray;
   Mountains, on whose barren breast
   The labouring clouds do often rest;
75 Meadows trim, with daisies pied,
   Shallow brooks, and rivers wide;
   Towers and battlements it sees
   Bosomed high in tufted trees,
   Where perhaps some beauty lies,
80 The cynosure of neighbouring eyes.
     Hard by a cottage chimney smokes
   From betwixt two aged oaks,
   Where Corydon and Thyrsis met,
   Are at their savoury dinner set
85 Of herbs, and other country messes,
   Which the neat-handed Phillis dresses;
   And then in haste her bower she leaves,
   With Thestylis to bind the sheaves;
   Or, if the earlier season lead,
90 To the tanned haycock in the mead.
     Sometimes, with secure delight,
   The upland hamlets will invite,
   When the merry bells ring round,
   And the jocund rebecks sound
95 To many a youth and many a maid
   Dancing in the checkered shade,

And young and old come forth to play
On a sunshine holyday,
Till the livelong daylight fail:
100 Then to the spicy nut-brown ale,
With stories told of many a feat,
How Faery Mab the junkets eat.
She was pinched and pulled, she said;
And he, by Friar's lantern led,
105 Tells how the drudging goblin sweat
To earn his cream-bowl duly set,
When in one night, ere glimpse of morn,
His shadowy flail hath threshed the corn
That ten day-labourers could not end;
110 Then lies him down the lubber fiend,
And, stretched out all the chimney's length,
Basks at the fire his hairy strength,
And crop-full out of doors he flings,
Ere the first cock his matin rings.
115 Thus done the tales, to bed they creep,
By whispering winds soon lulled asleep.
   Towered cities please us then,
And the busy hum of men,
Where throngs of knights and barons bold,
120 In weeds of peace, high triumphs hold,
With store of ladies, whose bright eyes
Rain influence, and judge the prize
Of wit or arms, while both contend
To win her grace whom all commend.
125 There let Hymen oft appear
In saffron robe, with taper clear,
And pomp, and feast, and revelry,
With mask and antique pageantry;
Such sights as youthful poets dream
130 On summer eves by haunted stream.
Then to the well-trod stage anon,
If Jonson's learned sock be on,
Or sweetest Shakespeare, Fancy's child,
Warble his native wood-notes wild.

135   And ever, against eating cares,
       Lap me in soft Lydian airs,
       Married to immortal verse,
       Such as the meeting soul may pierce,
       In notes with many a winding bout
140 Of linked sweetness long drawn out,
       With wanton heed and giddy cunning,
       The melting voice through mazes running,
       Untwisting all the chains that tie
       The hidden soul of harmony;
145 That Orpheus' self may heave his head
       From golden slumber on a bed
       Of heaped Elysian flowers, and hear
       Such strains as would have won the ear
       Of Pluto to have quite set free
150 His half-regained Eurydice.
       These delights if thou canst give,
       Mirth, with thee I mean to live.

IL PENSEROSO

(1634)

    Hence, vain deluding Joys,
    The brood of Folly without father bred!
      How little you bested,
        Or fill the fixèd mind with all your toys!
5   Dwell in some idle brain,
        And fancies fond with gaudy shapes possess,
    As thick and numberless
    As the gay motes that people the sun-beams,
    Or likest hovering dreams,
10   The fickle pensioners of Morpheus' train.
    But, hail! thou Goddess sage and holy,
    Hail, divinest Melancholy!
    Whose saintly visage is too bright
    To hit the sense of human sight,

15 And therefore to our weaker view
O'erlaid with black, staid Wisdom's hue;
Black, but such as in esteem
Prince Memnon's sister might beseem,
Or that starred Ethiop queen that strove
20 To set her beauty's praise above
The Sea-Nymphs, and their powers offended.
Yet thou art higher far descended:
Thee bright-haired Vesta long of yore
To solitary Saturn bore;
25 His daughter she; in Saturn's reign
Such mixture was not held a stain.
Oft in glimmering bowers and glades
He met her, and in secret shades
Of woody Ida's inmost grove,
30 Whilst yet there was no fear of Jove.
    Come, pensive Nun, devout and pure,
Sober, steadfast, and demure,
All in a robe of darkest grain,
Flowing with majestic train,
35 And sable stole of cypress lawn
Over thy decent shoulders drawn.
Come; but keep thy wonted state,
With even step, and musing gait,
And looks commercing with the skies,
40 Thy rapt soul sitting in thine eyes:
There, held in holy passion still,
Forget thyself to marble, till
With a sad leaden downward cast
Thou fix them on the earth as fast.
45 And join with thee calm Peace and Quiet,
Spare Fast, that oft with gods doth diet,
And hears the Muses in a ring
Aye round about Jove's altar sing;
And add to these retired Leisure,
50 That in trim gardens takes his pleasure;
But, first and chiefest, with thee bring

Him that yon soars on golden wing,
Guiding the fiery-wheeled throne,
The Cherub Contemplation;
55 And the mute Silence hist along,
'Less Philomel will deign a song,
In her sweetest saddest plight,
Smoothing the rugged brow of Night,
While Cynthia checks her dragon yoke
60 Gently o'er the accustomed oak.
Sweet bird, that shunn'st the noise of folly,
Most musical, most melancholy!
Thee, chauntress, oft the woods among
I woo, to hear thy even-song;
65 And, missing thee, I walk unseen
On the dry smooth-shaven green,
To behold the wandering moon,
Riding near her highest noon,
Like one that had been led astray
70 Through the heaven's wide pathless way,
And oft, as if her head she bowed,
Stooping through a fleecy cloud.
     Oft, on a plat of rising ground,
I hear the far-off curfew sound,
75 Over some wide-watered shore,
Swinging slow with sullen roar;
Or, if the air will not permit,
Some still removèd place will fit,
Where glowing embers through the room
80 Teach light to counterfeit a gloom,
Far from all resort of mirth,
Save the cricket on the hearth,
Or the bellman's drowsy charm
To bless the doors from nightly harm.
85   Or let my lamp, at midnight hour,
Be seen in some high lonely tower,
Where I may oft outwatch the Bear,
With thrice great Hermes, or unsphere

The spirit of Plato, to unfold
90 What worlds or what vast regions hold
The immortal mind that hath forsook
Her mansion in this fleshly nook;
And of those demons that are found
In fire, air, flood, or underground,
95 Whose power hath a true consent
With planet or with element.
Sometime let gorgeous Tragedy
In sceptred pall come sweeping by,
Presenting Thebes, or Pelops' line,
100 Or the tale of Troy divine,
Or what (though rare) of later age
Ennobled hath the buskined stage.
But, O sad Virgin! that thy power
Might raise Musæus from his bower;
105 Or bid the soul of Orpheus sing
Such notes as, warbled to the string,
Drew iron tears down Pluto's cheek,
And made Hell grant what love did seek;
Or call up him that left half-told
110 The story of Cambuscan bold,
Of Camball, and of Algarsife,
And who had Canace to wife,
That owned the virtuous ring and glass,
And of the wondrous horse of brass
115 On which the Tartar king did ride;
And if aught else great bards beside
In sage and solemn tunes have sung,
Of turneys, and of trophies hung,
Of forests, and enchantments drear,
120 Where more is meant than meets the ear.
Thus, Night, oft see me in thy pale career,
Till civil-suited Morn appear,
Not tricked and frounced, as she was wont
With the Attic boy to hunt,
125 But kercheft in a comely cloud,

While rocking winds are piping loud,
Or ushered with a shower still,
When the gust hath blown his fill,
Ending on the rustling leaves,
130 With minute-drops from off the eaves.
And, when the sun begins to fling
His flaring beams, me, Goddess, bring
To archèd walks of twilight groves,
And shadows brown, that Sylvan loves,
135 Of pine, or monumental oak,
Where the rude axe with heavèd stroke
Was never heard the nymphs to daunt,
Or fright them from their hallowed haunt.
There, in close covert, by some brook,
140 Where no profaner eye may look,
Hide me from day's garish eye,
While the bee with honied thigh,
That at her flowry work doth sing,
And the waters murmuring,
145 With such consort as they keep,
Entice the dewy-feathered Sleep.
And let some strange mysterious dream
Wave at his wings, in airy stream
Of lively portraiture displayed,
150 Softly on my eyelids laid;
And, as I wake, sweet music breathe
Above, about, or underneath,
Sent by some Spirit to mortals good,
Or the unseen Genius of the wood.
155   But let my due feet never fail
To walk the studious cloister's pale,
And love the high embowèd roof,
With antique pillars massy-proof,
And storied windows richly dight,
160 Casting a dim religious light.
There let the pealing organ blow
To the full-voiced quire below,

In service high and anthems clear,
As may with sweetness, through mine ear,
165 Dissolve me into ecstasies,
And bring all heaven before mine eyes.
   And may at last my weary age
Find out the peaceful hermitage,
The hairy gown and mossy cell,
170 Where I may sit and rightly spell
Of every star that heaven doth shew,
And every herb that sips the dew,
Till old experience do attain
To something like prophetic strain.
175   These pleasures, Melancholy, give;
And I with thee will choose to live.

SONG. SWEET ECHO

(From *Comus*, acted 1634)

Sweet Echo, sweetest nymph, that liv'st unseen
    Within thy airy shell,
  By slow Meander's margent green,
And in the violet-embroidered vale
5   Where the love-lorn nightingale
Nightly to thee her sad song mourneth well:
Canst thou not tell me of a gentle pair
    That likest thy Narcissus are?
     O, if thou have
10   Hid them in some flowery cave,
    Tell me but where,
    Sweet Queen of Parley, Daughter of the
    Sphere!
So may'st thou be translated to the skies,
And give resounding grace to all heaven's harmonies.

SONG. SABRINA FAIR

(From the Same)

Sabrina fair,
  Listen where thou art sitting
Under the glassy, cool, translucent wave,
  In twisted braids of lilies knitting
5 The loose train of thy amber-dropping hair;
    Listen for dear honour's sake,
    Goddess of the silver lake,
      Listen and save!
Listen, and appear to us,
10 In name of great Oceanus.
By the earth-shaking Neptune's mace,
And Tethys' grave majestic pace;
By hoary Nereus' wrinkled look,
And the Carpathian wizard's hook;
15 By scaly Triton's winding shell,
And old soothsaying Glaucus' spell;
By Leucothea's lovely hands,
And her son that rules the strands;
By Thetis' tinsel-slippered feet,
20 And the songs of Sirens sweet;
By dead Parthenope's dear tomb,
And fair Ligea's golden comb,
Wherewith she sits on diamond rocks
Sleeking her soft alluring locks;
25 By all the Nymphs that nightly dance
Upon thy streams with wily glance;
Rise, rise, and heave thy rosy head
From thy coral-paven bed,
And bridle in thy headlong wave,
30 Till thou our summons answered have.
              Listen and save!

LYCIDAS

(1638)

Yet once more, O ye laurels, and once more,
Ye myrtles brown, with ivy never sere,
I come to pluck your berries harsh and crude,
And with forced fingers rude
5　Shatter your leaves before the mellowing year.
Bitter constraint and sad occasion dear
Compels me to disturb your season due;
For Lycidas is dead, dead ere his prime,
Young Lycidas, and hath not left his peer.
10　Who would not sing for Lycidas? He knew
　Himself to sing, and build the lofty rhyme.
He must not float upon his watery bier
Unwept, and welter to the parching wind,
Without the meed of some melodious tear.
15　　Begin, then, Sisters of the sacred well
That from beneath the seat of Jove doth spring;
Begin, and somewhat loudly sweep the string.
Hence with denial vain and coy excuse:
So may some gentle Muse
20　With lucky words favour *my* destined urn,
And as he passes turn,
And bid fair peace be to my sable shroud!
　For we were nursed upon the self-same hill,
Fed the same flock, by fountain, shade, and rill;
25　Together both, ere the high lawns appeared
Under the opening eyelids of the Morn,
We drove a-field, and both together heard
What time the gray-fly winds her sultry horn,
Battening our flocks with the fresh dews of night,
30　Oft till the star that rose at evening bright
　Toward heaven's descent had sloped his westering
　　　　wheel.
Meanwhile the rural ditties were not mute;

Tempered to the oaten flute,
Rough Satyrs danced, and Fauns with cloven heel
35 From the glad sound would not be absent long;
And old Damœtas loved to hear our song.
    But, oh! the heavy change, now thou art gone,
Now thou art gone and never must return!
Thee, Shepherd, thee the woods and desert caves,
40 With wild thyme and the gadding vine o'ergrown,
And all their echoes, mourn.
The willows, and the hazel copses green,
Shall now no more be seen
Fanning their joyous leaves to thy soft lays.
45 As killing as the canker to the rose,
Or taint-worm to the weanling herds that graze,
Or frost to flowers that their gay wardrobe wear,
When first the white-thorn blows;
Such, Lycidas, thy loss to shepherd's ear.
50   Where were ye, Nymphs, when the remorseless
      deep
Closed o'er the head of your loved Lycidas?
For neither were ye playing on the steep
Where your old bards, the famous Druids, lie,
Nor on the shaggy top of Mona high,
55 Nor yet where Deva spreads her wizard stream.
Ay me! I fondly dream
"Had ye been there," . . . for what could that
      have done?
What could the Muse herself that Orpheus bore,
The Muse herself, for her enchanting son,
60 Whom universal nature did lament,
When, by the rout that made the hideous roar,
His gory visage down the stream was sent,
Down the swift Hebrus to the Lesbian shore?
    Alas! what boots it with uncessant care
65 To tend the homely, slighted, shepherd's trade,
And strictly meditate the thankless Muse?
Were it not better done, as others use,

To sport with Amaryllis in the shade,
Or with the tangles of Neæra's hair?
70 Fame is the spur that the clear spirit doth raise
(That last infirmity of noble mind)
To scorn delights and live laborious days;
But the fair guerdon when we hope to find,
And think to burst out into sudden blaze,
75 Comes the blind Fury with the abhorrèd shears,
And slits the thin-spun life. "But not the
        praise,"
Phœbus replied, and touched my trembling ears:
"Fame is no plant that grows on mortal soil,
Nor in the glistering foil
80 Set off to the world, nor in broad rumour lies,
But lives and spreads aloft by those pure eyes
And perfect witness of all-judging Jove:
As he pronounces lastly on each deed,
Of so much fame in heaven expect thy meed."
85   O fountain Arethuse, and thou honoured flood,
Smooth-sliding Mincius, crowned with vocal
        reeds,
That strain I heard was of a higher mood.
But now my oat proceeds,
And listens to the Herald of the Sea,
90 That came in Neptune's plea.
He asked the waves, and asked the felon winds,
What hard mishap hath doomed this gentle
        swain?
And questioned every gust of rugged wings
That blows from off each beakèd promontory.
95 They knew not of his story;
And sage Hippotades their answer brings,
That not a blast was from his dungeon strayed:
The air was calm, and on the level brine
Sleek Panope with all her sisters played.
100 It was that fatal and perfidious bark,
Built in the eclipse, and rigged with curses dark,
That sunk so low that sacred head of thine.

Next, Camus, reverend sire, went footing slow,
His mantle hairy, and his bonnet sedge,
105 Inwrought with figures dim, and on the edge
Like to that sanguine flower inscribed with woe.
"Ah! who hath reft," quoth he, "my dearest
                pledge?"
Last came, and last did go,
The Pilot of the Galilean Lake;
110 Two massy keys he bore of metals twain
(The golden opes, the iron shuts amain.)
He shook his mitred locks, and stern bespake:—
"How well could I have spared for thee, young
                swain,
Enow of such as, for their bellies' sake,
115 Creep, and intrude, and climb into the fold!
Of other care they little reckoning make
Than how to scramble at the shearers' feast,
And shove away the worthy bidden guest.
Blind mouths! that scarce themselves know how
                to hold
120 A sheep-hook, or have learnt aught else the
                least
That to the faithful herdman's art belongs!
What recks it them? What need they? They
                are sped;
And, when they list, their lean and flashy songs
Grate on their scrannel pipes of wretched straw;
125 The hungry sheep look up, and are not fed,
But, swoln with wind and the rank mist they
                draw,
Rot inwardly, and foul contagion spread;
Besides what the grim wolf with privy paw,
Daily devours apace, and nothing said.
130 But that two-handed engine at the door
Stands ready to smite once, and smite no more."
    Return, Alpheus; the dread voice is past
That shrunk thy streams; return Sicilian Muse,

And call the vales, and bid them hither cast
135　Their bells and flowerets of a thousand hues.
Ye valleys low, where the mild whispers use
Of shades, and wanton winds, and gushing
　　　brooks,
On whose fresh lap the swart star sparely looks,
Throw hither all your quaint enamelled eyes,
140　That on the green turf suck the honeyed showers,
And purple all the ground with vernal flowers.
Bring the rathe primrose that forsaken dies,
The tufted crow-toe, and pale jessamine,
The white pink, and the pansy freaked with jet,
145　The glowing violet,
The musk-rose, and the well-attired woodbine,
With cowslips wan that hang the pensive head,
And every flower that sad embroidery wears;
Bid amaranthus all his beauty shed,
150　And daffadillies fill their cups with tears,
To strew the laureate hearse where Lycid lies.
For so, to interpose a little ease,
Let our frail thoughts dally with false surmise,
Ay me! whilst thee the shores and sounding seas
155　Wash far away, where'er thy bones are hurled;
Whether beyond the stormy Hebrides,
Where thou perhaps under the whelming tide
Visit'st the bottom of the monstrous world;
Or whether thou, to our moist vows denied,
160　Sleep'st by the fable of Bellerus old,
Where the great Vision of the guarded mount
Looks toward Namancos and Bayona's hold.
Look homeward, Angel, now, and melt with ruth.
And, O ye dolphins, waft the hapless youth.
165　　Weep no more, woeful shepherds, weep no more,
For Lycidas, your sorrow, is not dead,
Sunk though he be beneath the watery floor.
So sinks the day-star in the ocean bed,
And yet anon repairs his drooping head,

170 And tricks his beams, and with new-spangled
  ore
  Flames in the forehead of the morning sky:
  So Lycidas sunk low, but mounted high,
  Through the dear might of Him that walked the
  waves,
  Where, other groves and other streams along,
175 With nectar pure his oozy locks he laves,
  And hears the unexpressive nuptial song,
  In the blest kingdoms meek of joy and love.
  There entertain him all the saints above,
  In solemn troops, and sweet societies,
180 That sing, and singing in their glory move,
  And wipe the tears for ever from his eyes.
  Now, Lycidas, the shepherds weep no more;
  Henceforth thou art the genius of the shore,
  In thy large recompense, and shalt be good
185 To all that wander in that perilous flood.

  Thus sang the uncouth swain to the oaks and
  rills,
  While the still morn went out with sandals gray:
  He touched the tender stops of various quills,
  With eager thought warbling his Doric lay:
190 And now the sun had stretched out all the hills,
  And now was dropt into the western bay.
  At last he rose, and twitched his mantle blue:
  To-morrow to fresh woods, and pastures new.

SONNET

ON HIS HAVING ARRIVED AT THE AGE OF TWENTY-THREE
(1631)

How soon hath Time, the subtle thief of youth,
  Stolen on his wing my three-and-twentieth year!
  My hasting days fly on with full career,
  But my late spring no bud nor blossom shew'th.

Perhaps my semblance might deceive the truth   5
    That I to manhood am arrived so near;
    And inward ripeness doth much less appear,
    That some more timely-happy spirits endu'th.
Yet, be it less or more, or soon or slow,
    It shall be still in strictest measure even   10
    To that same lot, however mean or high,
Towards which Time leads me, and the will of Heaven.
    All is, if I have grace to use it so,
    As ever in my great Task-Master's eye.

SONNET

ON THE LATE MASSACRE IN PIEDMONT

(1655)

Avenge, O Lord, thy slaughtered saints, whose bones
    Lie scattered on the Alpine mountains cold;
    Even them who kept thy truth so pure of old,
    When all our fathers worshiped stocks and stones,
Forget not: in thy book record their groans   5
    Who were thy sheep, and in their ancient fold
    Slain by the bloody Piedmontese, that rolled
    Mother with infant down the rocks.   Their moans
The vales redoubled to the hills, and they
    To heaven.   Their martyred blood and ashes sow   10
    O'er all the Italian fields, where still doth sway
The triple Tyrant; that from these may grow
    A hundredfold who, having learnt thy way,
    Early may fly the Babylonian woe.

SONNET

ON HIS BLINDNESS

(From *Poems*, etc., 1673.   Written *cir.* 1655?)

When I consider how my light is spent
    Ere half my days in this dark world and wide,
    And that one talent which is death to hide

Lodged with me useless, though my soul more
    bent
5 To serve therewith my Maker, and present
    My true account, lest He returning chide;
    "Doth God exact day-labour, light denied?"
    I fondly ask. But Patience, to prevent
That murmur, soon replies, "God doth not need
10   Either man's work or his own gifts. Who best
    Bear his mild yoke, they serve him best. His
      state
Is kingly: thousands at his bidding speed,
    And post o'er land and ocean without rest;
    They also serve who only stand and wait."

SONNET

TO CYRIACK SKINNER

(First printed in Phillips' *Life of Milton*, 1694. Written *cir.*
1655)

Cyriack, this three years' day these eyes, though
    clear,
    To outward view, of blemish or of spot,
    Bereft of light, their seeing have forgot;
    Nor to their idle orbs doth sight appear
5 Of sun, or moon, or star, throughout the year,
    Or man, or woman. Yet I argue not
    Against Heaven's hand or will, nor bate a jot
    Of heart or hope, but still bear up and steer
Right onward. What supports me, dost thou
    ask?
10   The conscience, friend, to have lost them over-
    plied
    In Liberty's defence, my noble task,
Of which all Europe rings from side to side.
    This thought might lead me through the world's
    vain mask,
    Content, though blind, had I no better guide.

Andrew Marvell

1621–1678

THE GARDEN

(Written *cir.* 1650, published first in first collected edition
of Marvell's *Poems*, 1681)

How vainly men themselves amaze,
To win the palm, the oak, or bays,
And their incessant labours see
Crowned from some single herb, or tree,
5 Whose short and narrow-verged shade
Does prudently their toils upbraid,
While all the flowers and trees do close,
To weave the garlands of repose!

Fair Quiet, have I found thee here,
10 And Innocence, thy sister dear?
Mistaken long, I sought you then
In busy companies of men.
Your sacred plants, if here below,
Only among the plants will grow;
15 Society is all but rude
To this delicious solitude.

No white nor red was ever seen
So amorous as this lovely green.
Fond lovers, cruel as their flame,
20 Cut in these trees their mistress' name,
Little, alas! they know or heed,
How far these beauties her exceed!
Fair trees! where'er your barks I wound,
No name shall but your own be found.

25 When we have run our passion's heat,
  Love hither makes his best retreat.
  The gods, who mortal beauty chase,
  Still in a tree did end their race;
  Apollo hunted Daphne so,
30 Only that she might laurel grow;
  And Pan did after Syrinx speed,
  Not as a nymph, but for a reed.

  What wondrous life is this I lead!
  Ripe apples drop about my head;
35 The luscious clusters of a vine
  Upon my mouth do crush their wine;
  The nectarine, and curious peach,
  Into my hands themselves do reach;
  Stumbling on melons, as I pass,
40 Ensnared with flowers, I fall on grass.

  Meanwhile the mind, from pleasure less,
  Withdraws into its happiness;—
  The mind, that ocean where each kind
  Does straight its own resemblance find;
45 Yet it creates, transcending these,
  Far other worlds, and other seas,
  Annihilating all that's made
  To a green thought in a green shade.

  Here at the fountain's sliding foot,
50 Or at some fruit-tree's mossy root,
  Casting the body's vest aside,
  My soul into the boughs does glide:
  There, like a bird, it sits and sings,
  Then whets and claps its silver wings,
55 And, till prepared for longer flight,
  Waves in its plume the various light.

Such was that happy garden-state,
While man there walked without a mate:
After a place so pure and sweet,
60 What other help could yet be meet!
But 'twas beyond a mortal's share
To wander solitary there:
Two paradises are in one,
To live in paradise alone.

65 How well the skilful gardener drew
Of flowers, and herbs, this dial new,
Where, from above, the milder sun
Does through a fragrant zodiac run,
And, as it works, the industrious bee
70 Computes its time as well as we!
How could such sweet and wholesome hours
Be reckoned but with herbs and flowers?

PART THIRD

DRYDEN TO THOMSON

Cir. 1660—*Cir.* 1730

John Dryden

1631–1700

MAC-FLECKNOE; OR, A SATIRE ON THE TRUE BLUE PROTESTANT POET, T. S.

(1682)

ALL human things are subject to decay,
And, when fate summons, monarchs must obey.
This Flecknoe found, who, like Augustus, young
Was called to empire, and had governed long;
5 In prose and verse was owned, without dispute,
Through all the realms of Nonsense, absolute.
This aged prince, now flourishing in peace,
And blest with issue of a large increase,
Worn out with business, did at length debate
10 To settle the succession of the state;
And, pondering which of all his sons was fit
To reign, and wage immortal war with wit,
Cried, "'Tis resolved! for Nature pleads, that he
Should only rule, who most resembles me.
15 Shadwell alone my perfect image bears,
Mature in dulness from his tender years;
Shadwell alone, of all my sons, is he,

Who stands confirmed in full stupidity.
The rest to some faint meaning make pretence,
20 But Shadwell never deviates into sense;
Some beams of wit on other souls may fall,
Strike through, and make a lucid interval;
But Shadwell's genuine night admits no ray,
His rising fogs prevail upon the day.
25 Besides, his goodly fabric fills the eye,
And seems designed for thoughtless majesty;
Thoughtless as monarch oaks, that shade the
    plain,
And, spread in solemn state, supinely reign.
Heywood and Shirley were but types of thee,
30 Thou last great prophet of tautology!
Even I, a dunce of more renown than they,
Was sent before but to prepare thy way;
And, coarsely clad in Norwich drugget, came
To teach the nations in thy greater name.
35 My warbling lute,—the lute I whilom strung,
When to King John of Portugal I sung,—
Was but the prelude to that glorious day,
When thou on silver Thames didst cut thy way,
With well-timed oars, before the royal barge,
40 Swelled with the pride of thy celestial charge;
And big with hymn, commander of an host,—
The like was ne'er in Epsom blankets tost.
Methinks I see the new Arion sail,
The lute still trembling underneath thy nail.
45 At thy well-sharpened thumb, from shore to
    shore,
The trebles squeak for fear, the basses roar;

   .   .   .   .   .   .

   .   .   .   .   .   .

About thy boat the little fishes throng,
50 As at the morning toast that floats along.
Sometimes, as prince of thy harmonious band,
Thou wield'st thy papers in thy threshing hand;

St. André's feet ne'er kept more equal time,
Not even the feet of thy own Psyche's rhyme:
55 Though they in number as in sense excel;
So just, so like tautology, they fell,
That, pale with envy, Singleton forswore
The lute and sword, which he in triumph bore,
And vowed he ne'er would act Villerius more."
60   Here stopt the good old sire and wept for joy,
In silent raptures of the hopeful boy.
All arguments, but most his plays, persuade,
That for anointed dulness he was made.
     Close to the walls which fair Augusta bind,
65 (The fair Augusta much to fears inclined),
An ancient fabric raised to inform the sight,
There stood of yore, and Barbican it hight;
A watch-tower once, but now, so fate ordains,
Of all the pile an empty name remains;

.   .   .   .

.   .   .   .

Near it a Nursery erects its head,
Where queens are formed and future heroes bred,
Where unfledged actors learn to laugh and cry,

.   .   .   .

And little Maximins the gods defy.
Great Fletcher never treads in buskins here,
80 Nor greater Jonson dares in socks appear;
But gentle Simkin just reception finds
Amidst this monument of vanished minds;
Pure clinches the suburban muse affords,
And Panton waging harmless war with words.
85 Here Flecknoe, as a place to fame well known,
Ambitiously designed his Shadwell's throne.
For ancient Decker prophesied long since,
That in this pile should reign a mighty prince,
Born for a scourge of wit, and flail of sense;
90 To whom true dulness should some Psyches owe,

But worlds of Misers from his pen should flow;
Humorists and Hypocrites, it should produce,—
Whole Raymond families, and tribes of Bruce.
   Now empress Fame had published the renown
95 Of Shadwell's coronation through the town.
Roused by report of fame, the nations meet,
From near Bunhill, and distant Watling Street.
No Persian carpets spread the imperial way,
But scattered limbs of mangled poets lay.

.   .   .   .   .   .

    .   .   .   .   .

Much Heywood, Shirley, Ogleby there lay,
But loads of Shadwell almost choked the way;
Bilked stationers for yeomen stood prepared,
105 And Herringman was captain of the guard.
The hoary prince in majesty appeared,
High on a throne of his own labours reared.
At his right hand our young Ascanius sate,
Rome's other hope, and pillar of the state.
110 His brows thick fogs, instead of glories, grace,
And lambent dulness played around his face.
As Hannibal did to the altars come,
Sworn by his sire, a mortal foe to Rome,
So Shadwell swore, nor should his vow be vain,
115 That he till death true dulness would maintain;
And, in his father's right, and realm's defence,
Ne'er to have peace with wit, nor truce with
    sense.
The king himself the sacred unction made,
As king by office, and as priest by trade.
120 In his sinister hand, instead of ball,
He placed a mighty mug of potent ale;
"Love's kingdom" to his right he did convey,
At once his sceptre, and his rule of sway;
Whose righteous lore the prince had practised
    young,
125 And from whose loins recorded Psyche sprung.

His temples, last, with poppies were o'erspread,
That nodding seemed to consecrate his head.
Just at the point of time, if fame not lie,
On his left hand twelve reverend owls did fly;
130 So Romulus, 'tis sung, by Tiber's brook,
Presage of sway from twice six vultures took.
The admiring throng loud acclamations make,
And omens of his future empire take.
The sire then shook the honours of his head,
135 And from his brows damps of oblivion shed
Full on the filial dulness: long he stood,
Repelling from his breast the raging god;
At length burst out in this prophetic mood:—
"Heavens bless my son! from Ireland let him
    reign,
140 To far Barbadoes on the western main;
Of his dominion may no end be known,
And greater than his father's be his throne;
Beyond love's kingdom let him stretch his pen!"
He paused, and all the people cried, "Amen."
145 Then thus continued he: "My son, advance
Still in new impudence, new ignorance.
Success let others teach, learn thou from me
Pangs without birth, and fruitless industry.
Let Virtuosos in five years be writ,
150 Yet not one thought accuse thy toil of wit.
Let gentle George in triumph tread the stage,
Make Dorimant betray, and Loveit rage;
Let Cully, Cockwood, Fopling, charm the pit,
And in their folly show the writer's wit;
155 Yet still thy fools shall stand in thy defence,
And justify their author's want of sense.
Let them be all by thy own model made
Of dulness, and desire no foreign aid,
That they to future ages may be known,
160 Not copies drawn, but issue of thy own:
Nay, let thy men of wit too be the same,

All full of thee, and differing but in name,
But let no alien Sedley interpose,
To lard with wit thy hungry Epsom prose.
165 And when false flowers of rhetoric thou wouldst
　　　　cull,
Trust nature; do not labour to be dull,
But write thy best, and top; and, in each line,
Sir Formal's oratory will be thine:
Sir Formal, though unsought, attends thy quill,
170 And does thy northern dedications fill.
Nor let false friends seduce thy mind to fame,
By arrogating Jonson's hostile name;
Let father Flecknoe fire thy mind with praise,
And uncle Ogleby thy envy raise.
175 Thou art my blood, where Jonson has no part:
What share have we in nature, or in art?
Where did his wit on learning fix a brand,
And rail at arts he did not understand?
Where made he love in Prince Nicander's vein,
180 Or swept the dust in Psyche's humble strain?

.　　　　.　　　　.　　　　.

When did his muse from Fletcher scenes purloin,
As thou whole Etherege dost transfuse to thine?
185 But so transfused, as oil and waters flow,
His always floats above, thine sinks below.
This is thy province, this thy wondrous way,
New humours to invent for each new play:
This is that boasted bias of thy mind,
190 By which one way to dulness 'tis inclined;
Which makes thy writings lean on one side still,
And, in all changes, that way bends thy will.
Nor let thy mountain belly make pretence
Of likeness; thine's a tympany of sense.
195 A tun of man in thy large bulk is writ,
But sure thou art but a kilderkin of wit.
Like mine, thy gentle numbers feebly creep;

Thy tragic muse gives smiles, thy comic sleep.
With whate'er gall thou setst thyself to write,
200 Thy inoffensive satires never bite;
In thy felonious heart though venom lies,
It does but touch thy Irish pen, and dies.
Thy genius calls thee not to purchase fame
In keen iambics, but mild anagram.
205 Leave writing plays, and choose for thy command,
Some peaceful province in Acrostic land.
There thou may'st wings display, and altars raise,
And torture one poor word ten thousand ways;
Or, if thou wouldst thy different talents suit,
210 Set thy own songs, and sing them to thy lute."
    He said: but his last words were scarcely
        heard;
For Bruce and Longvil had a trap prepared,
And down they sent the yet declaiming bard.
Sinking he left his drugget robe behind,
215 Borne upwards by a subterranean wind.
The mantle fell to the young prophet's part;
With double portion of his father's art.

ACHITOPHEL

(From *Absalom and Achitophel*, 1681)

150   Of these the false Achitophel was first;
A name to all succeeding ages curst:
For close designs, and crooked counsels fit;
Sagacious, bold, and turbulent of wit;
Restless, unfixed in principles and place;
155 In power unpleased, impatient of disgrace;
A fiery soul, which, working out its way,
Fretted the pigmy-body to decay,
And o'er-informed the tenement of clay.
A daring pilot in extremity,
160 Pleased with the danger, when the waves went
       high,

He sought the storms; but for a calm unfit,
Would steer too nigh the sands, to boast his wit.
Great wits are sure to madness near allied,
And thin partitions do their bounds divide;
165 Else, why should he, with wealth and honour
        blest,
Refuse his age the needful hours of rest?
Punish a body which he could not please;
Bankrupt of life, yet prodigal of ease?
And all to leave what with his toil he won,
170 To that unfeathered two-legged thing, a son;
Got, while his soul did huddled notions try;
And born a shapeless lump, like anarchy.
In friendship false, implacable in hate;
Resolved to ruin, or to rule the state.
175 To compass this the triple bond he broke;
The pillars of the public safety shook;
And fitted Israel for a foreign yoke;
Then, seized with fear, yet still affecting fame,
Usurped a patriot's all-atoning name.
180 So easy still it proves in factious times,
With public zeal to cancel private crimes.
How safe is treason, and how sacred ill,
Where none can sin against the people's will,
Where crowds can wink, and no offence be known,
185 Since in another's guilt they find their own?
Yet fame deserved no enemy can grudge;
The statesman we abhor, but praise the judge.
In Israel's courts ne'er sat an Abbethdin
With more discerning eyes, or hands more clean,
190 Unbribed, unsought, the wretched to redress;
Swift of despatch, and easy of access.
Oh! had he been content to serve the crown,
With virtue only proper to the gown;
Or had the rankness of the soil been freed
195 From cockle, that oppressed the noble seed;
David for him his tuneful harp had strung,

And heaven had wanted one immortal song.
But wild ambition loves to slide, not stand,
And fortune's ice prefers to virtue's land.
Achitophel, grown weary to possess   200
A lawful fame, and lazy happiness,
Disdained the golden fruit to gather free,
And lent the crowd his arm to shake the tree.

A SONG FOR ST. CECILIA'S DAY, 22ND NOVEMBER.

1687

I.

From harmony, from heavenly harmony,
    This universal frame began:
  When nature underneath a heap
    Of jarring atoms lay,
  And could not heave her head,   5
The tuneful voice was heard from high,
    "Arise, ye more than dead."
Then cold, and hot, and moist, and dry,
In order to their stations leap,
    And Music's power obey.   10
From harmony, from heavenly harmony,
    This universal frame began;
  From harmony to harmony
  Through all the compass of the notes it ran,
    The diapason closing full in man.   15

II.

What passion cannot music raise and quell?
  When Jubal struck the chorded shell,
    His listening brethren stood around,
And, wondering, on their faces fell
    To worship that celestial sound: 20

Less than a God they thought there could not dwell
    Within the hollow of that shell,
    That spoke so sweetly, and so well.
What passion cannot music raise and quell?

III.

    The trumpet's loud clangour   25
      Excites us to arms,
    With shrill notes of anger
      And mortal alarms.
The double, double, double beat
    Of the thundering drum,   30
    Cries, hark! the foes come:
Charge, charge! 'tis too late to retreat.

IV.

    The soft complaining flute,
      In dying notes, discovers
      The woes of hopeless lovers;   35
Whose dirge is whispered by the warbling lute.

V.

    Sharp violins proclaim
    Their jealous pangs and desperation,
    Fury, frantic indignation,
    Depth of pains, and height of passion,   40
      For the fair, disdainful dame.

VI.

    But, oh! what art can teach,
    What human voice can reach,
    The sacred organ's praise?
      Notes inspiring holy love,   45
Notes that wend their heavenly ways
    To mend the choirs above.

VII.

Orpheus could lead the savage race;
  And trees unrooted left their place,
    Sequacious of the lyre: 50
But bright Cecilia raised the wonder higher;
  When to her organ vocal breath was given,
An angel heard, and straight appeared,
  Mistaking earth for heaven.

GRAND CHORUS

As from the power of sacred lays   55
  The spheres began to move,
And sung the great Creator's praise
  To all the blessed above;
So when the last and dreadful hour
This crumbling pageant shall devour,   60
The trumpet shall be heard on high,
The dead shall live, the living die,
And Music shall untune the sky.

ALEXANDER'S FEAST, OR THE POWER OF MUSIC: AN ODE IN HONOUR OF ST. CECILIA'S DAY, 1697

I.

'Twas at the royal feast, for Persia won
  By Philip's warlike son:
    Aloft, in awful state,
    The godlike hero sate
On his imperial throne.   5
  His valiant peers were placed around;
Their brows with roses and with myrtles bound:
  (So should desert in arms be crowned.)
  The lovely Thais, by his side,
Sate like a blooming eastern bride,   10
  In flower of youth and beauty's pride.

Happy, happy, happy pair!
None but the brave,
None but the brave,
None but the brave deserves the fair.   15

CHORUS

Happy, happy, happy pair!
None but the brave,
None but the brave,
None but the brave deserves the fair.

II.

Timotheus, placed on high   20
   Amid the tuneful quire,
      With flying fingers touched the lyre:
The trembling notes ascend the sky,
      And heavenly joys inspire.
The song began from Jove,   25
Who left his blissful seats above,
(Such is the power of mighty love.)
A dragon's fiery form belied the god;
   Sublime on radiant spires he rode;
      When he to fair Olympia pressed,   30
      And while he sought her snowy breast;
Then, round her slender waist he curled,
And stamped an image of himself, a sovereign of the
      world.
The listening crowd admire the lofty sound,
A present deity! they shout around;   35
A present deity! the vaulted roofs rebound.
      With ravished ears,
      The monarch hears;
      Assumes the god,
      Affects to nod,   40
   And seems to shake the spheres.

CHORUS

With ravished ears,
The monarch hears;
Assumes the god,
Affects to nod, 45
And seems to shake the spheres.

III.

The praise of Bacchus then the sweet musician sung;
  Of Bacchus ever fair, and ever young.
    The jolly god in triumph comes;
    Sound the trumpets, beat the drums; 50
      Flushed with a purple grace
      He shows his honest face:
Now, give the hautboys breath; he comes, he comes.
    Bacchus, ever fair and young,
      Drinking joys did first ordain; 55
    Bacchus' blessings are a treasure,
    Drinking is the soldier's pleasure;
      Rich the treasure,
      Sweet the pleasure,
Sweet is pleasure after pain. 60

CHORUS

Bacchus' blessings are a treasure,
Drinking is the soldier's pleasure;
    Rich the treasure,
    Sweet the pleasure,
Sweet is pleasure after pain. 65

IV.

  Soothed with the sound, the king grew vain:
    Fought all his battles o'er again;
And thrice he routed all his foes, and thrice he slew the
    slain.

The master saw the madness rise,
His glowing cheeks, his ardent eyes;   70
And, while he heaven and earth defied,
Changed his hand, and checked his pride.
    He chose a mournful muse,
      Soft pity to infuse,
He sung Darius great and good,   75
    By too severe a fate,
Fallen, fallen, fallen, fallen,
Fallen from his high estate,
    And weltering in his blood:
Deserted, at his utmost need,   80
By those his former bounty fed;
On the bare earth exposed he lies,
With not a friend to close his eyes.
With downcast looks the joyless victor sate,
  Revolving, in his altered soul,   85
    The various turns of chance below;
And, now and then, a sigh he stole,
    And tears began to flow.

CHORUS

Revolving, in his altered soul,
  The various turns of chance below;   90
And, now and then, a sigh he stole;
  And tears began to flow.

V.

The mighty master smiled, to see
That love was in the next degree;
'Twas but a kindred-sound to move,   95
For pity melts the mind to love.
    Softly sweet, in Lydian measures,
      Soon he soothed his soul to pleasures:
War, he sung, is toil and trouble;
Honour, but an empty bubble;   100

Never ending, still beginning,
Fighting still, and still destroying:
　If the world be worth thy winning,
Think, O think it worth enjoying;
　Lovely Thais sits beside thee,   105
　Take the good the gods provide thee—
The many rend the skies with loud applause;
So Love was crowned, but Music won the cause.
　　The prince, unable to conceal his pain,
　　　Gazed on the fair,   110
　　　Who caused his care,
　And sighed and looked, sighed and looked,
　　Sighed and looked, and sighed again;
At length, with love and wine at once oppressed,
The vanquished victor sunk upon her breast.   115

CHORUS

The prince, unable to conceal his pain,
*　Gazed on the fair*
*　Who caused his care,*
And sighed and looked, sighed and looked,
*　Sighed and looked, and sighed again;*   120
At length, with love and wine at once oppressed,
The vanquished victor sunk upon her breast.

VI.

Now strike the golden lyre again;
A louder yet, and yet a louder strain.
Break his bands of sleep asunder,   125
And rouse him, like a rattling peal of thunder.
　　Hark, hark! the horrid sound
　　　Has raised up his head;
　　　As awaked from the dead,
　　And amazed, he stares around.   130
Revenge, revenge! Timotheus cries,
　See the furies arise;

See the snakes, that they rear,
How they hiss in their hair,
And the sparkles that flash from their eyes!   135
Behold a ghastly band,
Each a torch in his hand!
Those are Grecian ghosts, that in battle were slain,
And, unburied, remain
Inglorious on the plain: 140
Give the vengeance due
To the valiant crew.
Behold how they toss their torches on high,
How they point to the Persian abodes,
And glittering temples of their hostile gods.—   145
The princes applaud, with a furious joy,
And the king seized a flambeau with zeal to destroy;
Thais led the way,
To light him to his prey,
And, like another Helen, fired another Troy.   150

CHORUS

And the King seized a flambeau with zeal to destroy;
Thais led the way,
To light him to his prey,
And, like another Helen, fired another Troy.

VII.

Thus, long ago,   155
Ere heaving bellows learned to blow,
While organs yet were mute,
Timotheus, to his breathing flute,
And sounding lyre,
Could swell the soul to rage, or kindle soft desire.   160
At last divine Cecilia came,
Inventress of the vocal frame;
The sweet enthusiast, from her sacred store,
Enlarged the former narrow bounds,
And added length to solemn sounds,   165

With nature's mother-wit, and arts unknown before.
    Let old Timotheus yield the prize,
      Or both divide the crown;
    He raised a mortal to the skies,
      She drew an angel down.   170

GRAND CHORUS

*   At last divine Cecilia came,*
*   Inventress of the vocal frame :*
The sweet enthusiast, from her sacred store,
*   Enlarged the former narrow bounds,*
*   And added length to solemn sounds,*   *175*
With nature's mother-wit, and arts unknown before,
*   Let old Timotheus yield the prize,*
*   Or both divide the crown ;*
*   He raised a mortal to the skies,*
*   She drew an angel down.*   *180*

UNDER MR. MILTON'S PICTURE

Three poets, in three distant ages born,
Greece, Italy, and England, did adorn.
The first, in loftiness of thought surpassed;
The next, in majesty; in both the last.
The force of Nature could no further go;   5
To make a third, she joined the former two.

Matthew Prior

1664–1721

TO A CHILD OF QUALITY FIVE YEARS OLD.
MDCCIV

THE AUTHOR THEN FORTY

(From *Poems on Several Occasions*, 1709)

Lords, knights, and 'squires the numerous band,
    That wear the fair Miss Mary's fetters,
Were summoned by her high command,
    To show their passions by their letters.

5 My pen among the rest I took,
    Lest those bright eyes that cannot read
Should dart their kindling fires, and look
    The power they have to be obeyed.

Nor quality, nor reputation,
10   Forbid me yet my flame to tell,
Dear five years old befriends my passion,
    And I may write till she can spell.

For, while she makes her silk-worm's beds,
    With all the tender things I swear;
15 Whilst all the house my passion reads,
    In papers round her baby's hair;

She may receive and own my flame,
    For though the strictest prudes should know it,
She'll pass for a most virtuous dame,
20   And I for an unhappy poet.

Then, too, alas! when she shall tear
    The lines some younger rival sends;
She'll give me leave to write, I fear,
    And we shall still continue friends.

25 For, as our different ages move,
    'Tis so ordained, (would Fate but mend it!)
That I shall be past making love,
    When she begins to comprehend it.

A BETTER ANSWER

Dear Chloe, how blubbered is that pretty face!
    Thy cheek all on fire, and thy hair all uncurled:
Pr'ythee quit this caprice; and (as old Falstaff
    says),
    Let us e'en talk a little like folks of this world.

5 How cans't thou presume, thou hast leave to de-
    stroy
    The beauties, which Venus but lent to thy
    keeping?
Those looks were designed to inspire love and joy:
    More ordinary eyes may serve people for weep-
    ing.

To be vexed at a trifle or two that I writ,
10   Your judgment at once, and my passion you
    wrong:
You take that for fact, which will scarce be found
    wit:
    Od's life! must one swear to the truth of a
    song?

What I speak, my fair Chloe, and what I write,
    shows
    The difference there is betwixt nature and art:
15 I court others in verse; but I love thee in prose:
    And they have my whimsies; but thou hast my
    heart.

The god of us verse-men (you know, Child) the
    sun,
    How after his journeys he sets up his rest;
If at morning o'er earth 'tis his fancy to run;
20   At night he reclines on his Thetis's breast.

So when I am wearied with wandering all day;
    To thee, my delight, in the evening I come:
No matter what beauties I saw in my way:
    They were but my visits, but thou art my home.

25 Then finish, dear Chloe, this pastoral war;
    And let us like Horace and Lydia agree:
For thou art a girl as much brighter than her,
    As he was a poet sublimer than me.

Joseph Addison

1672–1719

ODE

THE SPACIOUS FIRMAMENT
(1712)

I.

The spacious firmament **on** high,
With all the blue ethereal sky,
And spangled heavens, a shining frame,
Their great Original proclaim:
5 Th' unwearied sun, from day to day,
Does his Creator's power display,
And publishes to every land
The work of an Almighty hand.

II.

Soon as the evening shades prevail,
10 The moon takes up the wondrous tale,

And, nightly, to the listening earth,
Repeats the story of her birth:
While all the stars that round her burn,
And all the planets in their turn,
15 Confirm the tidings as they roll,
And spread the truth from pole to pole.

III.

What though, in solemn silence, all
Move round the dark terrestrial ball?
What though nor real voice nor sound
20 Amid their radiant orbs be found?
In reason's ear they all rejoice,
And utter forth a glorious voice,
For ever singing as they shine,
"The hand that made us is divine."

John Gay

1688–1732

FABLE XVIII

THE PAINTER WHO PLEASED NOBODY AND EVERYBODY

(From *Fables*, 1727)

Lest men suspect your tale untrue,
Keep probability in view.
The traveller leaping o'er those bounds,
The credit of his book confounds.
5 Who with his tongue hath armies routed,
Makes ev'n his real courage doubted.
But flattery never seems absurd;
The flatter'd always take your word:
Impossibilities seem just:
10 They take the strongest praise on trust.

Hyperboles, though ne'er so great,
Will still come short of self-conceit.
　So very like a Painter drew,
That every eye the picture knew;
15 He hit complexion, feature, air,
So just, the life itself was there.
No flattery with his colours laid,
To bloom restor'd the faded maid;
He gave each muscle all its strength;
20 The mouth, the chin, the nose's length;
His honest pencil touch'd with truth,
And mark'd the date of age and youth.

　He lost his friends, his practice fail'd;
Truth should not always be reveal'd;
25 In dusty piles his pictures lay,
For no one sent the second pay.
Two bustos, fraught with every grace,
A Venus' and Apollo's face,
He plac'd in view; resolv'd to please,
30 Who ever sat he drew from these,
From these corrected every feature,
And spirited each awkward creature.

　All things were set; the hour was come,
His palette ready o'er his thumb,
35 My Lord appear'd; and, seated right,
In proper attitude and light,
The Painter look'd, he sketch'd the piece,
Then dipt his pencil, talk'd of Greece,
Of Titian's tints, of Guido's air;
40 'Those eyes, my Lord, the spirit there,
Might well a Raphael's hand require,
To give them all the native fire;
The features, fraught with sense and wit,
You'll grant are very hard to hit;
45 But yet with patience you shall view,
As much as paint and art can do.'
　Observe the work. My Lord replied,

'Till now I thought my mouth was wide;
Besides, my nose is somewhat long;
50 Dear sir, for me, 'tis far too young!'
  'Oh! pardon me, (the artist cried)
In this we Painters must decide.
The piece ev'n common eyes must strike,
I warrant it extremely like.'
55   My Lord examin'd it a-new;
No looking-glass seem'd half so true.
  A lady came, with borrow'd grace,
He from his Venus form'd her face.
Her lover prais'd the Painter's art;
60 So like the picture in his heart!
To every age some charm he lent;
Ev'n beauties were almost content.
  Through all the town his art they prais'd;
His custom grew, his price was rais'd.
65 Had he the real likeness shown,
Would any man the picture own?
But when thus happily he wrought,
Each found the likeness in his thought.

ON A LAP DOG

Shock's fate I mourn; poor Shock is now no
    more!
Ye Muses! mourn, ye Chambermaids! deplore.
Unhappy Shock! Yet more unhappy fair,
Doom'd to survive thy joy and only care.
5 Thy wretched fingers now no more shall deck,
And tie the favorite ribband round his neck;
No more thy hand shall smooth his glossy hair,
And comb the wavings of his pendent ear.
Let cease thy flowing grief, forsaken maid!
10 All mortal pleasures in a moment fade:
Our surest hope is in an hour destroy'd,
And love, best gift of Heaven, not long enjoy'd.

Methinks I see her frantic with despair,
Her streaming eyes, wrung hands, and flowing
hair;
15 Her Mechlin pinners, rent, the floor bestrow,
And her torn face gives real signs of woe.
Hence, Superstition! that tormenting guest,
That haunts with fancied fears the coward breast;
No dread events upon this fate attend,
20 Stream eyes no more, no more thy tresses rend.
Though certain omens oft forwarn a state,
And dying lions show the monarch's fate,
Why should such fears bid Celia's sorrow rise?
For when a lap dog falls, no lover dies.
25 　Cease, Celia, cease; restrain thy flowing tears,
Some warmer passion will dispel thy cares.
In man you'll find a more substantial bliss,
More grateful toying and a sweeter kiss.
　He's dead.　Oh! lay him gently in the ground!
30 And may his tomb be by this verse renown'd.
Here Shock, the pride of all his kind, is laid,
Who fawn'd like man, but ne'er like man betray'd.

Alexander Pope

1688-1744

THE RAPE OF THE LOCK

(Enlarged version published 1714)

CANTO I.

What dire offence from am'rous causes springs,
What mighty contests rise from trivial things,
I sing.—This verse to Caryll, Muse! is due;
This, ev'n Belinda may vouchsafe to view;
5 Slight is the subject, but not so the praise,
If she inspire, and he approve my lays.

Say what strange motive, goddess! could compel
A well-bred lord t' assault a gentle belle?
O say what stranger cause, yet unexplored,
10 Could make a gentle belle reject a lord?
In tasks so bold, can little men engage,
And in soft bosoms, dwells such mighty rage?
   Sol through white curtains shot a tim'rous ray,
And op'd those eyes that must eclipse the day;
15 Now lap-dogs give themselves the rousing shake,
And sleepless lovers, just at twelve, awake:
Thrice rung the bell, the slipper knock'd the ground,
And the pressed watch returned a silver sound.
Belinda still her downy pillow pressed,
20 Her guardian sylph prolonged the balmy rest:
'Twas he had summoned to her silent bed
The morning dream that hovered o'er her head,
A youth more glitt'ring than a birth-night beau,
(That ev'n in slumber caused her cheek to glow)
25 Seemed to her ear his winning lips to lay,
And thus in whispers said, or seemed to say.
   "Fairest of mortals, thou distinguished care
Of thousand bright inhabitants of air!
If e'er one vision touched thy infant thought,
30 Of all the nurse and all the priest have taught;
Of airy elves by moonlight shadows seen,
The silver token, and the circled green,
Or virgins visited by angel-pow'rs,
With golden crowns and wreaths of heav'nly flow'rs;
35 Hear and believe! thy own importance know,
Nor bound thy narrow views to things below.
Some secret truths, from learned pride concealed,
To maids alone and children are revealed.
What though no credit doubting wits may give?
40 The fair and innocent shall still believe.

Know then, unnumbered spirits round thee fly,
The light militia of the lower sky:
These, though unseen, are ever on the wing,
Hang o'er the box, and hover round the ring.
45 Think what an equipage thou hast in air,
And view with scorn two pages and a chair.
As now your own, our beings were of old,
And once inclosed in woman's beauteous mould;
Thence, by a soft transition, we repair
50 From earthly vehicles to these of air.
Think not, when woman's transient breath is
       fled,
That all her vanities at once are dead;
Succeeding vanities she still regards,
And though she plays no more, o'erlooks the
       cards.
55 Her joy in gilded chariots, when alive,
And love of ombre, after death survive.
For when the fair in all their pride expire,
To their first elements, their souls retire:
The sprites of fiery termagants in flame
60 Mount up, and take a salamander's name.
Soft yielding minds to water glide away,
And sip, with nymphs, their elemental tea.
The graver prude sinks downward to a gnome,
In search of mischief still on earth to roam.
65 The light coquettes in sylphs aloft repair,
And sport and flutter in the fields of air.
   "Know further yet; whoever fair and chaste
Rejects mankind, is by some sylph embraced:
For spirits, freed from mortal laws, with ease
70 Assume what sexes and what shapes they please.
What guards the purity of melting maids,
In courtly balls, and midnight masquerades,
Safe from the treach'rous friend, the daring
       spark,
The glance by day, the whisper in the dark,

75 When kind occasion prompts their warm de-
        sires,
  When music softens, and when dancing fires?
  'Tis but their sylph, the wise celestials know,
  Though honour is the word with men below.
      Some nymphs there are, too conscious of their
          face,
80 For life predestined to the gnomes' embrace.
  These swell their prospects and exalt their pride,
  When offers are disdained, and love denied:
  Then gay ideas crowd the vacant brain,
  While peers, and dukes, and all their sweeping
          train,
85 And garters, stars, and coronets appear,
  And in soft sounds, 'Your Grace' salutes their
          ear.
  'Tis these that early taint the female soul,
  Instruct the eyes of young coquettes to roll,
  Teach infant-cheeks a bidden blush to know,
90 And little hearts to flutter at a beau.
      "Oft', when the world imagine women stray,
  The sylphs through mystic mazes guide their
          way;
  Through all the giddy circle they pursue,
  And old impertinence expel by new.
95 What tender maid but must a victim fall
  To one man's treat, but for another's ball?
  When Florio speaks what virgin could withstand,
  If gentle Damon did not squeeze her hand?
  With varying vanities, from ev'ry part,
100 They shift the moving toyshop of their heart;
  Where wigs with wigs, with sword-knots sword-
          knots strive,
  Beaus banish beaus, and coaches coaches drive.
  This erring mortals levity may call;
  Oh blind to truth! the sylphs contrive it all.
105   "Of these am I, who thy protection claim,

A watchful sprite, and Ariel is my name.
Late, as I ranged the crystal wilds of air,
In the clear mirror of thy ruling star
I saw, alas! some dread event impend,
110 Ere to the main this morning sun descend.
But heaven reveals not what, or how, or where:
Warned by the sylph, oh pious maid, beware!
This to disclose is all thy guardian can:
Beware of all, but most beware of man!"

115   He said; when Shock, who thought she slept
          too long,
Leaped up, and waked his mistress with his
          tongue;
'Twas then, Belinda, if report say true,
Thy eyes first opened on a billet-doux;
Wounds, charms, and ardours, were no sooner
          read,
120 But all the vision vanished from thy head.
    And now, unveiled, the toilet stands displayed,
Each silver vase in mystic order laid.
First, rob'd in white, the nymph intent adores,
With head uncover'd, the cosmetic pow'rs.

125 A heav'nly image in the glass appears,
To that she bends, to that her eyes she rears;
Th' inferior priestess, at her altar's side,
Trembling begins the sacred rites of pride.
Unnumbered treasures ope at once, and here
130 The various off'rings of the world appear;
From each she nicely culls with curious toil,
And decks the goddess with the glitt'ring spoil.
This casket India's glowing gems unlocks,
And all Arabia breathes from yonder box,
135 The tortoise here and elephant unite,
Transformed to combs, the speckled and the
          white.
Here files of pins extend their shining rows,
Puffs, powders, patches, Bibles, billets-doux.

Now awful beauty puts on all its arms;
140 The fair each moment rises in her charms,
Repairs her smiles, awakens ev'ry grace,
And calls forth all the wonders of her face;
Sees by degrees a purer blush arise,
And keener lightnings quicken in her eyes.
145 The busy sylphs surround their darling care,
These set the head, and those divide the hair,
Some fold the sleeve, whilst others plait the gown;
And Betty's praised for labors not her own.

CANTO II.

Not with more glories, in th' ethereal plain,
The sun first rises o'er the purpled main,
Than, issuing forth, the rival of his beams
Launched on the bosom of the silver Thames.
5 Fair nymphs, and well-dressed youths around
        her shone,
But ev'ry eye was fixed on her alone.
On her white breast a sparkling cross she wore,
Which Jews might kiss, and infidels adore.
Her lively looks a sprightly mind disclose,
10 Quick as her eyes, and as unfixed as those.
Favours to none, to all she smiles extends;
Oft she rejects, but never once offends.
Bright as the sun, her eyes the gazers strike,
And, like the sun, they shine on all alike.
15 Yet graceful ease, and sweetness void of pride,
Might hide her faults, if belles had faults to hide;
If to her share some female errors fall,
Look on her face, and you'll forget 'em all.
    This nymph, to the destruction of mankind,
20 Nourished two locks, which graceful hung behind
In equal curls, and well conspired to deck,
With shining ringlets, the smooth iv'ry neck.

Love in these labyrinths his slaves detains,
And mighty hearts are held in slender chains.
25 With hairy springes we the birds betray,
Slight lines of hair surprise the finny prey,
Fair tresses man's imperial race insnare,
And beauty draws us with a single hair.
    Th' advent'rous baron the bright locks ad
        mired;
30 He saw, he wished, and to the prize aspired.
Resolv'd to win, he meditates the way,
By force to ravish, or by fraud betray;
For when success a lover's toil attends,
Few ask, if fraud or force attained his ends.
35   For this, ere Phœbus rose, he had implored
Propitious heav'n, and ev'ry pow'r adored,
But chiefly Love—to Love an altar built,
Of twelve vast French romances, neatly gilt.
There lay three garters, half a pair of gloves,
40 And all the trophies of his former loves;
With tender billets-doux he lights the pyre,
And breathes three am'rous sighs to raise the fire.
Then prostrate falls, and begs with ardent eyes
Soon to obtain, and long possess the prize:
45 The pow'rs gave ear, and granted half his pray'r,
The rest, the winds dispersed in empty air.
    But now secure the painted vessel glides,
The sun-beams trembling on the floating tides:
While melting music steals upon the sky,
50 And softened sounds along the waters die;
Smooth flow the waves, the zephyrs gently play,
Belinda smiled, and all the world was gay.
All but the sylph—with careful thoughts op-
      pressed,
Th' impending woe sat heavy on his breast.
55 He summons strait his denizens of air;
The lucid squadrons round the sails repair:
Soft o'er the shrouds aërial whispers breathe,

That seemed but zephyrs to the train beneath.
Some to the sun their insect-wings unfold,
60 Waft on the breeze, or sink in clouds of gold;
Transparent forms, too fine for mortal sight,
Their fluid bodies half dissolv'd in light,
Loose to the wind their airy garments flew,
Thin glitt'ring textures of the filmy dew,
65 Dipped in the richest tincture of the skies,
Where light disports in ever-mingling dyes;
While ev'ry beam new transient colours flings,
Colours that change whene'er they wave their
            wings.
Amid the circle, on the gilded mast,
70 Superior by the head, was Ariel plac'd;
His purple pinions opening to the sun,
He raised his azure wand, and thus begun:
    "Ye sylphs and sylphids, to your chief give ear!
Fays, fairies, genii, elves, and demons, hear!
75 Ye know the spheres and various tasks assigned
By laws eternal to th' aërial kind.
Some in the fields of purest ether play,
And bask and whiten in the blaze of day.
Some guide the course of wandering orbs on high,
80 Or roll the planets through the boundless sky;
Some less refined, beneath the moon's pale light
Pursue the stars that shoot athwart the night,
Or suck the mists in grosser air below,
Or dip their pinions in the painted bow,
85 Or brew fierce tempests on the wintry main,
Or o'er the glebe distil the kindly rain.
Others on earth o'er human race preside,
Watch all their ways, and all their actions guide:
Of these the chief the care of nations own,
90 And guard with arms divine the British throne.
    "Our humbler province is to tend the fair,
Not a less pleasing, though less glorious care;
To save the powder from too rude a gale,

Nor let th' imprisoned essences exhale;
95 To draw fresh colours from the vernal flow'rs,
To steal from rainbows ere they drop in show'rs
A brighter wash to curl their waving hairs,
Assist their blushes, and inspire their airs;
Nay, oft, in dreams, invention we bestow,
100 To change a flounce, or add a furbelow.
    "This day, black omens threat the brightest
       fair
That e'er deserved a watchful spirit's care;
Some dire disaster, or by force, or slight;
But what, or where, the fates have wrapped in
    night.
105 Whether the nymph shall break Diana's law,
Or some frail China jar receive a flaw;
Or stain her honour, or her new brocade;
Forget her pray'rs, or miss a masquerade;
Or lose her heart, or necklace, at a ball;
110 Or whether heav'n has doom'd that Shock must
    fall.
Haste, then, ye spirits! to your charge repair:
The flutt'ring fan be Zephyretta's care;
The drops to thee, Brillante, we consign;
And, Momentilla, let the watch be thine;
115 Do thou, Crispissa, tend her fav'rite lock;
Ariel himself shall be the guard of Shock.
    "To fifty chosen Sylphs, of special note,
We trust th' important charge, the petticoat:

Form a strong line about the silver bound,
And guard the wide circumference around.
    "Whatever spirit, careless of his charge,
His post neglects, or leaves the fair at large,
125 Shall feel sharp vengeance soon o'ertake his sins,
Be stopped in vials, or transfixed with pins;
Or plunged in lakes of bitter washes lie,
Or wedged, whole ages in a bodkin's eye;

Gums and pomatums shall his flight restrain,
130 While clogged he beats his silken wings in vain;
Or alum styptics with contracting pow'r,
Shrink his thin essence like a rivelled flower;
Or, as Ixion fixed, the wretch shall feel
The giddy motion of the whirling mill,
135 In fumes of burning chocolate shall glow,
And tremble at the sea that froths below!"
   He spoke; the spirits from the sails descend:
Some, orb in orb, around the nymph extend;
Some thrid the mazy ringlets of her hair;
140 Some hang upon the pendants of her ear;
With beating hearts the dire event they wait,
Anxious, and trembling for the birth of fate.

CANTO III.

Close by those meads, for ever crowned with
   flow'rs,
Where Thames with pride surveys his rising
   tow'rs,
There stands a structure of majestic frame,
Which from the neighb'ring Hampton takes its
   name.
5 Here Britain's statesmen oft the fall foredoom
Of foreign tyrants, and of nymphs at home;
Here thou, great ANNA! whom three realms obey,
Dost sometimes counsel take—and sometimes tea.
   Hither the heroes and the nymphs resort,
10 To taste a while the pleasures of a court;
In various talk th' instructive hours they passed,
Who gave the ball, or paid the visit last;
One speaks the glory of the British Queen,
And one describes a charming Indian screen;
15 A third interprets motions, looks, and eyes;
At ev'ry word a reputation dies.

Snuff, or the fan, supply each pause of chat,
With singing, laughing, ogling, and all that.
　　Meanwhile, declining from the noon of day,
20 The sun obliquely shoots his burning ray;
The hungry judges soon the sentence sign,
And wretches hang that jury-men may dine;
The merchant from th' Exchange returns in
　　　peace,
And the long labours of the toilet cease.
25 Belinda now, whom thirst of fame invites,
Burns to encounter two advent'rous knights,
At ombre singly to decide their doom;
And swells her breast with conquests yet to come.
Straight the three bands prepare in arms to join,
30 Each band the number of the sacred nine.
Soon as she spreads her hand, th' aërial guard
Descend, and sit on each important card:
First Ariel perched upon a Matadore,
Then each according to the rank they bore;
35 For sylphs, yet mindful of their ancient race,
Are, as when women, wondrous fond of place.
　　Behold four kings in majesty revered,
With hoary whiskers and a forky beard;
And four fair queens whose hands sustain a
　　　flow'r,
40 Th' expressive emblem of their softer pow'r;
Four knaves in garbs succinct, a trusty band;
Caps on their heads, and halberts in their hand;
And parti-coloured troops, a shining train,
Draw forth to combat on the velvet plain.
45 The skilful nymph reviews her force with
　　　care:
Let spades be trumps! she said, and trumps they
　　　were.
　　Now move to war her sable Matadores,
In show like leaders of the swarthy Moors.
Spadillio first, unconquerable lord!

50 Led off two captive trumps, and swept the board.
  As many more Manillio forced to yield,
  And marched a victor from the verdant field.
  Him Basto followed, but his fate more hard
  Gained but one trump and one plebeian card.
55 With his broad sabre next, a chief in years,
  The hoary majesty of spades appears,
  Puts forth one manly leg, to sight revealed,
  The rest his many coloured robe concealed.
  The rebel knave, who dares his prince engage,
60 Proves the just victim of his royal rage.
    Ev'n mighty Pam, that kings and queens
        o'erthrew,
  And mowed down armies in the fights of loo,
  Sad chance of war! now destitute of aid,
  Falls undistinguished by the victor spade!
65   Thus far both armies to Belinda yield;
  Now to the baron fate inclines the field.
  His warlike Amazon her host invades,
  Th' imperial consort of the crown of spades.
  The club's black tyrant first her victim died,
70 Spite of his haughty mien, and barb'rous pride:
  What boots the regal circle on his head,
  His giant limbs, in state unwieldy spread;
  That long behind he trails his pompous robe,
  And of all monarchs only grasps the globe?
75   The baron now his diamonds pours apace!
  Th' embroidered king who shows but half his
        face,
  And his refulgent queen, with pow'rs combined,
  Of broken troops, an easy conquest find.
  Clubs, diamonds, hearts, in wild disorder seen,
80 With throngs promiscuous strew the level green.
  Thus when dispersed a routed army runs,
  Of Asia's troops, and Afric's sable sons,
  With like confusion different nations fly,
  Of various habit, and of various dye;

85 The pierced battalions disunited fall,
 In heaps on heaps; one fate o'erwhelms them all.
  The knave of diamonds tries his wily arts,
 And wins (oh shameful chance!) the queen of
   hearts.
 At this, the blood the virgin's cheek forsook,
90 A livid paleness spreads o'er all her look;
 She sees, and trembles at th' approaching ill,
 Just in the jaws of ruin, and codille.
 And now (as oft in some distempered state)
 On one nice trick depends the gen'ral fate:
95 An ace of hearts steps forth: The king unseen
 Lurked in her hand, and mourned his captive
   queen:
 He springs to vengeance with an eager pace,
 And falls like thunder on the prostrate ace.
 The nymph exulting fills with shouts the sky;
100 The walls, the woods, and long canals reply.
  Oh thoughtless mortals! ever blind to fate,
 Too soon dejected, and too soon elate.
 Sudden these honours shall be snatched away,
 And cursed for ever this victorious day.
105 For lo! the board with cups and spoons is
   crowned,
 The berries crackle, and the mill turns round;
 On shining altars of japan they raise
 The silver lamp; the fiery spirits blaze:
 From silver spouts the grateful liquors glide,
110 While China's earth receives the smoking tide:
 At once they gratify their scent and taste,
 And frequent cups prolong the rich repast.
 Straight hover round the fair her airy band;
 Some, as she sipped, the fuming liquor fanned,
115 Some o'er her lap their careful plumes displayed,
 Trembling, and conscious of the rich brocade.
 Coffee (which makes the politician wise,
 And see through all things with his half-shut
  eyes)

Sent up in vapours to the baron's brain
120 New stratagems, the radiant lock to gain.
Ah cease, rash youth! desist ere 'tis too late,
Fear the just gods, and think of Scylla's fate!
Changed to a bird, and sent to flit in air,
She dearly pays for Nisus' injured hair!
125   But when to mischief mortals bend their will,
How soon they find fit instruments of ill!
Just then, Clarissa drew with tempting grace
A two-edged weapon from her shining case:
So ladies in romance assist their knight,
130 Present the spear, and **arm** him for the fight.
He takes the gift with rev'rence, and extends
The little engine on his fingers' ends;
This just behind Belinda's neck he spread,
As o'er the fragrant steams she bends her head.
135 Swift to the lock a thousand sprites repair;
A thousand wings, by turns, blow back the hair;
And thrice they twitched the diamond in her ear;
Thrice she looked back, and thrice the foe
      drew near.
Just in that instant, anxious Ariel sought
140 The close recesses of the virgin's thought;
As on the nosegay in her breast reclined,
He watched th' ideas rising in her mind,
Sudden he viewed in spite of all her art,
An earthly lover lurking at her heart.
145 Amazed, confused, he found his pow'r expired,
Resigned to fate, and with a sigh retired.
    The peer now spreads the glitt'ring forfex wide
T' inclose the lock; now joins it, to divide.
Ev'n then, before the fatal engine closed,
150 A wretched sylph too fondly interposed;
Fate urged the shears, and cut the sylph in twain,
(But airy substance soon unites again,)
The meeting points the sacred hair dissever
From the fair head, for ever, and for ever!

155   Then flashed the living lightning from her
          eyes,
     And screams of horror rend th' affrighted skies.
     Not louder shrieks to pitying heav'n are cast,
     When husbands, or when lap-dogs breathe their
          last;
     Or when rich China vessels fall'n from high,
160 In glitt'ring dust, and painted fragments lie!
       "Let wreaths of triumph now my temples
          twine,"
     (The victor cried,) "the glorious prize is mine!
     While fish in streams, or birds delight in air,
     Or in a coach and six the British fair,
165 As long as Atalantis shall be read,
     Or the small pillow grace a lady's bed,
     While visits shall be paid on solemn days,
     When num'rous wax-lights in bright order blaze,
     While nymphs take treats, or assignations give,
170 So long my honour, name, and praise shall live!"
       What time would spare, from steel receives its
          date,
     And monuments, like men, submit to fate!
     Steel could the labour of the gods destroy,
     And strike to dust th' imperial tow'rs of Troy;
175 Steel could the works of mortal pride confound,
     And hew triumphal arches to the ground.
     What wonder then, fair nymph! thy hair should
          feel
     The conqu'ring force of unresisted steel?

CANTO IV.

But anxious cares the pensive nymph oppressed,
And secret passions laboured in her breast.
Not youthful kings in battle seized alive,
Not scornful virgins who their charms survive,

 5 Not ardent lovers robbed of all their bliss,
   Not ancient ladies when refused a kiss,
   Not tyrants fierce that unrepenting die,
   Not Cynthia when her manteau's pinned awry,
   E'er felt such rage, resentment, and despair,
10 As thou, sad virgin! for thy ravished hair.
       For, that sad moment, when the sylphs with-
           drew,
   And Ariel weeping from Belinda flew,
   Umbriel, a dusky, melancholy sprite,
   As ever sullied the fair face of light,
15 Down to the central earth, his proper scene,
   Repaired to search the gloomy cave of Spleen.
       Swift on his sooty pinions flits the gnome,
   And in a vapour reached the dismal dome.
   No cheerful breeze this sullen region knows,
20 The dreaded east is all the wind that blows,
   Here in a grotto, sheltered close from air,
   And screened in shades from day's detested glare,
   She sighs for ever on her pensive bed,
   Pain at her side, and Megrim at her head.
25   Two handmaids wait the throne; alike in place,
   But diff'ring far in figure and in face.
   Here stood Ill-nature like an ancient maid,
   Her wrinkled form in black and white arrayed;
   With store of pray'rs, for mornings, nights, and
           noons,
30 Her hand is filled; her bosom with lampoons.
       There Affectation, with a sickly mien,
   Shows in her cheek the roses of eighteen,
   Practised to lisp and hang the head aside,
   Faints into airs, and languishes with pride,
35 On the rich quilt sinks with becoming woe,
   Wrapt in a gown, for sickness, and for show.
   The fair ones feel such maladies as these,
   When each new night-dress gives a new disease.
   A constant vapour o'er the palace flies;

40 Strange phantoms rising as the mists arise;
   Dreadful, as hermit's dreams in haunted shades,
   Or bright, as visions of expiring maids.
   Now glaring fiends, and snakes on rolling spires,
   Pale spectres, gaping tombs, and purple fires;
45 Now lakes of liquid gold, Elysian scenes,
   And crystal domes, and angels in machines.
   Unnumbered throngs on ev'ry side are seen,
   Of bodies changed to various forms by Spleen.
   Here living tea-pots stand, one arm held out,
50 One bent; the handle this, and that the spout;
   A pipkin there, like Homer's tripod walks;
   Here sighs a jar, and there a goose-pye talks;
   Men prove with child, as pow'rful fancy works,
   And maids turned bottles call aloud for corks.
55   Safe past the gnome through this fantastic band,
   A branch of healing spleenwort in his hand.
   Then thus addressed the pow'r—"Hail, wayward
             queen!
   Who rule the sex to fifty from fifteen;
   Parent of vapours and of female wit,
60 Who give th' hysteric, or poetic fit,
   On various tempers act by various ways,
   Make some take physic, others scribble plays;
   Who cause the proud their visits to delay,
   And send the godly in a pet to pray;
65 A nymph there is, that all thy pow'r disdains,
   And thousands more in equal mirth maintains.
   But, oh! if e'er thy gnome could spoil a grace,
   Or raise a pimple on a beauteous face,
   Like citron-waters matrons' cheeks inflame,
70 Or change complexions at a losing game;

   .   .   .   .

   Or caus'd suspicion when no soul was rude,
   Or discompos'd the head-dress of a prude,
75 Or e'er to costive lapdog gave disease,
   Which not the tears of brightest eyes could ease,

Hear me, and touch Belinda with chagrin,
That single act gives half the world the spleen."
   The goddess with a discontented air
80 Seems to reject him, though she grants his pray'r.
A wond'rous bag with both her hands she binds,
Like that where once Ulysses held the winds;
There she collects the force of female lungs,
Sighs, sobs, and passions, and the war of tongues.
85 A phial next she fills with fainting fears,
Soft sorrows, melting griefs, and flowing tears.
The gnome rejoicing bears her gifts away,
Spreads his black wings, and slowly mounts to
     day.
   Sunk in Thalestris' arms the nymph he found.
90 Her eyes dejected, and her hair unbound.
Full o'er their heads the swelling bag he rent,
And all the furies issued at the vent.
Belinda burns with more than mortal ire,
And fierce Thalestris fans the rising fire.
95 "O wretched maid!" she spread her hands, and
     cried,
(While Hampton's echoes "Wretched maid!"
     replied,)
"Was it for this you took such constant care
The bodkin, comb, and essence to prepare?
For this your locks in paper durance bound?
100 For this with tort'ring irons wreathed around?
For this with fillets strained your tender head,
And bravely bore the double loads of lead?
Gods! shall the ravisher display your hair,
While the fops envy, and the ladies stare!
105 Honour forbid! at whose unrivalled shrine
Ease, pleasure, virtue, all our sex resign.
Methinks already I your tears survey,
Already hear the horrid things they say,
Already see you a degraded toast,
110 And all your honour in a whisper lost!

How shall I, then, your helpless fame defend?
'Twill then be infamy to seem your friend!
And shall this prize, th' inestimable prize,
Exposed through crystal to the gazing eyes,
115 And heightened by the diamond's circling rays,
On that rapacious hand for ever blaze?
Sooner shall grass in Hyde Park Circus grow,
And wits take lodgings in the sound of Bow;
Sooner let earth, air, sea, to chaos fall,
120 Men, monkeys, lap-dogs, parrots, perish all!"
     She said; then raging to Sir Plume repairs,
And bids her beau demand the precious hairs:
(Sir Plume, of amber snuff-box justly vain,
And the nice conduct of a clouded cane)
125 With earnest eyes, and round unthinking face,
He first the snuff-box opened, then the case,
And thus broke out—"My Lord, why, what the
          devil!
Zounds! damn the lock! 'fore Gad, you must be
          civil.
Plague on 't! 'tis past a jest—nay prithee, pox!
130 Give her the hair"—he spoke, and rapped his box.
     "It grieves me much," replied the peer again,
"Who speaks so well should ever speak in vain,
But by this lock, this sacred lock I swear,
(Which never more shall join its parted hair;
135 Which never more its honours shall renew,
Clipped from the lovely head where late it grew)
That, while my nostrils draw the vital air,
This hand, which won it, shall for ever wear."
He spoke, and speaking, in proud triumph spread
140 The long-contended honours of her head.
     But Umbriel, hateful gnome! forbears not so;
He breaks the phial whence the sorrows flow.
Then see! the nymph in beauteous grief appears,
Her eyes half-languishing, half-drowned in tears;
145 On her heaved bosom hung her drooping head,

Which, with a sigh, she raised; and thus she said.
"For ever cursed be this detested day,
Which snatched my best, my fav'rite curl away!
Happy! ah ten times happy had I been,
150 If Hampton-Court these eyes had never seen!
Yet am not I the first mistaken maid,
By love of courts to num'rous ills betrayed.
Oh had I rather unadmired remained
In some lone isle, or distant northern land,
155 Where the gilt chariot never marks the way,
Where none learn ombre, none e'er taste bohea!
There kept my charms concealed from mortal eye,
Like roses, that in deserts bloom and die.
What moved my mind with youthful lords to
roam?
160 Oh had I stayed, and said my pray'rs at home!
'Twas this, the morning omens seemed to tell,
Thrice from my trembling hand the patch-box
fell;
The tott'ring china shook without a wind,
Nay, Poll sat mute, and Shock was most unkind!
165 A sylph too warned me of the threats of fate,
In mystic visions, now believed too late!
See the poor remnants of these slighted hairs!
My hands shall rend what ev'n thy rapine spares:
These in two sable ringlets taught to break,
170 Once gave new beauties to the snowy neck;
The sister-lock now sits uncouth, alone,
And in its fellow's fate foresees its own;
Uncurled it hangs, the fatal shears demands,
And tempts, once more, thy sacrilegious hands.
175 Oh hadst thou, cruel! been content to seize
Hairs less in sight, or any hairs but these!"

CANTO V.

She said: the pitying audience melt in tears,
But fate and Jove had stopped the baron's ears.
In vain Thalestris with reproach assails,
For who can move when fair Belinda fails?
5 Not half so fixed the Trojan could remain,
While Anna begged and Dido raged in vain.
Then grave Clarissa graceful waved her fan;
Silence ensued, and thus the nymph began:
    "Say, why are beauties praised and honoured
        most,
10 The wise man's passion, and the vain man's toast?
Why decked with all that land and sea afford,
Why angels called, and angel-like adored?
Why round our coaches crowd the white-gloved
        beaux,
Why bows the side-box from its inmost rows?
15 How vain are all these glories, all our pains,
Unless good sense preserve what beauty gains;
That men may say, when we the front box grace,
Behold the first in virtue as in face!
Oh! if to dance all night, and dress all day,
20 Charmed the small-pox, or chased old age away;
Who would not scorn what housewife's cares pro-
        duce,
Or who would learn one earthly thing of use?
To patch, nay ogle, might become a saint,
Nor could it sure be such a sin to paint.
25 But since, alas! frail beauty must decay,
Curled or uncurled, since locks will turn to gray;
Since painted, or not painted, all shall fade,
And she who scorns a man, must die a maid;
What then remains but well our pow'r to use,
30 And keep good-humour, still whate'er we lose?
And trust me, dear! good-humour can prevail,
When airs, and flights, and screams, and scolding
        fail.

Beauties in vain their pretty eyes may roll;
Charms strike the sight, but merit wins the soul."
35   So spoke the dame, but no applause ensued;
Belinda frowned, Thalestris called her prude.
"To arms, to arms!" the fierce virago cries,
And swift as lightning to the combat flies.
All side in parties, and begin th' attack;
40 Fans clap, silks rustle, and tough whalebones
     crack;
Heroes' and heroines' shouts confus'dly rise,
And base and treble voices strike the skies.
No common weapons in their hands are found,
Like gods they fight, nor dread a mortal wound.
45   So when bold Homer makes the gods engage,
And heav'nly breasts with human passions rage;
'Gainst Pallas, Mars; Latona, Hermes arms;
And all Olympus rings with loud alarms:
Jove's thunder roars, heav'n trembles all around,
50 Blue Neptune storms, the bellowing deeps re-
     sound:
Earth shakes her nodding tow'rs, the ground gives
     way,
And the pale ghosts start at the flash of day!
   Triumphant Umbriel on a sconce's height
Clapped his glad wings, and sate to view the
     fight.
55 Propped on their bodkin spears, the sprites survey
The growing combat, or assist the fray.
   While through the press enraged Thalestris
     flies,
And scatters death around from both her eyes,
A beau and witling perished in the throng,
60 One died in metaphor, and one in song.
"O cruel nymph! a living death I bear,"
Cried Dapperwit, and sunk beside his chair.
A mournful glance Sir Fopling upward cast,
"Those eyes are made so killing"—was his last.

65 Thus on Meander's flow'ry margin lies
   Th' expiring swan, and as he sings he dies.
     When bold Sir Plume had drawn Clarissa
       down,
   Chloe stepped in, and killed him with a frown;
   She smiled to see the doughty hero slain,
70 But, at her smile, the beau revived again.
     Now Jove suspends his golden scales in air,
   Weighs the men's wits against the lady's hair;
   The doubtful beam long nods from side to side;
   At length the wits mount up, the hairs subside.
75   See fierce Belinda on the baron flies,
   With more than usual lightning in her eyes:
   Nor fear'd the chief th' unequal fight to try,
   Who sought no more than on his foe to die.
   But this bold lord with manly strength endued,
80 She with one finger and a thumb subdued;
   Just where the breath of life his nostrils drew,
   A charge of snuff the wily virgin threw;
   The gnomes direct, to ev'ry atom just,
   The pungent grains of titillating dust.
85 Sudden, with starting tears each eye o'erflows,
   And the high dome re-echoes to his nose.
     "Now meet thy fate," incensed Belinda cried,
   And drew a deadly bodkin from her side.
   (The same, his ancient personage to deck,
90 Her great-great-grandsire wore about his neck,
   In three seal-rings; which after, melted down,
   Formed a vast buckle for his widow's gown:
   Her infant grandame's whistle next it grew,
   The bells she jingled, and the whistle blew;
95 Then in a bodkin graced her mother's hairs,
   Which long she wore, and now Belinda wears.)
     "Boast not my fall," he cried, "insulting foe!
   Thou by some other shalt be laid as low:
   Nor think, to die dejects my lofty mind;
100 All that I dread is leaving you behind!

Rather than so, ah let me still survive,
And burn in Cupid's flames—but burn alive."
  "Restore the lock!" she cries; and all around
"Restore the lock!" the vaulted roofs rebound.
105 Not fierce Othello in so loud a strain
Roared for the handkerchief that caused his pain.
But see how oft' ambitious aims are crossed,
And chiefs contend till all the prize is lost!
The lock, obtained with guilt, and kept with pain,
110 In ev'ry place is sought, but sought in vain:
With such a prize no mortal must be blest,
So heav'n decrees: with heav'n who can contest?
  Some thought it mounted to the lunar sphere,
Since all things lost on earth are treasured there.
115 There heroes' wits are kept in pond'rous vases,
And beaus' in snuff-boxes and tweezer-cases.
There broken vows, and death-bed alms are found,
And lovers' hearts with ends of ribbon bound,
The courtier's promises, and sick man's pray'rs,
120 The smiles of harlots, and the tears of heirs,
Cages for gnats, and chains to yoke a flea,
Dried butterflies, and tomes of casuistry.
  But trust the Muse—she saw it upward rise,
Tho' mark'd by none but quick, poetic eyes:
125 (So Rome's great founder to the heav'ns with-
    drew,
To Proculus alone confessed in view)
A sudden star, it shot through liquid air,
And drew behind a radiant trail of hair.
Not Berenice's locks first rose so bright,
130 The heav'ns bespangling with disheveled light.
The sylphs behold it kindling as it flies,
And pleased pursue its progress through the skies.
  This the beau monde shall from the Mall
    survey,
And hail with music its propitious ray;
135 This the bless'd lover shall for Venus take,

And send up vows from Rosamonda's lake;
This Partridge soon shall view in cloudless skies,
When next he looks through Galileo's eyes;
And hence th' egregious wizard shall foredoom
140 The fate of Louis, and the fall of Rome.
    Then cease, bright nymph! to mourn thy rav-
        ished hair,
Which adds new glory to the shining sphere!
Not all the tresses that fair head can boast,
Shall draw such envy as the Lock you lost.
145 For after all the murders of your eye,
When, after millions slain, yourself shall die;
When those fair suns shall set, as set they must,
And all those tresses shall be laid in dust,
This lock the Muse shall consecrate to fame,
150 And 'midst the stars inscribe Belinda's name.

ELEGY TO THE MEMORY OF AN UNFORTU-
NATE LADY.
(1717)

What beck'ning ghost, along the moon-light shade
Invites my steps, and points to yonder glade?
'Tis she!—but why that bleeding bosom gored?
Why dimly gleams the visionary sword?
5 Oh ever beauteous, ever friendly! tell,
Is it, in heav'n, a crime to love too well?
To bear too tender, or too firm a heart,
To act a lover's or a Roman's part?
Is there no bright reversion in the sky,
10 For those who greatly think, or bravely die?
    Why bade ye else, ye pow'rs! her soul aspire
Above the vulgar flight of low desire?
Ambition first sprung from your blessed abodes;
The glorious fault of angels and of gods:
15 Thence to their images on earth it flows,
And in the breasts of kings and heroes glows.

Most souls, 'tis true, but peep out once an age,
Dull sullen pris'ners in the body's cage:
Dim lights of life, that burn a length of years
20 Useless, unseen, as lamps in sepulchres;
Like Eastern kings a lazy state they keep,
And, close confined to their own palace, sleep.
  From these perhaps (ere nature bade her die)
Fate snatched her early to the pitying sky.
25 As into air the purer spirits flow,
And sep'rate from their kindred dregs below;
So flew the soul to its congenial place,
Nor left one virtue to redeem her race.
  But thou, false guardian of a charge too good,
30 Thou mean deserter of thy brother's blood!
See on these ruby lips the trembling breath,
These cheeks now fading at the blast of death;
Cold is that breast which warmed the world be-
    fore,
And those love-darting eyes must roll no more.
35 Thus, if eternal justice rules the ball,
Thus shall your wives, and thus your children
    fall:
On all the line a sudden vengeance waits,
And frequent hearses shall besiege your gates;
Their passengers shall stand, and pointing say,
40 (While the long fun'rals blacken all the way)
  "Lo! these were they, whose souls the furies
    steeled,
  "And cursed with hearts unknowing how to
    yield."
Thus unlamented passed the proud away,
The gaze of fools, and pageant of a day!
45 So perish all, whose breast ne'er learned to glow
For others' good, or melt at others' woe.
  What can atone, oh ever-injured shade!
Thy fate unpitied, and thy rites unpaid?
No friend's complaint, no kind domestic tear

50 Pleased thy pale ghost, or graced thy mournful
    bier.
By foreign hands thy dying eyes were closed,
By foreign hands thy decent limbs composed,
By foreign hands thy humble grave adorned,
By strangers honoured and by strangers mourned!
55 What though no friends in sable weeds appear,
Grieve for an hour, perhaps, then mourn a year,
And bear about the mockery of woe
To midnight dances, and the public show?
What though no weeping loves thy ashes grace,
60 Nor polished marble emulate thy face?
What though no sacred earth allow thee room,
Nor hallowed dirge be muttered o'er thy tomb?
Yet shall thy grave with rising flowers be dressed,
And the green turf lie lightly on thy breast:
65 There shall the morn her earliest tears bestow,
There the first roses of the year shall blow;
While angels with their silver wings o'ershade
The ground, now sacred by thy reliques made.
    So peaceful rests, without a stone, a name,
70 What once had beauty, titles, wealth, and fame.
How loved, how honoured once, avails thee not,
To whom related, or by whom begot;
A heap of dust alone remains of thee;
'Tis all thou art, and all the proud shall be!
75   Poets themselves must fall like those they sung,
Deaf the praised ear, and mute the tuneful
    tongue.
Even he, whose soul now melts in mournful lays,
Shall shortly want the gen'rous tear he pays;
Then from his closing eyes thy form shall part,
80 And the last pang shall tear thee from his heart,
Life's idle business at one gasp be o'er,
The muse forgot, and thou beloved no more!

UNIVERSAL PRAYER
(Published 1738)

Father of all! in ev'ry age,
   In ev'ry clime adored,
By saint, by savage, and by sage,
   Jehovah, Jove, or Lord!

5 Thou Great First Cause, least understood!
   Who all my sense confined
To know but this, that Thou art good,
   And that myself am blind;

Yet gave me in this dark estate,
10   To see the good from ill:
And binding nature fast in fate,
   Left free the human will.

What conscience dictates to be done,
   Or warns me not to do,
15 This teach me more than hell to shun,
   That, more than heav'n pursue.

What blessings thy free bounty gives
   Let me not cast away;
For God is paid when man receives:
20   T' enjoy is to obey.

Yet not to earth's contracted span
   Thy goodness let me bound,
Or think Thee Lord alone of man,
   When thousand worlds are round:

25 Let not this weak, unknowing hand
   Presume thy bolts to throw,
And deal damnation round the land
   On each I judge thy foe.

If I am right, thy grace impart
30   Still in the right to stay:
If I am wrong, oh teach my heart
    To find that better way.

Save me alike from foolish pride,
    Or impious discontent,
35 At aught thy wisdom has denied,
    Or aught thy goodness lent.

Teach me to feel another's woe,
    To hide the fault I see;
That mercy I to others show,
40   That mercy show to me.

Mean though I am, not wholly so,
    Since quickened by thy breath:
Oh lead me wheresoe'er I go,
    Through this day's life or death.

45 This day be bread and peace my lot:
    All else beneath the sun,
Thou know'st if best bestowed or not,
    And let thy will be done.

To Thee, whose temple is all space,
50   Whose altar, earth, sea, skies,
One chorus let all being raise;
    All nature's incense rise!

EPISTLE TO DR. ARBUTHNOT

BEING THE PROLOGUE TO THE SATIRES
(Published 1735)

P. Shut, shut the door, good John! fatigued I said:
  Tie up the knocker, say I'm sick, I'm dead.
  The Dog-star rages! nay, 'tis past a doubt,
  All Bedlam, or Parnassus is let out:

5 Fire in each eye, and papers in each hand,
  They rave, recite, and madden round the land.
  What walls can guard me, or what shades can
        hide?
  They pierce my thickets, through my grot they
        glide,
  By land, by water, they renew the charge,
10 They stop the chariot, and they board the barge.
  No place is sacred, not the church is free,
  Ev'n Sunday shines no Sabbath-day to me:
  Then from the Mint walks forth the man of
        rhyme,
  Happy! to catch me, just at dinner-time.
15 Is there a parson, much be-mus'd in beer,
  A maudlin poetess, a rhyming peer;
  A clerk, foredoomed his father's soul to cross,
  Who pens a stanza, when he should engross?
  Is there, who, locked from ink and paper, scrawls
20 With desperate charcoal round his darkened
       walls?
  All fly to Twit'nam, and in humble strain
  Apply to me, to keep them mad or vain.
  Arthur, whose giddy son neglects the laws,
  Imputes to me and my damned works the cause:
25 Poor Cornus sees his frantic wife elope,
  And curses wit, and poetry, and Pope.
    Friend to my life! (which did not you prolong,
  The world had wanted many an idle song),
  What drop or nostrum can this plague remove?
30 Or which must end me, a fool's wrath or love?
  A dire dilemma! either way I'm sped,
  If foes, they write, if friends, they read me dead.
  Seized and tied down to judge, how wretched I!
  Who can't be silent, and who will not lie:
35 To laugh, were want of goodness and of grace,
  And to be grave, exceeds all power of face.
  I sit with sad civility, I read

With honest anguish, and an aching head;
And drop at last, but in unwilling ears,
40 This saving counsel—"Keep your piece nine
    years."
  "Nine years!" cries he, who, high in Drury
    Lane,
Lulled by soft zephyrs through the broken pane,
Rhymes ere he wakes, and prints before Term
    ends,
Obliged by hunger and request of friends:
45   "The piece you think is incorrect? why take it;
I'm all submission; what you'd have it, make it."
  Three things another's modest wishes bound,
My friendship, and a prologue, and ten pound.
  Pitholeon sends to me: "You know his grace,
50 I want a patron; ask him for a place."
Pitholeon libelled me—"but here's a letter
Informs you, sir, 'twas when he knew no better.
Dare you refuse him? Curll invites to dine;
He'll write a journal, or he'll turn divine."
55   Bless me! a packet. "'Tis a stranger sues,
A virgin tragedy, an orphan Muse."
If I dislike it, "Furies, death, and rage!"
If I approve, "Commend it to the stage."
There (thank my stars) my whole commission
    ends,
60 The players and I are, luckily, no friends.
Fired that the house reject him, "'Sdeath I'll
    print it,
And shame the fools—your interest, sir, with
    Lintot."
Lintot, dull rogue, will think your price too
    much:
"Not, sir, if you revise it, and retouch."
65 All my demurs but double his attacks:
At last he whispers, "Do; and we go snacks."
Glad of a quarrel, straight I clap the door:

"Sir, let me see your works and you no more."

. . . .

One dedicates in high heroic prose,
110 And ridicules beyond a hundred foes:
One from all Grubstreet will my fame defend,
And, more abusive, calls himself my friend.
This prints my letters, that expects a bribe,
And others roar aloud, "Subscribe, subscribe!"
115 There are who to my person pay their court:
I cough like Horace, and, though lean, am short.
Ammon's great son one shoulder had too high,—
Such Ovid's nose,—and, "sir, you have an eye."
Go on, obliging creatures, make me see
120 All that disgraced my betters met in me.
Say, for my comfort, languishing in bed,
"Just so immortal Maro held his head:"
And, when I die, be sure you let me know
Great Homer died three thousand years ago.
125 Why did I write? what sin to me unknown
Dipped me in ink, my parents', or my own?
As yet a child, nor yet a fool to fame,
I lisped in numbers, for the numbers came.
I left no calling for this idle trade,
130 No duty broke, no father disobeyed:
The muse but served to ease some friend, not wife,
To help me through this long disease, my life;
To second, Arbuthnot! thy art and care,
And teach the being you preserved to bear.

. . . .

Soft were my numbers; who could take offence
While pure description held the place of sense?

Did some more sober critic come abroad—
If wrong, I smiled; if right, I kissed the rod.
Pains, reading, study, are their just pretence,
160 And all they want is spirit, taste, and sense.
Commas and points they set exactly right,

And 't were a sin to rob them of their mite.

. . . .

Were others angry—I excused them too;
Well might they rage, I gave them but their due.
175 A man's true merit 'tis not hard to find;
But each man's secret standard in his mind,
That casting-weight pride adds to emptiness,
This, who can gratify, for who can guess?
The bard whom pilfered Pastorals renown,
180 Who turns a Persian tale for half-a-crown,
Just writes to make his barrenness appear,
And strains from hard-bound brains, eight lines
a-year;
He, who still wanting, though he lives on theft,
Steals much, spends little, yet has nothing left:
185 And he, who now to sense, now nonsense leaning,
Means not, but blunders round about a meaning:
And he, whose fustian's so sublimely bad,
It is not poetry but prose run mad:
All these, my modest satire bade translate,
190 And owned that nine such poets made a Tate.
How did they fume, and stamp, and roar, and
chafe!
And swear, not Addison himself was safe.

Peace to all such! but were there one whose
fires
True genius kindles, and fair fame inspires;
195 Blest with each talent, and each art to please,
And born to write, converse, and live with ease:
Should such a man, too fond to rule alone,
Bear, like the Turk, no brother near the throne,
View him with scornful, yet with jealous eyes,
200 And hate for arts that caused himself to rise;
Damn with faint praise, assent with civil leer,
And without sneering, teach the rest to sneer;
Willing to wound, and yet afraid to strike,
Just hint a fault, and hesitate dislike,

205 Alike reserved to blame, or to commend,
    A timorous foe, and a suspicious friend;
    Dreading e'en fools, by flatterers besieged,
    And so obliging, that he ne'er obliged;
    Like Cato, give his little senate laws,
210 And sit attentive to his own applause;
    While wits and templars every sentence raise,
    And wonder with a foolish face of praise—
    Who but must laugh, if such a man there be?
    Who would not weep, if Atticus were he?

     .   o   .   .   .   .   o

PART FOURTH

THOMSON TO TENNYSON

Cir. 1730–Cir. 1830

James Thomson

1700–1748

SPRING

(1728)

(From *The Seasons*)

Come, gentle Spring, etherial mildness, come,
And from the bosom of yon dropping cloud,
While music wakes around, veil'd in a shower
Of shadowing roses, on our plains descend.

   .   .   .   .   .

   And see where surly Winter passes off,
Far to the north, and calls his ruffian blasts:
His blasts obey, and quit the howling hill,
The shatter'd forest, and the ravag'd vale;
15 While softer gales succeed, at whose kind touch,
Dissolving snows in livid torrents lost,
The mountains lift their green heads to the sky.
As yet the trembling year is unconfirm'd,
And Winter oft at eve resumes the breeze,
20 Chills the pale morn, and bids his driving sleets
Deform the day delightless; so that scarce
The bittern knows his time, with bill engulf'd

To shake the sounding marsh; or from the shore
The plovers when to scatter o'er the heath,
25 And sing their wild notes to the listening waste.
At last from Aries rolls the bounteous Sun,
And the bright Bull receives him. Then no more
Th' expansive atmosphere is cramp'd with cold;
But, full of life and vivifying soul,
30 Lifts the light clouds sublime, and spreads them
        thin,
Fleecy and white, o'er all-surrounding heaven.
Forth fly the tepid airs; and unconfin'd,
Unbinding earth, the moving softness strays.
Joyous, the impatient husbandman perceives
35 Relenting Nature, and his lusty steers
Drives from their stalls, to where the well-us'd
        plough
Lies in the furrow, loosen'd from the frost.
There, unrefusing, to the harness'd yoke
They lend their shoulder, and begin their toil,
40 Cheer'd by the simple song and soaring lark.
Meanwhile incumbent o'er the shining share
The master leans, removes th' obstructing clay,
Winds the whole work, and sidelong lays the
        glebe.
    While thro' the neighb'ring fields the sower
        stalks,
45 With measur'd step; and liberal throws the grain
Into the faithful bosom of the ground:
The harrow follows harsh, and shuts the scene.
    Be gracious, Heaven! for now laborious Man
Has done his part. Ye fostering breezes, blow!
50 Ye softening dews, ye tender showers, descend!
And temper all, thou world-reviving sun,
Into the perfect year! Nor ye who live
In luxury and ease, in pomp and pride,
Think these lost themes unworthy of your ear:
55 Such themes as these the rural Maro sung

To wide imperial Rome, in the full height
Of elegance and taste, by Greece refin'd.
In ancient times, the sacred plough employ'd
The kings and awful fathers of mankind:
60 And some, with whom compar'd your insect-tribes
Are but the beings of a summer's day,
Have held the scale of empire, rul'd the storm
Of mighty war; then, with victorious hand,
Disdaining little delicacies, seiz'd
65 The plough, and greatly independent, scorn'd
All the vile stores Corruption can bestow.
    Ye generous Britons, venerate the plough;
And o'er your hills, and long-withdrawing vales,
Let Autumn spread his treasures to the sun,
70 Luxuriant and unbounded: as the Sea,
Far thro' his azure turbulent domain,
Your empire owns, and from a thousand shores
Wafts all the pomp of life into your ports;
So with superior boon may your rich soil,
75 Exuberant, Nature's better blessings pour
O'er every land, the naked nations clothe,
And be th' exhaustless granary of a world!

.   .   .   .

    From the moist meadow to the wither'd hill,
Led by the breeze, the vivid verdure runs
And swells, and deepens, to the cherish'd eye.
90 The hawthorn whitens; and the juicy groves
Put forth their buds, unfolding by degrees,
Till the whole leafy forest stands display'd,
In full luxuriance to the sighing gales;
Where the deer rustle through the twining brake,
95 And the birds sing conceal'd. At once array'd
In all the colours of the flushing year,
By Nature's swift and secret-working hand,
The garden glows, and fills the liberal air
With lavish fragrance; while the promis'd fruit
100 Lies yet a little embryo, unperceiv'd,

Within its crimson fold. Now from the town,
Buried in smoke, and sleep, and noisome damps,
Oft let me wander o'er the dewy fields,
Where freshness breathes, and dash the trem-
        b'ling drops
105 From the bent bush, as thro' the verdant maze
Of sweet-briar hedges I pursue my walk;
Or taste the smell of dairy, or ascend
Some eminence, AUGUSTA, in thy plains,
And see the country, far diffused around,
110 One boundless blush, one white empurpled
        shower
Of mingled blossoms; where the raptur'd eye
Hurries from joy to joy, and, hid beneath
The fair profusion, yellow Autumn spies.

SUMMER

(1827)

From brightening fields of ether fair disclos'd,
Child of the Sun, refulgent Summer comes,
In pride of youth, and felt through Nature's
        depth:
He comes attended by the sultry Hours,
5 And ever-fanning breezes, on his way;
While, from his ardent look, the turning Spring,
Averts her blushful face; and earth, and skies,
All-smiling, to his hot dominion leaves.
    Hence, let me haste into the mid-wood shade,
10 Where scarce a sunbeam wanders thro' the
        gloom;
And on the dark-green grass, beside the brink
Of haunted stream, that by the roots of oak
Rolls o'er the rocky channel, lie at large,
And sing the glories of the circling year.

    .   .   .   .   .   .

Now swarms the village o'er the joyful mead:

The rustic youth, brown with meridian toil,
Healthful and strong; full as the summer rose
355 Blown by prevailing suns, the ruddy maid,
Half naked, swelling on the sight, and all
Her kindled graces burning o'er her cheek.
E'en stooping age is here; and infant hands
Trail the long rake, or, with the fragrant load
360 O'ercharg'd, amid the kind oppression roll.
Wide flies the tedded grain; all in a row
Advancing broad, or wheeling round the field,
They spread their breathing harvest to the sun,
That throws refreshful round a rural smell.
365 Or, as they take the green-appearing ground,
And drive the dusky wave along the mead,
The russet hay-cock rises thick behind,
In order gay: While, heard from dale to dale,
Waking the breeze, resounds the blended voice
370 Of happy labour, love, and social glee.
　　Or rushing thence, in one diffusive band,
They drive the troubled flocks, by many a dog
Compell'd, to where the mazy-running brook
Forms a deep pool: this bank abrupt and high,
375 And that fair spreading in a pebbled shore.
Urg'd to the giddy brink, much is the toil,
The clamour much, of men, and boys, and dogs,
Ere the soft fearful people to the flood
Commit their woolly sides. And oft the swain,
380 On some impatient seizing, hurls them in:
Embolden'd then, nor hesitating more,
Fast, fast, they plunge amid the flashing wave,
And, panting, labour to the farther shore.
Repeated this till deep the well-wash'd fleece
385 Has drunk the flood, and from his lively haunt
The trout is banish'd by the sordid stream;
Heavy, and dripping to the breezy brow
Slow move the harmless race; where, as they
　　　spread

Their swelling treasures to the sunny ray,
390 Inly disturb'd, and wond'ring what this wild
Outrageous tumult means, their loud complaints
The country fill; and, tost from rock to rock,
Incessant bleatings run around the hills.
At last, of snowy white, the gather'd flocks
395 Are in the wattled pen innumerous press'd,
Head above head: and, rang'd in lusty rows,
The shepherds sit, and whet the sounding shears.
The housewife waits to roll her fleecy stores,
With all her gay-drest maids attending round.
400 One, chief, in gracious dignity enthron'd,
Shines o'er the rest, the pastoral queen, and rays
Her smiles, sweet beaming, on her shepherd king;
While the glad circle round them yield their souls
To festive mirth, and wit that knows no gall.

AUTUMN

(1730)

Crown'd with the sickle and the wheaten sheaf,
While Autumn, nodding o'er the yellow plain,
Comes jovial on; the Doric reed once more,
Well pleas'd, I tune. Whate'er the Wintry frost
5 Nitrous prepar'd, the various-blossom'd Spring
Put in white promise forth; and Summer's suns
Concocted strong; rush boundless now to view,
Full, perfect all, and swell my glorious theme.

.   .   .   .

But see, the fading many-colour'd woods,
950 Shade deepening over shade, the country round
Imbrown; a crowded umbrage, dusk, and dun,
Of every hue, from wan declining green
To sooty dark. These now the lonesome Muse,
Low-whispering, lead into their leaf-strown
walks,
955 And give the season in its latest view.
Meantime, light shadowing all, a sober calm

Fleeces unbounded ether; whose least wave
Stands tremulous, uncertain where to turn
The gentle current; while, illumin'd wide,
960 The dewy-skirted clouds imbibe the sun,
And thro' their lucid veil his soften'd force
Shed o'er the peaceful world. Then is the time,
For those whom Wisdom and whom Nature
    charm,
To steal themselves from the degenerate crowd,
965 And soar above this little scene of things;
To tread low-thoughted Vice beneath their feet;
To soothe the throbbing passions into peace,
And woo lone Quiet in her silent walks.
    Thus solitary, and in pensive guise,
970 Oft let me wander o'er the russet mead,
And thro' the sadden'd grove, where scarce is
    heard
One dying strain, to cheer the woodman's toil.
Haply some widow'd songster pours his plaint,
Far, in faint warblings, thro' the tawny copse;
975 While congregated thrushes, linnets, larks,
And each wild throat, whose artless strains so
    late
Swell'd all the music of the swarming shades,
Robb'd of their tuneful souls, now shivering sit
On the dead tree, a dull despondent flock;
980 With not a brightness waving o'er their plumes,
And nought save chattering discord in their note.
Oh, let not, aim'd from some inhuman eye,
The gun the music of the coming year
Destroy; and harmless, unsuspecting harm,
985 Lay the weak tribes a miserable prey,
In mingled murder, fluttering on the ground!
    The pale descending year, yet pleasing still,
A gentler mood inspires; for now the leaf
Incessant rustles from the mournful grove;
990 Oft startling such as, studious, walk below,

And slowly circles thro' the waving air.
But should a quicker breeze amid the boughs
Sob, o'er the sky the leafy deluge streams;
Till chok'd, and matted with the dreary shower,
995 The forest-walks, at every rising gale,
Roll wide the wither'd waste, and whistle bleak
Fled is the blasted verdure of the fields:
And, shrunk into their beds, the flowery race
Their sunny robes resign. Even what remain'd
1000 Of stronger fruits fall from the naked tree;
And woods, fields, gardens, orchards, all around
The desolated prospect thrills the soul.

WINTER

(1726)

See, Winter comes, to rule the varied year,
Sullen and sad, with all his rising train—
Vapours, and clouds, and storms. Be these my
     theme;
These, that exalt the soul to solemn thought,
5 And   heavenly   musing.   Welcome,   kindred
     glooms!
Congenial horrors, hail! With frequent foot,
Pleas'd have I, in my cheerful morn of life,
When nurs'd by careless Solitude I liv'd,
And sung of Nature with unceasing joy,—
10 Pleas'd have I wander'd through your rough
     domain;
Trod the pure virgin-snows, myself as pure;
Heard the winds roar, and the big torrent burst;
Or seen the deep-fermenting tempest brew'd,
In the grim evening sky. Thus pass'd the time,
15 Till through the lucid chambers of the South
Look'd out the joyous Spring, look'd out, and
     smil'd.

The keener tempests come: and fuming dun
From all the livid East, or piercing North,
225 Thick clouds ascend; in whose capacious womb
A vapoury deluge lies, to snow congeal'd.
Heavy they roll their fleecy world along,
And the sky saddens with the gather'd storm.
Thro' the hush'd air the whitening shower descends,
230 At first thin-wavering; till at last the flakes
Fall broad and wide, and fast, dimming the day
With a continual flow. The cherish'd fields
Put on their winter-robe of purest white.
'Tis brightness all; save where the new snow melts
235 Along the mazy current. Low the woods
Bow their hoar head; and, ere the languid Sun
Faint from the West emits his evening ray,
Earth's universal face, deep-hid, and chill,
Is one wild dazzling waste, that buries wide
240 The works of Man. Drooping, the labourer-ox
Stands cover'd o'er with snow, and then demands
The fruit of all his toil. The fowls of heaven,
Tam'd by the cruel season, crowd around
The winnowing store, and claim the little boon
245 Which Providence assigns them. One alone,
The red-breast, sacred to the household gods,
Wisely regardful of th' embroiling sky,
In joyless fields and thorny thickets leaves
His shivering mates, and pays to trusted man
250 His annual visit. Half afraid, he first
Against the window beats; then, brisk, alights
On the warm hearth; then, hopping o'er the floor,
Eyes all the smiling family askance,
And pecks, and starts, and wonders where he is:
255 Till, more familiar grown, the table-crumbs
Attract his slender feet. The foodless wilds
Pour forth their brown inhabitants. The hare,
Though timorous of heart, and hard beset

By death in various forms—dark snares, and dogs,
260 And more unpitying men—the garden seeks,
Urg'd on by fearless want. The bleating kind
Eye the bleak heaven, and next the glistening
earth,
With looks of dumb despair; then, sad-dispers'd,
Dig for the wither'd herb thro' heaps of snow.

.   .   .   .

Ah! little think the gay licentious proud,
Whom pleasure, pow'r, and affluence surround;
They who their thoughtless hours in giddy mirth
325 And wanton, often cruel, riot waste;—
Ah! little think they, while they dance along,
How many feel, this very moment, death
And all the sad variety of pain.
How many sink in the devouring flood,
330 Or more devouring flame; how many bleed,
By shameful variance betwixt man and man:
How many pine in want and dungeon glooms,
Shut from the common air, and common use
Of their own limbs: How many drink the cup
335 Of baleful grief, or eat the bitter bread
Of misery: sore pierc'd by wintry winds,
How many shrink into the sordid hut
Of cheerless poverty: how many shake
With all the fiercer tortures of the mind,—
340 Unbounded passion, madness, guilt, remorse;
Whence tumbled headlong from the height of life,
They furnish matter for the tragic Muse:
Ev'n in the vale where wisdom loves to dwell,
With Friendship, Peace, and Contemplation
join'd,
345 How many, rack'd with honest passions, droop
In deep-retir'd distress: how many stand
Around the death-bed of their dearest friends,
And point the parting anguish. Thought fond
man

Of these, and all the thousand nameless-ills,
350 That one incessant struggle render life,
One scene of toil, of suff'ring, and of fate;
Vice in his high career would stand appall'd,
And heedless rambling Impulse learn to think;
The conscious heart of Charity would warm,
355 And her wide wish Benevolence dilate;
The social tear would rise, the social sigh;
And into clear perfection, gradual bliss,
Refining still, the social passions work.
And here can I forget the generous band,
360 Who, touch'd with human woe, redressive
            search'd
Into the horrors of the gloomy jail?
Unpitied and unheard, where misery moans;
Where Sickness pines; where Thirst and Hunger
            burn,
And poor Misfortune feels the lash of Vice.
365 While in the land of liberty—the land
Whose every street and public meeting glow
With open freedom—little tyrants rag'd;
Snatch'd the lean morsel from the starving
            mouth;
Tore from cold wintry limbs the tatter'd weed;
370 Even robb'd them of the last of comforts, sleep;
The free-born Briton to the dungeon chain'd,
Or, as the lust of cruelty prevail'd,
At pleasure mark'd him with inglorious stripes;
And crush'd out lives, by secret barbarous ways,
375 That for their country would have toil'd, or bled.
Oh great design! if executed well,
With patient care and wisdom-temper'd zeal.
Ye sons of mercy! yet resume the search;
Drag forth the legal monsters into light,
380 Wrench from their hands Oppression's iron rod,
And bid the cruel feel the pangs they give.
Much still untouch'd remains; in this rank age,

Much is the patriot's weeding hand requir'd.
The toils of law,—what dark insidious men
835 Have cumbrous added, to perplex the truth,
And lengthen simple justice into trade,—
How glorious were the day that saw these broke,
And every man within the reach of right!

RULE BRITANNIA

(1740)

When Britain first at Heaven's command
   Arose from out the azure main,
This was the charter of her land,
   And guardian angels sung the strain:
5 Rule, Britannia! Britannia rules the waves!
   Britons never shall be slaves.

The nations not so blest as thee
   Must in their turn to tyrants fall,
While thou shalt flourish great and free,
10   The dread and envy of them all.

Still more majestic shalt thou rise,
   More dreadful from each foreign stroke;
As the loud blast that tears the skies
   Serves but to root thy native oak.

15 Thee haughty tyrants ne'er shall tame;
   All their attempts to bend thee down
Will but arouse thy generous flame,
   And work their woe and thy renown.

To thee belongs the rural reign;
20   Thy cities shall with commerce shine;
All thine shall be the subject main,
   And every shore it circles thine!

The Muses, still with Freedom found,
  Shall to thy happy coast repair;
25 Blest Isle, with matchless beauty crown'd
  And manly hearts to guard the fair:—
Rule, Britannia! Britannia rules the waves!
  Britons never shall be slaves!

William Collins

1721-1759.

ODE TO EVENING

(From *Odes*, 1746)

If aught of oaten stop, or pastoral song,
May hope, chaste eve, to soothe thy modest ear,
    Like thy own solemn springs,
    Thy springs, and dying gales,

5 O nymph reserved, while now the bright-haired
        sun,
Sits in yon western tent, whose cloudy skirts,
    With brede ethereal wove,
    O'erhang his wavy bed:

Now air is hushed, save where the weak-eyed bat
10 With short, shrill shriek, flits by on leathern
        wing;
    Or where the beetle winds
    His small but sullen horn,

As oft he rises 'midst the twilight path,
Against the pilgrim borne in heedless hum:
15   Now teach me, maid composed,
    To breath some softened strain,

Whose numbers, stealing through thy darkening
          vale,
May, not unseemly, with its stillness suit,
          As, musing slow, I hail
20   Thy genial loved return!

For when thy folding star arising shows
His paly circlet, at his warning lamp
          The fragrant hours, and elves
          Who slept in flowers the day,

25 And many a nymph who wreathes her brows with
          sedge,
And sheds the freshening dew, and, lovelier still,
          The pensive pleasures sweet
          Prepare thy shadowy car.

Then lead, calm votaress, where some sheety lake
30 Cheers the lone heath, or some time-hallowed pile,
          Or up-land fallows grey
          Reflect its last cool gleam.

But when chill blustering winds, or driving rain,
Forbid my willing feet, be mine the hut,
35   That from the mountain's side,
          Views wilds, and swelling floods,

And hamlets brown, and dim-discovered spires;
And hears their simple bell, and marks o'er all
          Thy dewy fingers draw
40   The gradual dusky veil.

While spring shall pour his showers, as oft he
          wont,
And bathe thy breathing tresses, meekest eve!
          While summer loves to sport
          Beneath thy lingering light;

45 While sallow autumn fills thy lap with leaves;
   Or winter yelling through the troublous air,
        Affrights thy shrinking train,
        And rudely rends thy robes;

   So long, sure-found beneath the sylvan shed,
50 Shall   fancy,   friendship,   science,   rose-lipp'd
        health,
        Thy gentlest influence own,
        And hymn thy favorite name!

THE PASSIONS

AN ODE FOR MUSIC

(From the same)

   When music, heavenly maid, was young,
   While yet in early Greece she sung,
   The passions oft, to hear her shell,
   Thronged around her magic cell,
5 Exulting, trembling, raging, fainting,
   Possest beyond the muse's painting:
   By turns they felt the glowing mind
   Disturbed, delighted, raised, refined;
   Till once, 'tis said, when all were fired,
10 Filled with fury, rapt, inspired,
   From the supporting myrtles round
   They snatched her instruments of sound;
   And, as they oft had heard apart
   Sweet lessons of her forceful art,
15 Each (for madness ruled the hour)
   Would prove his own expressive power.
   First fear, his hand, its skill to try,
        Amid the chords bewildered laid,
   And back recoiled, he knew not why,
20   Even at the sound himself had made.

Next anger rushed; his eyes on fire,
    In lightnings owned his secret stings:
In one rude clash he struck the lyre,
    And swept, with hurried hand, the strings.

25 With woful measures wan despair
    Low, sullen sounds his grief beguiled;
A solemn, strange, and mingled air;
    'Twas sad by fits, by starts 'twas wild.

But thou, O hope, with eyes so fair,
30   What was thy delightful measure?
Still it whispered promised pleasure,
    And bade the lovely scenes at distance hail!
Still would her touch the strain prolong;
    And from the rocks, the woods, the vale,
35 She called on echo still, through all the song;
    And, where her sweetest theme she chose,
    A soft responsive voice was heard at every close,
And hope enchanted smiled, and waved her golden
      hair.

And longer had she sung;—but, with a frown,
40   Revenge impatient rose:
He threw his blood-stained sword, in thunder,
      down;
    And with a withering look,
    The war-denouncing trumpet took,
And blew a blast so loud and dread,
45 Were ne'er prophetic sounds so full of woe!
    And, ever and anon, he beat
    The doubling drum, with furious heat;
And though sometimes, each dreary pause be-
      tween,
    Dejected pity, at his side,
50   Her soul-subduing voice applied,
Yet still he kept his wild unaltered mien,
While each strained ball of sight seemed burst-
      ing from his head.

Thy numbers, jealousy, to naught were fixed;
    Sad proof of thy distressful state;
55 Of differing themes the veering song was mixed;
    And now it courted love, now raving called on hate.
With eyes upraised, as one inspired,
Pale melancholy sat retired;
And, from her wild sequestered seat,
60 In notes by distance made more sweet,
Poured through the mellow horn her pensive soul:
    And, dashing soft from rocks around,
    Bubbling runnels joined the sound;
Through glades and glooms the mingled measure stole,
65 Or, o'er some haunted stream, with fond delay,
    Round an holy calm diffusing,
    Love of peace, and lonely musing,
In hollow murmurs died away.
But O! how altered was its sprightlier tone,
70 When cheerfulness, a nymph of healthiest hue,
    Her bow across her shoulder flung,
    Her buskins gemmed with morning dew,
Blew an inspiring air, that dale and thicket rung,
The hunter's call, to faun and dryad known!
75 The oak-crowned sisters, and their chaste-eyed queen,
    Satyrs and sylvan boys, were seen,
    Peeping from forth their alleys green:
Brown exercise rejoiced to hear;
    And sport leapt up, and seized his beechen spear.
80 Last came joy's ecstatic trial:
    He, with viny crown advancing,
    First to the lively pipe his hand addrest;
But soon he saw the brisk awakening viol,
    Whose sweet entrancing voice he loved the best;

85 They would have thought who heard the strain
    They saw, in Tempe's vale, her native maids,
    Amidst the festal sounding shades,
To some unwearied minstrel dancing,
    While, as his flying fingers kissed the strings,
90   Love framed with mirth a gay fantastic
      round:
    Loose were her tresses seen, her zone un-
      bound;
    And he, amidst his frolic play,
    As if he would the charming air repay,
Shook thousand odours from his dewy wings.

95 O music! sphere-descended maid,
    Friend of pleasure, wisdom's aid!
    Why, goddess! why, to us denied,
    Lay'st thou thy ancient lyre aside?
    As, in that loved Athenian bower,
100 You learned an all-commanding power,
    Thy mimic soul, O nymph endeared,
    Can well recall what then it heard;
    Where is thy native simple heart,
    Devote to virtue, fancy, art?
105 Arise, as in that elder time,
    Warm, energetic, chaste, sublime!
    Thy wonders, in that godlike age,
    Fill thy recording sister's page—
    'Tis said, and I believe the tale,
110 Thy humblest reed could more prevail,
    Had more of strength, diviner rage,
    Than all which charms this laggard age;
    E'en all at once together found,
    Cecilia's mingled world of sound—
115 O bid our vain endeavours cease;
    Revive the just designs of Greece:
    Return in all thy simple state!
    Confirm the tales her sons relate!

ODE

WRITTEN IN THE BEGINNING OF THE YEAR 1746

How sleep the brave who sink to rest,
By all their country's wishes blessed!
When spring, with dewy fingers cold,
Returns to deck their hallowed mould,
5 She there shall dress a sweeter sod
Than fancy's feet have ever trod.

By fairy hands their knell is rung;
By forms unseen their dirge is sung;
There honour comes, a pilgrim grey,
10 To bless the turf that wraps their clay;
And freedom shall awhile repair,
To dwell, a weeping hermit, there!

DIRGE IN CYMBELINE

SUNG BY GUIDERUS AND ARVIRAGUS OVER FIDELE, SUPPOSED TO BE DEAD

(First published in *The Gentleman's Magazine*, for October
1749)

To fair Fidele's grassy tomb
  Soft maids and village hinds shall bring
Each opening sweet of earliest bloom,
  And rifle all the breathing spring.

5 No wailing ghost shall dare appear
  To vex with shrieks this quiet grove;
But shepherd lads assemble here,
  And melting virgins own their love.

No withered witch shall here be seen;
10   No goblins lead their nightly crew:
The female fays shall haunt the green,
    And dress thy grave with pearly dew!

The redbreast oft, at evening hours,
    Shall kindly lend his little aid,
15 With hoary moss, and gathered flowers,
    To deck the ground where thou art laid.

When howling winds and beating rain,
    In tempests shake the sylvan cell;
Or 'midst the chase, on every plain,
20   The tender thought on thee shall dwell;

Each lonely scene shall thee restore;
    For thee the tear be duly shed;
Beloved till life can charm no more,
    And mourned till pity's self be dead.

Thomas Gray

1716–1771

ODE ON A DISTANT PROSPECT OF ETON COLLEGE

(1747)

Ye distant spires, ye antique towers,
    That crown the watry glade,
Where grateful Science still adores
    Her HENRY's holy Shade;
5 And ye, that from the stately brow
Of WINDSOR's heights th' expanse below
    Of grove, of lawn, of mead survey,
Whose turf, whose shade, whose flowers among
Wanders the hoary Thames along
10   His silver-winding way:

Ah, happy hills, ah, pleasing shade,
   Ah, fields belov'd in vain,
Where once my careless childhood stray'd,
   A stranger yet to pain!
15 I feel the gales, that from ye blow,
A momentary bliss bestow,
   As waving fresh their gladsome wing,
My weary soul they seem to soothe,
And, redolent of joy and youth,
20   To breathe a second spring.

Say, father THAMES, for thou hast seen
   Full many a sprightly race
Disporting on thy margent green
   The paths of pleasure trace,
25 Who foremost now delight to cleave
With pliant arm thy glassy wave?
   The captive linnet which enthral?
What idle progeny succeed
To chase the rolling circle's speed,
30   Or urge the flying ball?

While some on earnest business bent
   Their murm'ring labours ply
'Gainst graver hours, that bring constraint,
   To sweeten liberty: ·
35 Some bold adventurers disdain
The limits of their little reign,
   And unknown regions dare descry:
Still as they run they look behind,
They hear a voice in every wind,
40   And snatch a fearful joy.

Gay hope is theirs by fancy fed,
   Less pleasing when possest;
The tear forgot as soon as shed,
   The sunshine of the breast:

45 Theirs buxom health of rosy hue,
   Wild wit, invention ever-new,
     And lively chear of vigour born;
   The thoughtless day, the easy night,
   The spirits pure, the slumbers light,
50   That fly th' approach of morn.

   Alas, regardless of their doom
     The little victims play!
   No sense have they of ills to come,
     Nor care beyond to-day:
55 Yet see how all around 'em wait
   The Ministers of human fate,
     And black Misfortune's baleful train!
   Ah, show them where in ambush stand
   To seize their prey the murth'rous band!
60   Ah, tell them, they are men!

   These shall the fury Passions tear,
     The vulturs of the mind,
   Disdainful Anger, pallid Fear,
     And Shame that sculks behind;
65 Or pineing Love shall waste their youth,
   Or Jealousy with rankling tooth,
     That inly gnaws the secret heart,
   And Envy wan, and faded Care,
   Grim-visag'd comfortless Despair,
70   And Sorrow's piercing dart.

   Ambition this shall tempt to rise,
     Then whirl the wretch from high,
   To bitter Scorn a sacrifice,
     And grinning Infamy.
75 The stings of Falsehood those shall try,
   And hard Unkindness' alter'd eye,
     That mocks the tear it forc'd to flow;
   And keen Remorse with blood defil'd,

And moody Madness laughing wild
80   Amid severest woe.

Lo, in the vale of years beneath
   A griesly troop are seen,
The painful family of Death,
   More hideous than their Queen:
85 This racks the joints, this fires the veins,
That every labouring sinew strains,
   Those in the deeper vitals rage:
Lo, Poverty, to fill the band,
That numbs the soul with icy hand,
90   And slow-consuming Age.

To each his suff'rings: all are men,
   Condemn'd alike to groan,
The tender for another's pain;
   Th' unfeeling for his own.
95 Yet, ah! why should they know their fate?
Since sorrow never comes too late,
   And happiness too swiftly flies,
Thought would destroy their paradise.
No more; where ignorance is bliss,
100   'Tis folly to be wise.

ELEGY WRITTEN IN A COUNTRY CHURCHYARD
(1751)

The curfew tolls the knell of parting day,
   The lowing herd wind slowly o'er the lea,
The plowman homeward plods his weary way,
   And leaves the world to darkness and to me.

5 Now fades the glimmering landscape on the
      sight,
   And all the air a solemn stillness holds,
Save where the beetle wheels his droning flight,
   And drowsy tinklings lull the distant folds:

    Save that from yonder ivy-mantled tower,
10   The moping owl does to the moon complain
    Of such as, wandering near her secret bower,
        Molest her ancient solitary reign.

    Beneath those rugged elms, that yew-tree's shade
        Where heaves the turf in many a mouldering
            heap,
15 Each in his narrow cell forever laid
        The rude forefathers of the hamlet sleep.

    The breezy call of incense-breathing Morn,
        The swallow twittering from the straw-built
            shed,
    The cock's shrill clarion, or the echoing horn,
20   No more shall rouse them from their lowly bed.

    For them no more the blazing hearth shall burn,
        Or busy housewife ply her evening care:
    No children run to lisp their sire's return,
        Or climb his knees the envied kiss to share.

25 Oft did the harvest to their sickle yield,
        Their furrow oft the stubborn glebe has broke:
    How jocund did they drive their team afield!
        How bow'd the woods beneath their sturdy
            stroke!

    Let not Ambition mock their useful toil,
30   Their homely joys, and destiny obscure;
    Nor Grandeur hear with a disdainful smile
        The short and simple annals of the poor.

    The boast of heraldry, the pomp of power,
        And all that beauty, all that wealth e'er gave,
35 Await alike th' inevitable hour.
        The paths of glory lead but to the grave.

Nor you, ye Proud, impute to these the fault,
   If Mem'ry o'er their tomb no trophies raise,
Where through the long-drawn aisle and fretted
      vault
40   The pealing anthem swells the note of praise.

Can storied urn or animated bust
   Back to its mansion call the fleeting breath?
Can Honour's voice provoke the silent dust,
   Or Flatt'ry soothe the dull cold ear of death?

45 Perhaps in this neglected spot is laid
   Some heart once pregnant with celestial fire;
Hands, that the rod of empire might have
      sway'd,
   Or waked to ecstasy the living lyre.

But Knowledge to their eyes her ample page
50   Rich with the spoils of time did ne'er unroll;
Chill Penury repress'd their noble rage,
   And froze the genial current of the soul.

Full many a gem of purest ray serene
   The dark unfathom'd caves of ocean bear:
55 Full many a flower is born to blush unseen,
   And waste its sweetness on the desert air.

Some village Hampden, that with dauntless
      breast
   The little tyrant of his fields withstood,
Some mute inglorious Milton here may rest,
60   Some Cromwell guiltless of his country's blood.

Th' applause of list'ning senates to command,
   The threats of pain and ruin to despise,
To scatter plenty o'er a smiling land,
   And read their hist'ry in a nation's eyes,

65 Their lot forbad: nor circumscrib'd alone
        Their growing virtues, but their crimes con-
            fin'd;
    Forbad to wade through slaughter to a throne,
        And shut the gates of mercy on mankind,

    The struggling pangs of conscious truth to hide,
70   To quench the blushes of ingenuous shame,
    Or heap the shrine of Luxury and Pride
        With incense kindled at the Muse's flame.

    Far from the madding crowd's ignoble strife,
        Their sober wishes never learn'd to stray;
75 Along the cool sequester'd vale of life
        They kept the noiseless tenor of their way.

    Yet ev'n these bones from insult to protect
        Some frail memorial still erected nigh,
    With uncouth rhymes and shapeless sculpture
            deck'd,
80   Implores the passing tribute of a sigh.

    Their name, their years, spelt by th' unletter'd
            muse,
        The place of fame and elegy supply:
    And many a holy text around she strews,
        That teach the rustic moralist to die.

85 For who to dumb Forgetfulness a prey,
        This pleasing anxious being e'er resign'd,
    Left the warm precincts of the cheerful day,
        Nor cast one longing ling'ring look behind?

    On some fond breast the parting soul relies,
90   Some pious drops the closing eye requires;
    E'en from the tomb the voice of Nature cries,
        E'en in our ashes live their wonted fires.

For thee, who mindful of th' unhonour'd dead,
  Dost in these lines their artless tale relate;
95 If chance, by lonely contemplation led,
  Some kindred spirit shall inquire thy fate,—

Haply some hoary-headed Swain may say,
  "Oft have we seen him at the peep of dawn
Brushing with hasty steps the dews away
100 To meet the sun upon the upland lawn.

"There at the foot of yonder nodding beech,
  That wreathes its old fantastic roots so high,
His listless length at noontide would he stretch,
  And pore upon the brook that babbles by.

105 "Hard by yon wood, now smiling as in scorn,
  Mutt'ring his wayward fancies he would rove,
Now drooping, woful-wan; like one forlorn,
  Or craz'd with care, or cross'd in hopeless love.

"One morn I missed him on the custom'd hill,
110 Along the heath, and near his fav'rite tree;
Another came; nor yet beside the rill,
  Nor up the lawn, nor at the wood was he:

"The next, with dirges due in sad array
  Slow through the church-way path we saw him
     borne:
115 Approach and read (for thou canst read) the lay,
  Grav'd on the stone beneath yon aged thorn."

THE EPITAPH

Here rests his head upon the lap of Earth
  A Youth, to Fortune and to Fame unknown;
Fair Science frown'd not on his humble birth,
120 And Melancholy mark'd him for her own.

Large was his bounty, and his soul sincere,
    Heav'n did a recompense as largely send:
He gave to Mis'ry all he had, a tear,
    He gain'd from heav'n ('twas all he wish'd) a
        friend.

125 No farther seek his merits to disclose,
    Or draw his frailties from their dread abode,
    (There they alike in trembling hope repose,)
    The bosom of his Father and his God.

THE BARD

(From *Odes*, 1757)

I. 1.

    " Ruin seize thee, ruthless King!
Confusion on thy banners wait,
Tho' fann'd by Conquest's crimson wing
    They mock the air with idle state.
5 Helm, nor Hauberk's twisted mail,
    Nor even thy virtues, Tyrant, shall avail
        To save thy secret soul from nightly fears,
        From Cambria's curse, from Cambria's
            tears! "
Such were the sounds, that o'er the crested pride
10   Of the first Edward scatter'd wild dismay,
As down the steep of Snowdon's shaggy side
        He wound with toilsome march his long
            array.
Stout Glo'ster stood aghast in speechless trance:
    " To arms! " cried Mortimer, and couch'd his
        quiv'ring lance.

I. 2.

15   On a rock, whose haughty brow
Frowns o'er old Conway's foaming flood,
    Robed in the sable garb of woe,
With haggard eyes the Poet stood;
(Loose his beard, and hoary hair
20   Stream'd, like a meteor, to the troubled air,)
And with a Master's hand, and Prophet's fire,
Struck the deep sorrows of his lyre.
    "Hark, how each giant-oak, and desert cave,
Sighs to the torrent's awful voice beneath!
25 O'er thee, oh King! their hundred arms they
      wave,
    Revenge on thee in hoarser murmurs
      breathe;
Vocal no more, since Cambria's fatal day,
To high-born Hoel's harp, or soft Llewellyn's
    lay."

I. 3.

    "Cold is Cadwallo's tongue,
30   That hush'd the stormy main:
Brave Urien sleeps upon his craggy bed:
      Mountains, ye mourn in vain
      Modred, whose magic song
Made huge Plinlimmon bow his cloud-top'd head.
35   On dreary Arvon's shore they lie,
Smear'd with gore, and ghastly pale:
Far, far aloof th' affrighted ravens sail;
    The famish'd Eagle screams, and passes by.
Dear lost companions of my tuneful art,
40   Dear, as the light that visits these sad eyes,
Dear, as the ruddy drops that warm my heart,
    Ye died amidst your dying country's cries—
No more I weep. They do not sleep.
    On yonder cliffs, a griesly band,

45 I see them sit, they linger yet,
     Avengers of their native land:
With me in dreadful harmony they join,
And weave with bloody hands the tissue of thy
    line."

II. 1.

  "Weave the warp, and weave the woof,
50 The winding-sheet of Edward's race.
     Give ample room, and verge enough
The characters of hell to trace.
Mark the year, and mark the night,
When Severn shall re-echo with affright
55 The shrieks of death, thro' Berkley's roofs that
    ring,
Shrieks of an agonizing King!
     She-Wolf of France, with unrelenting fangs,
That tear'st the bowels of thy mangled Mate,
     From thee be born, who o'er thy country
     hangs
60 The scourge of Heav'n.   What Terrors round
    him wait!
Amazement in his van, with Flight combined,
And Sorrow's faded form, and Solitude behind."

II. 2.

  "Mighty Victor, mighty Lord!
Low on his funeral couch he lies!
65   No pitying heart, no eye, afford
A tear to grace his obsequies.
     Is the sable Warriour fled?
Thy son is gone.   He rests among the Dead.
The Swarm, that in thy noontide beam were
    born?
70 Gone to salute the rising Morn.
Fair laughs the Morn, and soft the Zephyr blows,
    While proudly riding o'er the azure realm

In gallant trim the gilded Vessel goes;
　　Youth on the prow, and Pleasure at the
　　　　helm;
75 Regardless of the sweeping Whirlwind's sway,
That, hush'd in grim repose, expects his even-
　　　ing prey."

II. 3.

　"Fill high the sparkling bowl,
The rich repast prepare,
　　Reft of a crown, he yet may share the feast:
80 Close by the regal chair
　　Fell Thirst and Famine scowl
　　A baleful smile upon their baffled Guest.
Heard ye the din of battle bray,
　　Lance to lance, and horse to horse?
85　　Long years of havoc urge their destined
　　　　course,
And thro' the kindred squadrons mow their way.
　　Ye Towers of Julius, London's lasting
　　　　shame,
With many a foul and midnight murther fed,
　　Revere his Consort's faith, his Father's
　　　　fame,
90 And spare the meek Usurper's holy head.
Above, below, the rose of snow,
　　Twined with her blushing foe, we spread:
The bristled Boar in infant gore
　　Wallows beneath the thorny shade.
95 Now, Brothers, bending o'er th' accursed loom
Stamp we our vengeance deep, and ratify his
　　　doom."

III. 1.

　"Edward, lo! to sudden fate
(Weave we the woof.　The thread is spun.)
　　Half of thy heart we consecrate.

100 (The web is wove. The work is done.)
    Stay, oh stay! nor thus forlorn
    Leave me unbless'd, unpitied, here to mourn:
    In yon bright track, that fires the western skies,
    They melt, they vanish from my eyes.
105 But oh! what solemn scenes on Snowdon's height
        Descending slow their glitt'ring skirts un-
            roll?
    Visions of glory, spare my aching sight,
        Ye unborn Ages, crowd not on my soul!
    No more our long-lost Arthur we bewail.
110 All hail, ye genuine Kings, Britannia's Issue,
        hail!"

III. 2.

    " Girt with many a Baron bold
        Sublime their starry fronts they rear;
    And gorgeous Dames, and Statesmen old
    In bearded majesty, appear.
115 In the midst a Form divine!
    Her eye proclaims her of the Briton-line;
    Her lyon-port, her awe-commanding face,
    Attemper'd sweet to virgin-grace.
    What strings symphonious tremble in the air,
120   What strains of vocal transport round her
            play.
    Hear from the grave, great Taliessin, hear;
        They breathe a soul to animate thy clay.
    Bright Rapture calls, and soaring, as she sings,
    Waves in the eye of Heav'n her many-colour'd
        wings."

III. 3.

125   " The verse adorn again
        Fierce War, and faithful Love,
    And Truth severe, by fairy Fiction drest.
        In buskin'd measures move

Pale Grief, and Pleasing Pain,
130 With Horrour, Tyrant of the throbbing breast.
      A Voice, as of the Cherub-Choir,
    Gales from blooming Eden bear;
    And distant warblings lessen on my ear,
      That lost in long futurity expire.
135 Fond impious Man, think'st thou, yon sanguine
        cloud,
        Rais'd by thy breath, has quench'd the Orb
          of day?
    To-morrow he repairs the golden flood,
        And warms the nations with redoubled ray.
    Enough for me: With joy I see
140   The different doom our Fates assign.
    Be thine Despair, and sceptr'd Care,
    To triumph, and to die, are mine."
    He spoke, and headlong from the mountain's
        height
    Deep in the roaring tide he plung'd to endless
        night.

Oliver Goldsmith

1728–1774

THE DESERTED VILLAGE

(1770)

Sweet Auburn! loveliest village of the plain,
Where health and plenty cheer'd the labouring
    swain,
Where smiling spring its earliest visit paid,
And parting summer's lingering blooms delay'd:
5 Dear lovely bowers of innocence and ease,
Seats of my youth, when every sport could please,
How often have I loiter'd o'er thy green,
Where humble happiness endear'd each scene!

How often have I paus'd on every charm,
10 The shelter'd cot, the cultivated farm,
The never-failing brook, the busy mill,
The decent church that topt the neighbouring
    hill,
The hawthorn bush with seats beneath the shade,
For talking age and whispering lovers made!
15 How often have I blest the coming day
When toil remitting lent its turn to play,
And all the village train from labour free,
Led up their sports beneath the spreading tree;
While many a pastime circled in the shade,
20 The young contending as the old survey'd,
And many a gambol frolick'd o'er the ground,
And sleights of art and feats of strength went
    round!
And still, as each repeated pleasure tir'd,
Succeeding sports the mirthful band inspir'd;
25 The dancing pair that simply sought renown
By holding out to tire each other down,
The swain mistrustless of his smutted face,
While secret laughter titter'd round the place,
The bashful virgin's sidelong looks of love,
30 The matron's glance that would those looks
    reprove.
These were thy charms, sweet village! sports like
    these,
With sweet succession, taught even toil to please;
These round thy bowers their cheerful influence
    shed;
These were thy charms—but all these charms are
    fled.
35   Sweet smiling village, loveliest of the lawn,
Thy sports are fled, and all thy charms with-
    drawn;
Amidst thy bowers the tyrant's hand is seen,
And desolation saddens all thy green;

One only master grasps the whole domain,
40 And half a tillage stints thy smiling plain.
No more thy glassy brook reflects the day,
But chok'd with sedges, works its weedy way;
Along thy glades, a solitary guest,
The hollow-sounding bittern guards its nest;
45 Amidst thy desert walks the lapwing flies,
And tires their echoes with unvaried cries:
Sunk are thy bowers in shapeless ruin all,
And the long grass o'ertops the mouldering wall;
And, trembling, shrinking from the spoiler's hand,
50 Far, far away thy children leave the land.

Ill fares the land, to hastening ills a prey,
Where wealth accumulates and men decay;
Princes and lords may flourish, or may fade—
A breath can make them, as a breath has made—
55 But a bold peasantry, their country's pride,
When once destroy'd, can never be supplied.

A time there was, ere England's griefs began,
When every rood of ground maintain'd its man:
For him light labour spread her wholesome store,
60 Just gave what life requir'd, but gave no more;
His best companions, innocence and health,
And his best riches, ignorance of wealth.

But times are alter'd; trade's unfeeling train
Usurp the land, and dispossess the swain:
65 Along the lawn where scatter'd hamlets rose,
Unwieldy wealth and cumbrous pomp repose,
And every want to opulence allied,
And every pang that folly pays to pride.
Those gentle hours that plenty bade to bloom,
70 Those calm desires that ask'd but little room,
Those healthful sports that grac'd the peaceful
        scene,
Liv'd in each look and brighten'd all the green—
These, far departing, seek a kinder shore,
And rural mirth and manners are no more.

75　　Sweet Auburn! parent of the blissful hour,
　　　Thy glades forlorn confess the tyrant's power.
　　　Here, as I take my solitary rounds
　　　Amidst thy tangling walks and ruin'd grounds,
　　　And, many a year elaps'd, return to view
80　Where once the cottage stood, the hawthorn
　　　　　grew,
　　　Remembrance wakes with all her busy train,
　　　Swells at my breast, and turns the past to pain.
　　　　In all my wanderings round this world of care,
　　　In all my griefs—and God has given my share—
85　I still had hopes, my latest hours to crown,
　　　Amidst these humble bowers to lay me down;
　　　To husband out life's taper at the close,
　　　And keep the flame from wasting by repose.
　　　I still had hopes, for pride attends us still,
90　Amidst the swains to show my book-learn'd skill,
　　　Around my fire an evening group to draw,
　　　And tell of all I felt, and all I saw;
　　　And as an hare whom hounds and horns pursue
　　　Pants to the place from whence at first she flew,
95　I still had hopes, my long vexations past,
　　　Here to return—and die at home at last.
　　　　O blest retirement, friend to life's decline,
　　　Retreats from care, that never must be mine!
　　　How happy he who crowns, in shades like these,
100　A youth of labour with an age of ease;
　　　Who quits a world where strong temptations try,
　　　And, since 'tis hard to combat, learns to fly!
　　　For him no wretches, born to work and weep,
　　　Explore the mine, or tempt the dangerous deep;
105　Nor surly porter stands, in guilty state,
　　　To spurn imploring famine from the gate;
　　　But on he moves to meet his latter end,
　　　Angels around befriending virtue's friend,
　　　Bends to the grave with unperceiv'd decay,
110　While resignation gently slopes the way,

And, all his prospects brightening to the last,
His heaven commences ere the world be past.
   Sweet was the sound, when oft at evening's
     close
Up yonder hill the village murmur rose.
115 There as I passed with careless steps and slow,
The mingling notes came soften'd from below:
The swain responsive as the milkmaid sung,
The sober herd that low'd to meet their young,
The noisy geese that gabbled o'er the pool,
120 The playful children just let loose from school,
The watch-dog's voice that bay'd the whispering
     wind,
And the loud laugh that spoke the vacant mind—
These all in sweet confusion sought the shade,
And fill'd each pause the nightingale had made.
125 But now the sounds of population fail,
No cheerful murmurs fluctuate in the gale,
No busy steps the grass-grown footway tread,
For all the bloomy flush of life is fled—
All but yon widow'd, solitary thing,
130 That feebly bends beside the plashy spring;
She, wretched matron—forc'd in age, for bread,
To strip the brook with mantling cresses spread,
To pick her wintry faggot from the thorn,
To seek her nightly shed, and weep till morn—
135 She only left of all the harmless train,
The sad historian of the pensive plain!
   Near yonder copse, where once the garden
     smil'd,
And still where many a garden-flower grows wild,
There, where a few torn shrubs the place disclose,
140 The village preacher's modest mansion rose.
A man he was to all the country dear,
And passing rich with forty pounds a year.
Remote from towns he ran his godly race,
Nor e'er had chang'd, nor wish'd to change his
     place;

145 Unpractis'd he to fawn, or seek for power
    By doctrines fashion'd to the varying hour;
    Far other aims his heart had learn'd to prize,
    More skill'd to raise the wretched than to rise.
    His house was known to all the vagrant train,
150 He chid their wanderings, but reliev'd their pain;
    The long-remember'd beggar was his guest,
    Whose beard descending swept his aged breast;
    The ruin'd spendthrift, now no longer proud,
    Claim'd kindred there, and had his claims al-
        low'd;
155 The broken soldier, kindly bade to stay,
    Sat by his fire, and talk'd the night away,
    Wept o'er his wounds, or, tales of sorrow done,
    Shoulder'd his crutch and show'd how fields were
        won.
    Pleas'd with his guests, the good man learn'd to
        glow,
160 And quite forgot their vices in their woe;
    Careless their merits or their faults to scan,
    His pity gave ere charity began.
      Thus to relieve the wretched was his pride,
    And even his failings lean'd to virtue's side;
165 But in his duty prompt at every call,
    He watch'd and wept, he pray'd and felt for all:
    And, as a bird each fond endearment tries
    To tempt its new-fledg'd offspring to the skies,
    He tried each art, reprov'd each dull delay,
170 Allur'd to brighter worlds, and led the way.
      Beside the bed where parting life was laid,
    And sorrow, guilt, and pain by turns dismay'd,
    The reverend champion stood: at his control
    Despair and anguish fled the struggling soul;
175 Comfort came down the trembling wretch to
      raise,
    And his last faltering accents whisper'd praise.
    At church, with meek and unaffected grace,

His looks adorn'd the venerable place;
Truth from his lips prevail'd with double sway,
180 And fools who came to scoff remained to pray.
The service past, around the pious man,
With ready zeal, each honest rustic ran;
Even children follow'd, with endearing wile,
And pluck'd his gown, to share the good man's
    smile:
185 His ready smile a parent's warmth exprest,
Their welfare pleas'd him, and their cares dis-
    trest.
To them his heart, his love, his griefs were given,
But all his serious thoughts had rest in heaven:
As some tall cliff, that lifts its awful form,
190 Swells from the vale, and midway leaves the
    storm,
Though round its breast the rolling clouds are
    spread,
Eternal sunshine settles on its head. ·
   Beside yon straggling fence that skirts the way,
With blossom'd furze unprofitably gay,
195 There, in his noisy mansion, skill'd to rule,
The village master taught his little school.
A man severe he was, and stern to view;
I knew him well, and every truant knew:
Well had the boding tremblers learn'd to trace
200 The day's disasters in his morning face;
Full well they laugh'd with counterfeited glee
At all his jokes, for many a joke had he;
Full well the busy whisper, circling round,
Convey'd the dismal tidings when he frown'd;
205 Yet he was kind, or if severe in aught,
The love he bore to learning was in fault.
The village all declar'd how much he knew;
'Twas certain he could write, and cipher too,
Lands he could measure, terms and tides presage,
210 And even the story ran that he could gauge,

In arguing too the parson own'd his skill,
For even though vanquish'd, he could argue still;
While words of learned length and thundering
    sound
Amaz'd the gazing rustics rang'd around;
215 And still they gaz'd, and still the wonder grew
That one small head could carry all he knew.
    But past is all his fame: the very spot,
Where many a time he triumph'd, is forgot.
Near yonder thorn, that lifts its head on high,
220 Where once the sign-post caught the passing eye,
Low lies that house where nut-brown draughts
       inspir'd,
Where gray-beard mirth and smiling toil retir'd,
Where village statesmen talk'd with looks pro-
    found,
And news much older than their ale went round.
225 Imagination fondly stoops to trace
The parlour splendours of that festive place:
The whitewash'd wall, the nicely sanded floor,
The varnish'd clock that click'd behind the door;
The chest contriv'd a double debt to pay,
230 A bed by night, a chest of drawers by day;
The pictures plac'd for ornament and use,
The twelve good rules, the royal game of goose;
The hearth, except when winter chill'd the day,
With aspen boughs, and flowers, and fennel gay,
235 While broken tea-cups, wisely kept for show,
Rang'd o'er the chimney, glisten'd in a row.
    Vain transitory splendours! could not all
Reprieve the tottering mansion from its fall?
Obscure it sinks, nor shall it more impart
240 An hour's importance to the poor man's heart.
Thither no more the peasant shall repair
To sweet oblivion of his daily care;
No more the farmer's news, the barber's tale,
No more the woodman's ballad shall prevail;

245 No more the smith his dusky brow shall clear,
    Relax his ponderous strength, and lean to hear;
    The host himself no longer shall be found
    Careful to see the mantling bliss go round;
    Nor the coy maid, half willing to be prest,
250 Shall kiss the cup to pass it to the rest.
        Yes! let the rich deride, the proud disdain,
    These simple blessings of the lowly train;
    To me more dear, congenial to my heart,
    One native charm, than all the gloss of art;
255 Spontaneous joys, where nature has its play,
    The soul adopts, and owns their first-born sway;
    Lightly they frolic o'er the vacant mind,
    Unenvied, unmolested, unconfin'd.
    But the long pomp, the midnight masquerade,
260 With all the freaks of wanton wealth array'd,
    In these, ere triflers half their wish obtain,
    The toiling pleasure sickens into pain;
    And, even while fashion's brightest arts decoy,
    The heart distrusting asks, if this be joy?
265   Ye friends to truth, ye statesmen who survey
    The rich man's joys increase, the poor's decay,
    'Tis yours to judge how wide the limits stand
    Between a splendid and a happy land.
    Proud swells the tide with loads of freighted ore,
270 And shouting Folly hails them from her shore;
    Hoards even beyond the miser's wish abound,
    And rich men flock from all the world around;
    Yet count our gains: this wealth is but a name
    That leaves our useful products still the same.
275 Not so the loss. The man of wealth and pride
    Takes up a space that many poor supplied—
    Space for his lake, his park's extended bounds,
    Space for his horses, equipage, and hounds:
    The robe that wraps his limbs in silken sloth
280 Has robbed the neighbouring fields of half their
      growth;

His seat, where solitary spots are seen,
Indignant spurns the cottage from the green;
Around the world each needful product flies,
For all the luxuries the world supplies.
285 While thus the land, adorn'd for pleasure, all
In barren splendour feebly waits the fall.
As some fair female, unadorn'd and plain,
Secure to please while youth confirms her reign,
Slights every borrow'd charm that dress supplies,
290 Nor shares with art the triumph of her eyes;
But when those charms are past, for charms are
          frail,
When time advances, and when lovers fail,
She then shines forth, solicitous to bless,
In all the glaring impotence of dress:
295 Thus fares the land, by luxury betray'd;
In nature's simplest charms at first array'd,
But verging to decline, its splendours rise,
Its vistas strike, its palaces surprise;
While, scourg'd by famine from the smiling land,
300 The mournful peasant leads his humble band;
And while he sinks, without one arm to save,
The country blooms—a garden, and a grave.
Where then, ah! where shall poverty reside,
To 'scape the pressure of contiguous pride?
305 If to some common's fenceless limits stray'd
He drives his flock to pick the scanty blade,
Those fenceless fields the sons of wealth divide,
And even the bare-worn common is denied.
If to the city sped—what waits him there?
310 To see profusion that he must not share;
To see ten thousand baneful arts combin'd
To pamper luxury, and thin mankind;
To see each joy the sons of pleasure know,
Extorted from his fellow-creature's woe.
315 Here, while the courtier glitters in brocade,
There the pale artist plies the sickly trade;

Here, while the proud their long-drawn pomps
    display,
There, the black gibbet glooms beside the way.
The dome where pleasure holds her midnight
    reign,
320 Here, richly deck'd, admits the gorgeous train;
Tumultuous grandeur crowds the blazing square,
The rattling chariots clash, the torches glare.
Sure scenes like these no troubles e'er annoy!
Sure these denote one universal joy!
325 Are these thy serious thoughts? Ah, turn thine
    eyes
Where the poor houseless shivering female lies.
She once, perhaps, in village plenty blest,
Has wept at tales of innocence distrest;
Her modest looks the cottage might adorn,
330 Sweet as the primrose peeps beneath the thorn;
Now lost to all—her friends, her virtue fled—
Near her betrayer's door she lays her head,
And, pinch'd with cold, and shrinking from the
    shower,
With heavy heart deplores that luckless hour
335 When idly first, ambitious of the town,
She left her wheel, and robes of country brown.
    Do thine, sweet Auburn, thine, the loveliest
    train,
Do thy fair tribes participate her pain?
Even now, perhaps, by cold and hunger led,
340 At proud men's doors they ask a little bread.
    Ah, no! To distant climes, a dreary scene,
Where half the convex world intrudes between,
Through torrid tracts with fainting steps they go,
Where wild Altama murmurs to their woe.
345 Far different there from all that charm'd before,
The various terrors of that horrid shore:
Those blazing suns that dart a downward ray,
And fiercely shed intolerable day;

Those matted woods where birds forget to sing,
350 But silent bats in drowsy clusters cling;
Those poisonous fields with rank luxuriance
          crown'd,
Where the dark scorpion gathers death around;
Where at each step the stranger fears to wake
The rattling terrors of the vengeful snake;
355 Where crouching tigers wait their hapless prey,
And savage men more murderous still than they;
While oft in whirls the mad tornado flies,
Mingling the ravag'd landscape with the skies.
Far different these from every former scene,
360 The cooling brook, the grassy-vested green,
The breezy covert of the warbling grove,
That only shelter'd thefts of harmless love.
     Good Heaven! what sorrows gloom'd that part-
          ing day,
That call'd them from their native walks away;
365 When the poor exiles, every pleasure past,
Hung round the bowers, and fondly look'd their
          last,
And took a long farewell, and wish'd in vain
For seats like these beyond the western main;
And shuddering still to face the distant deep,
370 Return'd and wept, and still return'd to weep.
The good old sire the first prepar'd to go
To new-found worlds, and wept for other's woe;
But for himself, in conscious virtue brave,
He only wish'd for worlds beyond the grave.
375 His lovely daughter, lovelier in her tears,
The fond companion of his helpless years,
Silent went next, neglectful of her charms,
And left a lover's for a father's arms.
With louder plaints the mother spoke her woes,
380 And blest the cot where every pleasure rose,
And kiss'd her thoughtless babes with many a
          tear,

And clasp'd them close, in sorrow doubly dear;
Whilst her fond husband strove to lend relief
In all the silent manliness of grief.
385　　O Luxury! thou curst by Heaven's decree,
How ill exchang'd are things like these for thee!
How do thy potions, with insidious joy,
Diffuse their pleasures only to destroy!
Kingdoms by thee, to sickly greatness grown,
390　Boast of a florid vigour not their own:
At every draught more large and large they grow,
A bloated mass of rank, unwieldy woe;
Till **sapp'd** their strength, and every part un-
　　sound,
Down, down they sink, and spread a ruin round.
395　　Even now the devastation is begun,
And half the business of destruction done;
Even now, methinks, as pondering here I stand,
I see the rural Virtues leave the land.
Down where yon anchoring vessel spreads the sail
400　That idly waiting **flaps** with every gale,
Downward they move, a melancholy band,
Pass from the shore, and darken all the strand.
Contented Toil, and hospitable Care,
And kind connubial Tenderness are there;
405　And Piety with wishes placed above,
And steady Loyalty, and faithful Love.
And thou, sweet Poetry, thou loveliest maid,
Still first to fly where sensual joys invade;
Unfit in these degenerate times of shame
410　To catch the heart, or strike for honest fame;
Dear, charming nymph, neglected and decried,
My shame in crowds, my solitary pride,
Thou source of all my bliss, and all my woe,
Thou found'st me poor at first, and keep'st me so;
415　Thou guide by which the noble arts excel,
Thou nurse of every virtue, fare thee well!
Farewell! and O where'er thy voice be tried,

On Torno's cliffs or Pambamarca's side,
Whether where equinoctial fervours glow,
420 Or winter wraps the polar world in snow,
Still let thy voice, prevailing over time,
Redress the rigours of the inclement clime;
Aid slighted truth with thy persuasive strain;
Teach erring man to spurn the rage of gain;
425 Teach him, that states of native strength possest,
Though very poor, may still be very blest;
That trade's proud empire hastes to swift decay,
As ocean sweeps the labour'd mole away;
While self-dependent power can time defy,
430 As rocks resist the billows and the sky.

Thomas Chatterton

1752–1770

MINSTREL'S ROUNDELAY

(From *Aella*, 1770)

O sing unto my roundelay,
  O drop the briny tear with me,
Dance no more at holy-day,
  Like a running river be.
5   My love is dead,
     Gone to his death-bed,
      All under the willow-tree.

Black his locks as the winter night
  White his skin as the summer snow,
10 Red his face as the morning light,
  Cold he lies in the grave below.
     My love is dead,
     Gone to his death-bed,
      All under the willow-tree.

15 Sweet his tongue as the throstle's note,
       Quick in dance as thought can be,
Deft his tabor, cudgel stout,
       O he lies by the willow-tree!
       My love is dead,
20   Gone to his death-bed,
           All under the willow-tree.

Hark! the raven flaps his wing
       In the briar'd dell below;
Hark! the death-owl loud doth sing
25   To the nightmares as they go.
       My love is dead,
       Gone to his death-bed,
           All under the willow-tree.

See! the white moon shines on high;
30   Whiter is my true love's shroud;
Whiter than the morning sky,
       Whiter than the evening cloud.
       My love is dead,
       Gone to his death-bed,
35   All under the willow-tree.

Here upon my true love's grave
       Shall the barren flowers be laid:
Not one holy Saint to save
       All the coldness of a maid!
40   My love is dead,
       Gone to his death-bed,
           All under the willow-tree.

With my hands I'll gird the briars
       Round his holy corse to grow.
45 Elfin Faëry, light your fires;
       Here my body still shall bow.
       My love is dead,
       Gone to his death-bed,
           All under the willow-tree.

50 Come, with acorn-cup and thorn,
      Drain my hearte's blood away;
Life and all its good I scorn,
      Dance by night or feast by day.
      My love is dead,
55   Gone to his death-bed,
        All under the willow-tree.

THE BALADE OF CHARITIE

(From *Poems* collected 1777)

In Virginè the sultry Sun 'gan sheene
      And hot upon the meads did cast his ray:
The apple ruddied from its paly green,
      And the soft pear did bend the leafy spray;
5   The pied chelàndry sang the livelong day:
      'Twas now the pride, the manhood of the year,
   And eke the ground was dight in its most deft
        aumere.

The sun was gleaming in the mid of day,
      Dead still the air and eke the welkin blue,
10 When from the sea arist in drear array
      A heap of clouds of sable sullen hue,
      The which full fast unto the woodland drew,
   Hiding at once the sunnè's festive face;
   And the black tempest swelled and gathered up
        apace.

15 Beneath an holm, fast by a pathway side
      Which did unto Saint Godwyn's convent lead,
A hapless pilgrim moaning did abide,
      Poor in his view, ungentle in his weed,
      Long breast-full of the miseries of need.
20 Where from the hailstorm could the beggar fly?
He had no housen there, nor any convent nigh.

Look in his gloomèd face; his sprite there scan,
  How woe-begone, how withered, sapless, dead!
Haste to thy church-glebe-house, accursèd man,
25 Haste to thy coffin, thy sole slumbering-bed!
    Cold as the clay which will grow on thy head
  Are Charity and Love among high elves;
  The Knights and Barons live for pleasure and
    themselves.

  The gathered storm is ripe; the big drops fall;
30 The sunburnt meadows smoke and drink the
    rain;
  The coming ghastness dothe the cattle appal,
    And the full flocks are driving o'er the plain;
    Dashed from the clouds, the waters gush
      again;
  The welkin opes, the yellow levin flies,
35 And the hot fiery steam in the wide flame-lowe
    dies.

  List! now the thunder's rattling clamouring
    sound
  Moves slowly on, and then upswollen clangs,
  Shakes the high spire, and lost, dispended,
    drown'd,
    Still on the affrighted ear of terror hangs;
40 The winds are up; the lofty elm-tree swangs;
  Again the levin and the thunder pours,
  And the full clouds are burst at once in stormy
    showers.

  Spurring his palfrey o'er the watery plain,
    The Abbot of Saint Godwyn's convent came;
45 His chapournette was drenchèd with the rain,
    His painted girdle met with mickle shame;
    He backwards told his bederoll at the same.

The storm increasèd, and he drew aside,
  With the poor alms-craver near to the holm to
      bide.

50 His cope was all of Lincoln cloth so fine,
    With a gold button fastened near his chin;
  His autremete was edged with golden twine,
    And his peaked shoe a lordling's might have
      been;
  Full well it showed he counted cost no sin:
55 The trammels of the palfrey pleased his sight,
  For the horse-milliner his head with roses dight.

"An alms, Sir Priest!" the drooping pilgrim
      said,
  "O let me wait within your convent-door
  Till the sun shineth high above our head
60   And the loud tempest of the air is o'er.
  Helpless and old am I, alas! and poor:
  No house, nor friend, no money in my pouch;
  All that I call my own is this my silver crouch."

"Varlet," replied the Abbot, "cease your din;
65   This is no season alms and prayers to give;
  My porter never lets a beggar in;
    None touch my ring who not in honour live."
    And now the sun with the black clouds did
      strive,
  And shot upon the ground his glaring ray:
70 The Abbot spurred his steed, and eftsoons rode
    away.

Once more the sky was black, the thunder roll'd:
  Fast running o'er the plain a priest was seen,
  Not dight full proud nor buttoned up in gold;
    His cope and jape were grey, and eke were
      clean;
75   A Limitour he was, of order seen;

And from the pathway side then turned he,
Where the poor beggar lay beneath the holmen
tree.

"An alms, Sir Priest," the drooping pilgrim
said,
"For sweet Saint Mary and your order's
sake!"
80 The Limitour then loosened his pouch-thread
And did thereout a groat of silver take;
The needy pilgrim did for gladness shake.
"Here, take this silver, it may ease thy care;
We are God's stewards all,—nought of our own
we bear.

85 "But ah! unhappy pilgrim, learn of me,
Scarce any give a rentroll to their Lord:
Here, take my semicope,—thou'rt bare, I see;
'Tis thine; the Saints will give me my re-
ward!"
He left the pilgrim and his way aborde.
90 Virgin and holy Saints who sit in gloure,
Or give the mighty will, or give the good man
power.

William Cowper
1731–1800

THE TASK
(1785)
(Selections from Book I. *The Sofa*)

But though true worth and virtue, in the mild
And genial soil of cultivated life,
680 Thrive most, and may perhaps thrive only there,
Yet not in cities oft: in proud and gay

And gain-devoted cities.   Thither flow,
As to a common and most noisome sewer,
The dregs and feculence of every land.
685 In cities foul example on most minds
Begets its likeness.   Rank abundance breeds
In gross and pampered cities sloth and lust,
And wantónness and gluttonous excess.
In cities vice is hidden with most ease,
690 Or seen with least reproach; and virtue, taught
By frequent lapse, can hope no triumph there
Beyond the achievement of successful flight.
I do confess them nurseries of the arts,
In which they flourish most; where, in the beams
695 Of warm encouragement, and in the eye
Of public note, they reach their perfect size.
Such London is, by taste and wealth proclaimed
The fairest capital of all the world,
By riot and incontinence the worst.
700 There, touched by Reynolds, a dull blank becomes
A lucid mirror, in which Nature sees
All her reflected features.   Bacon there
Gives more than female beauty to a stone,
And Chatham's eloquence to marble lips.
705 Nor does the chisel occupy alone
The powers of sculpture, but the style as much;
Each province of her art her equal care.
With nice incision of her guided steel
She ploughs a brazen field, and clothes a soil
710 So sterile, with what charms soe'er she will,
The richest scenery and the loveliest forms.
Where finds Philosophy her eagle eye,
With which she gazes at yon burning disk
Undazzled, and detects and counts his spots?
715 In London.   Where her implements exact,
With which she calculates, computes, and scans
All distance, motion, magnitude, and now
Measures an atom, and now girds a world?

In London. Where has commerce such a mart,
720 So rich, so thronged, so drained, and so supplied,
As London, opulent, enlarged, and still
Increasing London? Babylon of old
Not more the glory of the earth than she,
A more accomplished world's chief glory now.
725   She has her praise. Now mark a spot or two
That so much beauty would do well to purge;
And show this queen of cities, that so fair
May yet be foul, so witty yet not wise.
It is not seemly, nor of good report,
730 That she is slack in discipline; more prompt
To avenge than to prevent the breach of law;
That she is rigid in denouncing death
On petty robbers, and indulges life
And liberty, and oftimes honour too,
735 To peculators of the public gold;
That thieves at home must hang, but he that puts
Into his overgorged and bloated purse
The wealth of Indian provinces, escapes.
Nor is it well, nor can it come to good,
740 That, through profane and infidel contempt
Of Holy Writ, she has presumed to annul
And abrogate, as roundly as she may,
The total ordinance and will of God;
Advancing Fashion to the post of Truth,
745 And centering all authority in modes
And customs of her own, till Sabbath rites
Have dwindled into unrespected forms,
And knees and hassocks are well-nigh divorced.
    God made the country, and man made the
        town:
750 What wonder then, that health and virtue, gifts
That can alone make sweet the bitter draught
That life holds out to all, should most abound
And least be threatened in the fields and groves?
Possess ye therefore, ye who, borne about

755 In chariots and sedans, know no fatigue
    But that of idleness, and taste no scenes
    But such as art contrives, possess ye still
    Your element; there only ye can shine,
    There only minds like yours can do no harm.
760 Our groves were planted to console at noon
    The pensive wanderer in their shades. At eve
    The moonbeam, sliding softly in between
    The sleeping leaves, is all the light they wish,
    Birds warbling all the music. We can spare
765 The splendour of your lamps, they but eclipse
    Our softer satellite. Your songs confound
    Our more harmonious notes: the thrush departs
    Scared, and the offended nightingale is mute.
    There is a public mischief in your mirth,
770 It plagues your country. Folly such as yours
    Graced with a sword, and worthier of a fan,
    Has made, what enemies could ne'er have done,
    Our arch of empire, steadfast but for you,
    A mutilated structure, soon to fall.

            .   .   .   .

BOOK II.—THE TIME-PIECE

    Oh for a lodge in some vast wilderness,
    Some boundless contiguity of shade,
    Where rumour of oppression and deceit,
    Of unsuccessful or successful war,
  5 Might never reach me more! My ear is pained,
    My soul is sick with every day's report
    Of wrong and outrage with which earth is filled.
    There is no flesh in man's obdurate heart,
    It does not feel for man; the natural bond
 10 Of brotherhood is severed as the flax
    That falls asunder at the touch of fire.
    He finds his fellow guilty of a skin
    Not coloured like his own, and having power
    To enforce the wrong, for such a worthy cause

15 Dooms and devotes him as his lawful prey.
   Lands intersected by a narrow frith
   Abhor each other.   Mountains interposed
   Make enemies of nations who had else
   Like kindred drops been mingled into one.
20 Thus man devotes his brother, and destroys;
   And worse than all, and most to be deplored,
   As human nature's broadest, foulest blot,
   Chains him, and tasks him, and exacts his sweat
   With stripes that Mercy, with a bleeding heart,
25 Weeps when she sees inflicted on a beast.
   Then what is man?   And what man seeing this,
   And having human feelings, does not blush
   And hang his head, to think himself a man?
   I would not have a slave to till my ground,
30 To carry me, to fan me while I sleep,
   And tremble when I wake, for all the wealth
   That sinews bought and sold have ever earned.
   No: dear as freedom is, and in my heart's
   Just estimation prized above all price,
35 I had much rather be myself the slave
   And wear the bonds, than fasten them on him.
   We have no slaves at home.—Then why abroad?
   And they themselves once ferried o'er the wave
   That parts us, are emancipate and loosed.
40 Slaves cannot breathe in England; if their lungs
   Receive our air, that moment they are free;
   They touch our country, and their shackles fall.
   That's noble, and bespeaks a nation proud
   And jealous of the blessing.   Spread it then,
45 And let it circulate through every vein
   Of all your empire; that where Britain's power
   Is felt, mankind may feel her mercy too.

.   .   .   .   .   .

BOOK III.—THE GARDEN

.   .   .   .

   I was a stricken deer that left the herd
Long since; with many an arrow deep infixed

110 My panting side was charged, when I withdrew
To seek a tranquil death in distant shades.
There was I found by One who had Himself
Been hurt by the archers. In His side He bore,
And in His hands and feet, the cruel scars.
115 With gentle force soliciting the darts,
He drew them forth, and healed, and bade me live.
Since then, with few associates, in remote
And silent woods I wander, far from those
My former partners of the peopled scene;
120 With few associates, and not wishing more.
Here much I ruminate, as much I may,
With other views of men and manners now
Than once, and others of a life to come.

. . . .

. . . .

BOOK IV.—THE WINTER'S EVENING

Hark! 'tis the twanging horn! O'er yonder
bridge,
That with its wearisome but needful length
Bestrides the wintry flood, in which the moon
Sees her unwrinkled face reflected bright,
5 He comes, the herald of a noisy world,
With spattered boots, strapped waist, and frozen
locks,
News from all nations lumbering at his back.
True to his charge, the close-packed load behind,
Yet careless what he brings, his one concern
10 Is to conduct it to the destined inn,
And having dropped the expected bag—pass on.
He whistles as he goes, light-hearted wretch,
Cold and yet cheerful: messenger of grief
Perhaps to thousands, and of joy to some,
15 To him indifferent whether grief or joy.
Houses in ashes, and the fall of stocks,
Births, deaths, and marriages, epistles wet

With tears that trickled down the writer's cheeks
Fast as the periods from his fluent quill,
20 Or charged with amorous sighs of absent swains,
Or nymphs responsive, equally affect
His horse and him, unconscious of them all.
But oh the important budget! ushered in
With such heart-shaking music, who can say
25 What are its tidings? have our troops awaked?
Or do they still, as if with opium drugged,
Snore to the murmurs of the Atlantic wave?
Is India free? and does she wear her plumed
And jewelled turban with a smile of peace,
30 Or do we grind her still?   The grand debate,
The popular harangue, the tart reply,
The logic, and the wisdom, and the wit,
And the loud laugh—I long to know them all;
I burn to set the imprisoned wranglers free,
35 And give them voice and utterance once again.
     Now stir the fire, and close the shutters fast,
Let fall the curtains, wheel the sofa round,
And while the bubbling and loud hissing urn
Throws up a steamy column, and the cups
40 That cheer but not inebriate, wait on each,
So let us welcome peaceful evening in.

.   .   .   .

.   .   .   .

120   Oh Winter! ruler of the inverted year,
Thy scattered hair with sleet like ashes filled,
Thy breath congealed upon thy lips, thy cheeks
Fringed with a beard made white with other
          snows
Than those of age, thy forehead wrapt in clouds,
125 A leafless branch thy sceptre, and thy throne
A sliding car, indebted to no wheels,
But urged by storms along its slippery way;
I love thee, all unlovely as thou seemest,
And dreaded as thou art.   Thou holdest the sun

130 A prisoner in the yet undawning east,
  Shortening his journey between morn and noon,
  And hurrying him, impatient of his stay,
  Down to the rosy west; but kindly still
  Compensating his loss with added hours
135 Of social converse and instructive ease,
  And gathering, at short notice, in one group
  The family dispersed, and fixing thought,
  Not less dispersed by daylight and its cares.
  I crown thee King of intimate delights,
140 Fireside enjoyments, home-born happiness,
  And all the comforts that the lowly roof
  Of undisturbed retirement, and the hours
  Of long uninterrupted evening know.

  .   .   .   .

  Come, Evening, once again, season of peace;
  Return, sweet Evening, and continue long!
245 Methinks I see thee in the streaky west,
  With matron step slow moving, while the Night
  Treads on thy sweeping train; one hand employed
  In letting fall the curtain of repose
  On bird and beast, the other charged for man
250 With sweet oblivion of the cares of day;
  Not sumptuously adorned, nor needing aid,
  Like homely-featured Night, of clustering gems;
  A star or two just twinkling on thy brow
  Suffices thee; save that the moon is thine
255 No less than hers, not worn indeed on high
  With ostentatious pageantry, but set
  With modest grandeur in thy purple zone,
  Resplendent less, but of an ample round.
  Come then, and thou shalt find thy votary calm,
260 Or make me so. Composure is thy gift:
  And whether I devote thy gentler hours
  To books, to music, or the poet's toil;
  To weaving nets for bird-alluring fruit;

Or twining silken threads round ivory reels,
265 When they command whom man was born to
          please:
I slight thee not, but make thee welcome still.

          .   .   .   .

          .   .   .   .

     In such a world, so thorny, and where none
Finds happiness unblighted, or, if found,
335 Without some thistly sorrow at its side,
It seems the part of wisdom, and no sin
Against the law of love, to measure lots
With less distinguished than ourselves, that thus
We may with patience bear our moderate ills,
340 And sympathize with others, suffering more.
Ill fares the traveller now, and he that stalks
In ponderous boots beside his reeking team.
The wain goes heavily, impeded sore
By congregated loads adhering close
345 To the clogged wheels; and in its sluggish pace
Noiseless appears a moving hill of snow.
The toiling steeds expand the nostril wide,
While every breath, by respiration strong
Forced downward, is consolidated soon
350 Upon their jutting chests. He, formed to bear
The pelting brunt of the tempestuous night,
With half-shut eyes and puckered cheeks, and
          teeth
Presented bare against the storm, plods on.
One hand secures his hat, save when with both
355 He brandishes his pliant length of whip,
Resounding oft, and never heard in vain.
Oh happy! and in my account, denied
The sensibility of pain with which
Refinement is endued, thrice happy thou.
360 Thy frame, robust and hardy, feels indeed
The piercing cold, but feels it unimpaired.
The learnèd finger never need explore

Thy vigorous pulse; and the unhealthful east,
That breathes the spleen, and searches every bone
365 Of the infirm, is wholesome air to thee.
Thy days roll on exempt from household care;
Thy waggon is thy wife; and the poor beasts,
That drag the dull companion to and fro,
Thine helpless charge, dependent on thy care.
370 Ah, treat them kindly! rude as thou appearest,
Yet show that thou hast mercy, which the great,
With needless hurry whirled from place to place,
Humane as they would seem, not always show.
Poor, yet industrious, modest, quiet, neat,
375 Such claim compassion in a night like this,
And have a friend in every feeling heart.

. . . . . .

BOOK VI.—THE WINTER WALK AT NOON

. . . . . .

The night was winter in his roughest mood,
The morning sharp and clear. But now at noon,
Upon the southern side of the slant hills,
60 And where the woods fence off the northern blast,
The season smiles, resigning all its rage,
And has the warmth of May. The vault is blue
Without a cloud, and white without a speck
The dazzling splendour of the scene below.
65 Again the harmony comes o'er the vale,
And through the trees I view the embattled
tower
Whence all the music. I again perceive
The soothing influence of the wafted strains,
And settle in soft musings as I tread
70 The walk, still verdant, under oaks and elms,
Whose outspread branches overarch the glade.
The roof, though moveable through all its length
As the wind sways it, has yet well sufficed,
And intercepting in their silent fall
75 The frequent flakes, has kept a path for me.

No noise is here, or none that hinders thought.
The redbreast warbles still, but is content
With slender notes, and more than half sup-
　　pressed:
Pleased with his solitude, and flitting light
80 From spray to spray, where'er he rests he shakes
From many a twig the pendant drops of ice,
That tinkle in the withered leaves below.
Stillness, accompanied with sounds so soft,
Charms more than silence.　Meditation here
85 May think down hours to moments.　Here the
　　　heart
May give a useful lesson to the head,
And learning wiser grow without his books.
Knowledge and wisdom, far from being one,
Have oftimes no connection.　Knowledge dwells
90 In heads replete with thoughts of other men,
Wisdom in minds attentive to their own.
Knowledge, a rude unprofitable mass,
The mere materials with which wisdom builds,
Till smoothed and squared and fitted to its place,
95 Does but encumber whom it seems to enrich.
Knowledge is proud that he has learned so much;
Wisdom is humble that he knows no more.

　　·　　　·　　　·　　　·　　　·　　　·　　　·

560　I would not enter on my list of friends
(Though graced with polished manners and fine
　　　sense,
Yet wanting sensibility) the man
Who needlessly sets foot upon a worm.
An inadvertent step may crush the snail
565 That crawls at evening in the public path;
But he that has humanity, forewarned,
Will tread aside, and let the reptile live.
The creeping vermin, loathsome to the sight,
And charged perhaps with venom, that intrudes,
570 A visitor unwelcome, into scenes

Sacred to neatness and repose, the alcove,
The chamber, or refectory, may die:
A necessary act incurs no blame.
Not so when, held within their proper bounds,
575 And guiltless of offence, they range the air,
Or take their pastime in the spacious field:
There they are privileged: and he that hunts
Or harms them there is guilty of a wrong,
Disturbs the economy of nature's realm,
580 Who, when she formed, designed them an abode.
The sum is this: if man's convenience, health,
Or safety interfere, his rights and claims
Are paramount, and must extinguish theirs.
Else they are all—the meanest things that are—
585 As free to live, and to enjoy that life,
As God was free to form them at the first,
Who in His sovereign wisdom made them all.
Ye therefore who love mercy, teach your sons
To love it too. The spring-time of our years
590 Is soon dishonoured and defiled in most
By budding ills, that ask a prudent hand
To check them.   But, alas! none sooner shoots,
If unrestrained, into luxuriant growth,
Than cruelty, most devilish of them all.
595 Mercy to him that shows it, is the rule
And righteous limitation of its act,
By which Heaven moves in pardoning guilty
          man,
And he that shows none, being ripe in years,
And conscious of the outrage he commits,
600 Shall seek it and not find it in his turn.
     Distinguished much by reason, and still more
By our capacity of grace divine,
From creatures that exist but for our sake,
Which, having served us, perish, we are held
605 Accountable, and God, some future day,
Will reckon with us roundly for the abuse

Of what He deems no mean or trivial trust.
Superior as we are, they yet depend
Not more on human help than we on theirs.
610 Their strength, or speed, or vigilance, were given
In aid of our defects. In some are found
Such teachable and apprehensive parts,
That man's attainments in his own concerns,
Matched with the expertness of the brutes in
   theirs,
615 Are oftimes vanquished and thrown far behind.

. . . .

. . . .

ON THE RECEIPT OF MY MOTHER'S PICTURE
OUT OF NORFOLK
(*Cir.* 1790)

THE GIFT OF MY COUSIN, ANN BODHAM

O That those lips had language! Life has passed
With me but roughly since I heard thee last.
Those lips are thine—thy own sweet smile I see,
The same that oft in childhood solaced me;
5 Voice only fails, else how distinct they say,
" Grieve not, my child, chase all thy fears away! "
The meek intelligence of those dear eyes
(Blessed be the art that can immortalize,
The art that baffles Time's tyrannic claim
10 To quench it) here shines on me still the same.
 Faithful remembrancer of one so dear,
O welcome guest, though unexpected here!
Who bidst me honour with an artless song,
Affectionate, a mother lost so long,
15 I will obey, not willingly alone,
But gladly, as the precept were her own:
And, while that face renews my filial grief,
Fancy shall weave a charm for my relief,
Shall steep me in Elysian revery,
20 A momentary dream, that thou art she.

My mother! when I learnt that thou wast dead,
Say, wast thou conscious of the tears I shed?
Hovered thy spirit o'er thy sorrowing son,
Wretch even then, life's journey just begun?
25 Perhaps thou gavest me, though unfelt, a kiss:
Perhaps a tear, if souls can weep in bliss—
Ah, that maternal smile! it answers—Yes.
I heard the bell tolled on thy burial day,
I saw the hearse that bore thee slow away,
30 And, turning from my nursery window, drew
A long, long sigh, and wept a last adieu!
But was it such? It was.—Where thou art gone
Adieus and farewells are a sound unknown.
May I but meet thee on that peaceful shore,
35 The parting word shall pass my lips no more!
Thy maidens, grieved themselves at my concern,
Oft gave me promise of thy quick return.
What ardently I wished I long believed,
And, disappointed still, was still deceived.
40 By expectation every day beguiled,
Dupe of *to-morrow* even from a child.
Thus many a sad to-morrow came and went,
Till, all my stock of infant sorrow spent,
I learnt at last submission to my lot;
45 But, though I less deplored thee, ne'er forgot.
    Where once we dwelt our name is heard no
        more,
Children not thine have trod my nursery floor;
And where the gardener Robin, day by day,
Drew me to school along the public way,
50 Delighted with my bauble coach, and wrapped
In scarlet mantle warm, and velvet capped,
'Tis now become a history little known,
That once we called the pastoral house our own.
Short-lived possession! But the record fair
55 That memory keeps, of all thy kindness there,
Still outlives many a storm that has effaced

A thousand other themes less deeply traced.
Thy nightly visits to my chamber made,
That thou mightst know me safe and warmly
          laid;
60 Thy morning bounties ere I left my home,
The biscuit, or confectionery plum;
The fragrant waters on my cheeks bestowed
By thy own hand, till fresh they shone and
          glowed;
All this, and more endearing still than all,
65 Thy constant flow of love, that knew no fall,
Ne'er roughened by those cataracts and breaks
That humour interposed too often makes;
All this still legible in memory's page,
And still to be so to my latest age,
70 Adds joy to duty, makes me glad to pay
Such honours to thee as my numbers may;
Perhaps a frail memorial, but sincere,
Not scorned in heaven, though little noticed here.
     Could Time, his flight reversed, restore the
          hours,
75 When, playing with thy vesture's tissued flow-
          ers,
The violet, the pink, and jessamine,
I pricked them into paper with a pin,
(And thou wast happier than myself the while,
Wouldst softly speak, and stroke my head and
          smile.)
80 Could those few pleasant days again appear,
Might one wish bring them, would I wish them
          here?
I would not trust my heart—the dear delight
Seems so to be desired, perhaps I might.—
But no—what here we call our life is such,
85 So little to be loved, and thou so much,
That I should ill requite thee to constrain
Thy unbounded spirit into bonds again.

  Thou, as a gallant bark from Albion's coast
  (The storms all weathered and the ocean crossed)
90 Shoots into port at some well-haven'd isle,
  Where spices breathe, and brighter seasons smile,
  There sits quiescent on the floods, that show
  Her beauteous form reflected clear below,
  While airs impregnated with incense play
95 Around her, fanning light her streamers gay;
  So thou, with sails how swift! hast reached the
    shore,
  " Where tempests never beat nor billows roar,"
  And thy loved consort on the dangerous tide
  Of life long since has anchored by thy side.
100 But me, scarce hoping to attain that rest,
  Always from port withheld, always distressed—
  Me howling blasts drive devious, tempest-tosst,
  Sails ripped, seams opening wide, and compass
    lost,
  And day by day some current's thwarting force
105 Sets me more distant from a prosperous course.
  Yet, Oh, the thought that thou art safe, and he!
  That thought is joy, arrive what may to me.
  My boast is not, that I deduce my birth
  From loins enthroned and rulers of the earth;
110 But higher far my proud pretensions rise—
  The son of parents passed into the skies!
  And now, farewell—Time unrevoked has run
  His wonted course, yet what I wished is done.
  By contemplation's help, not sought in vain,
115 I seem to have lived my childhood o'er again;
  To have renewed the joys that once were mine,
  Without the sin of violating thine:
  And, while the wings of Fancy still are free,
  And I can view this mimic show of thee,
120 Time has but half succeeded in his theft—
  Thy self removed, thy power to soothe me left.

ON THE LOSS OF THE "ROYAL GEORGE"

WRITTEN WHEN THE NEWS ARRIVED, SEPTEMBER, 1782, TO
THE MARCH IN "SCIPIO"

Toll for the brave!
The brave that are no more!
All sunk beneath the wave,
Fast by their native shore!

5 Eight hundred of the brave,
Whose courage well was tried,
Had made the vessel heel,
And laid her on her side.

A land-breeze shook the shrouds,
10 And she was overset;
Down went the *Royal George*,
With all her crew complete.

Toll for the brave!
Brave Kempenfelt is gone;
15 His last sea-fight is fought;
His work of glory done.

It was not in the battle;
No tempest gave the shock;
She sprang no fatal leak;
20 She ran upon no rock.

His sword was in its sheath;
His fingers held the pen,
When Kempenfelt went down
With twice four hundred men.

25 Weigh the vessel up,
Once dreaded by our foes!
And mingle with our cup
The tear that England owes.

Her timbers yet are sound,
30 And she may float again
Full-charged with England's thunder,
And plough the distant main.

But Kempenfelt is gone,
His victories are o'er;
35 And he and his eight hundred
Shall plough the wave no more.

THE CAST-AWAY

(March 20, 1799)

Obscurest night involved the sky,
The Atlantic billows roared,
When such a destined wretch as I,
Washed headlong from on board,
5 Of friends, of hope, of all bereft,
His floating home forever left.

No braver chief could Albion boast
Than he with whom he went,
Nor ever ship left Albion's coast
10 With warmer wishes sent.
He loved them both, but both in vain,
Nor him beheld, nor her again.

Not long beneath the whelming brine,
Expert to swim, he lay;
15 Nor soon he felt his strength decline,
Or courage die away;
But waged with death a lasting strife,
Supported by despair of life.

He shouted: nor his friends had failed
20 To check the vessel's course,
But so the furious blast prevailed,

That, pitiless perforce,
They left their outcast mate behind,
And scudded still before the wind.

25 Some succor yet they could afford;
And such as storms allow,
The cask, the coop, the floated cord,
Delayed not to bestow.
But he (they knew) nor ship nor shore,
30 What e'er they gave, should visit more.

Nor, cruel as it seemed, could he
Their haste himself condemn,
Aware that flight, in such a sea,
Alone could rescue them;
35 Yet bitter felt it still to die
Deserted, and his friends so nigh.

He long survives, who lives an hour
In ocean, self-upheld:
And so long he, with unspent power,
40 His destiny repelled;
And ever, as the minutes flew,
Entreated help, or cried—"Adieu!"

At length, his transient respite past,
His comrades, who before
45 Had heard his voice in every blast,
Could catch the sound no more:
For then, by toil subdued, he drank
The stifling wave, and then he sank.

No poet wept him; but the page
50 Of narrative sincere,
That tells his name, his worth, his age,
Is wet with Anson's tear:
And tears by bards or heroes shed
Alike immortalize the dead.

55 I therefore purpose not, or dream,
    Descanting on his fate,
To give the melancholy theme
    A more enduring date:
But misery still delights to trace
60 Its semblance in another's case.

No voice divine the storm allayed,
    No light propitious shone,
When, snatched from all effectual aid,
    We perished, each alone:
65 But I beneath a rougher sea,
    And whelmed in deeper gulfs than he.

William Blake

1757-1827

TO THE MUSES

(From *Poetical Sketches,* 1783)

Whether on Ida's shady brow,
    Or in the chambers of the East,
The chambers of the sun that now
    From ancient melody have ceased;

5 Whether in Heaven ye wander fair,
    Or the green corners of the earth,
Or the blue regions of the air,
    Where the melodious winds have birth;

Whether on crystal rocks ye rove
10 Beneath the bosom of the sea,
    Wandering in many a coral grove;
    Fair Nine, forsaking Poetry;

How have you left the ancient love
That bards of old enjoy'd in you!
15 The languid strings do scarcely move,
The sound is forced, the notes are few.

TO THE EVENING STAR

(From the same)

Thou fair-haired angel of the evening,
Now, whilst the sun rests on the mountain, light
Thy brilliant torch of love; thy radiant crown
Put on, and smile upon our evening bed!
5 Smile on our loves; and whilst thou drawest
    round
The curtains of the sky, scatter thy dew
On every flower that closes its sweet eyes
In timely sleep. Let thy west wind sleep on
The lake; speak silence with thy glimmering eyes,
10 And wash the dusk with silver. Soon, full soon
Dost thou withdraw; then the wolf rages wide,
And then the lion glares through the dun forest.
The fleeces of our flocks are covered with
Thy sacred dew: protect them with thine in-
    fluence.

INTRODUCTION

(From *Songs of Innocence*, 1787)

Piping down the valleys wild,
Piping songs of pleasant glee,
On a cloud I saw a child,
And he, laughing, said to me:

5 'Pipe a song about a Lamb!'
So I piped with merry cheer.
'Piper, pipe that song again;'
So I piped: he wept to hear.

'Drop thy pipe, thy happy pipe;
10 Sing thy songs of happy cheer!'
So I sang the same again,
While he wept with joy to hear.

'Piper, sit thee down and write
In a book, that all may read.'
15 So he vanish'd from my sight;
And I plucked a hollow reed,

And I made a rural pen,
And I stain'd the water clear,
And I wrote my happy songs
20 Every child may joy to hear.

THE LAMB

(From the same)

Little lamb, who made thee?
Dost thou know who made thee?
Gave thee life, and bade thee feed
By the stream and o'er the mead;
5 Gave thee clothing of delight,
Softest clothing, woolly, bright;
Gave thee such a tender voice,
Making all the vales rejoice?
Little lamb, who made thee?
10   Dost thou know who made thee?

Little lamb, I'll tell thee;
Little lamb, I'll tell thee:
He is callèd by thy name,
For He calls Himself a Lamb.
15 He is meek, and He is mild,
He became a little child.

I a child and thou a lamb,
We are callèd by His name.
    Little lamb, God bless thee!
20   Little lamb, God bless thee!

NIGHT

(From the same)

The sun descending in the west,
The evening star does shine,
The birds are silent in their nest,
And I must seek for mine.
5   The moon, like a flower
    In heaven's high bower,
    With silent delight,
    Sits and smiles on the night.

Farewell, green fields and happy grove,
10 Where flocks have ta'en delight;
Where lambs have nibbled, silent move
The feet of angels bright;
    Unseen, they pour blessing,
    And joy without ceasing,
15   On each bud and blossom,
    And each sleeping bosom.

They look in every thoughtless nest,
Where birds are covered warm;
They visit caves of every beast,
20 To keep them all from harm.
    If they see any weeping
    That should have been sleeping,
    They pour sleep on their head,
    And sit down by their bed.

25 When wolves and tigers howl for prey
     They pitying stand and weep,
     Seeking to drive their thirst away,
     And keep them from the sheep.
       But if they rush dreadful,
30   The angels, most heedful,
       Receive each mild spirit,
       New worlds to inherit.

     And there the lion's ruddy eyes
     Shall flow with tears of gold:
35 And pitying the tender cries,
     And walking round the fold:
       Saying: 'Wrath by His meekness,
       And by His health, sickness,
       Are driven away
40   From our immortal day.

     'And now beside thee, bleating lamb,
     I can lie down and sleep,
     Or think on Him who bore thy name,
     Graze after thee, and weep.
45   For wash'd in life's river,
       My bright mane forever
       Shall shine like the gold,
       As I guard o'er the fold.'

TO THE DIVINE IMAGE

(From the same)

To mercy, pity, peace, and love,
    All pray in their distress,
And to these virtues of delight
    Return their thankfulness.

5 For mercy, pity, peace, and love,
　　Is God our Father dear;
　And mercy, pity, peace, and love,
　　Is man, His child and care.

　For Mercy has a human heart,
10　　Pity, a human face;
　And Love, the human form divine;
　　And Peace, the human dress.

　Then every man, of every clime,
　　That prays in his distress,
15 Prays to the human form divine;
　　Love, Mercy, Pity, Peace.

　And all must love the human form,
　　In heathen, Turk, or Jew;
　Where mercy, love, and pity dwell,
20　　There God is dwelling too.

ON ANOTHER'S SORROW

(From the same)

　Can I see another's woe,
　　And not be in sorrow too?
　Can I see another's grief,
　　And not seek for kind relief?

5 Can I see a falling tear,
　　And not feel my sorrow's share?
　Can a father see his child
　　Weep, nor be with sorrow fill'd?

　Can a mother sit and hear,
10 An infant groan, an infant fear?
　No, no! never can it be!
　Never, never can it be!

And can He, who smiles on all,
Hear the wren, with sorrow small,
15 Hear the small bird's grief and care,
Hear the woes that infants bear?

And not sit beside the nest,
Pouring Pity in their breast,
And not sit the cradle near,
20 Weeping tear on infant's tear?

And not sit both night and day,
Wiping all our tears away?
Oh, no! never can it be!
Never, never can it be!

25 He doth give His joy to all:
He becomes an infant small
He becomes a man of woe,
He doth feel the sorrow too.

Think not thou canst sigh a sigh,
30 And thy Maker is not by:
Think not thou canst weep a tear,
And thy Maker is not near.

Oh! He gives to us His joy,
That our griefs He may destroy,
35 Till our grief is fled and gone
He doth sit by us and moan.

THE TIGER

(From *The Songs of Experience*, 1794)

Tiger, Tiger, burning bright
In the forest of the night,
What immortal hand or eye
Framed thy fearful symmetry?

5 In what distant deeps or skies
  Burned that fire within thine eyes?
  On what wings dared he aspire?
  What the hand dared seize the fire?

  And what shoulder, and what art,
10 Could twist the sinews of thy heart?
  When thy heart began to beat,
  What dread hand and what dread feet?

  What the hammer, what the chain,
  Knit thy strength and forged thy brain?
15 What the anvil? What dread grasp
  Dared thy deadly terrors clasp?

  When the stars threw down their spears,
  And water'd heaven with their tears,
  Did He smile His work to see?
20 Did He who made the lamb make thee?

AH! SUNFLOWER

(From the same)

Ah! Sunflower! weary of time,
  Who countest the steps of the sun,
Seeking after that sweet golden prime
  Where the traveller's journey is done;
5 Where the Youth pined away with desire,
  And the pale virgin shrouded in snow,
Arise from their graves, and aspire
  Where my sunflower wishes to go!

Robert Burns

(1759–1796)

THE COTTER'S SATURDAY NIGHT

(1785)

"Let not Ambition mock their useful toil,
    Their homely joys, and destiny obscure ;
Nor Grandeur hear, with a disdainful smile,
    The short and simple annals of the poor."—*Gray.*

My lov'd, my honour'd, much respected friend!
    No mercenary bard his homage pays;
With honest pride, I scorn each selfish end,
    My dearest meed, a friend's esteem and
        praise:
5   To you I sing, in simple Scottish lays,
    The lowly train in life's sequester'd scene;
        The native feelings strong, the guileless
            ways,
What Aiken in a cottage would have been;
Ah! tho' his worth unknown, far happier there I
    ween!

10   November chill blaws loud wi' angry sugh;
    The short'ning winter-day is near a close;
The miry beasts retreating frae the pleugh;
    The black'ning trains o' craws to their repose:
    The toil-worn Cotter frae his labour goes,—
15   This night his weekly moil is at an end,
        Collects his spades, his mattocks, and his
            hoes,
Hoping the morn in ease and rest to spend,
And weary, o'er the moor, his course does hame-
    ward bend.

At length his lonely cot appears in view,
20   Beneath the shelter of an aged tree;
Th' expectant wee-things, toddlin', stacher
     through
     To meet their dad, wi' flichterin' noise and
     glee.
His wee bit ingle, blinkin' bonily,
His clean hearth-stane, his thrifty wifie's smile,
25   The lisping infant, prattling on his knee,
Does a' his weary kiaugh and care beguile,
And makes him quite forget his labour and his
     toil.

Belyve, the elder bairns come drapping in,
     At service out, amang the farmers roun';
30 Some ca' the pleugh, some herd, some tentie rin
     A cannie errand to a neebor town:
     Their eldest hope, their Jenny, woman-
     grown,
In youthfu' bloom,—love sparkling in her e'e—
     Comes hame, perhaps to shew a braw new
     gown,
35 Or deposit her sair-won penny-fee,
To help her parents dear, if they in hardship be.

With joy unfeign'd, brothers and sisters meet,
     And each for other's weelfare kindly spiers:
The social hours, swift-wing'd, unnotic'd fleet:
40   Each tells the uncos that he sees or hears;
     The parents partial eye their hopeful years;
Anticipation forward points the view;
     The mother, wi' her needle and her shears,
Gars auld claes look amaist as weel's the new,
45 The father mixes a' wi' admonition due.

Their master's and their mistress's command,
     The younkers a' are warned to obey:
And mind their labors wi' an eydent hand,

And ne'er, tho' out o' sight, to jauk or play;
50   "And O! be sure to fear the Lord alway,
And mind your duty, duly, morn and night;
   Lest in temptation's path ye gang astray,
Implore His counsel and assisting might:
They never sought in vain that sought the Lord
   aright."

55 But, hark! a rap comes gently to the door;
   Jenny, wha kens the meaning o' the same,
Tells how a neibor lad came o'er the moor,
   To do some errands, and convoy her hame.
   The wily mother sees the conscious flame
60 Sparkle in Jenny's e'e, and flush her cheek;
   With heart-struck anxious care enquires his
     name,
While Jenny hafflins is afraid to speak;
Weel-pleased the mother hears it's nae wild,
   worthless rake.

Wi' kindly welcome, Jenny brings him ben;
65   A strappin youth, he takes the mother's eye;
Blythe Jenny sees the visit's no ill-ta'en;
   The father cracks of horses, pleughs, and kye.
   The youngster's artless heart o'erflows wi'
     joy,
But blate an' laithfu', scarce can weel behave;
70   The mother, wi' a woman's wiles, can spy
What makes the youth sae bashfu' and sae
   grave,
Weel-pleas'd to think her bairn's respected like
   the lave.

Oh, happy love! where love like this is found!
   Oh, heart-felt raptures! bliss beyond com-
     pare!
75 I've pacèd much this weary, mortal round,
   And sage experience bids mè this declare;—

"If Heaven a draught of heavenly pleasure
    spare—
One cordial in this melancholy vale,
    'Tis when a youthful, loving, modest pair
80 In other's arms breathe out the tender tale,
    Beneath the milk-white thorn that scents the
        evening gale."

Is there, in human form, that bears a heart,
    A wretch! a villain! lost to love and truth!
That can, with studied, sly, ensnaring art,
85   Betray sweet Jenny's unsuspecting youth?
    Curse on his perjur'd arts! dissembling
        smooth!
    Are honour, virtue, conscience, all exil'd?
    Is there no pity, no relenting ruth,
    Points to the parents fondling o'er their child?
90 Then paints the ruin'd maid, and their distrac-
        tion wild?

But now the supper crowns their simple board,
    The halesome parritch, chief o' Scotia's food;
The soupe their only hawkie does afford,
    That, 'yont the hallan snugly chows her cood:
95   The dame brings forth, in complimental
        mood,
    To grace the lad, her weel-hain'd kebbuck, fell;
    And aft he's prest, and aft he ca's it guid:
    The frugal wifie, garrulous, will tell
    How 't was a towmond auld, sin' lint was i' the
        bell.

100   The cheerfu' supper done, wi' serious face,
        They, round the ingle, form a circle wide;
    The sire turns o'er, with patriarchal grace,
        The big ha'-bible, ance his father's pride;

His bonnet rev'rently is laid aside,
105 His lyart haffets wearing thin and bare;
    Those strains that once did sweet in Zion
    glide,
    He wales a portion with judicious care;
And "Let us worship God!" he says, with solemn
    air.

They chant their artless notes in simple guise,
110   They tune their hearts, by far the noblest
    aim;
    Perhaps 'Dundee's' wild-warbling measures
    rise,
    Or plaintive 'Martyrs,' worthy of the name;
    Or noble 'Elgin' beets the heaven-ward
    flame,
The sweetest far of Scotia's holy lays:
115   Compar'd with these, Italian trills are tame;
    The tickl'd ears no heart-felt raptures raise;
Nae unison hae they with our Creator's praise.

The priest-like father reads the sacred page,
    How Abram was the friend of God on high;
120 Or Moses bade eternal warfare wage
    With Amalek's ungracious progeny;
    Or how the royal bard did groaning lie
Beneath the stroke of Heaven's avenging ire;
    Or Job's pathetic plaint, and wailing cry;
125   Or rapt Isaiah's wild, seraphic fire;
Or other holy seers that tune the sacred lyre.

Perhaps the Christian volume is the theme,
    How guiltless blood for guilty man was shed;
How He, who bore in Heaven the second name,
130   Had not on earth whereon to lay His head;
    How His first followers and servants sped;

The precepts sage they wrote to many a land:
How he, who lone in Patmos banishèd,
Saw in the sun a mighty angel stand,
135 And heard great Bab'lon's doom pronounc'd by
Heaven's command.

Then kneeling down, to Heaven's Eternal King,
The saint, the father, and the husband prays:
Hope "springs exulting on triumphant wing,"
That thus they all shall meet in future days,
140 There, ever bask in uncreated rays,
No more to sigh, or shed the bitter tear,
Together hymning their Creator's praise,
In such society, yet still more dear;
While circling Time moves round in an eternal
sphere.

145 Compar'd with this, how poor Religion's pride,
In all the pomp of method, and of art;
When men display to congregations wide
Devotion's ev'ry grace, except the heart!
The Power, incens'd, the pageant will desert,
150 The pompous strain, the sacerdotal stole;
But haply, in some cottage far apart,
May hear, well pleas'd, the language of the
soul;
And in His Book of Life the inmates poor enroll.

Then homeward all take off their sev'ral way;
155 The youngling cottagers retire to rest:
The parent-pair their secret homage pay,
And proffer up to Heaven the warm request,
That He who stills the raven's clam'rous nest,
And decks the lily fair in flow'ry pride,
160 Would, in the way His wisdom sees the best,
For them and for their little ones provide;
But chiefly, in their hearts with grace divine pre-
side.

From scenes like these, old Scotia's grandeur
    springs,
    That makes her lov'd at home, rever'd abroad:
165 Princes and lords are but the breath of kings,
    " An honest man's the noblest work of God;"
    And certes, in fair virtue's heavenly road,
The cottage leaves the palace far behind;
    What is a lordling's pomp? a cumbrous load,
170 Disguising oft the wretch of human kind,
Studied in arts of hell, in wickedness refin'd!

O Scotia! my dear, my native soil!
    For whom my warmest wish to Heaven is
    sent,
Long may thy hardy sons of rustic toil
175   Be blest with health, and peace, and sweet
    content!
    And O! may Heaven their simple lives pre-
    vent
From luxury's contagion, weak and vile!
    Then, howe'er crowns and coronets be rent,
A virtuous populace may rise the while,
180 And stand a wall of fire around their much-lov'd
    isle.

O Thou! who pour'd the patriotic tide,
    That stream'd thro' great unhappy Wallace'
    heart,
Who dar'd to nobly stem tyrannic pride,
    Or nobly die, the second glorious part:
185   (The patriot's God, peculiarly Thou art,
His friend, inspirer, guardian, and reward!)
    Oh never, never Scotia's realm desert;
But still the patriot, and the patriot-bard
In bright succession raise, her ornament and
    guard!

TO A MOUSE, ON TURNING HER UP IN HER NEST, WITH THE PLOUGH, NOVEMBER, 1785

Wee, sleekit, cowrin, tim'rous beastie,
O, what a panic's in thy breastie!
Thou need na start awa sae hasty,
      Wi' bickering brattle!
5 I wad be laith to rin an' chase thee,
        Wi' murd'ring pattle!

I'm truly sorry man's dominion,
Has broken Nature's social union,
An' justifies that ill opinion,
10   Which makes thee startle
At me, thy poor, earth-born companion,
        An' fellow-mortal!

I doubt na, whyles, but thou may thieve;
What then? poor beastie, thou maun live!
15 A daimen icker in a thrave
      'S a sma' request;
I'll get a blessin wi' the lave,
      And never miss't!

Thy wee bit housie, too, in ruin!
20 It's silly wa's the win's are strewin!
An' naething now to big a new ane,
      O' foggage green!
An' bleak December's winds ensuin,
      Baith snell an' keen!

25 Thou saw the fields laid bare an' waste,
An' weary winter comin fast,
An' cozie here, beneath the blast,
      Thou thought to dwell—
Till, crash! the cruel coulter past
30   Out thro' thy cell.

That wee bit heap o' leaves an' stibble
Has cost thee mony a weary nibble!
Now thou's turned out, for a' thy trouble,
          But house or hald,
35 To thole the winter's sleety dribble,
              An' cranreuch cauld!

But Mousie, thou art no thy lane,
In proving foresight may be vain;
The best laid schemes o' mice an' men
40   Gang aft agley,
An' lea'e us nought but grief an' pain
          For promis'd joy!

Still, thou art blest, compar'd wi' me!
The present only toucheth thee:
45 But, och! I backward cast my e'e,
          On prospects drear!
An' forward, tho' I canna see,
          I guess an' fear!

TO A MOUNTAIN DAISY, ON TURNING ONE DOWN WITH THE PLOUGH IN APRIL, 1786

Wee, modest, crimson-tippèd flow'r,
Thou's met me in an evil hour;
For I maun crush amang the stour
          Thy slender stem:
5 To spare thee now is past my pow'r,
          Thou bonie gem.

Alas! it's no thy neibor sweet,
The bonie lark, companion meet,
Bending thee 'mang the dewy weet,
10   Wi' spreckl'd breast!
When upward-springing, blythe, to greet
          The purpling east.

Cauld blew the bitter-biting north
Upon thy early, humble birth;
15 Yet cheerfully thou glinted forth
   Amid the storm,
Scarce rear'd above the parent-earth
   Thy tender form.

The flaunting flow'rs our gardens yield,
20 High shelt'ring woods and wa's maun shield;
But thou, beneath the random bield
   O' clod or stane,
Adorns the histy stibble-field,
   Unseen, alane.

25 There, in thy scanty mantle clad,
Thy snawie bosom sun-ward spread,
Thou lifts thy unassuming head
   In humble guise;
But now the share upturns thy bed,
30   And low thou lies!

Such is the fate of artless maid,
Sweet flow'ret of the rural shade!
By love's simplicity betray'd,
   And guileless trust,
35 Till she, like thee, all soil'd is laid,
   Low i' the dust.

Such is the fate of simple bard,
On life's rough ocean luckless starr'd!
Unskilful he to note the card
40   Of prudent lore,
Till billows rage, and gales blow hard,
   And whelm him o'er!

Such fate to suffering worth is given,
Who long with wants and woes has striv'n,

45 By human pride or cunning driv'n,
        To mis'ry's brink;
    Till, wrench'd of ev'ry stay but Heav'n
        He, ruin'd, sink!

    Ev'n thou who mourn'st the Daisy's fate,
50 That fate is thine—no distant date;
    Stern Ruin's plough-share drives, elate,
        Full on thy bloom,
    Till crush'd beneath the furrow's weight,
        Shall be thy doom!

TAM O' SHANTER

(First published 1791)

"Of Brownyis and of Bogillis full is this Buke."—*Gawin Douglas*

    When chapman billies leave the street,
    And drouthy neibors, neibors meet;
    As market days are wearing late,
    And folk begin to tak the gate,
 5 While we sit bousing at the nappy,
    An' getting fou and unco happy,
    We think na on the lang Scots miles,
    The mosses, waters, slaps, and stiles,
    That lie between us and our hame,
10 Where sits our sulky, sullen dame,
    Gathering her brows like gathering storm,
    Nursing her wrath to keep it warm.

    This truth fand honest TAM O' SHANTER,
    As he frae Ayr ae night did canter:
15 (Auld Ayr, wham ne'er a town surpasses,
    For honest men and bonie lasses).

    O Tam! had'st thou but been sae wise,
    As ta'en thy ain wife Kate's advice!

She tauld thee weel thou wast a skellum;
20 A blethering, blustering, drunken blellum;
That frae November till October,
Ae market-day thou wasna sober;
That ilka melder wi' the Miller,
Thou sat as lang as thou had siller;
25 That ev'ry naig was ca'd a shoe on
The Smith and thee gat roarin fou on;
That at the Lord's house, ev'n on Sunday,
Thou drank wi' Kirkton Jean till Monday;
She prophesied that late or soon,
30 Thou wad be found deep drown'd in Doon,
Or catch'd wi' warlocks in the mirk,
By Alloway's auld haunted kirk.

Ah, gentle dames! it gars me greet,
To think how mony counsels sweet,
35 How mony lengthen'd sage advices,
The husband frae the wife despises!

But to our tale:—Ae market night,
Tam had got planted unco right,
Fast by an ingle, bleezing finely,
40 Wi' reaming swats, that drank divinely;
And at his elbow, Souter Johnie,
His ancient, trusty, drouthy crony:
Tam lo'ed him like a very brither;
They had been fou for weeks thegither.
45 The night drave on wi' sangs an' clatter;
And aye the ale was growing better:
The Landlady and Tam grew gracious,
Wi' favours secret, sweet, and precious:
The Souter tauld his queerest stories;
50 The Landlord's laugh was ready chorus:
The storm without might rair and rustle,
Tam did na mind the storm a whistle.

Care, mad to see a man sae happy,
E'en drown'd himsel amang the nappy.
55 As bees flee hame wi' lades o' treasure,
The minutes wing'd their way wi' pleasure:
Kings may be blest, but Tam was glorious,
O'er a' the ills o' life victorious!

But pleasures are like poppies spread,
60 You seize the flow'r, its bloom is shed;
Or like the snow falls in the river,
A moment white—then melts forever;
Or like the Borealis race,
That flit ere you can point their place;
65 Or like the Rainbow's lovely form,
Evanishing amid the storm.—
Nae man can tether Time or Tide;
The hour approaches Tam maun ride:
That hour, o' night's black arch the key-stane,
70 That dreary hour he mounts his beast in;
And sic a night he taks the road in,
As ne'er poor sinner was abroad in.
The wind blew as 't wad blawn its last;
The rattling showers rose on the blast;
75 The speedy gleams the darkness swallow'd;
Loud, deep, and lang the thunder bellow'd:
That night, a child might understand,
The deil had business on his hand.
Weel-mounted on his gray mare Meg,
80 A better never lifted leg,
Tam skelpit on thro' dub and mire,
Despising wind, and rain, and fire;
Whiles holding fast his gude blue bonnet,
Whiles crooning o'er some auld Scots sonnet,
85 Whiles glow'rin round wi' prudent cares,
Lest bogles catch him unawares;
Kirk-Alloway was drawing nigh,
Where ghaists and houlets nightly cry.

By this time he was cross the ford,
90 Where in the snaw the chapman smoor'd;
And past the birks and meikle stane,
Where drunken Charlie brak's neck-bane;
And thro' the whins, and by the cairn,
Where hunters fand the murder'd bairn;
95 And near the thorn, aboon the well,
Where Mungo's mither hang'd hersel'.
Before him Doon pours all his floods;
The doubling storm roars thro' the woods,
The lightnings flash from pole to pole,
100 Near and more near the thunders roll,
When, glimmering thro' the groaning trees,
Kirk-Alloway seem'd in a bleeze,
Thro' ilka bore the beams were glancing,
And loud resounded mirth and dancing.

105 Inspiring bold John Barleycorn!
What dangers thou canst make us scorn!
Wi' tippenny, we fear nae evil;
Wi' usquebae, we'll face the devil!
The swats sae ream'd in Tammie's noddle,
110 Fair play, he car'd na deils a boddle,
But Maggie stood, right sair astonish'd,
Till, by the heel and hand admonish'd,
She ventur'd forward on the light;
And, wow! Tam saw an unco sight!

115 Warlocks and witches in a dance:
Nae cotillion, brent new frae France,
But hornpipes, jigs, strathspeys, and reels,
Put life and mettle in their heels.
A winnock-bunker in the east,
120 There sat auld Nick, in shape o' beast;
A towzie tyke, black, grim, and large,
To gie them music was his charge;
He screw'd the pipes and gart them skirl,

Till roof and rafters a' did dirl.
125 Coffins stood round, like open presses,
    That shaw'd the Dead in their last dresses;
    And (by some devilish cantraip sleight)
    Each in its cauld hand held a light.
    By which heroic Tam was able
130 To note upon the haly table,
    A murderer's banes, in gibbet-airns;
    Twa span-lang, wee, unchristened bairns;
    A thief, new-cutted frae a rape,
    Wi' his last gasp his gab did gape;
135 Five tomahawks, wi' blude red-rusted;
    Five scimitars, wi' murder crusted;
    A garter which a babe had strangled:
    A knife, a father's throat had mangled,
    Whom his ain son of life bereft,
140 The gray-hairs yet stack to the heft;
    Wi' mair of horrible and awfu',
    Which even to name wad be unlawfu'.

    As Tammie glowr'd amaz'd, and curious,
    The mirth and fun grew fast and furious;
145 The Piper loud and louder blew,
    The dancers quick and quicker flew;
    They reel'd, they set, they cross'd, they cleekit,
    Till ilka carlin swat and reekit,
    And coost her duddies to the wark,
150 And linket at it in her sark!

    Now Tam, O Tam! had thae been queans,
    A' plump and strapping in their teens!
    Their sarks, instead o' creeshie flainen,
    Been snaw-white seventeen-hunder linen!—
155 Thir breeks o' mine, my only pair,
    That ance were plush, o' guid blue hair,
    I wad hae gi'en them off my hurdies,
    For ae blink o' the bonie burdies!

But wither'd beldams, auld and droll,
160 Rigwoodie hags wad spean a foal,
Louping an' flinging on a crummock,
I wonder didna turn thy stomach.
 But Tam kennt what was what fu' brawlie;
There was ae winsome wench and waulie,
165 That night enlisted in the core,
Lang after ken'd on Carrick shore;
(For mony a beast to dead she shot,
And perish'd mony a bonie boat,
And shook baith meikle corn and bear,
170 And kept the country-side in fear);
Her cutty sark, o' Paisley harn,
That while a lassie she had worn,
In longitude tho' sorely scanty,
It was her best, and she was vauntie.
175 Ah! little ken'd thy reverend grannie,
That sark she coft for her wee Nannie,
Wi' twa pund Scots ('twas a' her riches),
Wad ever grac'd a dance o' witches!
 But here my Muse her wing maun cour,
180 Sic flights are far beyond her power;
To sing how Nannie lap and flang,
(A souple jade she was and strang),
And how Tam stood, like ane bewitch'd,
And thought his very een enrich'd:
185 Even Satan glowr'd and fidg'd fu' fain,
And hotch'd and blew wi' might and main:
Till first ae caper, syne anither,
Tam tint his reason a' thegither,
And roars out, "Weel done, Cutty-sark!"
190 And in an instant all was dark:
And scarcely had he Maggie rallied,
When out the hellish legion sallied.

 As bees bizz out wi' angry fyke,
When plundering herds assail their byke;

195 As open pussie's mortal foes,
    When, pop! she starts before their nose;
    As eager runs the market-crowd,
    When "Catch the thief!" resounds aloud;
    So Maggie runs, the witches follow,
200 Wi' mony an eldritch skreich and hollow.

    Ah, Tam! ah, Tam! thou 'll get thy fairin!
    In hell they 'll roast thee like a herrin!
    In vain thy Kate awaits thy comin!
    Kate soon will be a woefu' woman!
205 Now, do thy speedy-utmost, Meg,
    And win the key-stane o' the brig;
    There, at them thou thy tail may toss,
    A running stream they darena cross!
    But ere the key-stane she could make,
210 The fient a tail she had to shake!
    For Nannie, far before the rest,
    Hard upon noble Maggie prest,
    And flew at Tam wi' furious ettle;
    But little wist she Maggie's mettle!
215 Ae spring brought off her master hale,
    But left behind her ain gray tail:
    The carlin claught her by the rump,
    And left poor Maggie scarce a stump.

    Now, wha this tale o' truth shall read,
220 Ilk man, and mother's son, take heed:
    Whene'er to Drink you are inclin'd,
    Or Cutty-sarks rin in your mind,
    Think ye may buy the joys o'er dear;
    Remember Tam o' Shanter's mare.

BRUCE'S ADDRESS TO HIS ARMY AT BANNOCKBURN

(1793)

Scots, wha hae wi' WALLACE bled,
Scots, wham BRUCE has often led;
Welcome to your gory bed,
      Or to Victorie!

5 Now's the day, and now's the hour;
See the front o' battle lour;
See approach proud EDWARD'S power—
      Chains and Slaverie!

Wha will be a traitor knave?
10 Wha can fill a coward's grave?
Wha sae base as be a slave?
      Let him turn and flee!

Wha, for Scotland's King and Law,
Freedom's sword will strongly draw,
15 FREEMAN stand, or FREEMAN fa',
      Let him on wi' me!

By Oppression's woes and pains!
By your Sons in servile chains!
We will drain our dearest veins,
20   But they shall be free!

Lay the proud Usurpers low!
Tyrants fall in every foe!
LIBERTY'S in every blow!—
      Let us Do or Die!

THE BANKS OF DOON

(Second version, 1791)

Ye flowery banks o' bonie Doon,
 How can ye blume sae fair?
How can ye chant, ye little birds,
 And I sae fu' o' care!

5 Thou'll break my heart, thou bonie bird,
 That sings upon the bough!
Thou minds me o' the happy days
 When my fause Luve was true.

Thou'll break my heart, thou bonie bird,
10 That sings beside thy mate;
For sae I sat, and sae I sang,
 And wist na o' my fate.

Aft hae I rov'd by bonie Doon,
 To see the woodbine twine;
15 And ilka bird sang o' its Luve,
 And sae did I o' mine.

Wi' lightsome heart I pu'd a rose,
 Upon its thorny tree;
But my fause Luver staw the rose,
20 And left the thorn wi' me.

Wi' lightsome heart I pu'd a rose,
 Upon a morn in June;
And sae I flourished on the morn,
 And sae was pu'd or noon.

A RED, RED ROSE

(1793)

O my Luve's like a red, red rose,
  That's newly sprung in June:
O my Luve's like the melodie
  That's sweetly play'd in tune.

5 As fair art thou, my bonie lass,
  So deep in luve am I;
And I will luve thee still, my dear,
  Till a' the seas gang dry.

Till a' the seas gang dry, my dear,
10   And the rocks melt wi' the sun:
And I will luve thee still, my dear,
  While the sands o' life shall run.

And fare-thee-weel, my only Luve!
  And fare-thee-weel awhile!
15 And I will come again, my Luve,
  Tho' 't were ten thousand mile!

IS THERE, FOR HONEST POVERTY

(1795)

(Tune—" For a' that ")

Is there for honest Poverty,
  That hings his head, an' a' that;
The coward slave—we pass him by,
  We dare be poor for a' that!
5 For a' that, an' a' that,
  Our toils obscure an' a' that,
The rank is but the guinea's stamp,
  The Man's the gowd for a' that.

What though on hamely fare we dine,
10　Wear hoddin grey, an' a' that;
Gie fools their silks, and knaves their wine,
A Man's a Man for a' that:
For a' that, an' a' that,
　　Their tinsel show, an' a' that;
15 The honest man, tho' e'er sae poor,
　　Is king o' men for a' that.

Ye see yon birkie ca'd a lord,
　　Wha struts, an' stares an' a' that;
Tho' hundreds worship at his word,
20　He's but a coof for a' that:
For a' that, an' a' that,
　　His ribband, star, an' a' that:
The man o' independent mind,
　　He looks an' laughs at a' that.

25 A prince can mak a belted knight,
　　A marquis, duke, an' a' that;
But an honest man's aboon his might,
　　Guid faith, he maunna fa' that!
For a' that, an' a' that,
30　Their dignities an' a' that;
The pith o' sense, an' pride o' worth,
　　Are higher rank than a' that.

Then let us pray that come it may,
　　(As come it will for a' that,)
35 That Sense and Worth, o'er a' the earth,
　　Shall bear the gree, an' a' that.
For a' that, an' a' that,
　　It's coming yet for a' that,
That Man to Man, the warld o'er,
40　Shall brothers be for a' that.

O, WERT THOU IN THE CAULD BLAST

(1796)

O wert thou in the cauld blast,
   On yonder lea, on yonder lea,
My plaidie to the angry airt,
   I'd shelter thee, I'd shelter thee;
5 Or did Misfortune's bitter storms
   Around thee blaw, around thee blaw,
Thy bield should be my bosom,
   To share it a', to share it a'.

Or were I in the wildest waste,
10   Sae black and bare, sae black and bare,
The desert were a Paradise,
   If thou wert there, if thou wert there;
Or were I monarch o' the globe,
   Wi' thee to reign, wi' thee to reign,
15 The brightest jewel in my Crown
   Wad be my Queen, wad be my Queen.

William Wordsworth

1770–1850

LINES

**COMPOSED A FEW MILES ABOVE TINTERN ABBEY, ON RE-
VISITING THE BANKS OF THE WYE DURING A TOUR**
(July 13, 1798)

Five years have past; five summers, with the
   length
Of five long winters! and again I hear
These waters, rolling from their mountain-springs
With a sweet inland murmur.—Once again
5 Do I behold these steep and lofty cliffs,

That on a wild secluded scene impress
Thoughts of more deep seclusion; and connect
The landscape with the quiet of the sky.
The day is come when I again repose
10 Here, under this dark sycamore, and view
These plots of cottage-ground, these orchard-
       tufts,
Which at this season, with their unripe fruits,
Are clad in one green hue, and lose themselves
'Mid groves and copses.   Once again I see
15 These hedge-rows, hardly hedge-rows, little lines
Of sportive wood run wild; these pastoral farms,
Green to the very door; and wreaths of smoke
Sent up, in silence, from among the trees!
With some uncertain notice, as might seem
20 Of vagrant dwellers in the houseless woods,
Or of some hermit's cave, where by his fire
The hermit sits alone.
               These beauteous forms,
Through a long absence, have not been to me
As is a landscape to a blind man's eye:
25 But oft, in lonely rooms, and 'mid the din
Of towns and cities, I have owed to them,
In hours of weariness, sensations sweet,
Felt in the blood, and felt along the heart;
And passing even into my purer mind,
30 With tranquil restoration:—feelings too
Of unremembered pleasure: such, perhaps,
As have no slight or trivial influence
On that best portion of a good man's life,
His little, nameless, unremembered, acts
35 Of kindness and of love.   Nor less, I trust,
To them I may have owed another gift,
Of aspect more sublime; that blessed mood,
In which the burden of the mystery,
In which the heavy and the weary weight
40 Of all this unintelligible world,

Is lightened:—that serene and blessed mood,
In which the affections gently lead us on,—
Until, the breath of this corporeal frame
And even the motion of our human blood
45 Almost suspended, we are laid asleep
In body, and become a living soul;
While with an eye made quiet by the power
Of harmony, and the deep power of joy,
We see into the life of things.

                            If this
50 Be but a vain belief, yet, oh! how oft—
In darkness and amid the many shapes
Of joyless daylight; when the fretful stir
Unprofitable, and the fever of the world,
Have hung upon the beatings of my heart—
55 How oft, in spirit, have I turned to thee,
O sylvan Wye! Thou wanderer thro' the woods,
How often has my spirit turned to thee!

   And now, with gleams of half-extinguished
      thought,
With many recognitions dim and faint,
60 And somewhat of a sad perplexity,
The picture of the mind revives again:
While here I stand, not only with the sense
Of present pleasure, but with pleasing thoughts
That in this moment there is life and food
35 For future years. And so I dare to hope,
Though changed, no doubt, from what I was when
     first
I came among these hills; when like a roe
I bounded o'er the mountains, by the sides
Of the deep rivers, and the lonely streams,
70 Wherever nature led: more like a man
Flying from something that he dreads than one
Who sought the thing he loved. For Nature
     then

(The coarser pleasures of my boyish days,
And their glad animal movements all gone by)
75 To me was all in all.—I cannot paint
What then I was. The sounding cataract
Haunted me like a passion: the tall rock,
The mountain, and the deep and gloomy wood,
Their colours and their forms, were then to me
80 An appetite; a feeling and a love,
That had no need of a remoter charm,
By thought supplied, nor any interest
Unborrowed from the eye.—That time is past,
And all its aching joys are now no more,
85 And all its dizzy raptures. Nor for this
Faint I, nor mourn nor murmur; other gifts
Have followed; for such loss, I would believe,
Abundant recompense. For I have learned
To look on nature, not as in the hour
90 Of thoughtless youth; but hearing oftentimes
The still, sad music of humanity,
Nor harsh nor grating, though of ample power
To chasten and subdue. And I have felt
A presence that disturbs me with the joy
95 Of elevated thoughts; a sense sublime
Of something far more deeply interfused,
Whose dwelling is the light of setting suns,
And the round ocean and the living air,
And the blue sky, and in the mind of man:
100 A motion and a spirit, that impels
All thinking things, all objects of all thought,
And rolls through all things. Therefore am I
        still
A lover of the meadows and the woods,
And mountains; and of all that we behold
105 From this green earth; of all the mighty
        world
Of eye, and ear,—both what they half create,
And what perceive; well pleased to recognize

In nature and the language of the sense,
The anchor of my purest thoughts, the nurse,
110 The guide, the guardian of my heart, and soul
Of all my moral being.
                              Nor perchance,
If I were not thus taught, should I the more
Suffer my genial spirits to decay:
For thou art with me here upon the banks
115 Of this fair river; thou, my dearest Friend,
My dear, dear Friend; and in thy voice I catch
The language of my former heart, and read
My former pleasures in the shooting lights
Of thy wild eyes. Oh! yet a little while
120 May I behold in thee what I was once,
My dear, dear Sister! and this prayer I make,
Knowing that Nature never did betray
The heart that loved her; 'tis her privilege
Through all the years of this our life, to lead
125 From joy to joy: for she can so inform
The mind that is within us, so impress
With quietness and beauty, and so feed
With lofty thoughts, that neither evil tongues,
Rash judgments, nor the sneers of selfish men,
130 Nor greetings where no kindness is, nor all
The dreary intercourse of daily life,
Shall e'er prevail against us, or disturb
Our cheerful faith, that all which we behold
Is full of blessings. Therefore let the moon
135 Shine on thee in thy solitary walk;
And let the misty mountain-winds be free
To blow against thee: and, in after years,
When these wild ecstasies shall be matured
Into a sober pleasure; when thy mind
140 Shall be a mansion for all lovely forms,
Thy memory be as a dwelling-place
For all sweet sounds and harmonies; oh! then,
If solitude, or fear, or pain, or grief,

Should be thy portion, with what healing
    thoughts
145 Of tender joy wilt thou remember me,
And these my exhortations! Nor, perchance—
If I should be where I no more can hear
Thy voice, nor catch from thy wild eyes these
    gleams
Of past existence—wilt thou then forget
150 That on the banks of this delightful stream
We stood together; and that I, so long
A worshipper of Nature, hither came
Unwearied in that service: rather say
With warmer love—oh! with far deeper zeal
155 Of holier love. Nor will thou then forget,
That after many wanderings, many years
Of absence, these steep woods and lofty cliffs,
And this green pastoral landscape, were to me
More dear, both for themselves and for thy
    sake!

EXPOSTULATION AND REPLY

(1798)

"Why, William, on that old gray stone
Thus for the length of half a day,
Why, William, sit you thus alone,
And dream your time away?

5 Where are your books?—that light bequeathed
To Beings else forlorn and blind!
Up! up! and drink the spirit breathed
From dead men to their kind.

You look round on your Mother Earth,
10 As if she for no purpose bore you;
As if you were her first-born birth,
And none had lived before you!"

One morning thus, by Esthwaite lake,
When life was sweet, I knew not why,
15 To me my good friend Matthew spake,
And thus I made reply:

" The eye—it cannot choose but see;
We cannot bid the ear be still;
Our bodies feel, where'er they be,
20 Against or with our will.

Nor less I deem that there are Powers
Which of themselves our minds impress;
That we can feed this mind of ours
In a wise passiveness.

25 Think you, 'mid all this mighty sum
Of things forever speaking,
That nothing of itself will come,
But we must still be seeking?

—Then ask not wherefore, here, alone,
30 Conversing as I may,
I sit upon this old gray stone,
And dream my time away."

THE TABLES TURNED

AN EVENING SCENE ON THE SAME SUBJECT
(1798)

Up! up! my Friend, and quit your books;
Or surely you 'll grow double:
Up! up! my Friend, and clear your looks;
Why all this toil and trouble?

5 The sun, above the mountain's head,
A freshening lustre mellow
Through all the long green fields has spread,
His first sweet evening yellow.

Books! 'tis a dull and endless strife:
10 Come, hear the woodland linnet,
How sweet his music! on my life,
There's more of wisdom in it.

And hark! how blithe the throstle sings!
He, too, is no mean preacher:
15 Come forth into the light of things,
Let Nature be your teacher.

She has a world of ready wealth,
Our minds and hearts to bless—
Spontaneous wisdom breathed by health,
20 Truth breathed by cheerfulness.

One impulse from a vernal wood
May teach you more of man,
Of moral evil and of good,
Than all the sages can.

25 Sweet is the lore which Nature brings;
Our meddling intellect
Mis-shapes the beauteous forms of things:—
We murder to dissect.

Enough of Science and of Art;
30 Close up those barren leaves;
Come forth, and bring with you a heart
That watches and receives.

THREE YEARS SHE GREW
(1799)

Three years she grew in sun and shower,
Then Nature said, "A lovelier flower
On earth was never sown;
This Child I to myself will take;
5 She shall be mine, and I will make
A Lady of my own.

Myself will to my darling be
Both law and impulse: and with me
The Girl, in rock and plain,
10 In earth and heaven, in glade and bower,
Shall feel an overseeing power
To kindle or restrain.

She shall be sportive as the fawn
That wild with glee across the lawn
15 Or up the mountain springs;
And hers shall be the breathing balm,
And hers the silence and the calm
Of mute insensate things.

The floating clouds their state shall lend
20 To her; for her the willow bend;
Nor shall she fail to see
Even in the motions of the Storm,
Grace that shall mold the Maiden's form
By silent sympathy.

25 The stars of midnight shall be dear
To her; and she shall lean her ear
In many a secret place
Where rivulets dance their wayward round,
And beauty born of murmuring sound
30 Shall pass into her face.

And vital feelings of delight
Shall rear her form to stately height,
Her virgin bosom swell;
Such thoughts to Lucy I will give
35 While she and I together live
Here in this happy dell."

Thus Nature spake—The work was done—
How soon my Lucy's race was run!

        She died, and left to me
40 This heath, this calm, and quiet scene;
   The memory of what has been,
   And never more will be.

SHE DWELT AMONG THE UNTRODDEN WAYS

(1799)

      She dwelt among the untrodden ways
        Beside the springs of Dove,
      A Maid whom there were none to praise,
        And very few to love:

   5 A violet by a mossy stone
        Half hidden from the eye!
      —Fair as a star, when only one
        Is shining in the sky.

      She lived unknown, and few could know
   10   When Lucy ceased to be;
      But she is in her grave, and, oh,
        The difference to me!

MICHAEL

A Pastoral Poem

(1800)

   If from the public way you turn your steps
   Up the tumultuous brook of Green-head Ghyll,
   You will suppose that with an upright path
   Your feet must struggle; in such bold ascent
 5 The pastoral mountains front you, face to face.
   But, courage! for around that boisterous brook
   The mountains have all opened out themselves,
   And made a hidden valley of their own.

No habitation can be seen; but they
10 Who journey thither find themselves alone
With a few sheep, with rocks and stones, and
   kites
That overhead are sailing in the sky.
It is in truth an utter solitude;
Nor should I have made mention of this Dell
15 But for one object which you might pass by,
Might see and notice not.   Beside the brook
Appears a straggling heap of unhewn stones:
And to that simple object appertains
A story unenriched with strange events,
20 Yet not unfit, I deem, for the fireside,
Or for the summer shade.   It was the first
Of those domestic tales that spake to me
Of Shepherds, dwellers in the valleys, men
Whom I already loved:—not verily
25 For their own sakes, but for the fields and hills
Where was their occupation and abode.
And hence this Tale, while I was yet a Boy
Careless of books, yet having felt the power
Of Nature, by the gentle agency
30 Of natural objects, led me on to feel
For passions that were not my own, and think
(At random and imperfectly indeed)
On man, the heart of man, and human life.
Therefore, although it be a history
35 Homely and rude, I will relate the same
For the delight of a few natural hearts;
And, with yet fonder feeling, for the sake
Of youthful Poets, who among these hills
Will be my second self when I am gone.

40   Upon the forest-side in Grasmere Vale
There dwelt a Shepherd, Michael was his name;
An old man, stout of heart, and strong of limb.
His bodily frame had been from youth to age

Of an unusual strength: his mind was keen,
45 Intense, and frugal, apt for all affairs,
And in his shepherd's calling he was prompt
And watchful more than ordinary men.
Hence had he learned the meaning of all winds,
Of blasts of every tone; and, oftentimes,
50 When others heeded not, he heard the South
Make subterraneous music, like the noise
Of bagpipers on distant Highland hills.
The Shepherd, at such warning, of his flock
Bethought him, and he to himself would say,
55 "The winds are now devising work for me!"
And, truly, at all times, the storm, that drives
The traveller to a shelter, summoned him
Up to the mountains: he had been alone
Amid the heart of many thousand mists,
60 That came to him, and left him, on the heights.
So lived he till his eightieth year was past.
And grossly that man errs, who should suppose
That the green valleys, and the streams and rocks,
Were things indifferent to the Shepherd's
　　　thoughts.
65 Fields, where with cheerful spirits he had
　　　breathed
The common air; hills, which with vigorous step
He had so often climbed; which had impressed
So many incidents upon his mind
Of hardship, skill or courage, joy or fear;
70 Which, like a book, preserved the memory
Of the dumb animals whom he had saved,
Had fed or sheltered, linking to such acts
The certainty of honourable gain,
Those fields, those hills—what could they less?
　　　had laid
75 Strong hold on his affections, were to him
A pleasurable feeling of blind love,
The pleasure which there is in life itself.

His days had not been passed in singleness.
His Helpmate was a comely matron, old—
80 Though younger than himself full twenty years.
She was a woman of a stirring life,
Whose heart was in her house: two wheels she had
Of antique form; this large, for spinning wool;
That small, for flax; and if one wheel had rest,
85 It was because the other was at work.
The Pair had but one inmate in their house,
An only Child, who had been born to them
When Michael, telling o'er his years, began
To deem that he was old,—in shepherd's phrase,
90 With one foot in the grave. This only Son,
With two brave sheep-dogs tried in many a storm,
The one of an inestimable worth,
Made all their household. I may truly say
That they were as a proverb in the vale
95 For endless industry. When day was gone,
And from their occupations out of doors
The Son and Father were come home, even then,
Their labor did not cease; unless when all
Turned to the cleanly supper-board, and there,
100 Each with a mess of pottage and skimmed milk,
Sat round the basket piled with oaten cakes,
And their plain home-made cheese. Yet when
          the meal
Was ended, Luke (for so the Son was named)
And his old Father both betook themselves
105 To such convenient work as might employ
Their hands by the fire-side; perhaps to card
Wool for the Housewife's spindle, or repair
Some injury done to sickle, flail, or scythe,
Or other implement of house or field.

110   Down from the ceiling, by the chimney's edge,
That in our ancient uncouth country style
With huge and black projection overbrowed

Large space beneath, as duly as the light
Of day grew dim the Housewife hung a lamp;
115 An aged utensil, which had performed
Service beyond all others of its kind.
Early at evening did it burn—and late,
Surviving comrade of uncounted hours,
Which, going by from year to year, had found,
120 And left the couple neither gay perhaps
Nor cheerful, yet with objects and with hopes,
Living a life of eager industry.
And now, when Luke had reached his eighteenth
    year,
There by the light of this old lamp they sat,
125 Father and Son, while far into the night
The Housewife plied her own peculiar work,
Making the cottage through the silent hours
Murmur as with the sound of summer flies.
This light was famous in its neighborhood,
130 And was a public symbol of the life
That thrifty Pair had lived. For, as it chanced,
Their cottage on a plot of rising ground
Stood single, with large prospect, north and south,
High into Easedale, up to Dunmail-Raise,
135 And westward to the village near the lake;
And from this constant light, so regular
And so far seen, the House itself, by all
Who dwelt within the limits of the vale,
Both old and young, was named The Evening
    Star.
140   Thus living on through such a length of years,
The Shepherd, if he loved himself, must needs
Have loved his Helpmate; but to Michael's heart
This son of his old age was yet more dear—
Less from instinctive tenderness, the same
145 Fond spirit that blindly works in the blood of
    all—
Than that a child, more than all other gifts

That earth can offer to declining man,
Brings hope with it, and forward-looking
thoughts,
And stirrings of inquietude, when they
150 By tendency of nature needs must fail.
Exceeding was the love he bare to him,
His heart and his heart's joy! For oftentimes
Old Michael, while he was a babe in arms,
Had done him female service, not alone
155 For pastime and delight, as is the use
Of fathers, but with patient mind enforced
To acts of tenderness; and he had rocked
His cradle, as with a woman's gentle hand.
    And, in a later time, ere yet the Boy
160 Had put on boy's attire, did Michael love,
Albeit of a stern unbending mind,
To have the Young one in his sight, when he
Wrought in the field, or on his shepherd's stool
Sate with a fettered sheep before him stretched
165 Under the large old oak, that near his door
Stood single, and, from matchless depth of shade,
Chosen for the Shearer's covert from the sun,
Thence in our rustic dialect was called
The Clipping Tree, a name which yet it bears.
170 There while they two were sitting in the shade,
With others round them, earnest all and blithe,
Would Michael exercise his heart with looks
Of fond correction and reproof bestowed
Upon the Child, if he disturbed the sheep
175 By catching at their legs, or with his shouts
Scared them, while they lay still beneath the
shears.

And when by Heaven's good grace the boy
grew up
A healthy Lad, and carried in his cheek
Two steady roses that were five years old;

180 Then Michael from a winter coppice cut
　　With his own hand a sapling, which he hooped
　　With iron, making it throughout in all
　　Due requisites a perfect shepherd's staff,
　　And gave it to the Boy; wherewith equipt
185 He as a watchman oftentimes was placed
　　At gate or gap, to stem or turn the flock;
　　And, to his office prematurely called,
　　There stood the urchin, as you will divine,
　　Something between a hindrance and a help;
190 And for this cause not always, I believe,
　　Receiving from his Father hire of praise;
　　Though naught was left undone which staff, or
　　　　voice,
　　Or looks, or threatening gestures, could perform.

　　But soon, as Luke, full ten years old, could
　　　　stand
195 Against the mountain blasts, and to the heights,
　　Not fearing toil, nor length of weary ways,
　　He with his Father daily went, and they
　　Were as companions, why should I relate
　　That objects which the Shepherd loved before
200 Were dearer now? that from the Boy there came
　　Feelings and emanations—things which were
　　Light to the sun and music to the wind:
　　And that the old Man's heart seemed born again?

　　Thus in his Father's sight the Boy grew up;
205 And now, when he had reached his eighteenth
　　　　year,
　　He was his comfort and his daily hope.

　　While in this sort the simple household lived
　　From day to day, to Michael's ear there came
　　Distressful tidings. Long before the time
210 Of which I speak, the Shepherd had been bound

In surety for his brother's son, a man
Of an industrious life, and ample means;
But unforeseen misfortunes suddenly
Had prest upon him; and old Michael now
215 Was summoned to discharge the forfeiture,
A grievous penalty, but little less
Than half his substance. This unlooked-for
   claim,
At the first hearing, for a moment took
More hope out of his life than he supposed
220 That any old man ever could have lost.
As soon as he had armed himself with strength
To look his trouble in the face, it seemed
The Shepherd's sole resource to sell at once
A portion of his patrimonial fields.
225 Such was his first resolve; he thought again,
And his heart failed him. "Isabel," said he,
Two evenings after he had heard the news,
"I have been toiling more than seventy years,
And in the open sunshine of God's love
230 Have we all lived; yet if these fields of ours
Should pass into a stranger's hand, I think
That I could not lie quiet in my grave.
Our lot is a hard lot; the sun himself
Has scarcely been more diligent than I;
235 And I have lived to be a fool at last
To my own family. An evil man
That was, and made an evil choice, if he
Were false to us; and if he were not false,
There are ten thousand to whom loss like this
240 Had been no sorrow. I forgive him;—but
'Twere better to be dumb than to talk thus.

When I began, my purpose was to speak
Of remedies and of a cheerful hope.
Our Luke shall leave us, Isabel; the land
245 Shall not go from us, and it shall be free;

He shall possess it free as is the wind
That passes over it.   We have, thou know'st,
Another kinsman—he will be our friend
In this distress.   He is a prosperous man,
250 Thriving in trade—and Luke to him shall go,
And with his kinsman's help and his own thrift
He quickly will repair this loss, and then
He may return to us.   If here he stay,
What can be done?   Where everyone is poor,
255 What can be gained?"

                 At this the old Man paused,
And Isabel sat silent, for her mind
Was busy, looking back into past times.
There's Richard Bateman, thought she to herself,
He was a parish-boy—at the church-door
260 They made a gathering for him, shillings, pence
And   half   pennies,   wherewith   the   neighbors
           bought
A basket, which they filled with peddler's wares;
And, with this basket on his arm, the lad
Went up to London, found a master there,
265 Who, out of many, chose the trusty boy
To go and overlook his merchandise
Beyond the seas; where he grew wondrous rich,
And left estates and moneys to the poor,
And, at his birth-place, built a chapel, floored
270 With marble, which he sent from foreign lands.
These thoughts, and many others of like sort,
Passed quickly through the mind of Isabel,
And her face brightened.   The old Man was glad,
And thus resumed:—" Well, Isabel! this scheme
275 These two days, has been meat and drink to me.
Far more than we have lost is left us yet.
—We have enough—I wish indeed that I
Were younger;—but this hope is a good hope.
—Make ready Luke's best garments, of the best
280 Buy for him more, and let us send him forth

To-morrow, or the next day, or to-night:
If he *could* go, the boy should go to-night."
Here Michael ceased, and to the fields went forth
With a light heart. The Housewife for five days
285 Was restless morn and night, and all day long
Wrought on with her best fingers to prepare
Things needful for the journey of her son.
But Isabel was glad when Sunday came
To stop her in her work: for, when she lay
290 By Michael's side, she through the last two
   nights
Heard him, how he was troubled in his sleep:
And when they rose at morning she could see
That all his hopes were gone. That day at noon
She said to Luke, while they two by themselves
295 Were sitting at the door, "Thou must not go:
We have no other Child but thee to lose,
None to remember—do not go away;
For if thou leave thy Father, he will die."
The youth made answer with a jocund voice;
300 And Isabel, when she had told her fears,
Recovered heart. That evening her best fare
Did she bring forth, and all together sat
Like happy people round a Christmas fire.
 With daylight Isabel resumed her work
305 And all the ensuing week the house appeared
As cheerful as a grove in Spring: at length
The expected letter from their kinsman came,
With kind assurances that he would do
His utmost for the welfare of the Boy;
310 To which, requests were added, that forthwith
He might be sent to him. Ten times or more
The letter was read over; Isabel
Went forth to show it to the neighbors round;
Nor was there at that time on English land
315 A prouder heart than Luke's. When Isabel
Had to her house returned, the old Man said,

"He shall depart to-morrow." To this word
The Housewife answered, talking much of things
Which, if at such short notice he should go,
320 Would surely be forgotten. But at length
She gave consent, and Michael was at ease.
    Near the tumultuous brook of Green-head
        Ghyll,
In that deep valley, Michael had designed
To build a Sheep-fold; and, before he heard
325 The tidings of his melancholy loss,
For this same purpose he had gathered up
A heap of stones, which by the streamlet's edge
Lay thrown together, ready for the work.
With Luke that evening thitherward he walked:
330 And soon as they had reached the place he
        stopped,
And thus the old Man spake to him: "My Son,
To-morrow thou wilt leave me: with full heart
I look upon thee, for thou art the same
That wert a promise to me ere thy birth
335 And all thy life hast been my daily joy.
I will relate to thee some little part
Of our two histories; 'twill do thee good
When thou art from me, even if I should touch
On things thou canst not know of.—After thou
340 First camest into the world—as oft befalls
To new-born infants—thou didst sleep away
Two days, and blessings from thy Father's tongue
Then fell upon thee. Day by day passed on,
And still I loved thee with increasing love.
345 Never to living ear came sweeter sounds
Than when I heard thee by our own fire-side
First uttering, without words, a natural tune;
While thou, a feeding babe, didst in thy joy
Sing at thy mother's breast. Month followed
        month,
350 And in the open fields my life was passed

And on the mountains; else I think that thou
Hadst been brought up upon thy Father's knees.
But we were playmates, Luke: among these hills,
As well thou knowest, in us the old and young
355 Have played together, nor with me didst thou
Lack any pleasure which a boy can know."
Luke had a manly heart; but at these words
He sobbed aloud. The old Man grasped his hand,
And said, "Nay, do not take it so—I see
360 That these are things of which I need not speak.
Even to the utmost I have been to thee
A kind and a good Father: And herein
I but repay a gift which I myself
Received at others' hands; for, though now old
365 Beyond the common life of man, I still
Remember them who loved me in my youth.
Both of them sleep together: here they lived,
As all their Forefathers had done; and when
At length their time was come, they were not loth
370 To give their bodies to the family mould.
I wished that thou shouldst live the life they
    lived:
But, 'tis a long time to look back, my Son,
And see so little gain from threescore years.
These fields were burdened when they came
    to me;
375 Till I was forty years of age, not more
Than half of my inheritance was mine.
I toiled and toiled; God blessed me in my work,
And till these three weeks past the land was free.
It looks as if it never could endure
380 Another Master. Heaven forgive me, Luke,
If I judge ill for thee, but it seems good
That thou should'st go."
                At this the old man paused.
Then, pointing to the stones near which they
    stood

Thus, after a short silence, he resumed:
385 " This was a work for us; and now, my Son,
It is a work for me.   But, lay one stone—
Here, lay it for me, Luke, with thine own hands.
Nay, Boy, be of good hope;—we both may live
To see a better day.   At eighty-four
390 I am strong and hale;—Do thou thy part;
I will do mine.—I will begin again
With many tasks that were resigned to thee:
Up to the heights, and in among the storms,
Will I without thee go again, and do
395 All works which I was wont to do alone,
Before I knew thy face.—Heaven bless thee, Boy!
Thy heart these two weeks has been beating fast
With many hopes; it should be so—yes—yes—
I knew that thou couldst never have a wish
400 To leave me, Luke: thou hast been bound to me
Only by links of love: When thou art gone,
What will be left to us!—But, I forget
My purposes.   Lay now the corner-stone,
As I requested; and hereafter, Luke,
405 When thou art gone away, should evil men
Be thy companions, think of me, my Son,
And of this moment: hither turn thy thoughts,
And God will strengthen thee: amid all fear
And all temptation, Luke, I pray that thou
410 Mayst bear in mind the life thy Fathers lived,
Who, being innocent, did for that cause
Bestir them in good deeds.   Now, fare thee well—
When thou return'st, thou in this place wilt see
A work which is not here—a covenant
415 'Twill be between us; but, whatever fate
Befall thee, I shall love thee to the last,
And bear thy memory with me to the grave."

The Shepherd ended here; and Luke stooped
down,

And, as his Father had requested, laid
420 The first stone of the Sheep-fold. At the sight
The old Man's grief broke from him; to his heart
He pressed his Son, he kissèd him and wept;
And to the house together they returned.
Hushed was that House in peace, or seeming
        peace,
425 Ere the night fell:—with morrow's dawn the Boy
Began his journey, and when he had reached
The public way, he put on a bold face;
And all the neighbors, as he passed their doors,
Came forth with wishes and with farewell prayers,
430 That followed him till he was out of sight.

    A good report did from their Kinsman come,
Of Luke and his well-doing: and the Boy
Wrote loving letters, full of wondrous news,
Which, as the Housewise phrased it, were
        throughout
435 "The prettiest letters that were ever seen."
Both parents read them with rejoicing hearts.
So, many months passed on; and once again
The Shepherd went about his daily work
With confident and cheerful thoughts; and now
440 Sometimes when he could find a leisure hour
He to that valley took his way, and there
Wrought at the Sheep-fold. Meantime Luke
        began
To slacken in his duty; and, at length,
He in the dissolute city gave himself
445 To evil courses: ignominy and shame
Fell on him, so that he was driven at last
To seek a hiding-place beyond the seas.

    There is a comfort in the strength of love;
'Twill make a thing endurable, which else
450 Would overset the brain, or break the heart:
I have conversed with more than one who well
Remember the old Man, and what he was

Years after he had heard this heavy news.
His bodily frame had been from youth to age
455 Of an unusual strength. Among the rocks
He went, and still looked up to sun and cloud,
And listened to the wind; and, as before,
Performed all kinds of labor for his sheep,
And for the land, his small inheritance.
460 And to that hollow dell from time to time
Did he repair, to build the Fold of which
His flock had need. 'Tis not forgotten yet
The pity which was then in every heart
For the old Man—and 'tis believed by all
465 That many and many a day he thither went,
And never lifted up a single stone.

There, by the Sheep-fold, sometimes was he
    seen,
Sitting alone, or with his faithful Dog,
Then old, beside him, lying at his feet.
470 The length of full seven years, from time to time,
He at the building of this Sheep-fold wrought,
And left the work unfinished when he died.
Three years, or little more, did Isabel
Survive her husband: at her death the estate
475 Was sold, and went into a stranger's hand.
The Cottage which was named The Evening Star
Is gone—the plowshare has been through the
    ground
On which it stood; great changes have been
    wrought
In all the neighborhood:—yet the oak is left
480 That grew beside their door; and the remains
Of the unfinished Sheep-fold may be seen
Beside the boisterous brook of Green-head Ghyll.

MY HEART LEAPS UP
(1807)

My heart leaps up when I behold
    A rainbow in the sky:
So was it when my life began;
So is it now I am a man;
5 So be it when I shall grow old,
    Or let me die!
The Child is father of the Man;
And I could wish my days to be
Bound each to each by natural piety.

THE SOLITARY REAPER
(1807)

Behold her, single in the field,
Yon solitary Highland Lass!
Reaping and singing by herself;
Stop here, or gently pass!
5 Alone she cuts and binds the grain,
And sings a melancholy strain;
O, listen! for the Vale profound
Is overflowing with the sound.

No nightingale did ever chaunt
10 More welcome notes to weary bands
Of travellers in some shady haunt,
Among Arabian sands:
A voice so thrilling ne'er was heard
In spring-time from the cuckoo-bird,
15 Breaking the silence of the seas
Among the farthest Hebrides.

Will no one tell me what she sings?—
Perhaps the plaintive numbers flow
For old, unhappy, far-off things,
20 And battles long ago:

Or is it some more humble lay,
Familiar matter of to-day?
Some natural sorrow, loss, or pain,
That has been, and may be again?

25 Whate'er the theme, the Maiden sang
As if her song could have no ending;
I saw her singing at her work,
And o'er the sickle bending;—
I listened, motionless and still;
30 And, as I mounted up the hill,
The music in my heart I bore,
Long after it was heard no more.

ODE

INTIMATIONS OF IMMORTALITY FROM RECOLLECTIONS OF EARLY CHILDHOOD.

(1803–6)

I.

There was a time when meadow, grove, and stream,
The earth, and every common sight,
          To me did seem
          Apparelled in celestial light,
5 The glory and the freshness of a dream.
It is not now as it hath been of yore;—
          Turn wheresoe'er I may,
          By night or day,
The things which I have seen I now can see no
          more.

II.

10   The Rainbow comes **and** goes,
          And lovely is the Rose,
          The Moon doth with delight
Look round her when the heavens are bare,
          Waters on a starry night
15   Are beautiful and fair;

The sunshine is a glorious birth;
But yet I know, where'er I go,
That there hath passed away a glory from the
    earth.

III.

Now, while the birds thus sing a joyous song,
20   And while the young lambs bound
        As to the tabor's sound,
To me alone there came a thought of grief:
A timely utterance gave that thought relief,
        And I again am strong:
25 The cataracts blow their trumpets from the steep;
No more shall grief of mine the season wrong;
I hear the Echoes through the mountains throng,
The Winds come to me from the fields of sleep,
        And all the earth is gay;
30   Land and sea
      Give themselves up to jollity,
        And with the heart of May
    Doth every Beast keep holiday;—
        Thou Child of Joy,
35 Shout round me, let me hear thy shouts, thou
    happy Shepherd-boy!

IV.

Ye blessèd Creatures, I have heard the call
    Ye to each other make; I see
The heavens laugh with you in your jubilee;
    My heart is at your festival,
40   My head hath its coronal,
The fulness of your bliss, I feel—I feel it all.
    O evil day! if I were sullen
    While Earth herself is adorning,
      This sweet May-morning,
45   And the Children are culling
      On every side,

In a thousand valleys far and wide,
 Fresh flowers; while the sun shines warm,
And the Babe leaps up on his Mother's arm:—
50 I hear, I hear, with joy I hear!
  —But there's a Tree, of many, one,
A single Field which I have looked upon,
Both of them speak of something that is gone:
   The Pansy at my feet
55   Doth the same tale repeat:
Whither is fled the visionary gleam?
Where is it now, the glory and the dream?

V.

Our birth is but a sleep and a forgetting:
The Soul that rises with us, our life's Star,
60 Hath had elsewhere its setting,
   And cometh from afar:
  Not in entire forgetfulness,
  And not in utter nakedness,
But trailing clouds of glory do we come
65 From God, who is our home:
Heaven lies about us in our infancy!
Shades of the prison-house begin to close
   Upon the growing Boy,
But He beholds the light, and whence it flows,
70 He sees it in his joy;
The Youth, who daily farther from the east
  Must travel, still is Nature's Priest,
   And by the vision splendid
   Is on his way attended;
75 At length the Man perceives it die away,
And fade into the light of common day.

VI.

Earth fills her lap with pleasures of her own;
Yearnings she hath in her own natural kind,

And, even with something of a Mother's mind,
80   And no unworthy aim,
   The homely Nurse doth all she can
To make her Foster-child, her Inmate Man,
    Forget the glories he hath known,
And that imperial palace whence he came.

VII.

85 Behold the Child among his new-born blisses,
A six years' Darling of a pigmy size!
See, where 'mid work of his own hand he lies,
Fretted by sallies of his mother's kisses,
With light upon him from his father's eyes!
90 See, at his feet, some little plan or chart,
Some fragment from his dream of human life,
Shaped by himself with newly-learned art;
     A wedding or a festival,
     A mourning or a funeral;
95   And this hath now his heart,
    And unto this he frames his song:
       Then will he fit his tongue
To dialogues of business, love, or strife;
     But it will not be long
100   Ere this be thrown aside,
    And with new joy and pride
The little Actor cons another part;
Filling from time to time his "humorous stage"
With all the Persons, down to palsied Age,
105 That Life brings with her in her equipage;
     As if his whole vocation
     Were endless imitation.

VIII.

Thou, whose exterior semblance doth belie
     Thy Soul's immensity;
110 Thou best Philosopher, who yet dost keep
Thy heritage, thou Eye among the blind,

That, deaf and silent, read'st the eternal deep,
Haunted forever by the eternal mind,—
      Mighty Prophet! Seer blest!
115   On whom those truths do rest,
Which we are toiling all our lives to find,
In darkness lost, the darkness of the grave;
Thou, over whom thy Immortality
Broods like the Day, a Master o'er a Slave,
120 A Presence which is not to be put by;
Thou little Child, yet glorious in the might
Of heaven-born freedom on thy being's height,
Why with such earnest pains dost thou provoke
The years to bring the inevitable yoke,
125 Thus blindly with thy blessedness at strife?
Full soon thy Soul shall have her earthly freight,
And custom lie upon thee with a weight,
Heavy as frost, and deep almost as life!

IX.

    O joy! that in our embers
130   Is something that doth live,
    That nature yet remembers
    What was so fugitive!
The thought of our past years in me doth breed
Perpetual benediction: not indeed
135 For that which is most worthy to be blest;
Delight and liberty, the simple creed
Of Childhood, whether busy or at rest,
With new-fledged hope still fluttering in his
      breast:—
    Not for these I raise
140   The song of thanks and praise;
    But for those obstinate questionings
    Of sense and outward things,
    Fallings from us, vanishings;
    Blank misgivings of a Creature
145 Moving about in worlds not realized,

High instincts before which our mortal Nature
Did tremble like a guilty thing surprised:
    But for those first affections,
    Those shadowy recollections,
150   Which, be they what they may,
Are yet the fountain light of all our day,
Are yet a master light of all our seeing;
    Uphold us, cherish, and have power to make
Our noisy years seem moments in the being
155 Of the eternal Silence: truths that wake,
    To perish never;
Which neither listlessness, nor mad endeavor,
    Nor Man nor Boy,
Nor all that is at enmity with joy,
160 Can utterly abolish or destroy!
    Hence in a season of calm weather
    Though inland far we be,
Our Souls have sight of that immortal sea
    Which brought us hither,
165   Can in a moment travel thither,
And see the Children sport upon the shore,
And hear the mighty waters rolling evermore.

X.

Then sing, ye Birds, sing, sing a joyous song!
    And let the young Lambs bound
170   As to the tabor's sound!
We in thought will join your throng,
    Ye that pipe and ye that play,
    Ye that through your hearts to-day
    Feel the gladness of the May!
175 What though the radiance which was once so bright
Be now forever taken from my sight,
    Though nothing can bring back the hour
Of splendour in the grass, of glory in the flower;
    We will grieve not, rather find

180   Strength in what remains behind;
           In the primal sympathy
           Which having been must ever be;
           In the soothing thoughts that spring
           Out of human suffering;
185   In the faith that looks through death
     In years that bring the philosophic mind.

                    XI.

     And O, ye Fountains, Meadows, Hills and
                    Groves,
     Forebode not any severing of our loves!
     Yet in my heart of hearts I feel your might;
190 I only have relinquished one delight
     To live beneath your more habitual sway.
     I love the Brooks which down their channels fret,
     Even more than when I tripped lightly as they;
     The innocent brightness of a new-born Day
195   Is lovely yet;
     The Clouds that gather round the setting sun
     Do take a sober colouring from an eye
     That hath kept watch o'er man's mortality;
     Another race hath been, and other palms are won.
200 Thanks to the human heart by which we live,
     Thanks to its tenderness, its joys, and fears,
     To me the meanest flower that blows can give
     Thoughts that do often lie too deep for tears.

     "I WANDERED LONELY AS A CLOUD"
                  (1807)

     I wandered lonely as a cloud
        That floats on high o'er vales and hills,
     When all at once I saw a crowd,
        A host, of golden daffodils;
5   Beside the lake, beneath the trees,
        Fluttering and dancing in the breeze.

Continuous as the stars that shine
And twinkle on the milky way,
They stretched in never-ending line
10 Along the margin of a bay:
Ten thousand saw I at a glance,
Tossing their heads in sprightly dance.

The waves beside them danced; but they
Out-did the sparkling waves in glee:
15 A poet could not but be gay,
In such a jocund company:
I gazed—and gazed—but little thought
What wealth the show to me had brought:

For oft, when on my couch I lie
20 In vacant or in pensive mood,
They flash upon that inward eye
Which is the bliss of solitude:
And then my heart with pleasure fills,
And dances with the daffodils.

"SHE WAS A PHANTOM OF DELIGHT"
(1807)

She was a Phantom of delight
When first she gleamed upon my sight;
A lovely Apparition, sent
To be a moment's ornament;
5 Her eyes are stars of Twilight fair;
Like Twilight's, too, her dusky hair;
But all things else about her drawn
From May-time and the cheerful Dawn;
A dancing Shape, an Image gay,
10 To haunt, to startle, and way-lay.

I saw her upon nearer view,
A Spirit, yet a Woman too!
Her household motions light and free,
And steps of virgin-liberty;

15 A countenance in which did meet
   Sweet records, promises as sweet;
   A Creature not too bright or good
   For human nature's daily food;
   For transient sorrows, simple wiles,
20 Praise, blame, love, kisses, tears, and smiles.

   And now I see with eyes serene
   The very pulse of the machine;
   A Being breathing thoughtful breath,
   A traveller between life and death;
25 The reason firm, the temperate will,
   Endurance, foresight, strength, and skill;
   A perfect Woman, nobly planned,
   To warn, to comfort, and command;
   And yet a Spirit still, and bright
30 With something of an angel light.

ODE TO DUTY

(1807)

   Stern Daughter of the Voice of God!
   O Duty! if that name thou love
   Who art a light to guide, a rod
   To check the erring, and reprove;
5 Thou, who art victory and law
   When empty terrors overawe;
   From vain temptations dost set free;
   And calm'st the weary strife of frail humanity!

   There are who ask not if thine eye
10 Be on them; who, in love and truth,
   Where no misgiving is, rely
   Upon the genial sense of youth:
   Glad Hearts! without reproach or blot;
   Who do thy work, and know it not.
15 Long may the kindly impulse last!
   But thou, if they should totter, teach them to
      stand fast!

Serene will be our days and bright,
And happy will our nature be,
When love is an unerring light,
20 And joy its own security.
And they a blissful course may hold
Even now, who, not unwisely bold,
Live in the spirit of this creed;
Yet seek thy firm support according to their need.

25 I, loving freedom, and untried;
No sport of every random gust,
Yet being to myself a guide,
Too blindly have reposed my trust:
And oft, when in my heart was heard
30 Thy timely mandate, I deferred
The task, in smoother walks to stray;
But thee I now would serve more strictly, if I
          may.

Through no disturbance of my soul,
Or strong compunction in me wrought,
35 I supplicate for thy control;
But in the quietness of thought:
Me this unchartered freedom tires;
I feel the weight of chance-desires:
My hopes no more must change their name,
40 I long for a repose that ever is the same.

Stern Lawgiver! yet thou dost wear
The Godhead's most benignant grace;
Nor know we anything so fair
As is the smile upon thy face:
45 Flowers laugh before thee on their beds
And fragrance in thy footing treads;
Thou dost preserve the stars from wrong;
And the most ancient heavens, through Thee, are
          fresh and strong.

To humbler functions, awful Power!
50 I call thee: I myself commend
Unto thy guidance from this hour;
Oh, let my weakness have an end!
Give unto me, made lowly wise,
The spirit of self-sacrifice;
55 The confidence of reason give;
And in the light of truth thy Bondman let me
    live!

SONNETS

WRITTEN IN LONDON, SEPTEMBER, 1802

O Friend! I know not which way I must look
For comfort, being, as I am, opprest,
To think that now our life is only drest
For show; mean handy-work of craftsman, cook,
5 Or groom!—We must run glittering like a brook
In the open sunshine, or we are unblest:
The wealthiest man among us is the best:
No grandeur now in nature or in book
Delights us. Rapine, avarice, expense,
10 This is idolatry: and these we adore:
Plain living and high thinking are no more:
The homely beauty of the good old cause
Is gone; our peace, our fearful innocence,
And pure religion breathing household laws.

LONDON, 1802

Milton! thou shouldst be living at this hour:
England hath need of thee: she is a fen
Of stagnant waters: altar, sword, and pen,
Fireside, the heroic wealth of hall and bower,
Have forfeited their ancient English dower   5
Of inward happiness. We are selfish men;
Oh! raise us up, return to us again;
And give us manners, virtue, freedom, power.

Thy soul was like a Star, and dwelt apart:
Thou hadst a voice whose sound was like the sea:
Pure as the naked heavens, majestic, free, 11
So didst thou travel on life's common way,
In cheerful godliness; and yet thy heart
The lowliest duties on herself did lay.

"WHEN I HAVE BORNE IN MEMORY"
(1802)

When I have borne in memory what has tamed
Great Nations, how ennobling thoughts depart
When men change swords for ledgers, and desert
The student's bower for gold, some fears unnamed
I had, my Country!—am I to be blamed? 5
Now, when I think of Thee, and what Thou art,
Verily, in the bottom of my heart,
Of those unfilial fears I am ashamed,
For dearly must we prize thee; we who find
In thee a bulwark for the cause of men; 10
And I by my affection was beguiled:
What wonder if a Poet now and then,
Among the many movements of his mind,
Felt for thee as a lover or a child!

COMPOSED UPON WESTMINSTER BRIDGE,
SEPTEMBER 3, 1802

Earth has not anything to show more fair:
Dull would he be of soul who could pass by
A sight so touching in its majesty:
This City now doth, like a garment, wear
The beauty of the morning; silent, bare, 5
Ships, towers, domes, theatres, and temples lie
Open unto the fields, and to the sky;
All bright and glittering in the smokeless air.
Never did sun more beautifully steep
In his first splendour valley, rock, or hill; 10
Ne'er saw I, never felt, a calm so deep!

The river glideth at his own sweet will:
Dear God! the very houses seem asleep;
And all that mighty heart is lying still!

COMPOSED UPON THE BEACH, NEAR CALAIS,
August, 1802

It is a beauteous evening, calm and free;
The holy time is quiet as a Nun
Breathless with adoration; the broad sun
Is sinking down in its tranquillity;
The gentleness of heaven broods o'er the Sea. 5
Listen! the mighty Being is awake,
And doth with his eternal motion make
A sound like thunder—everlastingly.
Dear Child! dear Girl! that walkest with me here,
If thou appear untouched by solemn thought, 10
Thy nature is not therefore less divine.
Thou liest in Abraham's bosom all the year;
And worship'st at the Temple's inner shrine,
God being with thee when we know it not.

"THE WORLD IS TOO MUCH WITH US"
(1806)

The world is too much with us: late and soon,
Getting and spending, we lay waste our powers:
Little we see in Nature that is ours;
We have given our hearts away, a sordid boon!
The Sea that bares her bosom to the moon; 5
The winds that will be howling at all hours,
And are up-gathered now like sleeping flowers;
For this, for everything, we are out of tune;
It moves us not.—Great God! I'd rather be
A Pagan suckled in a creed outworn; 10
So might I, standing on this pleasant lea,
Have glimpses that would make me less forlorn;
Have sight of Proteus rising from the sea;
Or hear old Triton blow his wreathèd horn.

Samuel Taylor Coleridge
1772–1834

THE RIME OF THE ANCIENT MARINER
IN SEVEN PARTS

(From the *Lyrical Ballads*, 1798)

Argument

How a Ship having passed the Line was driven by
storms to the cold Country towards the South Pole;
and how from thence she made her course to the tropical Latitude of the Great Pacific Ocean; and of the
strange things that befell; and in what manner the
Ancyent Marinere came back to his own Country.

PART I.

An ancient Ma-
riner meeteth
three Gallants
bidden to a wed-
ding-feast, and
detaineth one.

It is an ancient Mariner,
And he stoppeth one of three,
'By thy long gray beard and glittering eye,
Now wherefore stopp'st thou me?

The Bridegroom's doors are opened wide,
And I am next of kin;   6
The guests are met, the feast is set:
May'st hear the merry din.'

He holds him with his skinny hand,
'There was a ship,' quoth he.   10
'Hold off! unhand me, gray-beard loon!'
Eftsoons his hand dropt he.

The Wedding-
Guest is spell-
bound by the
eye of the old
seafaring man,
and constrained
to hear his tale.

He holds him with his glittering eye—
The Wedding-Guest stood still,
And listens like a three years' child: 15
The Mariner hath his will.

The Wedding-Guest sat on a stone:
He cannot choose but hear;
And thus spake on that ancient man,
The bright-eyes Mariner.   20

'The ship was cheered, the harbour
        cleared,
Merrily did we drop
Below the kirk, below the hill,
Below the lighthouse top.

The Mariner tells how the ship sailed southward with a good wind and fair weather, till it reached the line.

The sun came up upon the left   25
Out of the sea came he!
And he shone bright, and on the right
Went down into the sea.

Higher and higher every day,
Till over the mast at noon—'   30
The Wedding-Guest here beat his breast,
For he heard the loud bassoon.

The Wedding-Guest heareth the bridal music; but the Mariner continueth his tale.

The bride hath paced into the hall,
Red as a rose is she;
Nodding their heads before her goes   35
The merry minstrelsy.

The Wedding-Guest he beat his breast,
Yet he cannot choose but hear;
And thus spake on that ancient man,
The bright-eyed Mariner.   40

The ship driven by a storm toward the south pole.

'And now the Storm-blast came, and he
Was tyrannous and strong:
He struck with his o'ertaking wings,
And chased us south along.

With sloping masts and dipping prow,   45
As who pursued with yell and blow

Still treads the shadow of his foe,
And forward bends his head,
The ship drove fast, loud roared the blast,
And southward aye we fled.   50

And now there came both mist and snow
And it grew wondrous cold:
And ice, mast-high, came floating by,
As green as emerald.

The land of ice, and of fearful sounds where no living thing was to be seen.

And through the drifts the snowy
     clifts   55
Did send a dismal sheen:
Nor shapes of men nor beasts we ken—
The ice was all between.

The ice was here, the ice was there,
The ice was all around: 60
It cracked and growled, and roared and
     howled,
Like noises in a swound!

Till a great sea-bird, called the Albatross, came through the snow-fog, and was received with great joy and hospitality.

At length did cross an Albatross,
Thorough the fog it came;
As if it had been a Christian soul,   65
We hailed it in God's name.

It ate the food it ne'er had eat,
And round and round it flew.
The ice did split with a thunder-fit;
The helmsman steered us through!   70

And lo! the Albatross proveth a bird of good omen, and followeth the ship as it returned northward through fog and floating ice.

And a good south wind sprung up behind;
The Albatross did follow,
And every day, for food or play,
Came to the mariners' hollo!

In mist or cloud, on mast or shroud,   75
It perched for vespers nine;
Whiles all the night, through fog-smoke
    white,
Glimmered the white moon-shine.'

The ancient Mariner inhospitably killeth the pious bird of good omen.

'God save thee, ancient Mariner!
From the fiends, that plague thee
    thus!—   80
Why look'st thou so?'—With my cross-
    bow
I shot the Albatross.

PART II.

The Sun now rose upon the right;
Out of the sea came he,
Still hid in mist, and on the left   85
Went down into the sea.

And the good south wind still blew behind,
But no sweet bird did follow,
Nor any day for food or play
Came to the mariners' hollo!   90

His shipmates cry out against the ancient Mariner, for killing the bird of good luck.

And I had done a hellish thing,
And it would work 'em woe:
For all averred, I had killed the bird
That made the breeze to blow.
Ah wretch! said they, the bird to slay,   95
That made the breeze to blow!

But when the fog cleared off, they justify the same, and thus make themselves accomplices in the crime,

Nor dim nor red, like God's own head,
The glorious Sun uprist:
Then all averred, I had killed the bird
That brought the fog and mist.   100
'Twas right, said they, such birds to slay,
That bring the fog and mist.

The fair breeze blew, the white foam flew,
The furrow followed free;
We were the first that ever burst   105
Into that silent sea.

Down dropt the breeze, the sails dropt
          down,
'Twas sad as sad could be;
And we did speak only to break
The silence of the sea!   110

All in a hot and copper sky,
The bloody Sun, at noon,
Right up above the mast did stand,
No bigger than the Moon.

Day after day, day after day,   115
We stuck, nor breath nor motion;
As idle as a painted ship
Upon a painted ocean.

Water, water, everywhere,
And all the boards did shrink;   120
Water, water, everywhere,
Nor any drop to drink.

The very deep did rot: O Christ!
That ever this should be!
Yea, slimy things did crawl with legs 125
Upon the slimy sea.

About, about, in reel and rout
The death-fires danced at night;
The water, like a witch's oils,
Burnt green, and blue, and white.   130

A spirit had fol-
lowed them;
one of the in-
visible inhabi-
tants of this
planet, neither
departed souls
nor angels; con-
cerning whom
the learned Jew,
Josephus, and
the Platonic
Constantino-
politan Michael
Psellus, may be
consulted. They
are very numer-
ous, and there is
no climate or
element without
one or more.

The shipmates,
in their sore dis-
tress, would fain
throw the whole
guilt on the an-
cient Mariner:
in sign whereof
they hang the
dead sea-bird
round his neck.

And some in dreams assured were
Of the Spirit that plagued us so
Nine fathom deep he had followed us
From the land of mist and snow.

And   every   tongue,   through   utter
          drought,   135
Was withered at the root;
We could not speak, no more than if
We had been choked with soot.

Ah! well-a-day! what evil looks
Had I from old and young!   140
Instead of the cross, the Albatross
About my neck was hung.

PART III.

There passed a weary time. Each throat
Was parched, and glazed each eye.
A weary time! a weary time!   145
How glazed each weary eye,
When looking westward, I beheld
A something in the sky.

The ancient Ma-
riner beholdeth
a sign in the
element afar off.

At first it seemed a little speck,
And then it seemed a mist;   150
It moved and moved, and took at last
A certain shape, I wist.

A speck, a mist, a shape, I wist!
And still it neared and neared:
As if it dodged a water-sprite,   155
It plunged and tacked and veered.

At its nearer ap-
proach, it seem-
eth him to be a
ship; and at a
dear ransom he

With throats unslaked, with black lips
          baked,
We could nor laugh nor wail;

freeth his
speech from the
bonds of thirst.

Through utter drought all dumb we stood!
I bit my arm, I sucked the blood,   160
And cried, A sail! a sail!

With throats unslaked, with black lips
  baked,
Agape they heard me call:

A flash of joy.

Gramercy! they for joy did grin,
And all at once their breath drew in,   165
As they were drinking all.

And horror fol-
lows ; for can it
be a ship that
comes onward
without wind or
tide ?

See! see! (I cried) she tacks no more!
Hither to work us weal;
Without a breeze, without a tide,
She steadies with upright keel!   170

The western wave was all a-flame.
The day was well-nigh done!
Almost upon the western wave
Rested the broad bright Sun;
When that strange shape drove sud-
  denly   175
Betwixt us and the Sun.

It seemeth him
but the skele-
ton of a ship.

And straight the Sun was flecked with
  bars,
(Heaven's Mother send us grace!)
As if through a dungeon-grate he peered
With broad and burning face.   180

Alas! (thought I, and my heart beat loud)
How fast she nears and nears!
Are those her sails that glance in the sun,
Like restless gossameres?

And its ribs are seen as bars on the face of the setting Sun. The Spectre-Woman and her death-mate, and no other on board the skeleton ship. Like vessel, like crew!

Are those her ribs through which the sun   185
Did peer, as through a grate?
And is that Woman all her crew?
Is that a Death? and are there two?
Is Death that woman's mate?

Her lips were red, her looks were free, 190
Her locks were yellow as gold:
Her skin was as white as leprosy,
The Night-mare Life-in-Death was she,
Who thicks man's blood with cold.

Death and Life-in-Death have diced for the ship's crew, and she (the latter) winneth the ancient Mariner.

The naked hulk alongside came,   195
And the twain were casting dice;
'The game is done! I've won! I've won!'
Quoth she, and whistles thrice.

No twilight within the courts of the Sun.

The Sun's rim dips; the stars rush out;
At one stride comes the dark;   200
With far-heard whisper, o'er the sea,
Off shot the spectre-bark.

At the rising of the Moon,

We listened and looked sideways up!
Fear at my heart, as at a cup,
My life-blood seemed to sip!   205
The stars were dim, and thick the night,
The steersman's face by his lamp gleamed white;
From the sails the dew did drip—
Till clomb above the eastern bar
The horned Moon, with one bright star   210
Within the nether tip.

one after another;

One after one, by the star-dogged Moon.
Too quick for groan or sigh,

Each turned his face with a ghastly pang,
And cursed me with his eye.   215

his shipmates
drop down
dead.

Four times fifty living men,
(And I heard nor sigh nor groan)
With heavy thump, a lifeless lump,
They dropped down one by one.

But Life-in-
Death begins
her work on the
ancient Ma-
riner.

The souls did from their bodies fly,— 220
They fled to bliss or woe!
And every soul, it passed me by,
Like the whizz of my cross-bow!

PART IV.

The Wedding-
Guest feareth
that a spirit is
talking to him;

'I fear thee, ancient Mariner!
I fear thy skinny hand!   225
And thou art long, and lank, and brown,
As is the ribbed sea-sand.

I fear thee and thy glittering eye,
And thy skinny hand, so brown.'—

but the ancient
Mariner as-
sureth him of
his bodily life,
and proceedeth
to relate his
horrible pen-
ance.

Fear not, fear not, thou Wedding-
          Guest!   230
This body dropt not down.

Alone, alone, all, all alone,
Alone on a wide wide sea!
And never a saint took pity on
My soul in agony.   235

He despiseth
the creatures of
the calm.

The many men, so beautiful!
And they all dead did lie:
And a thousand thousand slimy things
Lived on; and so did I.

and envieth that they should live, and so many lie dead.

I looked upon the rotting sea,   240
And drew my eyes away;
I looked upon the rotting deck,
And there the dead men lay.

I looked to heaven, and tried to pray;
But or ever a prayer had gusht,   245
A wicked whisper came, and made
My heart as dry as dust.

I closed my lids, and kept them close,
And the balls like pulses beat;
For the sky and the sea, and the sea and
    the sky   250
Lay like a load on my weary eye,
And the dead were at my feet.

But the curse liveth for him in the eye of the dead men.

The cold sweat melted from their limbs,
Nor rot nor reek did they:
The look with which they looked on
    me   255
Had never passed away.

An orphan's curse would drag to hell
A spirit from on high;

In his loneliness and fixedness he yearneth towards the journeying Moon, and the stars that still sojourn, yet still move onward; and everywhere the blue sky belongs to them, and is their appointed rest, a d their native country and their own natural homes, which they enter unannounced, as

But oh! more horrible than that
Is a curse in a dead man's eye!   260
Seven days, seven nights, I saw that curse,
And yet I could not die.

The moving Moon went up the sky,
And nowhere did abide:
Softly she was going up,   265
And a star or two beside—

Her beams bemocked the sultry main,
Like April hoar-frost spread;

lords that are certainly expected and yet there is a silent joy at their arrival.

But where the ship's huge shadow lay,
The charmed water burnt alway   270
A still and awful red.

By the light of the Moon he beholdeth God's creatures of the great calm.

Beyond the shadow of the ship,
I watched the water-snakes:
They moved in tracks of shining white,
And when they reared, the elfish light 275
Fell off in hoary flakes.

Within the shadow of the ship
I watched their rich attire:
Blue, glossy green, and velvet black,
They coiled and swam; and every
        track   280
Was a flash of golden fire.

Their beauty and their happiness.

O happy living things! no tongue
Their beauty might declare:
A spring of love gushed from my heart,

He blesseth them in his heart.

And I blessed them unaware: 285
Sure my kind saint took pity on me,
And I blessed them unaware.

The spell begins to break.

The selfsame moment I could pray;
And from my neck so free
The Albatross fell off, and sank   290
Like lead into the sea.

PART V.

Oh sleep! it is a gentle thing,
Beloved from pole to pole!
To Mary Queen the praise be given!
She   sent   the   gentle   sleep   from
        heaven,   295
That slid into my soul.

By grace of the
holy Mother,
the ancient Ma-
riner is re-
freshed with
rain.

The silly buckets on the deck,
That had so long remained,
I dreamt that they were filled with dew;
And when I awoke, it rained.   300

My lips were wet, my throat was cold,
My garments all were dank;
Sure I had drunken in my dreams,
And still my body drank.

I moved, and could not feel my limbs: 305
I was so light—almost
I thought that I had died in sleep,
And was a blessed ghost.

He heareth
sounds and
seeth strange
sights and com-
motions in the
sky and the ele-
ment.

And soon I heard a roaring wind:
It did not come anear;   310
But with its sound it shook the sails,
That were so thin and sere.

The upper air burst into life!
And a hundred fire-flags sheen,
To and fro they were hurried about!   315
And to and fro, and in and out,
The wan stars danced between.
And the coming wind did roar more loud,
And the sails did sigh like sedge;
And the rain poured down from one black
          cloud;   320
The Moon was at its edge.

The thick black cloud was cleft, and still
The Moon was at its side:
Like waters shot from some high crag,
The lightning fell with never a jag,   325
A river steep and wide.

The bodies of
the ship's crew
are inspired, and
the ship moves
on;

The loud wind never reached the ship,
Yet now the ship moved on!
Beneath the lightning and the Moon
The dead men gave a groan.   330

They groaned, they stirred, they all up-
          rose,
Nor spake, nor moved their eyes;
It had been strange, even in a dream,
To have seen those dead men rise.

The helmsman steered, the ship moved
          on;   335
Yet never a breeze up blew;
The mariners all 'gan work the ropes,
Where they were wont to do;
They raised their limbs like lifeless
          tools—
We were a ghastly crew.   340

The body of my brother's son
Stood by me, knee to knee:
The body and I pulled at one rope
But he said nought to me.

but not by the
souls of the
men, nor by
dæmons of
earth or middle
air, but by a
blessed troop of
angelic spirits,
sent down by
the invocation
of the guardian
saint.

'I fear thee, ancient Mariner!'   345
Be calm, thou Wedding-Guest!
'Twas not those souls that fled in pain,
Which to their corses came again,
But a troop of spirits blest:

For when it dawned—they dropped their
          arms,   350
And clustered round the mast;
Sweet sounds rose slowly through their
          mouths,
And from their bodies passed.

Around, around, flew each sweet sound,
Then darted to the Sun;   355
Slowly the sounds came back again,
Now mixed, now one by one.

Sometimes a-dropping from the sky
I heard the sky-lark sing;
Sometimes all little birds that are,   360
How they seemed to fill the sea and air
With their sweet jargoning!

And now 'twas like all instruments,
Now like a lonely flute;
And now it is an angel's song,   365
That makes the heavens be mute.

It ceased; yet still the sails made on
A pleasant noise till noon,
A noise like of a hidden brook
In the leafy month of June,   370
That to the sleeping woods all night
Singeth a quiet tune.

Till noon we quietly sailed on,
Yet never a breeze did breathe:
Slowly and smoothly went the ship,   375
Moved onward from beneath.

The lonesome
Spirit from the
south-pole car-
ries on the ship
as far as the
line, in obedi-
ence to the
angelic troop,
but still re-
quireth ven-
geance.

Under the keel nine fathom deep,
From the land of mist and snow,
The spirit slid: and it was he
That made the ship to go.   380
The sails at noon left off their tune,
And the ship stood still also.

The Sun, right up above the mast,
Had fixed her to the ocean:

But in a minute she 'gan stir, 385
With a short uneasy motion—
Backwards and forwards half her length
With a short uneasy motion.

Then like a pawing horse let go,
She made a sudden bound: 390
It flung the blood into my head,
And I fell down in a swound.

The Polar Spirit's fellow-dæmons, the invisible inhabitants of the element, take part in his wrong; and two of them relate one to the other, that penance long and heavy for the ancient Mariner hath been accorded to the Polar Spirit, who returneth southward.

How long in that same fit I lay,
I have not to declare;
But ere my living life returned, 395
I heard and in my soul discerned,
Two voices in the air.

' Is it he? ' quoth one, ' Is this the man?
By Him who died on cross,
With his cruel bow he laid full low 400
The harmless Albatross.

' The spirit who bideth by himself
In the land of mist and snow,
He loved the bird that loved the man
Who shot him with his bow.' 405

The other was a softer voice,
As soft as honey-dew:
Quoth he, ' The man hath penance done,
And penance more will do.'

PART VI.

FIRST VOICE

' But tell me, tell me! speak again, 410
Thy soft response renewing—
What makes that ship drive on so fast?
What is the ocean doing?'

SECOND VOICE

'Still as a slave before his lord,
The ocean hath no blast;   415
His great bright eye most silently
Up to the Moon is cast—

If he may know which way to go;
For she guides him smooth or grim.
See, brother, see! how graciously   420
She looketh down on him.'

FIRST VOICE

'But why drives on that ship so fast,
Without or wave or wind?'

SECOND VOICE

'The air is cut away before,
And closes from behind.   425

Fly, brother, fly! more high, more high!
Or we shall be belated:
For slow and slow that ship will go,
When the Mariner's trance is abated.'

The Mariner hath been cast into a trance; for the angelic power causeth the vessel to drive northward faster than human life could endure.

I woke, and we were sailing on   430
As in a gentle weather:
'Twas night, calm night, the Moon was
high,
The dead men stood together.

The supernatural motion is retarded; the Mariner awakes, and his penance begins anew.

All stood together on the deck,
For a charnel-dungeon fitter: 435
All fixed on me their stony eyes,
That in the Moon did glitter.

The pang, the curse, with which they died,
Had never passed away:
I could not draw my eyes from theirs, 440
Nor turn them up to pray.

The curse is finally expiated.

And now this spell was snapt: once more
I viewed the ocean green,
And looked far forth, yet little saw
Of what had else been seen— 445

Like one, that on a lonesome road
Doth walk in fear and dread,
And having once turned round walks on,
And turns no more his head;
Because he knows, a frightful fiend 450
Doth close behind him tread.

But soon there breathed a wind on me,
Nor sound nor motion made:
Its path was not upon the sea,
In ripple or in shade. 455

It raised my hair, it fanned my cheek
Like a meadow-gale of spring—
It mingled strangely with my fears,
Yet it felt like a welcoming.

Swiftly, swiftly flew the ship, 460
Yet she sailed softly too:
Sweetly, sweetly blew the breeze—
On me alone it blew.

And the ancient Mariner beholdeth his native country.

Oh! dream of joy! is this indeed
The lighthouse top I see? 465
Is this the hill? is this the kirk?
Is this mine own countree?

We drifted o'er the harbour-bar,
And I with sobs did pray—
O let me be awake, my God!   470
Or let me sleep alway.

The harbour-bay was clear as glass,
So smoothly it was strewn!
And on the bay the moonlight lay,
And the shadow of the Moon.   475

The rock shone bright, the kirk no less,
That stands above the rock:
The moonlight steeped in silentness
The steady weathercock.

The angelic
spirits leave the
dead bodies,

And the bay was white with silent
            light   480
Till rising from the same,
Full many shapes, that shadows were,
In crimson colours came.

and appear in
their own forms
of light.

A little distance from the prow
Those crimson shadows were: 485
I turned my eyes upon the deck—
Oh Christ! what saw I there!

Each corse lay flat, lifeless and flat,
And, by the holy rood!
A man all light, a seraph-man,   490
On every corse there stood.

This seraph-band, each waved his hand:
It was a heavenly sight!
They stood as signals to the land,
Each one a lovely light;   495

This seraph-band, each waved his hand,
No voice did they impart—

No voice; but oh! the silence sank
Like music on my heart.

But soon I heard the dash of oars, 500
I heard the Pilot's cheer;
My head was turned perforce away,
And I saw a boat appear.
The Pilot and the Pilot's boy,
I heard them coming fast: 505
Dear Lord in Heaven! it was a joy
The dead men could not blast.

I saw a third—I heard his voice:
It is the Hermit good!
He singeth loud his godly hymns 510
That he makes in the wood.
He'll shrieve my soul, he'll wash away
The Albatross's blood.

PART VII.

The Hermit of
the wood

This Hermit good lives in that wood
Which slopes down to the sea. 515
How loudly his sweet voice he rears!
He loves to talk with marineres
That come from a far countree.

He kneels at morn, and noon, and eve—
He hath a cushion plump: 520
It is the moss that wholly hides
The rotted old oak-stump.

The skiff-boat neared: I heard them talk,
'Why, this is strange, I trow!
Where are those lights so many and
    fair, 525
That signal made but now?'

approacheth
the ship with
wonder.

'Strange, by my faith!' the Hermit
                                    said—
'And they answered not our cheer!
The planks look warped! and see those
                                    sails,
How thin they are and sere!   530
I never saw aught like to them,
Unless perchance it were

'Brown skeletons of leaves that lag
My forest-brook along;
When the ivy-tod is heavy with snow, 535
And the owlet whoops to the wolf below,
That eats the she-wolf's young.'

'Dear Lord! it hath a fiendish look—
(The Pilot made reply)
I am a-feared'—'Push on, push on!' 540
Said the Hermit cheerily.

The boat came closer to the ship,
But I nor spake nor stirred;
The boat came close beneath the ship,
And straight a sound was heard.   545

The ship sud-
denly sinketh.

Under the water it rumbled on,
Still louder and more dread:
It reached the ship, it split the bay;
The ship went down like lead.

The ancient
Mariner is saved
in the Pilot's
boat.

Stunned by that loud and dreadful
                        sound,   550
Which sky and ocean smote,
Like one that hath been seven days
                        drowned
My body lay afloat;
But swift as dreams, myself I found
Within the Pilot's boat.   555

Upon the whirl, where sank the ship,
The boat spun round and round;
And all was still, save that the hill
Was telling of the sound.

I moved my lips—the Pilot shrieked   560
And fell down in a fit;
The holy Hermit raised his eyes,
And prayed where he did sit.

I took the oars: the Pilot's boy,
Who now doth crazy go,   565
Laughed loud and long, and all the while
His eyes went to and fro.
'Ha! ha!' quoth he, 'full plain I see,
The Devil knows how to row.'

And now, all in my own countree,   570
I stood on the firm land!
The Hermit stepped forth from the boat,
And scarcely he could stand.

The ancient Mariner earnestly entreateth the Hermit to shrieve him; and the penance of life falls on him.

'O shrieve me, shrieve me, holy man!'
The Hermit crossed his brow.   575
'Say quick,' quoth he, 'I bid thee say—
What manner of man art thou?'

Forthwith this frame of mine was
        wrenched
With a woful agony,
Which forced me to begin my tale;   580
And then it left me free.

And ever and anon throughout his future life an agony constraineth him to travel from land to land,

Since then, at an uncertain hour,
That agony returns:
And till my ghastly tale is told,
This heart within me burns.   585

I pass, like night, from land to land;
I have strange power of speech;
That moment that his face I see,
I know the man that must hear me:
To him my tale I teach.   590

What loud uproar bursts from that door!
The wedding-guests are there:
But in the garden-bower the bride
And bride-maids singing are:
And hark the little vesper bell,   595
Which biddeth me to prayer!

O Wedding-Guest! this soul hath been
Alone on a wide, wide sea:
So lonely 'twas, that God himself
Scarce seemed there to be.   600

O sweeter than the marriage-feast,
'Tis sweeter far to me,
To walk together to the kirk
With a goodly company!—

To walk together to the kirk,   605
And all together pray,
While each to his great Father bends,
Old men, and babes, and loving friends
And youths and maidens gay!

and to teach,
by his own ex-
ample, love and
reverence
to all things
that God made
and loveth.

Farewell, farewell! but this I tell   610
To thee, thou Wedding-Guest!
He prayeth well, who loveth well
Both man and bird and beast.

He prayeth best, who loveth best
All things both great and small;   615
For the dear God who loveth us,
He made and loveth all.

The Mariner, whose eye is bright,
Whose beard with age is hoar,
620 Is gone: and now the Wedding-Guest
Turned from the bridegroom's door.

He went like one that hath been stunned,
And is of sense forlorn:
A sadder and a wiser man,
625 He rose the morrow morn.

THE GOOD GREAT MAN

(1802)

COMPLAINT

'How seldom, friend! a good great man inherits
Honour or wealth with all his worth and pains!
It sounds like stories from the land of spirits
If any man obtain that which he merits
5   Or any merit that which he obtains.'

REPLY

For shame, dear friend, renounce this canting
            strain!
What would'st thou have a good great man ob-
            tain?
Place? titles? salary? a gilded chain?
Or throne of corses which his sword had slain?
10 Greatness and goodness are not *means*, but *ends*!
Hath he not always treasures, always friends,
The good great man? *three* treasures, LOVE and
            LIGHT,
And CALM THOUGHTS, regular as infants' breath:
And three firm friends, more sure than day and
            night—
15 HIMSELF, his MAKER, and the ANGEL DEATH!

YOUTH AND AGE
(1822–1832)

Verse, a breeze mid blossoms straying,
Where Hope clung feeding, like a bee—
Both were mine! Life went a-maying
    With Nature, Hope, and Poesy,
5   When I was young!
When I was young?—Ah, woful When!
Ah! for the change 'twixt Now and Then!
This breathing house not built with hands,
This body that does me grievous wrong,
10 O'er aery cliffs and glittering sands,
How lightly *then* it flashed along:—
Like those trim skiffs, unknown of yore,
On winding lakes and rivers wide,
That ask no aid of sail or oar,
15 That fear no spite of wind or tide!
Nought cared this body for wind or weather
When Youth and I lived in't together.

Flowers are lovely; Love is flower-like;
Friendship is a sheltering tree;
20 O! the joys, that came down shower-like,
Of Friendship, Love, and Liberty,
    Ere I was old.

Ere I was old? Oh woful Ere,
Which tells me, Youth's no longer here!
25 O Youth! for years so many and sweet,
'Tis known, that Thou and I were one,
I'll think it but a fond conceit—
It cannot be that Thou art gone!
Thy vesper-bell hath not yet toll'd:—
30 And thou wert aye a masker bold!
What strange disguise hast now put on,
To *make believe*, that Thou art gone?

I see these locks in silvery slips,
This drooping gait, this altered size:
35 But Spring-tide blossoms on thy lips
And tears take sunshine from thine eyes!
Life is but thought: so think I will
That Youth and I are house-mates still.

Dew-drops are the gems of morning,
40 But the tears of mournful eve!
Where no hope is, life's a warning
That only serves to make us grieve,
    When we are old:
That only serves to make us grieve
45 With oft and tedious taking-leave,
Like some poor nigh-related guest,
That may not rudely be dismist;
Yet hath outstay'd his welcome while,
And tells the jest without the smile.

WORK WITHOUT HOPE

(February 21st, 1827)

All Nature seems at work. Slugs leave their
    lair—
The bees are stirring—birds are on the wing—
And Winter slumbering in the open air,
Wears on his smiling face a dream of Spring!
5 And I the while, the sole unbusy thing,
Nor honey make, nor pair, nor build, nor sing.
    Yet well I ken the banks where amaranths
      blow,
Have traced the fount whence streams of nectar
    flow.
Bloom, O ye amaranths! bloom for whom ye may,
10 For me ye bloom not! Glide, rich streams, away!
With lips unbrightened, wreathless brow, I stroll:

And would you learn the spells that drowse my
    soul?
Work without Hope draws nectar in a sieve,
And Hope without an object cannot live.

Robert Southey

1774–1843

THE BATTLE OF BLENHEIM

(Written at Westbury, 1798)

I.

It was a summer evening,
    Old Kaspar's work was done,
And he before his cottage door
    Was sitting in the sun,
5 And by him sported on the green
His little grandchild Wilhelmine.

II.

She saw her brother Peterkin
    Roll something large and round,
Which he beside the rivulet
10   In playing there had found;
He came to ask what he had found,
That was so large, and smooth, and round.

III.

Old Kaspar took it from the boy,
    Who stood expectant by;
15 And then the old man shook his head,
    And with a natural sigh,
" 'Tis some poor fellow's skull," said he,
" Who fell in the great victory.

IV.

"I find them in the garden,
20   For there's many hereabout;
And often when I go to plough,
    The ploughshare turns them out!
For many thousand men," said he,
"Were slain in that great victory."

V.

25 "Now tell us what 't was all about,"
    Young Peterkin, he cries;
And little Wilhelmine looks up
    With wonder-waiting eyes;
"Now tell us all about the war,
30 And what they fought each other for."

VI.

"It was the English," Kaspar cried,
    "Who put the French to rout;
But what they fought each other for,
    I could not well make out;
35 But every body said," quoth he,
    "That 'twas a famous victory.

VII.

"My father lived at Blenheim then,
    Yon little stream hard by;
They burnt his dwelling to the ground,
40   And he was forced to fly;
So with his wife and child he fled,
Nor had he where to rest his head.

VIII.

"With fire and sword the country round
    Was wasted far and wide,
45 And many a childing mother then

And new-born baby died;
But things like that, you know, must be
At every famous victory.

IX.

"They say it was a shocking sight
50   After the field was won;
For many thousand bodies here
    Lay rotting in the sun;
But things like that, you know, must be
After a famous victory.

X.

55 "Great praise the Duke of Marlboro' won,
    And our good Prince Eugene."
"Why 'twas a very wicked thing!"
    Said little Wilhelmine.
    "Nay . . nay . . my little girl," quoth he,
60 "It was a famous victory.

XI.

"And every body praised the Duke
    Who this great fight did win."
"But what good came of it at last?"
    Quoth little Peterkin.
65 "Why that I cannot tell," said he,
"But 'twas a famous victory."

MY DAYS AMONG THE DEAD ARE PAST

(Written at Keswick, 1818)

I.

My days among the Dead are past;
    Around me I behold,
Where'er these casual eyes are cast,

The mighty minds of old;
5 My never-failing friends are they,
With whom I converse day by day.

II.

With them I take delight in weal,
　　And seek relief in woe;
And while I understand and feel
10　　How much to them I owe,
My cheeks have often been bedew'd
With tears of thoughtful gratitude.

III.

My thoughts are with the Dead; with them
　　I live in long-past years;
15 Their virtues love, their faults condemn,
　　Partake their hopes and fears,
And from their lessons seek and find
Instruction with an humble mind.

IV.

My hopes are with the Dead; anon
20　　My place with them will be,
And I with them shall travel on
　　Through all Futurity:
Yet leaving here a name, I trust,
That will not perish in the dust.

Joseph Blanco White

1775-1841

SONNET TO NIGHT

(First published 1828)

Mysterious Night! when our first parent knew
Thee by report Divine, and heard thy name,
Did he not tremble for this goodly frame,
This glorious canopy of light and blue?
5 But through a curtain of translucent dew,
Bathed in the hues of the great setting flame,
Hesperus with the Host of Heaven came,
And lo! creation broadened to man's view.
Who could have guessed such darkness lay con-
      cealed
10 Within thy beams, O Sun! or who divined
Whilst bud, and flower, and insect stood revealed,
Thou to such countless worlds hadst made us
      blind?
Why should we, then, shun death with anxious
      strife,
If Light conceals so much, wherefore not Life?

Sir Walter Scott

1771-1832

HAROLD'S SONG TO ROSABELLE

(From *Lay of the Last Minstrel*)

CANTO VI.–XXIII.

(1805)

" O listen, listen, ladies gay!
      No haughty feat of arms I tell;
Soft is the note, and sad the lay,
      That mourns the lovely Rosabelle.

5 " Moor, moor the barge, ye gallant crew!
    And, gentle ladye, deign to stay!
Rest thee in Castle Ravensheuch,
    Nor tempt the stormy firth to-day.

" The blackening wave is edged with white;
10   To inch and rock the sea-mews fly;
The fishers have heard the Water-Sprite,
    Whose screams forebode that wreck is nigh.

" Last night the gifted Seer did view
    A wet shrowd swathed round ladye gay;
15 Then stay thee, Fair, in Ravensheuch:
    Why cross the gloomy firth to-day?"—

" 'Tis not because Lord Lindesay's heir
    To-night at Roslin leads the ball,
But that my ladye-mother there
20   Sits lonely in her castle-hall.

" 'Tis not because the ring they ride,
    And Lindesay at the ring rides well,
But that my sire the wine will chide,
    If 'tis not fill'd by Rosabelle.—"

25 O'er Roslin all that dreary night,
    A wondrous blaze was seen to gleam;
'Twas broader than the watch-fire's light,
    And redder than the bright moonbeam.

It glared on Roslin's castled rock,
30   It ruddied all the copse-wood glen;
'Twas seen from Dryden's groves of oak,
    And seen from cavern'd Hawthornden.

Seem'd all on fire that chapel proud,
    Where Roslin's chiefs uncoffin'd lie,
35 Each Baron, for a sable shroud,
    Sheathed in his iron panoply.

Seem'd all on fire within, around,
　　Deep sacristy and altar's pale;
Shone every pillar foliage-bound,
40　　And glimmer'd all the dead men's mail.

Blazed battlement and pinnet high,
　　Blazed every rose-carved buttress fair—
So still they blaze, when fate is nigh
　　The lordly line of high St. Clair.

45 There are twenty of Roslin's barons bold
　　Lie buried within that proud chapelle;
Each one the holy vault doth hold—
　　But the sea holds lovely Rosabelle!

And each St. Clair was buried there,
50　　With candle, with book, and with knell;
But the sea-caves rung, and the wild winds sung,
　　The dirge of lovely Rosabelle.

BALLAD

ALICE BRAND

(From *The Lady of the Lake*, 1810)

CANTO IV.

XII.

Merry it is in the good greenwood,
　　When the mavis and merle are singing,
When the deer sweeps by, and the hounds are in
　　　　cry,
　　And the hunter's horn is ringing.

5 "O Alice Brand, my native land
　　Is lost for love of you;
And we must hold by wood and wold,
　　As outlaws wont to do.

" O Alice, 'twas all for thy locks so bright,
10   And 'twas all for thine eyes so blue,
That on the night of our luckless flight,
    Thy brother bold I slew.

" Now must I teach to hew the beech
    The hand that held the glave,
15 For leaves to spread our lowly bed,
    And stakes to fence our cave.

" And for vest of pall, thy fingers small,
    That wont on harp to stray,
A cloak must shear from the slaughter'd deer,
20   To keep the cold away."——

" O Richard! if my brother died,
    'Twas but a fatal chance;
For darkling was the battle tried,
    And fortune sped the lance.

25 " If pall and vair no more I wear,
    Nor thou the crimson sheen,
As warm, we'll say, is the russet grey,
    As gay the forest green.

" And, Richard, if our lot be hard,
30   And lost thy native land,
Still Alice has her own Richard,
    And he his Alice Brand."

XIII.

'Tis merry, 'tis merry, in good greenwood,
    So blithe Lady Alice is singing;
35 On the beech's pride, and oak's brown side,
    Lord Richard's axe is ringing.

Up spoke the moody Elfin King,
　　Who won'd within the hill,—
Like wind in the porch of a ruin'd church,
40　　His voice was ghostly shrill.

" Why sounds yon stroke on beech and oak,
　　Our moonlight circle's screen?
Or who comes here to chase the deer,
　　Beloved of our Elfin Queen?
45 Or who may dare on wold to wear
　　The fairies' fatal green?

" Up, Urgan, up! to yon mortal hie,
　　For thou wert christen'd man;
For cross or sign thou wilt not fly,
50　　For mutter'd word or ban.

" Lay on him the curse of the wither'd heart,
　　The curse of the sleepless eye;
Till he wish and pray that his life would part,
　　Nor yet find leave to die."

XIV.

55 'Tis merry, 'tis merry, in good greenwood,
　　Though the birds have still'd their singing;
The evening blaze doth Alice raise,
　　And Richard is fagots bringing.

Up Urgan starts, that hideous dwarf,
60　　Before Lord Richard stands,
And, as he cross'd and bless'd himself,
" I fear not sign," quoth the grisly elf,
　　" That is made with bloody hands."

But out then spoke she, Alice Brand,
65　　That woman void of fear,—
" And if there's blood upon his hand,
　　'Tis but the blood of deer."—

"Now loud thou liest, thou bold of mood!
  It cleaves unto his hand,
70 The stain of thine own kindly blood,
  The blood of Ethert Brand."

Then forward stepp'd she, Alice Brand,
  And made the holy sign,—
"And if there's blood on Richard's hand,
75 A spotless hand is mine.

"And I conjure thee, Demon elf,
  By Him whom Demons fear,
To show us whence thou art thyself,
  And what thine errand here?"—

xv.

80 "'Tis merry, 'tis merry, in Fairy-land,
  When fairy birds are singing,
When the court doth ride by their monarch's side,
  With bit and bridle ringing:

"And gaily shines the Fairy-land—
85 But all is glistening show,
Like the idle gleam that December's beam
  Can dart on ice and snow.

"And fading, like that varied gleam,
  Is our inconstant shape,
90 Who now like knight and lady seem,
  And now like dwarf and ape.

"It was between the night and day,
  When the Fairy King has power,
That I sunk down in a sinful fray,
95 And, 'twixt life and death, was snatch'd away,
  To the joyless Elfin bower.

"But wist I of a woman bold,
　　Who thrice my brow durst sign,
I might regain my mortal mold,
100　　As fair a form as thine."

She cross'd him once—she cross'd him twice—
　　That lady was so brave;
The fouler grew his goblin hue,
　　The darker grew the cave.

105　She cross'd him thrice, that lady bold;
　　He rose beneath her hand
The fairest knight on Scottish mold,
　　Her brother, Ethert Brand!

Merry it is in good greenwood,
110　　When the mavis and merle are singing,
But merrier were they in Dunfermeline gray
　　When all the bells were ringing.

EDMUND'S SONG

(From *Rokeby*, 1812)

CANTO III. XVI.

O, Brignall banks are wild and fair,
　　And Greta woods are green,
And you may gather garlands there,
　　Would grace a summer queen.
5　And as I rode by Dalton-hall,
　　Beneath the turrets high,
A Maiden on the castle wall
　　Was singing merrily,—

CHORUS

"O, Brignall banks are fresh and fair,
10　　And Greta woods are green;
I'd rather rove with Edmund there,
　　Than reign our English queen."—

"If, maiden, thou wouldst wend with me,
      To leave both tower and town,
15 Thou first must guess what life lead we,
      That dwell by dale and down?
And if thou canst that riddle read,
      As read full well you may,
Then to the greenwood shalt thou speed,
20   As blithe as Queen of May."—

CHORUS

Yet sung she, "Brignall banks are fair,
      And Greta woods are green;
I'd rather rove with Edmund there,
      Than reign our English queen.

25 "I read you, by your bugle-horn,
      And by your palfrey good,
I read you for a Ranger sworn,
      To keep the king's greenwood.—
"A Ranger, lady, winds his horn,
30   And 'tis at peep of light;
His blast is heard at merry morn,
      And mine at dead of night."—

CHORUS

Yet sung she, "Brignall banks are fair,
      And Greta woods are gay;
35 I would I were with Edmund there,
      To reign his Queen of May!

"With burnish'd brand and musketoon,
      So gallantly you come,
I read you for a bold dragoon,
40   That lists the tuck of drum."—

"I list no more the tuck of drum,
　No more the trumpet hear;
But when the beetle sounds his hum,
　My comrades take the spear.

CHORUS

45 "And, O! though Brignall banks be fair,
　And Greta woods be gay,
Yet mickle must the maiden dare,
　Would reign my Queen of May!

"Maiden! a nameless life I lead,
50　A nameless death I'll die;
The fiend, whose lantern lights the mead,
Were better mate than I!
And when I'm with my comrades met,
　Beneath the greenwood bough,
55 What once we were we all forget,
　Nor think what we are now.

CHORUS

"Yet Brignall banks are fresh and fair,
　And Greta woods are green,
And you may gather garlands there
60　Would grace a summer queen."—

SONG

A WEARY LOT IS THINE

(From the same)

CANTO III. XXVIII.

"A weary lot is thine, fair maid,
　A weary lot is thine!
To pull the thorn thy brow to braid,
　And press the rue for wine!

5 A lightsome eye, a soldier's mien,
 A feather of the blue,
A doublet of the Lincoln green,—
 No more of me you knew
  My love!
10 No more of me you knew.

 "This morn is merry June, I trow,
  The rose is budding fain;
 But she shall bloom in winter snow,
  Ere we two meet again."
15 He turn'd his charger as he spake,
  Upon the river shore,
 He gave his bridle-reins a shake,
  Said, "Adieu forever more,
   My love!
20 And adieu forever more."—

SONG

ALLAN-A-DALE

(From the same)

CANTO III. XXX.

Allan-a-Dale has no faggots for burning,
Allan-a-Dale has no furrow for turning,
Allan-a-Dale has no fleece for the spinning,
Yet Allan-a-Dale has red gold for the winning.
5 Come, read me my riddle! come, harken my tale!
And tell me the craft of bold Allan-a-Dale.

The Baron of Ravensworth prances in pride,
And he views his domains upon Arkindale side.
The mere for his net, and the land for his game,
10 The chase for the wild, and the park for the
  tame;
Yet the fish of the lake, and the deer of the vale,
Are less free to Lord Dacre than Allan-a-Dale!

Allan-a-Dale was ne'er belted a knight,
Though his spur be as sharp, and his blade be as
    bright;
15 Allan-a-Dale is no baron or lord,
Yet twenty tall yeoman will draw at his word;
And the best of our nobles his bonnet will vail,
Who at Rere-cross on Stanmore meets Allan-a-
    Dale.

Allan-a-Dale to his wooing is come;
20 The mother, she ask'd of his household and home:
"Though the castle of Richmond stand fair on
    the hill,
My hall," quoth bold Allan, "shows gallanter
    still;
'Tis the blue vault of heaven, with its crescent
    so pale,
And with all its bright spangles!" said Allan-a-
    Dale.

25 The father was steel, and the mother was stone;
They lifted the latch, and they bade him begone;
But loud, on the morrow, their wail and their
    cry:
He has laugh'd on the lass with his bonny black
    eye,
And she fled to the forest to hear a love-tale,
30 And the youth it was told by was Allan-a-Dale!

SONG

THE CAVALIER

(From the same)

CANTO V. XX

While the dawn on the mountain was misty and
    gray,
My true love has mounted his steed and away,

Over hill, over valley, o'er dale, and o'er down;
Heaven shield the brave Gallant that fights for
the Crown!

5 He has doff'd the silk doublet the breast-plate to
bear,
He has placed the steel-cap o'er his long flowing
hair,
From his belt to his stirrup his broadsword hangs
down,—
Heaven shield the brave Gallant that fights for
the Crown!

For the rights of fair England that broadsword
he draws;
10 Her King is his leader, her Church is his cause;
His watchword is honour, his pay is renown,—
God strike with the Gallant that strikes for
the Crown!

They may boast of their Fairfax, their Waller,
and all
The round-headed rebels of Westminster Hall;
15 But tell those bold traitors of London's proud
town,
That the spears of the North have encircled the
Crown.

There's Derby and Cavendish, dread of their
foes;
There's Erin's high Ormond, and Scotland's
Montrose!
Would you match the base Skippon, and Massey,
and Brown,
20 With the Barons of England, that fight for the
Crown?

Now joy to the crest of the brave Cavalier!
Be his banner unconquer'd, resistless his spear,
Till in peace and in triumph his toils he may
    drown,
In a pledge to fair England, her Church, and her
    Crown.

HUNTING SONG

(1808)

Waken, lords and ladies gay,
  On the mountain dawns the day;
  All the jolly chase is here
  With hawk, and horse, and hunting-spear;
5 Hounds are in their couples yelling,
  Hawks are whistling, horns are knelling,
  Merrily, merrily, mingle they,
      "Waken, lords and ladies gay."

Waken, lords and ladies gay,
10 The mist has left the mountain gray,
  Springlets in the dawn are steaming,
  Diamonds on the brake are gleaming;
  And foresters have busy been
  To track the buck in thicket green;
15 Now we come to chant our lay,
      "Waken, lords and ladies gay."

Waken, lords and ladies gay,
  To the green-wood haste away;
  We can show you where he lies,
20 Fleet of foot, and tall of size;
  We can show the marks he made,
  When 'gainst the oak his antlers frayed;
  You shall see him brought to bay,
      "Waken, lords and ladies gay."

25 Louder, louder chant the lay,
   Waken, lords and ladies gay!
Tell them youth, and mirth, and glee,
Run a course as well as we;
Time, stern huntsman! who can baulk,
30 Stanch as hound, and fleet as hawk;
Think of this, and rise with day,
   Gentle lords and ladies gay.

JOCK OF HAZELDEAN

(1816)

I.

   "Why weep ye by the tide, ladie?
   Why weep ye by the tide?
I'll wed ye to my youngest son,
   And ye sall be his bride:
5 And ye sall be his bride, ladie,
   Sae comely to be seen"—
But aye she loot the tears down fa'
   For Jock of Hazeldean.

II.

   "Now let this wilfu' grief be done,
10   And dry that cheek so pale;
Young Frank is chief of Errington
   And lord of Langley-dale;
His step is first in peaceful ha',
   His sword in battle keen"—
15 But aye she loot the tears down fa'
   For Jock of Hazeldean.

III.

   "A chain of gold ye sall not lack,
   Nor braid to bind your hair;
Nor mettled hound, nor managed hawk,
20   Nor palfrey fresh and fair;

And you, the foremost of them a',
　　Shall ride our forest-queen "—
But aye she loot the tears down fa'
　　For Jock of Hazeldean.

IV.

25　　The kirk was deck'd at morning-tide,
　　　The tapers glimmered fair;
The priest and bridegroom wait the bride
　　　And dame and knight are there:
They sought her baith by bower and ha';
30　　The ladie was not seen!
She's o'er the border and awa'
　　Wi' Jock of Hazeldean.

MADGE WILDFIRE'S SONG

(From *The Heart of Midlothian*, 1818)

" Proud Maisie is in the wood,
　　Walking so early;
Sweet Robin sits on the bush,
　　Singing so rarely.

5　" ' Tell me, thou bonny bird,
　　When shall I marry me? '
' When six braw gentlemen
　　Kirkward shall carry ye.'

　　　.　　.　　.　　.　　.

" ' Who makes the bridal bed,
10　　Birdie, say truly? '—
' The grey-headed sexton,
　　That delves the grave duly.

　　　.　　.　　.　　.

The glow-worm o'er grave and stone
 Shall light thee steady;
15 The owl from the steeple sing,
 'Welcome, proud lady.'"

BORDER BALLAD

(From *The Monastery*, 1820)

I.

March, march, Ettrick and Teviotdale,
 Why the deil dinna ye march forward in order?
March, march, Eskdale and Liddesdale,
 All the Blue Bonnets are bound for the Border.
5 Many a banner spread,
  Flutters above your head,
 Many a crest that is famous in story;
  Mount and make ready then,
  Sons of the mountain glen,
10 Fight for the Queen and the old Scottish glory!

II.

Come from the hills where the hirsels are graz-
   ing,
 Come from the glen of the buck and the roe;
Come to the crag where the beacon is blazing,
 Come with the buckler, the lance, and the bow.
15 Trumpets are sounding,
  War-steeds are bounding,
Stand to your arms then, and march in good
   order;
  England shall many a day
  Tell of the bloody fray,
20 When the Blue Bonnets came over the Border!

COUNTY GUY

(From *Quentin Durward*, 1823)

" Ah! County Guy, the hour is nigh,
　　The sun has left the lea,
The orange-flower perfumes the bower,
　　The breeze is on the sea.
5 The lark, his lay who thrill'd all day,
　　Sits hush'd his partner nigh;
Breeze, bird, and flower, confess the hour,
　　But where is County Guy?

" The village maid steals through the shade,
10　　Her shepherd's suit to hear;
To beauty shy, by lattice high,
　　Sings high-born Cavalier.
The star of Love, all stars above,
　　Now reigns o'er earth and sky;
15 And high and low the influence know—
　　But where is County Guy?"

Thomas Campbell

1777–1844

YE MARINERS OF ENGLAND

(1800)

Ye mariners of England
That guard our native seas,
Whose flag has braved a thousand years
The battle and the breeze!
5 Your glorious standard launch again
To match another foe,
And sweep through the deep,

While the stormy winds do blow;
While the battle rages loud and long,
10 And the stormy winds do blow.

The spirits of your fathers
Shall start from every wave!—
For the deck it was their field of fame,
And Ocean was their grave:
15 Where Blake and mighty Nelson fell
Your manly hearts shall glow,
As ye sweep through the deep,
While the stormy winds do blow;
While the battle rages loud and long,
20 And the stormy winds do blow.

Britannia needs no bulwark,
No towers along the steep;
Her march is o'er the mountain waves,
Her home is on the deep.
25 With thunders from her native oak
She quells the floods below—
As they roar on the shore,
Where the stormy winds do blow;
When the battle rages loud and long,
30 And the stormy winds do blow.

The meteor flag of England
Shall yet terrific burn,
Till danger's troubled night depart
And the star of peace return.
35 Then, then, ye ocean warriors!
Our song and feast shall flow
To the fame of your name,
When the storm has ceased to blow;
When the fiery fight is heard no more,
40 And the storm has ceased to blow.

HOHENLINDEN

(1802)

On Linden, when the sun was low,
All bloodless lay th' untrodden snow,
And dark as winter was the flow
  Of Iser, rolling rapidly.

5 But Linden saw another sight,
When the drum beat at dead of night,
Commanding fires of death to light
  The darkness of her scenery.

By torch and trumpet fast arrayed,
10 Each horseman drew his battle blade,
And furious every charger neighed,
  To join the dreadful revelry.

Then shook the hills with thunder riven,
Then rushed the steed to battle driven,
15 And louder than the bolts of heaven,
  Far flashed the red artillery.

But redder yet that light shall glow,
On Linden's hills of stainèd snow,
And bloodier yet the torrent flow
20   Of Iser, rolling rapidly.

'Tis morn, but scarce yon level sun
Can pierce the war-clouds, rolling dun,
Where furious Frank, and fiery Hun,
  Shout in their sulphurous canopy.

25 The combat deepens. On, ye brave,
Who rush to glory, or the grave!
Wave, Munich! all thy banners wave,
  And charge with all thy chivalry!

Few, few, shall part where many meet!
30 The snow shall be their winding sheet,
   And every turf beneath their feet
      Shall be a soldier's sepulchre.

BATTLE OF THE BALTIC
(1809)

Of Nelson and the North
Sing the glorious day's renown,
When to battle fierce came forth
All the might of Denmark's crown,
5 And her arms along the deep proudly shone;
By each gun the lighted brand
In a bold determin'd hand,
And the Prince of all the land
Led them on.

10 Like leviathans afloat
Lay their bulwarks on the brine,
While the sign of battle flew
On the lofty British line:
It was ten of April morn by the chime;
15 As they drifted on their path,
There was silence deep as death,
And the boldest held his breath
For a time.

But the might of England flushed
20 To anticipate the scene,
And her van the fleeter rushed
O'er the deadly space between—
"Hearts of oak," our captains cried, when each
      gun
From its adamantine lips
25 Spread a death-shade round the ships,
Like the hurricane eclipse
Of the sun.

Again! again! again!
And the havoc did not slack,
30 Till a feeble cheer the Dane
To our cheering sent us back;—
Their shots along the deep slowly boom:—
Then ceased—and all is wail,
As they strike the shattered sail,
35 Or in conflagration pale
Light the gloom.

Out spoke the victor then,
As he hailed them o'er the wave;
"Ye are brothers! ye are men!
40 And we conquer but to save;
So peace instead of death let us bring:
But yield, proud foe, thy fleet
With the crews, at England's feet,
And make submission meet
45 To our King."

Then Denmark blest our chief,
That he gave her wounds repose;
And the sounds of joy and grief,
From her people wildly rose,
50 As death withdrew his shades from the day;
While the sun looked smiling bright
O'er a wide and woeful sight,
Where the fires of funeral light
Died away.

55 Now joy, old England, raise
For the tidings of thy might,
By the festal cities' blaze,
While the wine cup shines in light;
And yet amidst that joy and uproar,

60 Let us think of them that sleep,
   Full many a fathom deep,
   By thy wild and stormy steep,
   Elsinore!

   Brave hearts! to Britain's pride
65 Once so faithful and so true,
   On the deck of fame that died,
   With the gallant good Riou,
   Soft sigh the winds of heaven o'er their grave!
   While the billow mournful rolls,
70 And the mermaid's song condoles,
   Singing glory to the souls
   Of the brave!

SONG

"MEN OF ENGLAND"

Men of England! who inherit
   Rights that cost your sires their blood,
Men whose undegenerate spirit
   Has been proved on land and flood:

5 By the foes ye've fought uncounted,
   By the glorious deeds ye've done,
Trophies captured—breaches mounted,
   Navies conquered—kingdoms won!

Yet, remember, England gathers
10   Hence but fruitless wreaths of fame,
If the patriotism of your fathers
   Glow not in your hearts the same.

What are monuments of bravery,
   Where no public virtues bloom?
15 What avail in lands of slavery,
   Trophied temples, arch and tomb?

Pageants!—Let the world revere us
  For our people's rights and laws,
And the breasts of civic heroes
20   Bared in Freedom's holy cause.

Yours are Hampden's, Russell's glory,
  Sydney's matchless fame is yours,—
Martyrs in heroic story,
  Worth a hundred Agincourts!

25 We're the sons of sires that baffled
  Crowned and mitred tyranny:
They defied the field and scaffold
  For their birthrights—so will we!

SONG

TO THE EVENING STAR

Star that bringest home the bee,
And sett'st the weary labourer free!
If any star shed peace, 'tis thou,
  That send'st it from above,
5 Appearing when Heaven's breath and brow,
  Are sweet as her's we love.

Come to the luxuriant skies,
Whilst the landscape's odours rise,
Whilst far-off lowing herds are heard,
10   And songs, when toil is done,
From cottages whose smoke unstirred
  Curls yellow in the sun.

Star of love's soft interviews,
Parted lovers on thee muse;
15 Their remembrancer in Heaven
  Of thrilling vows thou art,
Too delicious to be riven
  By absence from the heart.

Thomas Moore

1779-1852

AS SLOW OUR SHIP
(From *Irish Melodies*, 1807-1834)

As slow our ship her foamy track
    Against the wind was cleaving,
Her trembling pennant still look'd back
    To that dear isle 'twas leaving.
5 So loath we part from all we love,
    From all the links that bind us;
So turn our hearts, where'er we rove,
    To those we've left behind us!

When, round the bowl, of vanish'd years
10   We talk, with joyous seeming,
And smiles that might as well be tears,
    So faint, so sad their beaming;
While mem'ry brings us back again
    Each early tie that twin'd us,
15 Oh, sweet's the cup that circles then
    To those we've left behind us!

And, when in other climes we meet
    Some isle or vale enchanting,
Where all looks flow'ry, mild and sweet,
20   And nought but love is wanting;
We think how great had been our bliss,
    If Heav'n had but assign'd us
To live and die in scenes like this,
    With some we've left behind us!

25 As trav'llers oft look back at eve,
    When eastward darkly going,
To gaze upon the light they leave
    Still faint behind them glowing—

So, when the close of pleasure's day
30　To gloom hath near consign'd us,
We turn to catch one fading ray
　Of joy that's left behind us.

THE HARP THAT ONCE THROUGH TARA'S HALLS

(From the same)

The harp that once, through Tara's Halls
　The soul of music shed,
Now hangs as mute on Tara's walls,
　As if that soul were fled:—
5 So sleeps the pride of former days,
　So glory's thrill is o'er;
And hearts, that once beat high for praise,
　Now feel that pulse no more!

No more to chiefs and ladies bright
10　The harp of Tara swells;
The chord, alone, that breaks the night,
　Its tale of ruin tells:—
Thus freedom now so seldom wakes,
　The only throb she gives
15 Is when some heart indignant breaks,
　To show that still she lives!

George Gordon Byron

1788-1824

STANZAS FOR MUSIC

(1815)

> " O Lachrymarum fons, tenero sacros
>   Ducentium ortus ex animo : quater
>   Felix! in imo qui scatentem
>   Pectore te, pia Nympha, sensit."
>   —*Gray's Poemata.*

I.

There's not a joy the world can give like that it takes
        away,
When the glow of early thought declines in feeling's
        dull decay;
'Tis not on youth's smooth cheek the blush alone, which
        fades so fast,
But the tender bloom of heart is gone, e'er youth itself
        be past.

II.

Then the few whose spirits float above the wreck of
        happiness   5
Are driven o'er the shoals of guilt or ocean of excess:
The magnet of their course is gone, or only points in
        vain
The shore to which their shiver'd sail shall never
        stretch again.

III.

Then the mortal coldness of the soul like death itself
        comes down;
It cannot feel for others' woes, it dare not dream its
        own;   10

That heavy chill has frozen o'er the fountain of our
  tears,
And though the eye may sparkle still, 'tis where the ice
  appears.

IV.

Though wit may flash from fluent lips, and mirth dis-
  tract the breast,
Through midnight hours that yield no more their
   former hope of rest;   14
'Tis but as ivy leaves around the ruin'd turret wreath,
All green and wildly fresh without, but worn and **gray**
  beneath.

V.

Oh could I feel as I have felt,—or be what I have been,
Or weep as I could once have wept o'er many a vanish'd scene:
As springs in deserts found seem sweet, all brackish
  though they be,
So midst the wither'd waste of life, those tears would
  flow to me.   20

SHE WALKS IN BEAUTY

(From *Hebrew Melodies*, 1815)

I.

She walks in beauty, like the night
 Of cloudless climes and starry skies;
And all that's best of dark and bright
 Meet in her aspect and her eyes:
5 Thus mellow'd to that tender light
 Which heaven to gaudy day denies.

II.

One shade the more, one ray the less,
　　Had half impair'd the nameless grace
Which waves in every raven tress,
10　　Or softly lightens o'er her face;
　　Where thoughts serenely sweet express
　　How pure, how dear, their dwelling-place.

III.

And on that cheek, and o'er that brow,
　　So soft, so calm, yet eloquent,
15 The smiles that win, the tints that glow,
　　But tell of days in goodness spent,
A mind at peace with all below,
　　A heart whose love is innocent!

SONNET ON CHILLON

(Introduction to *The Prisoner of Chillon*)

(1816)

Eternal spirit of the chainless mind!
　　Brightest in dungeons, Liberty! thou art,
　　For there thy habitation is the heart—
　　The heart which love of thee alone can bind;
And when thy sons to fetters are consign'd—　　5
　　To fetters, and the damp vault's dayless gloom
　　Their country conquers with their martyrdom,
　　And Freedom's fame finds wings on every wind.
Chillon! thy prison is a holy place,
　　And thy sad floor an altar—for 'twas trod,　　10
　　Until his very steps have left a trace
Worn, as if thy cold pavement were a sod,
　　By Bonnivard!—May none those marks efface!
　　For they appeal from tyranny to God.

CHILDE HAROLD'S PILGRIMAGE

(1816)

CANTO III.

III.

In my youth's summer I did sing of One,
The wandering outlaw of his own dark mind;   20
Again I seize the theme, then but begun,
And bear it with me, as the rushing wind
Bears the cloud onwards: in that Tale I find
The furrows of long thought, and dried-up tears,
Which, ebbing, leave a sterile track behind,   25
O'er which all heavily the journeying years
Plod the last sands of life,—where not a flower appears.

.   .   .   .

VIII.

Something too much of this:—but now 'tis past,
And the spell closes with its silent seal.   65
Long absent Harold re-appears at last;
He of the breast which fain no more would feel,
Wrung with the wounds which kill not, but ne'er
    heal;
Yet Time, who changes all, had altered him
In soul and aspect as in age: years steal   70
Fire from the mind as vigour from the limb;
And life's enchanted cup but sparkles near the brim.

IX.

His had been quaff'd too quickly, and he found
The dregs were wormwood; but he fill'd again,
And from a purer fount, on holier ground,   75
And deem'd its spring perpetual; but in vain!
Still round him clung invisibly a chain

Which gall'd forever, fettering though unseen,
And heavy though it clank'd not; worn with pain,
Which pined although it spoke not, and grew keen,
Entering with every step he took through many a
    scene.   81

.   .   .   .

XII.

But soon he knew himself the most unfit   100
Of men to herd with Man; with whom he held
Little in common; untaught to submit
His thoughts to others, though his soul was quell'd
In youth by his own thoughts; still uncompell'd,
He would not yield dominion of his mind   105
To spirits against whom his own rebell'd;
Proud though in desolation; which could find
A life within itself, to breathe without mankind.

XIII.

Where rose the mountains, there to him were friends;
Where roll'd the ocean, thereon was his home;   110
Where a blue sky, and glowing clime, extends,
He had the passion and the power to roam;
The desert, forest, cavern, breaker's foam,
Were unto him companionship; they spake
A mutual language, clearer than the tome   115
Of his land's tongue, which he would oft forsake
For Nature's pages glass'd by sunbeams on the lake.

XIV.

Like the Chaldean, he could watch the stars,
Till he had peopled them with beings bright
As their own beams; and earth, and earth-born jars,
And human frailties, were forgotten quite: 121
Could he have kept his spirit to that flight

He had been happy; but this clay will sink
Its spark immortal, envying it the light
To which it mounts, as if to break the link   125
That keeps us from yon heaven which woos us to its
        brink.

XV.

But in Man's dwellings he became a thing
Restless and worn, and stern and wearisome,
Droop'd as a wild-born falcon with clipt wing,
To whom the boundless air alone were home: 130
Then came his fit again, which to o'ercome,
As eagerly the barr'd-up bird will beat
His breast and beak against his wiry dome
Till the blood tinge his plumage, so the heat
Of his impeded soul would through his bosom eat. 135

XVI.

Self-exiled Harold wanders forth again,
With naught of hope left, but with less of gloom;
The very knowledge that he lived in vain,
That all was over on this side the tomb,
Had made Despair a smilingness assume,   140
Which, though 'twere wild,—as on the plunder'd
        wreck
When mariners would madly meet their doom
With draughts intemperate on the sinking deck,—
Did yet inspire a cheer, which he forbore to check.

    .   .   .   .

XVIII.

And Harold stands upon this place of skulls,
The grave of France, the deadly Waterloo;   155
How in an hour the power which gave annuls
Its gifts, transferring fame as fleeting too!
In "pride of place" here last the eagle flew,

Then tore with bloody talon the rent plain,
Pierced by the shaft of banded nations through;   160
Ambition's life and labours all were vain;
He wears the shatter'd links of the world's broken
    chain.

.   .   .   .   .   .

XXI.

There was a sound of revelry by night,
And Belgium's capital had gather'd then
Her Beauty and her Chivalry, and bright
The lamps shone o'er fair women and brave men;
A thousand hearts beat happily; and when   185
Music arose with its voluptuous swell,
Soft eyes look'd love to eyes which spake again,
And all went merry as a marriage-bell;
But hush! hark! a deep sound strikes like a rising
    knell!

XXII.

Did ye not hear it?—No; 'twas but the wind,   190
Or the car rattling o'er the stony street;
On with the dance! let joy be unconfined;
No sleep till morn, when Youth and Pleasure meet
To chase the glowing Hours with flying feet—
But, Hark!—that heavy sound breaks in once more
As if the clouds its echo would repeat;   196
And nearer, clearer, deadlier than before!
Arm! Arm! it is—it is—the cannon's opening roar!

XXIII.

Within a window'd niche of that high hall
Sate Brunswick's fated chieftain; he did hear   200
That sound the first amidst the festival,
And caught its tone with Death's prophetic ear;
And when they smiled because he deem'd it near,

His heart more truly knew that peal too well
Which stretch'd his father on a bloody bier,   205
And roused the vengeance blood alone could quell:
He rush'd into the field, and, foremost fighting, fell.

XXIV.

Ah! then and there was hurrying to and fro,
And gathering tears, and tremblings of distress,
And cheeks all pale, which but an hour ago   210
Blush'd at the praise of their own loveliness;
And there were sudden partings, such as press
The life from out young hearts, and choking sighs
Which ne'er might be repeated; who could guess
If ever more should meet those mutual eyes,   215
Since upon night so sweet such awful morn could rise?

XXV.

And there was mounting in hot haste: the steed,
The mustering squadron, and the clattering car,
Went pouring forward with impetuous speed,
And swiftly forming in the ranks of war;   220
And the deep thunder peal on peal afar;
And near, the beat of the alarming drum
Roused up the soldier ere the morning star;
While throng'd the citizens with terror dumb,
Or whispering, with white lips—"The foe! They
come! they come!"   225

XXVI.

And wild and high the "Cameron's gathering" rose!
The war-note of Lochiel, which Albyn's hills
Have heard, and heard, too, have her Saxon foes:—
How in the noon of night that pibroch thrills,   229
Savage and shrill! But with the breath which fills

Their mountain-pipe, so fill the mountaineers
With the fierce native daring which instils
The stirring memory of a thousand years,
And Evan's, Donald's fame rings in each clansmen's
ears!

XXVII.

And Ardennes waves above them her green leaves,
Dewy with nature's tear-drops, as they pass,   236
Grieving, if aught inanimate e'er grieves,
Over the unreturning brave,—alas!
Ere evening to be trodden like the grass
Which now beneath them, but above shall grow 240
In its next verdure, when this fiery mass
Of living valour, rolling on the foe
And burning with high hope, shall moulder cold and
low.

XXVIII.

Last noon beheld them full of lusty life,
Last eve in Beauty's circle proudly gay,   245
The midnight brought the signal-sound of strife,
The morn the marshalling in arms,—the day
Battle's magnificently-stern array!
The thunder-clouds close o'er it, which when rent
The earth is cover'd thick with other clay,   250
Which her own clay shall cover, heap'd and pent,
Rider and horse,—friend, foe,—in one red burial
blent!

.   .   .   .   .   .

LXXXV.

Clear, placid Leman! thy contrasted lake,
With the wild world I dwell in, is a thing
Which warns me, with its stillness, to forsake
Earth's troubled waters for a purer spring.   760
This quiet sail is as a noiseless wing

To waft me from distraction; once I loved
Torn ocean's roar, but thy soft murmuring
  Sounds sweet as if a sister's voice reproved,
That I with stern delights should e'er have been so
      moved.   765

LXXXVI.

It is the hush of night, and all between
Thy margin and the mountains, dusk, yet clear,
Mellow'd and mingling, yet distinctly seen,
Save darken'd Jura, whose capt heights appear
Precipitously steep; and drawing near,   770
There breathes a living fragrance from the shore,
Of flowers yet fresh with childhood; on the ear
Drops the light drip of the suspended oar,
Or chirps the grasshopper one good-night carol more;

LXXXVII.

He is an evening reveller, who makes   775
His life an infancy, and sings his fill;
At intervals, some bird from out the brakes
Starts into voice a moment, then is still.
There seems a floating whisper on the hill,
But that is fancy, for the starlight dews   780
All silently their tears of love instil,
Weeping themselves away, till they infuse
Deep into Nature's breast the spirit of her hues.

LXXXVIII.

Ye stars! which are the poetry of heaven!
If in your bright leaves we would read the fate 785
Of men and empires,—'tis to be forgiven,
That in our aspirations to be great,
Our destinies o'erleap their mortal state,

And claim a kindred with you; for ye are
A beauty and a mystery, and create   790
In us such love and reverence from afar,
That fortune, fame, power, life, have named them-
        selves a star.

LXXXIX.

All heaven and earth are still—though not in sleep,
But breathless, as we grow when feeling most;
And silent, as we stand in thoughts too deep:—   795
All heaven and earth are still: From the high host
Of stars, to the lull'd lake and mountain-coast,
All is concentr'd in a life intense,
Where not a beam, nor air, nor leaf is lost,
But hath a part of being, and a sense   800
Of that which is of all Creator and defence.

XC.

Then stirs the feeling infinite, so felt
In solitude, where we are *least* alone;
A truth, which through our being then doth melt
And purifies from self: it is a tone,   805
The soul and source of music, which makes known
Eternal harmony, and sheds a charm,
Like to the fabled Cytherea's zone,
Binding all things with beauty;—'twould disarm 809
The spectre Death, had he substantial power to harm.

XCI.

Not vainly did the early Persian make
His altar the high places and the peak
Of earth-o'ergazing mountains, and thus take
A fit and unwall'd temple, there to seek

The spirit, in whose honour shrines are weak,   815
Uprear'd of human hands.   Come, and compare
Columns and idol-dwellings, Goth or Greek,
With Nature's realms of worship, earth and air,
Nor fix on fond abodes to circumscribe thy pray'r!

XCII.

The sky is changed!—and such a change—
            Oh night,   820
And storm, and darkness, ye are wondrous strong,
Yet lovely in your strength, as is the light
Of a dark eye in woman!   Far along,
From peak to peak, the rattling crags among
Leaps the live thunder!   Not from one lone cloud,
But every mountain now hath found a tongue,   826
And Jura answers, through her misty shroud,
Back to the joyous Alps, who call to her aloud!

XCIII.

And this is in the night:—Most glorious night!
Thou wert not sent for slumber! let me be   830
A sharer in thy fierce and far delight,—
A portion of the tempest and of thee!
How the lit lake shines, a phosphoric sea,
And the big rain comes dancing to the earth!
And now again 'tis black,—and now, the glee   835
Of the loud hills shakes with its mountain-mirth,
As if they did rejoice o'er a young earthquake's birth.

XCIV.

Now, where the swift Rhone cleaves his way between
Heights which appear as lovers who have parted
In hate, whose mining depths so intervene,   840
That they can meet no more, though broken-hearted!

Though in their souls, which thus each other
  thwarted:
Love was the very root of the fond rage
Which blighted their life's **bloom,** and then de-
  parted:
  Itself expired, but leaving them an age   845
Of years all winters,—war within themselves to wage.

XCV.

Now, where the quick Rhone thus hath cleft his way,
The mightiest of the storms hath ta'en his stand:
For here, not one, but many, make their play,
And fling their thunderbolts from hand to hand, 850
Flashing and cast around: of all the band,
The brightest through these parted hills hath fork'd
His lightnings,—as if he did understand,
That in such gaps as desolation work'd,
There the hot shaft should blast whatever therein
  lurk'd.   855

XCVI.

Sky, mountains, river, winds, lake, lightnings! Ye!
With night, and clouds, and thunder, and a soul
To make these felt and feeling, well may be
Things that have made me watchful; the far roll
Of your departing voices, is the knoll   860
Of what in me is sleepless,—if I rest.
But where of ye, oh tempests! is the goal?
Are ye like those within the human breast?
Or do ye find, at length, like eagles, some high nest?

XCVII.

Could I embody and unbosom now   865
That which is most within me,—could I wreak
My thoughts upon expression, and thus throw
Soul, heart, mind, passions, feelings, strong or weak,

All that I would have sought, and all I seek,
Bear, know, feel, and yet breathe—into *one* word, 870
And that one word were Lightning, I would speak;
But as it is, I live and die unheard,
With a most voiceless thought, sheathing it as a sword.

CANTO IV.
(1818)

LXXVIII.

Oh Rome! my country! city of the soul!
The orphans of the heart must turn to thee, 695
Lone mother of dead empires! and control
In their shut breasts their petty misery.
What are our woes and sufferance? Come and see
The cypress, hear the owl, and plod your way
O'er steps of broken thrones and temples, Ye! 700
Whose agonies are evils of a day—
A world is at our feet as fragile as our clay.

LXXIX.

The Niobe of nations! there she stands,
Childless and crownless, in her voiceless woe,
An empty urn within her wither'd hands, 705
Whose holy dust was scatter'd long ago;
The Scipio's tomb contains no ashes now;
The very sepulchres lie tenantless
Of their heroic dwellers: dost thou flow,
Old Tiber! through a marble wilderness? 710
Rise, with thy yellow waves, and mantle her distress.

LXXX.

The Goth, the Christian, Time, War, Flood, and
Fire,
Have dealt upon the seven-hill'd city's pride;
She saw her glories star by star expire,
And up the steep, barbarian monarchs ride, 715

Where the car climb'd the Capitol; far and wide
Temple and tower went down, nor left a site:—
Chaos of ruins! who shall trace the void,
O'er the dim fragments cast a lunar light,
And say, "here was, or is," where all is doubly night?

LXXXI.

The double night of ages, and of her,   721
Night's daughter, Ignorance, hath wrapt and wrap
All round us; we but feel our way to err:
The ocean hath his chart, the stars their map,
And Knowledge spreads them on her ample lap; 725
But Rome is as the desert, where we steer
Stumbling o'er recollections; now we clap
Our hands, and cry "Eureka!" it is clear—
Where but some false mirage of ruin rises near.

LXXXII.

Alas! the lofty city! and alas!   730
The trebly hundred triumphs! and the day
When Brutus made the dagger's edge surpass
The conqueror's sword in bearing fame away!
Alas, for Tully's voice, and Virgil's lay,
And Livy's pictured page!—but these shall be   735
Her resurrection; all beside—decay.
Alas for earth, for never shall we see
That brightness in her eye she bore when Rome was
    free!

.   .   .   .

CLXXV.

But I forget.—My Pilgrim's shrine is won,
And he and I must part,—so let it be,—
His task and mine alike are nearly done;
Yet once more let us look upon the sea;   1570

The midland ocean breaks on him and me,
And from the Alban Mount we now behold
Our friend of youth, that ocean, which when we
Beheld it last by Calpe's rock unfold
Those waves, we follow'd on till the dark Euxine roll'd

CLXXVI.

Upon the blue Symplegades: long years—   1576
Long, though not very many, since have done
Their work on both; some suffering and some tears
Have left us nearly where we had begun:
Yet not in vain our mortal race hath run,   1580
We have had our reward—and it is here;
That we can yet feel gladden'd by the sun,
And reap from earth, sea, joy almost as dear
As if there were no man to trouble what is clear.

CLXXVII.

Oh! that the Desert were my dwelling-place,   1585
With one fair Spirit for my minister,
That I might all forget the human race,
And, hating no one, love but only her!
Ye Elements!—in whose ennobling stir
I feel myself exalted—Can ye not   1590
Accord me such a being? Do I err
In deeming such inhabit many a spot?
Though with them to converse can rarely be our lot.

CLXXVIII.

There is a pleasure in the pathless woods,
There is a rapture on the lonely shore,   1595
There is society, where none intrudes,
By the deep Sea, and music in its roar:
I love not Man the less, but Nature more,
From these our interviews, in which I steal
From all I may be, or have been before,   1600

To mingle with the Universe, and feel
What I can ne'er express, yet cannot all conceal.

CLXXIX.

Roll on, thou deep and dark blue Ocean—roll!
Ten thousand fleets sweep over thee in vain;
Man marks the earth with ruin—his control   1605
Stops with the shore;—upon the watery plain
The wrecks are all thy deed, nor doth remain
A shadow of man's ravage, save his own,
When, for a moment, like a drop of rain,
He sinks into thy depths with bubbling groan,   1610
Without a grave, unknell'd, uncoffin'd, and unknown.

CLXXX.

His steps are not upon thy paths,—thy fields
Are not a spoil for him,—thou dost arise
And shake him from thee; the vile strength he wields
For earth's destruction thou dost all despise,   1615
Spurning him from thy bosom to the skies,
And send'st him, shivering in thy playful spray
And howling, to his Gods, where haply lies
His petty hope in some near port or bay,
And dashest him again to earth:—there let him lay.

CLXXXI.

The armaments which thunderstrike the walls   1621
Of rock-built cities, bidding nations quake,
And monarchs tremble in their capitals,
The oak leviathans, whose huge ribs make
Their clay creator the vain title take   1625
Of lord of thee, and arbiter of war;
These are thy toys, and, as the snowy flake,
They melt into thy yeast of waves, which mar
Alike the Armada's pride, or spoils of Trafalgar.

CLXXXII.

Thy shores are empires, changed in all save thee—
Assyria, Greece, Rome, Carthage, what are they?
Thy waters wasted them while they were free,   1632
And many a tyrant since; their shores obey
The stranger, slave, or savage; their decay
Has dried up realms to deserts:—not so thou,   1635
Unchangeable save to thy wild waves' play—
Time writes no wrinkle on thine azure brow—
Such as creation's dawn beheld, thou rollest now.

CLXXXIII.

Thou glorious mirror, where the Almighty's form
Glasses itself in tempests; in all time   1640
Calm or convulsed—in breeze, or gale, or storm,
Icing the pole, or in the torrid clime
Dark-heaving;—boundless, endless, and sublime—
The image of Eternity—the throne
Of the Invisible; even from out thy slime   1645
The monsters of the deep are made; each zone
Obeys thee; thou goest forth, dread, fathomless, alone.

CLXXXIV.

And I have loved thee, Ocean! and my joy
Of youthful sports was on thy breast to be
Borne, like thy bubbles, onward: from a boy   1650
I wanton'd with thy breakers—they to me
Were a delight; and if the freshening sea
Made them a terror—'twas a pleasing fear,
For I was as it were a child of thee,
And trusted to thy billows far and near   1655
And laid my hand upon thy mane—as I do here.

DON JUAN

(1821)

CANTO III.

XC.

And glory long has made the sages smile;
  'Tis something, nothing, words, illusion, wind—
Depending more upon the historian's style   715
  Than on the name a person leaves behind:
Troy owes to Homer what whist owes to Hoyle:
  The present century was growing blind
To the great Marlborough's skill in giving knocks
Until his late Life by Archdeacon Coxe.   720

XCI.

Milton's the prince of poets—so we say;
  A little heavy, but no less divine:
An independent being in his day—
  Learn'd, pious, temperate in love and wine;
But his life falling into Johnson's way,   725
  We're told this great high-priest of all the Nine
Was whipt at college—a harsh sire—odd spouse,
For the first Mrs. Milton left his house.

XCII.

All these are, *certes*, entertaining facts,
  Like Shakespeare's stealing deer, Lord Bacon's
      bribes;   730
Like Titus' youth, and Caesar's earliest acts;
  Like Burns (whom Dr. Currie well describes)
Like Cromwell's pranks;—but although truth exacts
  These amiable descriptions from the scribes,
As most essential to their hero's story,   735
They do not much contribute to his glory.

XCIII.

All are not moralists, like Southey, when
    He prated to the world of "Pantisocracy;"
Or Wordsworth unexcised, unhir'd, who then
    Season'd his pedlar poems with democracy;   740
Or Coleridge, long before his flighty pen
    Let to the Morning Post its aristocracy;
When he and Southey, following the same path,
Espoused two partners (milliners of Bath).

XCIV.

Such names at present cut a convict figure,   745
    The very Botany Bay in moral geography;
Their loyal treason, renegado vigour,
    Are good manure for their more bare biography.
Wordsworth's last quarto, by the way, is bigger
    Than any since the birthday of typography;   750
A clumsy, frowzy poem, call'd the "Excursion"
Writ in a manner which is my aversion.

XCV.

He there builds up a formidable dyke
    Between his own and others' intellect;
But Wordsworth's poem, and his followers, like   755
    Joanna Southcote's Shiloh, and her sect,
Are things which in this century don't strike
    The public mind,—so few are the elect;
And the new births of both their stale virginities
Have proved but dropsies taken for divinities.   760

.   .   .   .   .   .

CI.

T' our tale.—The feast was over, the slaves gone,
    The dwarfs and dancing girls had all retir'd;
The Arab lore and poet's song were done,
    And every sound of revelry expir'd;

The lady and her lover, left alone,   805
  The rosy flood of twilight sky admir'd;—
Ave Maria! o'er the earth and sea,
That heavenliest hour of Heaven is worthiest thee!

CII.

Ave Maria! blessed be the hour!
  The time, the clime, the spot, where I so oft   810
Have felt that moment in its fullest power
  Sink o'er the earth so beautiful and soft,
While swung the deep bell in the distant tower,
  Or the faint dying day-hymn stole aloft,
  And not a breath crept through the rosy air,   815
And yet the forest leaves seem stirr'd with prayer.

  .   .   .   .

CV.

Sweet hour of twilight!—in the solitude
  Of the pine forest, and the silent shore
Which bounds Ravenna's immemorial wood,   835
  Rooted where once the Adrian wave flow'd o'er,
To where the last Cæsarean fortress stood,
  Evergreen forest! which Boccaccio's lore
And Dryden's lay made haunted ground to me,
How have I loved the twilight hour and thee!   840

CVI.

The shrill cicalas, people of the pine,
  Making their summer lives one ceaseless song,
Were the sole echoes, save my steed's and mine,
  And vesper-bell's that rose the boughs along;
The spectre huntsman of Onesti's line,   845
  His hell-dogs, and their chase, and the fair throng
Which learn'd from this example not to fly
From a true lover, shadow'd my mind's eye.

CVII.

Oh, Hesperus! thou bringest all good things—
  Home to the weary, to the hungry cheer,   850
To the young bird the parent's brooding wings,
  The welcome stall to the o'erlabour'd steer;
Whate'er of peace about our hearthstone clings,
  Whate'er our household gods protect of dear,
Are gather'd round us by thy look of rest;   855
Thou bring'st the child, too, to the mother's breast.

CVIII.

Soft hour! which wakes the wish and melts the heart
  Of those who sail the seas, on the first day
When they from their sweet friends are torn apart;
  Or fills with love the pilgrim on his way   860
As the far bell of vesper makes him start,
  Seeming to weep the dying day's decay;
Is this a fancy which our reason scorns?
Ah! surely nothing dies but something mourns!

Percy Bysshe Shelley

1792–1822

ODE TO THE WEST WIND
(1819)

I.

O wild West Wind, thou breath of Autumn's
        being,
  Thou, from whose unseen presence the leaves dead
Are driven, like ghosts from an enchanter fleeing,

  Yellow, and black, and pale, and hectic red,
5 Pestilence-stricken multitudes: O thou,
  Who chariotest to their dark wintry bed

The wingèd seeds, where they lie cold and low,
Each like a corpse within its grave, until
Thine azure sister of the Spring shall blow

10 Her clarion o'er the dreaming earth, and fill
(Driving sweet buds like flocks to feed in air)
With living hues and odours plain and hill:

Wild Spirit, which art moving every where;
Destroyer and preserver; hear, oh, hear!

II.

15 Thou on whose stream, 'mid the steep sky's com-
       motion,
Loose clouds like earth's decaying leaves are shed,
Shook from the tangled boughs of Heaven and
       Ocean,

Angels of rain and lightning: there are spread
On the blue surface of thine airy surge,
20 Like the bright hair uplifted from the head

Of some fierce Mænad, even from the dim verge
Of the horizon to the zenith's height,
The locks of the approaching storm.   Thou dirge

Of the dying year, to which this closing night
25 Will be the dome of a vast sepulchre,
Vaulted with all thy congregated might

Of vapours, from whose solid atmosphere
Black rain, and fire, and hail will burst: oh, hear!

III.

Thou who didst waken from his summer dreams
30 The blue Mediterranean, where he lay,
Lulled by the coil of his crystalline streams,

Beside a pumice isle in Baiae's bay,
And saw in sleep old palaces and towers
Quivering within the wave's intenser day,

35 All overgrown with azure moss, and flowers
So sweet the sense faints picturing them! Thou
For whose path the Atlantic's level powers

Cleave themselves into chasms, while far below
The sea-blooms and the oozy woods which wear
40 The sapless foliage of the ocean know

Thy voice, and suddenly grow gray with fear,
And tremble and despoil themselves: oh, hear!

IV.

If I were a dead leaf thou mightest bear;
If I were a swift cloud to fly with thee;
45 A wave to pant beneath thy power, and share

The impulse of thy strength, only less free
Than thou, O uncontrollable! If even
I were as in my boyhood, and could be

The comrade of thy wanderings over heaven,
50 As then, when to outstrip thy skyey speed
Scarce seemed a vision; I would ne'er have
striven

As thus with thee in prayer in my sore need.
Oh, lift me as a wave, a leaf, a cloud!
I fall upon the thorns of life! I bleed!

55 A heavy weight of hours has chained and bowed
One too like thee: tameless, and swift, and proud.

V.

Make me thy lyre, even as the forest is:
What if my leaves are falling like its own!
The tumult of thy mighty harmonies

60 Will take from both a deep, autumnal tone,
Sweet though in sadness. Be thou, Spirit fierce
My spirit! Be thou me, impetuous one!

Drive my dead thoughts over the universe
Like withered leaves to quicken a new birth!
65 And, by the incantation of this verse,

Scatter, as from an unextinguished hearth
Ashes and sparks, my words among mankind!
Be through my lips to unawakened earth

The trumpet of a prophecy! O wind,
70 If Winter comes, can Spring be far behind?

TO A SKYLARK

(1820)

Hail to thee, blithe Spirit!
   Bird thou never wert,
That from Heaven, or near it,
   Pourest thy full heart
5 In profuse strains of unpremeditated art.

Higher still and higher
   From the earth thou springest
Like a cloud of fire;
   The blue deep thou wingest,
10 And singing still dost soar, and soaring ever
     singest.

In the golden lightning
   Of the sunken sun,
O'er which clouds are bright'ning,
   Thou dost float and run;
15 Like an unbodied joy whose race is just begun.

The pale purple even
   Melts around thy flight;
Like a star of heaven,
   In the broad day-light
20 Thou art unseen,—but yet I hear thy shrill
     delight,

Keen as are the arrows
   Of that silver sphere,
Whose intense lamp narrows
   In the white dawn clear
25 Until we hardly see—we feel that it is there.

All the earth and air
   With thy voice is loud,
As, when Night is bare,
   From one lonely cloud
30 The moon rains out her beams, and Heaven is
     overflowed.

What thou art we know not;
   What is most like thee?
From rainbow clouds there flow not
   Drops so bright to see
35 As from thy presence showers a rain of melody.

Like a Poet hidden
   In the light of thought,
Singing hymns unbidden
   Till the world is wrought
40 To sympathy with hopes and fears it heeded not:

Like a high-born maiden
    In a palace tower,
Soothing her love-laden
    Soul in secret hour
45 With music sweet as love,—which overflows her
        bower:

Like a glow-worm golden
    In a dell of dew,
Scattering unbeholden
    Its aërial hue
50 Among the flowers and grass which screen **it from**
        the view:

Like a rose embowered
    In its own green leaves,
By warm winds deflowered,
    Till the scent it gives
55 Makes faint with too much sweet those **heavy-**
        wingèd thieves:

Sound of vernal showers
    On the twinkling grass,
Rain-awakened flowers,
    All that ever was
60 Joyous and clear and fresh, thy music doth sur-
        pass.

Teach us, Sprite or Bird,
    What sweet thoughts are thine;
I have never heard
    Praise of love or wine
65 That panted forth a flood of rapture so divine.

Chorus Hymenæal,
    Or triumphal chaunt,

Matched with thine, would be all
　　But an empty vaunt,
70 A thing wherein we feel there is some hidden
　　　want.

What objects are the fountains
　　Of thy happy strain?
What fields or waves or mountains?
　　What shapes of sky or plain?
75 What love of thine own kind? what ignorance of
　　　pain?

With thy clear keen joyance
　　Languor cannot be;
Shadow of annoyance
　　Never came near thee;
80 Thou lovest—but ne'er knew love's sad satiety.

Waking or asleep
　　Thou of death must deem
Things more true and deep
　　Than we mortals dream—
85 Or how could thy notes flow in such a crystal
　　　stream?

We look before and after,
　　And pine for what is not;
Our sincerest laughter
　　With some pain is fraught;
90 Our sweetest songs are those that tell of saddest
　　　thought.

Yet if we could scorn
　　Hate and pride and fear;
If we were things born
　　Not to shed a tear,
95 I know not how thy joy we ever should come near.

Better than all measures
 Of delightful sound,
Better than all treasures
 That in books are found,
100 Thy skill to poet were, thou scorner of the
  ground!

Teach me half the gladness
 That thy brain must know,
Such harmonious madness
 From my lips would flow,
105 The world should listen then—as I am listening
  now.

THE CLOUD

(1820)

I bring fresh showers for the thirsting flowers,
 From the seas and the streams;
I bear light shade for the leaves when laid
 In their noonday dreams.
5 From my wings are shaken the dews that waken
 The sweet buds every one,
When rocked to rest on their mother's breast,
 As she dances about the sun.
I wield the flail of the lashing hail,
10 And whiten the green plains under,
And then again I dissolve it in rain,
 And laugh as I pass in thunder.

I sift the snow on the mountains below,
 And their great pines groan aghast;
15 And all the night 'tis my pillow white,
 While I sleep in the arms of the blast.
Sublime on the towers of my skyey bowers,
 Lightning my pilot sits;
In a cavern under is fettered the thunder,
20 It struggles and howls by fits;

Over earth and ocean, with gentle motion,
    This pilot is guiding me,
Lured by the love of the genii that move
    In the depths of the purple sea;
25 Over the rills, and the crags, and the hills,
    Over the lakes and the plains,
Wherever he dream, under mountain or stream,
    The Spirit he loves remains;
And I all the while bask in heaven's blue smile,
30   Whilst he is dissolving in rains.

The sanguine sunrise, with his meteor eyes,
    And his burning plumes outspread,
Leaps on the back of my sailing rack,
    When the morning star shines dead;
35 As on the jag of a mountain crag,
    Which an earthquake rocks and swings,
An eagle alit one moment may sit
    In the light of its golden wings.
And when sunset may breathe, from the lit sea
      beneath,
40   Its ardours of rest and of love,
And the crimson pall of eve may fall
    From the depth of heaven above,
With wings folded I rest, on mine airy nest,
    As still as a brooding dove.

45 That orbèd maiden, with white fire laden,
    Whom mortals call the Moon,
Glides glimmering o'er my fleece-like floor,
    By the midnight breezes strewn;
And wherever the beat of her unseen feet,
50   Which only the angels hear,
May have broken the woof of my tent's thin roof,
    The stars peep behind her and peer;
And I laugh to see them whirl and flee,

Like a swarm of golden bees,
55 When I widen the rent in my wind-built tent,
    Till the calm rivers, lakes, and seas,
Like strips of the sky fallen through me on high,
    Are each paved with the moon and these.

I bind the sun's throne with a burning zone,
60   And the moon's with a girdle of pearl;
The volcanos are dim, and the stars reel and
      swim,
    When the whirlwinds my banner unfurl.
From cape to cape, with a bridge-like shape,
    Over a torrent sea,
65 Sunbeam-proof, I hang like a roof,—
    The mountains its columns be.
The triumphal arch, through which I march,
    With hurricane, fire, and snow,
When the powers of the air are chained to my
      chair,
70   Is the million-colored bow;
The sphere-fire above its soft colors wove,
    While the moist earth was laughing below.

I am the daughter of earth and water,
    And the nursling of the sky;
75 I pass through the pores of the ocean and shores;
    I change, but I cannot die.
For after the rain, when with never a stain
    The pavilion of heaven is bare,
And the winds and sunbeams with their convex
      gleams,
80   Build up the blue dome of air,
I silently laugh at my own cenotaph,
    And out of the caverns of rain,
Like a child from the womb, like a ghost from the
      tomb,
    I arise and unbuild it again.

ADONAIS

(1821)

I.

I weep for Adonais—he is dead!
Oh, weep for Adonais! though our tears
Thaw not the frost which binds so dear a head!
And thou, sad Hour, selected from all years
5   To mourn our loss, rouse thy obscure compeers,
And teach them thine own sorrow; Say: "With
    me
Died Adonais; till the Future dares
Forget the Past, his fate and fame shall be
An echo and a light unto eternity!"

II.

10   Where wert thou, mighty Mother, when he lay,
When thy Son lay, pierced by the shaft
    which flies
In darkness? where was lorn Urania
When Adonais died? With veilèd eyes,
'Mid listening Echoes, in her Paradise
15   She sate, while one, with soft enamoured
    breath,
Rekindled all the fading melodies,
With which, like flowers that mock the corse
    beneath,
He had adorned and hid the coming bulk of
    death.

III.

Oh, weep for Adonais—he is dead!
20   Wake, melancholy Mother, wake and weep!
Yet wherefore? Quench within their burning
    bed
Thy fiery tears, and let thy loud heart keep

Like his a mute and uncomplaining sleep;
For he is gone where all things wise and fair
25   Descend. Oh, dream not that the amorous
          Deep
Will yet restore him to the vital air;
Death feeds on his mute voice, and laughs at our
          despair.

IV.

Most musical of mourners, weep again!
Lament anew, Urania!—He died,
30   Who was the sire of an immortal strain,
Blind, old, and lonely, when his country's pride
The priest, the slave, and the liberticide
Trampled and mocked with many a loathèd rite
Of lust and blood; he went, unterrified,
35   Into the gulf of death; but his clear Sprite
Yet reigns o'er earth, the third among the sons of
          light.

V.

Most musical of mourners, weep anew!
Not all to that bright station dared to climb;
And happier they their happiness who knew,
40   Whose tapers yet burn through that night of
          time
In which suns perished; others more sublime,
Struck by the envious wrath of man or God,
Have sunk, extinct in their refulgent prime;
And some yet live, treading the thorny road,
45 Which leads, through toil and hate, to Fame's
          serene abode.

VI.

But now, thy youngest, dearest one has
          perished,
The nursling of thy widowhood, who grew,
Like a pale flower by some sad maiden cherished
And fed with true-love tears instead of dew;

50   Most musical of mourners, weep anew!
      Thy extreme hope, the loveliest and the last,
      The bloom, whose petals, nipt before they blew,
      Died on the promise of the fruit, is waste;
The broken lily lies—the storm is overpast.

VII.

55   To that high Capital, where kingly Death
      Keeps his pale court in beauty and decay,
      He came; and bought, with price of purest
              breath,
      A grave among the eternal.—Come away!
      Haste, while the vault of blue Italian day
60   Is yet his fitting charnel-roof! while still
      He lies, as if in dewy sleep he lay;
      Awake him not! surely he takes his fill
Of deep and liquid rest, forgetful of all ill.

VIII.

      He will awake no more, oh, never more!
65   Within the twilight chamber spreads apace
      The shadow of white Death, and at the door
      Invisible Corruption waits to trace
      His extreme way to her dim dwelling-place;
      The eternal Hunger sits, but pity and awe
70   Soothe her pale rage, nor dares she to deface
      So fair a prey, till darkness and the law
Of change, shall o'er his sleep the mortal curtain
      draw.

IX.

      Oh, weep for Adonais!—The quick Dreams,
      The passion-wingèd ministers of thought,
75   Who were his flocks, whom near the living
              streams
      Of his young spirit he fed, and whom he taught

The love which was its music, wander not,—
Wander no more, from kindling brain to brain,
But droop there, whence they sprung; and
    mourn their lot
80 Round the cold heart, where, after their sweet
    pain,
They ne'er will gather strength, or find a home
    again.

X.

And one with trembling hands clasps his cold
    head,
And fans him with her moonlight wings, and
    cries,
" Our love, our hope, our sorrow, is not dead;
85 See, on the silken fringe of his faint eyes,
Like dew upon a sleeping flower, there lies
A tear some Dream has loosened from his
    brain."
Lost Angel of a ruined Paradise!
She knew not 'twas her own; as with no stain
90 She faded, like a cloud which had outwept its
    rain.

XI.

One from a lucid urn of starry dew
Washed his light limbs as if embalming them;
Another clipt her profuse locks, and threw
The wreath upon him, like an anadem,
95 Which frozen tears instead of pearls begem;
Another in her wilful grief would break
Her bow and wingèd reeds, as if to stem
A greater loss with one which was more weak;
And dull the barbèd fire against his frozen cheek.

XII.

100　Another Splendour on his mouth alit,
　　　　That mouth, whence it was wont to draw the
　　　　　　breath
　　　Which gave it strength to pierce the guarded
　　　　　　wit,
　　　And pass into the panting heart beneath
　　　With lightning and with music: the damp
　　　　　death
105 Quenched its caress upon his icy lips;
　　　　And, as a dying meteor stains a wreath
　　　Of moonlight vapour, which the cold night clips,
　　It flushed through his pale limbs, and past to its
　　　　eclipse.

XIII.

　　　And others came . . . Desires and Adorations,
110　Wingèd Persuasions and veiled Destinies,
　　　Splendours, and Glooms, and glimmering In-
　　　　carnations
　　　Of hopes and fears, and twilight Fantasies;
　　　And Sorrow, with her family of Sighs,
　　　And Pleasure, blind with tears, led by the
　　　　gleam
115　Of her own dying smile instead of eyes,
　　　　Came in slow pomp;—the moving pomp might
　　　　seem
　　Like pageantry of mist on an autumnal stream.

XIV.

　　　All he had loved, and molded into thought,
　　　From shape, and hue, and odour, and sweet
　　　　sound,
120　Lamented Adonais. Morning sought
　　　Her eastern watch tower, and her hair un-
　　　　bound,

Wet with the tears which should adorn the
　　　ground,
　Dimmed the aërial eyes that kindle day;
　Afar the melancholy thunder moaned,
125　Pale Ocean in unquiet slumber lay,
And the wild winds flew round, sobbing in their
　　　dismay.

XV.

Lost Echo sits amid the voiceless mountains,
And feeds her grief with his remembered lay,
And will no more reply to winds or fountains,
130　Or amorous birds perched on the young green
　　　spray,
Or herdsman's horn, or bell at closing day;
Since she can mimic not his lips, more dear
Than those for whose disdain she pined away
Into a shadow of all sounds:—a drear
135 Murmur, between their songs, is all the woodmen
　　　hear.

XVI.

Grief made the young Spring wild, and she
　　　threw down
　Her kindling buds, as if she Autumn were,
　Or they dead leaves; since her delight is
　　　flown,
　For whom should she have waked the sullen
　　　year?
140　To Phœbus was not Hyacinth so dear,
　Nor to himself Narcissus, as to both
　Thou, Adonais; wan they stand and sere
　Amid the faint companions of their youth,
With dew all turned to tears; odour, to sighing
　　　ruth.

XVII.

145 Thy spirit's sister, the lorn nightingale,
  Mourns not her mate with such melodious pain;
  Not so the eagle, who like thee could scale
  Heaven, and could nourish in the sun's domain
  Her mighty youth with morning, doth complain,
150 Soaring and screaming round her empty nest,
  As Albion wails for thee: the curse of Cain
  Light on his head who pierced thy innocent breast,
  And scared the angel soul that was its earthly guest!

XVIII.

  Ah woe is me! Winter is come and gone,
155 But grief returns with the revolving year;
  The airs and streams renew their joyous tone;
  The ants, the bees, the swallows reappear;
  Fresh leaves and flowers deck the dead Seasons' bier;
  The amorous birds now pair in every brake,
160 And build their mossy homes in field and brere;
  And the green lizard and the golden snake,
  Like unimprisoned flames, out of their trance awake.

XIX.

  Through wood and stream and field and hill and Ocean,
  A quickening life from the Earth's heart has burst,
165 As it has ever done, with change and motion,
  From the great morning of the world when first

God dawned on Chaos; in its stream immersed
The lamps of Heaven flash with a softer light;
All baser things pant with life's sacred thirst,
170 Diffuse themselves, and spend in love's delight,
The beauty and the joy of their renewèd might.

XX.

The leprous corpse touched by this spirit
    tender,
Exhales itself in flowers of gentle breath;
Like incarnations of the stars, when splendour
175 Is changed to fragrance, they illumine death
And mock the merry worm that wakes beneath.
Nought we know dies. Shall that alone which
    knows
Be as a sword consumed before the sheath
By sightless lightning?—the intense atom
    glows
180 A moment, then is quenched in a most cold
    repose.

XXI.

Alas! that all we loved of him should be,
But for our grief, as if it had not been,
And grief itself be mortal! Woe is me!
Whence are we, and why are we? of what scene
185 The actors or spectators? Great and mean
Meet massed in death, who lends what life must
    borrow.
As long as skies are blue, and fields are green,
Evening must usher night, night urge the
    morrow,
Month follow month with woe, and year wake
    year to sorrow.

XXII.

190   *He* will awake no more, oh, never more!
     "Wake thou," cried Misery, "childless Mother, rise
     Out of thy sleep, and slake, in thy heart's core,
     A wound more fierce than his with tears and sighs."
     And all the Dreams that watched Urania's eyes,
195   And all the Echoes whom their sister's song
     Had held in holy silence, cried, "Arise!"
     Swift as a Thought by the snake Memory stung,
    From her ambrosial rest the fading Splendour sprung.

XXIII.

     She rose like an autumnal night, that springs
200   Out of the East, and follows wild and drear
     The golden Day, which, on eternal wings,
     Even as a ghost abandoning a bier,
     Had left the Earth a corpse,—sorrow and fear
     So struck, so roused, so rapt Urania;
205   So saddened round her like an atmosphere
     Of stormy mist; so swept her on her way
    Even to the mournful place where Adonais lay.

XXIV.

     Out of her secret Paradise she sped,
     Through camps and cities rough with stone, and steel,
210   And human hearts which, to her airy tread
     Yielding not, wounded the invisible

Palms of her tender feet where'er they fell;
And barbèd tongues, and thoughts more sharp
than they,
Rent the soft Form they never could repel,
215 Whose sacred blood, like the young tears of
May,
Paved with eternal flowers that undeserving
way.

XXV.

In the death-chamber for a moment Death,
Shamed by the presence of that living Might,
Blushed to annihilation, and the breath
220 Revisited those lips, and life's pale light
Flashed through those limbs, so late her dear
delight.
"Leave me not wild and drear and comfortless,
As silent lightning leaves the starless night!
Leave me not!" cried Urania; her distress
225 Roused Death; Death rose and smiled, and met
her vain caress.

XXVI.

"Stay yet awhile! speak to me once again;
Kiss me, so long but as a kiss may live;
And in my heartless breast and burning brain
That word, that kiss, shall all thoughts else
survive,
230 With food of saddest memory kept alive,
Now thou art dead, as if it were a part
Of thee, my Adonais! I would give
All that I am to be as thou now art!
But I am chained to Time, and cannot thence
depart!

XXVII.

235   " O gentle child, beautiful as thou wert,
       Why didst thou leave the trodden paths of men
       Too soon, and with weak hands though mighty
           heart
       Dare the unpastured dragon in his den?
       Defenceless as thou wert, oh, where was then
240   Wisdom the mirrored shield, or scorn the spear?
       Or hadst thou waited the full cycle, when
       Thy spirit should have filled its crescent sphere,
   The monsters of life's waste had fled from thee
           like deer.

XXVIII.

     " The herded wolves, bold only to pursue;
245   The obscene ravens, clamorous o'er the dead;
       The vultures, to the conqueror's banner true,
       Who feed where Desolation first has fed,
       And whose wings rain contagion;—how they
           fled,
       When, like Apollo, from his golden bow
250   The Pythian of the age one arrow sped
       And smiled!—The spoilers tempt no second
           blow,
   They fawn on the proud feet that spurn them ly-
           ing low.

XXIX.

     " The sun comes forth, and many reptiles
           spawn;
       He sets, and each ephemeral insect then
255   Is gathered into death without a dawn,
       And the immortal stars awake again;

So is it in the world of living men:
A godlike mind soars forth, in its delight
Making earth bare and veiling heaven, and
    when
260 It sinks, the swarms that dimmed or shared
    its light
Leave to its kindred lamps the spirit's awful
    night."

XXX.

Thus ceased she: and the mountain shepherds
    came,
Their garlands sere, their magic mantles rent;
The Pilgrim of Eternity, whose fame
265 Over his living head like Heaven is bent,
An early but enduring monument,
Came, veiling all the lightnings of his song
In sorrow; from her wilds Ierne sent
The sweetest lyrist of her saddest wrong,
270 And love taught grief to fall like music from his
    tongue.

XXXI.

Midst others of less note, came one frail Form,
A phantom among men; companionless
As the last cloud of an expiring storm
Whose thunder is its knell; he, as I guess,
275 Had gazed on Nature's naked loveliness,
Acteon-like, and now he fled astray
With feeble steps o'er the world's wilderness,
And his own thoughts, along that rugged way,
Pursued, like raging hounds, their father and
    their prey.

XXXII.

280　　A pardlike Spirit beautiful and swift—
　　　　A Love in desolation masked;—a Power
　　　　Girt round with weakness;—it can scarce uplift
　　　　The weight of the superincumbent hour;
　　　　It is a dying lamp, a falling shower,
285　　A breaking billow;—even whilst we speak
　　　　Is it not broken? On the withering flower
　　　　The killing sun smiles brightly: on a cheek
　　The life can burn in blood, even while the heart
　　　　　may break.

XXXIII.

　　　　His head was bound with pansies overblown,
290　　And faded violets, white, and pied, and blue;
　　　　And a light spear topped with a cypress cone,
　　　　Round whose rude shaft dark ivy tresses grew
　　　　Yet dripping with the forest's noonday dew,
　　　　Vibrated, as the ever-beating heart
295　　Shook the weak hand that grasped it; of that
　　　　　crew
　　　　He came the last, neglected and apart;
　　A herd-abandoned deer struck by the hunter's
　　　　dart.

XXXIV.

　　　　All stood aloof, and at his partial moan
　　　　Smiled through their tears; well knew that
　　　　　gentle band
300　　Who in another's fate now wept his own,
　　　　As in the accents of an unknown land
　　　　He sung new sorrow; sad Urania scanned
　　　　The Stranger's mien, and murmured: "Who
　　　　　art thou?"
　　　　He answered not, but with a sudden hand

305 Made bare his branded and ensanguined brow,
Which was like Cain's or Christ's—oh! that it
should be so!

XXXV.

What softer voice is hushed over the dead?
Athwart what brow is that dark mantle thrown?
What form leans sadly o'er the white death-
bed,
310 In mockery of monumental stone,
The heavy heart heaving without a moan?
If it be He, who, gentlest of the wise,
Taught, soothed, loved, honoured the departed
one;
Let me not vex with inharmonious sighs
315 The silence of that heart's accepted sacrifice.

XXXVI.

Our Adonais has drunk poison—oh,
What deaf and viperous murderer could crown
Life's early cup with such a draught of woe?
The nameless worm would now itself disown;
320 It felt, yet could escape the magic tone
Whose prelude held all envy, hate and wrong,
But what was howling in one breast alone,
Silent with expectation of the song,
Whose master's hand is cold, whose silver lyre
unstrung.

XXXVII.

325 Live thou, whose infamy is not thy fame!
Live! fear no heavier chastisement from me,
Thou noteless blot on a remembered name!
But be thyself, and know thyself to be!

And ever at thy season be thou free
330   To spill the venom when thy fangs o'erflow;
Remorse and Self-contempt shall cling to thee;
Hot Shame shall burn upon thy secret brow,
And like a beaten hound tremble thou shalt—as
    now.

XXXVIII.

Nor let us weep that our delight is fled
335   Far from these carrion kites that scream below;
He wakes or sleeps with the enduring dead;
Thou canst not soar where he is sitting now.
Dust to the dust! but the pure spirit shall flow
Back to the burning fountain whence it came,
340   A portion of the Eternal, which must glow
Through time and change, unquenchably the
    same,
Whilst thy cold embers choke the sordid hearth
    of shame.

XXXIX.

Peace, peace! he is not dead, he doth not
    sleep—
He hath awakened from the dream of life—
345   'Tis we, who, lost in stormy visions, keep
With phantoms an unprofitable strife,
And in mad trance, strike with our spirit's
    knife
Invulnerable nothings. *We* decay
Like corpses in a charnel; fear and grief
350   Convulse us and consume us day by day,
And cold hopes swarm like worms within our liv-
    ing clay.

XL.

He has outsoared the shadow of our night;
Envy and calumny and hate and pain,
And that unrest which men miscall delight,
355 Can touch him not and torture not again;
From the contagion of the world's slow stain
He is secure, and now can never mourn
A heart grown cold, a head grown gray in vain;
Nor, when the spirit's self has ceased to burn,
360 With sparkless ashes load an unlamented urn.

XLI.

He lives, he wakes—'tis Death is dead, not he;
Mourn not for Adonais.—Thou young Dawn,
Turn all thy dew to splendour, for from thee
The spirit thou lamentest is not gone;
365 Ye caverns and ye forests, cease to moan!
Cease, ye faint flowers and fountains, and thou
Air,
Which like a mourning veil thy scarf hadst
thrown
O'er the abandoned Earth, now leave it bare
Even to the joyous stars which smile on its
despair!

XLII.

370 He is made one with Nature: there is heard
His voice in all her music, from the moan
Of thunder, to the song of night's sweet bird;
He is a presence to be felt and known
In darkness and in light, from herb and stone,
375 Spreading itself where'er that Power may move
Which has withdrawn his being to its own;
Which wields the world with never wearied
love,
Sustains it from beneath, and kindles it above.

XLIII.

He is a portion of the loveliness
380 Which once he made more lovely: he doth bear
His part, while the one Spirit's plastic stress
Sweeps through the dull dense world, compel-
    ling there,
All new successions to the forms they wear;
Torturing th' unwilling dross that checks its
    flight
385 To its own likeness, as each mass may bear,
And bursting in its beauty and its might
From trees and beasts and men into the Heaven's
    light.

XLIV.

The splendours of the firmament of time
May be eclipsed, but are extinguished not;
390 Like stars to their appointed height they climb,
And death is a low mist which cannot blot
The brightness it may veil. When lofty
    thought
Lifts a young heart above its mortal lair,
And love and life contend in it for what
395 Shall be its earthly doom, the dead live there
And move like winds of light on dark and stormy
    air.

XLV.

The inheritors of unfulfilled renown
Rose from their thrones, built beyond mortal
    thought,
Far in the Unapparent. Chatterton
400 Rose pale,—his solemn agony had not
Yet faded from him; Sidney, as he fought
And as he fell and as he lived and loved,
Sublimely mild, a Spirit without spot,

Arose; and Lucan, by his death approved;
405 Oblivion as they rose shrank like a thing re-
          proved.

XLVI.

And many more, whose names on Earth are
          dark,
    But whose transmitted effluence cannot die
    So long as fire outlives the parent spark,
    Rose, robed in dazzling immortality.
410   "Thou art become as one of us," they cry;
    "It was for thee yon kingless sphere has long
    Swung blind in unascended majesty,
    Silent alone amid an Heaven of song.
Assume thy wingèd throne, thou Vesper of our
          throng!"

XLVII.

415 Who mourns for Adonais? oh, come forth,
    Fond wretch! and know thyself and him aright.
    Clasp with thy panting soul the pendulous
          Earth;
    As from a centre, dart thy spirit's light
    Beyond all worlds, until its spacious might
420 Satiate the void circumference; then shrink
    Even to a point within our day and night;
    And keep thy heart light lest it make thee sink
When hope has kindled hope, and lured thee to
          the brink.

XLVIII.

Or go to Rome, which is the sepulchre
425 Oh, not of him, but of our joy: 'tis naught
    That ages, empires, and religions there
    Lie buried in the ravage they have wrought;

For such as he can lend,—they borrow not
Glory from those who made the world thei.
   prey;
430 And he is gathered to the kings of thought
Who waged contention with their time's decay,
And of the past are all that cannot pass away.

XLIX.

Go thou to Rome,—at once the Paradise,
The grave, the city, and the wilderness;
435 And where its wrecks like shattered mountains
   rise,
And flowering weeds, and fragrant copses dress
The bones of Desolation's nakedness,
Pass, till the Spirit of the spot shall lead
Thy footsteps to a slope of green access,
440 Where, like an infant's smile, over the dead
A light of laughing flowers along the grass is
   spread.

L.

And gray walls moulder round, on which dull
   Time
Feeds, like slow fire upon a hoary brand:
And one keen pyramid with wedge sublime,
445 Pavilioning the dust of him who planned
This refuge for his memory, doth stand
Like flame transformed to marble; and beneath
A field is spread, on which a newer band
Have pitched in Heaven's smile their camp of
   death,
450 Welcoming him we lose with scarce extinguished
   breath.

LI.

Here pause: these graves are all too young as
    yet
To have outgrown the sorrow which consigned
Its charge to each; and if the seal is set,
Here, on one fountain of a mourning mind,
455 Break it not thou! too surely shalt thou find
Thine own well full, if thou returnest home,
Of tears and gall. From the world's bitter
    wind
Seek shelter in the shadow of the tomb.
What Adonais is, why fear we to become?

LII.

460 The One remains, the many change and pass;
Heaven's light forever shines, Earth's shadows
    fly;
Life, like a dome of many-coloured glass,
Stains the white radiance of Eternity,
Until Death tramples it to fragments.—Die,
465 If thou wouldst be with that which thou dost
    seek!
Follow where all is fled!—Rome's azure sky,
Flowers, ruins, statues, music, words, are weak
The glory they transfuse with fitting truth to
    speak.

LIII.

Why linger, why turn back, why shrink, my
    Heart?
470 Thy hopes are gone before; from all things here
They have departed; thou shouldst now depart!
A light is past from the revolving year,

And man, and woman; and what still is dear
Attracts to crush, repels to make thee wither.
475 The soft sky smiles,—the low wind whispers
          near;
'Tis Adonais calls! oh, hasten thither,
No more let Life divide what Death can join
          together.

LIV.

That Light whose smile kindles the Universe,
That Beauty in which all things work and
          move,
480 That Benediction which the eclipsing Curse
Of birth can quench not, that sustaining Love
Which through the web of being blindly wove
By man and beast and earth and air and sea,
Burns bright or dim, as each are mirrors of
485 The fire for which all thirst, now beams on me,
Consuming the last clouds of cold mortality.

LV.

The breath whose might I have invoked in
          song
Descends on me; my spirit's bark is driven
Far from the shore, far from the trembling
          throng
490 Whose sails were never to the tempest given;
The massy earth and spherèd skies are riven!
I am borne darkly, fearfully, afar;
Whilst, burning through the inmost veil of
          Heaven,
The soul of Adonais, like a star,
495 Beacons from the abode where the Eternal are.

TIME
(1821)

Unfathomable Sea! whose waves are years,
  Ocean of Time, whose waters of deep woe
Are brackish with the salt of human tears!
  Thou shoreless flood, which in thy ebb and flow
5 Claspest the limits of mortality,
  And sick of prey, yet howling on for more,
Vomitest thy wrecks on its inhospitable shore;
  Treacherous in calm, and terrible in storm,
    Who shall put forth on thee,
10   Unfathomable Sea?

TO ——
(1821)

Music, when soft voices die,
Vibrates in the memory;
Odours, when sweet violets sicken;
Live within the sense they quicken.

5 Rose leaves, when the rose is dead,
Are heaped for the beloved's bed;
And so thy thoughts, when thou are gone,
Love itself shall slumber on.

TO NIGHT
(1821)

I.

Swiftly walk over the western wave,
  Spirit of Night!
Out of the misty eastern cave,
Where all the long and lone daylight
5 Thou wovest dreams of joy and fear,
Which make thee terrible and dear,—
  Swift be thy flight!

II.

Wrap thy form in a mantle gray,
    Star-inwrought!
10 Blind with thine hair the eyes of Day;
Kiss her until she be wearied out;
Then wander o'er city, and sea, and land,
Touching all with thine opiate wand—
    Come, long-sought!

III.

15 When I arose and saw the dawn,
    I sighed for thee;
When light rode high, and the dew was gone,
And noon lay heavy on flower and tree,
And the weary Day turned to his rest,
20 Lingering like an unloved guest,
    I sighed for thee.

IV.

Thy brother Death came, and cried,
    Wouldst thou me?
Thy sweet child Sleep, the filmy-eyed,
25 Murmured like a noontide bee,
Shall I nestle at thy side?
Would'st thou me?—and I replied,
    No, not thee!

V.

Death will come when thou art dead,
30   Soon, too soon;
Sleep will come when thou art fled;
Of neither would I ask the boon
I ask of thee, beloved Night,—
. Swift be thine approaching flight,
35   Come soon, soon!

A LAMENT
(1821)

I.

O world! O life! O time!
On whose last steps I climb,
   Trembling at that where I had stood before;
When will return the glory of your prime?
5   No more—oh, never more!

II.

Out of the day and night
A joy has taken flight;
   Fresh spring, and summer, and winter hoar,
Move my faint heart with grief, but with delight
10   No more—oh, never more!

TO ——
(1821)

I.

One word is too often profaned
   For me to profane it,
One feeling too falsely disdained
   For thee to disdain it;
5 One hope is too like despair
   For prudence to smother,
And pity from thee more dear
   Than that from another.

II.

I can give not what men call love,
10   But wilt thou accept not
The worship the heart lifts above
   And the Heavens reject not,—

The desire of the moth for the star,
Of the night for the morrow,
15 The devotion to something afar
From the sphere of our sorrow?

John Keats
1795-1821

THE EVE OF ST. AGNES
(1820)

I.

St. Agnes' Eve—Ah, bitter chill it was!
The owl, for all his feathers, was a-cold;
The hare limp'd trembling through the frozen
grass,
And silent was the flock in woolly fold:
5 Numb were the Beadsman's fingers, while he
told
His rosary, and while his frosted breath,
Like pious incense from a censer old,
Seem'd taking flight for heaven, without a
death,
Past the sweet Virgin's picture, while his prayer
he saith.

II.

10 His prayer he saith, this patient, holy man;
Then takes his lamp, and riseth from his knees,
And back returneth, meagre, barefoot, wan,
Along the chapel aisle by slow degrees:
The sculptur'd dead, on each side, seem to
freeze,
15 Emprison'd in black, purgatorial rails:
Knights, ladies, praying in dumb orat'ries,

He passeth by; and his weak spirit fails
To think how they may ache in icy hoods and
mails.

III.

Northward he turneth through a little door,
20 And scarce three steps, ere Music's golden
tongue
Flatter'd to tears this aged man and poor;
But no—already had his deathbell rung;
The joys of all his life were said and sung;
His was harsh penance on St. Agnes' eve:
25 Another way he went, and soon among
Rough ashes sat he for his soul's reprieve,
And all night kept awake, for sinners' sake to
grieve.

IV.

That ancient Beadsman heard the prelude soft;
And so it chanc'd, for many a door was wide,
30 From hurry to and fro. Soon, up aloft,
The silver, snarling trumpets 'gan to chide:
The level chambers, ready with their pride,
Were glowing to receive a thousand guests:
The carved angels, ever eager-ey'd,
35 Star'd, where upon their heads the cornice rests,
With hair blown back, and wings put cross-wise
on their breasts.

V.

At length burst in the argent revelry,
With plume, tiara, and all rich array,
Numerous as shadows haunting faerily
40 The brain, newstuff'd in youth, with triumphs
gay

Of old romance. These let us wish away,
And turn, sole-thoughted, to one Lady there,
Whose heart had brooded, all that wintry day,
On love, and wing'd St. Agnes' saintly care,
45 As she had heard old dames full many times
      declare.

VI.

They told her how, upon St. Agnes' eve,
Young virgins might have visions of delight,
And soft adorings from their loves receive
Upon the honey'd middle of the night,
50 If ceremonies due they did aright;
    As, supperless to bed they must retire,
And couch supine their beauties, lily white;
Nor look behind, nor sideways, but require
Of Heaven with upward eyes for all that they
      desire.

VII.

55 Full of this whim was thoughtful Madeline:
The music, yearning like a God in pain,
She scarcely heard: her maiden eyes divine
Fix'd on the floor, saw many a sweeping train
Pass by—she heeded not at all: in vain
60 Came many a tiptoe, amorous cavalier,
And back retir'd; not cool'd by high disdain,
But she saw not: her heart was otherwhere:
She sigh'd for Agnes' dreams, the sweetest of the
     year.

VIII.

She danc'd along with vague, regardless eyes,
65 Anxious her lips, her breathing quick and
     short:
The hallow'd hour was near at hand: she sighs
Amid the timbrels, and the throng'd resort

Of whisperers in anger, or in sport;
'Mid looks of love, defiance, hate, and scorn,
70   Hoodwink'd with faery fancy; all amort,
Save to St. Agnes and her lambs unshorn,
And all the bliss to be before to-morrow morn.

IX.

So, purposing each moment to retire,
She linger'd still. Meantime, across the
moors,
75   Had come young Porphyro, with heart on fire
For Madeline. Beside the portal doors,
Buttress'd from moonlight, stands he, and im-
plores
All saints to give him sight of Madeline,
But for one moment in the tedious hours,
80   That he might gaze and worship all unseen;
Perchance speak, kneel, touch, kiss—in sooth such
things have been.

X.

He ventures in: let no buzz'd whisper tell:
All eyes be muffled, or a hundred swords
Will storm his heart, Love's fev'rous citadel:
85   For him, those chambers held barbarian hordes,
Hyena foemen, and hot-blooded lords,
Whose very dogs would execrations howl
Against his lineage: not one breast affords
Him any mercy, in that mansion foul,
90 Save one old beldame, weak in body and in soul.

XI.

Ah, happy chance! the aged creature came,
Shuffling along with ivory-headed wand,
To where he stood, hid from the torch's flame,
Behind a broad hall-pillar, far beyond

95   The sound of merriment and chorus bland:
        He startled her; but soon she knew his face,
        And grasp'd his fingers in her palsied hand,
        Saying, "Mercy, Porphyro! hie thee from this
                place;
    "They are all here to-night, the whole blood-
                thirsty race!

XII.

100   "Get hence! get hence! there's dwarfish Hilde-
                brand;
        "He had a fever late, and in the fit
        "He cursed thee and thine, both house and
                land:
        "Then there's that old Lord Maurice, not a
                whit
        "More tame for his grey hairs—Alas me! flit!
105   "Flit like a ghost away."—"Ah, Gossip dear,
        "We're safe enough; here in this armchair sit,
        "And tell me how"— "Good Saints not
                here, not here:
    "Follow me, child, or else these stones will be thy
                bier."

XIII.

        He follow'd through a lowly arched way,
110   Brushing the cobwebs with his lofty plume,
        And as she mutter'd "Well-a-well-a-day!"
        He found him in a little moonlight room,
        Pale, lattic'd, chill, and silent as a tomb.
        "Now tell me where is Madeline," said he,
115   "O tell me, Angela, by the holy loom
        "Which none but secret sisterhood may see,
    "When they St. Agnes' wool are weaving
                piously."

XIV.

  " St. Agnes! Ah! it is St. Agnes' Eve—
  " Yet men will murder upon holy days:
120 " Thou must hold water in a witch's sieve,
  " And be liege-lord of all the Elves and Fays,
  " To venture so: it fills me with amaze
  " To see thee, Porphyro!—St. Agnes' Eve!
  " God's help! my lady fair the conjurer plays
125 " This very night: good angels her deceive!
  " But let me laugh awhile, I've mickle time to grieve."

XV.

  Feebly she laugheth in the languid moon,
  While Porphyro upon her face doth look,
  Like puzzled urchin on an aged crone
130 Who keepeth clos'd a wondrous riddle-book,
  As spectacled she sits in chimney nook.
  But soon his eyes grew brilliant, when she told
  His lady's purpose; and he scarce could brook
  Tears, at the thought of those enchantments cold,
135 And Madeline asleep in lap of legends old.

XVI.

  Sudden a thought came like a full-blown rose,
  Flushing his brow, and in his pained heart
  Made purple riot: then doth he propose
  A stratagem, that makes the beldame start:
140 " A cruel man and impious thou art:
  " Sweet lady, let her pray, and sleep, and dream
  " Alone with her good angels, far apart
  " From wicked men like thee. Go, go!—I deem
  " Thou canst not surely be the same that thou didst seem."

XVII.

145 "I will not harm her, by all saints I swear,"
 Quoth Porphyro: "O may I ne'er find grace
 "When my weak voice shall whisper its last
   prayer,
 "If one of her soft ringlets I displace,
 "Or look with ruffian passion in her face;
150 "Good Angela, believe me by these tears;
 "Or I will, even in a moment's space,
 "Awake, with horrid shout, my foemen's ears,
"And beard them, though they be more fang'd
   than wolves and bears."

XVIII.

 "Ah! why wilt thou affright a feeble soul?
155 "A poor, weak, palsy-stricken, churchyard
   thing,
 "Whose passing-bell may ere the midnight toll;
 "Whose prayers for thee, each morn and even-
   ing,
 "Were never miss'd."—Thus plaining, doth
   she bring
 A gentler speech from burning Porphyro;
160 So woful, and of such deep sorrowing,
 That Angela gives promise she will do
Whatever he shall wish, betide her weal or woe.

XIX.

 Which was, to lead him, in close secrecy,
 Even to Madeline's chamber, and there hide
165 Him in a closet, of such privacy
 That he might see her beauty unespy'd,
 And win perhaps that night a peerless bride,
 While legion'd fa'ries pac'd the coverlet,
 And pale enchantment held her sleepy-ey'd.

170   Never on such a night have lovers met,
       Since Merlin paid his Demon all the monstrous
          debt.

XX.

    " It shall be as thou wishest," said the Dame:
    " All cates and dainties shall be stored there
    " Quickly on this feast-night: by the tambour
       frame
175 " Her own lute thou wilt see: no time to spare,
    " For I am slow and feeble, and scarce dare
    " On such a catering trust my dizzy head.
    " Wait here, my child, with patience; kneel in
       prayer
    " The while: Ah! thou must needs the lady wed,
180 " Or may I never leave my grave among the
       dead."

XXI.

    So saying, she hobbled off with busy fear.
    The lover's endless minutes slowly pass'd;
    The dame return'd and whisper'd in his ear
    To follow her; with aged eyes aghast
185 From fright of dim espial. Safe at last,
    Through many a dusky gallery, they gain
    The maiden's chamber, silken, hush'd, and
       chaste;
    Where Porphyro took covert, pleas'd amain.
 His poor guide hurried back with agues in her
       brain.

XXII.

190 Her falt'ring hand upon the balustrade,
    Old Angela was feeling for the stair,
    When Madeline, St. Agnes' charmed maid,
    Rose, like a mission'd spirit, unaware:

With silver taper's light, and pious care,
195 She turn'd, and down the aged gossip led
To a safe level matting. Now prepare,
Young Porphyro, for gazing on that bed;
She comes, she comes again, like ring-dove fray'd
and fled.

XXIII.

Out went the taper as she hurried in;
200 Its little smoke, in pallid moonshine, died:
She clos'd the door, she panted, all akin
To spirits of the air, and visions wide:
No uttered syllable, or, woe betide!
But to her heart, her heart was voluble,
205 Paining with eloquence her balmy side;
As though a tongueless nightingale should swell
Her throat in vain, and die, heart-stifled, in her
dell.

XXIV.

A casement high and triple-arch'd there was,
All garlanded with carven imag'ries
210 Of fruits, and flowers, and bunches of knot-
grass,
And diamonded with panes of quaint device,
Innumerable of stains and splendid dyes,
As are the tiger-moth's deep-damask'd wings;
And in the midst, 'mong thousand heraldries,
215 And twilight saints, and dim emblazonings,
A shielded scutcheon blush'd with blood of
queens and kings.

XXV.

Full on this casement shone the wintry moon,
And threw warm gules on Madeline's fair
breast,
As down she knelt for heaven's grace and boon;
220 Rose-bloom fell on her hands, together prest,

And on her silver cross soft amethyst,
And on her hair a glory, like a saint:
She seem'd a splendid angel, newly drest,
Save wings, for heaven:—Porphyro grew faint:
225 She knelt, so pure a thing, so free from mortal taint.

XXVI.

Anon his heart revives: her vespers done,
Of all its wreathed pearls her hair she frees;
Unclasps her warmed jewels one by one;
Loosens her fragrant bodice; by degrees
230 Her rich attire creeps rustling to her knees:
Half-hidden, like a mermaid in sea-weed,
Pensive awhile she dreams awake, and sees,
In fancy, fair St. Agnes in her bed,
But dares not look behind, or all the charm is fled.

XXVII.

235 Soon, trembling in her soft and chilly nest,
In sort of wakeful swoon, perplex'd she lay,
Until the poppied warmth of sleep oppress'd
Her soothed limbs, and soul fatigued away;
Flown, like a thought, until the morrow-day;
240 Blissfully haven'd both from joy and pain;
Clasp'd like a missal where swart Paynims pray;
Blinded alike from sunshine and from rain,
As though a rose should shut, and be a bud again.

XXVIII.

Stol'n to this paradise, and so entranced,
245 Porphyro gaz'd upon her empty dress,
And listened to her breathing, if it chanced
To wake into a slumberous tenderness;

Which when he heard, that minute did he bless
And breath'd himself: then from the closet crept,
250   Noiseless as fear in a wide wilderness,
And over the hush'd carpet, silent, stept,
And 'tween the curtains peep'd, where, lo!—how fast she slept.

XXIX.

Then by the bed-side where the faded moon
Made a dim, silver twilight, soft he set
255   A table, and, half anguish'd, threw thereon
A cloth of woven crimson, gold, and jet:—
O for some drowsy Morphean amulet!
The boisterous, midnight, festive clarion,
The kettle-drum and far-heard clarionet,
260   Affray his ears, though but in dying tone:—
The hall-door shuts again, and all the noise is gone.

XXX.

And still she slept an azure-lidded sleep,
In blanched linen, smooth, and lavender'd,
While he forth from the closet brought a heap
265   Of candied apple, quince, and plum, and gourd;
With jellies soother than the creamy curd,
And lucent syrops, tinct with cinnamon;
Manna and dates, in argosy transferr'd
From Fez; and spiced dainties, every one,
270 From silken Samarcand to cedar'd Lebanon.

XXXI.

These delicates he heap'd with glowing hand
On golden dishes and in baskets bright
Of wreathed silver: sumptuous they stand
In the retired quiet of the night,

275 Filling the chilly room with perfumed light—
 " And now, my love, my seraph fair, awake!
 " Thou art my heaven, and I thine eremite:
 " Open thine eyes, for meek St. Agnes' sake,
 " Or I shall drowse beside thee, so my soul doth
     ache."

XXXII.

280 Thus whispering, his warm, unnerved arm
 Sank in her pillow. Shaded was her dream
 By the dusk curtains:—'twas a midnight
     charm
 Impossible to melt as iced stream:
 The lustrous salvers in the moonlight gleam;
285 Broad golden fringe upon the carpet lies:
 It seem'd he never, never could redeem
 From such a steadfast spell his lady's eyes;
 So mus'd awhile, entoil'd in woofed phantasies.

XXXIII.

 Awakening up, he took her hollow lute,—
290 Tumultuous,—and,—in chords that tender-
     est be,
 He play'd an ancient ditty, long since mute,
 In Provence call'd, " La belle dame sans
     mercy:"
 Close to her ear touching the melody;—
 Wherewith disturb'd, she utter'd a soft moan:
295 He ceas'd—she panted quick—and suddenly
 Her blue affrayed eyes wide open shone:
 Upon his knees he sank, pale as smooth-
     sculptured-stone.

XXXIV.

 Her eyes were open, but she still beheld,
 Now wide awake, the vision of her sleep:
300 There was a painful change, that nigh expell'd
 The blisses of her dream so pure and deep;

At which fair Madeline began to weep,
And moan forth witless words with many a
    sigh,
While still her gaze on Porphyro would keep;
305   Who knelt, with joined hands and piteous eye,
Fearing to move or speak, she look'd so drean-
    ingly.

XXXV.

"Ah, Porphyro!" said she, "but even now
"Thy voice was at sweet tremble in mine ear,
"Made tuneable with every sweetest vow;
310   "And those sad eyes were spiritual and clear:
"How chang'd thou art! how pallid, chill, and
    drear!
"Give me that voice again, my Porphyro,
"Those looks immortal, those complaining
    dear!
"Oh leave me not in this eternal woe,
315 "For if thou diest, my Love, I know not where
    to go."

XXXVI.

Beyond a mortal man impassion'd far
At these voluptuous accents, he arose,
Ethereal, flush'd, and like a throbbing star
Seen 'mid the sapphire heaven's deep repose;
320   Into her dream he melted, as the rose
Blended its odour with the violet,—
Solution sweet: meantime the frost-wind blows
Like Love's alarum pattering the sharp sleet
Against the window-panes; St. Agnes' moon hath
    set.

XXXVII.

325   'Tis dark: quick pattereth the flaw-blown sleet:
"This is no dream, my bride, my Madeline!"
'Tis dark: the iced gusts still rave and beat:
"No dream, alas! alas! and woe is mine!

"Porphyro will leave me here to fade and
  pine.—
330 " Cruel! what traitor could thee hither bring?
" I curse not, for my heart is lost in thine,
" Though thou forsakest a deceived thing;—
 " A dove forlorn and lost with sick unpruned
  wing."

XXXVIII.

" My Madeline! sweet dreamer! lovely bride!
335 " Say, may I be for aye thy vassal blest?
" Thy beauty's shield, heart-shap'd and vermeil
  dy'd?
" Ah, silver shrine, here will I take my rest
" After so many hours of toil and quest,
" A famish'd pilgrim,—sav'd by miracle.
340 " Though I have found, I will not rob thy nest
" Saving of thy sweet self; if thou think'st well
 " To trust, fair Madeline, to no rude infidel.

XXXIX.

" Hark! 'tis an elfin-storm from faery land,
" Of haggard seeming, but a boon indeed:
345 " Arise—arise! the morning is at hand;—
" The bloated wassailers will never heed:—
" Let us away, my love, with happy speed;
" There are no ears to hear, or eyes to see,—
" Drown'd all in Rhenish and the sleepy mead:
350 " Awake! arise! my love, and fearless be,
 " For o'er the southern moors I have a home for
  thee."

XL.

She hurried at his words, beset with fears,
For there were sleeping dragons all around,
At glaring watch, perhaps, with ready spears—
355 Down the wide stairs a darkling way they
  found.—

In all the house was heard no human sound.
A chain-droop'd lamp was flickering by each
door;
The arras rich with horseman, hawk, and
hound,
Flutter'd in the besieging wind's uproar;
360 And the long carpets rose along the gusty floor.

XLI.

They glide, like phantoms, into the wide hall;
Like phantoms, to the iron porch, they glide;
Where lay the Porter, in uneasy sprawl,
With a huge empty flagon by his side:
365 The wakeful bloodhound rose, and shook his
hide,
But his sagacious eye an inmate owns:
By one, and one, the bolts full easy slide:—
The chains lie silent on the footworn stones;—
The key turns, and the door upon its hinges
groans.

XLII.

370 And they are gone: ay, ages long ago
These lovers fled away into the storm.
That night the Baron dreamt of many a woe,
And all his warrior-guests, with shade and
form
Of witch, and demon, and large coffin-worm,
375 Were long be-nightmar'd. Angela the old
Died palsy-twitch'd, with meagre face deform;
The Beadsman, after thousand aves told,
For aye unsought-for slept amongst his ashes
cold.

ODE TO A NIGHTINGALE

(1819)

I.

My heart aches, and a drowsy numbness pains
  My sense, as though of hemlock I had drunk,
Or emptied some dull opiate to the drains
  One minute past, and Lethe-wards had sunk:
5 'Tis not through envy of thy happy lot,
  But being too happy in thine happiness,—
    That thou, light-winged Dryad of the trees,
    In some melodious plot
Of beechen green, and shadows numberless,
10 Singest of summer in full-throated ease.

II.

O, for a draught of vintage! that hath been
  Cool'd a long age in the deep-delved earth,
Tasting of Flora and the country green,
  Dance, and Provençal song, and sunburnt
    mirth!
15 O for a beaker full of the warm South,
  Full of the true, the blushful Hippocrene,
    With beaded bubbles winking at the brim,
    And purple-stained mouth;
That I might drink, and leave the world unseen,
20 And with thee fade away into the forest dim:

III.

Fade far away, dissolve, and quite forget
  What thou among the leaves hast never known,
The weariness, the fever, and the fret
  Here, where men sit and hear each other groan;

25 Where palsy shakes a few, sad, last gray hairs,
    Where youth grows pale, and spectre-thin, and
        dies;
      Where but to think is to be full of sorrow
        And leaden-ey'd despairs,
    Where Beauty cannot keep her lustrous eyes,
30   Or new Love pine at them beyond to-morrow.

IV.

Away! away! for I will fly to thee,
    Not charioted by Bacchus and his pards,
But on the viewless wings of Poesy,
    Though the dull brain perplexes and retards:
35 Already with thee! tender is the night,
    And haply the Queen-Moon is on her throne,
      Cluster'd around by all her starry Fays;
        But here there is no light,
Save what from heaven is with the breezes blown
40   Through verdurous glooms and winding mossy
        ways.

V.

I cannot see what flowers are at my feet,
    Nor what soft incense hangs upon the boughs,
But, in embalmed darkness, guess each sweet
    Wherewith the seasonable month endows
45 The grass, the thicket, and the fruit-tree wild;
    White hawthorn, and the pastoral eglantine;
      Fast fading violets cover'd up in leaves;
        And mid-May's eldest child,
The coming musk-rose, full of dewy wine,
50   The murmurous haunt of flies on summer eves.

VI.

Darkling I listen; and, for many a time
    I have been half in love with easeful Death,
Call'd him soft names in many a mused rhyme,
    To take into the air my quiet breath;

55   Now more than ever seems it rich to die,
    To cease upon the midnight with no pain,
        While thou art pouring forth thy soul abroad
            In such an ecstasy!
    Still wouldst thou sing, and I have ears in vain—
60   To thy high requiem become a sod.

VII.

    Thou wast not born for death, immortal Bird!
        No hungry generations tread thee down;
    The voice I hear this passing night was heard
        In ancient days by emperor and clown:
65 Perhaps the self-same song that found a path
        Through the sad heart of Ruth, when, sick for
            home,
            She stood in tears amid the alien corn;
                The same that oft-times hath
    Charm'd magic casements, opening on the foam
70   Of perilous seas, in faery lands forlorn.

VIII.

    Forlorn! the very word is like a bell
        To toll me back from thee to my sole self!
    Adieu! the fancy cannot cheat so well
        As she is fam'd to do, deceiving elf.
75 Adieu! adieu! thy plaintive anthem fades
        Past the near meadows, over the still stream,
            Up the hill-side; and now 'tis buried deep
                In the next valley-glades:
    Was it a vision, or a waking dream?
80   Fled is that music:—Do I wake or sleep?

ODE ON A GRECIAN URN
(Written 1819)

I.

Thou still unravish'd bride of quietness,
   Thou foster-child of silence and slow time,
Sylvan historian, who canst thus express
   A flowery tale more sweetly than our rhyme:
5 What leaf-fring'd legend haunts about thy shape
   Of deities or mortals, or of both,
     In Tempe or the dales of Arcady?
   What men or gods are these? What maidens
     loth?
What mad pursuit? What struggle to escape?
10   What pipes and timbrels? What wild ecstasy?

II.

Heard melodies are sweet, but those unheard
   Are sweeter; therefore, ye soft pipes, play on;
Not to the sensual ear, but, more endear'd,
   Pipe to the spirit ditties of no tone:
15 Fair youth, beneath the trees, thou canst not leave
   Thy song, nor ever can those trees be bare;
     Bold Lover, never, never canst thou kiss,
   Though winning near the goal—yet, do not
     grieve;
     She cannot fade, though thou hast not thy bliss,
20   For ever wilt thou love, and she be fair!

III.

Ah! happy, happy boughs! that cannot shed
   Your leaves, nor ever bid the Spring adieu;
And, happy melodist, unwearied,
   For ever piping songs for ever new;

25 More happy love! more happy, happy love!
      For ever warm and still to be enjoy'd,
         For ever panting, and for ever young;
   All breathing human passion far above,
      That leaves a heart high-sorrowful and cloy'd,
30   A burning forehead, and a parching tongue.

                          IV.

   Who are these coming to the sacrifice?
      To what green altar, O mysterious priest,
   Lead'st thou that heifer lowing at the skies,
      And all her silken flanks with garlands drest?
35 What little town by river or sea shore,
      Or mountain-built with peaceful citadel,
         Is emptied of this folk, this pious morn?
   And, little town, thy streets for evermore
      Will silent be; and not a soul to tell
40   Why thou art desolate, can e'er return.

                          V.

   O Attic shape! Fair attitude! with brede
      Of marble men and maidens overwrought,
   With forest branches and the trodden weed;
      Thou, silent form, dost tease us out of thought
45 As doth eternity: Cold Pastoral!
      When old age shall this generation waste,
         Thou shalt remain, in midst of other woe
   Than ours, a friend to man, to whom thou say'st,
      "Beauty is truth, truth beauty,"—that is all
50   Ye know on earth, and all ye need to know.

TO AUTUMN
(Written 1819 ?)

I.

Season of mists and mellow fruitfulness,
  Close bosom-friend of the maturing sun;
Conspiring with him how to load and bless
    With fruit the vines that round the thatch-
      eaves run;
5 To bend with apples the moss'd cottage-trees,
    And fill all fruit with ripeness to the core;
      To swell the gourd, and plump the hazel
        shells
With a sweet kernel; to set budding more,
    And still more, later flowers for the bees,
10   Until they think warm days will never cease,
      For Summer has o'er-brimm'd their clammy
        cells.

II.

Who hath not seen thee oft amid thy store?
  Sometimes whoever seeks abroad may find
Thee sitting careless on a granary floor,
15   Thy hair soft-lifted by the winnowing wind;
Or on a half-reap'd furrow sound asleep,
    Drows'd with the fume of poppies, while thy
      hook
      Spares the next swath and all its twined
        flowers:
And sometimes like a gleaner thou dost keep
20   Steady thy laden head across a brook;
    Or by a cyder-press, with patient look,
      Thou watchest the last oozings hours by
        hours.

III.

Where are the songs of Spring? Ay, where are
    they?
  Think not of them, thou hast thy music too,—
25 While barred clouds bloom the soft-dying day,
  And touch the stubble-plains with rosy hue;
Then in a wailful choir the small gnats mourn
  Among the river sallows, borne aloft
    Or sinking as the light wind lives or dies;
30 And full-grown lambs loud bleat from hilly
    bourn;
    Hedge-crickets sing; and now with treble soft
  The red-breast whistles from a garden croft;
    And gathering swallows twitter in the skies.

LA BELLE DAME SANS MERCI
(1820)

I.

Ah, what can ail thee, wretched wight,
  Alone and palely loitering;
The sedge is wither'd from the lake,
  And no birds sing.

II.

5 Ah, what can ail thee, wretched wight,
  So haggard and so woe-begone?
The squirrel's granary is full,
  And the harvest's done.

III.

I see a lily on thy brow,
10 With anguish moist and fever dew;
And on thy cheek a fading rose
  Fast withereth too.

IV.

I met a lady in the meads,
    Full beautiful, a faery's child;
15 Her hair was long, her foot was light,
    And her eyes were wild.

V.

I set her on my pacing steed,
    And nothing else saw all day long;
For sideways would she lean and sing
20   A faery's song.

VI.

I made a garland for her head,
    And bracelets too, and fragrant zone;
She look'd at me as she did love,
    And made sweet moan.

VII.

25 She found me roots of relish sweet,
    And honey wild, and manna dew;
And sure in language strange she said,
    I love thee true.

VIII.

She took me to her elfin grot,
30   And there she gaz'd and sighed deep;
And there I shut her wild sad eyes—
    So kissed to sleep.

IX.

And there we slumber'd on the moss,
    And there I dream'd, ah woe betide,
35 The latest dream I ever dream'd,
    On the cold hill side.

X.

I saw pale kings, and princes too,
  Pale warriors, death-pale were they all;
Who cry'd—" La belle Dame sans merci
40 Hath thee in thrall!"

XI.

I saw their starv'd lips in the gloom,
  With horrid warning gaped wide,
And I awoke, and found me here
  On the cold hill side.

XII.

45 And this is why I sojourn here
  Alone and palely loitering,
Though the sedge is wither'd from the lake
  And no birds sing.

SONNETS

ON FIRST LOOKING INTO CHAPMAN'S HOMER
(Written 1816)

XI.

Much have I travell'd in the realms of gold,
  And many goodly states and kingdoms seen;
  Round many western islands have I been
Which bards in fealty to Apollo hold.
5 Oft of one wide expanse had I been told
  That deep-brow'd Homer rul'd as his demesne;
  Yet did I never breathe its pure serene
Till I heard Chapman speak out loud and bold:

Then felt I like some watcher of the skies
10   When a new planet swims into his ken;
Or like stout Cortez when with eagle eyes
    He star'd at the Pacific—and all his men
Look'd at each other with a wild surmise—
    Silent, upon a peak in Darien.

SONNET

(June, 1816)

To one who has been long in city pent,
    'Tis very sweet to look into the fair
    And open face of heaven,—to breathe a prayer
Full in the smile of the blue firmament.
5 Who is more happy, when, with heart's content,
    Fatigued he sinks into some pleasant lair
    Of wavy grass, and reads a debonair
And gentle tale of love and languishment?
Returning home at evening, with an ear
10   Catching the notes of Philomel,—an eye
Watching the sailing cloudlets' bright career,
    He mourns that day so soon has glided by:
E'en like the passage of an angel's tear
    That falls through the clear ether silently.

xv.

ON THE GRASSHOPPER AND CRICKET

(Written December 30th, 1816)

The poetry of earth is never dead:
    When all the birds are faint with the hot sun,
    And hide in cooling trees, a voice will run
From hedge to hedge about the new-mown mead;
5 That is the Grasshopper's—he takes the lead
    In summer luxury,—he has never done
    With his delights; for when tired out with fun
He rests at ease beneath some pleasant weed.

The poetry of earth is ceasing never:
10   On a lone winter evening, when the frost
        Has wrought a silence, from the stove there
          shrills
The Cricket's song, in warmth increasing ever,
    And seems to one in drowsiness half lost,
        The Grasshopper's among some grassy hills.

LAST SONNET

(Written on a Blank Page in Shakespeare's Poems, Facing
"A Lover's Complaint")

(Written 1820)

Bright star, would I were steadfast as thou art—
    Not in lone splendour hung aloft the night
And watching, with eternal lids apart,
    Like nature's patient, sleepless Eremite,
5 The moving waters at their priestlike task
    Of pure ablution round earth's human shores,
Or gazing on the new soft-fallen mask
    Of snow upon the mountains and the moors—
No—yet still steadfast, still unchangeable,
10   Pillow'd upon my fair love's ripening breast,
To feel for ever its soft fall and swell,
    Awake for ever in a sweet unrest,
Still, still to hear her tender-taken breath,
And so live ever—or else swoon to death.

James Henry Leigh Hunt
1784–1859

TO THE GRASSHOPPER AND THE CRICKET
(1816)

Green little vaulter in the sunny grass,
Catching your heart up at the feel of June,
Sole voice that's heard amidst the lazy noon,
When even the bees lag at the summoning brass;

5 And you, warm little housekeeper, who class
   With those who think the candles come too soon,
   Loving the fire, and with your tricksome tune
   Nick the glad silent moments as they pass;

   Oh sweet and tiny cousins, that belong,
10 One to the fields, the other to the hearth,
   Both have your sunshine; both, though small, are
        strong
   At your clear hearts; and both seem giv'n to earth
   To sing in thoughtful ears this natural song—
   In doors and out, summer and winter, Mirth.

Walter Savage Landor
1775–1864
MILD IS THE PARTING YEAR, AND SWEET
(Collected Works, 1846)

   Mild is the parting year, and sweet
      The odour of the falling spray;
   Life passes on more rudely fleet,
      And balmless is its closing day.
5 I wait its close, I court its gloom,
      But mourn that never must there fall
   Or on my breast or on my tomb
      The tear that would have sooth'd it all.

AH WHAT AVAILS THE SCEPTERED RACE
(From the same)

   Ah what avails the sceptered race,
      Ah what the form divine!
   What every virtue, every grace!
      Rose Aylmer, all were thine,
5 Rose Aylmer, whom these wakeful eyes
      May weep, but never see,
   A night of memories and of sighs
      I consecrate to thee.

YES; I WRITE VERSES

(From the same)

Yes; I write verses now and then,
But blunt and flaccid is my pen,
No longer talkt of by young men
             As rather clever:
5 In the last quarter are my eyes,
You see it by their form and size;
Is it not time then to be wise?
             Or now or never.
Fairest that ever sprang from Eve!
10 While Time allows the short reprieve,
Just look at me! would you believe
             'Twas once a lover?
I cannot clear the five-bar gate
But, trying first its timber's state,
15 Climb stiffly up, take breath, and wait
             To trundle over.
Thro' gallopade I cannot swing
The entangling blooms of Beauty's spring:
I cannot say the tender thing,
20   Be't true or false,
And am beginning to opine
Those girls are only half-divine
Whose waists yon wicked boys entwine
             In giddy waltz.
25 I fear that arm above that shoulder,
I wish them wiser, graver, older,
Sedater, and no harm if colder
             And panting less.
Ah! people were not half so wild
30 In former days, when starchly mild,
Upon her high-heel'd Essex smiled
             The Brave Queen Bess.

TO ROBERT BROWNING
(From the same)

There is delight in singing, tho' none hear
Beside the singer; and there is delight
In praising, tho' the praiser sit alone
And see the prais'd far off him, far above.
5 Shakespeare is not our poet, but the world's,
Therefore on him no speech! and brief for thee,
Browning! Since Chaucer was alive and hale,
No man hath walkt along our roads with step
So active, so inquiring eye, or tongue
10 So varied in discourse. But warmer climes
Give brighter plumage, stronger wing: the breeze
Of Alpine heights thou playest with, borne on
Beyond Sorrento and Amalfi, where
The Siren waits thee, singing song for song.

INTRODUCTION TO
THE LAST FRUIT OFF AN OLD TREE
(1853)

I strove with none, for none was worth my strife.
Nature I loved, and, next to Nature, Art;
I warmed both hands before the fire of Life;
It sinks, and I am ready to depart.

Bryan Waller Procter
(Barry Cornwall)
1787-1874

A PETITION TO TIME
(From *Poems*, 1850)

Touch us gently, Time!
　Let us glide adown thy stream
Gently,—as we sometimes glide
　Through a quiet dream!

5 Humble voyagers are We,
  Husband, wife, and children three—
  (One is lost,—an angel, fled
    To the azure overhead!)

  Touch us gently, Time!
10   We've not proud nor soaring wings:
  Our ambition, *our* content
    Lies in simple things.
  Humble voyagers are We,
  O'er Life's dim unsounded sea,—
15 Seeking only some calm clime:—
  Touch us *gently*, gentle Time!

Hartley Coleridge

1796–1849

SONG

(From *Poems*, 1833)

  She is not fair to outward view
    As many maidens be,
  Her loveliness I never knew
    Until she smiled on me;
5 Oh! then I saw her eye was bright,
  A well of love, a spring of light.

  But now her looks are coy and cold,
    To mine they ne'er reply,
  And yet I cease not to behold
10   The love-light in her eye:
  Her very frowns are fairer far,
  Than smiles of other maidens are.

Charles Lamb

1775–1834

TO HESTER

(1805)

When maidens such as Hester die,
Their place ye may not well supply,
Though ye among a thousand try,
      With vain endeavour.

5 A month or more hath she been dead,
Yet cannot I by force be led
To think upon the wormy bed,
      And her together.

A springy motion in her gait,
10 A rising step, did indicate
Of pride and joy no common rate,
      That flushed her spirit.

I know not by what name beside
I shall it call;—if 'twas not pride,
15 It was a joy to that allied,
      She did inherit.

Her parents held the Quaker rule,
Which doth the human feeling cool,
But she was train'd in Nature's school,
20   Nature had blest her.

A waking eye, a prying mind,
A heart that stirs, is hard to bind,
A hawk's keen sight ye cannot blind,
      Ye could not Hester.

25 My sprightly neighbour, gone before
  To that unknown and silent shore,
  Shall we not meet, as heretofore,
      Some summer morning,

  When from thy cheerful eyes a ray
30 Hath struck a bliss upon the day,
  A bliss that would not go away,
      A sweet fore-warning?

Thomas Hood

1798–1845

THE DEATH BED

(From *Poems*, 1825)

We watched her breathing thro' the night,
  Her breathing soft and low,
As in her breast the wave of life
  Kept heaving to and fro.

5 So silently we seemed to speak,
  So slowly moved about,
As we had lent her half our powers
  To eke her living out.

Our very hopes belied our fears,
10 Our fears our hopes belied—
We thought her dying when she slept,
  And sleeping when she died.

For when the morn came dim and sad,
  And chill with early showers,
15 Her quiet eyelids closed—she had
  Another morn than ours.

THE BRIDGE OF SIGHS

("Drowned! drowned!"—*Hamlet*)

(First published in *Hood's Magazine*, 1844)

One more Unfortunate,
Weary of breath,
Rashly importunate,
Gone to her death!

5 Take her up tenderly,
Lift her with care;
Fashioned so slenderly,
Young, and so fair!

Look at her garments
10 Clinging like cerements;
Whilst the wave constantly
Drips from her clothing;
Take her up instantly,
Loving, not loathing.—

15 Touch her not scornfully;
Think of her mournfully,
Gently and humanly;
Not of the stains of her,
All that remains of her
20 Now is pure womanly.

Make no deep scrutiny
Into her mutiny
Rash and undutiful:
Past all dishonor,
25 Death has left on her
Only the beautiful.

Still, for all slips of hers,
One of Eve's family—
Wipe those poor lips of hers
30 Oozing so clammily.

Loop up her tresses
Escaped from the comb,
Her fair auburn tresses;
Whilst wonderment guesses
35 Where was her home?

Who was her father?
Who was her mother?
Had she a sister?
Had she a brother?
40 Or was there a dearer one
Still, and a nearer one
Yet, than all other?

Alas! for the rarity
Of Christian charity
45 Under the sun!
Oh! it was pitiful!
Near a whole city full,
Home she had none.

Sisterly, brotherly,
50 Fatherly, motherly
Feelings had changed:
Love, by harsh evidence,
Thrown from its eminence;
Even God's providence
55 Seeming estranged.

Where the lamps quiver
So far in the river,
With many a light
From window and casement,
60 From garret to basement,
She stood, with amazement,
Houseless by night.

The bleak wind of March
Made her tremble and shiver;
65 But not the dark arch,
Or the black flowing river:
Mad from life's history,
Glad to death's mystery,
Swift to be hurled—
70 Anywhere, anywhere
Out of the world.

In she plunged boldly,
No matter how coldly
The rough river ran,—
75 Over the brink of it,
Picture it—think of it,
Dissolute Man!
Lave in it, drink of it,
Then, if you can!

80 Take her up tenderly,
Lift her with care;
Fashioned so slenderly,
Young, and so fair!

Ere her limbs frigidly
85 Stiffen too rigidly,
Decently,—kindly,—
Smooth, and compose them;
And her eyes, close them,
Staring so blindly!

90 Dreadfully staring
Thro' muddy impurity,
As when with the daring
Last look of despairing
Fix'd on futurity.

95 Perishing gloomily,
Spurred by contumely,
Cold inhumanity,
Burning insanity,
Into her rest.—
100 Cross her hands humbly
As if praying dumbly,
Over her breast.

Owning her weakness,
Her evil behavior,
105 And leaving, with meekness,
Her sins to her Saviour!

PART FIFTH

VICTORIAN VERSE

Thomas Babington Macaulay

1800–1859

BATTLE OF IVRY

(1842)

Now glory to the Lord of Hosts, from whom all
    glories are!
And glory to our Sovereign Liege, King Henry
    of Navarre!
Now let there be the merry sound of music and
    of dance,
Through thy corn-fields green and sunny vines,
5 O pleasant land of France!
And thou, Rochelle, our own Rochelle, proud city
    of the waters,
Again let rapture light the eyes of all thy mourn-
    ing daughters.
As thou wert constant in our ills, be joyous in
    our joy;
For cold and stiff and still are they who wrought
    thy walls annoy.
10 Hurrah! hurrah! a single field hath turn'd the
    chance of war!
Hurrah! hurrah! for Ivry, and King Henry of
    Navarre.
Oh! how our hearts were beating, when, at the
    dawn of day,
We saw the army of the League drawn out in
    long array;

With all its priest-led citizens, and all its rebel
  peers,
15 And Appenzel's stout infantry, and Egmont's
  Flemish spears;
There rode the blood of false Lorraine, the curses
  of our land;
And dark Mayenne was in the midst, a truncheon
  in his hand;
And, as we look'd on them, we thought of Seine's
  empurpled flood,
And good Coligni's hoary hair all dabbled with his
  blood;
20 And we cried unto the living God, who rules the
  fate of war,
To fight for His own holy name, and Henry of
  Navarre.

The king is come to marshal us, in all his armor
  drest;
And he has bound a snow-white plume upon his
  gallant crest.
He look'd upon his people, and a tear was in his
  eye;
25 He look'd upon the traitors, and his glance was
  stern and high.
Right graciously he smil'd on us, as roll'd from
  wing to wing,
Down all our line, in deafening shout: "God save
  our lord, the king!"
"And if my standard-bearer fall, as fall full well
  he may,
For never saw I promise yet of such a bloody
  fray,
30 Press where ye see my white plume shine amidst
  the ranks of war,
And be your oriflamme to-day the helmet of
  Navarre."

Hurrah! the foes are moving. Hark to the mingled din,
Of fife, and steed, and trump, and drum, and
roaring culverin.
The fiery duke is pricking fast across St. Andre's
plain,
35 With all the hireling chivalry of Guelders and
Almayne.
Now by the lips of those ye love, fair gentlemen
of France,
Charge for the golden lilies now upon them with
the lance!
A thousand spurs are striking deep, a thousand
spears in rest,
A thousand knights are pressing close behind the
snow-white crest;
40 And in they burst, and on they rush'd, while, like
a guiding star,
Amidst the thickest carnage blaz'd the helmet of
Navarre.

Now, God be prais'd, the day is ours: Mayenne
hath turn'd his rein,
D'Aumale hath cried for quarter; the Flemish
Count is slain,
Their ranks are breaking like thin clouds before
a Biscay gale;
45 The field is heap'd with bleeding steeds, and flags,
and cloven mail;
And then we thought on vengeance, and all along
our van,
"Remember St. Bartholomew!" was pass'd from
man to man.
But out spake gentle Henry—"No Frenchman is
my foe:
Down, down with every foreigner, but let your
brethren go."

50 Oh! was there ever such a knight, in friendship
    or in war,
  As our sovereign lord, King Henry, the soldier of
    Navarre?

Right well fought all the Frenchmen who fought
    for France to-day;
And many a lordly banner God gave them for a
    prey.
But we of the religion have borne us best in fight;
55 And the good lord of Rosny hath ta'en the cor-
    net white—
Our own true Maximilian the cornet white hath
    ta'en;
The cornet white, with crosses black the flag of
    false Lorraine.
Up with it high; unfurl it wide;—that all the
    host may know
How God hath humbled the proud house which
    wrought His Church such woe.
60 Then on the ground, while trumpets sound their
    loudest point of war,
Fling the red shreds a footcloth meet for Henry
    of Navarre.

Ho! maidens of Vienna; ho! matrons of Luzerne,
Weep, weep, and rend your hair for those who
    never shall return.
Ho! Philip, send, for charity, thy Mexican
    pistoles,
65 That Antwerp monks may sing a mass for thy
    poor spearmen's souls.
Ho! gallant nobles of the League, look that your
    arms be bright;
Ho! burghers of St. Genevieve, keep watch and
    ward to-night;
For our God hath crush'd the tyrant, our God
    hath rais'd the slave,

And mock'd the counsel of the wise and the valor
    of the brave.
70 Then glory to His holy name, from whom all
    glories are;
And glory to our sovereign lord, King Henry of
    Navarre!

Alfred Tennyson

1809–1892

LOCKSLEY HALL

(From *Poems*, 1842)

COMRADES, leave me here a little, while as yet
    'tis early morn:
Leave me here, and when you want me, sound
    upon the bugle-horn.

'Tis the place, and all around it, as of old, the
    curlews call,
Dreary gleams about the moorland flying over
    Locksley Hall;

5 Locksley Hall, that in the distance overlooks the
    sandy tracts,
And the hollow-ocean ridges roaring into cata-
    racts.

Many a night from yonder ivied casement, ere I
    went to rest,
Did I look on great Orion sloping slowly to the
    West.

Many a night I saw the Pleiads, rising thro' the
    mellow shade,
10 Glitter like a swarm of fire-flies tangled in a silver
    braid.

Here about the beach I wander'd, nourishing a
    youth sublime
With the fairy tales of science, and the long result
    of Time;

When the centuries behind me like a fruitful land
    reposed;
When I clung to all the present for the promise
    that it closed.

15 When I dipt into the future far as human eye
    could see;
Saw the Vision of the world, and all the wonder
    that would be.—

In the Spring a fuller crimson comes upon the
    robin's breast;
In the Spring the wanton lapwing gets himself
    another crest;

In the Spring a livelier iris changes on the bur-
    nish'd dove;
20 In the Spring a young man's fancy lightly turns
    to thoughts of love.

Then her cheek was pale and thinner than should
    be for one so young,
And her eyes on all my motions with a mute
    observance hung.

And I said, 'My Cousin Amy, speak, and speak
    the truth to me,
Trust me, cousin, all the current of my being sets
    to thee.'

25 On her pallid cheek and forehead came a colour
    and a light,
As I have seen the rosy red flushing in the
    northern night.

And she turn'd—her bosom shaken with a sudden
    storm of sighs—
All the spirit deeply dawning in the dark of hazel
    eyes—

Saying, 'I have hid my feelings, fearing they
    should do me wrong;'
30 Saying, 'Dost thou love me, cousin?' weeping,
    'I have loved thee long.'

Love took up the glass of Time, and turn'd it in
    his glowing hands
Every moment, lightly shaken, ran itself in golden
    sands.

Love took up the harp of Life, and smote on all
    the chords with might;
Smote the chord of Self, that, trembling, pass'd
    in music out of sight.

35 Many a morning on the moorland did we hear
    the copses ring,
And her whisper throng'd my pulses with the full-
    ness of the Spring.

Many an evening by the waters did we watch the
    stately ships,
And our spirits rush'd together at the touching
    of the lips.

O my cousin, shallow-hearted! O my Amy, mine
    no more!
40 O the dreary, dreary moorland! O the barren,
    barren shore!

Falser than all fancy fathoms, falser than all
    songs have sung,
Puppet to a father's threat, and servile to a
    shrewish tongue!

Is it well to wish thee happy?—having known me
　　—to decline
On a range of lower feelings and a narrower heart
　　than mine!

45 Yet it shall be: thou shalt lower to his level day
　　by day,
What is fine within thee growing coarse to sym-
　　pathise with clay.

As the husband is, the wife is: thou art mated
　　with a clown,
And the grossness of his nature will have weight
　　to drag thee down.

He will hold thee, when his passion shall have
　　spent its novel force,
50 Something better than his dog, a little dearer
　　than his horse.

What is this? his eyes are heavy: think not they
　　are glazed with wine.
Go to him: it is thy duty: kiss him: take his hand
　　in thine.

It may be my lord is weary, that his brain is over-
　　wrought:
Soothe him with thy finer fancies, touch him with
　　thy lighter thought.

55 He will answer to the purpose, easy things to
　　understand—
Better thou wert dead before me, tho' I slew thee
　　with my hand!

Better thou and I were lying, hidden from the
　　heart's disgrace,
Roll'd in one another's arms, and silent in a last
　　embrace.

Cursed be the social wants that sin against the
  strength of youth!
60 Cursed be the social lies that warp us from the
  living truth!

Cursed be the sickly forms that err from honest
  Nature's rule!
Cursed be the gold that gilds the straitened fore-
  head of the fool!

Well—'tis well that I should bluster!—Hadst thou
  less unworthy proved—
Would to God—for I had loved thee more than
  ever wife was loved.

65 Am I mad, that I should cherish that which bears
  but bitter fruit?
I will pluck it from my bosom, tho' my heart be
  at the root.

Never, tho' my mortal summers to such length of
  years should come
As the many-winter'd crow that leads the clanging rookery home.

Where is comfort? in division of the records of
  the mind?
70 Can I part her from herself, and love her, as I
  knew her, kind?

I remember one that perish'd: sweetly did she
  speak and move:
Such a one do I remember, whom to look at was
  to love.

Can I think of her as dead, and love her for the
  love she bore?
No—she never loved me truly: love is love for-
  evermore.

75 Comfort? comfort scorn'd of devils! this is truth
　　　the poet sings,
　That a sorrow's crown of sorrow is remembering
　　　happier things.

　Drug thy memories, lest thou learn it, lest thy
　　　heart be put to proof,
　In the dead unhappy night, and when the rain is
　　　on the roof.

　Like a dog, he hunts in dreams, and thou art
　　　staring at the wall,
80 Where the dying night-lamp flickers, and the
　　　shadows rise and fall.

　Then a hand shall pass before thee, pointing to
　　　his drunken sleep,
　To thy widow'd marriage-pillows, to the tears that
　　　thou wilt weep.

　Thou shalt hear the ' Never, never,' whisper'd by
　　　the phantom years,
　And a song from out the distance in the ringing
　　　of thine ears;

85 And an eye shall vex thee, looking ancient kind-
　　　ness on thy pain.
　Turn thee, turn thee on thy pillow: get thee to
　　　thy rest again.

　Nay, but Nature brings thee solace; for a tender
　　　voice will cry.
　'Tis a purer life than thine; a lip to drain thy
　　　trouble dry.

　Baby lips will laugh me down: my latest rival
　　　brings thee rest.
90 Baby fingers, waxen touches, press me from the
　　　mother's breast.

O, the child too clothes the father with a dearness
  not his due.
Half is thine and half is his: it will be worthy of
  the two.

O, I see thee, old and formal, fitted to thy petty
  part,
With a little hoard of maxims preaching down a
  daughter's heart.

95 'They were dangerous guides the feelings—she
  herself was not exempt—
Truly, she herself had suffer'd'—Perish in thy
  self-contempt!

Overlive it—lower yet—be happy! wherefore
  should I care?
I myself must mix with action, lest I wither by
  despair.

What is that which I should turn to, lighting
  upon days like these?
100 Every door is barr'd with gold, and opens but to
  golden keys.

Every gate is throng'd with suitors, all the mar-
  kets overflow.
I have but an angry fancy: what is that which
  I should do?

I had been content to perish, falling on the foe-
  man's ground,
When the ranks are roll'd in vapour, and the
  winds are laid with sound.

105 But the jingling of the guinea helps the hurt that
  Honour feels,
And the nations do but murmur, snarling at each
  other's heels.

Can I but relive in sadness? I will turn that
    earlier page.
Hide me from my deep emotion, O thou wondrous
    Mother-Age!

Make me feel the wild pulsation that I felt before
    the strife,
110 When I heard my days before me, and the tumult
    of my life;

Yearning for the large excitement that the com-
    ing years would yield,
Eager-hearted as a boy when first he leaves his
    father's field.

And at night along the dusky highway near and
    nearer drawn,
Sees in heaven the light of London flaring like
    a dreary dawn;

115 And his spirit leaps within him to be gone before
    him then,
Underneath the light he looks at, in among the
    throngs of men;

Men, my brothers, men the workers, ever reaping
    something new:
That which they have done but earnest of the
    things that they shall do:

For I dipt into the future, far as human eye
    could see,
120 Saw the Vision of the world, and all the wonder
    that would be;

Saw the heavens fill with commerce, argosies of
    magic sails,
Pilots of the purple twilight, dropping down with
    costly bales;

Heard the heavens fill with shouting, and there
    rain'd a ghastly dew
From the nations' airy navies grappling in the
    central blue;

125 Far along the world-wide whisper of the south-
    wind rushing warm,
With the standards of the peoples plunging thro'
    the thunder-storm;

Till the war-drum throbb'd no longer, and the
    battle-flags were furl'd,
In the Parliament of man, the Federation of the
    world.

There the common sense of most shall hold a fret-
    ful realm in awe,
130 And the kindly earth shall slumber, lapt in uni-
    versal law.

So I triumph'd ere my passion sweeping thro' me
    left me dry,
Left me with the palsied heart, and left me with
    the jaundiced eye;

Eye, to which all order festers, all things here are
    out of joint:
Science moves, but slowly, slowly, creeping on
    from point to point:

135 Slowly comes a hungry people, as a lion creeping
    nigher,
Glares at one that nods and winks behind a
    slowly-dying fire.

Yet I doubt not thro' the ages one increasing
    purpose runs,
And the thoughts of men are widen'd with the
    process of the suns.

What is that to him that reaps not harvest of his
    youthful joys,
140 Tho' the deep heart of existence beat forever like
    a boy's?

Knowledge comes, but wisdom lingers, and I
    linger on the shore,
And the individual withers, and the world is more
    and more.

Knowledge comes, but wisdom lingers, and he
    bears a laden breast,
Full of sad experience, moving toward the still-
    ness of his rest.

145 Hark, my merry comrades call me, sounding on
    the bugle-horn,
They to whom my foolish passion were a target
    for their scorn:

Shall it not be scorn to me to harp on such a
    moulder'd string?
I am shamed thro' all my nature to have loved
    so slight a thing.

Weakness to be wroth with weakness! woman's
    pleasure, woman's pain—
150 Nature made them blinder motions bounded in
    a shallower brain:

Woman is the lesser man, and all thy passions,
    match'd with mine,
Are as moonlight unto sunlight, and as water
    unto wine—

Here at least, where nature sickens, nothing.
    Ah for some retreat
Deep in yonder shining Orient, where my life be-
    gan to beat;

155 Where in wild Mahratta-battle fell my father,
      evil-starr'd;—
    I was left a trampled orphan, and a selfish uncle's
      ward.

    Or to burst all links of habit—there to wander
      far away,
    On from island unto island at the gateways of
      the day.

    Larger constellations burning, mellow moons and
      happy skies,
160 Breadths of tropic shade and palms in cluster,
      knots of Paradise.

    Never comes the trader, never floats an European
      flag,
    Slides the bird o'er lustrous woodland, swings
      the trailer from the crag;

    Droops the heavy-blossom'd bower, hangs the
      heavy-fruit'd tree—
    Summer isles of Eden lying in dark-purple
      spheres of sea.

165 There methinks would be enjoyment more than in
      this march of mind,
    In the steamship, in the railway, in the thoughts
      that shake mankind.

    There the passions cramp'd no longer shall have
      scope and breathing space;
    I will take some savage woman, she shall rear my
      dusky race.

    Iron-jointed, supple-sinew'd, they shall dive, and
      they shall run,
170 Catch the wild goat by the hair, and hurl their
      lances in the sun;

Whistle back the parrot's call, and leap the rainbows of the brooks,
Not with blinded eyesight poring over miserable
books—

Fool, again the dream, the fancy! but I *know* my
words are wild,
But I count the gray barbarian lower than the
Christian child.

175 I, to herd with narrow foreheads, vacant of our
glorious gains,
Like a beast with lower pleasures, like a beast
with lower pains!

Mated with a squalid savage—what to me were
sun or clime?
I the heir of all the ages, in the foremost files of
time—

I that rather held it better men should perish
one by one,
180 Than that earth should stand at gaze like
Joshua's moon in Ajalon!

Not in vain the distance beacons. Forward, forward let us range,
Let the great world spin forever down the ringing grooves of change.

Thro' the shadow of the globe we sweep into the
younger day:
Better fifty years of Europe than a cycle of
Cathay.

185 Mother-Age (for mine I knew not) help me as
when life begun:
Rift the hills, and roll the waters, flash the
lightnings, weigh the Sun,

O, I see the crescent promise of my spirit hath
    not set.
Ancient founts of inspiration well thro' all my
    fancy yet.

Howsoever these things be, a long farewell to
    Locksley Hall!
190 Now for me the woods may wither, now for me
    the roof-tree fall.

Comes a vapour from the margin, blackening
    over heath and holt,
Cramming all the blast before it, in its breast a
    thunderbolt.

Let it fall on Locksley Hall, with rain or hail, or
    fire or snow;
For the mighty wind arises, roaring seaward, and
    I go.

ULYSSES

(From the same)

It little profits that an idle king,
By this still hearth, among these barren crags,
Match'd with an aged wife, I mete and dole
Unequal laws unto a savage race,
5 That hoard, and sleep, and feed, and know not me.
I cannot rest from travel: I will drink
Life to the lees: all times I have enjoy'd
Greatly, have suffer'd greatly, both with those
That loved me, and alone; on shore, and when
10 Thro' scudding drifts the rainy Hyades
Vext the dim sea: I am become a name;
For always roaming with a hungry heart

Much have I seen and known; cities of men
And manners, climates, councils, governments,
15 Myself not least, but honour'd of them all;
And drunk delight of battle with my peers,
Far on the ringing plains of windy Troy.
I am a part of all that I have met;
Yet all experience is an arch wherethro'
20 Gleams that untravell'd world, whose margin
    fades
Forever and forever when I move.
How dull it is to pause, to make an end,
To rust unburnished, not to shine in use!
As tho' to breathe were life. Life piled on life
25 Were all too little, and of one to me
Little remains: but every hour is saved
From that eternal silence, something more,
A bringer of new things; and vile it were
For some three suns to store and hoard myself,
30 And this gray spirit yearning in desire
To follow knowledge like a sinking star,
Beyond the utmost bound of human thought.
This is my son, mine own Telemachus,
To whom I leave the sceptre and the isle—
35 Well-loved of me, discerning to fulfil
This labour, by slow prudence to make mild
A rugged people, and thro' soft degrees
Subdue them to the useful and the good.
Most blameless is he, centred in the sphere
40 Of common duties, decent not to fail
In offices of tenderness, and pay
Meet adoration to my household gods,
When I am gone. He works his work, I mine.
    There lies the port; the vessel puffs her sail:
45 There gloom the dark broad seas. My mariners,
Souls that have toil'd and wrought, and thought
    with me—
That ever with a frolic welcome took

The thunder and the sunshine, and opposed
Free hearts, free foreheads—you and I are old;
50 Old age hath yet his honour and his toil;
Death closes all: but something ere the end,
Some work of noble note, may yet be done,
Not unbecoming men that strove with Gods.
The lights begin to twinkle from the rocks:
55 The long day wanes: the slow moon climbs: the
        deep
Moans round with many voices. Come, my
        friends,
'Tis not too late to seek a newer world.
Push off, and sitting well in order smite
The sounding furrows; for my purpose holds
60 To sail beyond the sunset, and the baths
Of all the western stars, until I die.
It may be that the gulfs will wash us down:
It may be we shall touch the Happy Isles,
And see the great Achilles, whom we knew.
65 Tho' much is taken, much abides; and tho'
We are not now that strength which in old days
Moved earth and heaven; that which we are, we
        are;
One equal temper of heroic hearts,
Made weak by time and fate, but strong in will
70 To strive, to seek, to find, and not to yield.

THE EPIC

(INTRODUCTION TO MORTE D'ARTHUR)

(From *Poems*, 1842)

At Francis Allen's on the Christmas-eve,—
The game of forfeits done—the girls all kiss'd
Beneath the sacred bush and past away—
The parson Holmes, the poet Everard Hall,

5 The host, and I sat round the wassail-bowl,
  Then half-way ebb'd: and there we held a talk,
  How all the old honour had from Christmas gone,
  Or gone or dwindled down to some old games
  In some odd nooks like this; till I, tired out
10 With cutting eights that day upon the pond,
  Where, three times slipping from the outer edge,
  I bump'd the ice into three several stars,
  Fell in a doze; and half-awake I heard
  The parson taking wide and wider sweeps,
15 Now harping on the church-commissioners,
  Now hawking at Geology and schism;
  Until I woke, and found him settled down
  Upon the general decay of faith
  Right thro' the world, 'at home was little left,
20 And none abroad: there was no anchor, none,
  To hold by.' Francis, laughing, clapt his hand
  On Everard's shoulder, with 'I hold by him.'
  'And I,' quoth Everard, 'by the wassail-bowl.'
  'Why yes,' I said, 'we knew your gift that way
25 At college: but another which you had,
  I mean of verse (for so we held it then),
  What came of that?' 'You know,' said Frank,
    'he burnt
  His epic, his King Arthur, some twelve books'—
  And then to me demanding why? 'Oh, sir,
30 He thought that nothing new was said, or else
  Something so said 'twas nothing—that a truth
  Looks freshest in the fashion of the day:
  God knows: he has a mint of reasons: ask.
  It pleased *me* well enough.' 'Nay, nay,' said
    Hall,
35 'Why take the style of those heroic times?
  For nature brings not back the Mastodon,
  Nor we those times; and why should any man
  Remodel models? these twelve books of mine
  Were faint Homeric echoes, nothing-worth,

40 Mere chaff and draff, much better burnt.'
      'But I,'
  Said Francis, 'pick'd the eleventh from this
      hearth
  And have it; keep a thing, its use will come.
  I hoard it as a sugar-plum for Holmes.'
  He laugh'd, and I, tho' sleepy, like a horse
45 That hears the corn-bin open, prick'd my ears;
  For I remember'd Everard's college fame
  When we were Freshmen: then at my request
  He brought; and the poet little urged,
  But with some prelude of disparagement,
50 Read, mouthing out his hollow oes and aes,
  Deep-chested music, and to this result.

MORTE D'ARTHUR

  So all day long the noise of battle roll'd
  Among the mountains by the winter sea;
  Until King Arthur's table, man by man,
  Had fallen in Lyonesse about their Lord,
5 King Arthur: then, because his wound was deep,
  The bold Sir Bedivere uplifted him,
  Sir Bedivere, the last of all his knights,
  And bore him to a chapel nigh the field,
  A broken chancel with a broken cross,
10 That stood on a dark strait of barren land.
  On one side lay the Ocean, and on one
  Lay a great water, and the moon was full.
  Then spake King Arthur to Sir Bedivere:
  'The sequel of to-day unsolders all
15 The goodliest fellowship of famous knights
  Whereof this world holds record. Such a sleep
  They sleep—the men I loved. I think that we

Shall never more, at any future time,
Delight our souls with talk of knightly deeds,
20 Walking about the gardens and the halls
Of Camelot, as in the days that were.
I perish by this people which I made,—
Tho' Merlin sware that I should come again
To rule once more—but let what will be, be,
25 I am so deeply smitten thro' the helm
That without help I cannot last till morn.
Thou therefore take my brand Excalibur,
Which was my pride: for thou rememberest how
In those old days, one summer noon, an arm
30 Rose up from out the bosom of the lake,
Clothed in white samite, mystic, wonderful,
Holding the sword—and how I row'd across
And took it, and have worn it, like a king:
And, wheresoever I am sung or told
35 In after time, this also shall be known:
But now delay not: take Excalibur,
And fling him far into the middle mere:
Watch what thou seëst, and lightly bring me
word.'
To him replied the bold Sir Bedivere:
40 'It is not meet, Sir King, to leave thee thus,
Aidless, alone, and smitten thro' the helm.
A little thing may harm a wounded man.
Yet I thy hest will all perform at full,
Watch what I see, and lightly bring thee word.'
45 So saying, from the ruin'd shrine he stept
And in the moon athwart the place of tombs,
Where lay the mighty bones of ancient men,
Old knights, and over them the sea-wind sang
Shrill, chill, with flakes of foam. He, stepping
down
50 By zigzag paths, and juts of pointed rock,
Came on the shining levels of the lake.
There drew he forth the brand Excalibur,

And o'er him, drawing it, the winter moon,
Brightening the skirts of a long cloud, ran forth
55 And sparkled keen with frost against the hilt:
For all the haft twinkled with diamond sparks,
Myriads of topaz-lights, and jacinth-work
Of subtlest jewellery. He gazed so long
That both his eyes were dazzled, as he stood,
60 This way and that dividing the swift mind,
In act to throw: but at the last it seem'd
Better to leave Excalibur conceal'd
There in the many-knotted waterflags,
That whistled stiff and dry about the marge.
65 So strode he back slow to the wounded King.
　　Then spake King Arthur to Sir Bedivere:
'Hast thou perform'd my mission which I gave?
What is it thou hast seen? or what hast heard?'
　　And answer made the bold Sir Bedivere:
70 'I heard the ripple washing in the reeds,
And the wild water lapping on the crags.'
　　To whom replied King Arthur, faint and pale:
'Thou hast betray'd thy nature and thy name,
Not rendering true answer, as beseem'd
75 Thy fealty, nor like a noble knight:
For surer sign had follow'd, either hand,
Or voice, or else a motion of the mere.
This is a shameful thing for men to lie.
Yet now, I charge thee, quickly go again
80 As thou art lief and dear, and do the thing
I bade thee, watch, and lightly bring me word.'
　　Then went Sir Bedivere the second time
Across the ridge, and paced beside the mere,
Counting the dewy pebbles, fix'd in thought;
85 But when he saw the wonder of the hilt,
How curiously and strangely chased, he smote
His palms together, and he cried aloud,
'And if indeed I cast the brand away,
Surely a precious thing, one worthy note

90 Should thus be lost forever from the earth,
    Which might have pleased the eyes of many men
    What good should follow this, if this were done?
    What harm, undone? deep harm to disobey,
    Seeing obedience is the bond of rule.
95 Were it well to obey then, if a king demand
    An act unprofitable, against himself?
    The King is sick, and knows not what he does.
    What record, or what relic of my lord
    Should be to aftertime, but empty breath
100 And rumours of a doubt? but were this kept,
    Stored in some treasure-house of mighty kings,
    Some one might show it at a joust of arms,
    Saying, " King Arthur's sword, Excalibur,
    Wrought by the lonely maiden of the Lake.
105 Nine years she wrought it, sitting in the deeps
    Upon the hidden bases of the hills."
    So might some old man speak in the aftertime
    To all the people, winning reverence.
    But now much honour and much fame were lost.'
110   So spake he, clouded with his own conceit,
    And hid Excalibur the second time,
    And so strode back slow to the wounded king.
      Then spoke King Arthur, breathing heavily:
    ' What is it thou hast seen? or what hast heard?'
115 And answer made the bold Sir Bedivere:
    ' I heard the water lapping on the crag
    And the long ripple washing in the reeds.'
      To whom replied King Arthur, much in wrath:
    ' Ah, miserable and unkind, untrue,
120 Unknightly, traitor-hearted! Woe is me!
    Authority forgets a dying king,
    Laid widow'd of the power in his eye
    That bow'd the will. I see thee what thou art,
    For thou, the latest-left of all my knights,
125 In whom should meet the offices of all,
    Thou would'st betray me for the precious hilt;

Either from lust of gold, or like a girl
Valuing the giddy pleasure of the eyes.
Yet, for a man may fail in duty twice,
130 And the third time may prosper, get thee hence:
But, if thou spare to fling Excalibur,
I will arise and slay thee with my hands.'
    Then quickly rose Sir Bedivere, and ran,
And, leaping down the ridges lightly, plunged
135 Among the bulrush-beds, and clutch'd the sword,
And strongly wheel'd and threw it. The great
        brand
Made lightnings in the splendour of the moon,
And flashing round and round, and whirl'd in an
        arch,
Shot like a streamer of the northern morn,
140 Seen where the moving isles of winter shock
By night, with noises of the northern sea.
So flash'd and fell the brand Excalibur:
But ere he dipt the surface, rose an arm
Clothed in white samite, mystic, wonderful,
145 And caught him by the hilt, and brandished him
Three times, and drew him under in the mere.
And lightly went the other to the King.
    Then spoke King Arthur, drawing thicker
        breath:
' Now see I by thy eyes that this is done.
150 Speak out: what is it thou hast heard, or seen?'
    And answer made the bold Sir Bedivere:
' Sir king, I closed mine eyelids, lest the gems
Should blind my purpose, for I never saw,
Nor shall see, here or elsewhere, till I die,
155 Not tho' I live three lives of mortal men,
So great a miracle as yonder hilt.
    Then with both hands I flung him, wheeling
        him;
But when I look'd again, behold an arm,
Clothed in white samite, mystic, wonderful,

160 That caught him by the hilt, and brandish'd him
  Three times, and drew him under in the mere.'
      And answer made King Arthur, breathing
          hard:
  ' My end draws nigh; 'tis time that I were gone.
  Make broad thy shoulders to receive my weight,
165 And bear me to the margin; yet I fear
  My wound hath taken cold, and I shall die.'
      So saying, from the pavement he half rose,
  Slowly, with pain, reclining on his arm,
  And looking wistfully with wide blue eyes
170 As in a picture. Him Sir Bedivere
  Remorsefully regarded thro' his tears,
  And would have spoken, but he found not words,
  Then took with care, and kneeling on one knee,
  O'er both his shoulders drew the languid hands,
175 And rising bore him thro' the place of tombs.
  But, as he walk'd, King Arthur panted hard,
  Like one that feels a nightmare on his bed
  When all the house is mute. So sigh'd the king,
  Muttering and murmuring at his ear, ' Quick,
          quick!
180 I fear it is too late, and I shall die.'
  But the other swiftly strode from ridge to ridge,
  Clothed with his breath, and looking, as he walk'd,
  Larger than human on the frozen hills.
  He heard the deep behind him, and a cry
185 Before. His own thoughts drove him, like a goad.
  Dry clash'd his harness in the icy caves
  And barren chasms, and all to left and right
  The bare black cliff clang'd round him, as he based
  His feet on juts of slippery crag that rang
190 Sharp-smitten with the dint of armed heels—
  And on a sudden, lo! the level lake,
  And the long glories of the winter moon.
      Then saw they how there hove a dusky barge,
  Dark as a funeral scarf from stem to stern,

195 Beneath them; and descending they were ware
   That all the decks were dense with stately forms
   Black-stoled, black-hooded, like a dream—by
      these
   Three Queens with crowns of gold—and from
      them rose
   A cry that shiver'd to the tingling stars,
200 And, as it were one voice an agony
   Of lamentation, like a wind, that shrills
   All night in a waste land, where no one comes,
   Or hath come, since the making of the world.
      Then murmur'd Arthur, 'Place me in the
      barge,'
205 And to the barge they came. There those three
      Queens
   Put forth their hands, and took the king, and
      wept.
   But she, that rose the tallest of them all
   And fairest, laid his head upon her lap,
   And loosed the shatter'd casque, and chafed his
      hands,
210 And call'd him by his name, complaining loud,
   And dropping bitter tears against his brow
   Striped with dark blood: for his face was white
   And colourless, and like the wither'd moon
   Smote by the fresh beam of the springing east;
215 And all his greaves and cuisses dash'd with drops
   Of onset; and the light and lustrous curls—
   That made his forehead like a rising sun
   High from the dais-throne—were parch'd with
      dust;
   Or, clotted into points and hanging loose,
220 Mix'd with the knightly growth that fringed his
      lips.
   So like a shatter'd column lay the king;
   Not like that Arthur who, with lance in rest,
   From spur to plume a star of tournament,

Shot thro' the lists at Camelot, and charged
225 Before the eyes of ladies and of kings.
  Then loudly cried the bold Sir Bedivere,
'Ah! my Lord Arthur, whither shall I go?
Where shall I hide my forehead and my eyes?
For now I see the true old times are dead,
230 When every morning brought a noble chance,
And every chance brought out a noble knight.
Such times have been not since the light that led
The holy Elders with the gift of myrrh.
But now the whole ROUND TABLE is dissolved
235 Which was an image of the mighty world;
And I, the last, go forth companionless,
And the days darken round me, and the years,
Among new men, strange faces, other minds.'
  And slowly answered Arthur from the barge:
240 'The old order changeth, yielding place to new,
And God fulfils Himself in many ways,
Lest one good custom should corrupt the world.
Comfort thyself: what comfort is in me?
I have lived my life, and that which I have done
245 May He within Himself make pure! but thou,
If thou shouldst never see my face again,
Pray for my soul. More things are wrought by
      prayer
Than this world dreams of. Wherefore, let thy
      voice
Rise like a fountain for me night and day.
250 For what are men better than sheep or goats
That nourish a blind life within the brain,
If, knowing God, they lift not hands of prayer
Both for themselves and those who call them
      friend?
For so the whole round earth is every way
255 Bound by gold chains about the feet of God.
But now farewell. I am going a long way
With these thou seëst—if indeed I go—

(For all my mind is clouded with a doubt)
To the island valley of Avilion;
260 Where falls not hail, or rain, or any snow,
Nor ever wind blows loudly; but it lies
Deep-meadow'd, happy, fair with orchard-lawns
And bowery hollows crown'd with summer sea,
Where I will heal me of my grievous wound.'
265   So said he, and the barge with oar and sail
Moved from the brink, like some full-breasted
          swan
That, fluting a wild carol ere her death,
Ruffles her pure cold plume, and takes the flood
With swarthy webs.   Long stood Sir Bedivere
270 Revolving many memories, till the hull
Look'd one black dot against the verge of dawn,
And on the mere the wailing died away.

Here ended Hall, and our last light, that long
Had wink'd and threaten'd darkness, flared and
          fell:
275 At which the Parson, sent to sleep with sound,
And waked with silence, grunted 'Good!' but we
Sat rapt: it was the tone with which he read—
Perhaps some modern touches here and there
Redeem'd it from the charge of nothingness—
280 Or else we loved the man, and prized his work;
I know not: but we sitting, as I said,
The cock crew loud; as at that time of year
The lusty bird takes every hour for dawn:
Then Francis, muttering, like a man ill-used,
285 'There now—that's nothing!' drew a little back,
And drove his heel into the smoulder'd log,
That sent a blast of sparkles up the flue:
And so to bed; where yet in sleep I seem'd
To sail with Arthur under looming shores,
290 Point after point; till on to dawn, when dreams,
Began to feel the truth and stir of day,

To me, methought, who waited with a crowd,
There came a bark that, blowing forward, bore
King Arthur, like a modern gentleman
295 Of stateliest port; and all the people cried,
'Arthur is come again; he cannot die.'
Then those that stood upon the hills behind
Repeated—'Come again, and thrice as fair;'
And, further inland, voices echoed—'Come
300 With all good things, and war shall be no more.'
At this a hundred bells began to peal,
That with the sound I woke, and heard indeed
The clear church-bells ring in the Christmas
    morn.

SIR GALAHAD

(From the same)

My good blade carves the casques of men,
    My tough lance thrusteth sure,
My strength is as the strength of ten,
    Because my heart is pure.
5 The shattering trumpet shrilleth high,
    The hard brands shiver on the steel,
The splinter'd spear-shafts crack and fly,
    The horse and rider reel:
They reel, they roll in clanging lists,
10   And when the tide of combat stands,
Perfume and flowers fall in showers,
    That lightly rain from ladies' hands.

How sweet are looks that ladies bend
    On whom their favours fall!
15 For them I battle till the end,
    To save from shame and thrall:

But all my heart is drawn above,
  My knees are bow'd in crypt and shrine;
I never felt the kiss of love,
20   Nor maiden's hand in mine.
More bounteous aspects on me beam,
  Me mightier transports move and thrill;
So keep I fair thro' faith and prayer
  A virgin heart in work and will.

25 When down the stormy crescent goes,
  A light before me swims,
Between dark stems the forest glows,
  I hear a noise of hymns:
Then by some secret shrine I ride;
30   I hear a voice but none are there;
The stalls are void, the doors are wide,
  The tapers burning fair.
Fair gleams the snowy altar-cloth,
  The silver vessels sparkle clean,
35 The shrill bell rings, the censer swings,
  And solemn chaunts resound between.

Sometimes on lonely mountain-meres
  I find a magic bark;
I leap on board: no helmsman steers:
40   I float till all is dark.
A gentle sound, an awful light!
  Three angels bear the holy Grail:
With folded feet, in stoles of white,
  On sleeping wings they sail.
45 Oh, blessed vision! blood of God!
  My spirit beats her mortal bars,
As down dark tides the glory slides,
  And star-like mingles with the stars.

When on my goodly charger borne
50   Thro' dreaming towns I go,

The cock crows ere the Christmas morn,
   The streets are dumb with snow.
The tempest crackles on the leads,
   And, ringing, springs from brand and mail;
55 But o'er the dark a glory spreads,
   And gilds the driving hail.
I leave the plain, I climb the height;
   No branchy thicket shelter yields;
But blessed forms in whistling storms
60   Fly o'er waste fens and windy fields.

A maiden knight—to me is given
   Such hope, I know not fear;
I yearn to breathe the airs of heaven
   That often meet me here.
65 I muse on joy that will not cease,
   Pure spaces clothed in living beams,
Pure lilies of eternal peace,
   Whose odours haunt my dreams;
And, stricken by an angel's hand,
70   This mortal armour that I wear,
This weight and size, this heart and eyes,
   Are touch'd, are turn'd to finest air.

The clouds are broken in the sky,
   And thro' the mountain-walls
75 A rolling organ-harmony
   Swells up, and shakes and falls.
Then move the trees, the copses nod,
   Wings flutter, voices hover clear:
'O just and faithful knight of God!
80   Ride on! the prize is near.'
So pass I hostel, hall, and grange;
   By bridge and ford, by park and pale,
All-arm'd I ride, whate'er betide
   Until I find the holy Grail.

BREAK, BREAK, BREAK

(From the same)

Break, break, break,
  On thy cold gray stones, O Sea!
And I would that my tongue could utter
  The thoughts that arise in me.

5 O well for the fisherman's boy,
  That he shouts with his sister at play!
O well for the sailor lad,
  That he sings in his boat on the bay!

And the stately ships go on
10 To their haven under the hill;
But O for the touch of a vanish'd hand
  And the sound of a voice that is still!

Break, break, break,
  At the foot of thy crags, O Sea!
15 But the tender grace of a day that is dead
  Will never come back to me.

TEARS, IDLE TEARS

(Song from *The Princess*, edition 1850)

' Tears, idle tears, I know not what they mean,
Tears from the depth of some divine despair
Rise in the heart, and gather to the eyes,
In looking on the happy Autumn-fields,
5 And thinking of the days that are no more.

' Fresh as the first beam glittering on a sail,
That brings our friends up from the underworld,

Sad as the last which reddens over one
That sinks with all we love below the verge;
10 So sad, so fresh, the days that are no more.

'Ah, sad and strange as in dark summer dawns
The earliest pipe of half-awaken'd birds
To dying ears, when unto dying eyes
The casement slowly grows a glimmering square;
15 So sad, so strange, the days that are no more.

'Dear as remembered kisses after death,
And sweet as those by hopeless fancy feign'd
On lips that are for others; deep as love,
Deep as first love, and wild with all regret;
20 O Death in Life, the days that are no more.'

BUGLE SONG

(From the same)

The splendour falls on castle walls
  And snowy summits old in story:
The long light shakes across the lakes,
  And the wild cataract leaps in glory.
5 Blow, bugle, blow, set the wild echoes flying,
Blow, bugle; answer, echoes, dying, dying, dying.

O hark, O hear! how thin and clear,
  And thinner, clearer, farther going!
O sweet and far from cliff and scar
10 The horns of Elfland faintly blowing!
Blow, let us hear the purple glens replying:
Blow, bugle; answer, echoes, dying, dying, dying.

O love, they die in yon rich sky,
  They faint on hill or field or river:

15   Our echoes roll from soul to soul,
        And grow forever and forever.
    Blow, bugle, blow, set the wild echoes flying,
    And answer, echoes, answer, dying, dying, dying.

IN MEMORIAM

(From *In Memoriam*, 1850)

    Strong Son of God, immortal Love,
        Whom we, that have not seen thy face,
        By faith, and faith alone, embrace,
    Believing where we cannot prove;

5   Thine are these orbs of light and shade;
        Thou madest Life in man and brute;
        Thou madest Death; and lo, thy foot
    Is on the skull which thou hast made.

    Thou wilt not leave us in the dust:
10   Thou madest man, he knows not why,
        He thinks he was not made to die;
    And thou hast made him: thou art just.

    Thou seemest human and divine,
        The highest, holiest manhood, thou:
15   Our wills are ours, we know not how;
    Our wills are ours, to make them thine.

    Our little systems have their day;
        They have their day and cease to be:
        They are but broken lights of thee,
20 And thou, O Lord, art more than they.

    We have but faith: we cannot know;
        For knowledge is of things we see;
        And yet we trust it comes from thee,
    A beam in darkness: let it grow

25 Let knowledge grow from more to more,
    But more of reverence in us dwell;
    That mind and soul, according well,
May make one music as before,

    But vaster. We are fools and slight;
30   We mock thee when we do not fear:
    But help thy foolish ones to bear;
Help thy vain worlds to bear thy light.

Forgive what seem'd my sin in me;
    What seem'd my worth since I began;
35   For merit lives from man to man,
And not from man, O Lord, to thee.

Forgive my grief for one removed,
    Thy creature, whom I found so fair.
    I trust he lives in thee, and there
40 I find him worthier to be loved.

Forgive these wild and wandering cries,
    Confusions of a wasted youth;
    Forgive them where they fail in truth,
And in thy wisdom make me wise.

MAUD

(From *Maud*, 1855)

XVIII.

I.

I have led her home, my love, my only friend.
There is none like her, none.
And never yet so warmly ran my blood
And sweetly, on and on
5 Calming itself to the long-wish'd-for end,
    Full to the banks, close on the promised good.

II.

None like her, none.
Just now the dry-tongued laurels' pattering talk
Seem'd her light foot along the garden walk,
10 And shook my heart to think she comes once
    more;
But even then I heard her close the door,
The gates of Heaven are closed, and she is gone.

III.

There is none like her, none.
Nor will be when our summers have deceased.
15 O, art thou sighing for Lebanon
In the long breeze that streams to thy delicious
    East,
Sighing for Lebanon,
Dark cedar, tho' thy limbs have here increased,
Upon a pastoral slope as fair,
20 And looking to the South, and fed
With honey'd rain and delicate air,
And haunted by the starry head
Of her whose gentle will has changed my fate,
And made my life a perfumed altar-flame;
25 And over whom thy darkness must have spread
With such delight as theirs of old, thy great
Forefathers of the thornless garden, there
Shadowing the snow-limb'd Eve from whom she
    came.

IV.

Here will I lie, while these long branches sway,
30 And yon fair stars that crown a happy day
Go in and out as if at merry play,
Who am no more so all forlorn,
As when it seem'd far better to be born

To labour and the mattock-harden'd hand,
35 Than nursed at ease and brought to understand
A sad astrology, the boundless plan
That makes you tyrants in your iron skies,
Innumerable, pitiless, passionless eyes,
Cold fires, yet with power to burn and brand
40 His nothingness into man.

V.

But now shine on, and what care I,
Who in this stormy gulf have found a pearl
The countercharm of space and hollow sky,
And do accept my madness, and would die
45 To save from some slight shame one simple girl.

VI.

Would die; for sullen-seeming Death may give
More life to Love than is or ever was
In our low world, where yet 'tis sweet to live.
Let no one ask me how it came to pass;
50 It seems that I am happy, that to me
A livelier emerald twinkles in the grass,
A purer sapphire melts into the sea.

VII.

Not die; but live a life of truest breath,
And teach true life to fight with mortal wrongs.
55 O why should Love, like men in drinking-songs,
Spice his fair banquet with the dust of death?
Make answer, Maud my bliss,
Maud made my Maud by that long loving kiss,
Life of my life, wilt thou not answer this?
60 'The dusky strand of Death inwoven here
    With dear Love's tie, makes Love himself more
        dear'

VIII.

Is that enchanted moan only the swell
Of the long waves that roll in yonder bay?
And hark the clock within, the silver knell
65 Of twelve sweet hours that past in bridal white,
And died to live, long as my pulses play;
But now by this my love has closed her sight
And given false death her hand, and stol'n away
To dreamful wastes where footless fancies dwell
70 Among the fragments of the golden day.
May nothing there her maiden grace affright!
Dear heart, I feel with thee the drowsy spell.
My bride to be, my evermore delight,
My own heart's heart, my ownest own, farewell;
75 It is but for a little space I go:
And ye meanwhile far over moor and fell
Beat to the noiseless music of the night!
Has our whole earth gone nearer to the glow
Of your soft splendours that you look so bright?
80 *I* have climbed nearer out of lonely Hell.
Beat, happy stars, timing with things below,
Beat with my heart more blest than heart can tell,
Blest, but for some dark undercurrent woe
That seems to draw—but it shall not be so:
85 Let all be well, be well.

CROSSING THE BAR

(1889)

Sunset and evening star,
    And one clear call for me!
And may there be no moaning of the bar,
    When I put out to sea,

5 But such a tide as moving seems asleep,
   Too full for sound and foam,
When that which drew from out the boundless
      deep
   Turns again home.

Twilight and evening bell,
10   And after that the dark!
And may there be no sadness of farewell,
   When I embark;

For tho' from out our bourne of Time and Place
   The flood may bear me far,
15 I hope to see my Pilot face to face
   When I have crost the bar.

Robert Browning

1812-1889

MY LAST DUCHESS

FERRARA

(First published, 1836)

That's my last Duchess painted on the wall,
Looking as if she were alive. I call
That piece a wonder, now; Frà Pandolf's hands
Worked busily a day, and there she stands.
5 Will 't please you sit and look at her? I said
"Frà Pandolf" by design, for never read
Strangers like you that pictured countenance,
The depth and passion of its earnest glance,
But to myself they turned (since none puts by
10 The curtain I have drawn for you, but I)
And seemed as they would ask me, if they durst,
How such a glance came there; so, not the first

Are you to turn and ask thus. Sir, 'twas not
Her husband's presence only, called that spot
15 Of joy into the Duchess' cheek: perhaps
Frà Pandolf chanced to say "Her mantle laps
Over my lady's wrist too much," or "Paint
Must never hope to reproduce the faint
Half-flush that dies along her throat:" such stuff
20 Was courtesy, she thought, and cause enough
For calling up that spot of joy. She had
A heart—how shall I say?—too soon made glad,
Too easily impressed; she liked whate'er
She looked on, and her looks went everywhere.
25 Sir, 'twas all one! My favor at her breast,
The dropping of the daylight in the West,
The bough of cherries some officious fool
Broke in the orchard for her, the white mule
She rode with round the terrace—all and each
30 Would draw from her alike the approving speech,
Or blush, at least. She thanked men,—good! but
        thanked
Somehow—I know not how—as if she ranked
My gift of a nine-hundred-years-old name
With anybody's gift. Who'd stoop to blame
35 This sort of trifling? Even had you skill
In speech—(which I have not)—to make your will
Quite clear to such an one, and say, "Just this
Or that in you disgusts me; here you miss,
Or there exceed the mark"—and if she let
40 Herself be lessoned so, nor plainly set
Her wits to yours, forsooth, and made excuse,
—E'en then would be some stooping; and I choose
Never to stoop. Oh, sir, she smiled, no doubt,
Whene'er I passed her; but who passed without
45 Much the same smile? This grew; I gave com-
        mands;
Then all smiles stopped together. There she
        stands

As if alive. Will 't please you rise? We'll meet
The company below, then. I repeat
The Count your master's known munificence
50 Is ample warrant that no just pretense
Of mine for dowry will be disallowed;
Though his fair daughter's self, as I avowed
At starting, is my object. Nay, we'll go
Together down, sir. Notice Neptune, though,
55 Taming a sea-horse, thought a rarity,
Which Claus of Innsbruck cast in bronze for
     me!

SONG

(From *Pippa Passes*, 1841)

The year 's at the spring
The day 's at the morn;
Morning 's at seven;
The hillside 's dew-pearled;
5 The lark 's on the wing;
The snail 's on the thorn:
God 's in his heaven—
All 's right with the world!

HOME THOUGHTS, FROM ABROAD

(From *Bells and Pomegranates* No. VII., 1845)

I.

Oh, to be in England now that April's there,
And whoever wakes in England sees, some morn-
     ing, unaware,
That the lowest boughs and the brush-wood sheaf
Round the elm-tree bole are in tiny leaf,
5 While the chaffinch sings on the orchard bough
In England—now!

II.

And after April, when May follows,
    And the whitethroat builds, and all the swallows!
Hark, where my blossomed pear-tree in the hedge
10 Leans to the field and scatters on the clover
    Blossoms and dewdrops—at the bent spray's
        edge—
That's the wise thrush; he sings each song twice
    over
Lest you should think he never could recapture
    The first fine careless rapture!
15 And though the fields look rough with hoary dew,
    All will be gay when noontide wakes anew
    The buttercups, the little children's dower
    —Far brighter than this gaudy melon-flower!

THE GUARDIAN-ANGEL:

A PICTURE AT FANO

(From *Men and Women*, 1855)

I.

Dear and great Angel, wouldst thou only leave
    That child, when thou hast done with him,
        for me!
Let me sit all the day here, that when eve
    Shall find performed thy special ministry,
5 And time come for departure, thou, suspending
Thy flight, may'st see another child for tending,
    Another still, to quiet and retrieve.

II.

Then I shall feel thee step one step, no more,
    From where thou stand'st now, to where I gaze,
10 And suddenly my head be covered o'er

With those wings, white above the child who
   prays
Now on that tomb—and I shall feel thee guard-
   ing
Me, out of all the world; for me, discarding
   Yon heaven thy home, that waits and opes its
    door!

III.

15 I would not look up thither past thy head
   Because the door opes, like that child, I know,
For I should have thy gracious face instead,
   Thou bird of God! And wilt thou bend me
    low
Like him, and lay, like his, my hands together,
20 And lift them up to pray, and gently tether
   Me as thy lamb there, with thy garment's
    spread?

IV.

If this was ever granted, I would rest
   My head beneath thine, while thy healing
    hands
Close-covered both my eyes beside thy breast,
25   Pressing the brain which too much thought ex-
    pands
Back to its proper size again, and smoothing
Distortion down till every nerve had soothing,
   And all lay quiet, happy and supprest.

V.

How soon all worldly wrong would be repaired!
30   I think how I should view the earth and skies
And sea, when once again my brow was bared
   After thy healing, with such different eyes.

O world, as God has made it! all is beauty;
And knowing this, is love, and love is duty.
35 What further may be sought for or declared?

. . . .
. . . .

ANDREA DEL SARTO

CALLED "THE FAULTLESS PAINTER"

(From *Men and Women*, 1855)

But do not let us quarrel any more,
No, my Lucrezia; bear with me for once:
Sit down and all shall happen as you wish.
You turn your face, but does it bring your heart?
5 I'll work then for your friend's friend, never fear,
Treat his own subject after his own way,
Fix his own time, accept too his own price,
And shut the money into this small hand
When next it takes mine. Will it? tenderly?
10 Oh, I'll content him,—but to-morrow, Love!
I often am much wearier than you think,
This evening more than usual, and it seems
As if—forgive now—should you let me sit
Here by the window with your hand in mine
15 And look a half hour forth on Fiesole,
Both of one mind, as married people use,
Quietly, quietly the evening through,
I might get up to-morrow to my work
Cheerful and fresh as ever. Let us try.
20 To-morrow, how you shall be glad for this!
Your soft hand is a woman of itself,
And mine the man's bared breast she curls inside.
Don't count the time lost, neither; you must
    serve
For each of the five pictures we require:

25 It saves a model.   So! keep looking so—
My serpentining beauty, rounds on rounds!
—How could you ever prick those perfect ears,
Even to put the pearl there! oh, so sweet—
My face, my moon, my everybody's moon,

30 Which everybody looks on and calls his,
And, I suppose, is looked on by in turn,
While she looks—no one's: very dear, no less.
You smile? why, there's my picture ready made,
There's what we painters call our harmony!

35 A common grayness silvers every thing,—
All in a twilight, you and I alike
—You, at the point of your first pride in me
(That's gone, you know),—but I, at every point;
My youth, my hope, my art, being all toned down

40 To yonder sober pleasant Fiesole.
There's the bell clinking from the chapel-top;
That length of convent-wall across the way
Holds the trees safer, huddled more inside;
The last monk leaves the garden; days decrease,

45 And autumn grows, autumn in every thing.
Eh? the whole seems to fall into a shape
As if I saw alike my work and self
And all that I was born to be and do,
A twilight-piece.   Love, we are in God's hand.

50 How strange now looks the life he makes us lead;
So free we seem, so fettered fast we are!
I feel he laid the fetter: let it lie!
This chamber for example—turn your head—
All that's behind us!   You don't understand

55 Nor care to understand about my art,
But you can hear at least when people speak:
And that cartoon, the second from the door
—It is the thing, Love! so such things should
    be—
Behold Madonna!—I am bold to say.

60 I can do with my pencil what I know,

What I see, what at bottom of my heart
I wish for, if I ever wish so deep—
Do easily, too—when I say, perfectly,
I do not boast, perhaps: yourself are judge
65 Who listened to the Legate's talk last week,
And just as much they used to say in France.
At any rate 'tis easy, all of it!
No sketches first, no studies, that's long past:
I do what many dream of all their lives.
70 —Dream? strive to do, and agonize to do,
And fail in doing. I could count twenty such
On twice your fingers, and not leave this town,
Who strive—you don't know how the others strive
To paint a little thing like that you smeared
75 Carelessly passing with your robes afloat,—
Yet do much less, so much less, Someone says,
(I know his name, no matter)—so much less!
Well, less is more, Lucrezia: I am judged.
There burns a truer light of God in them,
80 In their vexed beating stuffed and stopped-up
        brain,
Heart, or whate'er else, than goes on to prompt
This low-pulsed forthright craftsman's hand of
        mine.
Their works drop groundward, but themselves, I
        know,
Reach many a time a heaven that's shut to me,
85 Enter and take their place there sure enough,
Though they come back and cannot tell the world.
My works are nearer heaven, but I sit here.
The sudden blood of these men! at a word—
Praise them, it boils, or blame them, it boils too.
90 I, painting from myself and to myself,
Know what I do, am unmoved by men's blame
Or their praise either. Somebody remarks
Morello's outline there is wrongly traced,
His hue mistaken; what of that? or else,

95 Rightly traced and well ordered; what of that?
Speak as they please, what does the mountain
care?
Ah, but a man's reach should exceed his grasp,
Or what's a heaven for? All is silver-gray,
Placid and perfect with my art: the worse!
100 I know both what I want and what might gain;
And yet how profitless to know, to sigh
"Had I been two, another and myself,
Our head would have o'erlooked the world—" No
doubt.
Yonder's a work now, of that famous youth
105 The Urbinate who died five years ago.
('Tis copied, George Vasari-sent it me.)
Well, I can fancy how he did it all,
Pouring his soul, with kings and popes to see,
Reaching, that heaven might so replenish him,
110 Above and through his art—for it gives way;
That arm is wrongly put—and there again—
A fault to pardon in the drawing's lines,
Its body, so to speak: its soul is right,
He means right—that, a child may understand.
115 Still, what an arm! and I could alter it:
But all the play, the insight and the stretch—
Out of me, out of me! And wherefore out?
Had you enjoined them on me, given me soul,
We might have risen to Rafael, I and you!
120 Nay, Love, you did give all I asked, I think—
More than I merit, yes, by many times.
But had you—oh, with the same perfect brow,
And perfect eyes, and more than perfect mouth,
And the low voice my soul hears, as a bird
125 The fowler's pipe, and follows to the snare—
Had you, with these the same, but brought a
mind!
Some women do so. Had the mouth there urged,
"God and the glory! never care for gain.

The present by the future, what is that?
130 Live for fame, side by side with Agnolo!
Rafael is waiting: up to God, all three!"
I might have done it for you. So it seems:
Perhaps not. All is as God overrules.
Beside, incentives come from the soul's self:
135 The rest avail not. Why do I need you?
What wife had Rafael, or has Agnolo?
In this world, who can do a thing, will not;
And who would do it, cannot, I perceive:
Yet the will's somewhat—somewhat, too, the
    power—
140 And thus we half-men struggle. At the end,
God, I conclude, compensates, punishes.
'Tis safer for me, if the award be strict,
That I am something underrated here,
Poor this long while, despised, to speak the truth.
145 I dared not, do you know, leave home all day,
For fear of chancing on the Paris lords.
The best is when they pass and look aside;
But they speak sometimes; I must bear it all.
Well may they speak! That Francis, that first
    time,
150 And that long festal year at Fontainebleau!
I surely then could sometimes leave the ground,
Put on the glory, Rafael's daily wear,
In that humane great monarch's golden look,—
One finger in his beard or twisted curl
155 Over his mouth's good mark that made the smile,
One arm about my shoulder, round my neck,
The jingle of his gold chain in my ear,
I painting proudly with his breath on me,
All his court round him, seeing with his eyes,
160 Such frank French eyes, and such a fire of souls
Profuse, my hand kept plying by those hearts,—
And, best of all, this, this, this face beyond,
This in the background, waiting on my work,

To crown the issue with a last reward!
165 A good time, was it not, my kingly days?
And had you not grown restless . . . but I
know—
'Tis done and past; 'twas right, my instinct said;
Too live the life grew, golden and not gray,
And I'm the weak-eyed bat no sun should tempt
170 Out of the grange whose four walls make his
world.
How could it end in any other way?
You called me, and I came home to your heart.
The triumph was, to have ended there; then, if
I reached it ere the triumph, what is lost?
175 Let my hands frame your face in your hair's
gold,
You beautiful Lucrezia that are mine!
" Rafael did this, Andrea painted that;
The Roman's is the better when you pray,
But still the other's Virgin was his wife "—
180 Men will excuse me. I am glad to judge
Both pictures in your presence; clearer grows
My better fortune, I resolve to think.
For, do you know, Lucrezia, as God lives,
Said one day Agnolo, his very self,
185 To Rafael . . . I have known it all these
years . . .
(When the young man was flaming out his
thoughts
Upon a palace-wall for Rome to see,
Too lifted up in heart because of it)
" Friend, there's a certain sorry little scrub
190 Goes up and down our Florence, none cares how,
Who, were he set to plan and execute
As you are, pricked on by your popes and kings,
Would bring the sweat into that brow of yours! "
To Rafael's!—And indeed the arm is wrong.
195 I hardly dare . . . yet, only you to see,

Give the chalk here—quick, thus the line should
     go!
Ay, but the soul! he's Rafael! rub it out!
Still, all I care for, if he spoke the truth,
(What he? why, who but Michel Agnolo?
200 Do you forget already words like those?)
If really there was such a chance, so lost,—
Is, whether you're—not grateful—but more
     pleased.
Well, let me think so. And you smile indeed!
This hour has been an hour! Another smile?
205 If you would sit thus by me every night
I should work better, do you comprehend?
I mean that I should earn more, give you more.
See, it is settled dusk now; there's a star;
Morello's gone, the watch-lights show the wall,
210 The cue-owls speak the name we call them by.
Come from the window, Love,—come in, at last,
Inside the melancholy little house
We built to be so gay with. God is just.
King Francis may forgive me: oft at nights
215 When I look up from painting, eyes tired out,
The walls become illumined, brick by brick
Distinct, instead of mortar, fierce bright gold,
That gold of his I did cement them with!
Let us but love each other. Must you go?
220 That Cousin here again? he waits outside?
Must see you—you, and not with me? Those
     loans?
More gaming debts to pay? you smiled for that?
Well, let smiles buy me! have you more to spend?
While hand and eye and something of a heart
225 Are left me, work's my ware, and what's it worth?
I'll pay my fancy. Only let me sit
The gray remainder of the evening out,
Idle, you call it, and muse perfectly
How I could paint, were I but back in France,

230 One picture, just one more—the Virgin's face,
    Not yours this time! I want you at my side
    To hear them—that is, Michel Agnolo—
    Judge all I do and tell you of its worth.
    Will you? To-morrow, satisfy your friend.
235 I take the subjects for his corridor,
    Finish the portrait out of hand—there, there,
    And throw him in another thing or two
    If he demurs; the whole should prove enough
    To pay for this same Cousin's freak. Beside,
240 What's better and what's all I care about,
    Get you the thirteen scudi for the ruff!
    Love, does that please you? Ah, but what does
        he,
    The Cousin! what does he to please you more?

      I am grown peaceful as old age to-night.
245 I regret little, I would change still less.
    Since there my past life lies, why alter it?
    The very wrong to Francis!—it is true
    I took his coin, was tempted and complied,
    And built this house and sinned, and all is said.
250 My father and my mother died of want.
    Well, had I riches of my own? you see
    How one gets rich! Let each one bear his lot.
    They were born poor, lived poor, and poor they
        died:
    And I have labored somewhat in my time
255 And not been paid profusely. Some good son
    Paint my two hundred pictures—let him try!
    No doubt, there's something strikes a balance.
        Yes,
    You love me quite enough, it seems to-night.
    This must suffice me here. What would one
        have?
260 In heaven, perhaps, new chances, one more
        chance—

Four great walls in the New Jerusalem
Meted on each side by the angel's reed,
For Leonard, Rafael, Agnolo and me
To cover—the three first without a wife,
265 While I have mine! So—still they overcome
Because there's still Lucrezia,—as I choose.

Again the Cousin's whistle! Go, my Love.

PROSPICE

(From *Dramatis Personæ*, 1864)

Fear death?—to feel the fog in my throat,
    The mist in my face,
When the snows begin, and the blasts denote
    I am nearing the place,
5 The power of the night, the press of the storm,
    The post of the foe;
Where he stands, the Arch Fear in a visible form,
    Yet the strong man must go;
For the journey is done and the summit attained,
10   And the barriers fall,
Though a battle's to fight ere the guerdon be
    gained,
    The reward of it all.
I was ever a fighter, so—one fight more,
    The best and the last!
15 I would hate that death bandaged my eyes, and
    forebore,
    And bade me creep past.

No! let me taste the whole of it, fare like my
    peers,
    The heroes of old,
Bear the brunt, in a minute pay glad life's arrears
20   Of pain, darkness and cold.

For sudden the worst turns the best to the brave,
    The black minute's at end,
And the elements' rage, the fiend-voices that rave,
    Shall dwindle, shall blend,
25 Shall change, shall become first a peace out of
        pain,
    Then a light, then thy breast,
O thou soul of my soul! I shall clasp thee again,
    And with God be the rest!

RABBI BEN EZRA

(From the same)

I.

Grow old along with me!
The best is yet to be,
The last of life, for which the first was made:
    Our times are in His hand
5   Who saith, "A whole I planned,
Youth shows but half; trust God: see all, nor be
        afraid!"

II.

Not that, amassing flowers,
Youth sighed, "Which rose make ours,
Which lily leave and then as best recall?"
10 Not that, admiring stars,
    It yearned, "Nor Jove, nor Mars;
Mine be some figured flame which blends, trans-
        scends them all!"

III.

Not for such hopes and fears
Annulling youth's brief years,

15 Do I remonstrate; folly wide the mark!
   Rather I prize the doubt
   Low kinds exist without,
   Finished and finite clods, untroubled by a spark.

IV.

   Poor vaunt of life indeed,
20 Were man but formed to feed
   On joy, to solely seek and find and feast;
   Such feasting ended, then
   As sure an end to men;
   Irks care the crop-full bird? Frets doubt the
      maw-crammed beast?

V.

25 Rejoice we are allied
   To That which doth provide
   And not partake, effect and not receive!
   A spark disturbs our clod;
   Nearer we hold of God
30 Who gives, than of His tribes that take, I must
      believe.

VI.

   Then, welcome each rebuff
   That turns earth's smoothness rough,
   Each sting that bids nor sit nor stand but go!
   Be our joys three-parts pain!
35 Strive, and hold cheap the strain;
   Learn, nor account the pang; dare, never grudge
      the throe!

VII.

   For thence,—a paradox
   Which comforts while it mocks,—

Shall life succeed in that it seems to fail:
40 What I aspired to be,
And was not, comforts me:
A brute I might have been, but would not sink
         i' the scale.

VIII.

What is he but a brute
Whose flesh hath soul to suit,
45 Whose spirit works lest arms and legs want play?
To man, propose this test—
Thy body at its best,
How far can that project thy soul on its lone
         way?

IX.

Yet gifts should prove their use:
50 I own the Past profuse
Of power each side, perfection every turn:
Eyes, ears took in their dole,
Brain treasured up the whole;
Should not the heart beat once "How good to
         live and learn?"

X.

55 Not once beat "Praise be Thine!
I see the whole design,
I, who saw Power, see now Love perfect too:
Perfect I call Thy plan:
Thanks that I was a man!
60 Maker, remake complete,—I trust what Thou
         shalt do!"

XI.

For pleasant is this flesh;
Our soul, in its rose-mesh

Pulled ever to the earth, still yearns for rest:
Would we some prize might hold
65 To match those manifold
Possessions of the brute,—gain most, as we did
    best!

XII.

Let us not always say,
"Spite of this flesh to-day
I strove, made head, gained ground upon the
    whole!"
70 As the bird wings and sings,
Let us cry "All good things
Are ours, nor soul helps flesh more, now, than
    flesh helps soul!"

XIII.

Therefore I summon age
To grant youth's heritage,
75 Life's struggle having so far reached its term:
Thence shall I pass, approved
A man, for aye removed
From the developed brute; a God though in the
    germ.

XIV.

And I shall thereupon
80 Take rest, ere I be gone
Once more on my adventure brave and new:
Fearless and unperplexed,
When I wage battle next,
What weapons to select, what armor to indue.

XV.

85 Youth ended, I shall try
My gain or loss thereby;

Leave the fire-ashes, what survives is gold:
And I shall weigh the same,
Give life its praise or blame:
90 Young, all lay in dispute; I shall know, being old.

XVI.

For note, when evening shuts,
A certain moment cuts
The deed off, calls the glory from the gray:
A whisper from the west
95 Shoots—" Add this to the rest,
Take it and try its worth: here dies another day."

XVII.

So, still within this life,
Though lifted o'er its strife,
Let me discern, compare, pronounce at last,
100 " This rage was right i' the main,
That acquiescence vain:
The Future I may face now I have proved the
Past."

XVIII.

For more is not reserved
To man with soul just nerved
105 To act to-morrow what he learns to-day:
Here, work enough to watch
The Master work, and catch
Hints of the proper craft, tricks of the tool's true
play.

XIX.

As it was better, youth
110 Should strive, through acts uncouth,
Toward making, than repose on aught found
made!

So, better, age, exempt
From strife, should know, than tempt
Further. Thou waitedst age: wait death, nor be
    afraid!

XX.

115 Enough now, if the Right
And Good and Infinite
Be named here, as thou callest thy hand thine
    own,
With knowledge absolute,
Subject to no dispute
120 From fools that crowded youth, nor let thee feel
    alone.

XXI.

Be there, for once and all,
Severed great minds from small,
Announced to each his station in the Past!
Was I, the world arraigned,
125 Were they, my soul disdained,
Right? Let age speak the truth and give us
    peace at last!

XXII.

Now, who shall arbitrate?
Ten men love what I hate,
Shun what I follow, slight what I receive;
130 Ten, who in ears and eyes
Match me: we all surmise,
They, this thing, and I, that: whom shall my soul
    believe?

XXIII.

Not on the vulgar mass
Called "work," must sentence pass,

135 Things done, that took the eye and had the price;
  O'er which, from level stand,
  The low world laid its hand,
Found straightway to its mind, could value in
    a trice:

XXIV.

  But all, the world's coarse thumb
140 And finger failed to plumb,
So passed in making up the main account;
  All instincts immature,
  All purposes unsure,
That weighed not as his work, yet swelled the
    man's amount:

XXV.

145 Thoughts hardly to be packed
  Into a narrow act,
Fancies that broke through language and es-
    caped;
  All I could never be,
  All, men ignored in me,
150 This, I was worth to God, whose wheel the pitcher
    shaped.

XXVI.

  Ay, note that Potter's wheel,
  That metaphor! and feel
Why time spins fast, why passive lies our clay,—
  Thou, to whom fools propound,
155 When the wine makes its round,
  "Since life fleets, all is change; the Past gone,
    seize to-day!"

XXVII.

Fool! All that is, at all,
Lasts ever, past recall;
Earth changes, but thy soul and God stand sure:
160 What entered into thee,
That was, is, and shall be:
Time's wheel runs back or stops: Potter and clay
     endure.

XXVIII.

He fixed thee mid this dance
Of plastic circumstance,
165 This Present, thou, forsooth, wouldst fain arrest:
Machinery just meant
To give thy soul its bent,
Try thee and turn thee forth, sufficiently im-
     pressed.

XXIX.

What though the earlier grooves,
170 Which ran the laughing loves,
Around thy base, no longer pause and press?
What though, about thy rim,
Skull-things in order grim
Grow out, in graver mood, obey the sterner stress?

XXX.

175 Look not thou down but up!
To uses of a cup,
The festal board, lamp's flash and trumpet's peal,
The new wine's foaming flow,
The Master's lips aglow!
180 Thou, heaven's consummate cup, what needst
     thou with earth's wheel?

XXXI.

But I need, now as then,
Thee, God, who moldest men;
And since, not even while the whirl was worst,
Did I—to the wheel of life
185 With shapes and colors rife,
Bound dizzily—mistake my end, to slake Thy
      thirst:

XXXII.

So, take and use Thy work:
Amend what flaws may lurk,
What strain o' the stuff, what warpings past the
      aim!
190 My times be in Thy hand!
Perfect the cup as planned!
Let age approve of youth, and death complete the
      same!

EPILOGUE

(From *Asolando*, 1890)

At the midnight in the silence of the sleep-time,
    When you set your fancies free,
Will they pass to where—by death, fools think,
    imprisoned—
Low he lies who once so loved you, whom you
    loved so,
5   —Pity me?

Oh to love so, be so loved, yet so mistaken!
    What had I on earth to do
With the slothful, with the mawkish, the un-
    manly?
Like the aimless, helpless, hopeless did I drivel
10   —Being—who?

One who never turned his back but marched
    breast forward,
    Never doubted clouds would break,
Never dreamed, though right were worsted, wrong
    would triumph,
Held we fall to rise, are baffled to fight better,
15   Sleep to wake.

No, at noonday in the bustle of man's work-time
    Greet the unseen with a cheer!
Bid him forward, breast and back as either should
    be,
"Strive and thrive!" cry "Speed,—fight on, fare
    ever
20   There as here!"

Elizabeth Barrett Browning

1809–1861

A MUSICAL INSTRUMENT

(From *Poems*, 1844)

I.

What was he doing, the great god Pan,
    Down in the reeds by the river?
Spreading ruin and scattering ban,
Splashing and paddling with hoofs of a goat,
5 And breaking the golden lilies afloat
    With the dragon-fly on the river.

II.

He tore out a reed, the great god Pan,
    From the deep cool bed of the river:

The limpid water turbidly ran,
10 And the broken lilies a-dying lay,
And the dragon-fly had fled away,
   Ere he brought it out of the river.

III.

High on the shore sat the great god Pan,
   While turbidly flowed the river;
15 And hacked and hewed as a great god can,
With his hard bleak steel at the patient reed,
Till there was not a sign of the leaf indeed
   To prove it fresh from the river.

IV.

He cut it short, did the great god Pan
20   (How tall it stood in the river!),
Then drew the pith, like the heart of a man,
Steadily from the outside ring,
And notched the poor dry empty thing
   In holes, as he sat by the river.

V.

25 " This is the way," laughed the great god Pan
   (Laughed while he sat by the river),
" The only way, since gods began
To make sweet music, they could succeed."
Then, dropping his mouth to a hole in the reed,
30   He blew in power by the river.

VI.

Sweet, sweet, sweet, O Pan!
   Piercing sweet by the river!
Blinding sweet, O great god Pan!
The sun on the hill forgot to die,
35 And the lilies revived, and the dragon-fly
   Came back to dream on the river.

VII.

Yet half a beast is the great god Pan,
   To laugh as he sits by the river,
Making a poet out of a man:
40 The true gods sigh for the cost and pain,—
   For the reed which grows nevermore again
   As a reed with the reeds in the river.

SONNETS

CHEERFULNESS TAUGHT BY REASON

I think we are too ready with complaint
In this fair world of God's. Had we no hope
Indeed beyond the zenith and the slope
Of yon grey blank of sky, we might grow faint
5 To muse upon eternity's constraint
Round our aspirant souls; but since the scope
Must widen early, is it well to droop,
For a few days consumed in loss and taint?
O pusillanimous Heart, be comforted
10 And, like a cheerful traveller, take the road,
Singing beside the hedge. What if the bread
Be bitter in thine inn, and thou unshod
To meet the flints? At least it may be said,
"Because the way is *short*, I thank thee, God."

THE PROSPECT

Methinks we do as fretful children do,
Leaning their faces on the window-pane
To sigh the glass dim with their own breath's
    stain,
And shut the sky and landscape from their view:
5 And thus, alas, since God the maker drew
A mystic separation 'twixt those twain,
The life beyond us, and our souls in pain,

We miss the prospect which we are called unto
By grief we are fools to use.   Be still and strong,
10 O man, my brother! hold thy sobbing breath,
And keep thy soul's large window pure from
    wrong
That so, as life's appointment issueth,
Thy vision may be clear to watch along
The sunset consummation-lights of death.

WORK

What are we set on earth for?   Say, to toil;
Nor seek to leave thy tending of the vines
For all the heat o' the day, till it declines,
And Death's mild curfew shall from work assoil.
5 God did anoint thee with His odorous oil,
To wrestle, not to reign; and He assigns
All thy tears over, like pure crystallines,
For younger fellow-workers of the soil
To wear for amulets.   So others shall
10 Take patience, labour, to their heart and hand,
From thy hand and thy heart and thy brave cheer,
And God's grace fructify through thee to all.
The least flower, with a brimming cup may stand,
And share its dew-drop with another near.

(From *Sonnets from the Portuguese,* 1850)

I.

I thought once how Theocritus had sung
Of the sweet years, the dear and wished-for years,
Who each one in a gracious hand appears
To bear a gift for mortals, old or young:
5 And, as I mused it in his antique tongue,
I saw, in gradual vision through my tears,
The sweet, sad years, the melancholy years,

Those of my own life, who by turns had flung
A shadow across me. Straightway I was 'ware,
10 So weeping, how a mystic Shape did move
Behind me, and drew me backward by the hair;
And a voice said in mastery, while I strove,—
" Guess now who holds thee? "—" Death," I said.
    But, there,
The silver answer rang,—" Not Death, but Love."

VI.

Go from me. Yet I feel that I shall stand
Henceforward in thy shadow. Nevermore
Alone upon the threshold of my door
Of individual life, I shall command
5 The uses of my soul, nor lift my hand
Serenely in the sunshine as before,
Without the sense of that which I forbore—
Thy touch upon the palm. The widest land
Doom takes to part us, leaves thy heart in mine
10 With pulses that beat double. What I do
And what I dream include thee, as the wine
Must taste of its own grapes. And when I sue
God for myself, He hears that name of thine,
And sees within my eyes the tears of two.

XXXV.

If I leave all for thee, wilt thou exchange
And be all to me? Shall I never miss
Home-talk and blessing and the common kiss
That comes to each in turn, nor count it strange,
5 When I look up, to drop on a new range
Of walls and floors, another home than this?
Nay, wilt thou fill that place by me which is
Filled by dead eyes too tender to know change?
That's hardest. If to conquer love, has tried,
10 To conquer grief, tries more, as all things prove;

For grief indeed is love and grief beside.
Alas, I have grieved so I am hard to love.
Yet love me—wilt thou?   Open thine heart wide,
And fold within the wet wings of thy dove.

XLIII.

How do I love thee?   Let me count the ways.
I love thee to the depth and breadth and height
My soul can reach, when feeling out of sight
For the ends of Being, and ideal Grace.
5 I love thee to the level of everyday's
Most quiet need, by sun and candlelight.
I love thee freely, as men strive for Right;
I love thee purely, as they turn from Praise.
I love thee with the passion put to use
10 In my old griefs, and with my childhood's faith.
I love thee with a love I seemed to lose
With my lost saints,—I love thee with the breath,
Smiles, tears, of all my life!—and, if God choose,
I shall but love thee better after death.

Charles Kingsley

1819-1875

SONG

(From *The Saint's Tragedy*, 1848)

Oh! that we two were Maying
Down the stream of the soft spring breeze;
Like children with violets playing
In the shade of the whispering trees.

5 Oh! that we two sat dreaming
On the sward of some sheep-trimmed down
Watching the white mist steaming
Over river and mead and town.

Oh! that we two lay sleeping
10 In our nest in the churchyard sod,
   With our limbs at rest on the quiet earth's breast,
   And our souls at home with God.

THE THREE FISHERS

(1851)

Three fishers went sailing away to the West,
   Away to the West as the sun went down;
Each thought on the woman who loved him the
     best,
   And the children stood watching them out of
     the town,
5   For men must work, and women must weep,
   And there's little to earn, and many to keep,
     Though the harbour bar be moaning.

Three wives sat up in the lighthouse tower,
   And they trimmed the lamps as the sun went
     down;
10 They looked at the squall, and they looked at the
     shower,
   And the night-rack came rolling up ragged and
     brown.
But men must work, and women must weep,
Though storms be sudden, and waters deep,
     And the harbour bar be moaning.

15 Three corpses lay out on the shining sands
   In the morning gleam as the tide went down,
And the women are weeping and wringing their
     hands
   For those who will never come home to the
     town;

20
For men must work, and women must weep,
And the sooner it's over, the sooner to sleep;
And good-bye to the bar and its moaning.

THE SANDS OF DEE

(From *Alton Locke*, 1849)

" O Mary, go and call the cattle home
And call the cattle home,
And call the cattle home
Across the sands of Dee; "
5 The western wind was wild and dank with foam
And all alone went she.

The western tide crept up along the sand,
And o'er and o'er the sand,
And round and round the sand,
10   As far as eye could see.
The rolling mist came down and hid the land:
And never home came she.

" Oh! is it weed, or fish, or floating hair—
A tress of golden hair,
15   A drownèd maiden's hair
Above the nets at sea?
Was never salmon yet that shone so fair
Among the stakes on Dee."

They rowed her in across the rolling foam,
20   The cruel crawling foam,
The cruel hungry foam,
To her grave beside the sea:
But still the boatmen hear her call the cattle
home
Across the sands of Dee.

CLEAR AND COOL

(Song from *The Water Babies*, 1863)

Clear and cool, clear and cool,
By laughing shallow, and dreaming pool;
Cool and clear, cool and clear,
By shining shingle, and foaming wear;
5 Under the crag where the ouzel sings,
And the ivied wall where the church-bell rings,
Undefiled, for the undefiled;
Play by me, bathe in me, mother and child.

Dank and foul, dank and foul,
10 By the smoky town in its murky cowl;
Foul and dank, foul and dank,
By wharf and sewer and slimy bank;
Darker and darker the further I go,
Baser and baser the richer I grow;
15   Who dare sport with the sin-defiled?
Shrink from me, turn from me, mother and child.

Strong and free, strong and free;
The floodgates are open, away to the sea.
Free and strong, free and strong,
20 Cleansing my streams as I hurry along
To the golden sands, and the leaping bar,
And the taintless tide that awaits me afar,
As I lose myself in the infinite main,
Like a soul that has sinned and is pardoned
again.
25   Undefiled, for the undefiled;
Play by me, bathe in me, mother and child.

Arthur Hugh Clough

1819–1861

QUA CURSUM VENTUS

(From *Ambarvalia*, 1843)

As ships, becalmed at eve, that lay
  With canvas drooping, side by side,
Two towers of sail at dawn of day
  Are scarce long leagues apart descried;

5 When fell the night, upsprung the breeze,
  And all the darkling hours they plied,
Nor dreamt but each the self-same seas
  By each was cleaving, side by side:

E'en so—but why the tale reveal
10 Of those, whom year by year unchanged,
Brief absence joined anew to feel,
  Astounded, soul from soul estranged?

At dead of night their sails were filled,
  And onward each rejoicing steered—
15 Ah, neither blame, for neither willed,
  Or wist, what first with dawn appeared

To veer, how vain! On, onward strain,
  Brave barks! In light, in darkness too,
Through winds and tides one compass guides—
20 To that, and your own selves, be true.

But O blithe breeze! and O great seas,
  Though ne'er, that earliest parting past,
On your wide plain they join again,
  Together lead them home at last.

25 One port, methought, alike they sought,
    One purpose hold where'er they fare,—
  O bounding breeze, O rushing seas!
    At last, at last, unite them there.

"WITH WHOM IS NO VARIABLENESS, NEITHER SHADOW OF TURNING"

(From the same)

  It fortifies my soul to know
  That, though I perish, Truth is so:
  That, howsoe'er I stray and range,
  Whate'er I do, Thou dost not change.
5 I steadier step when I recall
  That, if I slip Thou dost not fall.

SAY NOT, THE STRUGGLE NOUGHT AVAILETH

(From the same)

  Say not, the struggle nought availeth,
    The labour and the wounds are vain,
  The enemy faints not, nor faileth,
    And as things have been they remain.

5 If hopes were dupes, fears may be liars;
    It may be, in yon smoke concealed,
  Your comrades chase e'en now the fliers,
    And, but for you, possess the field.

  For while the tired waves, vainly breaking,
10   Seem here no painful inch to gain,
  Far back, through creeks and inlets making,
    Comes silent, flooding in, the main.

And not by eastern windows only,
    Where daylight comes, comes in the light,
15 In front, the sun climbs slow, how slowly,
    But westward, look, the land is bright.

THE STREAM OF LIFE

(From the same)

O stream descending to the sea,
    Thy mossy banks between,
The flow'rets blow, the grasses grow,
    The leafy trees are green.

5 In garden plots the children play,
    The fields the labourers till,
And houses stand on either hand,
    And thou descendest still.

O life descending unto death,
10   Our waking eyes behold,
Parent and friend thy lapse attend,
    Companions young and old.

Strong purposes our minds possess,
    Our hearts affections fill,
15 We toil and earn, we seek and learn,
    And thou descendest still.

O end to which our currents tend,
    Inevitable sea,
To which we flow, what do we know,
20   What shall we guess of thee?

A roar we hear upon thy shore,
    As we our course fulfil;
Scarce we divine a sun will shine
    And be above us still.

Matthew Arnold

1822–1888

STANZAS FROM THE GRANDE CHARTREUSE

(First published in *Fraser's Magazine*, 1855)

Through Alpine meadows soft-suffused
With rain, where thick the crocus blows,
Past the dark forges long disused,
The mule-track from Saint Laurent goes.
5 The bridge is cross'd, and slow we ride,
Through forest, up the mountain-side.

The autumnal evening darkens round,
The wind is up, and drives the rain;
While, hark! far down, with strangled sound
10 Doth the Dead Guier's stream complain,
Where that wet smoke, among the woods,
Over his boiling cauldron broods.

Swift rush the spectral vapours white
Past limestone scars with ragged pines,
15 Showing—then blotting from our sight!—
Halt—through the cloud-drift something shines!
High in the valley, wet and drear,
The huts of Courrerie appear.

Strike leftward! cries our guide; and higher
20 Mounts up the stony forest-way.
At last the encircling trees retire;
Look! through the showery twilight grey
What pointed roofs are these advance?—
A palace of the Kings of France?

25 Approach, for what we seek is here!
Alight, and sparely sup, and wait

For rest in this outbuilding near;
Then cross the sward and reach that gate;
Knock; pass the wicket! Thou art come
30 To the Carthusians' world-famed home.

The silent courts, where night and day
Into their stone-carved basins cold
The splashing icy fountains play—
The humid corridors behold,
35 Where, ghostlike in the deepening night,
Cowl'd forms brush by in gleaming white!

The chapel, where no organ's peal
Invests the stern and naked prayer!—
With penitential cries they kneel
40 And wrestle; rising then, with bare
With white uplifted faces stand
Passing the Host from hand to hand;

Each takes, and then his visage wan
Is buried in his cowl once more.
45 The cells!—the suffering Son of Man
Upon the wall—the knee-worn floor—
And where they sleep, that wooden bed,
Which shall their coffin be, when dead!

The library, where tract and tome
50 Not to feed priestly pride are there,
To hymn the conquering march of Rome,
Nor yet to amuse, as ours are!
They paint of souls the inner strife,
Their drops of blood, their death in life.

55 The garden, overgrown—yet mild,
See, fragrant herbs are flowering there!

Strong children of the Alpine wild
Whose culture is the brethren's care;
Of human tasks their only one,
60 And cheerful works beneath the sun.

Those halls, too, destined to contain
Each its own pilgrim-host of old,
From England, Germany, or Spain—
All are before me! I behold
65 The House, the Brotherhood austere!—
And what am I, that I am here?

For rigorous teachers seized my youth,
And purged its faith, and trimm'd its fire,
Shew'd me the high, white star of Truth,
70 There bade me gaze, and there aspire.
Even now their whispers pierce the gloom:
What dost thou in this living tomb?

Forgive me, masters of the mind!
At whose behest I long ago
75 So much unlearnt, so much resign'd—
I come not here to be your foe!
I seek these anchorites, not in ruth,
To curse and to deny your truth;

Not as their friend, or child, I speak!
80 But as, on some far northern strand,
Thinking of his own Gods, a Greek
In pity and mournful awe might stand
Before some fallen Runic stone—
For both were faiths, and both are gone.

85 Wandering between two worlds, one dead,
The other powerless to be born,

With nowhere yet to rest my head,
Like these, on earth I wait forlorn.
Their faith, my tears, the world deride—
90 I come to shed them at their side.

Oh, hide me in your gloom profound,
Ye solemn seats of holy pain!
Take me, cowl'd forms, and fence me round,
Till I possess my soul again;
95 Till free my thoughts before me roll,
Not chafed by hourly false control!

For the world cries your faith is now
But a dead time's exploded dream;
My melancholy, sciolists say,
100 Is a pass'd mode, an outworn theme,—
As if the world had ever had
A faith, or sciolists been sad!

Ah, if it *be* pass'd, take away,
At least, the restlessness, the pain!
105 Be man henceforth no more a prey
To these out-dated stings again!
The nobleness of grief is gone—
Ah, leave us not the fret alone!

But—if you cannot give us ease—
110 Last of the race of them who grieve
Here leave us to die out with these
Last of the people who believe!
Silent, while years engrave the brow;
Silent—the best are silent now.

115 Achilles ponders in his tent,
The kings of modern thought are dumb;

Silent they are, though not content,
And wait to see the future come.
They have the grief men had of yore,
120 But they contend and cry no more.

Our fathers water'd with their tears
This sea of time whereon we sail;
Their voices were in all men's ears
Who pass'd within their puissant hail.
125 Still the same ocean round us raves,
But we stand mute, and watch the waves.

For what avail'd it, all the noise
And outcry of the former men?—
Say, have their sons achieved more joys,
130 Say, is life lighter now than then?
The sufferers died, they left their pain—
The pangs which tortured them remain.

What helps it now, that Byron bore,
With haughty scorn which mock'd the smart,
135 Through Europe to the Ætolian shore
The pageant of his bleeding heart?
That thousands counted every groan,
And Europe made his woe her own?

What boots it, Shelley! that the breeze
140 Carried thy lovely wail away,
Musical through Italian trees
Which fringe thy soft blue Spezzian bay?
Inheritors of thy distress
Have restless hearts one throb the less?

145 Or are we easier, to have read,
O Obermann! the sad stern page,

Which tells us how thou hidd'st thy head
From the fierce tempest of thine age
In the lone brakes of Fontainebleau,
150 Or chalets near the Alpine snow?

Ye slumber in your silent grave!—
The world, which for an idle day
Grace to your mood of sadness gave,
Long since hath flung her weeds away.
155 The eternal trifler breaks your spell;
But we—we learnt your lore too well!

Years hence, perhaps, may dawn an age,
More fortunate, alas! than we,
Which without hardness will be sage,
160 And gay without frivolity.
Sons of the world, oh, speed those years;
But, while we wait, allow our tears!

Allow them! We admire with awe
The exulting thunder of your race;
165 You give the universe your law,
You triumph over time and space!
Your pride of life, your tireless powers,
We praise them, but they are not ours.

We are like children rear'd in shade
170 Beneath some old-world abbey wall,
Forgotten in a forest-glade,
And secret from the eyes of all.
Deep, deep the greenwood round them waves,
Their abbey, and its close of graves!

175 But, where the road runs near the stream,
Oft through the trees they catch a glance

Of passing troops in the sun's beam—
Pennon, and plume, and flashing lance!
Forth to the world those soldiers fare,
180 To life, to cities, and to war!

And through the wood, another way,
Faint bugle-notes from far are borne,
Where hunters gather, staghounds bay,
Round some old forest-lodge at morn.
185 Gay dames are there, in sylvan green;
Laughter and cries—those notes between!

The banners flashing through the trees
Make their blood dance and chain their eyes;
That bugle-music on the breeze
190 Arrests them with a charm'd surprise.
Banner by turns and bugle woo:
Ye shy recluses, follow too!

O children, what do ye reply?—
" Action and pleasure, will ye roam
195 Through these secluded dells to cry
And call us?—but too late ye come!
Too late for us your call ye blow,
Whose bent was taken long ago.

" Long since we pace this shadow'd nave;
200 We watch those yellow tapers shine,
Emblems of hope over the grave,
In the high altar's depth divine.
The organ carries to our ear
Its accents of another sphere.

205 " Fenced early in this cloistral round
Of reverie, of shade, of prayer,

How should we grow in other ground?
How can we flower in foreign air?
—Pass, banners, pass, and bugles, cease;
210 And leave our desert to its peace!"

GEIST'S GRAVE

(January, 1881)

Four years!—and didst thou stay above
The ground, which hides thee now, but four?
And all that life, and all that love,
Were crowded, Geist! into no more?

5 Only four years those winning ways,
Which make me for thy presence yearn,
Call'd us to pet thee or to praise,
Dear little friend! at every turn?

That loving heart, that patient soul,
10 Had they indeed no longer span,
To run their course, and reach their goal,
And read their homily to man?

That liquid, melancholy eye,
From whose pathetic, soul-fed springs
15 Seem'd surging the Virgilian cry,
The sense of tears in mortal things—

That steadfast, mournful strain, consoled
By spirits gloriously gay,
And temper of heroic mould—
20 What, was four years their whole short day?

Yes, only four!—and not the course
Of all the centuries yet to come,
And not the infinite resource
Of nature, with her countless sum

25 Of figures, with her fulness vast
   Of new creation evermore,
   Can ever quite repeat the past,
   Or just thy little self restore.

   Stern law of every mortal lot!
30 Which man, proud man, finds hard to bear,
   And builds himself I know not what
   Of second life I know not where.

   But thou, when struck thine hour to go,
   On us, who stood despondent by,
35 A meek last glance of love didst throw,
   And humbly lay thee down to die.

   Yet would we keep thee in our heart—
   Would fix our favourite on the scene,
   Nor let thee utterly depart
40 And be as if thou ne'er hadst been.

   And so there rise these lines of verse
   On lips that rarely form them now;
   While to each other we rehearse:
   Such ways, such arts, such looks hadst thou!

45 We stroke thy broad brown paws again,
   We bid thee to thy vacant chair,
   We greet thee by the window-pane,
   We hear thy scuffle on the stair;

   We see the flaps of thy large ears
50 Quick raised to ask which way we go;
   Crossing the frozen lake, appears
   Thy small black figure on the snow!

   Nor to us only art thou dear
   Who mourn thee in thine English home;
55 Thou hast thine absent master's tear,
   Dropt by the far Australian foam.

Thy memory lasts both here and there,
And thou shalt live as long as we.
And after that—thou dost not care!
60 In us was all the world to thee.

Yet, fondly zealous for thy fame,
Even to a date beyond our own
We strive to carry down thy name,
By mounded turf, and graven stone.

65 We lay thee, close within our reach,
Here, where the grass is smooth and warm,
Between the holly and the beech,
Where oft we watch'd thy couchant form,

Asleep, yet lending half an ear
70 To travellers on the Portsmouth road;—
There choose we thee, O guardian dear,
Mark'd with a stone, thy last abode!

Then some, who through this garden pass,
When we too, like thyself, are clay,
75 Shall see thy grave upon the grass,
And stop before the stone, and say:

People who lived here long ago
Did by this stone, it seems, intend
To name for future times to know
80 *The dachs-hound, Geist, their little friend.*

DOVER BEACH

(From *New Poems*, 1867)

The sea is calm to-night.
The tide is full, the moon lies fair
Upon the straits;—on the French coast the light
Gleams and is gone; the cliffs of England stand,
5 Glimmering and vast, out in the tranquil bay.

Come to the window, sweet is the night-air!
Only, from the long line of spray
Where the sea meets the moon-blanch'd sand,
Listen! you hear the grating roar
10 Of pebbles which the waves draw back, and fling,
At their return, up the high strand,
Begin, and cease, and then again begin,
With tremulous cadence slow, and bring
The eternal note of sadness in.

15 Sophocles long ago
Heard it on the Ægean, and it brought
Into his mind the turbid ebb and flow
Of human misery; we
Find also in the sound a thought,
20 Hearing it by this distant northern sea.

　　The sea of faith
Was once, too, at the full, and round earth's shore
Lay like the folds of a bright girdle furl'd.
But now I only hear
25 Its melancholy, long, withdrawing roar,
Retreating, to the breath
Of the night-wind, down the vast edges drear
And naked shingles of the world.

Ah, love, let us be true
30 To one another! for the world, which seems
To lie before us like a land of dreams,
So various, so beautiful, so new,
Hath really neither joy, nor love, nor light,
Nor certitude, nor peace, nor help for pain;
35 And we are here as on a darkling plain
Swept with confused alarms of struggle and
　　　flight,
Where ignorant armies clash by night.

LINES WRITTEN IN KENSINGTON GARDENS

(From *Empedocles on Etna and Other Poems*, 1852)

In this lone, open glade I lie,
Screen'd by deep boughs on either hand;
And at its end, to stay the eye,
Those black-crown'd, red-boled pine-trees stand!

5 Birds here make song, each bird has his,
Across the girdling city's hum.
How green under the boughs it is!
How thick the tremulous sheep-cries come!

Sometimes a child will cross the glade
10 To take his nurse his broken toy;
Sometimes a thrush flit overhead
Deep in her unknown day's employ.

Here at my feet what wonders pass,
What endless, active life is here!
15 What blowing daisies, fragrant grass!
An air-stirr'd forest, fresh and clear.

Scarce fresher is the mountain-sod
Where the tired angler lies, stretch'd out,
And, eased of basket and of rod,
20 Counts his day's spoil, the spotted trout.

In the huge world, which roars hard by,
Be others happy if they can!
But in my helpless cradle I
Was breathed on by the rural Pan.

25 I on men's impious uproar hurl'd,
Think often, as I hear them rave,
That peace has left the upper world
And now keeps only in the grave.

Yet here is peace for ever new!
30 When I who watch them am away,
Still all things in this glade go through
The changes of their quiet day.

Then to their happy rest they pass!
The flowers upclose, the birds are fed,
35 The night comes down upon the grass,
The child sleeps warmly in his bed.

Calm soul of all things! make it mine
To feel, amid the city's jar,
That there abides a peace of thine
40 Man did not make, and cannot mar.

The will to neither strive nor cry,
The power to feel with others give!
Calm, calm me more! nor let me die
Before I have begun to live.

SELF-DEPENDENCE

(From the same)

Weary of myself, and sick of asking
What I am, and what I ought to be,
At this vessel's prow I stand, which bears me
Forwards, forwards, o'er the starlit sea.

5 And a look of passionate desire
O'er the sea and to the stars I send:
" Ye who from my childhood up have calm'd me,
Calm me, ah, compose me to the end!

" Ah, once more," I cried, " ye stars, ye waters,
10 On my heart your mighty charm renew;
Still, still let me, as I gaze upon you,
Feel my soul becoming vast like you!"

From the intense, clear, star-sown vault of heaven,
Over the lit sea's unquiet way,
15 In the rustling night-air came the answer:
"Wouldst thou *be* as these are? *Live* as they.

"Unaffrighted by the silence round them,
Undistracted by the sights they see,
These demand not that the things without them
20 Yield them love, amusement, sympathy.

"And with joy the stars perform their shining,
And the sea its long moon-silver'd roll;
For self-poised they live, nor pine with noting
All the fever of some differing soul.

25 "Bounded by themselves, and unregardful
In what state God's other works may be,
In their own tasks all their powers pouring,
These attain the mighty life you see."

O air-born voice! long since, severely clear,
30 A cry like thine in mine own heart I hear:
"Resolve to be thyself; and know, that he
Who finds himself, loses his misery!"

SHAKSPEARE

(From *The Strayed Reveller and Other Poems*, 1849)

Others abide our question. Thou art free.
We ask and ask—Thou smilest and art still,
Out-topping knowledge. For the loftiest hill.
Who to the stars uncrowns his majesty,

5 Planting his steadfast footsteps in the sea,
Making the heaven of heavens his dwelling-place,
Spares but the cloudy border of his base
To the foil'd searching of mortality;

And thou, who didst the stars and sunbeams
    know,
10 Self-school'd, self-scann'd, self-honour'd, self-
    secure,
Didst tread on earth unguess'd at.—Better so!

All pains the immortal spirit must endure,
All weakness which impairs, all griefs which bow,
Find their sole speech in that victorious brow.

Gabriel Charles Dante Rossetti

1828–1882

THE BLESSED DAMOZEL

(Third Version, from *Poems*, 1870)

The blessed damozel leaned out
    From the gold bar of Heaven;
Her eyes were deeper than the depth
    Of waters stilled at even;
5 She had three lilies in her hand.
    And the stars in her hair were seven.

Her robe ungirt from clasp to hem,
    No wrought flowers did adorn,
But a white rose of Mary's gift,
10   For service meetly worn;
Her hair that lay along her back
    Was yellow like ripe corn.

Herseemed she scarce had been a day
    One of God's choristers;
15 The wonder was not yet quite gone
    From that still look of hers;
Albeit, to them she left, her day
    Had counted as ten years.

(To one, it is ten years of years.
20　. . . Yet now, and in this place,
　　Surely she leaned o'er me—her hair
　　　Fell all about my face. . .
　　Nothing: the autumn fall of leaves.
　　　The whole year sets apace.)

25 It was the rampart of God's house
　　　That she was standing on;
　　By God built over the sheer depth
　　　The which is Space begun;
　　So high, that looking downward thence
30　　She scarce could see the sun.

　　It lies in Heaven, across the flood
　　　Of ether, as a bridge.
　　Beneath, the tides of day and night
　　　With flame and darkness ridge
35 The void, as low as where this earth
　　　Spins like a fretful midge.

　　Around her, lovers, newly met
　　　'Mid deathless love's acclaims,
　　Spoke evermore among themselves
40　　Their heart-remembered names;
　　And the souls mounting up to God
　　　Went by her like thin flames.

　　And still she bowed herself and stooped
　　　Out of the circling charm;
45 Until her bosom must have made
　　　The bar she leaned on warm,
　　And the lilies lay as if asleep
　　　Along her bended arm.

　　From the fixed place of Heaven she saw
50　　Time like a pulse shake fierce

Through all the world.   Her gaze still strove
   Within the gulf to pierce
Its path; and now she spoke as when
   The stars sang in their spheres.

55 The sun was gone now; the curled moon
   Was like a little feather
Fluttering far down the gulf; and now
   She spoke through the still weather.
Her voice was like the voice the stars
60   Had when they sang together.

(Ah sweet!   Even now, in that bird's song,
   Strove not her accents there,
Fain to be harkened?   When those bells
   Possessed the mid-day air,
65 Strove not her steps to reach my side
   Down all the echoing stair?)

'I wish that he were come to me,
   For he will come,' she said.
'Have I not prayed in Heaven?—on earth,
70   Lord, Lord, has he not pray'd?
Are not two prayers a perfect strength?
   And shall I feel afraid?

'When round his head the aureole clings,
   And he is clothed in white,
75 I'll take his hand and go with him
   To the deep wells of light;
As unto a stream we will step down,
   And bathe there in God's sight.

'We two will stand beside that shrine,
80   Occult, withheld, untrod,

Whose lamps are stirred continually
    With prayer sent up to God;
And see our old prayers, granted, melt
    Each like a little cloud.

85 ' We two will lie i' the shadow of
    That living mystic tree
Within whose secret growth the Dove
    Is sometimes felt to be,
While every leaf that His plumes touch
90   Saith His name audibly.

' And I myself will teach to him,
    I myself, lying so,
The songs I sing here; which his voice
    Shall pause in, hushed and slow,
95 And find some knowledge at each pause,
    Or some new thing to know.'

(Alas! We two, we two, thou say'st!
    Yea, one wast thou with me
That once of old. But shall God lift
100   To endless unity
The soul whose likeness with thy soul
    Was but its love for thee?)

' We two,' she said, ' will seek the groves
    Where the lady Mary is,
105 With her five handmaidens, whose names
    Are five sweet symphonies,
Cecily, Gertrude, Magdalen,
    Margaret and Rosalys.

' Circlewise sit they, with bound locks
110   And foreheads garlanded;

Into the fine cloth white like flame
  Weaving the golden thread,
To fashion the birth-robes for them
  Who are just born, being dead.

115 'He shall fear, haply, and be dumb:
  Then will I lay my cheek
To his, and tell about our love,
  Not once abashed or weak:
And the dear Mother will approve
120   My pride, and let me speak.

  'Herself shall bring us, hand in hand,
    To Him round whom all souls
Kneel, the clear-ranged unnumbered heads
    Bowed with their aureoles:
125 And angels meeting us shall sing
    To their citherns and citoles.

  'There will I ask of Christ the Lord
    Thus much for him and me:—
Only to live as once on earth
130   With Love,—only to be,
As then awhile, forever now
    Together, I and he.'

She gazed and listened and then said,
  Less sad of speech than mild,—
135 'All this is when he comes.' She ceased.
  The light thrilled towards her, fill'd
With angels in strong level flight.
  Her eyes prayed, and she smil'd.

(I saw her smile.) But soon their path
140   Was vague in distant spheres:

And then she cast her arms along
   The golden barriers,
And laid her face between her hands,
   And wept.   (I heard her tears.)

THE SEA-LIMITS

(From the same)

Consider the sea's listless chime:
   Time's self it is, made audible,—
   The murmur of the earth's own shell.
Secret continuance sublime
5   Is the sea's end: our sight may pass
   No furlong further.   Since time was,
This sound hath told the lapse of time.

No quiet, which is death's,—it hath
   The mournfulness of ancient life,
10   Enduring always at dull strife.
As the world's heart of rest and wrath,
   Its painful pulse is in the sands.
Last utterly, the whole sky stands,
   Gray and not known, along its path.

15 Listen alone beside the sea,
   Listen alone among the woods;
   Those voices of twin solitudes
Shall have one sound alike to thee:
   Hark where the murmurs of thronged men
20   Surge and sink back and surge again,—
Still the one voice of wave and tree.

Gather a shell from the strown beach
   And listen at its lips: they sigh
   The same desire and mystery,

25 The echo of the whole sea's speech.
     And all mankind is thus at heart
     Not any thing but what thou art:
     And Earth, Sea, Man, are all in each.

SONNETS

SIBYLLA PALMIFERA

(For a Picture)

Under the arch of Life, where love and death,
     Terror and mystery, guard her shrine, I saw
     Beauty enthroned; and though her gaze struck
          awe,
I drew it in as simply as my breath.
5 Hers are the eyes which, over and beneath,
     The sky and sea bend on thee,—which can draw,
     By sea or sky or woman, to one law,
The allotted bondman of her palm and wreath.

This is that Lady Beauty, in whose praise
10   Thy voice and hand shake still,—long known to
          thee
     By flying hair and fluttering hem,—the beat
     Following her daily of thy heart and feet,
How passionately and irretrievably,
     In what fond flight, how many ways and days!

(From *The House of Life*, in *Ballads and Sonnets*, 1881)

SONNET XIX

SILENT NOON

Your hands lie open in the long fresh grass,—
     The finger-points look through like rosy blooms:
     Your eyes smile peace. The pasture gleams
          and glooms

'Neath billowing skies that scatter and amass.
5 All round our nest, far as the eye can pass,
    Are golden kingcup-fields with silver edge
      Where the cow-parsley skirts the hawthorn-
        hedge.
'Tis visible silence, still as the hour-glass.

Deep in the sun-searched growths the dragon-fly
10 Hangs like a blue thread loosened from the sky :—
    So this wing'd hour is dropt to us from above.
Oh! clasp we to our hearts, for deathless dower,
This close-companioned inarticulate hour
    When twofold silence was the song of love.

SONNET LXIII.

INCLUSIVENESS

The changing guests, each in a different mood,
    Sit at the roadside table and arise:
    And every life among them in likewise
Is a soul's board set daily with new food.
5 What man has bent o'er his son's sleep, to brood
    How that face shall watch his when cold it lies?
    Or thought, as his own mother kissed his eyes,
Of what her kiss was when his father wooed?

May not this ancient room thou sit'st in dwell
10   In separate living souls for joy or pain?
    Nay, all its corners may be painted plain
Where Heaven shows pictures of some life spent
      well;
    And may be stamped, a memory all in vain,
Upon the sight of lidless eyes in Hell.

SONNET XCVII.

A SUPERSCRIPTION

Look in my face; my name is Might-have-been;
   I am also called No-more, Too-late, Farewell;
   Unto thine ear I hold the dead-sea shell
Cast up thy Life's foam-fretted feet between;
5 Unto thine eyes the glass where that is seen
   Which had Life's form and Love's, but by my spell
   Is now a shaken shadow intolerable,
Of ultimate things unuttered the frail screen.

Mark me how still I am! But should there dart
10   One moment through thy soul the soft surprise
   Of that winged Peace which lulls the breath of sighs,—
Then shalt thou see me smile, and turn apart
Thy visage to mine ambush at thy heart
   Sleepless with cold commemorative eyes.

William Morris

1834–1896

AN APOLOGY

(From *The Earthly Paradise*, 1868–70)

Of Heaven or Hell I have no power to sing,
   I cannot ease the burden of your fears,
Or make quick-coming death a little thing,
   Or bring again the pleasure of past years,
5 Nor for my words shall ye forget your tears,
   Or hope again for aught that I can say,
   The idle singer of an empty day.

But rather, when aweary of your mirth,
From full hearts still unsatisfied ye sigh,
10 And, feeling kindly unto all the earth,
Grudge every minute as it passes by,
Made the more mindful that the sweet days die—
—Remember me a little then I pray,
The idle singer of an empty day.

15   The heavy trouble, the bewildering care
That weighs us down who live and earn our bread,
These idle verses have no power to bear;
So let me sing of names remembered,
Because they, living not, can ne'er be dead,
20 Or long time take their memory quite away
From us poor singers of an empty day.

Dreamer of dreams, born out of my due time,
Why should I strive to set the crooked straight?
Let it suffice me that my murmuring rhyme
25 Beats with light wing against the ivory gate,
Telling a tale not too importunate
To those who in the sleepy region stay,
Lulled by the singer of an empty day.

Folk say, a wizard to a northern king
30 At Christmas-tide such wondrous things did
      show,
That through one window men beheld the spring,
And through another saw the summer glow,
And through a third the fruited vines a-row,
While still, unheard, but in its wonted way,
35 Piped the drear wind of that December day.

So with this Earthly Paradise it is,
If ye will read aright, and pardon me,
Who strive to build a shadowy isle of bliss

Midmost the beating of the steely sea,
40 Where tossed about all hearts of men must be;
Whose ravening monsters mighty men shall slay,
Not the poor singer of an empty day.

THE DAY OF DAYS

(From *Poems by the Way*, 1892)

Each eve earth falleth down the dark,
As though its hope were o'er;
Yet lurks the sun where day is done
Behind to-morrow's door.

5 Grey grows the dawn while men-folk sleep,
Unseen spreads on the light,
Till the thrush sings to the coloured things,
And earth forgets the night.

No otherwise wends on our Hope:
10 E'en as a tale that's told
Are fair lives lost, and all the cost
Of wise and true and bold.

We've toiled and failed; we spake the word;
None hearkened; dumb we lie;
15 Our Hope is dead, the seed we spread
Fell o'er the earth to die.

What's this? For joy our hearts stand still,
And life is loved and dear,
The lost and found the Cause hath crowned,
20 The Day of Days is here.

DRAWING NEAR THE LIGHT

(From the same)

Lo, when we wade the tangled wood,
In haste and hurry to be there,
Nought seem its leaves and blossoms good,
For all that they be fashioned fair.

5 But looking up, at last we see
The glimmer of the open light,
From o'er the place where we would be:
Then grow the very brambles bright.

So now, amidst our day of strife,
10 With many a matter glad we play,
When once we see the light of life
Gleam through the tangle of to-day.

Rudyard Kipling

1865—

RECESSIONAL

(1897)

God of our fathers, known of old—
Lord of our far-flung battle-line—
Beneath Whose awful Hand we hold
Dominion over palm and pine—
5 Lord God of Hosts, be with us yet,
Lest we forget—lest we forget!

The tumult and the shouting dies—
The captains and the kings depart—

Still stands Thine ancient Sacrifice,
10   An humble and a contrite heart.
Lord God of Hosts, be with us yet,
Lest we forget—lest we forget!

Far-called our navies melt away—
    On dune and headland sinks the fire—
15 Lo, all our pomp of yesterday
    Is one with Nineveh and Tyre!
Judge of the Nations, spare us yet,
Lest we forget—lest we forget!

If, drunk with sight of power, we loose
20   Wild tongues that have not Thee in awe—
Such boasting as the Gentiles use
    Or lesser breeds without the Law—
Lord God of Hosts, be with us yet,
Lest we forget—lest we forget!

25 For heathen heart that puts her trust
    In reeking tube and iron shard
All valiant dust that builds on dust,
    And guarding calls not Thee to guard—
For frantic boast and foolish word,
30 Thy Mercy on Thy People, Lord!
                              Amen.

NOTES

The heavy-faced figures refer to pages, the ordinary figures to lines. Int. Eng. Lit. indicates the editor's *Introduction to English Literature*, revised edition, 1896.

BALLADS

(OF VARIOUS AND UNCERTAIN DATES.)

CHEVY CHASE.

1. This ballad, like its companion the still older *Batue of Otterbourne*, is a famous expression in popular song of the fierce antagonism, the jealousy, and the daring fostered and kept alive among the dwellers in the Borders, or Marches, between England and Scotland, by frequent wars and continual forays. Percy says, speaking of the origin of the poem: "The ballad, without being historical, may have had some foundation in fact. The law of the Marches interdicted either nation from hunting on the borders of the other, without leave from the proprietors, or their deputies. The long rivalry between the martial families of Percy and Douglas must have burst into many sharp feuds and little incursions not recorded in history; and the old ballad of the 'Hunting a' the Cheviat,' which was the original title, may have sprung out of such a quarrel." (*Reliques.*) *Chevy Chase*, now one of the most familiar and representative ballads, easily won a high place in the popular esteem. In 1711, Addison (who, however, knew the poem only in an inferior and more modern version) wrote: "The old Song of Chevy-Chase is the favorite ballad of the common people of England: and Ben Jonson used to say that he had rather have been the author of it than of all of his works." He then quotes the now-familiar passage from Sir Philip Sidney's *Defense of Poesie* (1581?): "I never heard the old song of Piercy and Douglas, that I found not my heart more moved than with a trumpet, etc." (*Spectator*, LXX. and LXXIV.) Prof. Child remarks that Sidney's words are equally applicable to the *Battle of Otterbourne*, at least so far as the subject is concerned, that being also a song of "Piercy and Douglas." Nevertheless, he thinks that the superior poetic quality of *Chevy Chase* makes it probable that

Sidney had that ballad in mind as is generally supposed.
(*Ballads*, Pt. VI. 305.)

DATE.—It has been thought that *Chevy Chase* is really a
modified account of the Battle of Otterbourne, celebrated in
the ballad of that name, which took place in 1388. Dr. Child
holds that the differences in the story of the two ballads are
not so great as to prevent us from holding this view. As James
of Scotland is mentioned, we know that it was not before 1424,
the date of the accession of James I. (Child, *ib.* p. 304.) The
date of actual composition was of course an indefinite time
after the occurrence of the event celebrated, while Sidney's
allusion makes it clear that the ballad was well known in 1580.

1.—5. **Magger** = mauger = in spite of, or against the will
of. (O. F. *malgré*.)—10. **Let** = prevent. (A. S. *laet* = slow.
Hence *to let* is to make later or to hinder.)—12. **Meany** = company, or following of retainers.

2.—20. **Reas** = rouse.—21. **Byckarte uppone the bent** =
skirmished upon the coarse grass, or the moor. Beaters appear to have been sent into the woods to drive the game into
the open, where the hunters awaited them.—23. **Wyld**, i.e.
the wild deer.—25. **glent** = flashed. The word, which is related
to glitter, glisten, etc., here includes the idea of rapid motion.
—31. **Mort** = the series of notes blown upon the horn to an-
nounce the death of the deer. (Fr. *mort* = death.)—32. **Shear**
= in different directions. *On sydis shear* = on all sides.—33.
Quyrry = the slaughtered game. See Skeat's *Etymol. Dict.*
— 34. **Bryttlynge** = the cutting, or, literally, the breaking up,
of the deer. (A. S. *brecan* = to break.)—37. **Verament** = truly.
(Fr. *vrai* = truth; *vraiment* = truly.)

3.—43. **Bylle** = bill, a battle-axe. **Brande** = a sword, v.
Skeat.—57. **Glede** = a glowing coal. (A. S. *glowan* = to glow.)
—72. **Ton of us** = one of us.—78. **Yerle** = earl.—81. **Cors** =
curse.

5.—110. **Wouche** = wrong, damage.—122. **Basnites** =
basinet, "a steel cap, originally of very simple form, named
from its resemblance to a little basin." (*Cent. Dict.*)—123.
Myneyeple = "manople, a gauntlet covering hand and fore-
arm" (Skeat.)—125. **Freyke** = man, a warrior. (A. S. *frecca* =
a bold man, analogous to Lat. *vir*. *Fre* = free-born, generous.)

6.—129. **Swapte** = struck, or slashed. (A. S. *swappen*, to
strike.)—130. **Myllan** = Milan steel.—133. **Sprente** = sprang.
(A. S. *sprengan* = to spring.)—140. **Hight** = promise. (A. S.
Haten.)—148. **Wane**: according to Skeat the word means here
a great number, hence "a single arrow out of a vast quantity."
Gummere suggests that *wane* "might = wone = one; a
mighty one," but declares this also to be unsatisfactory.

8.—194. **Stour** = conflict, battle.—201. **The tocke** . . .

Something is wanting here in the MS., and various guesses have been made as to the missing word. Probably Skeat's suggestion to supply "the fight" comes nearest. It may have been some equivalent expression as "hard strikes."—210. **On hy** = upright.

9.—213-234. **Thear was slayne with the lord Persé.** Percy says that most of these here mentioned belonged to distinguished families in the North. John Agertoun, or Haggerstoun, is supposed to have been one of the Rutherfords, then retained by the house of Douglas; "*ryche Rugbé*" is said to have been Ralph Neville of Raby Castle, cousin-german to Hotspur, etc. (See *Reliques*.)—217. **Loumle** = Lumley. There was a prominent family in Northumberland by this name, at least one of whom was a follower of the Percies. See Burke's *Extinct Peerages*; also Stephen's *Dict. Nat. Biog.*—236. **Makys**, or **make**, = mates.—237. **Carpe** = sing, talk. (*Carpen* = to talk, to speak.)

10.—242. **Jamy**, James I. (reigned 1424-1437.)—251. **Lyff-tenant of the marches** = lieutenant, or deputy, to guard the marches or borders between Scotland and England.—257. **Brook** = use, enjoy. See *Cent. Dict.*—262. **Hombyll-doun** = Hamildon. There was a battle of Homildon Hill in 1402, between the English and the Scotch, in which the former were victorious. Percy, called Hotspur, commanded the English forces, and Douglas the Scotch. The reference to the occasion of this battle in the text is without historical foundation, as a careful examination of the chronology of the events referred to will show.—265. "**Glendale** is the district or ward in which Homildon is situated." (Percy.)

11.—279. **Balys bete** = remedy our evils. (Percy.)

SIR PATRICK SPENS (OR SPENCE.)

The question as to whether this famous ballad had any historical foundation, and if so, as to the precise events with which it is connected, has been much discussed. Various theories and opinions on these points will be found in Percy's *Reliques*, Scott's *Minstrelsy of the Scottish Border*, Child's *Ballads*, etc., but as the matter remains unsettled the conflicting views need not be here entered upon. Fortunately the determination of such questions is not necessary for readers who value the ballad as poetry, not as a topic for debate. On the whole Allingham's conclusion seems the sensible one: "There is no old MS. of the ballad. All the foundation which really seems attainable is this, that in old times there was much intercourse between Scotland and Norway, and between the royal courts of the two countries, and that some shipwreck not altogether unlike this may probably have happened." (The *Ballad Book*, 377.) Coleridge, who takes the motto of his ode *Dejection* from this poem, then refers to it as "the grand old ballad of Sir Patrick Spens." The great antiquity generally claimed for it has been unsuccessfully disputed, but the exact date is not known.

1. **Dumferling** = Dumfermline, a town in Fifeshire, some sixteen miles N.W. of Edinburgh. It was a favorite residence of the early Scottish kings and contained a royal palace.—3 **Sailôr**, accented here on the second syllable, as is lettér. The practice is common in the old ballads.—9. **Braid lettér** = an open, or patent, letter; i.e. here, a public document under the royal seal.

12.—25. **Late late yestreen**, etc. inwards quotes this in his *Weather-Lore*, and calls attention to the popular belief that the new moon holding the old moon in her arms, or with the entire disk visible, is a sign of storm.—32. **Thair hats**, etc. Motherwell gives this line: "They wat their hats aboun," and adds another reading, "Their hair was wat aboun," in a note. In any case the meaning is the same: loath to wet their shoes they were at last in over their heads.

13.—41. **Aberdour**, an old town on the Frith of Forth, about ten miles to the north of Edinburgh. It was half-way from Norway to this town that Sir Patrick was lost.

WALY WALY, LOVE BE BONNY.

This ancient song is said to have been first published in Ramsay's *Tea Table Miscellany* (1724), but it is thought to have been part of another ballad, *Lord Jamie Douglas*, which closely resembles it in some particulars. Allingham says that some have placed it about the middle of the sixteenth century.

1. **Waly** = an interjection expressing grief, equivalent to alas. (See *Wella way*, of which it is an abbreviated form in *Cent. Dict.*)—8. **Lichtlie** = make light of, to use with disrespect.—17. **Arthur's-seat** = Arthur's Seat, a steep and rocky hill near Edinburgh. **St. Anton's Well** is about one third of the way up its side. (See description in Scott's *Heart of Midlothian*, Ch. VII.)

14.—32. **Cramasie** = cramoisy = crimson.

THE TWA SISTERS O'BINNORIE.

Dr. Child notes that this is one of the very few old ballads still alive in tradition in the British Isles. Under the title of *The Miller and the King's Daughter* it was printed as a broadside in 1656, and included in the miscellany *Wit Restored*

1658. (*Ballads*, V. I. Pt. I. 118.) The whole tone and character of the story make it highly representative of a large class of popular songs and legends dealing with love, tragedy, and the supernatural. (Cf. ballads dealing with the allied themes of fratricide, *The Twa Brothers*, *Edward Edward*, *Son Davie*.) Not only has the story of the two sisters been told with many variations in the British Isles, it has a place in the popular poetry of many of the Teutonic nations, as the Danish, Norwegian, Swedish, Icelandic, etc. (See Child. *ib. supra.*) The use of the refrain should be noted as a characteristic feature of early ballad poetry, imitated by certain modern poets. "The refrain," says Prof. Gummere, "is almost the only rudiment of choral poetry surviving to our own day, and it has come down to us a companion of the ballad and the dance." (*Old English Ballads*, xc.) For modern use of the refrain cf. Rossetti's *Troy Town*, *Eden Bower*, Tennyson's *Oriana*, etc., and for parody on the Preraphaelite or other revivals of it, see *Ballad* in C. S. Calverly's *Fly Leaves*.

BONNIE GEORGE CAMPBELL.

18. The historical basis for this lament is of little importance and not certainly known. Motherwell thinks that it may have been "a lament for one of the adherents of the house of Argyle who fell in the battle of Glenlivet, 1594."
10. Greeting = weeping.—**15. Toom** = empty.—**19. Big** = build.

HELEN OF KIRCONNEL.

19. The foundation of this lament as given by Scott is substantially as follows: Helen Irving or Bell, daughter of the laird of Kirconnel in Dumfriesshire, had two suitors; one of them, Adam Fleming, was preferred. During a secret interview between the lovers in Kirconnel Churchyard on the river Kirtle, the rejected suitor fired on his rival from the other side of the stream. Helen was shot in shielding her lover, and died in his arms. The poem is the lament of Fleming over Helen's grave. (*Minstrelsy*, etc., 324.) Wordsworth has treated this subject in a very inferior poem, *Ellen Irwin* (see Knight's *Wordsworth*, II. 191, and note) "choosing" (as he tells us) a different style "to preclude all comparison." A similar theme is handled more successfully by Tennyson in *The Ballad of Oriana*, but even this cannot equal the Scotch ballad of a nameless singer in pathetic interest.
7. Burd = *burde* = maid.

SPENSER TO DRYDEN

(CIR. 1579—CIR. 1660.)

EDMUND SPENSER

21. Edmund Spenser, b. London 1552 and d. London 1599. His first important work, *The Shepherds Calendar*, 1579, stands at the beginning of a great epoch in English poetry. The first three books of *The Faerie Queene* were published in 1590, and three additional books in 1596. Spenser follows Chaucer in the chronological succession of the greater English poets. He was born about twelve years before Shakespeare; he made his mark on English poetry about ten years before Shakespeare began his work; and he died about nine years before the birth of Milton.

THE FAERIE QUEENE.

The Faerie Queene, Spenser's longest and greatest work, bears a general resemblance to the romantic epics of Tasso and Ariosto. It differs from its Italian models, however, in the elevation of its tone and in the definiteness and importance of its moral purpose. It is not merely a romance, it is a religious or spiritual allegory. Its object is to aid in the formation of noble character,—"to fashion a gentleman or noble person, in virtuous and gentle discipline,"—by presenting the triumph of chivalric ideals of manhood over sin. Spenser accordingly takes the twelve "moral virtues" which he conceives to be the essential elements in the character of a true knight, or Christian gentleman, representing each virtue by a knight who is made "the patron and defender of the same, in whose actions and feates of armes and chivalry the operations of that virtue whereof he is the protector 'are expressed,' and the vices that oppose themselves against the same are beaten down and overcome." One book was to have been devoted to each of the twelve virtues, but only six were completed. These six treat respectively of *Holiness, Temperance, Chastity, Friendship, Justice,* and *Courtesy*. Each complete book is composed of twelve cantos, each canto containing from thirty-five to sixty nine-line stanzas. There are also some fragmentary cantos, which appeared after Spenser's death. Spenser hoped to add a second part, consisting likewise of twelve books, which should treat of the twelve public or "politick" virtues, i.e. those of a man in his relation to the state.

The Selections here given are from the first and second books, and are so arranged that they can be read and understood as a continuous narrative. That the underlying, or allegorical, meaning of the story may become plain, a few points should be grasped at the outset and kept in mind. The first book shows us the perils which "enfold" Holiness, or "the righteous man," who is brought before us in the person of the Red-Cross Knight. This knight may be further, as Hallam holds, "the militant Christian," or perhaps England, or the Reformed England of Elizabeth's time, or—as Dean Church suggests—"the commonalty of England." However this may be, the *Knight*, or Holiness, is shown to us as the proper mate and champion of *Una*, or Truth, but beguiled and deceived by the wiles of *Duessa*, or Falsehood. Further, we are to understand that *Una* is not only truth, but religious truth, especially as it is embodied in the Church of England, and that similarly *Duessa* is not only error, but those especial errors with which (as Spenser believed) the Church of Rome was identified. Briefly the subject of the book may then be said to be Righteousness, incomplete and misled if separated from Religion, betrayed by Error and ultimately restored by being reunited to the true Church. (See Bk. I. Cant. VIII. 1.)

"The second book, *Of Temperance*," (in the words of Dean Church,) "represents the internal conquests of self-mastery, the conquests of a man over his passions, his violence, his covetousness, his ambition, his despair, his sensuality." (See Life of Spenser, *E. M. L.* series, 125–6.) The first book thus deals mainly with faith, or religion, the second with practice, or morality, the outcome, or practical result, of religious belief in the struggle with the World, the Flesh, and the Devil. The two together thus contain, as Dean Kitchin observes, "the substance of man's faith and duty." (See Kitchin's ed. *Faerie Queene*, Bk. II., Introd.) The selections given in the text deal with the struggle with two out of these three foes ; viz., the struggle with *Mammon*, or the world, and the struggle with the *Flesh*, or the seductions of idle pleasures and self-indulgence.

1. BOOK I. (*Introductory Stanzas.*)—**Lo I the man**, etc. An allusion to Spenser's first important work, *The Shepherds Calendar*, a pastoral, 1579. The lines follow closely the opening of Vergils Ænead, "*Ille ego qui quondam,*"etc.—7. **Areeds** = directs, counsels,—10. **O holy virgin**, etc. The muse Clio. Why

is she especially invoked?—13. **Scryme** = a box or case for keeping books. (See Lat. *scrimium*.)—14. **Fayrest Tanaquill.** From Bk. II. C. X. 76, it is evident that Spenser refers to Queen Elizabeth under the name of *Tanaquill.* What induced Spenser to choose this name for the queen is uncertain. Kitchin and others assert that *Tanaquill* was a British princess, but I have been unable to find on what ground. Mr. J. B. Fletcher, Harvard, has kindly furnished me the following suggestion. He thinks it not improbable that Spenser may have had *Tanaquill,* the wife of *Tarquinius Priscus,* in mind. "Spenser the humanist," he says, "might not impossibly have thought to flatter the English queen by an association with the Roman one, especially when the peculiar eminence and influence of *Tanaquil,* is remembered."

22.—19. **Impe of highest Jove** = Cupid, or Eros. *Imp* (Lat. *impotus* = a graft) was formerly used in a good sense, and meant simply child, or scion. (Cf. Shaks. *Hen. IV.* IV. 1.) The word is found in the sense of child in some early English epitaphs. There are conflicting accounts of Cupid's parentage in classical mythology. Two distinct mythical accounts are here referred to; according to one he was the son of Jove, according to another of Venus, but no version makes him the child of Jove and Venus.—23. **Heben** = ebony.—25. **Mart** = Mars.—34. **Type of thine** = Una, the type or image of his "Godesse heavenly bright," Queen Elizabeth, as well as of Truth.

23. CANTO I.—44. **iolly** = gallant, handsome. (O. F. *joli.*) There is nothing here of the modern use, as we are told later that the knight's bearing was "solemne sad."—54. **ydrad** = dreaded. (*y* here a later form of *ye,* the prefix in M. E. of the past part.—56. **Greatest Glorianna**: Queen Elizabeth. Spenser says in the explanatory letter to Raleigh: "In that Faerie Queene I mean *Glory* in my general intention, but in my particular I conceive the most excellent and glorious person of our soveraine the Queen."—60. **Earne** = yearn.—63. A **dragon,** i.e. Error, or more particularly the false doctrines of the Romish Church which the Red-Cross Knight, or Reformed England, must combat.—64. **A lovely lady,** i.e. Una, or Truth, which is one, or single, in contrast to Duessa, Falsehood, or Doubleness. Una is also, in a more definite sense, Truth as embodied in the true Church, once supreme from East to West (see Bk. I. C. I. st. v.), but now "forwasted" by errors.

24.—82. A **dwarfe**—supposed by some to represent common sense or prudence. (See *Blackwood's Mag.,* Nov. 1834.) The explanation is not very satisfactory.—92. A **shadie grove** = the thick wood of Error, into which the heavenly light of the stars cannot penetrate.

25.—105. **The sayling pine** = "the pine whence sailing ships are made." Kitchin.—113. **Sallow for the mill.** I am indebted to Mr. J. B. Fletcher for the following explanation: "The allusion here *may* be as follows. *Sallow*—the *Salix cinerea* and *caprea*—has been recognized almost from the invention of gunpowder to the present day as the best "charcoal" wood for gunpowder. In 1414, Henry V. ordered 'twenty pipes of powder made of willow charcoal.'" Spenser has just referred to the willow in general, he then goes on to speak of a particular species of willow, the *sallow*, and of its most important use.—117. **The carver holme,** the holly, which is especially fit for carving.

27.—152. **Read** = *rede*, advice, counsel.—245. **To welke** = to fade. (M. E. *welken.*)

28.—257. **Lin** = cease. (M. E. *linnen*, A. S. *linnan*, Sc. *blin*.)

29.—391. **Plutoes griesly dame.** Proserpina had both a creative and a destroying power. As the daughter of Demeter we think of her in the first, and as the wife of Pluto and queen of Erebus, in the second capacity. She is here called *griesly* or terrible, because the poet has the dark and death-dealing side of her function in mind.—395. **Great Gorgon,** i e. Demogorgon, a mysterious divinity, associated with darkness and the under world, quite distinct from the *Gorgon* or *Medusa* of classical mythology. He reappears in *Faerie Queene,* IV. II., is introduced into Milton's *Paradise Lost,* II. 964, and into Shelley's *Prometheus Unbound.*

30.—415. **Double gates.** Spenser here follows Homer. *Od* XIX. 564, and Vergil, *Æn.* VI. 894. According to the idea of these poets, true dreams were supposed to pass through a gate of horn, false dreams through one of ivory. The second gate is here spoken of as "overcast" with silver; horn was probably selected by Homer because it was a translucent substance through which actual things beyond could be seen, if but dimly. Cf. Wm. Watson's poem "The Dream of Man."

31.—444. **Hecate,** a powerful female divinity supposed to have been introduced into the Greek from an earlier mythology. Like Demogorgon she is associated with night or darkness and the nether world. She presides over magic, phantoms, and nocturnal ceremonies, hence Shakespeare appropriately makes her the mistress of the witches in Macbeth.—447. **Archimago,** by whom Spenser means hypocrisy (*Arch* = chief, Gr. ἀρχι, and Lat. *imago* = image, form, semblance): an allusion to this chief dissembler's power of assuming various guises in order to deceive. Spenser also connects him with the Romish Church. 'He may be intended," says Kitchin, "either for the Pope, or the Spanish King (Philip II.), or for the general spirit

of lying and false religion." He is first introduced in Cant.
I. XXIX. as "an aged sire"; see connecting argument on p. 28.

33.—3. (CANTO III.) **Then** = than.—14. **True as touch.**
Touch here probably used for touchstone, as in Shakespeare's
Rich. III. IV. 2: "Now do I play the touch, to try," etc. The
touchstone used to test the purity of precious metals came to
symbolize the power to tell the false from the true.

21. **Preace** = press, a throng.

BOOK II.

40. CANTO VI. — 104. **Gondelay** = gondola. 109–126.
Note the formal and artificial character of the description.
The second line of the XII. stanza is, however, quoted by
Lowell as one of the three which "best characterize the feel-
ing that Spenser's poetry gives us." (See essay on *Spenser*.)

41, 42.—136–162. This song is a good example of the
smoothness and sweetness of Spenser's verse. It appears to
imitate Tasso's *Gerusalemme Liberata*, Bk. XIV. 62; but if an
imitation, it is superior to the original. Tennyson has followed
precisely the same line of thought in the *Lotus Eaters*, Stz.
II and III. Spenser's idea that all good things are given to be
enjoyed is a frequent one with the poets. Cf. Milton's *Comus*,
l. 706 ; *Sonnet I* of Shakespeare, etc.

BOOK II.

43, 44. CANTO VII.—19–36. **Mammon**, here introduced
as the "God of the world and worldlings," was not a
heathen divinity, but, as in the *New Testament*, a simple personification of money or worldly ambition, from the Syriac
word for riches. Cf. *St. Mark*, vi. 24, and *Par. Lost*, I. 678
et seq.—40. **Of Mulciber's**, etc. Mulciber was the name given
to Vulcan (Lat. *Mulceo*, to soften), as the smoother, or softener,
of metals by fire. Milton (*Par. Lost*, I. 740) identifies him
with Mammon. *Of*, here used in the sense of *by*, as is frequent
in the *Bible* and in Shakespeare ; "and should have been
killed of them." *Acts.* xxiii. 27.

45.—70. **Swink** = to toil. In Chaucer a swinker is a work-
man or ploughman.

46.—91. **Weet** = know. A. S *witan*, to know.

48.—194. **Payne**, "not suffering, but Poena, the avenging
punishing deity." (Kitchin.) — 199–225. This description,
marked by intensity, compression, and power, may be compared
with a similar passage in Vergil's *Æn.* VI. 273, and with the
fine personifications of Sorrow, Remorse of Conscience, and the
rest in the *Introduction* to Sackville's *Mirror for Magistrates*.

49.—213. **Celeno**, one of the Harpies ; filthy, vulture-like

creatures, with head and breast of a woman. Celæno is especially mentioned by Vergil (*Æn.* III. 245).—232. **For next to
Death is Sleep,** etc. *Somnus* (sleep) and *Mors* (death) were
the sons of *Nox* (night). The idea is a favorite one with the
classic and the English poets. Cf. Vergil, *Æn.* VI. 278, and
Shelley's *Queen Mab,* "Death and his brother Sleep." Sackville calls sleep "the cousin of Death"; B. Griffen, "brother
to quiet death," etc.

50.—264. **Breaches** = stalactites.—268. **Arachne** = spider.
Arachne was a skilful needlewoman changed into a spider by
Minerva.

52.—321. **Culver** = dove. Lat. *Columba.*

THE COURTIER.

(EXTRACT FROM "MOTHER HUBBARD'S TALE.")

53. The poem from which this extract is taken first appeared
in a miscellaneous collection entitled *Complaints* (1591). It was
in this year that Spenser returned to his home in Ireland, after
a stay in London of some two years. This visit to England had
been made under the encouragement of Raleigh, who, Spenser
tells us, secured his admission to the queen. The poet gives
us an account of this visit in his *Colin Clout's Come Home Again*
(pub. 1596), but in the lines here given we have probably an
insight into the real mood in which he left the court. For
this, as well as for the side-light it throws on Elizabeth as a
patron of letters, and for its satiric force, the passage is a
memorable one.

SONNETS.

54, 55. XL and LXXV. These are from a series of
eighty-eight sonnets entitled *Amoretti,* published together with
the splendid *Epithalamion,* or marriage hymn, in 1595. The
sonnets commemorate Spenser's courtship of, and the *Epithalamion* his marriage to, a certain Irish country girl whose
Christian name was certainly Elizabeth, and whose last name
(according to Grosart) was Boyle. The marriage was celebrated
June 11, 1595.

ELIZABETHAN SONGS AND LYRICS

(THE ELIZABETHAN SONNET)

56. The Elizabethan Age was notably a great lyric as well as a great dramatic period. The number of songs and sonnets produced was extraordinarily large, and the quality of these productions was on the whole exceedingly high. Numerous poetical *Miscellanies*, or collections of short poems by various authors, were put out by enterprising printers during the latter half of the sixteenth and the opening years of the seventeenth century. The earliest of these, commonly known as *Tottel's Miscellany*, appeared in 1557, the year before Elizabeth's accession, and *England's Helicon*, one of the most famous of the later collections, was published in 1600, or about three years before the close of her reign. Besides the *Miscellanies* there were a number of *Song-books*, or books containing the music as well as the words of the songs. The first of these, Byrd's *Psalms, Songs, and Sonnets of Sadness and Piety*, was published in 1588. No less than fifty-five such *Song-books* are definitely known to have been published between that date and 1624. To the lyrics of the *Miscellanies* and the *Song-books* we must add the innumerable charming songs which are embedded in the plays and romances of the time. Shakespeare's plays are, as we know, full of such songs, as are the plays of Ben Jonson, Beaumont and Fletcher, and many others. Beside this extraordinary chorus of song, we must place the equally notable productiveness of the time in the writing of sonnets. The earliest English sonnets, those of Wyatt and Surrey, appeared in *Tottel's Miscellany* in 1557, but it was not until about thirty years later that the sonnet became a widely popular poetic form. From about 1591, the year of the appearance of Sidney's *Astrophel and Stella*, and of the earliest form of Daniel's *Delia*, *Sonnet-sequences*, or books composed of a series of sonnets, began to be much in favor. Mr. Saintsbury remarks that "Between 1593 and 1596 there were published more than a dozen collections, chiefly or wholly of sonnets, and almost all bearing the name of a single person, in whose honor they were supposed to be composed."

(*Hist. Eliz. Lit.*, p. 97.) Among these sonnet-sequences are those of Sidney, Drayton, Spenser, and Shakespeare. To gain any notion of the wealth of this time in lyrical verse, in songs or sonnets, the student should consult the various collections of Mr. A. H. Bullen, Prof. Schelling's *Elizabethan Lyrics*, and some of the many collections of English sonnets. Only a few familiar examples can be here given.

LYLY.

JOHN LYLY (1553-4-1606) was prominent as a romance, writer and dramatist, and exercised a very considerable influence upon contemporary literature and the taste of the court. He gained immediate popularity by his two romances, *Euphues, the Anatomy of Wit* (1579) and its sequel, *Euphues and his England* (1580). These romances originated in England that peculiar style of expression known as *euphuism ;* a style which Scott has unsuccessfully attempted to reproduce in the character of Sir Piercie Shafton. In the drama, Lyly is among the immediate predecessors of Shakespeare, but from about 1590 his popularity declined. His works are now comparatively little read, but the grace and fancy of the lines on Cupid and Campaspe have made them almost universally known.

GREENE.

ROBERT GREENE (1560-1592), like Lyly, one of the immediate dramatic predecessors of Shakespeare, was a man of profligate and unhappy life. The fact that he lived friendless, as he tells us, "except it were in a fewe ale houses," and died miserably, gives a peculiar pathos to this expression of his longing for content.

CONTENT.

7. **Homely** = homelike.
57.—9. **The mean that grees** = the middle state, or modest circumstances. This best *agrees*, etc.

MARLOWE.

CHRISTOPHER MARLOWE (1564-1593) was the greatest of Shakespeare's forerunners in the drama. He wrote poems, and made translations from the classics, but the selection here given is his one notable lyric. This, as Prof. Schelling points out, is remarkable when we consider his marvellous passion and the suprising lyrical excellence of certain passages in his plays. The poem called forth a number of answers; one of the best known of which is given on p. 67.

THE PASSIONATE SHEPHERD TO HIS LOVE.

3 Groves : here a dissyllable.

58.—22. **Morning** should here be accented on the second syllable.

DEKKER.

THOMAS DEKKER (1570?–1640?) was a busy playwright and pamphleteer. He began to write towards the close of the reign of Elizabeth, and continued his literary activity during that of her successor. In some cases he collaborated with Middleton, Heywood, and other well-known dramatists, and his services were apparently in great request. (See Dryden's *Mac Flecknoe*, l. 87 and n.) Dekker so excelled in portraying the life of the London about him that he has been called the Dickens of the Elizabethan time. Constantly involved in money difficulties, he seems, like Greene, to have known little of that Sweet Content of which he sang. Dekker's authorship of this song seems to be generally conceded, although it is taken from a play (*The Pleasant Comedie of Patient Grissel*, 1599) which he wrote in conjunction with two other dramatists. It is among the most charming and famous of Elizabethan lyrics.

HEYWOOD.

59. THOMAS HEYWOOD (1581?–1640?), dramatist and miscellaneous writer, was probably the most voluminous author of a prolific age. He wrote a poem in seventeen cantos, numerous prose works, and boasted some years before the close of his labors that he was author or part author of two hundred and twenty plays.

CAMPION.

TO LESBIA.

60. THOMAS CAMPION (d. 1619), a physician, poet, and musician of the reigns of Elizabeth and James I., appears to have won considerable contemporary fame. After a long interval of neglect, his reputation as a lyric poet and the interest in his work have recently revived. He wrote masques, Latin poems, a prose work—*Observations in the Art of English Poesy*, etc., but is chiefly remembered by sundry exquisite songs scattered through his various books of airs. In the verses *To Lesbia* he follows and in part translates the ode of Catullus *Vivamus, mea Lesbia, atque amemus.* (*Car.* V). His works have been collected and edited by A. H. Bullen, Chiswick Press, London, 1889.

THE ARMOUR OF INNOCENCE.

This poem, which appears in *The First Book of Airs* (1601), was reprinted in the *Second* (*cir.* 1613) with some textual variations. It is one of the many modulations of the noble theme of Horace's *Integer Vitæ* (*Odes*, Bk. I. *Car.* XXIII.), but is free from the weak close which detracts from that splendid poem. The reader can readily bring together many parallel poems and passages. Bullen reminds us that the poem has been ascribed to Bacon, but entertains no doubt that Campion was its author.

FORTUNATI NIMIUM.

61. Fortunati nimium = happy beyond measure. *O fortunatos nimium sua si bona norint Agricolas !* (Vergil, *Georg.* II. 458.)

62.—8. **Silver penny.** Before the time of James I., or about 1609, English pennies were of silver. In that reign copper pennies were first struck.—9. **Nappy ale,** strong or fine ale. *Nappy* is often made to stand for *ale,* as in Burns' *Twa Dogs* "'twal penny worth o' nappy!" and n. to *Tam O'Shanter,* 5. 19. **Tutties** = nosegays, posies. (Prov. Eng.) See *Cent. Dict.*

BEAUMONT AND FLETCHER.

63. BEAUMONT AND FLETCHER. These two men, who have been called "the double star of our poetical firmament," wrote in collaboration during the closing years of the sixteenth and early part of the seventeenth century some of the most justly admired plays of the period. They probably afford the most remarkable example of joint authorship in the history of the literature. They stand admittedly in the front rank of the Elizabethan song-writers. Swinburne declares that in their compositions of this order they "equal all their compeers whom they do not excel." *John Fletcher* was born 1579 and died in 1625; *Francis Beaumont* was probably born in 1585 and died in 1616, the year of the death of Shakespeare. The best of their work is supposed to have been produced between 1608 and 1611.

SONG OF THE PRIEST OF PAN.

32. Fall in numbers = fall with a musical or rhythmical cadence. The verb " fall," says Mason, refers not to "silence," but to " slumbers," since "silence" falling in numbers would be "absolute nonsense." *And soft silence* = *with soft silence.*

SONG TO PAN.

64.—2. **Virtues and ye powers.** Here of course the naiads or water-nymphs. Milton has the same conjunction, when he speaks of "Princedoms, *Virtues,* Powers" (*Par. Lost,* Bk. V. 602), thus making the *virtues* part of the angelic hierarchy.

ON THE LIFE OF MAN.

65. Although this poem is included in the *Poems* of Francis Beaumont, it is also attributed to Bishop Henry King, and appears in his poems under the title *Sic Vita.* The lines have also been claimed for others, but their authorship has never been satisfactorily determined. For further information see Hannah's Ed. of King's *Poems.*—7. **Borrowed light.** Man will be required to repay at nightfall the light of life loaned him but for a day.—8. **To-night,** instead of *at night,* is more forcible as suggesting the quick coming of death.

ON THE TOMBS IN WESTMINSTER ABBEY.

13. **The bones of birth,** the ashes or remains of those of high or royal lineage.

WOTTON.

THE CHARACTER OF A HAPPY LIFE.

66. SIR HENRY WOTTON (1568–1639), the descendant of a Kentish family distinguished for its lack of self-seeking and its substantial public services, was a man of high character and cultivation. He was at one time secretary to the Earl of Essex, and he was engaged in diplomatic missions under James I. After twenty years of service he retired from public life (having obtained the Provostship of Eton College), "knowing experimentally," says Isaac Walton, "that the great blessing of sweet content was not to be found in multitudes of men or business." He wrote but little verse, and that but as an amateur, but the uprightness, placidity, and elevation of his character, and to some degree the traditional habit of his family, are well expressed in the familiar poem here given.

SIR WALTER RALEIGH. (?)

THE NYMPH'S REPLY TO THE PASSIONATE SHEPHERD.

67. (See n. to *The Passionate Shepherd, supra.*) The authorship of this poem is doubtful. On its first appearance in a complete form in *England's Helicon* (1600) it was signed with the initials W. R., and in *The Complete Angler* (1653) Isaac Walton quotes the poem and refers to it as "made by Sir Walter Raleigh in his younger daies."

JONSON.

68. BEN JONSON (1573–1637) was one of the greatest of the Elizabethan dramatists and, after the death of Shakespeare, the leading man of letters in England. His dramatic methods and ideals were different from those of Shakespeare, and as far back as the time of Thomas Fuller, Jonson's laborious learning and Shakespeare's native nimbleness of intellect have been contrasted. All the surrounding circumstances invest Jonson's tribute to Shakespeare with a peculiar interest; and when we remember that the two poets represented different schools of dramatic art, the praise of Shakespeare's genius must be regarded as both unstinted and discriminating. Under it all lay a basis of genuine personal affection. "I loved the man," Jonson wrote of Shakespeare, "and do honor his memory on this side of idolatry as much as any." (*Timber, or Discoveries, etc.*)

TO THE MEMORY OF SHAKESPEARE.

1. **To draw no envy**, etc. "While Ignorance, Affection, or Malice, by excessive, indiscriminate, or unjust praise, would be sure to provoke the detraction of envy,

> . . . . These ways
> Were not the paths I meant unto thy praise ';

for he could with full knowledge and strict impartiality award him the highest praise that could be expressed." (Pub. *New Shaks. Soc.*, Ser. IV. 2. p. 151.)—2. **Ample** = liberal, lavish in the praise of.—8. **Seeliest ignorance** = blindest ignorance. The verb *to seel*, which means to close up the eyes of, and hence *to blind*, was originally a term in falconry for the operation of closing the eyes of a hawk, or other bird, by thread until it should become tractable. (Through O. F. from Lat. *cilium* = an eyelid, or eyelash. Cf. *Macbeth*, III. 2. 46.)—

19. **I will not lodge thee,** etc. Chaucer, Spenser, and Beaumont are buried near to each other in the Poets' Corner in Westminster Abbey. Proximity to the tomb of Chaucer, the first great English poet, was considered as a great honor. Spenser had been granted this in 1599, and Beaumont in 1615; a year later came the death of Shakespeare. Shakespeare's claim to a place near the tombs of the three poets just mentioned was put forth by a certain William Basse (or Bas) in his *Epitaph on Shakespeare:*

> "Renownèd Spenser, lie a thought more nigh
> To learnèd Chaucer; and rare Beaumont, lie
> A little nearer Spenser, to make room
> For Shakespeare in your threefold fourfold tomb."

Jonson's words are obviously in the nature of an answer to this passage. (See Pub. *New Shaks. Soc.*, Ser. IV. 2. pp. 136 and 147, and Stanley's *Historical Memorials of Westminster Abbey*, 269, 270.)

69.—27. **Judgment were of years,** i.e. one that would last, or go down to posterity.—29. **Thou didst our Lyly outshine,** etc. We should be on our guard against assuming that we can gain from this poem any exact notion of Jonson's opinion of his contemporaries, as he wisely avoids all mention of poets then living. Fletcher, Chapman, Middleton, Dekker, Drayton, Donne, who might otherwise have been mentioned, are excluded on this score if on no other. His obvious purpose is merely to allude incidentally to a few of Shakespeare's competitors by way of illustration. To get at his real feelings towards his fellows, consult Drummond's *Notes of Ben Jonson's Conversations*, Shakespeare Soc. Publications, 1842.— 30. **Sporting Kyd.** A satirical play upon the dramatist's name, since Thomas Kyd was anything but "sporting," being chiefly known as the author of tragedies of the most blood-curdling and bombastic character. The oft-quoted reference to Marlowe, on the other hand, is remarkably felicitous.—31. **And though thou hadst small Latin,** etc. "The passage may be thus paraphrased: Even if thou hadst little scholarship, I would not seek to honor thee as others have done Ovid, Plautus, Terence, etc., i e. by the names of the classical poets, but would rather invite them to witness how far thou dost outshine them." (Pub. *New Shaks. Soc.*, Ser. IV. 2. 151.)— 33. Æschylus, etc. The three Greek poets *Æschylus, Sophocles,* and *Euripides* (to name them in their proper chronological order) represent three stages in the development of the Greek tragic drama; so *Pacuvius, Accius* (or *Attius*), and "him of Cordova" (or *Seneca*) stand in a similar manner for Roman tragedy-writing at successive epochs. The three Greek tragedians are among the greatest dramatists of the world; the three Roman, and especially the first two, are comparatively little known, and seem introduced rather to give a proper balance to the passage than because any one would really compare them with Shakespeare.—36, 37. **Buskin . . . socks**. The ancients are summoned to hear Shakespeare both as a tragic and a comic writer; the *buskin*, or shoe worn by Greek and Roman actors in tragedy, stands here for tragedy, as the *sock*, or shoe of comedians, stands for comedy. (See *L'Allegro*, l. 132 and n.).—55. **Thy Art**. This tribute to the art of Shakespeare, and to his care in composition, derives an added interest from the fact that such a view was unusual in Jonson's time and for long after. Milton inclined to the opposite opinion (see *L'Allegro*, l. 133 and n.). Pope expressed the same popular impression in the lines :

> "But Otway failed to polish or refine,
>   And fluent Shakespeare scarce effac'd a line." (*Ep.* I. 278.)

Jonson himself, according to Drummond, declared that Shakespeare "wanted [or lacked] arte." Shakespeare certainly wrote rapidly, and the impression seems to have been that he wrote carelessly. Jonson's own words on this point should be compared with those of Pope and placed in contrast with the passage in the text : "I remember the Players have often mentioned it as an honour to Shakespeare, that in his writing (whatsoever he penn'd) hee never blotted out a line. My answer hath beene, would he had blotted a thousand, which they thought a malevolent speech." (*Timber; or Discoveries upon Men and Matter*, etc.)

JONSON'S SONGS.

70. Jonson's character and genius are commonly described as "robust," "rugged," and "masculine," yet his songs are frequently remarkable for their grace, lightness, and delicacy. In this respect he is rightly regarded as the predecessor of Herrick and some of his lyric brethren.

SIMPLEX MUNDITIIS.

"**Simplex munditiis**" = plain, or unadorned, in thy neatness. The phrase is from Horace's famous and often-translated ode to Pyrrha (*Odes*, Lib. I. car. v.):

> "Cui flavam religas comam
>   Simplex munditiis ?"

SHAKESPEARE'S SONGS.

73. Shakespeare was born in 1564; came up to London to seek his fortune about 1587; began to write for the stage about 1588–90; ended his career about 1612–13, and died in 1616. The greater part of his energy was given to the stage,— as actor, as part-owner of a theatre, and as playwright; but apart from his dramas he wrote two narrative poems and a series of sonnets. The songs scattered through his plays, while introduced for a dramatic purpose, and often intimately and artistically interwoven with the action, would alone give him an assured place among the poets of his time. Had he written nothing but these songs he would have survived as one of the leading lyric poets of a great song-writing age. No words of comment are needed on the songs here given. As Prof. Dowden says : " Of the exquisite songs scattered through Shakespeare's plays it is almost an impertinence to speak. If they do not make their own way, like the notes in the wildwood, no words will open the dull ear to take them in."

HARK, HARK, THE LARK.

75.—5. Mary-bud = marigold.

ELIZABETHAN SONNETS

(See "Elizabethan Songs and Lyrics," p. 590 *supra*.)

SIDNEY.

77. SIR PHILIP SIDNEY (1554–1586), the pattern of noble knighthood, whose name is forever linked with an act of self-sacrifice and compassion, was not only the courtier, the soldier, the gallant gentleman, loved by his nation as few men have been loved, and mourned as few men have been mourned; he was also a true poet and an accomplished man of letters. Although he died at thirty-two, he was a leading spirit in England's literary advance when the nation was feeling its way towards the period of its greatest triumphs. Sidney's *Astrophel and Stella* (1591), the first great sonnet-sequence in the literature (see p. 590 *supra*), marks an epoch in the growth of the sonnet in England. The series, which consists of 110 sonnets, records the poet's hopeless passion (whether real or assumed for poetic purposes is a matter of dispute) for Penelope Devereux, who was sister to the Earl of Essex and who became Lady Rich.

SONNET XXXI.

This is probably the best known of Sidney's sonnets. Wordsworth admired it sufficiently to use the two opening lines for the beginning of a sonnet written in 1806.

DANIEL.

78. SAMUEL DANIEL (1562–1619), who gained the title of "the well-languaged Daniel," while lacking in some of the qualities which make a popular poet, yet shows an elevation of feeling, depth of thought, and a scholarly taste. His sonnets to *Delia*, which appeared in his first known book of poems, contain some of his most familiar if not his finest work.

DRAYTON.

79. (For Drayton, see p. 601, n. on *Agincourt*.)

DRUMMOND.

79. WILLIAM DRUMMOND (1558–1613), often spoken of as " Drummond of Hawthornden," was a Scottish poet of noble birth, who passed a meditative and studious life at his secluded and beautiful home near Edinburgh. His life was saddened by the death of the lady to whom he was engaged to be married, and his poetry is tinged by a gentle melancholy. He is numbered with the followers of Spenser, but he shows—as in his sonnets—such a sympathy with the Italian models that he has been styled " the Scottish Petrarch."

SHAKESPEARE'S SONNETS.

80. The sonnets of Shakespeare were first published in 1609. The exact date of their composition is not known, but they were probably composed at intervals (as was Tennyson's *In Memoriam*) during a number of years. The earliest mention of them is found in the *Palladis Tamia* of Francis Meres (1678), who speaks of Shakespeare's "sugred sonnets among his private friends." Two of the series (sonnets 138 and 144) appeared in *The Passionate Pilgrim* (1599), a poetical miscellany. Dowden believes them all to have been written "somewhere between 1595 and 1605." The entire series consists of 154 sonnets. Critics are still divided concerning the interpretation of the series as a whole, but fortunately all theories of interpretation are powerless to mar our enjoyment of the sonnets as single poems. (See Dowden's *Shakespeare Primer* and his edition of Shakespeare's *Sonnets*.)

DONNE.

83. (For Donne, see " Seventeenth century Lyrists," p. 603.)

DRAYTON.

83. MICHAEL DRAYTON (1563–1631) was one of the most voluminous poets of a time distinguished by the extraordinary productiveness of its writers. His huge descriptive and historical poems, the *Baron's Wars*, the *Polyolbion*, and the rest, are now but little read, but one of his sonnets (see p. 79), ranks with the finest in the language, while his ballad on *Agincourt* and his *Nymphidia* are not only famous, but are still comparatively familiar. Mr. Saintsbury says of the former: "The Agincourt ballad is quite at the head of its own class of verse in England—Campbell's two masterpieces (given here on pp. 376, 379) and the present poet laureate's direct imitation in the 'Six Hundred,' falling, the first somewhat, and the last considerably, short of it. The sweep of the metre, the martial glow of the sentiment, and the skill with which the names are wrought into the verse, are altogether beyond praise." (*Hist. Eliz. Lit.* 141.) The impetuous metrical rush of the poem, one of its chief merits, has also been imitated by Longfellow in *The Skeleton in Armour*.

AGINCOURT.

84.—Camber-Britans. Cambria was the Roman name for Wales; hence by *Camber-* (or *Cambro-*) *Britans* is meant the Britons who were in Wales, as distinguished from those of the same race in Cornwall or elsewhere. The Cambro-Britans appear to have been especially noted for their skill in chanting poems to the harp, while the poetic genius of the British in Cornwall was shown more particularly in the dramatic form. The concluding part of the dedication has consequently an especial appropriateness.

25. **And turning to his men,** etc. Henry is said to have exclaimed before the battle that he "did not wish a single man more." (See Green's *Hist. Eng. People*, I. 542.) Shakespeare makes effective use of this incident. *Hen. V.* IV. 3: "God's will ! I pray thee wish not one man more," etc.

85.—49. **The Duke of York,** i.e. Edward, second Duke of York, and grandson of King Edward III. The account in the text is here substantially accurate. York commanded the right wing, and was a little in advance of the line, Henry the centre, and Lord Camoys the left. (See Shakespeare's *Henry V.* IV. 3, when York asks and receives the right of "leading" the "vaward."—52. **Henchmen** = followers. (See Skeat's *Etymol. Dict.*)—65. **Noble Erpingham,** i.e. Sir Thomas Erpingham, "who threw up his truncheon as a signal to the English forces, who lay in ambush, to advance."

86.—82. **Bilbows** = swords. From *Bilboa*, a Spanish town famous for its blades. The word also means *fetters*, an especial kind of fetter being also manufactured at Bilboa. The word is used in both senses by Shakespeare.—89. **When now that noble king,** etc. Here again the poet keeps pretty

close to historic fact.   Henry was actually forced to his knees,
by a stroke from the Duke d'Alençon, "so violent that it
dented his helmet." (See Church's *Henry V.*, p. 81.)—
97. **Gloster**, i.e. Humphrey, Duke of Gloucester, younger
brother of the king.   Thomas, Duke of Clarence, alluded to
here as *Clarence*, was also the king's brother.

87.—113. **Crispin day** is on the 25th of October.   Cf.
Shakespeare's *Henry V.* IV. 3.   "This day is called the feast
of Crispian," etc.

THE SEVENTEENTH-CENTURY-LYRISTS

88. The selections in this group have been chosen primarily for their intrinsic interest, and secondarily because they illustrate the nature and course of English verse in its lighter and shorter forms, between the closing years of the Elizabethan period and the new era of the Restoration. The age of Shakespeare and Spenser is very far removed in spirit from that of Dryden and Pope. These intermediate poets for the most part show us the way by which English poetry passed from the earlier to the later time. *John Donne*, the first poet of the group, is, from one aspect, really an Elizabethan, since he was born in the same year as Ben Jonson and died six years before him; while *Edmund Waller* (1605–1687), the last poet on the list, lived twenty-seven years after the Restoration, and was farther removed from the Elizabethans than the earlier poets of the group, being related rather to Dryden and poets of the later day. (For account of this period see Masson's *Life and Times of Milton*, Vol. I. Ch. VI., and *The Age of Milton*, by J. H. B. Masterman.) Many of these poets affected a fantastic style, full of far-fetched images or "conceits." Their peculiarities are thus described by Dr. Samuel Johnson : "The most heterogeneous ideas are yoked by violence together ; nature and art are ransacked for illustrations, comparisons and allusions ; their learning instructs and their subtilty surprises, but the reader commonly thinks his improvement dearly bought, and, though he sometimes admires, is seldom pleased." ("Cowley," in *Lives of the Poets.*) The founder of this school (or at least the poet most influential in promoting this fashion) was *Dr. John Donne* (1573–1631), who, born of Roman Catholic parentage, became a clergyman of the Church of England, and at last Dean of St. Paul's Cathedral. With Donne may be associated his friend *George Herbert* (1573–1633), also a clergyman, who wrote some of the best religious poetry in the language, and two other writers of sacred poems, *Richard Crashaw* (1613–1650 ?) and *Henry*

Vaughan (1622-1695 ?), who may be classed as Herbert's followers. *Abraham Cowley* (1618-1667), a disciple of Donne, was a famous poet of his day, and *George Wither* (1588-1667), a satirist, Puritan, and follower of Cromwell, were other religious poets of the time. *James Shirley* (1596-1667), whose splendid *Dirge* (p. 103) may be appropriately compared with Beaumont's *Westminster Abbey* (p. 65), an imitative rather than an original poet, represented the traditions of the Elizabethan drama and carried them on into the Restoration time. In another group stand the *Cavalier Lyrists*, light, gay, and amorous, *Richard Lovelace* (1618-1658), *Thomas Carew* (1598-1639 ?), *Sir John Suckling* (1609-1641), and the London wit and Devonshire clergyman, *Robert Herrick* (1591-1674).

DONNE.

ELEGY ON LADY MARKHAM.

Lady Markham died May 4, 1609. She was the daughter of Sir James Harrington, and wife of Sir Anthony Markham. Francis Beaumont also wrote an elegy to her. This poem, which illustrates the subtle, over-elaborated quality of Donne's work, shows also the extraordinary, if occasional, poetic beauty which sometimes accompanies it. Note, for example, the fineness of description displayed in the allusion to the retiring tide leaving "*embroidered works upon the sand*," and the beautiful definition of tears as "*the common stairs of men*," by which they climb to heaven.

89.—28. Élixir.—The sense appears to be that the grave as a *limbec* (or *alembic*) shall transform her, or distill her substance, into something more precious, as buried clay is changed to porcelain. So that, when God annuls the world by fire to recompense it, her soul shall animate flesh of that spiritual quality which He shall then make and name the *Elixir*, or transforming agency of all things. (See n. on *The Elixir*, p. 606.)

A VALEDICTION FORBIDDING MOURNING.

90. These verses are quoted with especial commendation by Isaac Walton in his life of Donne. Donne wrote them to his wife when he was obliged to leave her to accompany an embassy to the French Court. His wife was reluctant to let him go, as "her divining soul boded her some ill in his absence." Walton, after relating the story, adds of the verses: "And I beg leave to tell that I have heard some writers, learned both in languages and poetry, say that none of the

Greek or Latin poets did ever equal them." (See *Walton's Lives*, "Donne.") Grosart remarks : "The metaphor of the compasses in the *Valediction* only so daring an imaginator as Donne would have attempted ; and the out-of-the-wayness of it is not more noticeable than the imaginativeness which glorified it." He quotes Coleridge as declaring that "nothing was ever more admirably made out than the figure of the compass." ("Donne's Poems" in *Fuller's Worthies Lib.*, Vol. II. p. xl.)

SONG, SWEETEST LOVE.

91. This song, while by no means the best, is among the most generally known of Donne's short poems. The reader, unless he is of the inner circle of Donne's admirers, will probably be more impressed by its singularity than its beauty. Saintsbury thinks that it was inspired by the same occasion as the *Valediction* and written at the same time. He quotes the two opening lines of the last stanza, and thinks that they should be taken in conjunction with the forebodings felt by Donne's wife at his departure for France. (See *A Valediction*, etc., *supra*.)

92.—34. **Forethink me any ill** = anticipate any ill for me, as Destiny may fulfil your presentiment.

A HYMN TO GOD THE FATHER.

93. This poem is also quoted by Walton, who after saying that Donne "in his penitential years" regretted some of the lighter verses of his youth, adds that he did not therefore forsake heavenly poetry in his age, but that "even on his former sick-bed he wrote this heavenly hymn, expressing the great joy that then possessed his soul in the assurance of God's favor to him when he composed it." He tells us further that Donne caused the *Hymn* "to be set to a most grand and solemn tune, and to be often sung to the organ by the choristers of St. Paul's Church, in his own hearing, especially at Evening Service."

HERBERT.

THE TEMPLE.

The Temple, from which the selections here given are taken, is the collection of poems on which Herbert's fame chiefly rests. Walton tells us how Herbert in his last illness sent the MS. to his friend Mr. Nicholas Ferrar, of the so-called Protestant Nunnery at Little Gidding, saying that it contained "a picture of the many spiritual subjects that have passed betwixt God and my soul," and requesting him to publish it or not as he saw fit. It appeared in 1633 shortly after Herbert's death, and at once took and retained a high place. The poem entitled *The Collar*, with its admirable force, truth, and passion, seems to point to one of those "spiritual conflicts" from which even the saintly Herbert tells us he was not exempt.

VERTUE.

94.—5. **Angrie and brave.** Angry = red, the color of the face of one flushed with passion. **Brave** = splendid, gaudy, etc.

THE ELIXIR

95. An *Elixir* was, in alchemy, a substance supposed to possess the power of transmuting the baser metals into gold. Chaucer speaks of it as identical with the *Philosopher's Stone*, and the *Great Elixir* (or *Philosopher's Stone*) was also called the *red tincture* (see n. on l. 15).—1–8. **Teach me,** etc. The sense is: Teach me to see Thee in all things, and by making Thee first in every action thus give *it his* (i.e. *its*) perfection. In Herbert's time *his* was still commonly used where we should use *its*. (See Craik's *English of Shakespeare*, Rolfe's Ed. § 54).—15. **With his tincture.** Tincture being here, as has been said, the same as the *Elixir*, the sense is, that there is no action however mean which, imbued or purified by his (i.e. *its*) tincture *for Thy sake*, will not grow bright. To do a thing *as for Thee* is to transmute the action from base metal to fine gold, and the talisman *for Thy sake* is the magic *tincture* or *Elixir* which can effect the change. (This passage is differently explained by Grosart, see his ed. of Herbert, I. 313.)—24. **Told** = counted. Cannot be counted less.

VAUGHAN.

97. In his love of nature, and his sense of the holiness of childhood with its mysterious nearness to the divine, Vaughan is the precursor of Wordsworth The substantial identity between the fundamental thought in *The Retreate* and that of Wordsworth's *Ode on the Intimations of Immortality* (p. 318) has been often pointed out, and some have even claimed that the great *ode* was consciously based upon the earlier poem. For this, however, there seems to be no better authority than conjecture. The resemblances are undoubtedly striking.

COWLEY.

A VOTE.

101. The poem from which these verses are taken first appeared in the second edition of Cowley's volume of juvenile verse entitled *Poetical Blossoms* (1636). The entire poem consisted of eleven stanzas, of which the last three are given here. These stanzas were quoted by Cowley with some trifling changes in his essay *Of Myself*. He there alludes to the poem as "an ode which I made when I was but thirteen years old." "The beginning of it," he adds, "is boyish : but of this part which I here set down (if a very little were corrected) I should hardly now be much ashamed." (See Cowley's *Essays*.)

THE GRASSHOPPER.

102. This is the tenth of a series of twelve short poems entitled *Anacreontiques ; or, Some Copies of Verses Translated Porophrastically out of Anacreon*, which appeared at the end of the *Miscellanies* in the collection of Cowley's *Poems* of 1656. "Cowley," says Leslie Stephen, "can only be said to survive in the few pieces where he condescends to be unaffected." The selection here given is a good example of his simpler verse. (See "Cowley" in Gosse's *Seventeenth-century Studies*.)—8. **Ganimed** = Ganymede, the cup-bearer of Zeus.

LOVELACE.

TO ALTHEA FROM PRISON.

105. This poem was composed in 1642 during the poet's confinement in the Gatehouse at Westminster. Lovelace, who was of Kentish family, had been chosen to present to Parliament a petition from the Kentish royalists on behalf of Charles I. The Parliament threw him into prison because of this advocacy of the royal cause.

HERRICK.

107. ROBERT HERRICK (1591–1674), after being neglected for more than a century, has been given a high place among the lyrists of his time. Indeed within his own sphere, as laureate of pastoral England, and master of the lighter lyric, he has nothing to fear from comparison with the poets

of any period of the literature.   The son of a London goldsmith, he came as a young man within the group that as-
sembled round Jonson and was "sealed of the tribe of Ben."
His presentation, in 1629, to the living of Dean Prior, near
Ashburton, Devonshire, set him in the midst of that rural
life in England that lives in so much of his best verse.   De-
prived of his living in 1647 because of his royalist sympathies, he returned to London, but was restored to his living
in 1662, and died in 1674.   *King Oberon's Feast*, the first of his
poems to get into print, appeared in 1635, and his *Hesperides,
or the works both Humane and Divine of Robert Herrick, Esq.,*
a collection containing many of his best-known poems, was
published in 1648.

ARGUMENT TO HESPERIDES.

3. **Hock-carts**, the last carts to return from the fields at
harvest-home.   Perhaps from *Hockey*, Prov. Eng. for Harvest-home.   For description of the ceremonies customary at
harvest festivals, see Herrick's poem *The Hock-cart, Hesperides*, No. 250.—3. **Wassails**.   It was a rural custom to drink
the health of or to *Wassail*, the fruit-trees on Christmas eve.
Herrick alludes to this in his poem *Ceremonies for Christmas,
Hesperides*, No. 786.   For account of similar ceremonies practised in Devonshire, Herrick's county, on the eve of Epiphany,
see also Chambers's *Book of Days*, I. 56.)—3. **Wakes**, originally
festivals held in celebration of the dedication of a church,
usually upon the day of the saint after whom the church was
named ; later these festivals became county fairs but still
retained the name of *wakes* (see Strutt's *Sports and Pastimes*,
§ XXVIII).   A good notion of the appropriate ceremonies of
May-day, the other country festival here alluded to, will be
found in the next selection, *Corinna Going a-Maying.*—8. **Times
rans-shifting**.   Herrick wrote in a period of political change
and excitement, but as his work is habitually removed from
such matters, he probably refers here merely to the succession
of the seasons.—12. **The Court of Mab**.   The fairy Mab, popularly associated with dreams and nightmare.   Although she is
here said to have a court, the earliest known instance of her
being called a Queen is in Shakespeare's *Romeo and Juliet*, I. 4.
See Furness's n. on this passage in *Variorium Ed.*, vol. I. p. 61,
and Milton's *L'Allegro*, l. 101. and n.

WALLER.

ON A GIRDLE.

113.—6. **The pale**, etc. *Pale* is used for that which encompasses, as well as in the more ordinary sense of *a fence* or *boundary*, as of a park. The well-worn pun on *d·er*, poor enough at best, is one of the few blemishes on the poem. The conceit shows that poor taste from which even the greatest Elizabethan poets are not exempt. Shakespeare himself makes this same wretched pun more than once.

ON THE FOREGOING DIVINE POEMS.

114. On the Foregoing Divine Poems, i.e. *On Divine Love* (1685) and *The Fear of God* (1686).—1. **When we for age.** If this was written in 1686, the date of the last poem above mentioned, Waller must have been eighty-one years old at this time.—11. **Clouds of Affection**, i.e. clouds of passion, or the passing impulses and desires of youth. Affection was originally used in a bad as well as in a good sense. Here the sense is that the thronging desires and longings of youth hide that emptiness of life which age descries.

MILTON.

115. JOHN MILTON was born in 1608, or eight years before the death of Shakespeare and about twenty-three years before the birth of Dryden,—the next great master in the poetic succession. He lived until 1674, or fourteen years after the Restoration. He thus grew up and began to write during the latter years of the Elizabethan period; he was closely identified with almost the whole course of the Puritan struggle for civil and religious liberty, and he lived on, a sublime and solitary figure, into the midst of that new literary and social epoch which dates from the accession of Charles II. He was therefore contemporaneous with *Suckling, Lovelace, Herbert,* and the lyrists grouped together in the last section, although differing widely from them in his genius and work. Milton's literary career falls naturally into three well-marked divisions. 1st. MINOR POETIC PERIOD, *cir.* 1624–1638–40, which includes *L'Allegro, Il Penseroso, Comus, Lycidas,* and many of the short poems; 2d. PERIOD OF PROSE AND OF PAMPHLET WARFARE, *cir.* 1640–1660, which includes his controversial writing, tracts, and a few sonnets, poetical translations, etc.; 3d. MAJOR POETIC PERIOD, *cir.* 1660–1674, the great period of *Paradise Lost, Samson Agonistes,* and *Paradise Regained.*

L'ALLEGRO AND IL PENSEROSO.

These companion poems, written while Milton was living in his father's house at Horton,—a village near Windsor,—or between about 1632–38,—are either studies of two contrasted characters, that of the mirthful and the meditative man, or, possibly, revelations of two contrasted moods felt by the same man at different times and under different circumstances. The two poems should consequently be read together and constantly compared. Dr. Garnett remarks that the poems are "complementary" rather than contrary, and in a sense may be regarded as one poem whose theme is the praise of the reasonable life. "Mirth has an undertone of gravity, and melancholy of cheerfulness. There is no antagonism between the states of mind depicted ; and no rational lover, whether of contemplation or recreation, would find any difficulty in combining the two." (Life of *Milton,* G. W. S., p. 49.) The natural background in each poem, is skilfully harmonized with the general impression Milton wished to produce ; that is, the aspects of Nature described in either case may be regarded either as informing us of the character and especial preferences of the speaker,—if two distinct persons are portrayed,—or as indicating the scenes which are most conducive to, or in keeping with, the cheerful and the thoughtful mood. Dr. Johnson says : "The author's design is not, what Theobald has remarked, merely to show how objects derive their color from the mind by representing the operation of the same things upon the gay and the melancholy temper, or upon the same man as he is differently disposed ; but rather how, among the successive variety of appearances, every disposition of mind takes hold on those by which it may be gratified." ("Milton," *Lives of the Poets* (M. Arnold's ed.), p. 44.) Whatever view we take, the two poems should be read carefully for the light they throw on Milton himself at this period. A man's character can be inferred from his tastes, and as Milton's genius was not of that dramatic and objective quality which effaces the writer's personality in the portrayal of alien characters, we are justified in assuming that Milton himself really cared for those things—the stage, the cathedral, etc.—in which he makes the two speakers delight.

The sources of these poems have been discussed by the critics. It has been urged that the theme may have been suggested by certain portions of Burton's *Anatomy of Melancholy*

(1621) and by a song in Beaumont and Fletcher's play of *Nice Valor* (played 1613 ?). The opening lines of this song are as follows:

> " Hence, all you vain delights,
>   As short as are the nights
> Wherein you spend your folly !
>   There's naught in this life sweet,
> If man were wise to see't,
>   But only melancholy,
>   O sweetest melancholy."

The resemblance here to *Il Penseroso* seems certainly to be more than merely fortuitous. Prof. Masson thinks, however, that "the help from any such quarters must have been very small." It certainly seems more important to note that in their lyrical movement, and in their love of splendor, romance, and stately ceremonial (e.g. *L'Allegro*, l. 117-135), we recognize Milton's close affinity to the Elizabethans, during his early years.

L'ALLEGRO.

5. **Uncouth**, probably used in its original meaning, *unknown*.
12. **Euphrosyne** (Gr. ευφροσύνη = cheerfulness, mirth, verb ευφραίνω = to cheer, to delight.) Euphrosyne or joy, mirth, was one of the three Graces. Two views are here advanced in regard to the parentage of Euphrosyne ; the first, that she is the daughter of Venus and Bacchus (or that Mirth springs from Love and Wine) ; the second (which Milton declares to be the "sager," or wiser, view), that she is born of Zephyr and Aurora ; or that true mirth, such as the poet wishes to celebrate, comes not from heated pleasures, but from the pure delight in the freshness of a spring morning and surrounded by the loveliness of nature.

116.—40. Unreprovèd. Note that even in the midst of his praise of mirth Milton never forgets those principles which guided his life. He grew more austere and restrained with years, but he was the Puritan from the first.—**41. To hear the Lark**. The mirthful man's day begins early (cf. account of genealogy of Euphrosyne and note *supra*); indeed morning and daytime are given the first place in this poem, as evening and night are in the companion study.—**45. To come** probably depends upon "to hear" (l. 41) ; i.e. to hear the lark begin his flight, and then descending come to the speaker's window in the spite of, or to spite, sorrow. Critics have pointed out that such a visit would be contrary to the habit of the skylark. Masson defends Milton by contending that it is not the skylark, but the speaker, *L'Allegro*, who comes back to his own window (*v.* Masson's ed.). "To come" is thus made to depend upon "Mirth admit me," l. 38. On this, Pattison says: "I cannot construe the lines as Mr. Masson does, even though the consequences were to convict Milton, a city-bred youth, of not knowing a skylark from a sparrow when he saw it."

117.—80. **Cynosure.** The Greek name for the constellation of the Lesser Bear, which contains the Pole-star. Sailors keep their eyes on this in steering, hence an object on which the eyes are fastened as a guide came to be called a *cynosure.* Milton was not the first to use the word in this secondary sense. (See Murray's *Dict.*)—94. **Rebecks,** a primitive form of violin ; the earliest known form of instrument of the viol class.

118.—101. **Stories.** The superstitious rustics tell their various adventures with supernatural beings. *Mab* eats the junkets (*v. post*); and pinches the idle servants ; Friar Rush, or Will-o'-the-wisp, leads the wayfarer into bogs ; the drudging goblin or "lubber" fiend performs household tasks for a "cream-bowl duly set" for him to drink. Mab is the fairy called " Queen Mab " by Shakespeare and elaborately described by him in *Romeo and Juliet,* I. 4.—102. **Junkets,** originally a kind of cream cheese served on rushes (Ital. *guinco,* a rush), is commonly thought to be here used in the more general sense of delicacies or sweetmeats. The word was thus used in Milton's time (see Herrick's *The Wake*), but there seems to be no objection to adopting the ordinary meaning of curds or clouted cream. Shakespeare describes Mab as mischievous, and Ben Jonson speaks of her (*The Satyr,* 1603) as "the mistress fairy that doth nightly rob the dairy." It is not unlikely that it is such surreptitious visits to the dairy that the word *junkets* is here intended to indicate.—105. **Drudging Goblin,** i.e. Robin Goodfellow, who appears in an idealised form as Puck in the *Midsummer Night's Dream.*—110. **Lubberfiend.** A lazy, clumsy, unwieldy creature. See *Cent. Dict.* for *lubber, lob,* etc. Warton quotes Beaumont and Fletcher, 'there's a pretty tale of a witch—that had a giant to her son that was called *Lob-lie-by-the-fire*" (*Knight of the Burning Pestle,* III, IV), and thinks Milton confounded this giant with Goodfellow. See n. to Furness's *Mid. Night's Dream*—on p. 50. Also Mrs. Ewing's story (*Lob-Lie-by the-Fire*).—120. **Weeds of peace.** Garments ; the garb of peace. This word survives in the phrase *widow's weeds.*—122. **Influence,** probably used in the old astrological sense as in the phrase " born under the influence " of a certain planet. The passage suggests a likeness between the ladies' eyes and the stars which were supposed to influence events.—132. **Learned Sock.** The sock, or *soccus,* being the light boot worn by comedy actors in the Classic Drama, is used to indicate here that it is Ben Jonson's comedies rather than his tragedies that the cheerful man delights in. The manner in which Shakespeare is referred to, as well as the whole context, shows that it is the Shakespeare of *As You Like It* and the comedies, and not of *Hamlet*, that Milton has in mind. In spite of the frequent objection that the reference to Shakespeare fails to do justice to that poet's consummate art, the passage sufficiently indicates an important distinction between him and Jonson ; the latter, a good classical scholar, being praised for his learning ; the former, with his "small Latin," for his untaught and native power. Such, as Hales remarks, was the recognized seventeenth-century opinion.

119.—136. **Lydian airs.** The Lydians, a people of Asia Minor, were noted for their effeminacy. Their music was soft and voluptuous, while the Dorian music was majestic and inspiring (see *Par. Lost*, Bk. I. 549) and adapted to the bass, as the Lydian to the tenor voice. Cf. the noble anthems and the pealing organ music which especially appeals to the meditative man; also Alexander's Feast, l. 79, Spenser's *Faerie Queene*, Bk. III. Cnt I. l. 40.

IL PENSEROSO.

Penseroso. Milton has here made a slip in his Italian; he should have written *pensieroso*. *Il Pensieroso*, the meditative or thoughtful man, or one who enjoys the delights of lofty contemplation —3. **Bested** = bestead. The meaning here is *profit, avail,* or *advantage,* but this is a peculiar use. (See Dictionaries of Richardson and Skeat, *Bible Word Book*, etc.)—6. **Fond,** i.e. foolish. Look up and cf. Shakespeare's use of this word.—12. **Melancholy.** The idea that Milton's conception of melancholy was suggested by Albert Durer's figure of *Melancholia* seems to be both erroneous and misleading. Milton's *Melancholy* is not the inaction of utter despair, but simply those high and holy musings, those solemn joys, that to the weak only, seem "overlaid with black."

120.—18. **Prince Memnon's Sister.** In Homeric mythology Prince Memnon was famous for his dusky beauty. Tradition represents him as an Ethiopian prince, killed in the Trojan war. As there seems little warrant for the belief that he *had* a sister, it may be assumed that Milton evolved her for his convenience, intending to suggest to us a feminine impersonation of Memnon's characteristics. — 19. **Ethiop Queen.** See *Cassiepea* or *Cassiopea* in *Class. Dict.* — 23. **Bright-haired Vesta.** Contrast the parentage ascribed to Mirth and to Melancholy. In both cases the poet invents a significant genealogy. For the latter he chooses *Saturn* (called "solitary" from his having devoured his own children), and *Vesta* or *Hestia*, among the Romans the goddess of the domestic hearth. Vesta, being dedicated to virginity, is probably here taken as a type of purity, while Saturn clearly represents solitude. Hence Milton apparently means that the elevating contemplation he wishes to describe springs from the solitary meditation of a pure mind. The epithet "bright-haired" may possibly have been suggested by the flames kept burning on the altars of Vesta.—33. **Grain** = Crimson or, as here, Tyrian purple. This color was obtained from a small insect which, when dried, had the appearance of a seed or grain. (See *Par. Lost*, Bk. V. 285, and *Mid. N. D.* I. 2. 95.)—35. **Stole.** The *stole* was a long robe worn by Roman ladies. *Stole* also means the scarf worn by a priest Spenser uses *stole* for hood or veil, in which sense it is here used. **Cipress lawn,** i.e. *cyprus lawn.* *Cyprus* was a thin material, generally black, similar to crape. (See *Winter's Tale,* IV. 4.)

121.—54. **Contemplation.** See *Ezekiel,* ch. x., and *Par. Lost,* Bk. VI. 750-759. Milton here gives the name *Contemplation* to one of the cherubs in Ezekiel's vision. With writers of Milton's time *Contemplation* was a word of high meaning, denoting the faculty by which the clearest notion of divine things could be attained.—55. **Hist.** Skeat takes this to be past part. meaning *hushed, silenced;* i.e. bring along with thee mute Silence hushed. (See *Etymol. Dict.*) As we cannot conceive of *Silence* as other than "mute," it surely seems unnecessary to tell us in addition that she was "hushed." Masson and Hales, on the other hand, take *hist* as an imperative, and would understand it as "*Bring silently* along." The latter interpretation, if it can be sustained etymologically, would seem to be the better.— 59. **Dragon yoke,** "i.e. while the Moon, entranced with the song, is seen to check the pace of her dragon-drawn chariot over a particular oak tree, that she may listen the longer." (Masson. See his entire note.)—83. **Bellman.** The watchman in olden times used a bell. "Half-past nine and a fine cloudy evening," may be remembered yet as a cry of the watchman in some towns before the time of gas; but the older watchmen mingled pious benedictions with their meteorological information." (Masson.)—87. **The Bear.** The constellation of Ursa Major, which never sets.—88. **Thrice-great Hermes,** i.e. *Hermes Trismegistus* (Τρισμέγιστος = superlatively, or thrice, great), the Egyptian *Thoth* or *Thot,* identified by the Greeeks with *Hermes,* or *Mercury.* Many mystical books were ascribed to him, and it is these books that the student is supposed to sit absorbed in reading until the stars disappear in the dawn. **Unsphere,** etc. That is, bring back **Plato's** spirit from the sphere which may hold it, by the study of his works; or, to commune with Plato through his books. References to the spheres are common in Milton, who apparently preferred the Ptolemaic system at least for poetic purposes.

122.—93. **Demons.** Demon, not a devil, but an indwelling spirit (Gr. δαίμων), meant originally an inferior god, or often a guardian spirit. The idea that the four elements (out of which the Greek philosopher Empodocles held the universe to be composed) were inhabited by indwelling spirits, or demons, belongs to post-classic times.—95. **Consent** = connection. The belief in astrology was very general in Milton's time.—98. **Sceptred pall,** i.e. royal robe, or perhaps, with sceptre and with pall, or robe (Lat. *palla* = a robe, or mantle). —99. **Thebes or Pelops' line.** *L'Allegro's* taste is for the modern forms and creations of dramatic art—masks, pageants, the comedies of Jonson and Shakespeare. *Il Penseroso's* tastes are chiefly classical, as the subjects here referred to (connected with the house of *Œdipus* of Thebes, of *Pelops* of Phrygia, or of the Trojan heroes) are the themes of some of the greatest of the Athenian tragedies. Besides these the excellence of the later, or modern, stage seems to him rare.— 104. **Raise Musæus,** etc. Masson thus paraphrases this passage: "Oh that we could recover the sacred hymns of the primitive, semi-mythical Musæus of the Greeks, or the similar poems by his contemporary Orpheus."—110. **Cambuscan** (said to be a corruption of *Cambus* or *Genghis Khan*). The poet referred to as leaving the story half-told is Chaucer, who related part of it in his unfinished *Squire's Tale* in the *Canterbury Tales.* Spenser completed it (*Faerie Queene,* IV. C's. II. and III.).—116. **Great bards.** Generally taken to refer to the great romantic poets Spenser, Ariosto, Tasso, of whom Milton was fond in his youth.—124. **Attic boy,** i.e. *Cephalus.* See *Class. Dict.*

123.—134. **Sylvan,** i.e. *Sylvanus,* the wood-god. Hales quotes *Par. Lost,* IV. 705, and Virgil, *Georg.* II. 393 —159. **Storied windows,** i.e. stained-glass windows with scenes or figures illustrative of sacred story.

SONG SWEET ECHO.

124.—2. **Thy airy shell,** "the hollow vault of the atmosphere." (Masson.)—3. **Slow Meander's.** The Mæander was a river in Asia Minor celebrated for its winding, tortuous course (hence our verb *to meander*). It is to this characteristic of the stream that the epithet *slow* refers.— 7. **Gentle pair.** The song is sung by a maiden who has lost her way in a forest, having been accidentally separated from her two brothers. They are the "gentle pair" for whom she inquires. —8. **Thy Narcissus.** Echo was in love with and slighted by the beautiful youth Narcissus. (See Ovid, *Met.* 3. 341 *et seq.*)

SONG, SABRINA FAIR.

125.—1. **Sabrina**, or **Sabre**, was a princess celebrated in the legendary history of Britain. She was the daughter of the King Locrine and the beautiful German Princess Estrildis, and was thrown with her mother into the river Severn by order of Queen Gwendolen, her mother's rival. In the passage preceding the song, Milton tells us how, in the waters of the Severn, Sabrina was kindly received by *Nereus*, the father of the water-nymphs, and how, undergoing " a quick immortal change," she became "goddess of the river." Milton tells the story in his *History of Britain.* Spenser makes use of the legend in *The Faerie Queene*, Bk. II. c. x., and Drayton in the Fifth Song of his *Polyolbion.*—10. **Oceanus** was the first-born of the Titans, and consequently an earlier deity than *Neptune.* His wife was *Tethys*, and their children the rivers and the *Oceanides*, or nymphs of the ocean.—14. **Carpathian wizard**, "the subtle *Proteus*, ever changing his shape: he dwelt in a cave in the island of Carpathus; and he had a 'hook,' because he was the shepherd of the sea-calves." (Masson.) For the rest, *Triton* and *Thetis*, mother of *Achilles*, were sea-deities, and *Glaucus*, *Leucothea* ("the white goddess"), and *Melicertes*, i.e. "her son that rules the strands," were originally mortals who, like Sabrina herself, had been drowned and converted into water-powers.

LYCIDAS.

126. *Lycidas* was written late in 1637. It is a lament for the death of Edward King, a young man of much promise, who had been a fellow student of Milton's at Cambridge some five years before. King was drowned while on his way to Ireland,—the ship striking a hidden rock off the Welsh coast and going down in a calm sea. A small memorial volume of poems in Greek, Latin, and English was prepared by King's friends, and *Lycidas* was Milton's contribution to the volume. The book was printed at Cambridge in 1638.

Lycidas is a *pastoral elegy*, made to conform in general to the classic models. It is not a passionate outburst of personal grief, like parts of *In Memoriam*, but rather as severely classic in its subdued tone and emotional restraint as it is in its refined beauty, its indescribable but inimitable justness of phrase, and its perfect proportion of form. It is likely that Milton and King had seen little or nothing of each other for some years, and Milton's grief probably did not go beyond a sincere regret. There is no reason to assume that he mourned as another Cambridge man, Alfred Tennyson, did almost exactly two centuries later for his fellow student's untimely death. But while Milton does not exaggerate his grief for the sake of poetic effect, his tribute to King and to the memories of their college-days is doubtless sincere as well as beautiful.

The deepest feeling of the poem, however, is not expended on the death of King, but is poured out in the two famous passages, the *first* touching on the state of contemporary poetry (ll. 64-84), the *second* on the corrupt condition of the Church (ll. 107-132), which break in as episodes upon the regular progress of the poem. Two facts gave Milton some pretext for thus leaving the purely personal, and therefore more restricted, side of his subject, to plunge into those broad issues which were then absorbing the best powers of earnest men. First, King had written verse, he "knew himself to sing," and second, he was destined for the Church. By these two slender threads the poem is connected with the mighty matters then pressing for solution, and to understand it we must imagine ourselves back in the England of 1637, when Charles was trying to force the English liturgy on the indignant Scots, and when Hampden was arousing the nation by his resistance to the payment of ship-money. In those days men's minds were growing more stern and uncompromising, the lines between the hostile forces of Puritan and Cavalier were becoming more sharply drawn, and already the country was moving towards revolution. The poem shows also a somewhat similar transition in Milton himself. In it he passes definitely from the poet of *L'Allegro*, with its touches of the romantic coloring of Spenser, to the sterner, severer, and sublimer poet of *Paradise Lost*.

Lycidas. "The name Lycidas, chosen by Milton for Edward King, is taken, as was customary in such elegies, from the classic pastorals. It occurs in Theocritus; and Virgil has the name for one of the speakers in his Ninth Eclogue." (Masson.) —1. **Yet once more.** Milton had probably written no poetry since *Comus*, produced three years earlier (1634). This period of his life was one of solemn and studious preparation for his work as a poet. He here indicates that although he did not feel himself prepared for his high task, yet the "bitter constraint" of this sad event has compelled him to turn again to poetry, unprepared as he was; or (in his figure) to pluck with "forced fingers" the laurel, myrtle, and ivy, the emblems of the poet's calling, "before the mellowing year."—6. **Occasion dear,** i.e. the extremity of the situation. "Dear" has here the force of a superlative, as in *Hamlet* I. 2, "My *dearest* foe," etc. —10. **Who would not sing,** etc. An imitation of Vergil; *Eclogues* X. 3 : *Negat quis carmina gallo?*—15. **Sisters of the sacred well** = the Muses. One of the two places particularly associated with the Muses was the slope of Mount Helicon in western Bœotia. Here were the fountains Aganippe and Hippocrene, sacred to the Muses. Hales quotes the opening of Hesiod's *Theogony*, where the Muses of Helicon are described as dancing about Aganippe and "the altar of the mighty Son of Kronos," i.e. "the Seat of Jove."—20. **Lucky words.** Rather to be taken in the sense of words favorable to the repose of the departed than as involving any idea of chance. Such, according to the Roman rite, were the words *sit tibi terra levis,* uttered by the mourner as he sprinkled the earth three times over the dead. (See Hor. *Odes* I. xxviii.)— 23. **For we were nursed,** etc. Under the imagery appropriate to a pastoral elegy, Milton now shadows forth the early companionship of King and himself at Cambridge. Thus the "Satyrs" and "Fauns" (34) are supposed to represent the undergraduates, and "Old Damætus" (36) one of the tutors of Christ's College.

127.—40. **Gadding** = to run about aimlessly here and there, to wander. The word here has both a freshness and exactness which show the master's hand.—50. **Where were ye nymphs.** After stating the occasion of his poem (1-15), invoking the Muse (15-23), recalling early companionship (23-50), Milton now passes to the fourth natural division of his poem ; the vain inquiry addressed to the indwelling spirits, rulers, or forces of Nature, asking why the loss of Lycidas was permitted, and endeavoring to find out to whom or to what it is attributable. This may be regarded as extending from 50 to 131, including the two episodes, or digressions (64-85 and 113- 131) already alluded to. The question to the nymphs is a reminiscence of Vergil, *Eclog* X. 9-12, and of Theocritus, *Idyls* I. 65-9 ; a background of Welsh scenery being substituted for classical localities. Thus "the steep" is one of the mountainous heights of the Welsh coast ; "Deva" is the Dee, out of the mouth of which King sailed on his way from Chester ; and "Mona" is Anglesey, a great centre of Druidic religion in early times. (See Tacitus, *Anal.* XIV. 30.)—58. **The Muse herself** = Calliope. According to some accounts, Orpheus was torn in pieces by the Thracian women at a Bacchanalian festival, his limbs strewn upon the plain, and his head cast into the river Hebrus.

128.—68, 69. **Amaryllis—Neæra.** No especial persons appear to have been intended. These names, borrowed from the classic pastorals, simply stand for young and beautiful maidens.—75. **The Blind Fury.** Milton departs here from the classic mythology, according to which the being whose office it was to cut the thread of life was *Atropos*, one of the *Fates*, and not one of the *Furies*. Milton not infrequently used the great poet's privilege of making, or altering, a myth to suit his purpose, and he doubtless had some definite purpose in this variation of the established version. His design is apparently to represent death as coming inopportunely, or blunderingly, marring what we would regard as the right order of events. Hence the vague image of a being "blind" and uncontrolled may have been selected as better suited to his purpose than one of the *Fates*, suggestive as she would be of conforming to an appointed and inevitable order.—85, 86. **Arethuse . . . Mincius.** The first is in Ortygia off the coast of Sicily, an island associated with Theocritus, the second in northern Italy near the birthplace of Vergil. The first, as Masson remarks, consequently suggests the Greek, the second the Latin, pastoral. In the preceding digression Milton has gone far beyond the proper limits of the pastoral elegy; his strain has been in a "higher mood." This address to the fountains, suggestive of the Greek and Latin masters of the pastoral, and the succeeding passage, inform us that he has resumed the oaten pipe of the true shepherd Muse.—89. **Herald of the sea** = Triton, who comes in behalf of Neptune.—96. **Hippotades** = the son of Hippotas, i.e. Æolus.—99. **Panope,** or Panopea, was one of the Nereïds (see Verg. *Æn.* V. 240, etc.). By describing her as "sleek" and at play with her sisters, Milton indicates the smoothness of the sea.

101. **Built in the Eclipse.** Eclipses were considered by the ancients as out of the order of nature, and were supposed to exert a mysterious and disastrous influence. T. Warton quotes *Mac.* IV. 28, and Hales, *Lear* I. 2. 112, and *Par. Lost*, I. 596–9.

129.—103. **Camus.** The god, or genius, of the Cam, the stream on which Cambridge is situated. "He comes attired in a mantle of the hairy river-weed that floats on the Cam; his bonnet is of the sedge of that river, which exhibits peculiar markings, something like the αἲ αἲ (alas! alas!) which the Greek detected on the leaves of the hyacinth, in token of the sad death of the Spartan youth from whose blood the flower had sprung." (Masson.) 109. **The Pilot of the Galilean Lake** = St. Peter; here represented, however, not as the fisherman of Galilee, but as the Bishop with mitre and keys of heaven (see St. Matt. xvi. 17–19 and St. Matt. xviii. 18.)

"Clearly this marked insistence on the power of the true episcopate is to make us feel more weightily what is to be charged against the false claimants of episcopate; or generally, against false claimants of power and rank in the body of the clergy." (Ruskin, *Sesame and Lilies*, §§ 20 et seq., q. v. for analysis of the entire passage,—111. **Amain** = forcibly, with power. It indicates, I suppose, the final, effective manner in which the door is closed. (*Amain* = A. S. *on, an,* or *a,* with, and *maegene* = strength)—122. **They are sped** = they are advanced in worldly prosperity. The original meaning of the noun *speed* is *success, riches,* and this word and the verb are connected with A. S. *spowan* = to succeed. The phrase "you are sped" is employed by Shakespeare in an entirely different sense. The ideal of success entertained by the corrupt clergy is thus precisely the reverse of that laid down in the preceding digression on *Fame,* and the two passages are in effective contrast.—124. **Scrannel** = lean, thin, or harsh sounding. A provincial word probably connected with "scrawny," but unusual in classic English. With "grates," "wretched," and "straw," "scrannel" obviously adds wonderfully to the grinding, jarring effect that the poet wished to produce.— 128. **The grim wolf,** i.e. the Romish Church.—130. **Two-handed engine.** This has been much discussed. The "engine" has been thought to be the executioner's axe, and the passage taken as a prophecy of the execution of Archbishop Laud; others have thought it the sword of St. Peter; others, the two Houses of Parliament (an untenable interpretation); and others again have seen in it an allusion to the axe metaphorically spoken of in St. Matt. iii. 10, St. Luke iii. 9, which was to be "laid to the root of the tree." The last interpretation is probably the least objectionable; nevertheless the passage remains obscure, the essential meaning being, of course, that the end is at hand, and the avenger with his instrument of destruction, a terrible and sudden weapon of retribution, stands even at the door.—132. **Return, Alpheus.** This invocation, like the preceding one to Arethuse (l. 85), sounds the note of recall to the stricter limits of the true pastoral. *Alpheus* likewise suggests the Sicilian muse. (See *Class. Dict.* for story of Alpheus and Arethusa, and Shelley's *Arethusa*.)

130.—138. **The swart star** = Sirius, or the Dog-star. Coming at a hot time of the year, this star was anciently associated with, and even supposed by the Romans to cause, sultry weather. Here called "swart," i.e. dark, or swarthy, because of the burning or tanning effect of the summer suns. —142. **Rathe** = early; the positive, now out of use, of *rather,* earlier, sooner.—148 **Sad embroidery,** i.e. the garb of mourning. Note how skilfully Milton has contrived to associate the most of these flowers with thoughts or hues of grief: the "forsaken" primrose; the "pale" jessamine and black-streaked pansy; the "wan" cowslips, with their "pensive" heads; and the daffodillies, their cups filled with tears.—153. **False surmise.** "Milton has been speaking of the hearse" (i.e. tomb, or coffin) "of Lycidas, and the flowers fit to be strewn upon it in mourning, when he suddenly reminds himself that all is but a fond fancy, inasmuch as Lycidas had perished at sea and his body had never been recovered." (Masson.)—158. **Monstrous world,** i.e., the world of monsters at the bottom of the sea.—160. **Bellerus.** Land's End, Cornwall, was called *Bellerium* by the Romans. Bellerus here does not appear to be a real personage; the name was apparently coined by Milton from that of the promontory, with the idea of raising the implication that the region was named after some one so called. The sense here is, or dost thou sleep by the fabled land of old Bellerus?—161. **The guarded mount** is St. Michael's Mount, a precipitous and rocky islet near the coast of Cornwall. It was supposed to be guarded by the Archangel Michael, who was reported to have been seen there seated on a high ledge of rock. Hence the form of the Archangel is "the great vision," to be imagined as seated on the ledge called St. Michael's chair, and gazing far across the sea towards *Namancos* and *Bayona's* hold" (the former being a town, the second a stronghold on the Spanish coast), i.e. looking in the direction of Spain. St. Michael is then implored to turn his distant gaze homeward, and pity the youth who has perished almost at his feet.—165. **Weep no more.** In entering upon this new natural division of the poem we pass into a strain of hope and cheerfulness. Some such transition to a consolatory and reassuring tone is found toward the end of most of the famous elegies, and may be regarded as analogous to the *allegro* movement of a sonata. The ground of hope here, unlike that in Shelley's *Adonais* or Arnold's *Thyrsis*, is distinctly Christian. (See also Spenser, *Eclog.* VII.)

131.—189. **Doric lay.** So-called because Lycidas follows the elegiac manner of Theocritus and Moschus, who wrote in Doric Greek.

MILTON'S SONNETS.

Milton's important relation to the history of the sonnet in England is thus summarized by Mark Pattison: "Milton's distinction in the history of the English sonnet is that, not overawed by the great name of Shakespeare, he emancipated this form of poem from the two vices which depraved the Elizabethan sonnet—from the vice of misplaced wit in substance, and of misplaced rime in form. . . . The tradition of the son-

net, coming from what had not ceased to be regarded as the
home of learning, appealed to his classical feeling. His exquisite ear for ryhthm dictated to him a recurrence to the Italian
type in the arrangement of the rimes." (Pattison's Ed. of *The
Sonnets of John Milton*, Int. 45, 46.)

ON HAVING ARRIVED AT THE AGE OF TWENTY-THREE.

Milton's twenty-third birthday was Dec. 9, 1631 ; it is consequently assumed that this sonnet was written on or about
that date. The poem was sent in a letter to a Cambridge
friend, who had dwelt upon the ineffectiveness of a life given
up to study, and had urged upon Milton the duty of his devoting himself to the Church, or to some active pursuit. In the
letter Milton takes the characteristic position that he did not
take "thought of being late (or backward in actually doing, or
producing something) so it gives the advantage to be more fit."
He adds : " Yet that you may see I am something suspicious
of myself, and do take notice of a certain *belatedness* in me, I
am the bolder to send you some of my nightward thoughts
somewhile since, because they come in not altogether unfitly,
made up in a Petrarchian stanza which I told you of." Then
follows the sonnet. (The letter is given in Masson's *Life and
Times of Milton*, Vol. I. 24-6.)

5. **My semblance**, i.e. my appearance, deceives, making me
seem younger than I really am. In his youth Milton was
slender in figure, and of a fair, delicate beauty. We know
that at forty he was taken for ten years younger, and at
twenty-three his almost feminine refinement of face and figure
must have been similarly misleading.

ON THE LATE MASSACRE IN PIEDMONT.

132. The subject of this sonnet is the atrocities committed
against a Protestant community known as the Waldenses or
Vaudois, who inhabited certain valleys in the Alps. In 1655
an edict of the Duke of Savoy commanded them either to
leave their homes, or become Roman Catholics within twenty
days. The command was disregarded and the horrible butch-
eries and outrages which followed aroused the indignation of
Europe. Cromwell caused Milton, then Latin Secretary of
the Commonwealth, to write letters of remonstrance to the
Duke of Savoy and other rulers. Milton's personal indignation found utterance in a sonnet, which remains one of the
most mighty and majestic in the language. (See Masson's
Life and Times of Milton, Vol. V. 38.)

ON HIS BLINDNESS.

Milton's sight began to be seriously impaired in 1651 and he had become blind by 1652 or 1653. This sonnet is but one among several famous poetic outbursts of Milton in regard to his affliction. (Cf. e.g. *Paradise Lost*, Bk. III. 1, etc., Bk. VII. 23, etc., and *Samson Agonistes*, 67, etc.) According to Masson it may have been written "any time between 1652 and 1655." Mark Pattison thinks that as it follows the sonnet on the Piedmontese massacre it may have been written in that year (1655).

2. **Ere half my days.** Milton was about forty-four when he became totally blind, or at the fulness of his powers.—3. **One talent.** See *St. Matt.* xxv.—8. **Fondly** = foolishly.

SONNET TO CYRIACK SKINNER.

133. CYRIACK SKINNER was a lawyer, a friend, and probably a frequent visitor of Milton's. He is also said to have been Milton's pupil at an earlier period. The date of the sonnet is approximately fixed by the opening announcement that it was written just three years from the day Milton's sight was finally extinguished, or about 1655.

1. **This three years day,** i.e. this day three years ago. Pattison quotes Shakespeare II. *Hen. VI.* II. 1 in justification of the idiom.—**Though clear,** etc. Pattison apparently regards this as a piece of vanity on Milton's part. There is, however, an added pathos about eyes that look as though they could see and yet see not. Milton wrote elsewhere of his eyes: "They are externally uninjured; they shine with a clear unclouded light, just like the eyes of those whose vision is most acute." (*Defensio Secunda* 4. 267, 1654.)—11. **My noble task,** i.e. his *Pro Populo Anglicano Defensio*, an answer to a work by Salmasius of Leyden (one of the greatest scholars of the time) in defence of Charles I. Milton gave the last of his failing eyesight to this reply to Salmasius. It was published in 1651, attracted great attention in England and on the Continent, and was regarded as a damaging blow to Milton's great antagonist.

MARVELL.

134. ANDREW MARVELL (1621–1678), poet, satirist, republican, and friend of Milton, was a man of wide learning, of high integrity, and pure life, in a time of political corruption and loose morals. As a satirist he was honored by the admiration of Dryden, who in some respects followed, while he greatly surpassed him as a satiric writer. Leading an active life in the midst of a vexed and ignoble time, he has written of the charms of quiet and country life with a genuine love and intimate knowledge of nature. The poems of this group— of which *The Garden* is one—were composed between about 1650-52, while he was at Nunappleton in Yorkshire, the seat of Lord Fairfax, to whose daughter he was tutor. Marvell wrote it first in Latin and then himself turned it into English.

THE GARDEN.

1. **Amaze** = bewilder, perplex.—2. **The palm, the oak, or bays.** These three symbols of distinction are not exactly identical. The *palm* apparently stands for victory in general, distinction without specifying in what province ; the *oak wreath* was the reward of *civic* merit among the Romans, and signifies the glory of the soldier or patriot; while the *bays* (the berry of the laurel, and hence the laurel, or laurel wreath) had come to be more particularly associated with fame as a poet, to win the bays being sometimes equivalent to gaining the laureateship.

135.—36. **Curious peach.** *Curious* here = delicious, an unusual and obsolete use. Cf. Mather, *Mag. Christi*, III. 1. i.: " He made a careful though not *curious* dish serve him." Swinburne *Poems and Ballads* : " I served her wine and *curious* meat." See Murray's *Eng. Dict.* for these and additional examples.—51. **The body's vest,** etc., i.e. casting aside as a garment this body which is the *vesture* of the soul. So Shakespeare calls the body " this muddy *vesture* of decay." (*Mercht. of Ven.* V. 1.)

DRYDEN TO THOMSON

DRYDEN.

137. JOHN DRYDEN (1631–1700) was incomparably the most vigorous poet and the most influential and accomplished man of letters in England from the death of Milton in 1674 to the end of the century. Sprung from a Puritan and anti-monarchical family, he first attracted attention as a poet by his *Heroic Stanzas* to the memory of Cromwell (1658). But neither his descent, nor his eulogy on the great Puritan, prevented him from employing his poetic gift to welcome Charles II. on his return. After the Restoration he showed himself politic rather than nobly independent, he forced himself to write plays in keeping with the corrupt taste of the time, and in 1681 threw his almost unrivalled powers of satire on the side of the king. Besides several satiric masterpieces, Dryden wrote long religious controversial poems and made numerous poetical translations from the classics. In many respects we can see that he was the precursor and the model of Pope; indeed he may be said to have done much by precept and example to make a new epoch in literature. "Perhaps no nation," says Dr. Johnson, "ever produced a writer that enriched his nation with such a variety of models."

MAC FLECKNOE.

Mac Flecknoe, by general consent one of the ablest satires in the entire range of English poetry, was directed against THOMAS SHADWELL (1640–1692), a minor poet and dramatist of the Restoration era. A coolness sprang up between Dryden and Shadwell, who were at one time on friendly terms, which grew into a bitter enmity. The breach, which appears to have begun in literary jealousy, was intensified by political antagonism, Shadwell being a poet of the Whig, and Dryden of the Tory party. Dryden's poem *The Medal* drew from Shadwell a venomous counter-attack, *The Medal of John Bayes* (i.e. Dryden). This Dryden answered in *Mac Flecknoe*. Shadwell was in reality a follower of Ben Jonson; and Dryden himself, when the relations between the two poets had been friendly, had spoken of him as "second but to Ben," but in this satire he is represented as the son, or the poetic successor, of a certain *Richard Flecknoe*, a contemporary poet and playwright, an Irishman, a Roman Catholic priest, and a Jesuit. This obscure and unfortunate writer, now remembered chiefly as the butt of Dryden's unsparing ridicule, seems to have had hard measure. His works, like many others that have been mercifully forgotten, while not immortal creations, are said to be by no means devoid of merit, yet their author, besides being pilloried by the greatest satirist of his time, was likewise made the object of an offensively personal attack by no less a poet than Andrew Marvell, in which Flecknoe's poverty, his dress, his mean lodgings, and emaciated appearance, were ridiculed with more bad taste than humor. Flecknoe, although not a genius, seems to have done nothing to deserve such merciless abuse, but it was a time of hard hitting and Dryden had no light hand. The enmity of the great satirist seems to have been inspired by nothing more than a petty resentment against Flecknoe for his well-merited attack upon the contemporary stage, of which Dryden was one of the pillars, for its immorality and worthlessness. The poem opens with the abdication of Flecknoe (who in fact had died shortly before) as absolute monarch of the kingdom of Nonsense in favor of Shadwell

Mac Flecknoe. RICHARD FLECKNOE, an Irish poet, wit, and playwright, who settled in London about the Restoration and became a minor figure in its literary life. He died about 1678. In the sub-title we find the real object of the satire, *T. S.* (Thomas Shadwell). THOMAS SHADWELL (1640–1692) was prominent among the Whig writers of the time, Dryden being identified with the champions of the opposing, or Tory, party. Contemptuous reference is accordingly made to Shadwell as the "true-blue Protestant poet," i.e. the *uncompromising*, or *thoroughgoing*, poetic advocate of the faction arrayed against Church and King. The phrase "true-blue" being usually associated with the Covenanters, or Presbyterians (see *Hudibras*, I 191, and Brewer's *Phrase and Fable*, "Blue"), the Puritan, or dissenting, element is probably here meant, as distinguished from the Anglican, or Church, party. Shadwell wrote some inferior verse, and seventeen comedies, which depict the social life of the time (and particularly its oddities, or "humors"), with more truth than decency. So far as the plays are concerned it is generally admitted that the charge of dulness is undeserved.

138.—25. Goodly fabrick. Shadwell was a man of huge, unwieldy bulk, and, apparently, of gross appearance. Dryden satirizes his corpulence in a famous description of him, under the name of Og, in the Second Part of *Absalom and Achitophel*, in which he is pictured as "rolling home" from a tavern "round as a globe and liquored every chink."—29. **Heywood and Shirley.** THOMAS HEYWOOD (1581 ?-1640 ?) and JAMES SHIRLEY (1596-1666) were voluminous dramatic writers. Shirley was the last representative of the Elizabethan drama (see p. 604, *supra*).—33. **Norwich drugget.** "This stuff appears to have been sacred to the poorer votaries of Parnassus ; and it is somewhat odd that it seems to have been the dress of our poet himself in the earlier stages of his fortune." (Scott.)—36. **King John of Portugal.** An allusion to some work of Flecknoe's of which, so far as I am aware, nothing is now known.—42. **Epsom blankets.** An obscure expression. One of Shadwell's plays was called *Epsom Wells*; to blanket, or toss in a blanket, was used in the general sense of to punish; possibly the meaning is, "such a ridiculous spectacle was never seen, not even in your *Epsom* when you toss, or punish, everything in your blankets," but the explanation is far from satisfactory.—50. **Morning toast.** In Dryden's day and for some time later, the Thames continued to be used as a great water-highway by the Londoners. It afforded an ordinary and convenient avenue of travel, and was also a resort of pleasure-seekers. The river was still clear ; and doubtless many who frequented it amused themselves by throwing bread or toast into the water, that they might watch the fish struggle for the fragments.

139.—53. **St. André.** A fashionable dancing-master of the time. 54. **Psyche.** The name of a very inferior opera by Shadwell, written in five weeks and produced in 1675 —57. **Singleton.** An opera-singer and musician then somewhat prominent. He took the part of *Vallerius* (see l. 59), one of the chief characters in Sir Wiliam Davenant's opera of *The Siege of Rhodes.*—64. **Augusta** was the title given by the Romans to London (*Londinium Augusta*) and to other cities in honor of the Emperor Augustus. The city is not infrequently thus referred to by the poets of the seventeenth and eighteenth centuries. (See Gay's *Trivia*, III. 145 ; Falconer's *Shipwreck*, 1. 3.)—65. **Fears inclined.** The Popish Plot, the apprehensions of civil war, the arrest of Shaftesbury, etc., had kept London in a panic of dread and feverish excitement.—67. **Barbican.** A round tower of Roman construction which stood near the junction of Barbican Street (to which it had given its name) and Aldgate Street. It was on the northern line of the old city wall. **Hight** = was called (*A. S. hátan*).—72. **A. Nursery.** A school of acting established in 1665 by Charles II. on petition of Thomas Killigrew and Sir William Davenant, and

designed to furnish actors for the theatres under the management of the petitioners. The right to "act plays and enter-
tainments of the stage" was given in the patent, and at the
Nursery youthful aspirants made their first crude attempts.
Pepys visited it and found "the music better than we looked
for, and the acting not worse, because I expected as bad as
could be; and I was not much mistaken, for it was so." *Diary*,
Feb. 24, 1678. See also *ib.*, Aug. 2, 1664, and Molloy's
Famous Plays, p. 13, etc.—78. **Maximius.** Maximin, the
defiant hero of Dryden's *Tyrannic Love.*—81. **Simkin** "was a
cobbler in an interlude of the day. Shoemaking was especially
styled 'the gentle craft.'" (Hales.)—83. **Clinches** = puns. (See
Johnson's *Dict.;* Popes *Dunciad*, I. 63.)—84. **Panton,** a noted
punster.—87. **Dekker** (Thomas), *cir.* 1570-1637, an Elizabethan
dramatist satirized by Ben Jonson in *The Poetaster.*

140.—91. **Worlds of Misers.** "Shadwell translated, or
rather imitated, Molière's *L'Avare*, under the title of *The
Miser.*" (Scott.) *The Humourists* is also the name of one of
Shadwell's plays; *Ramond* (l. 93) is a character in it, while
Bruce appears in another play, *The Virtuoso.* Both are
described as gentlemen of wit.—97. **Near Bunhill and distant
Watling Street.** Bunhill was in what were then the outskirts of
the City in a northerly direction. The Watling Street here
referred to is apparently the short street of that name that, in
Dryden's time as now, led into the open space back of St.
Paul's. The *Nursery*, the scene of MacFleknoe's abdication,
was, in general terms, between the two points (see n. to ll. 67
and 72, *supra*), but nearer to Bunhill. A good map of London
will make the exact relation of the places clear; the sense is
that they came from north and south.—102. **Ogleby** (John),
1600-1676. A Scotch versifier, now chiefly remembered by
the satiric allusions of Dryden and Pope (*Dunciad*, I. 141 and
328). He was dancing-master to the Earl of Strafford, and later
published translations of Vergil and Homer.—104. **Bilked** =
defrauded.—105. **Herringman** (Henry). A leading publisher
of the day.—108. **Young Ascanius.** The son of Æneas. On
Ascanius depended the succession and the future greatness
of Rome. (See Virgil's *Æneid, passim.*)—110. **Glories,** i.e. a
sacred light, or fire; often used to signify the *nimbus* of a
saint. The reference here is to the harmless flame that played
about the head of the young Iülus (Ascanius); a portent of
royal power (*Æn.* II. 682). Dryden in his translation of the
passage uses the same word, "lambent," to describe the flame
that he here applies to "dulness."—120. **Sinister.** Used here
in its primary meaning of *left* as opposed to *dexter,* right,
dextrius. The accent should be on the second syllable (see
Dict.). The *ball,* or *orb,* representing the world and hence

sometimes called the *mound* (Fr. *monde*), was an emblem of royal power borrowed from the Roman emperors. English sovereigns "held it in their right hand at coronation, and carried it in their *left* on their return to Westminster Hall." (Hare's *Walks in London*, 385.) (See also *Hen. V.* IV. 1. 277, and *Macbeth*, IV. 1. 121.)—125. **Recorded Psyche**, i.e. the opera of *Psyche* which was sung, or recorded. To *sing* is one of the accepted meanings of to *record*: "To hear the lark *record* her hymns." (Fairfax.) A *recorder* is a small flute, as in *Hamlet*.

141.—129. **Poppets.** "Perhaps in allusion to Shadwell's frequent use of opium as well as to his dulness." (Scott.)—149. **Virtuosos.** *The Virtuoso* was a comedy of Shadwell's, first produced in 1676. Poor Shadwell was accused by some of too much haste, hence the charge is that he wrote with the slowness that discloses incapacity.—151. **Gentle George,** i.e. Sir George Etheridge (*cir.* 1636–1689). He was a famous wit, fine gentleman, and comedy writer ; the companion of Sedley, Rochester, and other gay courtiers of Charles II.'s court. *Dorimant, Loveit,* etc., are characters in his comedies. The contrast is between the intentional frivolity of such young exquisites as Sir Fopling Flutter, or the gay and unprincipled Dorimant, who are at least amusing in their folly, and the unintentional but inevitable dulness of Shadwell's personages.

142.—163. **Alien Sedley,** i.e. Sir Charles Sedley (1639–1701), alluded to above as the companion of Etheridge, and like him a wit and patron of literature. He is called *alien* because he assisted Shadwell with his comedy of *Epsom Wells*, or, as Dryden insinuates, larded its prose with a wit alien to its native dulness.—168. **Sir Formal.** A grandiloquent and conceited character in *The Virtuoso.* The insinuation is that Shadwell himself wrote in the pompous style affected by this character, and that he uses it in his " northern dedications," i.e. certain dedications of his to the Duke and Duchess of Newcastle.—179. **Nicander,** a lover in the opera of *Psyche.*—188. **New humours** (see *Shadwell*, p. 625–6). To understand this passage and its context, we must remember that Shadwell aspired to be a follower of Ben Jonson, and that in presenting "humours," or types of eccentricity, he followed Jonson's lead. Dryden has particularly in mind some lines of eulogy on Jonson in the epilogue to Shadwell's *Humourists*, wherein a humour is described as "the bias of the mind " :—

> " By which with violence 'tis one way inclined ;
> It makes our actions lean on one side still,
> And in all changes that way bends our will."

Dryden, in paraphrasing this passage, declares that dulness is the weight, or *bias*, which inclines all Shadwell's writing toward stupidity. (See *Dict.* for original meaning of *bias*, and cf., e.g., *The Taming of the Shrew*, IV. 5. 25.)—193. **Mountain-belly.** The expression is taken from Ben Jonson's good-natured allusion to his own bulky person: "my mountain-belly and my rocky face." Dryden admits that Shadwell did indeed resemble Jonson in corpulence; but, unlike Jonson's, his is size without mind; his bloated form is but a "tympany of sense," i.e. it is empty or hollow, as a drum, but morbidly inflated by a windy distension." (See "Tympany," *Cent. Dict.*) A very hogshead, in this sense, in gross mass of flesh, he is in truth but a "kilderkin," or diminutive barrel, in wit, or intellect.

143.—204. **Mild anagram.** Anagrams, acrostics, poems in the shape of a cross, an altar, etc., and such other ingenious trifles, were common in the early seventeenth century. One of George Herbert's poems (*Easter Wings*) is in the form of a pair of wings. Hales refers us to *Spectator*, Nos. 58, 60, and Disraeli's *Curiosities of Literature*, "Literary Follies."— 212. **Bruce and Longville.** "Two very heavy characters in Shadwell's *Virtuoso*, whom he calls gentlemen of wit and good sense." (Derrick.) These two gentlemen dispose of Sir Formal Trifle in the midst of his declamation by unfastening a trap-door on which he is standing, whereupon he precipitately disappears.

ACHITOPHEL.

Absalom and Achitophel, from which this extract is taken, is the earliest of Dryden's satires, and among the greatest satires of the literature in brilliancy and incisive power. It was directed against the versatile, able, but unscrupulous politician, *Anthony Ashley Cooper, Lord Shaftesbury*, who appears in it under the name of Achitophel. The poem was written towards the close of 1681, at a critical juncture in public affairs. Shaftesbury (who had opposed the succession of the king's brother James, and favored that of the Duke of Monmouth) was then in the Tower awaiting his trial for high treason. Dryden, believing that Shaftesbury had nearly precipitated a civil war, found in the revolt of Absalom and Achitophel, the former counsellor of David (*II. Sam.* xv.), a Biblical parallel sufficiently close for his purpose. The tremendous indictment of Shaftesbury in the passage quoted is a masterpiece of pitiless analysis and satiric portraiture. Shaftesbury's character and career have been much discussed : the student should compare the views expressed by Dryden with those of Macaulay, W. D. Christie, H. D. Traill, and others.

154. **Unfixed in principles and place.** See any life of Lord Shaftesbury for an account of the daring changes which

marked his varied career.—157. **The pigmy body.** About twenty years before Dryden's satire, Shaftesbury, then Sir Ashley Cooper, suffered, in a carriage-accident, an injury from which he never entirely recovered.

144.—175. **The triple bond he broke.** A "Triple Alliance" was concluded between Holland, Sweden, and England in 1668. This "bond" was broken by an infamous secret treaty with France, known as the Treaty of Dover (1670). Shaftesbury was one of the signers of this treaty, although kept in ignorance of some of its provisions. Three years later he advocated a second war with the Dutch, one of the original parties to the "triple bond," in a famous speech. The "foreign yoke" referred to is that of France, really forwarded by the secret understanding between Charles and Louis at the Treaty of Dover.—188. **Abethdin.** A Hebrew word signifying "the fathers of the nation," i.e. the judges. As Lord Chancellor, Shaftesbury had a well-deserved reputation for uprightness and ability.

A SONG FOR ST. CECILIA'S DAY.

145. St. Cecilia, virgin, martyr, was a Roman lady of the third century. According to the legend, she sang hymns of praise to the accompaniment of an organ (by which we are to understand an instrument similar to the Pandean pipes), and so beautiful were her strains that an angel descended from the skies to listen to her. She has consequently been taken as the patron saint of sacred music, and in painting is commonly represented with her organ. (For a fuller account see Mrs. Jameson's *Sacred and Legendary Art.*) The poem is not merely nominally but literally a song, being composed for musical production at the festival of St. Cecilia's Day, November 22, 1687. A musical society had been formed in London which had a concert on that day every year, the first of their performances on record taking place in 1683. Dryden wrote his famous ode *Alexander's Feast*, 1697, for this same society. The subject was often attempted by succeeding poets. Addison wrote a *Song for St. Cecilia's Day*, a tame and very indifferent production, and Pope contributed a well-known ode on the same subject. (For fuller account, with a list of the poets and musicians who composed odes for this day, see Malone's Ed. of Dryden's *Prose Works*, II. 376.) Dryden's *Song* was first set to music by an Italian, one Giovanni Baptista Drayahi, and again in 1737 by Handel. The treatment of music in the *Song* is, on the whole, remarkably comprehensive. Beginning and closing with music in relation to the universe, as the originator and ender of the "frame" of things, the intermediate portion is devoted to music in its effects on human emotions, or as the raiser and queller of human passions.

1. From harmony, etc. This idea of the universe taking form out of a chaos of discordant atoms through the power of music, or harmony, is in general accord with the teachings of Pythagoras. That philosopher reverenced *order* as the central principle of the universe ; he consequently laid great stress on mathematics and on music, both being expressions of exact relations—or the *order* which he regarded as the basis of things. From these views grew his familiar doctrine of the " music of the spheres." (See Smith's *Class. Dict.*, " Pythagoras," and Plato's *Republic*, Bk. X.) These ideas seem to have been frequently referred to by the English poets preceding Dryden. (See *Mercht. of Ven.* V. 1. 66, and Milton's *Hymn on the Nativity*, XII., XIII.) In *Par. Lost* we have the same contrast between the order of creation and the warring elements of chaos. Dryden, l. 7, "hot, cold, moist, and dry," follows Milton's description of chaos word for word. (See *Par. Lost*, II. 878.)—**2. This universal frame**, i.e. the whole fabric of creation. (Cf. *Par Lost*, v. 153, "Thine *universal frame* thus wondrous fair," etc., and Addison, " The spacious firmament on high," p. 156.)—**15. Diapason**. (Gr. $\delta\iota\acute{a}$ = through, and $\pi\alpha\varsigma\tilde{\omega}\nu$ = all.) Nature, or creation, proceeds as through the seven notes of the musical scale, closing, or completing, the *diapson*, or octave, in man.—**17. Jubal**, the inventor of the lyre and flute. (See *Genesis* iv. 19-21.)

146.—**33. Flute.** The old English flute, or *flute-a-bec*, which was played from the end like our flageolet, must be here intended, as the modern, or German, flute did not come into use in England until some half a century later. This is worth noting, as one of the first occasions on which the modern flute was successfully introduced into an orchestral score was in Handel's musical setting of this *Ode* in 1739. He employed it for a solo in this stanza.—**47. To mend** = to *improve* or *complete*. The conceit is more daring than reverent.

147.—**50.—Sequacious.** (Lat. *sequax* = following after, pursuing.) The word, according to our modern taste, gives the line a pedantic and decidedly unpoetic character. It is notable here as just such a Latinism as disfigured much of the English poetry of the earlier eighteenth century. We cannot imagine that any poet from Chaucer to the last of the Elizabethans, or any poet (except a belated follower of Pope) from Wordsworth to our own day, would have employed such an expression : the brand of the eighteenth century is on it. Cf. Cowper, *Task :* "The stable yields a *stercoraceous* heap," etc., etc.—**52. Vocal breath.** The primitive nature of the so-called organ associated with St. Cecilia may throw some light on this passage. Raphael's picture of the saint with an organ made, like pipes, to be blown without any mechanical appliances, would make this idea familiar; on the other hand the organ is still said, in the language of organ-builders, to "speak" and to "be voiced."—53. **An angel heard.** This favorite incident in the legend of the saint is again alluded to by Dryden in the closing lines of *Alexander's Feast*, and by Tennyson in his *Palace of Art:*

> "Or in a clear-wall'd city on the sea,
>   Near gilded organ-pipes, her hair
> Wound with white roses, slept St. Cecily;
>   An angel look'd at her."

55. **Grand chorus.** This, by reverting again to the idea with which the poem began, gives a greater unity to the piece. Untune (l. 9) may really be considered as equivalent to *dissolve* or *discompose ;* music is the essential principle which brought order out of chaos; and music, at the sound of the last trump, shall be the signal for the destruction of the harmony of the universe.

ALEXANDER'S FEAST, OR THE POWER OF MUSIC.

The immediate occasion of the composition of this ode, which has probably retained its popularity better than any other single poem of its author, has been already stated (Int. note to *Song for St. Cecilia's Day*). According to Lord Bolingbroke, Dryden sat up all night to write it, being so struck with the subject that he could not leave the poem until it was completed. (See Warton's Essay on *Pope.*) The real theme of the ode is given in the sub-title, and the circumstances under which the power of music is displayed are well chosen and highly dramatic. The world-conqueror, at the pinnacle of his glory, is shown as himself conquered by and made subservient to the mightier power of song. Nevertheless, while the ode commands our admiration for its resounding lines and splendid, if somewhat pompous, rhetoric, it fails to arouse our deeper feelings. Mr. Churton Collins says with truth: "*Alexander's Feast* is a consummate example both of metrical skill and of what a combination of all the qualities which can enter into the compositition of rhetorical masterpieces can effect. But it is nothing more." (*Essays and Studies*, p. 89.)

1. **For Persia won,** i.e. the feast given on account of (or in celebration of) the conquest of Persia. The Persian Empire was finally overthrown by the battle of Arbela, B.C. 331, the third great battle of the invasion.—9. **Thais.** An Athenian noted for her wit and beauty who accompanied Alexander on his expedition against Persia. According to a story of doubt-

ful authority she beguiled Alexander into setting fire to the royal palace of Darius at Persepolis while a great festival was being held and the king was under the influence of wine. (See Dryden's allusion to this in stanza 6.)

148.—20. **Timotheus.** "A celebrated musician, a native of Thebes in Bœotia. He was one of those who were invited to attend at the celebration of the nuptials of Alexander the Great. He excelled particularly in playing on the flute ; and his performance is said to have animated the monarch in so powerful a degree that he started up and seized his arms—an incident which Dryden has beautifully introduced into English poetry." (Anthon's *Class. Dict.*)—25. **The song began from Jove**, etc. Alexander claimed to be the son not of Philip of Macedon, but of Zeus himself. Plutarch—who says that Jove is supposed to have visited Olympias, Alexander's mother, in the form of a serpent—quotes Eratosthenes as saying "that Olympias, when she attended Alexander on his way to the army in his first expedition, told him the secret of his birth, and bade him behave himself with courage suitable to his divine extraction." ("Life of Alexander.") Shortly before the battle of Arbela, Alexander, apparently intoxicated by his successes, had consulted the famous oracle of Jupiter Ammon in the Libyan desert, where his claim to be the son of Zeus had received due recognition. Timotheus, with skilful flattery, begins by assuming the truth of Alexander's pretensions.— 28. **Belied** = disguised.—30. **Olympia**, i.e. Olympias, perhaps changed *euphoniæ gratia* to avoid a too sibilant effect.

150.—108. **Lydian measures.** See *L'Allegro*, l. 136, and n.

152.—173. **Vocal frame** = " a speaking structure." (Hales.)

153.—181. **Drew an angel down.** See *Song for St. Cecilia's Day*, l. 53 and n.

PRIOR.

154. MATTHEW PRIOR (1664–1721) was a wit, ambassador, poet, story-writer, and man of affairs. Born shortly after the Restoration, he was employed in state affairs under William and during part of the reign of Anne. His first literary success was in *The City Mouse and the Country Mouse*, written in conjunction with his friend Montague (afterwards Earl of Halifax) to ridicule Dryden's *Hind and the Panther*. Prior's reputation as a poet now rests almost entirely upon his shorter and slighter verse. He was one of the earliest masters of society verse in England, and anticipated by many years the lightness and dexterity of such moderns as Praed, Locker, and Dobson. A recent writer has pointed out that Thomas Moore has "more than once" reproduced the

very trick and turn of Prior's verse. (See *A Better Answer*,
p. 155. Jno. Dennis, *The Age of Pope*, p. 68.) The verses *To
a Child of Quality* are less cynical and more pleasing than
most of his work, but *A Better Answer* is probably a more
representative example of his manner.

ADDISON.

156. JOSEPH ADDISON (1672–1719), although known to us
as a master of prose, gained through his verse some successes
which had a most important influence upon his career. This
was notably the case with his poem to Somers, his Latin
verses to Montague, his poem of *The Campaign*, which won
him the favor of a Prime Minister and £200 a year, and his
tragedy of *Cato*, which took the town by storm. These poems,
however, have had little lasting value. Outside of his
prose, Addison's most enduring work is probably as a hymn-
writer. Some of his hymns are still sung, and continue part
of the religious life of thousands, and in this province of
poetry he has been well called the forerunner of Watts and
Wesley. The *Hymn* or *Ode* selected as an example of Addison's verse, first appeared in *The Spectator*, No. 465. In the
essay which precedes the poem Addison is speaking of
the glories of nature as a confirmation of faith in a Supreme Creator. He then introduces the verses as follows:
". . . The psalmist has very beautiful strokes of poetry to this
purpose in that exalted strain, 'The heavens declare the glory
of God: and the firmament showeth his handiwork. One
day telleth another: and one night certifieth another. There
is neither speech nor language: but their voices are heard
among them. Their sound is gone out into all the lands:
and their words unto the ends of the world.' As such a bold
and sublime manner of thinking furnished very noble matter
for an ode, the reader may see it wrought into the following
one."

3. **Frame.** See *Song for St. Cecilia's Day*, l. 2, and note.
Cf. *Hamlet* II. 2: "This goodly *frame* the earth."—4. **Original** = originator, first cause. Thus Chaucer speaks of glut-
tony as the "*original* of our dampnacioun." (*Pardoner's Tale*,
l. 38.)

157.—21. **In reason's ear**, etc. Music has been associated
with the movements of the heavenly bodies by many writers
and in many ways. We are told in the Bible how "The morning stars sang together;" the Greeks philosophized about
the music of the spheres, and Shakespeare declares that only
the gross flesh prevents us from hearing each single orb in its

course, "still quiring to the young-eyed cherubim." But it was reserved for Addison, the sober prose-poet of an age of good sense, to declare that these celestial rejoicings are audible to the ear of reason. (See Dryden, *St. Cecilia's Day*, l. 1 and n.)

GAY.

JOHN GAY (1688–1732), a man of easy-going temperament and careless good nature, was a friend of Pope's and one of the most popular poets of his time. His mock-heroic poem, *Wine,* appeared in 1710. He wrote several comedies, and his *Beggars Opera* (1727) scored a great success. His minute descriptions of London life, as in his *Trivia, or the Art of Walking the Streets of London* (1716), have a permanent interest and value. Although his song of *Black-eyed Susan* has been widely popular, it is distinctly of an inferior quality. The *Fifty-one Fables in Verse* (1727) are mildly amusing and not devoid of cleverness.

FABLE XVIII. THE PAINTER, ETC.

158.—27. **Bustos** = busts (Ital. *busto*).

ON A LAP-DOG.

160.—15. **Mechlin pinners.** The long flaps belonging to a lady's headdress—which hang down each side of the face. These were made of, or sometimes trimmed with, lace. They are frequently mentioned in the literature of the period.—24. **For when a lap-dog falls,** etc. Cf. "Not louder shrieks to pitying heaven are cast, when husbands, or when lap-dogs breathe their last." (*Rape of the Lock,* III. 157.)

POPE.

160. ALEXANDER POPE, the poetic successor of Dryden and the representative poet of the Augustan Age, was born in 1688 and died in 1744. His *Essay on Criticism* (1711) was enthusiastically received, and *The Rape of the Lock* (1712) and other poems placed him in the front rank of the poets of his time. In many respects he is obviously a follower of Dryden; but he has more grace, sentiment, and delicacy of fancy, with far less intellectual force and masculine power. Both poets were satirists, both extensive translators from the classics; Dryden argued in verse on questions of theology, and Pope attempted to expound a system of philosophy. But the works of Dryden contain no parallel to *The Rape of the Lock*, which has the diaphanous hues and lightness of a soap-bubble, or to the sentiment of *The Elegy to an Unfortunate Lady*, or the *Epistle from Eloisa to Abelard*.

THE RAPE OF THE LOCK.

This poem belongs to the earlier part of Pope's career, preceding his satires and philosophic poems and his translations of Homer. In its original and shorter form it appeared in Bernard Lintot's *Miscellany* in 1711–12. It was well received, and Pope determined to alter and enlarge it. He introduced the supernatural "machinery" of the sylphs and sylphids, the game of Ombre, and other new features, thus increasing the original two cantos to five. This second version appeared in 1714. The poem, founded on an actual occurrence, was written at the request of a Mr. Caryl. One Lord Petre contrived to abstract a lock of Mistress Arabella Fermor's hair. The families of the daring lord and the offended beauty having been estranged, Mr. Caryl, anxious to restore peace, asked Pope to write a poem which should suggest to both sides the absurdity of quarrelling over so trifling an affair. The result was a masterpiece, which, if not his most ambitious, is probably Pope's most original and pleasing contribution to literature.

Canto I.—3. **Caryll**, a friend of Pope's who confided to him the incident on which the poem was founded.

161.—23. **Birth-night.** The dressing at court at the birth-night balls given to celebrate the birthdays of the members of the royal family, was unusually splendid.—32. **Silver token.** The piece of money which the fairies were believed to drop in the shoe of the diligent housemaid as a reward.

162.—44. **Box.** "The '*Box*' at the theatre and the '*Ring*' in Hyde Park are frequently mentioned as the two principal places for the display of beauty and fashion." (Elwin.) 62. **Tea.** Pronounced *tay* until the middle of the eighteenth century. (See *English Past and Present*, by R. C. Trench, p. 182.) In Canto III. l. 8, *tea* rhymes with *obey*.—58. **To their first elements**, etc. Pope here makes skilful use of the doctrine attributed to a sect known as the Rosicrucians, who held that each of the four elements was inhabited by a distinct order of spirits. The idea of substituting the souls of deceased mortals for the elemental spirits is an ingenious variation of Pope's.

163.—105. **Protection claim** = "claim to protect thee." The language here is, to say the least, ambiguous; on their face the words might mean "claim to be protected by thee."

165. CANTO II.—18. **Look on her face.** A better rendering has been suggested by Wakefield: "Look *in* her face, and you forget them all."

168.—100. **Furbelow.** A pleated or gathered flounce. Dr. Johnson gives an impromptu derivation of this word (*fur* and *below*), with the following definition: "fur sewed on the lower part of the garment; an ornament." (Johnson's *Dict.* See also *Spectator*, No. 129.)—113. **The drops,** "that is her ear-drops, set with brilliants." (Wakefield.)—263. **Do thou Crispissa.** Note that the names of these spirits correspond to their several charges. Wakefield says that "to crisp" was frequently used by the earlier writers for "to curl" (Lat. *crispo*).

169. CANTO III.—8. **Tea.** See C. I. l. 62 and n. *supra.*

170.—27. **Ombre.** A game of cards of Spanish origin. It was played by three persons, the one who named the trump (in this case Belinda) playing against the other two.—53. **Him Basto followed.** To understand the following passage, some knowledge of the game of ombre is required, for description of which see Hoyle's *Games*, under "Quadrille." The *Matadores—Spadille*, or "Spadillio," *Manille*, or " Manillio," and *Basto*—were the three principal cards, and ranked respectively as first, second, and third in power. *Spadille* was always the ace of spades, and *Basto* the ace of clubs; but *Manille* depended upon the trump. With a black trump (spades or clubs) Manille was the two of trumps; with a red trump (hearts or diamonds) Manille was the seven of trumps.

171.—61. **Pam,** the highest card in the game of *Loo*, is the knave of clubs, or sometimes the knave of the trump suit.

172.—92. **Codille.** "If either of the antagonists made more tricks than the ombre (see n. C. III. l. 27, *supra*) the winner took the pool and the ombre had to replace it for the next game. This was called *codille*." (Elwin.)

173. — 122. **Scylla.** See Anthon's *Class. Dict.* under "Nisus," and Ovid's *Metam.* VIII. The Scylla here mentioned must be distinguished from the monster of that name associated with Charybdis in the *Odyssey* and elsewhere.

174.—165. **Atalantis.** *The New Atlantis*, pub. 1709, was a popular and scandalous book, suited, according to Warburton, to the taste of the "better vulgar." Hales reminds us that it was one of the works in Leonora's library. (See *Spectator*, No. 37.)—178. **Unresisted.** That which cannot be resisted; irresistible.

CANTO IV. — 13. **Umbriel.** Lat. *umbra*, a shade, and *umbrifer*, shade-bringing.

175.—16. **Spleen.** An organ of the body whose function is uncertain; formerly supposed to be the seat of anger, caprice, and particularly low spirits, or, as we should say, "the blues." In Pope's time spleen was frequently used in the last sense, and Austin Dobson calls it the fashionable eighteenth-century disorder.— 20. **The dreaded east**, etc. Why the *east* wind? (See Cowper's *Task*, Bk. IV. 363.)—38. **Nightdress**. "The *gown* or *night-dress* of Pope is the dressing-gown of our day." (Elwin)

176.—46. **Angels in machines**, i.e., coming to the aid of mankind. In Pope's time "machine" signified the supernatural agency in a poem; thus in *The Rape of the Lock*, the *machinery* consists of sylphs and sylphides; in the *Iliad*, of gods and goddesses. "The changing of the Trojan fleet into water-nymphs is the most violent machine in the whole *Æneid*." (Addison.) Hales compares Lat. *Deus ex machina* and Greek Θεὸς ἀπομηχανῆς.—59. **Vapours** = spleen. Elwin says the disease was probably named from the atmospheric vapors which were reputed to be a principal cause of English melancholy. He quotes Cowper's *Task*, Bk. VI. 462.— 69. **Citron-waters**. A drink composed of wine with the rind of lemons and citron. Swift's *Modern Young Lady* takes a large dram of citron-water to cool her heated brains.

177.—99. **Locks in paper**. "The curl-papers of ladies' hair used to be fashioned with strips of pliant lead." (Croker.)

178.—118. **In the sound of Bow**, i.e., within the sound of the bells of St. Mary le Bow, an old and famous church in the heart of London. In Pope's time the *City*, or old part of London in the vicinity of this church, was avoided by fashion and the "wits." In Grub Street, in this locality, many starving hack writers and scribblers had lodgings.—121. **Sir Plume** = Sir George Brown. Speaking of the effect of the poem, Pope says: "Nobody but Sir George Brown was angry, and he was a good deal so and for a long time. He could not bear that Sir Plume should talk nothing but nonsense." (Spence's *Anecdotes*.)

179.—156. **Bohea**. Pronounced *bohay*. Compare *tea*, note to C. I. l. 62.

Canto V.—6. **Anna begg'd and Dido**, etc. Look up this allusion in *Æneid*, Bk. IV.—7. **Clarissa**. "A new character introduced in the subsequent editions, to open more clearly the moral of the poem, in a parody of the speech of Sarpedon to Glaucus in Homer." Pope. (See *Iliad*, Bk. XII. 310-328.)—14. **Side-box**. In the theatres the gentlemen occupied the side, and the ladies the front, boxes.

181.—45. **Homer**. Compare *Iliad*, Bk. VIII. 69-75; Verg. *Æneid*, Bk. XII. 725-727.—95. **Bodkin**. A large ornamental hairpin.

184.—136. **Rosamonda's Lake** was a "small oblong piece

of water near the Pimlico gate of St. James Park." (Croker.)
137. **Partridge.** John Partridge, an almanac-maker and
astrologer noted for his ridiculous predictions. He was
ridiculed by Swift, Steele, Addison, and others.

ELEGY TO THE MEMORY OF AN UNFORTUNATE LADY.

184.—This poem and the *Epistle of Eloisa to Abelard* are
memorable as excursions beyond the limits to which Pope's
verse is almost invariably confined. Critic, moralist, cynic,
satirist, clever trifler, or philosophic disputant, Pope here
comes before us as one who essays, at least, the language of
genuine pathos and passion. The feeling which animates
these poems has seemed to some to have the unmistakable
accent of sincerity; others, again, regard the poems as skilful poetic exercises, rather than the utterance of the heart. In
either case it can hardly be denied that they are distinguished
by a finish of workmanship which gives them a beauty of a
certain kind. The poems first appeared in a collected volume
of Pope's verse which was published in 1717. The subject of
the *Elegy* is not particularly clear, but we gather that it is
supposed to be founded upon the apparition of an unfortunate
lady who, persecuted by her guardian, has committed suicide
in a foreign land. Further than this the story is not told with
sufficient definiteness to be entirely clear. The lady's crime
is that she aspired too high and loved too well. The reason
for the guardian's alleged severity is not made apparent. Nor
are the obscurities of the story explainable upon the theory
that Pope's verses were inspired by some actual occurrence, the
details of which he did not choose to reveal. Numerous attempts were made by the earlier critics to ascertain or to manufacture the original of Pope's portrait, but with no satisfactory
result. It is, apparently, a "mere study in emotional charac-
terization," and if there are defects or obscurities in the narrative, Pope appears to be solely responsible for them. In
fact, the merit of the poem consists neither in its construction
nor in its morality, which, as Dr. Johnson pointed out, is faulty,
but in the sweetness of its rhythm and the general beauty of
its execution.

EPISTLE TO DR. ARBUTHNOT.

188.—The following brief account of this poem is taken
from Leslie Stephen's *Pope* (*E. M. L.* 182): "Bolingbroke,
coming one day in his (Pope's) room, took up a Horace, and
observed that the first satire of the second book would suit

Pope's style. Pope translated it in a morning or two, and sent it to press almost immediately (1733). . . . This again led to his putting together *The Epistle to Arbuthnot*, which includes the bitter attack upon Hervey, as part of a general *apologia pro vita sua*." **Dr. Arbuthnot.**—A Scotch physician, wit, and author, who had early settled in London and had become physician in ordinary to the Queen. He was one of the inner circle of London wits; intimate with Pope, Swift, Gay, and other men of letters, and—with Pope and Swift—one of the founders of the Scriblerus Club. As the poem intimates, he was Pope's own physician. 1. **Good John.**—Pope's faithful servant John Searle.

189.—8. **My grot.** Pope's famous grotto at Twickenham was really a tunnel, adorned with pieces of spar, mirrors, etc., leading under a public road that intersected the poet's grounds. (See Carruther's *Life of Pope*, V. I. 171-177, Bohn's ed.—13. **The Mint.** A district in Southwark, so called from a mint for coinage established here by Henry VIII. in Suffolk House. As persons were exempt from arrest within this district, it became another Alsatia, a place of refuge for insolvent debtors and criminals. As may be supposed, poor authors often had to take sanctuary there. A good account of it is given in Thornbury's *Old and New London*, V. VI. p. 60.—15. **Is there a parson**, etc. Supposed to be one Lawrence Eusden, rector of a parish in Lincolnshire.—**Bemused** = befogged, muddled.—23. **Arthur** = Arthur Moore, Esq., a prominent figure in the political and social life of the time. His *giddy son* was James Moore Smythe, a dissipated fop, who had excited Pope's petty and easily-provoked resentment by inserting without permission some then unpublished lines of Pope's into his comedy the *Rival Modes*. (See "Smythe" in L. Stephen's *Dict. Nat. Biog.*)—25. **Poor Cornus.** According to Horace Walpole, Cornus was Lord Robert Walpole, a son of the Prime Minister. Lord Robert's wife, Margaret, a daughter of Samuel Rolle, Esq., left her husband in 1734.—31. **I'm sped**, i.e., ruined, undone ; our modern phrase "done for" is perhaps the nearest equivalent. (Cf. Shaks. "I am sped," *Romeo and Juliet*, III. 1. 94 ; *Taming of the Shrew*, III. 2. 53 ; and see *Lycidas*, n. to l. 122, *supra*.)

190.—40. **Keep your piece,** etc. The famous precept of Horace, *Ars Poetica*, l. 388, "*nonumque prematur in annum.*" —41. **Drury Lane,** a fashionable quarter in the days of the Stuarts, had become the abode of vice, poverty, and impecunious authors, even before Pope's time. Gay speaks of the dangers of its "mazy courts and dark abodes," and Goldsmith alludes to it in uncomplimentary terms in his *Description of an Author's Bedchamber*.—43. **Before Term ends,** "i.e., before the end of the London Season. Trinity Term ended three weeks, or thereabouts, after Trinity Sunday." (Pattison.)—49. **Pitholeon.** The name is taken from Horace, *Sat.* I. 10, 22, where a certain Pitholeon of Rhodes, a poet who gloried in mixing Greek and Latin in his epigrams, is alluded to.—53. **Curll.** Edmund Curll (1675–1747), a contemptible bookseller, with whom Pope was on bad terms for twenty years. He published Pope's *Familiar Letters to Henry Cromwell* in 1726, as Pope affected to believe without authority. Pope attacks him in a disgusting passage in the *Dunciad.* He was notorious for his harsh treatment of the hack-writers whom he employed; for his unscrupulousness in business; and for the vile character of some of his publications.—56. **A Virgin tragedy.** "Alludes to a tragedy called *The Virgin Queen*, by M. R. Barford, published 1729, who displeased Pope by daring to adopt the fine machinery of his Sylphes in an heroi-comical poem called the Assembly." (Warton.)—62. **Lintot.** Bernard Lintot (1675–1736) was a leading bookseller of the day. He published Pope's *Rape of the Lock* and his translations of Homer. Pope quarrelled with him over some business in connection with the translation of the *Odyssey* and abused him in the *Dunciad.*—66. **Go snacks**, i.e., go shares, divide the spoils. *Snack* is a portion, or "literally a snatch or thing snatched up." (See Skeat, *Etymol. Dict.*)

191.—111. **One from all Grub Street.** Grub Street is defined by Dr. Johnson as "originally the name of a street in Moorfields in London, much inhabited by writers of small histories, dictionaries, and temporary poems; whence any mean production is called *Grub Street.*" According to Courthope the allusion here is probably "to the *Grub Street Journal*, the plan of which was to attack Pope's enemies by ironically praising them, and at the same time affecting to depreciate the poet's own works."—113. **This prints my letter.** Another thrust at Curll, see n. 53, *supra.*—116. **I cough like Horace**, etc. Direct evidence of Horace's cough appears to be wanting; we know, however, that he was short and fat. (Suetonius, *Vit. Horatii, Epistles* I. 20. 24, and I. 4. 15.)—117. **Ammon's great son**, i.e., Alexander the Great, who is known to have boasted that he was in reality the son of the Egyptian deity *Ammon* or *Amen*, the same god whom the Greeks identified with *Zeus* under the name of *Jupiter Ammon.* (See account of Alexander's visit to the oracle of Ammon.) Alexander's neck is reported to have been "a little inclined towards his left shoulder."—118. **Ovid's nose.** Apparently an allusion to the poet's family name. He was called P. Ovidius *Naso* (*nasus* = large-nosed).—161. **Commas and points.** Pope himself declared that his great ambition as a poet was to be correct and in this he merely represented the characteristic aspiration of his time. Yet even among the high priests of correctness we find the idea that correctness was the only essential, held up to ridicule. Cf. Addison's portrait of Ned Softly. *The Tatler*, No. 163.

192.—**179. The Bard**, etc., i.e., Ambrose Philips (1675?–1749), a poet and one of Pope's many enemies. Philips's *Pastorals* and Pope's *Pastorals* appeared in the same collection (*Tonson's Miscellany*, 1709), and certain compliments to this rival work of Philips' so excited Pope's morbidly jealous temper that he wrote a paper for *The Guardian*, in which Philips' *Pastorals* and his own were ironically compared.—**180. A Persian tale.** Philips was liberally paid (according to Dr. Johnson's opinion) for this work, since he may have received half a crown, not for the translation, but for each section into which it was divided. (See Johnson's *Lives of the Poets*, Life of Philips.)—**190. A Tate.** Nahum Tate (1652–1715) succeeded Shadwell as poet laureate in 1692. He wrote most of the second part of *Absalom and Achitophel* and made a number of translations from the classics. Pattison reminds us that, as Pope's own success had been largely due to his translations of Homer, the sneer at translators is particularly ill-timed.—**193. One whose fires.** This masterly but grossly unjust and mendacious attack upon Addison (Atticus), Pope's former friend, is one of the most justly familiar passages in all his work. Pattison says of these lines: "They are at once a masterpiece of Pope's skill as a poet, and his base disposition as a man. They unite the most exquisite finish of sarcastic expression with the venomous malignity of personal rancour." The lines were included in the *Prologue to the Satires* as an after-thought. They were written earlier and sent to Addison, and they were first published as a fragment in 1727. We are told that they were in great demand, and Atterbury was so much impressed by them that he advised Pope to devote his efforts to satire. Macaulay says of the passage: "One charge which Pope has enforced with great skill is probably not without foundation. Addison was, we are inclined to believe, too fond of presiding over a circle of humble friends. Of the other imputations which these famous lines are intended to convey, scarcely one has ever been proved to be just, and some are certainly false. That Addison was not in the habit of 'damning with faint praise' appears from innumerable passages in his writings, and from none more than from those in which he mentions Pope. And it is not merely unjust, but ridiculous, to describe a man who made the fortune of almost every one of his intimate friends, as ' so obliging that he ne'er obliged.'" (Essay on *Addison*. See also Spence's *Anecdotes*, and 'Pope' in Thackeray's *English Humorists*.)

THOMSON TO TENNYSON

(CIR. 1730—CIR. 1830.)

THE POETS OF THE MODERN PERIOD.

195.—The modern period of English poetry has its rise during the early half of the eighteenth century, in a divergence, more and more radical as the century advances, from the form, the spirit, and the literary standards exemplified by Pope and dominant in his time. It is customary to associate the beginning of this fresh poetic current with the work of two Scotchmen, *Allan Ramsay* (1685-1758) and *James Thomson* (1700-1748). Some of the distinctive qualities of this new poetry were a more genuine pleasure in nature and country-life, a deeper sympathy with all forms of suffering in man or in animals, a growing reverence for human nature, a revival of the old delight in Elizabethan literature, and the introduction of more varied and less mechanical metrical forms in place of the heroic couplet. (*Int. Eng. Lit.* 255-282.) The presence and increase of these and other allied qualities will be apparent from a careful consecutive reading of the selections. From Thomson to Burns the trend in the direction just indicated steadily becomes more apparent. All these poets are poets of nature, each in his own manner and degree : Collins, Gray, and Burns are manifestly preëminent in their lyrical gift ; while Thomson, Gray, Cowper, and Burns show both the gathering spirit of tenderness and the feeling of the new democracy. In Wordsworth, Coleridge, Southey, and Scott, the break with the outworn standards of Pope's day became complete. The poets from Byron to the advent of Tennyson may likewise be roughly grouped together. Many of them were obviously influenced by the spirit of that seething, rebellious, and morbidly melancholy time, when the agitations that followed the French Revolution were slowly subsiding, and democracy gathering force for another advance. With the advent of Tennyson, about 1830, we enter the threshold of our own time.

THOMSON.

195.—JAMES THOMSON (1700–1748) was born at Ednam, Roxburghshire, where his father was the parish minister. This Border region, separated from England by the Cheviot Hills, lies immediately to the east of Ayrshire, the district which fifty-nine years later gave birth to Burns. During his youth, spent in these unconfined and beautiful surroundings, Thomson was far removed from that circle of wits and satirists that from the heart of London dominated English letters. Thus early familiar with nature, it was Thomson's mission to freshen and sweeten the close and vitiated air of English poetry with the free air and wholesome sunshine of the open fields. "Winter," the first instalment of *The Seasons*, was published in 1726; "Spring" and "Summer" followed in 1727 and 1728, and the concluding part, "Autumn," in 1730. Like many other writers of his time, Thomson tried his hand at the drama, but with small success. *Rule Britannia*, the national song of England, appeared first in a masque produced by him in 1740, and has escaped the oblivion which has overtaken his dramatic productions. In *The Castle of Indolence* (1748) he employed the stanza of Spenser, and also followed him in diction and manner. This and *The Seasons* are his most important poems.

THE SEASONS.

SPRING.

16. **Livid.** The use of this word here is, from our associations with it, hardly a happy one. The idea appears to be that, contrasted with the white of the dissolving snows, the streams look lead-colored or bluish-black.

196.—26. **Aries,** the *Ram*, is the first of the signs of the Zodiac, and *Taurus*, or the *Bull*, the second. About thirty days would elapse between the time the sun is at the first point of *Aries* (or the time when the sun crosses the equator towards the north) and the time of its entrance into *Taurus*. Consequently the date the poet wishes to indicate is about a month after the vernal equinox (March 21st), or the latter part of April.—55. **Maro** = Vergil, whose full name was *Publius Vergilius Maronis*. The reference is to the *Georgics*.

197.—60. **And some,** etc. Probably a reference to the familiar story of Cincinnatus. The prophet Elisha (*I. Kings* xxx. 19) may have been one of those in the poet's mind in the earlier passage.—70–72. **As the sea ... your empire owns,** etc.

It should be remembered that England was not at this time (1728) the world-power which she was shortly destined to become. The fight for the supremacy in India and America had yet to be fought. Nevertheless, when Thomson wrote, the foundations of her world-trade were being laid under the sagacious management of Walpole, and the passage has an interest through its bearing on the commercial conditions of the time. Cf. *Autumn*, 117 *et seq.*

198.—108. **Augusta** = London. (See n. to Dryden's *Mac Flecknoe*, l. 64.) Many elevations on the outskirts of London would have afforded a good view of the fields in Thomson's time.

SUMMER.

199.—378. **People.** Seldom used except of human beings; compare, however, " The ants are a *people* not strong, yet they prepare their meats in the summer." (*Prov.* xxx. 25.)—386. **Sordid**, here = dirty (*obs.*).

AUTUMN.

200.—3. **The Doric reed**, i.e., the pipe, or oaten reed, of the pastoral poet. Rustic and pastoral poetry was associated with the Dorians, and especially with the Dorians in Sicily. See *Lycidas*, n. to l. 189.

201.—957. **Fleeces unbounded ether.** A unique, or at least an unusual, use of *fleeces*. The sense is that the calm spreads over the boundless atmosphere as soft as a fleece of wool. (See *Centy. Dict.*)

WINTER.

202.—5. **Welcome, kindred glooms!**, etc. *Winter* was the first of the four poems on *The Seasons* to be composed. It was begun in a period of depression, just after Thomson had given up a tutorship which he had regarded as a desirable opening. He was "without employment, without money, with few friends, [and] saddened by the loss of his mother." "This passage," says Minto, "expressed his own forlorn mood on the approach of the winter of 1725."—8. **Nursed by careless solitude**, etc. Thomson, born in the Scottish Border country near the waters of the Tweed, passed his youth in the freedom and beauty of that fascinating region. Dr. Johnson tells us that Thomson while a schoolboy at Jedburgh, a town in that vicinity, was given to poetical composition.

203.—224. **Livid.** See n. to *Spring*, l. 16, *supra.*—246. **The red-breast**, etc. To appreciate the accuracy of this beautiful description, we must remember that the English robin (which is, of course, the bird here referred to) is a different bird from its American namesake. Its trust in man, its timid entrance into human dwellings, enforced by the rigors of winter, are well-recognized facts. The peculiar understanding subsisting in England between man and this familiar bird is perhaps reflected in the well-known ballad, where the robins cover the lost children with leaves.

205.—356. **The social tear . . . the social sigh,** i.e., the tear or sigh prompted by sympathy with or compassion for society at large. Cf. Pope, *Essay on Man,* IV. 396. "That true self-love and *social* are the same."—359. **The generous band,** etc. That is, a Parliamentary Committee appointed at the instance of Oglethorpe (afterwards founder of Georgia) to investigate the condition of the Fleet and Marshalsea prisons. This committee began its work in 1729. Thomson does not exaggerate the horrors which this inquiry disclosed. In the allusion to "little tyrants" (367) the poet probably had in mind one, Thomas Bambridge, then warden of the Fleet, a brutal and despotic man who wrung exorbitant fees from the wretched inmates. This passage does not appear in the original version of *Winter,* 1726, which was considerably shorter than that with which we are familiar. The first version, it will be observed, was published some three years before the events here referred to took place, and the fact that these lines are a later insertion explains an apparent discrepancy in dates.

COLLINS.

207.—WILLIAM COLLINS (1721–1759), whose poetry, insignificant in amount and restricted in range, yet includes some of the most exquisitely finished and unobtrusively beautiful lyrics in the language, was born in Chichester, Sussex. His poetic faculty early declared itself. Born when the superiority of reason and "good sense" to emotion and imagination, was preached and exemplified in high places, Collins (in Dr. Johnson's phrase) "delighted to rove through the meanders of enchantment" and "gaze on the magnificence of golden palaces." The spell of the gorgeous East mysteriously took hold of him, and he wrote his *Persian Eclogues* (pub. 1742) while yet at school at Winchester. He came to London about 1744, determined to devote himself to literature and full of "projects." His *Odes on Several Descriptive and Allegoric Subjects, etc.,* appeared at the close of 1746 (dated 1747), preceding by a few months only the poetic advent of Gray. Wide as were the differences in life and character between these two poets, the two greatest lyric voices of their time, in their fame and in their work for English poetry they are not divided. Two of Collins' important odes, the one on the death of his friend the poet Thomson, the other *On the Popular Superstitions of the Highlands of Scotland*, belong to a later date (1748 and *cir.* 1749) than the collection first mentioned. Readers of Collins' own generation, accustomed to verse of a wholly different order, were naturally incapable of appreciating the subtle and elusive charm that emanates from his best work, but in our own time all true lovers of what is excellent in English poetry recognize and admire the soft and often intricate harmonies, the indescribable delicacy and refinement of his verse. The career of Collins was brief, his end melancholy. In less than ten years from the time he came to London, full of great plans, his life was shipwrecked, his health gone, his mind in ruins. After six years of a living death, he died in obscurity at the age of thirty-eight.

ODE TO EVENING. (*Odes*, 1746.)

207.—By our power to discern and to delight in the beauty of the *Ode to Evening*, we may test our power of apprehending and appreciating poetic excellence in its finer and less obvious forms. The poem has a marvellous and artistic harmony of tone and color : nowhere is there a discordant note, a too glaring tint. The "sedge," the "lone heath," the "cool gleam" of the lake among the gray uplands, the "hamlets brown," the "dim-discovered spires," all the elements in the landscape,—with its tender, neutral color-tones,—insensibly bring us into the living presence of Twilight. The spirit of Twilight, revealed under the varied aspects of the changing year,—with the stillness and diffused clearness of Summer's lingering light, with the showers of Spring, the heaped leaves of Autumn, or the blasts of Winter,—this spirit is part of the very breath and essence of the poem. No didactic moralizings, no appropriate reflections are needed: the poem itself awakens twilight-thoughts in us, it puts us into the twilight-mood as inevitably as Nature herself would do, and, as with Nature, an influence is communicated that cannot be formally expressed.

1. **Oaten stop.** Strictly speaking, the stops are the holes in a pipe, or " ventages " as Hamlet calls them, the opening and closing of which make the notes. *Oaten stop* here stands for the shepherd's pipe, made of the reed or oaten straw. It is the *Avena*, or oaten straw, of Vergil (*Ecl.* I. 2). Cf. also *Love's Lab. Lost*, V. 2. 913 : "When shepherds pipe on *oaten straws*"; and the *oaten flute* of Milton (*Lycidas*, l. 33).—15. **Now teach me**, etc. This is directly dependent on "If aught of oaten

stop," etc., but the number of intervening lines, and the intricacy of the construction, are apt to make a hasty reader overlook the connection and miss the sense. The idea is, if a pastoral song may soothe thee, now teach me, O Eve, as I hail thy return, to breathe some such softened strain.

THE PASSIONS : AN ODE FOR MUSIC.

209. This poem was included in the book of *Odes* of 1747. It was set to music by William Hayes, and produced at Oxford in 1750. Collins, says Lowell, was the first to rediscover "the long-lost secret of being classically elegant without being pedantically cold." From this aspect *The Passions* can be advantageously compared with the stiffer and more sonorous rhetoric of *Alexander's Feast.* The poem shows Collins' power of clothing abstractions with a definite form and personality, a power in which he follows Sackville and Spenser. But admirable as it is, *The Passions* is not the supreme effort of Collins' genius ; it is surpassed by the quieter beauty of such poems as the *Ode to Evening* and the *Ode Written in 1746*, a beauty which seems to shun rather than to challenge our admiration, and so wins us by its apparent unconsciousness.

3. **Shell** = lyre. The primitive lyre was supposed to have been made by drawing strings across the shell of a tortoise. (Cf. Dryden, *Song for St. Cecilia's Day,* l. 17.)

211.—58. **Melancholy.** This conception of Melancholy, with her love of solitude and her "pensive soul," follows closely after that of Milton's in *Il Penseroso.* (See note to that poem, l. 11.) Similarly the companion-figure of *Cheerfulness* (l. 70) may be compared with the *Mirth* of *L'Allegro.*

212.—95. **Sphere-descended maid.** See n. on Dryden's *Song for St. Cecilia's Day,* l.—105. **Arise, as in that elder time.** Poetry, the "recording sister," tells of such wonders wrought by music in the "god-like age" as the building of Thebes by the strains of Amphion's lyre, and Collins complains that then "the humblest reed" had more power than all "*Cecilia's mingled world of sound*" (i.e., the organ) in his own "laggard age." This is either a mere poetic exaggeration, introduced for effect, or else Collins was singularly uninformed or unappreciative of the advance which music was making in London at that very time. Three years before Collins published his *Odes* Handel's *Messiah* had been produced in London and was received with enthusiasm ; indeed most of Handel's greatest works were produced between 1739 and 1751.

ODE WRITTEN IN 1746.

213. This lament is considered by Mr. Edmund Gosse to be one of the two poems which "perhaps present" Collins' "delicate art of melody in its directest form." When it was composed, England was engaged in war both at home and abroad. She was taking part in the war of the Austrian Succession (1740–1748), and at home she was engaged in suppressing the Jacobite rebellion of 1745. The poem was written "in the beginning of 1746." The Jacobite victory of Falkirk was January 17th, and the crushing Jacobite defeat of Culloden April 16th, of that year.

DIRGE IN CYMBELINE.

For the event which gave rise to this poem, see *Cymbeline*, A. IV. Sc. 2. It may perhaps have been still more directly suggested by the following words of Arviragus over Fidele's (or Imogen's) grave, in the scene just referred to :

> "With fairest flowers,
> While summer lasts, and I live here, Fidele,
> I'll sweeten thy sad grave : thou shalt not lack
> The flower that's like thy face, pale primrose;" etc.

13. **The red-breast oft**, etc. See n. on the *The Seasons*, "Winter," l. 246.

GRAY.

214. THOMAS GRAY (1716–1771), the author of some of the most finished, famous, and familiar short poems in the language, was a man of delicate health, shy habit, and refined and scholarly tastes. He was sent to Eton in 1727, where Horace Walpole, the son of the great Prime Minister, and Richard West were among his most intimate friends. He left Eton in 1734, and after spending about five years at Cambridge, went on a European tour with Horace Walpole. He quarrelled with Walpole, and returned to England in 1741. In the year following he spent some time at Stoke Pogis, a village in Buckinghamshire, some four miles from Eton. Here is the old parish church with its "ivy-mantled tower" and peaceful graveyard, which is generally considered to have been the scene of his *Elegy*. Here he composed his *Ode on a Distant Prospect of Eton College*. We must try to enter into Gray's situation at this time, to take account of all the influences at work upon him, if we would understand the mood which inspired the poem last named. He had come back into the vicinity of his schoolboy days after an absence of eight years. While thus brought face to face with the past through the influence of association, the recollections of those early days thus vividly reawakened had been saddened and embittered by two painful occurrences. One of these had but just taken place, while the other was still comparatively recent. The first was the death of Richard West, with whom Gray had continued on terms of affectionate intimacy ; the second the breach with Walpole alluded to above. Memories of death and estrangement,—the sorrows which come as an inevitable sequence to the unreflecting happiness of boyhood,— thus give the poem its pervading and sombre coloring. The *Eton College* ode was published in 1747, and was Gray's first public appearance. It was received with coldness and indifference. Gray had settled again in Cambridge in 1742, and there (except for brief and occasional absences) he spent the remainder of his life; a shy, sensitive, secluded scholar, reading much and writing little. He was buried in the "country churchyard" at Stoke Pogis.

ODE ON A DISTANT PROSPECT OF ETON COLLEGE.

(See also remarks on this poem in sketch of Gray, *supra*.)

214.—1. **Ye distant spires.** Mr. Gosse says that in Gray's own MS , which he has examined, the title reads *Ode on a distant prospect of Eton College, Windsor, and the adjacent country.* The addition further emphasizes the fact that the poet views the scene from a sufficient distance to command a view not of Eton alone, but of a wide surrounding prospect. The towers of Windsor crown a height on the southern side of the Thames ; immediately across the stream is Eton College, with Stoke Pogis still farther to the north. There is a ridge in the neighborhood of that village from which the ground slopes southward to the river. From this ridge, therefore, Gray could command a view of the distant spires of Eton with the antique towers of Windsor rising behind.—4. **Henry's holy shade.** Eton College was founded in 1440, by Henry VI., whose mild and saintly character is here alluded to. Cf. Gray's reference to him in *The Bard:* "And spare the meek usurper's holy head."—9. **Father Thames.** Dr. Johnson has the following characteristic comment : "The ' Prospect of Eton College' suggests nothing to Gray which every beholder does not equally think and feel. His supplication to Father Thames, to tell him, who drives the hoop or tosses the ball, is useless and puerile. Father Thames has no better means of knowing than himself." ("Gray" in *Lives of the Poets.*)

215.—12. **Margent Green.** Milton's phrase. See Echo's Song in *Comus*, p. 124. **Murm'ring labours,** i.e., some are studying their lessons by the time-honored method of repeating them over and over in a monotonous sing-song.

ELEGY IN A COUNTRY CHURCHYARD.

217. This little masterpiece, which, it has been asserted, is "for its size the most popular poem ever written in any language," was elaborated with the most patient and fastidious care. Begun at Stoke Pogis in 1742, it was finished at the same place in 1750, Gray having apparently labored at it during the interval at Cambridge and, possibly, elswhere. It was published in 1751, and, unlike the *Eton College* ode, achieved a success which was as immediate as it was surprising to its author. From that time until now its fame has suffered none of the usual alternations, and it has continued to be the familiar delight of successive generations. Professor Henry Reed remarked that no English poem had been translated into so many languages ; while Professor Gosse has recently declared that it "has exercised an influence on all the poetry of Europe, from Denmark to Italy, from France to Russia." The famous line of Vergil's which Gray thought of adopting as a motto for the poem, "*Sunt lachrymæ rerum, et mentem mortalia tangunt*" (The tears of the world are here, and mortal things touch the mind), this line embodies, as Gray perceived, one great reason for the poem's popularity. But it is not merely that in the poem Death, the great unescapable fact of human life, makes its universal appeal to the mind ; it is the beauty and appropriateness of the time and place, in perfect keeping with these reflections, the hush of twilight and the nameless spell of rural England, that, pervading the whole poem, give it its distinctive charm. Notable also is the wholly democratic character of its feeling. Unlike Shirley's splendid lines, it shows us death as the conqueror, not of kings, but of peasants, and the deepest pathos of the poem is interwoven with the thought of the narrow interests, the restricted opportunities, of those whose little day is over. Perhaps Burns the ploughboy, with all his hearty human fellowship, never spoke so directly to the universal human sympathy as did Gray the scholar, alienated all his days from the common interests of the men about him, and thus reaching the general heart of man once and once only.

217.—1. **The curfew tolls,** etc. Gray acknowledged that this line was an imitation of the beautiful opening of the eighth canto of Dante's *Purgatorio :*

> " *Se ode squilla di lontano,*
> *Che paia il giorno pianger che si muore ;* "

i.e., the pilgrim thrills

> "If he hear the vesper bell from far
> That seems to mourn for the expiring day."
>
> (Cary's trans.)

The identity of Gray's image with that of Dante becomes more apparent when we realize that the word *parting* (or *departing*) is here used in the sense of *dying*, as *I. Henry VI.*, II. 5 : "And peace, no war, before thy *parting* soul." Gray told Nicholls that he had first written *dying* day and then changed it to *parting*. Cf. Byron, *Don Juan*, Canto III. 108, when the twilight hour

> "Fills with love the pilgrim on his way
> As the far bell of vesper makes him start,
> Seeming to weep the *dying day's* decay."

2. Wind. "*Wind*, not *winds*, is the reading of all the MSS. and of all the early editions,—that of 1768, Mason's, Wakefield's, Mathias's, etc.,—but we find no note of the fact in Mitford's or any other of the more recent editions, which have substituted *winds*. Whether the change was made as an amendment or accidentally we do not know ; but the original reading seems to us by far the better one. The poet does not refer to the herd as an aggregate, but to the animals that compose it. He sees, not *it*, but *them* on their winding way." (Rolfe.)

218.—13. **Beneath those rugged elms.** "As he stands in the churchyard, he thinks only of the poorer people . . . because the better-to-do lay interred inside the church. . . . In Gray's time, and long before, and some time after it, the former resting-place was for the poor, the latter for the rich." (Hales.)—20. **Their lowly bed.** This does not mean the grave, but is rather to be taken literally. The sense becomes clearer if we connect the verse, not with the "narrow cell" of the one preceding, but with the stanza immediately following.

219.—43. **Provoke**, i.e., call forth (Lat. *pro-vocare*).—59. **Milton.** This passage contains two of Gray's many alterations. According to Mitford the names of *Milton* and of *Cromwell* were here substituted for those of *Tully* (Cicero) and *Cæsar*. It must be remembered that when Gray wrote, and for long after, Cromwell was commonly regarded as a monster of hypocrisy and unscrupulous ambition.

220.—83. **Holy text.** Mitford says on this passage : "As this construction is not, as it now stands, correct, I think that Gray originally wrote '*to teach*,' but altered it afterwards *euphonia gratia*, and made the grammar give way to the sound." —85. **For who, to dumb forgetfulness**, etc. Cf. *Par. Lost*, Bk. II. l. 146.

221.—93. **For thee** ; that is, Gray himself. How far **we**

are justified in concluding that the poet intended here to describe his own life and character is an open question ; but the youth's brooding melancholy and his fondness for solitude and nature are certainly in keeping with Gray's character.—119. **Fair science,** i.e., knowledge, learning.

THE BARD.

222. *The Bard* was published with Gray's ode on *The Progress of Poesy* in 1757. Readers of that time, who passed for persons of some cultivation, found both poems very obscure, and Gray was induced to add explanatory notes to a subsequent edition (1768).

In form *The Bard* is *Pindaric*, that is, it follows the odes of Pindar in its general metrical arrangement. Many of the best English odes are *irregular*, the endeavor being to make the metrical movement vary with the emotion. *The Bard* is a *regular* ode ; but the regularity of its form does not consist in the uniformity of its stanzas, but in the uniformity of the groups of stanzas into which the poem is divided. There are three such stanzaic groups in the poem, each composed of three stanzas, and each group corresponding metrically with the rest. The form is a highly artificial one, and critics justly doubt whether it is one really adapted to our language. Theodore Watts has said that rhetoric is "the great vice of the English ode"; and from this vice Gray's most ambitious odes, with their touch of buckram and formality, are certainly not exempt. Nevertheless the poetic merits of *The Bard* and its place among notable English poems have long been beyond question.

"This ode," Gray writes, "is founded on a tradition current in Wales that Edward I., when he completed the conquest of that country, ordered all the bards that fell into his hands to be put to death." He gives the original argument of the poem in his *Commonplace Book* as follows : "The army of Edward I., as they march through a deep valley and approach Mount Snowdon, are suddenly stopped by the appearance of a venerable figure seated on the summit of an inaccessible rock, who, with a voice more than human, reproaches the king with all the desolation and misery which he had brought on his country ; foretells the misfortunes of the Norman race, and with prophetic spirit declares that all his cruelty shall never extinguish the noble ardour of poetic genius in this island ; and that men shall never be wanting to celebrate true virtue and valour in immortal strains, to expose vice and infamous pleasure, and boldly censure tyranny and oppression. His song ended, he precipitates himself from the mountain and is swallowed up by the river that rolls at its foot."

The story of Edward's edict seems to have been more than a local tradition, as it is given without question in Warrington's *Hist. of Wales*, Vol. II. 298 ; Jones's *Relicks of the Welsh Bards*, p. 38, and in other early authorities.

222.—8. **Cambria** = Wales. See Camber-Britans n. on title of Drayton's *Agincourt*, p. 601.—13. **Stout Glo'ster.** "Gilbert de Clare, Earl of Gloucester and Hereford, had, in 1282, conducted the war in South Wales ; and after overthrowing the enemy near Llandeilo Fawr, had reinforced the King in the northwest." (Hales.)—14. **Mortimer.** Edward de Mortimer actively co operated with the King in North Wales.

223.—16. **Conway's foaming flood.** A river in North Wales. Edward I. afterwards built Conway Castle near its mouth. The student should consult some good map for the general topography of the poem.—28. **High-born Hoel's harp,** etc. All the commentators assume that Gray gave to each of the slaughtered bards here mentioned the name of some veritable Welsh bard or ruler. They have accordingly taken great pains to identify the various persons whose names they think the poet here employed. In one instance it certainly seems probable that Gray thus borrowed the name of some actual person. In referring to the *high-born Hoel* it is likely that he had in mind *Howel ab Owain*, a bard of the latter twelfth century, who was one of the most melodious and unaffected of the Welsh singers. (Stephen's *Literature of the Kymrie*, 42; *Ency. Brit.*, "Celtic Lit." 319.) But the assumption that we are bound to thus furnish an original for each of the five bards referred to by name is entirely unnecessary and involves us in difficulties of our own creating. Thus as no *bard* could be found by the name of Llewyllen, we are told that some one *not* a bard must be intended. It has accordingly been held that by "soft Llewyllen's lay" we are to understand, not the songs composed by an imaginary bard whom Gray has chosen to distinguish by a representative Welsh name, but the lays sung *to* Llewyllen ap Gruffed, the last king of Wales and the antagonist of Edward I. This is a most strained and forced construction of a perfectly simple phrase: it totally overlooks the fact that the speaker, a bard, would hardly allude to his king as one of the "dear lost companions of his tuneful art" who has perished by the Edict; and it leads us to ask why a famous warrior king should be spoken of as "soft." Prof. Rolfe endeavors to extricate himself from this last difficulty by quoting from certain bardic tributes to Llewyllen, one of which states that though he "killed with fury in battle, yet he was a *mild* prince when the mead-horns were distributed." The simpler explanation would appear to be that, at least in the greater number of cases, Gray gave his dead bards names in keeping with their nationality, as a novelist of Scottish or Irish life would style one of his characters MacGregor or O'Rourke. —30. **That hushed the stormy main.** So far as I can ascertain, Gray had no particular incident or tradition in mind either here or in the following reference to Modred and Plinlimmon. He simply gave to the imaginary bard Cadwallo a power often attributed to poets of quieting the troubled waters by song. Mitford cites :

> "Uttering such dulcet and harmonious breath
> That the rude sea grew civil at her song."
> *Mid. N. Dream*, A. II. Sc. 1, l. 147.

35. **Arvon's shore,** i.e., on the coast of Carnarvonshire (Arvon = Caernarvon = Caer-yn-Arvon, the camp in Arvon).

224.—54. **Severn.** The river Severn flows near to Berkley Castle in Gloucestershire, where Edward II. was murdered. His shrieks are said by Holinshed to have been heard in the town of Berkley.—57. **She-wolf of France,** i.e., Isabelle, daughter of Philip the Fair, King of France, and wife of Edward II. She allied herself with Mortimer to compass the ruin of her husband. Cf. Shakespeare, *III. Henry VI.* I. 4. 111.—60. **Scourge of heaven.** Edward III., the invader of France, who, after his early triumphs, had an unhappy and solitary end.—67. **Sable warrior.** Edward the Black Prince, eldest son of Edward III. who died before his father.

225.—79. **Reft of a crown.** Richard II., who is said by the early writers to have been starved to death.—83. **Din of battle** The Wars of the Roses, 1455-1485.—87. **Towers of Julius.** The Tower of London, popularly supposed to have been first erected by Julius Cæsar but in reality not earlier than William the Conqueror.—90. **Meek usurper.** Henry VI. (See note on *Eton College Ode*, l. 4.) His consort was Margaret of Anjou, and his father Henry V., famous for his victories in France. — 93. **Bristled boar.** "The silver boar was the badge of Richard III., whence he was usually known in his own time by the name of *the Boar.*" (Gray.) — 97. **Sudden fate.** About five years after Edward's conquest of Wales his queen, Eleanor,—the half of his heart,—was taken ill during his absence and died before he could rejoin her. (Strickland's *Queens of England*, I. 291.)

226.—115 **Form divine.** i.e., Queen Elizabeth. She is of the "Briton line," being the granddaughter of Henry VII., who was descended, on his father's side, from the British, or Welsh, family of Tudor.—121. **Taliesin.** One of the most famous British bards of the sixth century.

227.—133. **Distant warblings,** etc., i.e., the poets succeeding Milton, who is referred to in the preceding lines. They grow more distant to the bard as they become farther away from him in point of time.

GOLDSMITH.

227. OLIVER GOLDSMITH was born in Pallas, Ireland, in 1728, and died in London in 1774. He had come to the capital in 1757, just twenty years later than Dr. Johnson. *The Traveller*, which laid the foundation of his fame as a poet, appeared in 1764, and was followed by *The Deserted Village* in 1770. The fifteen years of Goldsmith's literary activity were years of rapidly shifting standards in English society, literature, and politics. Goldsmith, surrounded by change, was not identified wholly with either the old order or the new.

THE DESERTED VILLAGE.

227. The didactic object of this poem, as Goldsmith explains in his letter of dedication to Sir Joshua Reynolds, is to call attention to the depopulation of England (which the poet erroneously believed to be then taking place) and to show the evil effects of luxury on the well-being of a State. It is the fashion to praise the poem for its character studies and its portrayal of village life, and either to condemn what is declared to be its fallacious political economy, or else to condone its economic errors as immaterial from a poetical point of view. Thus a recent biographer of Goldsmith remarks: "We must admit, after all, that it is a poetical exigency rather than a political economy that has decreed the destruction of the loveliest village of the plain." (Life in *E. M. L.* 120.) Long before this Macaulay complained (Essay on *Goldsmith*) that Auburn was an English village in its prosperity, but an Irish in its decay, and that by thus confusing the rural life of the two countries the poet had been so grossly untrue to fact as to seriously injure his poem as a work of art. Goldsmith himself says that he "has taken all possible pains" to be certain of his facts, and declares that his description of the village's decline is based upon his personal observation of conditions in England "for these four or five years past." In his opinion that England was becoming depopulated Goldsmith was entirely mistaken, the exact opposite being, in fact, the case. This, however, was a matter for the statistician, and beyond the sphere of the individual observer. On the other hand, when the conditions were ascertainable by personal observation, it will be found that Goldsmith was far truer to facts than his critics have commonly supposed.

We gather that the *Village* is ruined by a consolidation of the separate holdings of small owners in the hand of one tyrannical proprietor. The poet sees that throughout the land a new aristocracy of wealth is pushing aside the small farmer (ll. 65-69); that the great places of the large landowners take up a space " that many poor supplied " (ll. 270-280); and that the harvests are correspondingly diminished. He complains that even the commons, formerly open to the poor, are shut off, or "denied" (l. 307), and, finally, that the source of the national corruption is luxury, the outcome of a rapid growth in material prosperity. The latest researches confirm Goldsmith's substantial correctness on these points. The extinction of the small farmers through the enclosure of the commons, the acquisition of large tracts by wealthy proprietors, etc., and the breaking up of homes as a consequence of this change,—these are facts in the economic history of the time. "Multitudes of poor men who, without any legal right, had found a home upon the common land were driven away homeless and without conpensation." (Lecky, *Hist. Eng. in 18th Cent.* VI. 193-99; *Social England*, V. 337.) The hardships that Goldsmith pictured were not fanciful; where he erred was in asserting that the poor thus dispossessed were forced to emigrate in such numbers that the land was becoming depopulated. It is but just to a poet more distinguished, as a rule, for charm, than for exactness of statement, to show that in one case at least the inaccuracy is on the part of his critics. As poetry, *The Deserted Village* needs neither defence nor commendation. (See *Int. Eng. Lit.* 282-291.)

227.—1. **Sweet Auburn.** This village is not to be found on the map. There is, indeed, an Auburn in Wiltshire, but it is not Goldsmith's. Attempts have been made to show that the poem describes *Lissoy*, a town in Westmeath, Ireland, where Goldsmith's childish years were spent. Probably the poet used such of his early recollections as suited his purpose, idealizing them as he pleased, and not imposing on his imagination any slavish adherence to fact. (See Howitt's *Homes and Haunts of the British Poets*, 203.)—12. **Decent** = having a neat, uiobtrusive beauty (Lat. *decens*, involving the idea of symmetry and fitness). Cf. Milton, *Il Penseroso*, l. 36, and Pope, *Elegy on an Unfortunate Lady*, l. 52.

229.—53. **Princes and lords,** etc. See *Int. Eng. Lit.* 276. Hales refers to Burns's *Cotter's Saturday Night*, l. 165 (p. 278), "Princes and lords are but the breath of kings," and his *For a' that and a' that* (p. 291), " A prince can mak' a belted knight," etc.

230.—83. **In all my wand'rings.** See Thackeray's comment on this passage in *English Humorists*, 332.

231.—122. **Vacant** here does not mean lacking in intelligence, but free from worry or anxiety. — 126. **Fluctuate in the gale.** Note how exactly this is in the stereotyped early eighteenth-century manner of Pope and his followers, while the description immediately succeeding (129, etc.) is, in subject at least, akin to Wordsworth (cf. *The Leech-gatherer*). So Goldsmith touched both the past and the future.—140. **The village preacher.** A famous portrait of one of the lasting types in English society. Cf. Chaucer's *Prol.* to *Canterbury Tales*, 479–530, Fielding's Parson Adams, and Goldsmith's own *Vicar of Wakefield*. Irving says: "The picture of the village pastor, . . . taken in part from the character of his [Goldsmith's] father, embodied likewise recollections of his brother Henry: for the natures of the father and son seem to have been identical." Goldsmith had lost this brother recently, and the freshness of his grief doubtless gave an additional tenderness to the description.

233.—196. **The village master.** The original of the schoolmaster is supposed to be Goldsmith's own teacher in the village school at Lissoy, a certain Thomas (or, as he was irreverently nicknamed, Paddy) Byrne—an old soldier who had seen service. (See Irving's *Life of Goldsmith*.)

234.—232. **The twelve good rules.** "These were: '1. Urge no healths; 2. Profane no divine ordinances; 3. Touch no state matters; 4. Reveal no secrets; 5. Pick no quarrels; 6. Make no comparisons; 7. Maintain no ill opinions; 8. Keep no bad company; 9. Encourage no vice; 10. Make no long meals; 11. Repeat no grievances; 12. Lay no wagers.' These rules were ascribed to Charles I. Goldsmith in the fragment describing an author's bedchamber speaks of them as 'the twelve rules the royal martyr drew.' Cf. Crabbe, *Parish Register:*

> "There is King Charles and all his golden rules
> Who proved Misfortune's was the best of schools.'"

(Rolfe.)

232. **The royal game of goose.** Either a board for playing the game of fox and geese (see Strutt's *Sports and Pastimes*, Bk. IV. Ch. II. § XIV), or one for "The Game of Goose," a game entirely distinct from one the first named. (See *Ib.* Bk. IV. Ch. II. § XXV.)—244. **Woodman's ballad,** i.e., the forester's, or hunter's, song.

235.—257. **Vacant mind.** See n. to l. 122, *supra.*—266. **The rich man's joys increase,** etc. Goldsmith's anticipation of much of the modern feeling against wealth in certain quarters has not received sufficient attention. Careful examination of contemporary conditions shows that the poet's views were at

least not without some basis of fact. Gibben says : "The fact
has been that after the introduction of the new industrial system (i.e., cir. 1760), the condition of the working classes rapidly declined," etc. (*Industrial Hist. Eng.* 192, *Ib.* 186.) Lecky
says: "Shortly after the Peace of 1763, however, there were
evident signs that the population was beginning to press upon
the means of subsistence. The export of corn diminished ; the
price rose, and several temporary Acts were passed to relieve
the scarcity." (*Hist. of Eng. in the 18th Cent.*, VI. 193.)—269.
Proud swells the tide, etc. The idea apparently is, that while
more money comes into the country, it is received in return
for necessaries, some of which are needed for domestic consumption. As the money thus obtained goes to increase the
luxury of the rich, it does not add to the substantial prosperity of the community as a whole. The actual product of
the necessaries of life remains the same ; and the rich man
uses his superabundant wealth to encroach on the lands that
once supplied the needs of the poor.

236.—295. **By luxury betrayed.** The increase in luxury and
extravagance of living, among the industrial and trading, as
well as the upper, classes, was a prominent feature of the
time. "It was a change," says Lecky, "not without grave
social and moral evils." (See *Hist. of Eng. in the 18th Cent.*,
VI. 184 *et seq*) It is perhaps unkind to remember that poor
Goldsmith, with his fine clothes and his unpaid tailor's bill,
was an example of improvidence, not a type of frugality.
—308. **The bare-worn common,** etc. "No less than 700 Enclosure Acts were passed between 1760 and 1774. The old
common fields were beginning to disappear, and the working
classes also lost their rights of pasturing cattle on the wastes,
for the wastes were enclosed." (Gibben's *Industrial Hist. of
Eng.* 153.) "Districts once covered with small arable farms
were turned into immense pastures, and there were complaints that a single man monopolized a tract which had
formerly supported twelve or fourteen industrious families.
*Whole villages which had depended on free pasture-land and fuel
dwindled and perished, and a stream of emigrants passed to
America.*" (Lecky. *Hist. of Eng. in the 18th Cent.*, VI. 202
and n.)--316. **Artist** here means *artisan*, or *mechanic*—a
common use in Goldsmith's time.—325. **Houseless shivering
female.** Goldsmith's sympathy with the unfortunate did not
spend itself in poetical expressions. He once left the whist-
table and rushed into the street to relieve the misery of a
woman whom he heard "half singing and half sobbing" outside. (See Irving's *Life of Goldsmith*, Ch. XXXV.)

237.—344. "Wild Altama," i e., the river *Altamaha*, or
Alahamha, in Georgia. Oglethorpe secured Letters Patent

for the Colony of Georgia in 1732. As it was flourishing at the time Goldsmith wrote, and as it was started as an asylum for the oppressed, there is a special pertinence in the allusion.

238.—355. **Crouching tigers.** Some commentators object to this on the ground that there are no tigers in Georgia; Rolfe thinks that the reference is to the jaguar and the puma, "the American tigers." Probably the actual presence or absence of the tiger was a matter about which Goldsmith was utterly indifferent. There are similar errors in other parts of the description. Goldsmith wanted tigers for poetical purposes, as Shakespeare required lions in the forest of Arden.

239.—407. **And thou, sweet Poetry,** etc. Carlyle calls Goldsmith "the one only English poet of the period" (essay on *Goethe*); but while poetry was at a low ebb, the condition was not so bad as Carlyle asserts, for the tide had already turned. Gray, still living, had recently enriched English poetry, and Chatterton had published two notable poems shortly before this time. Percy's *Reliques* (1765) and *Ossian* (1762) may also be mentioned.

240.—418. **Torno's cliffs.** "There is a river Tornea (or Torneo, as it is sometimes written) flowing into the Gulf of Bothnia, and forming part of the boundary between Sweden and Russia. There is also a Lake Tornea in the extreme northern part of Sweden. Cf. Campbell : 'Cold as the rocks on Torneo's hoary brow.' *Pambamarca* is said to be a mountain near Quito." (Rolfe.)—427. **Trade's proud empire,** etc. "Goldsmith's fallacy," says Hales, "lies in identifying trade and luxury." The view is, of course, a partial one, the prosperity both of modern England and of the United States being largely founded on trade ; at the same time any impartial and clear-seeing American should admit that "the rage of gain" has its drawbacks.

CHATTERTON.

240.—THOMAS CHATTERTON (1752–1770) was the son of a schoolmaster at Bristol. An apparently instinctive delight in the romantic atmosphere of the Middle Ages was stimulated and developed by his earliest surroundings. His uncle was sexton of the beautiful old church of St. Mary Redcliffe, a position held by members of the family through many generations. This church, rich in relics of the past, was part of Chatterton's life from the first ; he learned his alphabet from the illustrated capitals of an old folio taken from its store of MSS. As a boy he dreamed himself back in the past, and between 1760 and 1770 he wrote poems which he pretended were the work of a monk of the fifteenth century, whom he called Thomas Rowley. After some unsuccessful attempts to bring his work before the public, he went up to London in 1770, resolved upon a literary career. He fought manfully for two months against the great city; but disappointment, poverty, and neglect were too strong for him. Hopeless, hungry to starvation, and too proud to accept charity, he poisoned himself and was found dead in a garret littered with the torn fragments of his verse. By promise, he is the most extraordinary poetic genius in the annals of the literature. In performance he is, if not, as Theodore Watts asserted, the father of that Romanticism which later found voice in Coleridge, Scott, and Keats, at least one of the earliest and most influential figures in the Mediæval Revival. It is noteworthy that the same decade which saw the composition of his mediæval poems saw also the publication of Horace Walpole's mediæval romance *The Castle of Otranto* and of Percy's *Reliques*.

THE BALLAD OF CHARITIE.

242.—The full title of this poem as originally given by Chatterton was, *An Excelente Balad of Charitie: As Wroten bie the Gode Prieste Thomas Rowleie, 1464.* Theodore Watts has pronounced it as perhaps "the most purely artistic work of Chatterton's time." After speaking of Chatterton as the successor in romanticism of Coleridge and others, he thus goes on to point out the close relationship between Chatterton and Keats. "It is difficult to express in words wherein lies the entirely spiritual kinship between Chatterton's *Ballad of Charity* and Keats's *Eve of St. Agnes*, yet I should be sceptical as to the insight of any critic who should fail to recognize that kinship. Not only are the beggar and the thunderstorm depicted with the sensuous sympathy and melodious insistence which is the great charm of *The Eve of St. Agnes*, but the movement of the lines is often the same. Take for instance the description of Keats's bedesman, 'meagre, barefoot, wan,' which is, in point of metrical movement, identical with Chatterton's description of the alms-craver, 'withered, for-wynd, dead.'"

242.—1. **In Virginè,** i.e., in the sign of the Zodiac known as *Virgo*, or the Virgin. That is, in September or at the time of the autumnal equinox. 5. **Chelandry** = goldfinch. Chatterton. *Chelaundre* is an obsolete form of *calandra*, a kind of lark.—7. **Aumere.** Here erroneously used as "a loose robe or mantle." The actual meaning is an almspurse or bag.—15. **Holm** = holly tree. (See *Faerie Queene*, Bk. I. C. I. 1. 81 and n.)

243.—31. **Ghastness** = terror. "Do you perceive the ghastness of her eye?" (*Othello*, V. 1.)—34. **Levin** = lightning. (M. E. *levene*, *levyn* = lightning.) *Faerie Queene*, Bk. V. C. VI. l. 40.—45. **Chapournette.** "A small round hat, . . . formerly worn by ecclesiastics and lawyers." (Chatterton.) (Fr. *chapournet* = a small hood.)—47. **Bederoll.** To tell one's beads backwards was "a figurative expression to signify cursing." (Chatterton.)

244.—50. **Cope** = cloak ; mantle. (See *Centy. Dict.*)—52. **Autremete.** Chatterton here means by this word "a loose white robe worn by priests."—63. **Crouch** = crucifix, cross (Lat. *crux*, M. E. *crouche*).—74. **Jape** = "a short surplice, worn by friars of an inferior class, and secular priests."—75. **Limitour.** A friar licensed to beg, and *limited* to a certain specified district. (See Chaucer's *Prologue* to *The Knight's Tale*, l. 209.)

245.—87. **Semi-cope** = "a short under-cloak."—90. **Glour** = glory (Fr. *gloire*).

COWPER.

245. In the succession of poets that prepared the way for Wordsworth, and those who came with and after him, WILLIAM COWPER (1731–1800) holds an honorable and important place. The close relations in which he stands to the poets who immediately precede or follow him are apparent to every thoughtful reader and cannot now be enlarged upon. *The Task*, for instance, may be appropriately placed between *The Seasons* on the one hand and *The Excursion* on the other. His relations to the new England springing up about him are equally important. He touches it at many points : its renewal of religious fervor ; its growing love of country-life ; its antagonism to the constraint and artificiality of great cities ; its love of animals ; its tender pity for suffering ; its generous championship of the wronged and the oppressed. To appreciate the real meaning of Cowper's work, we must remember his convictions and the spirit in which he wrote. The poems and passages given in the text are, in many cases, personal revelations, and they must be read in the light of our knowledge of the man and his time.

Cowper did not write of the country in the midst of the din of London : his poetry of nature was composed under the quieting influence of the scenes he describes. After failing to make his way in the capital, he retired into Huntingdonshire in 1765, leaving worldly ambition behind him, and leading (except for a few devoted friends) the life of a recluse. He had his dog and his pet hares, and he rambled through fields and woods, or meditated beside the lazy waters of his favorite Ouse. In 1779 he joined his friend Rev. John Newton in the publication of a book of hymns. Two volumes of verse followed, the second of which contained *John Gilpin* (1785). *The Task*, incomparably the best of his longer poems, appeared in 1785; in the year following Burns published his first volume, *Poems Chiefly in the Scotch Dialect*. The gloom that had long darkened Cowper's life deepened towards the close. His mind had long been affected, and at the last his state became pitiable in the extreme. Possessed by a marked religious melancholy, he looked upon himself as an outcast from the Divine mercy. Out of the darkness of his last years come two sad but beautiful poems, *Lines on the Receipt of my Mother's Picture* and *The Castaway*. The latter was his last original poem.

THE TASK.

BOOK I. THE SOFA.

700. Reynolds. At this time Sir Joshua Reynolds (1723–1792) was at the height of his fame as a painter. For about sixteen years he had been President of the Royal Academy, and the year before *The Task* was published had been appointed painter to the king.

246.—**702. Bacon.** John Bacon (1740–1799), who at this time held in sculpture a position somewhat comparable to that of Reynolds in painting.—**704. Chatham.** William Pitt, Earl of Chatham, one of the greatest of English orators. He had been dead for about six years when *The Task* appeared.

247.—**722 Increasing London.** The population of England increased rapidly toward the end of the eighteenth century; the greater part of the increase being in the towns. This of course was due to the growth of manufactures, commerce, and the Enclosure Acts. In 1750 the population of London was about 600,000; by 1801 it had increased to 864,035. (See note to Goldsmith's *Deserted Village*, l. 308.)—**732. In denouncing death**, etc. The penal laws, at this time, were both cruel and illogical. To give only a few illustrations: to steal a sheep or a horse, to cut down another's trees, to pick a man's pocket of more than twelve pence, were all crimes punishable with death. On the other hand, it was not a capital offence for a man to attempt to murder his father or to stab another severely, provided his victim did not die from his wounds. Sir Samuel Romilly (1757–1818) was the first to effect any important reforms in these barbarous laws. (See Lecky's *Hist. of Eng. in the 18th Centy.* Vol. VI. Ch. XXIII.)

248.—755. **Know no fatigue**, etc. Compare note to Goldsmith's *Deserted Village*, l. 266.

BOOK II. THE TIME-PIECE.

249.—40. **Slaves cannot breathe in England.** The question as to whether slaves were legally emancipated by being brought to England was not settled until 1772. Then a sick slave, named Somerset, was dismissed by the master who had brought him to England. When the slave recovered, his former master forcibly seized him, in order that he might sell him in Jamaica. The case was brought before Lord Mansfield, who decided in Somerset's favor, and held that every slave, as soon as he touched England, acquired his freedom. Wilberforce, Sharpe, and others, worked hard for the total abolition of slavery, and in 1787 the Society for the Suppression of Slavery was instituted. The Abolition Act, however, was not passed until 1807.

BOOK III. THE GARDEN.

108. **I was a stricken deer**, etc. Cowper suffered from attacks of terrible dejection, which several times resulted in insanity. After he had recovered from the worst of one of these, he gave up all hope of succeeding at the bar.

BOOK IV. THE WINTER'S EVENING.

250.—5. **He comes, the herald**, etc. Palmer's mail-coaches, which were started in 1784, considerably improved the postal service. There were many places, however, still dependent on postboys, who travelled on horseback over the rough and less frequented roads. In 1771 the press finally obtained the right to criticise and publish Parliamentary proceedings; and about and after that time many important newspapers were founded. —10. **Inn.** This was an inn in Olney called "The Swan." There is one there at the present time, of the same name, but not in the exact location of the one so called when Cowper wrote.

251.—28. **Is India free?** In 1784 Pitt introduced a bill for the government of India, which was a subject of much general interest and discussion. England was feeling the weight of her responsibilities in regard to it, and India had suffered much from oppression and injustice. Her cause, however, was soon to be investigated in the famous trial of Warren Hastings, which was begun in 1786. It is interesting to remember that Hastings was at one time a schoolfellow of Cowper's.—39. **The cups**, etc. Although there is mention made of tea by an Englishman as early as 1615, it does not seem to have been used in England until the middle of the seventeenth century. When first introduced, it was such an expensive luxury that it was not in general use until much later. By 1785, however, it could be bought for five or six shillings per pound.—120. **Oh Winter!** The fact that most of *The Task* was written during a particularly severe winter, accounts for the numerous and accurate descriptions of that season.

252.—243. **Come Evening**. Compare this with Milton's beautiful description, "Now came still Evening on", etc. (*Par. Lost*, Bk. IV. 598.)

254.—364. **That breathes the spleen.** Cf. n. to ll. 16 and 59, in C. IV. of *The Rape of the Lock.*—367. **The poor beasts.** Note here the care and sympathy shown for animals which appears so often in Cowper; see, e.g., the often-quoted passage beginning, "I would not enter on my list of friends" (Bk. VI. 560).

BOOK VI. THE WINTER WALK AT NOON.

66. **The embattled tower** is thought to refer to the church at Emberton, which is about a mile from Olney.

ON THE RECEIPT OF MY MOTHER'S PICTURE.

257. This picture was a miniature painted in oils by Heines. "In acknowledging the receipt of the gift, the poet says (February 27, 1790): 'The world could not have furnished you with a present so acceptable to me as the picture which you have so kindly sent me. I received it the night before last, and viewed it with a trepidation of nerves and spirits somewhat akin to what I should have felt had the dear original presented herself to my embraces. I kissed it and hung it where it is the last object that I see at night, and of course the first upon which I open my eyes in the morning. She died when I completed my sixth year, yet I remember her well and am an oracular witness of the great fidelity of the copy.'" (*The Life of William Cowper*, by Thomas Wright. 512.)

ON THE LOSS OF THE ROYAL GEORGE.

261. The Royal George, a vessel in the British navy, was lost off Spithead, August 29, 1792. The ship had been heeled over for repairs. While the crew were at dinner, she was struck by a sudden squall, and, the leeward deck-ports being left open, she rapidly filled and sank. From six to eight hundred men are said to have perished. Admiral Kempenfelt, who was in command, was the son of Col. Kempenfelt of

Sweden, immortalized by Addison in the *Sir Roger De Coverley Papers* under the name of Captain Sentry.

THE CASTAWAY.

262. This poem was written in 1799. It is founded on an incident related in *Anson's Voyages*, but those who know Cowper's history will have no difficulty in seeing that it is rather a touching record of the poet's own spiritual experience.

263.—25. **Some succor**, etc. In the early part of 1797 Cowper sank into a state of dejection, and the efforts of his friends to help him were like "the cask, the coop, the floated cord," of but temporary avail.

BLAKE.

264. WILLIAM BLAKE (1757-1827), painter, poet, and (as he esteemed himself) seer and prophet, had his own distinctive and recognized part and place in the rise of the new poetry. He was "at ten years of age an artist, at twelve a poet." His *Poetical Sketches* were published in 1783, his *Songs of Innocence* in 1789, and the companion volume, the *Songs of Experience*, in 1794. His best known and most intelligible poems are contained in one or the other of these three books, but besides these he produced a mass of poetry of an obscure and allegorical character. It is not in these so-called "prophetic books," fascinating as they may be to the enthusiastic or curious student, that we are to look for Blake's most vital contribution to literature; it is in his lyrics. There he touches the deepest questions with the simplicity of an inspired child; there, as the poet of the sacred mystery of childhood, he is the precursor of Wordsworth. Many of those new convictions which we have noted as dominating the poetry of Cowper and the poets of the new order, are found also in Blake, but impressed with the marks of his own peculiar personality.

TO THE MUSES.

264. This poem was written in 1783. The complaint of the dearth of poetic expression at this time is well founded, as Goldsmith and Gray were dead, and neither Burns nor Wordsworth had begun their work.

THE TIGER.

270. The unison of grace and malignity in the tiger confounds Blake, and he asks: "Did He who made the Lamb make thee?" Many men of diverging opinions have wondered over the presence of suffering and cruelty as part of the appointed order of the created world. (Cf. Tennyson's *In Memoriam*, LV., and *Maud*, IV., and also *Int. Eng. Lit.* 474–5.)

BURNS.

272. ROBERT BURNS, the greatest poet of Scotland, was born at Alloway in Ayrshire, January 25, 1759. His father held a small farm; his family had been farmers for generations. Burns, who thus came out of the great toiling mass of the Scottish people, was himself a farmer, sharing the toils, anxieties, hardships, and pleasures that were the common lot of the men of his class. It was a song-writing age in Scotland, and Burns wrote songs. His first poem is said to have been composed in 1775, when he was in his seventeenth year. Ten years later he entered upon a period of remarkable productiveness, and during 1785–6 produced an astonishing number of poems of high rank. These were included in his first volume of *Poems* (1786), which contained, among others, *The Cotter's Saturday Night*, *The Twa Dogs*, *The Jolly Beggars*, *The Mountain Daisy*. A second edition appeared in the following year, and a fuller collection in 1793. Burns died in 1796, at thirty-seven; it is astonishing to reflect that all the work on which his fame rests was produced within little more than ten years. Most of the longer poems belong to the earlier half of this brief period, while to the later belong many of his best songs. Sheer force—masculine, native, power—is perhaps the most predominant characteristic of the poems of the earlier time; melody, tenderness, intensity, of those of the later. This original power, manifest in such works as *The Jolly Beggars* and akin to that displayed in the prose of Fielding or the art of Hogarth, had long been absent from the poetry of England.

THE COTTER'S SATURDAY NIGHT.

272. According to Robert's brother Gilbert, this poem owes its existence to the deep impression made upon the poet by the simple family worship, regularly held in his own as in other Scotch households, before retiring for the night. From a child, Burns had watched his father hold this nightly service of Bible-reading and prayer, and after his father's death had himself—as eldest son—succeeded to this solemn duty. Gilbert says that Robert had frequently remarked to him "that he thought there was something peculiarly venerable in the phrase, 'Let us worship God!' used by a decent, sober head of a family introducing family worship. To this sentiment of the author the world is indebted for 'The Cotter's Saturday Night.'"

272.—1. **Much-respected friend.** Robert Aiken, a solicitor and tax-surveyor in Ayr, was a patron of Burns and an admirer of his poetry. He excelled as an orator and elocutionist, and rendered Burns' verses so effectively that the poet declared he "read him" into fame. There are numerous allusions to him scattered through Burns' poetry.—10. **Sugh** = a rustling sound, a rush of wind, or flaw.—15. **Moil** = drudgery. The original meaning of the verb to *moil* being to *moisten*, and secondarily to *dirty* or *bedaub*, the noun is naturally associated with toil of a grimy or dirty character.—16. **Mattocks.** Tools resembling a pickaxe.

273.—21. **Stacher** = stagger (also written *stacker, stakker*). —22. **Flichterin'** = fluttering.—23. **Ingle** = fireplace.—26. **Kiaugh** = carking.—28. **Belvye** = by-and-bye, presently. —30. **Ca'** = drive. This word is thought to be quite distinct from our verb *call*. To ca' a nail = to drive a nail (see Jamison's *Ety. Dict. of the Scottish Lang.*).—30. **Tentie rin a cannie errand** = careful run a quiet errand.—34. **Braw** = fine, gay. (Eng. *brave* = splendid, gorgeous).—35. **Sair won penny-fee** = hard-earned wages.—38. **Spiers** = enquires.—40. **Uncos** = strange happenings. *Unco* is primarily *unknown*, the equivalent of *uncouth*, for which see *Cent. Dict.*—44. **Gars** = makes. —48. **Eydent** = diligent.

274.—49. **Jauk** = trifle, or, as we would say, to fool.—62. **Hafflins** = half.—64. **Ben** = inside, or, more particularly, into the inner room. In two-roomed houses the outer apartment, or hall, was called the *but*, the inner, containing the fireside, *ben*. Hence, to be *far-ben* with any one meant to be on intimate terms.—67. **Cracks** = chats.—**Kye** = cows.—69. **Blate and laithfu'** = bashful and sheepish.—72. **Lave** = rest.

275.—92. **Halesome parritch** = wholesome porridge.—93. **Soupe** = liquid, i.e., the milk.—**Hawkie** = cow.—94. **Hallan** = wall. In Scotch cottages the hallan is the partition dividing the *but* from the *ben* (see note to l. 64, *supra*).—96. **Weel-hain'd kebbuck** = well-saved cheese.—**Fell** = strong, pungent. —99. **Sin' lint was i' the bell** = since flax was in the flower.— 103. **Ha' Bible** is literally *hall Bible*, i.e., the Bible of the household (ha', or hal = *hold*, or dwelling).

276.—104. **Bonnet.** In the English of Shakespeare and Milton *bonnet* often means a *cap* or *head-covering* worn by men or boys. In Scotland the use is still retained. The *Blue-bonnet*, a blue woollen cap, is so much used by the Scotch that "*the Blue-bonnets*" is sometimes equivalent to "*the Scotch*."

(See Scott's *Border Ballad*, p. 375.)—105. **Lyart haffets** = gray temples, i.e., the locks of gray about his temples.—107. **Wales** = selects.—111, 112, 113. **Dundee, Martyrs,** and **Elgin** are among the most familiar and characteristic of the Scottish hymn-tunes.—113. **Beets** = fans.

277.—135. **Bab'lon's doom.** See *Rev.* ch. xviii.—137. **The saint, the father, and the husband,** etc. The "priest-like father" of the simple home, worshipping with his family about him,—it is round this that the whole poem moves. Our conception of the Scotch peasant in his religious earnestness and patriarchal dignity is deepened and exalted by this noble and suggestive line.—138. **Springs exulting,** etc. Cf. Pope's *Windsor Forest*, l. 111, 112:

> "The whirring pheasant springs,
> And mounts exulting on triumphant wings:—"

278.—165. **Princes and lords,** etc. Cf. as another example of the rising tide of democratic feeling in the latter half of the eighteenth century, Goldsmith's *Deserted Village*, 53.

TO A MOUSE.

279.—4. **Bickerin' brattle.** 'Hurrying flight' is perhaps the nearest English equivalent, but it gives no notion of the force of the Scotch. Confusion and tumult are suggested, as well as rapid flight. Cf. for English use of *bicker*, Tennyson's *Brook.*—6. **Pattle** = "a stick with which the ploughman clears away the earth that adheres to the plough." (Jamieson.) —13. **Whyles** = sometimes.—15. **A daimen icker in a thrave** = an occasional ear in twenty-four sheaves. The *thraves*, as set up in the fields, consisted of two stooks, or shocks, of corn of twelve sheaves each.—21. **Big** = build.—22. **Foggage** = rank grass; growing here among the grain.—24. **Snell** = bitter, sharp.

280.—34. **But** = without.—36. **Cranreuch** = hoar-frost.— 40. **Agley** = askew. (Literally to go off the right line; glance obliquely.)

TO A MOUNTAIN DAISY.

3. **Stoure** = dust stirred up, or in motion. The primary idea of *stoure* is commotion, agitation; but the word is applied to objects, or to a number of persons in a state of disturbance. Here it is the moving dust, but it is similarly used of particles of water or flying spray.—9. **Weet** = wet.

281.—21. **Bield** = refuge, shelter.—23. **Histy** = dry, barren.—39. **Card,** possibly chart, but more probably used here for compass. The *card*, or compass-card, on which the points were given, was often used for the compass itself. Cf. *Macbeth*, I. 3: "All the quarters that they knew i' the *shipman's card*."

TAM O'SHANTER.

282. The original of *Tam O'Shanter* is supposed to be one Douglas Graham, tenant of the farm of Shanter. He is said to have been "noted for his convivial habits, which his wife's ratings tended rather to confirm than to eradicate." He had a long-tailed gray mare, whose tail was picked by certain jokers while she stood outside the tavern waiting for her master. Graham was sure that the mischief had been done by the witches at Alloway Kirk. (See Henley and Henderson's *Burns*, I. 437.)

The poem was composed in the autumn of 1790. According to Gilbert Burns its origin was as follows: Robert, having become intimate with a certain antiquarian named Captain Grose, asked him to make a drawing of Alloway Kirk, adding that there were many good witch-stories connected with it. The picture of the kirk Burns wished Grose to include in a book he was then engaged in preparing. The captain consented on condition that the poet would furnish a witch-poem to accompany the sketch. *Tam O'Shanter* was accordingly written, and published in Grose's *Antiquities of Scotland* in 1791. According to Lockhart the poem "was the work of one day."—**Of brownys**, etc. The motto of the poem is taken from the sixth prologue in Gawin Douglas's translation of the *Æneid.* cir. 1513.

1. **Chapman billies** = itinerant pedlars. A *chapman* is a hawker, and *billies* is a common term for young fellow or comrade.—2. **Drouthy** = thirsty, as after a drouth.—4. **Gate** = road.—5. **Bousing.** A slang nautical term; to "bouse up the jib" = to drink deeply.—5. **Nappy** = ale or strong drink. (See n. to *Fortunati nimium*, l. 9, *supra*.)—6. **Unco** = uncommonly.—7. **Scots miles.** The Scotch mile was several hundred yards longer than the English mile.—8. **Slaps** = gaps in a hedge or fence.

283.—19. **Skellum** = scoundrel, a worthless fellow.—20. **Blethering** and **blellum** = foolish talker. Both words mean the same. To *blether* = to talk nonsense.—23. **Melder.** "The quantity of meal ground at the mill at one time." (Jamieson.)—24. **Siller** = silver.—25 **Ca'd**, etc. See n. on *Cotter's Sat. Night*, l. 30, *supra*.—28. **Kirkton Jean**, i e., one Jean Kennedy, who kept a public house at the village of Kirkoswald. Kirkoswald is on the road from Portpatrick to Glasgow. Burns was at school there for some months in the summer of 1778, and there Graham (*Tam O'Shanter*) and John Davidson (who is supposed to have been the original of *Souter Johnnie*) are buried. (See *The Land of Burns*, by Prof. Wilson and Robert Chambers, I. 10.) —31. **Warlock** = a wizard ; one supposed to be in league with the devil. The word means primarily a traitor or deceiver.—31. **Mirk** = dark.—33. It **gars me greet** = it makes me weep. — 39. **Ingle** = fire. *Ingle-neuk* = fireside. — 40. **Reaming swats** = foaming new ale.—41. **Souter** or **soutar** = a cobbler.—51. **Rair** = roar.

284.—55. **Lades** = loads.—81. **Skelpit**, rode on fast. *Skelp* means to beat, so, probably, lashing his mare.—81. **Dub**, a small pool of water.—83. **Blue bonnet.** See n. on *Cotter's Sat. Night*, l. 104, *supra*. — 86. **Bogles** = spectres or hobgoblins. — 88. **Houlets** = owls.

285.—91. **Birks** = birches.—**Meikle stane** = large stone. *Meikle* = much, big.—93. **Cairn** = a heap of stones. These cairns are found throughout England and Scotland, and are conical in shape.—103. **Bore** = cranny.—105. **John Barleycorn** = Scotch whiskey. See Burns' poem entitled *John Barleycorn.* — 107. **Tippenny** = twopenny ale. — 108. **Usquebae** = whiskey.—110. **Boddle**, or *bodle*, or *bawbee*. A small Scotch copper coin issued under Charles II. and worth at that time twopence. The word is said to be a corruption of *Bothwell*, the name of the master of the mint at that time.—116. **Brent** = bright. *Brent new* = bran-new.—117. **Strathspey.** A dance invented in the eighteenth century in Strathspey, Scotland, somewhat like the reel, only slower and of a jerky measure.— 119. **Winnock-bunker** = window ledge or seat.—121. **Towzie tyke** = a shaggy unkempt cur.—123. **Gart them skirl** = made them scream. In speaking of bagpipes, they are always said to *scream*.

286.—124. **Dirl** = tremble, shake with noise.—127. **Cantrip**, or *cantraip* = spells or charms. *Cant* = incantation, *raip* = rope. In old times magicians used magic-ropes in performing their charms.—131. **Airns** = irons.—134. **Gab** = mouth.—147. **Cleekit** = linked their arms.—148. **Carlin** = an old crone. — 149. **Coost** = cast. —**Duddies** = rags. — 150. **Sark** = shirt. — 151. **Queans** = young women.—153. **Creeshie** = greasy. — 154. **Seventeen-hunder-linen** = fine linen. It is a weaving term, meaning so many threads to a certain measure; of course the quality becomes finer as the number of the threads increases. — 155. **Thir breeks** = these breeches. — 157. **Hurdies** = hips.—158. **Burdies** = lasses.

287.—160. **Rigwoodie hags.** Gallows-worthy hags, from *rig* = the back, and *widdy* or *woody* (Scotch *withy*) = a rope, to hang up by the back.—160. **Spean** = to wean.—161. **Crum-**

mock = staff ; a witch's stick. — 164. **Waulie** = strapping. — 165. **Core** = the heart, or innermost part of anything; here means she was the central figure.—171. **Cutty-sark** = short-shirt.—**Paisley harn** = Paisley linen, a kind of coarse linen. Paisley is noted for its manufacture of linen, shawls, etc. —176. **Coft** = bought.—179. **Cour** = cover.—186. **Hotch'd**, an awkward or ungainly mode of moving about. In Scotland, when potatoes are shaken together in a bag to pack them down, they are said to be *hotched.*—188. **Tint** = lost.—193. **Fyke** = fidget or nervous hurry.—194. **Byke** = hive.

288.—195. **Pussie's mortal foes.** *Puss* is here a hare, or rabbit. The word is often so used by Scott, etc.—200. **Eldritch** = ghastly.—201. **Fairin'**, a gift brought from a fair, but here used ironically, as an unwelcome gift.—206. **Keystone of the brig**, middle of the bridge, for the superstitious believe that if they can safely reach the middle of a stream of running water the fiends can then pursue them no further.—210. **Fient** = never, none.—213. **Ettle** = intent, aim.

BRUCE'S ADDRESS TO HIS ARMY AT BANNOCK-BURN.

289. This famous battle was fought on June 23, 1314. The English, under Edward II., were well equipped and numbered one hundred thousand men ; the Scotch forces, under Bruce, were poorly armed and outnumbered three to one by their formidable antagonists. Nevertheless, that patriotic courage to which Bruce appeals in the poem, won a victory for Scotland. "There is a tradition," says Burns, "that the old air, 'Hey, Tutti, Taiti,' was Robert Bruce's march at the battle of Bannockburn. This thought, in my solitary wanderings, has warmed me to a pitch of enthusiasm on the theme of liberty and independence, which I have thrown into a kind of Scottish ode," etc. "This ode," says Prof. Wilson—"the grandest out of the Bible—is sublime !"

BURNS' SONGS.

Although endowed with narrative, dramatic, and descriptive powers sufficient in themselves to place him among the great poets of the world, it was in his songs that the genius of Burns found its fullest and most inimitable medium of expression. His songs have in them an indescribable and varied melody; they are full of an intense and living humanity; they are marvellously simple and movingly sincere. These great qualities make Burns the song-writer, not of the cultured only, but of the world. His songs speak to all who have known the love of women, friends, or country, all who have enjoyed to-day, defied to-morrow, or looked back regretfully to the past.

THE BANKS OF DOON.

290. The first version of this song, commonly placed among Burns's three or four best lyrics, was written in March, 1791. It is said to have been suggested by an unfortunate love affair of a Miss Peggy Kennedy, a young girl of Ayrshire.

A RED, RED ROSE.

291. This lyric, one of the best of Burns' love-songs, is an astonishing example of the poet's power of using and improving upon the work of others. Like Shakespeare, Burns was a royal borrower, and like him he had that highest originality which is able to change borrowed materials into a new and higher thing. An interesting study of the sources of the poem will be found in Henley and Henderson's *Burns*, III. 402. The whole subject is far more than a mere matter of curious interest; it illustrates the general truth that Burns' poetry is not unrelated to what has gone before, but that it has absorbed and glorified the lilt and sentiment of many a forgotten song and many a nameless singer. Burns' songs are the finest and most consummate product of a song-making nation, and it takes nothing from our admiration of their author if we realize that a whole people, whose poetic utterance had been comparatively imperfect, spoke through him; that he was the real inheritor of his country's songs, because it was reserved for him to give them that final touch which made them immortal.

IS THERE FOR HONEST POVERTY.

291. This poem appeared in the *Glasgow Magazine* for August, 1795. Burns says of it, in a letter to George Thomson in January of that year that, according to the dicta of a great critic, it is "no song," but that it will nevertheless be allowed "to be two or three pretty good prose thoughts inverted into rhyme." Mr. John Maccuen gives certain passages from Paine's *Rights of Man*, which he seems to think similar enough to have been Burns' original. (See his *Ethics of Citizenship*, p. 64, or Wallace's *Life and Work of Burns*, IV. 186.) The close relation of the poem to the democratic trend of the time is significant and obvious. Cf. note to *Cotter's Saturday Night*, l. 165, and Goldsmith's *Deserted Village*, l. 53 and note, *supra*.

1–4. Is there, etc. "These four lines, the sense of which is often misunderstood, may be thus interpreted: Is there any one who hangs his head in shame at his poverty? If there is such a poor creature, we pass him by as a coward slave." (Wallace's *Burns*, IV. 186.)—7. **The rank is but the guinea's stamp,** etc. Some suppose the passage to have been suggested by the following from Wycherley's *Plain Dealer* (Act I. Sc. 1), pub. 1677: "I weigh the man with his title; 'tis not the king's stamp can make the metal better or heavier. Your lord is a leaden shilling, which you bend every way, and which debases the stamp he bears."

WORDSWORTH.

293. WILLIAM WORDSWORTH (1770–1850) was not only a writer of noble verse; he was also a revealer of a truth which he was the first great poet fully to perceive and express. He more than any other, made the growing love of nature not merely a matter of taste or of sentimental preference, but elevated it to a place in the spiritual or religious life; he made it "a revealing agency, like Love or Prayer." He came of good North-country stock; he was born at Cockermouth, Cumberland, in one of the loveliest regions of rural England. As child, boy, and youth the spirit of the country entered into his spirit, and as a man it was in the country that the greater part of his life was spent. His first published poem was *An Evening Walk* (1793). In 1798 he and Coleridge put forth *The Lyrical Ballads*—an epoch-making book. It is in his contributions to this joint venture that the poet Wordsworth,—in his weakness and his strength,—first definitely declared himself. Between this date and 1807 Wordsworth produced much of his best work. This period includes some of his masterpieces of short and simple narration (*Michael, The Brothers*, etc.), some of the best of his lyrics (*The Highland Girl, The Solitary Reaper*, etc.), and his two sublimest odes (*Duty* and *Intimations of Immortality*). To a later stage belong many poems which, if on the whole less spontaneous and consistently poetical, are nevertheless full of mature thought and characteristic beauty. Among these are *The Excursion, The White Doe of Rylston*,—a charming romantic narrative,—and the lofty classic poem *Laodamia*. Wordsworth's life was idyllically peaceful. Simple living, the constant companionship with nature in her fairest moods, the loving service of poetry, a home full of love and sympathy,—such were the elements of his life. Wordsworth was made Poet Laureate in 1843, and died in 1850. [*Int. Eng. Lit.*, 308.]

TINTERN ABBEY.

293. This poem was written in 1798 and published the same year in *The Lyrical Ballads*. Wordsworth had been at Bristol, arranging sundry details with Cottle, who was to publish the book. The business being completed, he left for a short trip. Crossing the Severn and proceeding up the river Wye, he stopped to see again the beautiful ruins of Tintern Abbey, which he had visited last in 1793. Wordsworth gives the following account of the composition of the poem thus suggested : "I began it upon leaving Tintern, after crossing the Wye, and concluded it just as I was entering Bristol in the evening, after a ramble of four or five days, with my sister. Not a line of it was altered, and not any part of it written down till I reached Bristol."

294.—12. **Which at this season.** Wordsworth's visit was made in the early part of July.—25. **But oft, in lonely rooms,** etc. Cf. "But oft when on my couch I lie," etc., in *I wandered lonely as a cloud*," and collect other instances in Wordsworth of the influence of natural scenes or sounds recollected at a later time.

295.—42. **The affections.** This appears to mean the feelings or emotions by which a thing is directly or intuitively perceived, as contrasted with the reason or intellect. "This term is applied to all the modes of the sensibility, or to all states of mind in which we are purely passive" (Krauth, *Vocab. of the Phil. Sciences.*) 45–49. **Laid asleep in body,** etc. This remarkable passage is perhaps the greatest description to be found in poetry of a state of *mystical exaltation* or *ecstasy*. The recognition of such a state, so far from being peculiar to Wordsworth, has entered into various philosophical systems or religions from an early period. This state has been well described in the article on "Mysticism" in *Enc. Brit.* XVII. 128. James Freeman Clarke says : "Mysticism may be called the belief that man can come into union with the Infinite Being by means of a wholly passive self-surrender to divine influence. The organ in man by which he thus communes with God is not will nor reason ; it is not moral nor intellectual, but a hidden faculty of the soul behind them all. In the ecstatic moment of this union, time, space, body, soul, personal existence, all disappear, and man becomes absorbed into the Divine Being." (*Events and Epochs in Religious History,* 276.) Wordsworth himself was a natural mystic, and his friend Coleridge was early fascinated by the writings of Plotinus, one of the Neo-Platonists.—67. **When like a roe,** etc. Cf. with this whole passage the contrast between the boyish and the mature feeling towards nature in *Ode on Intimations of Immortality*, especially stanzas x-xi.

296.—101. **All thinking things all objects of all thought,** etc. Wordsworth was naturally predisposed to dwell on the presence, or "immanence," of God in nature, i.e., in what we call the physical, or material, world; in this passage, however, he includes also the idea of God immanent in the soul, as an indwelling, impelling principle. The views of Carlyle and Browning on this whole matter may be advantageously compared with those of Wordsworth.—106. **Both what they half create,** etc. The total or ultimate effect of the sight of any aspect of nature upon each individual observer, is partly the result of a simple, sensuous perception, and partly of the emotional or intellectual state associated with that perception and largely modifying it. The images of objective phenomena, impressed upon the mind by the senses, are so clothed and colored by the personality of the observer, so endowed with sentiments, or mingled with associations, that each observer may be said to half perceive and half create the world, so far as he himself is concerned. Cf. Coleridge, *Dejection: an Ode.*

297.—121. **My dear, dear sister**! Dorothy Wordsworth, only sister of the poet, was between three and four years his senior. She also had a fine perception of natural beauty, and a true poetic feeling. She devoted her life to her brother, and was his almost constant helper and companion. Wordsworth's poetry is full of evidences of the extent of his indebtedness to her for suggestion, direct help, or sympathetic interest, and he has immortalized his appreciation of her devotion by poetic tributes like the one in question. It is of her that he says:

> "She gave me eyes, she gave me ears,
> And humble cares, and delicate fears:
> A heart the fountain of sweet tears,
> And love, and faith, and joy."

(See Dorothy Wordsworth's *Journal in Scotland*, and *Dorothy Wordsworth: The Story of a Sister's Love*, by Edmund Lee.)

298-9. *Expostulation and Reply* and *The Tables Turned* are companion-poems, presenting the same lesson from a slightly different aspect. In each poem the sixth stanza is especially well known and noteworthy. Both poems were written in 1798, and appeared in the *Lyrical Ballads* in that year.

300-2. *Three Years She Grew* and *She Dwelt among the Untrodden Ways.* These poems were written in 1799, during Wordsworth's stay in Germany. In the midst of strange surroundings his "mind recurred to his native land, and to the scenes of his early youth." Both poems belong to a re-

markable group relating to some one whom the poet calls
Lucy. It is noticeable that while Wordsworth's notes on his
other poems are usually full, he has passed over this group
without comment. A knowledge of the original of Lucy
(assuming that she existed outside of the imagination) and of
all the circumstances which may have suggested these poems,
while it might gratify curiosity, could hardly increase either
our understanding or our enjoyment. Lucy "lived unknown," and her poet seems to have fittingly chosen to hide
her from public view.

SHE DWELT AMONG THE UNTRODDEN WAYS.

302.—2. **The Springs of Dove.** There are at least two rivers
of this name in England, one in Yorkshire, the other in Derbyshire. I do not know which stream the poet had in mind, but
a German romancer, who has made this conjectured meeting
of Wordsworth with Lucy the theme of a novel, places the
scene of the novel in Yorkshire. (For Dovedale in Derbyshire
see *Prelude*, Bk. VI. 193.)

MICHAEL.

This poem was written at Town-end Grasmere in 1800, and
published in the second edition of the *Lyrical Ballads*, which
appeared in the same year. In a letter of dedication to Charles
James Fox, Wordsworth says that through the poems of *Michael* and *The Brothers* (which appeared in the same volume)
he wished to call attention to a matter of public interest to
statesmen. After lamenting the rapid decline of domestic
affection among the lower classes, Wordsworth attributes it, at
least in part, to the spread of manufactures, workhouses, shops,
etc.; the spirit of independence he believes to be rapidly dis-
appearing, but not extinct. He then proceeds: "In the two
poems *The Brothers* and *Michael* I have attempted to draw a
picture of the domestic affections as I know they exist among
a class of men who are now almost confined to the North of
England. They are small independent proprietors of land.
. . . The domestic affections will always be strong in men
who live in districts not crowded with population, if these
men are placed above poverty. . . . Their little tract of land
seems as a kind of permanent rallying-point for their domestic
feelings, . . . which makes them objects of memory in a
thousand instances, when they would otherwise be forgotten."
After intimating that the efforts of Fox have been given to
the preservation of this class, Wordsworth continues: "The
two poems which I have mentioned were written with a view

to show that men who do not wear fine clothes can feel deeply."

The exact spot in Greenhead Ghyll where the sheepfold stood cannot now be determined. When the poet and his sister visited it in 1800, the sheepfold was already "falling away." In the entry in her *Journal* (October 11, 1800) which records the after-dinner ramble to the scene of poor Michael's toils, Dorothy Wordsworth describes the sheepfold as "built in the form of a heart unequally divided."

2. **Green-head Ghyll.** Ghyll is a narrow valley or ravine; the word is used especially of those valleys which have streams rushing through them. (See *Cent. Dict.*)

303.—24, 25. **Not verily for their own sakes.** Notice here the characteristic order in which Wordsworth places first nature, then man, in his affections.

306.—134. **High into Easedale,** etc. Easedale is about half a mile from Grasmere, which was Wordsworth's home for many years; and from there begins a long ascent to the Pass of Dunmail-Raise, which is situated about three miles north from Grasmere.

308.—180. **Coppice** = a wood, or thicket formed of trees of small growth; *copse* is a contraction of coppice.—199. **Objects which the shepherd loved before.** Note that the relation between the sympathy with man and the sympathy with nature is a theme recurring through the poem. Wordsworth learns to love shepherds, from loving their haunts. The shepherd comes to love nature from daily companionship with her, and then loves her more and more, through his human affection for his son (the converse of the first instance)—209. **Distressful tidings,** etc. The pastoral peace in the poem is disturbed by the world of money-making without. Even in these hills it comes to destroy.

316.—455. **Among the rocks,** etc. We see in the end how the shepherd turns to nature for comfort; and notice also how the old man has sought to entwine pastoral association with his son's last recollections of home.

"MY HEART LEAPS UP WHEN I BEHOLD."

317. This was written at Town-end, Grasmere, in 1802. It is notable as a concise yet comprehensive statement of one of the important doctrines in Wordsworth's philosophy, which reappears in various poems with a great wealth of illustration. This doctrine is the importance of certain primitive emotions of childhood, and the desirability of retaining them through life, as an antidote to the effects of contact with the world. Wordsworth himself has pointed out the connection between

the concluding lines of this poem and his *Ode on the Intima-
tions of Immortality*. Cf. also *The Cuckoo, The Reverie of
Poor Susan, I Wandered Lonely as a Cloud* (p. 325), *Three
Years She Grew* (p. 300), and see *Int. Eng. Lit.* 315–16.

THE SOLITARY REAPER.

This poem, composed in 1803 and published in 1807, was
suggested (according to Dorothy Wordsworth) by a beautiful
sentence in Thomas Wilkinson's "Tour in Scotland." Prof.
Knight has succeeded in identifying the sentence referred to,
which is as follows: "Passed a female who was reaping
alone; she sung in Erac, as she bended over her sickle; the
sweetest human voice I ever heard: her strains were tenderly
melancholy, and felt delicious. *long after they were heard no
more.*" [Italics mine.] (See Knight's *Wordsworth*, II. 347.)

ODE. INTIMATIONS OF IMMORTALITY FROM RECOLLECTIONS OF EARLY CHILDHOOD.

318. This ode, one of the noblest in the language, was
written at Town-end, Grasmere, in 1803 and 1806. Wordsworth says that there was an interval of two years "between
the writing of the first four stanzas and the remaining parts."
(For fuller study of the poem, see *Int. Eng. Lit.* 319–22.)

319.—28. **The fields of sleep,** etc. The passage has been
thus explained: "The morning breeze blowing from the fields
that were dark during the hours of sleep." (Hawes Turner,
quoted by Knight.) I am inclined to think that Wordsworth
was thinking simply of the peaceful, quiet fields, as, e.g., in

> "The silence that is in the starry sky,
> The *sleep* that is among the lonely hills."
> *(Song at the Feast of Brougham Castle.)*

The "fields of sleep" are, in this view, not the fields lately
covered with darkness, for that is equally true of the whole
region, but the remote places full of this quiet of repose.

320.—72. **Nature's Priest.** Wordsworth himself has often
been spoken of as the "High-priest of Nature," and his poetic
disciple Matthew Arnold, says of him:

> "But he was a priest to us all
> Of the wonder and bloom of the world."
> *(The Youth of Nature.)*

321.—103. "Humorous stage," i.e., the stage on which
men and women are exhibited in the various moods, whims,
or caprices ("business, love, or strife"). The *persons* (i.e.,

the *dramatis personæ*), brought forward on this stage, not only thus show man in his diverse pursuits, or whims, but man at every stage of life.—105. **Equipage** = retinue, train.— 118. **Thy Immortality.** Immortality here, as throughout the poem, is used rather to describe the *eternal* sphere of things, as contrasted with the *temporal*, than in its ordinary sense of undying. The idea is that the light of this eternal sphere yet broods over the child.

322.—128. **Almost as life.** Note the force of the word "almost" here. It introduces the next stanza, which shows us that *custom*, however heavily it may lie on the soul, does not entirely obscure or extinguish the "something" of heavenly origin which still lives.—141. **But for those obstinate questionings.** One of the evidences, in Wordsworth's view, of our natural affinity with an eternal sphere or order of things is the child's imperfect accommodation to earthly conditions. Thus in the following passage a momentary doubt of the objective reality of the material world is described. In this state objective things seem falling away from his grasp, and the strangeness of a world in which he is but an alien fills him with "blank misgivings." Wordsworth, in explaining the passage, tells us that it is founded on experiences of his own childhood. He tells us that at times the external world became vague and unreal to him, and adds: "Many times while going to school have I grasped at a wall or tree to recall myself from this abyss of idealism to the reality."

I WANDERED LONELY AS A CLOUD.

324. Written at Town-end, Grasmere, in 1804, and published in 1807. Wordsworth tells us that "the daffodils grew, and still grow, on the margin of Ullswater, and probably may be seen to this day as beautiful in the month of March, nodding their golden heads beside the dancing and foaming waves."—21. **They flash upon that inward eye.** This line and the one following were composed by Mrs. Wordsworth. It is to this that the poet refers when he says of the poem: "The two best lines in it are by Mary."

SHE WAS A PHANTOM OF DELIGHT.

325. This poem was composed in 1804 and published in 1807. It is supposed to have been inspired by Wordsworth's wife, Mary Hutchinson. The poet's own comment on the verses is as follows: "Written at Town-end, Grasmere. The germ of this poem was four lines composed as a part of the verses on the Highland Girl. Though beginning in this way, it was written from my heart, as is sufficiently obvious."

ODE TO DUTY.

326. This ode was composed in 1805 and published in 1807. It ranks with Wordsworth's greatest works and is even placed by Swinburne above the yet more familiar *Immortality Ode* for pure poetic excellence. (Art. on "Wordsworth and Byron," in *Miscellanies*, 135.)

Wordsworth himself pointed out what may be called its poetic ancestry. "This ode is on the model," he remarks, "of Gray's Ode to Adversity, which is copied from Horace's Ode to Fortune." (I. xxxv.) "But," he adds in pencil, "is not the first stanza of Gray's from a chorus in Æschylus? And is not Horace's Ode also modelled on the Greek ?"

The ethical teaching of the *Ode to Duty* supplements and completes that of the *Ode on the Intimations of Immortality*. By combining the doctrines of the two poems we see that, in Wordsworth's view, there are two guides to conduct: first, natural emotion, or the impulse of an unspoilt nature; and second, conscience, the voice which prompts a deliberate choice of right, the *mens conscia recti*. Both of these guides may be said to be of a transcendental or superhuman character. The first, the kindly impulse, shows our original nearness to the Divine order, and is the "fountain-light of all our day"; the other, the appointed corrective of the first, is that sense of obedience to a Divine order, or law, which regulates the universe and "preserves the stars from wrong." This poem is an exception to Wordsworth's teaching, in that it emphasizes the importance of this second guide,—duty, or conscience,—as a restraining power. In most of his other poems, such as *Sonnet XXVII, The Mountain Echo*, etc., natural emotion or impulse is dwelt upon as all-sufficient.

15, 16. **Long may**, etc. Wordsworth altered these lines to :

"Oh ! if through confidence misplaced
They fail, thy saving arms, dread Power ! around them cast."

But I have ventured to retain the earlier version.

SONNETS.

328. Wordsworth holds his deservedly high place among English sonnet-writers for several distinct reasons. He has written some of the finest sonnets in the language ; sonnets comparable in force to the trumpet-notes of Milton, sonnets filled with a deep and quiet wisdom or a delicate beauty. But this is not all. Other English poets have produced some single sonnets of a high order : Wordsworth's place as sonnet-eer rests not merely on the excellence of certain individual sonnets, but on the magnitude and variety of his contributions to sonnet literature. Indeed, if numbers alone are considered, Wordsworth is probably not excelled by any other English sonneteer. Finally, Wordsworth bears an important relation to the history of sonnet-writing. The sonnet, cultivated in England during the sixteenth and the greater part of the seventeenth century, was neglected by Dryden, Pope, and their poetic kindred ; when an awakening England turned back to the verse of the Elizabethans, the sonnet, like the Spenserian stanza, was revived. Gray, Warton, Mason, and William Lisle Bowles, in turn assisted in thus restoring the sonnet to its lost dignity, but it is Wordsworth's distinction to be the first really great English sonnet-writer after Milton.

COLERIDGE.

331. SAMUEL TAYLOR COLERIDGE (1772–1834) was prob-ably the most variously gifted, brilliant, and inspiring Eng-lishman of his generation. Not only is he one of the glories of English poetry; in the philosophy, theology, literary criticism, and even the journalism of his time he was a force to be reck-oned with. Hardly less remarkable was his direct personal influence upon some of his greatest contemporaries, and through them upon his own and succeeding times. Many cir-cumstances connect Coleridge with the so-called "Lake Poets." He was a friend of Southey and of Wordsworth. He com-posed a youthful poem in conjunction with Southey, he united with Wordsworth in the production of *The Lyrical Ballads.* He wrote the best critical exposition of Wordsworth's poetic principles; he lived for some years near Southey in the Lake District. But the bond that united these three Lake poets was mainly that of friendly intercourse and congenial aims. The term "Lake School" is more truly applied to the poets than to their poetry: for while they were united in their lives, in their works they were sometimes widely divided. Thus Coleridge, although he sympathized with Wordsworth's theory of poetry, and himself employed the same general manner in some of his poems, yet won his most characteristic triumphs in poetry of a wholly different order. Wordsworth is in the direct line of succession from Thomson, Cowper, and Crabbe, while Coleridge's affiliations are rather with the old Ballads and Ossian, with Chatterton, Blake, and the great prophet of

Mediævalism, Walter Scott. In *The Ancient Mariner* and
Christabel, Coleridge takes the popular ballad,—with its simplicity and beauty, its primitive, haunting dread of the
unknown, its occasional crudity and vulgarity, — he takes
this rhyme of the people, and, preserving much of its force
and directness, he refines, glorifies, and lifts it up. To
at all appreciate Coleridge's poems of this order, we must
recognize their place in the history of English Romanticism,
connecting them with the publication of Percy's *Reliques* (1765)
on the one hand, and on the other with Keats' *Eve of St.
Agnes*, and with Morris, Rossetti, and the Pre-Raphaelites.

THE ANCIENT MARINER.

331. *The Ancient Mariner*, planned by Coleridge and
Wordsworth as they walked over the Quantock Hills in
Somersetshire, was begun in November, 1797, and completed
by the following March. In *The Prelude*, Wordsworth refers
as follows to the circumstances under which the poem took
shape :

> "That summer, under whose indulgent skies,
> Upon smooth Quantock's airy ridge we stood
> Unchecked, or loitered 'mid her sylvan combs,
> Thou in bewitching words, with happy heart,
> Didst chaunt the vision of that Ancient Man,
> The bright-eyed Mariner," etc.

The first idea of the two poets was to write the *Rime* together,
but the plan of joint composition soon proved to be imprac-
ticable. Wordsworth says that "the greatest part of the story
was Coleridge's invention," and in every way Wordsworth's
share in the work was comparatively trifling. Evidently Coleridge had found a subject particularly suited to his genius.
Wordsworth apparently recognized this, and left the poem in
his friend's hands. (See *Memoirs of William Wordsworth*, by
Christopher Wordsworth, D.D.; Coleridge's *Biographia
Literaria*, Ch. XIV.) The poem appeared in the first edition
of *The Lyrical Ballads* (1798); it was reprinted with considerable omissions and alterations in the second edition of that
memorable book in 1800. The marginal gloss, which taken
by itself is a singularly beautiful example of elevated and
imaginative prose, did not appear with it then or in the two
subsequent editions, and, according to Wordsworth, it was
not spoken of when the poem was planned.

The so-called "sources" of the poem have been frequently
commented upon and need not be again discussed here. (See
The Source of "The Ancient Mariner," by Ivor James, Car-
diff, 1890, and *The Poetical Works of Coleridge*, ed. by James

Dykes Campbell, 593 *et seq.*). That Coleridge did avail himself of various outside material in the composition of this poem is beyond question; how far such external hints were really suggestions to the poet's imagination is another matter. It is probably safe to say that after every known external suggestion has been taken into account—the friend's dream of a skeleton-ship, "with figures in it"; the passage in *Shelvocke's Voyages* which led Wordsworth to suggest the shooting of the albatross; the narrative of *The Strange and Dangerous Voyage of Captain Thomas James*—when all these are summed up and allowed for, we feel that the true sources of the poem were within, and that our wonder over it as an original imaginative creation remains unimpaired.

An elaborate attempt was made (*Journal of Speculative Philosophy*, July, 1880) to interpret the poem allegorically, and Mr. George Macdonald is credited with having expressed a similar view. While sound criticism forbids us to regard such attempts as more than ingenious speculations, there can be no doubt that the poem has a definite moral purpose and teaching. Coleridge himself settled this question when he told Mrs. Barbauld, who complained that the poem had no moral, that its chief fault was "the obtrusion of the moral sentiment" in a work "of pure imagination." (*Table Talk*, May 31, 1830.) Nor is the precise nature of this moral hard to discover. How shall a man love God who loves not his brother? or how shall he pray who sins against the law of love even in the world of God's lower creatures? Retribution for the violation of this law, and deliverance from the consequences of that violation, are the theme of the poem. (See *Int. Eng. Lit.* 332 *et seq.*)

The mood of the poet towards the unseen—a mood which we must throw ourselves into if we would get the full feeling of the poem—is indicated in the following motto, which was originally prefixed to it: "Facile credo, plures esse Naturas invisibiles in rerum universitate. Sed horum omnium familiam quis nobis enarrabit? et gradus et cognationes et discrimina et singulorum munera? Quid agunt? Quae loca habitant? Harum rerum notitiam semper ambivit ingenium humanum, nunquam attigit. Juvat, interea, non diffiteor, quandoque in animo, tanquam in Tabulâ, majoris et melioris mundi imaginem contemplari: ne mens assuefacta hodiernae vitae minutiis se contrahat nimis, et tota subsidat in pusillas cogitationes. Sed veritati interea invigilandum est, modusque servandus, ut certa ab incertis diem a nocte, distinguamus." (T. Burnet, *Archaeol. Phil.* p. 68.) (That there are in the universe more invisible than visible Natures, I readily believe. But who shall declare to us the family, the ranks, the relationships, the differences, the respective functions of all these creatures? What do they? Where do they inhabit? Human nature hath ever circled about, but hath never attained this knowledge. Meanwhile it is profitable, I doubt not, to contemplate at seasons with the mind's eye, as in a picture, the vision of this greater and better world, lest the mind, accustomed to the petty concerns of daily life, grow too narrow, and sink altogether into trifling thoughts. But, at the same time, we must be watchful for truth and observe restraint, that we may distinguish certain from uncertain, day from night.)

The feeling that there are more things in heaven and earth than are dreamt of in our philosophy, the suggestion of a world of mysterious presences, too fine in general for our limited perceptions, but here revealed through an exceptional situation—all this is impressed upon the poem. A few allusions to familiar things—the harbor, the hill which overlooks it, the kirk, and the lighthouse—skilfully place the ordinary in contrast with those remote ocean-solitudes beyond the reach of common experience. These unknown regions form an appropriate setting for the wonders of the story. We are led to invest the Mariner with something of that awe with which in old times men regarded the traveller returned from a far country full of a store of marvellous experiences.

331.—12. **Eftsoons** = soon after, after awhile. (*Eft* = after, again; *sone* = soon.)—13. **Glittering eye.** The Mariner first arrests the Wedding Guest by a physical grasp, then—that proving ineffectual—by a purely spiritual power. It is through the eye that mind speaks most directly to mind; through the eye that the imperative compelling force of the human will is exerted with the least physical intervention. The belief in this mysterious, compelling power is ancient and wide-spread. Even animals are supposed to be unable to resist it. Cf. also the power by which the cat and the serpent fascinate their victim.

333.—63. **An Albatross.** The albatross was considered by sailors a bird of good omen. The Mariner's crime is made blacker by this and other circumstances which are carefully enumerated. It comes in a time of danger, and responds to the sailors' welcome by trusting them, by eating their food, then it delivers them from their perils. Moreover, we are told (l. 404) that the bird "*loved the man* that shot him with his bow."

334.—83. **Upon the right,** i.e., the ship was now going northward (cf. l. 25).—120. **And all the boards,** etc. "And" here is used rather in the sense of *but* or *notwithstanding*. (Cf. the instances of the *adversative* use of *and* in Murray's *Eng.*

Dict., "And," II. 7, 8.)—132. **The spirit**, etc. The tutelary spirit of this Southern Polar region, who *loved* the albatross. (Cf. l. 404-5)

336.—141. **Instead of the cross**, etc. The dead albatross is the visible sign of the Mariner's transgression; his burden of sin, it takes the place of the sign of man's deliverance from sin.

337.—164. **Gramercy.** Literally "Many thanks" (*Grand merci*).

338.—193. **Life-in-Death.** The casting of the dice results in Life-in-Death winning the Mariner. He is reserved, that is, for a living death. Death, apparently by a previous throw, has won his comrades. It is difficult to reconcile the description of *Life-in-Death* with the subsequent adventures of the Mariner. She is apparently a personification of lawless pleasure, and has a bold and evil beauty. Apart from the sequence, it would seem as though the text, "She that liveth in pleasure is dead while she liveth" (*I. Tim.* v. 6), had been in the poet's mind. Perhaps Coleridge wished to bring her before us as a general embodiment of one dead in sin, without regard to her particular part in the poem.—212. **Star-dogged Moon.** "It is a common superstition among sailors that something evil is about to happen whenever a star dogs the moon." (Coleridge.)

339.—232. **Alone, alone.** Loneliness is the inevitable consequence of a sin against the law of love, the bond of brotherhood. The Mariner again recurs to his loneliness in the final summing up of his experience (ll. 597-610), evidently regarding it as the essential element in his sufferings.

341.—284. **A spring of love.** The power to pray, lost by wanton cruelty to one of God's creatures, is regained by a spontaneous impulse of love towards the "happy living things."

342.—297. **The silly buckets.** The exact sense of "silly" here is not easy to determine. The original meaning of the word is *happy* (A. S. *sælig* = happy), then *simple* or *innocent*, then *foolish*. Spenser also uses it, in the sense of *helpless* or *frail*, of a ship long storm-beaten. Coleridge may mean that the buckets are *blessed* or *happy*, because they are again being filled with water, or that they were *foolish* because they, whose office it was to hold water, had stood so long empty, as if in an absurd mockery.

350.—535. **Ivy tod** = ivy bush.

352.—601-609. **O sweeter than**, etc. Note that as the worst penance of the Mariner is *loneliness*, alienation from God and man, so the sweetest thing for him in life is *fellowship* with man and the nearness to God through prayer. The two following verses (ll. 610–617) sum up the essential teaching of the poem. (See *Int. Eng. Lit.* 334.)

YOUTH AND AGE. WORK WITHOUT HOPE.

354–5. Nearly all of Coleridge's best poetry was written between 1796 and 1801. This brief period includes *Kubla Khan*, *The Ancient Mariner*, *Christabel*, and the translation of *Wallenstein*. That Coleridge should have produced so much noble poetry in five years is surprising, but that he should have produced so little poetry in the remaining fifty-seven years of his life is more surprising still. But during the period of over thirty years that succeeded this time of poetic productiveness, Coleridge produced at long intervals a few poems of an exceedingly high order. Among these are the touchingly personal revelations, *Youth and Age*, and *Work Without Hope*, both of which express hopeless resignation, the pathetic patience which marked his closing years. "The first draft of the exquisite *Youth and Age*," says Mr. James Dykes Campbell, "is dated September 10, 1823, and seems to have been inspired by a day-dream of happy Quantock times." As at first printed in 1828, it closed at the thirty-eighth line. The last fourteen lines were composed in 1832, and added to the poem two years later. *Work Without Hope* was written in 1827. Mr. Campbell well says, in speaking of the poems of this period, "although now 'a common grayness silvers everything,' the old magic still mingles with the colors on the palette. Coleridge's attitude as he now looked over the wide landscape, where all nature seemed at work, and he, held in the bondage of a spell of his own creating, the sole unbusy thing, recalls Browning's picture of Andrea del Sarto watching the lights of Fiesole die out one by one, like his own hopes and ambitions. Coleridge also remembered days when he could leave the ground and 'put on the glory, Raphael's daily wear'—now he, himself a very Raphael, asks only to 'sit the gray remainder of his evening out,' and 'muse perfectly how he could paint—were he but back in France.'"

SOUTHEY.

356. ROBERT SOUTHEY, the youngest of the three poets of the "Lake School," was born at Bristol in 1774. As a young man he shared in the boundless hopes and passionate enthusiasms engendered in so many generous spirits by the beginning of the French Revolution; in later life he became an extreme conservative. By the time he was twenty he had begun his career as a poet by the publication, with R. Lovell, of a volume of *Poems* (1794). In 1804 he established himself near Coleridge at Greta Hall, Keswick, and settled down to a life of painstaking and incessant literary labor. His life was in many respects that of a typical man of letters. He accumulated a library of 14,000 volumes; he was an enormous reader and an industrious writer. He planned and partially completed a series of epics to illustrate the great religions of the world; he wrote histories, biographies, and innumerable magazine articles; he edited and collected other men's poetry, and all the while wrote poetry himself. He became famous, but remained poor; hampered by narrow means, he lost neither his high aims nor his confidence in himself. He was chosen Poet Laureate in 1813, and died in 1843.

Southey's poetry, admired by some of his greatest contemporaries, is now generally ignored by readers and slighted by critics, and it is not likely that his long poems will ever hold more than a nominal place in our literature. Yet Southey had something, at least, of the true poet in him, and out of the diffuse mass of his verse some of the short poems are certainly likely to long survive. In prose he is admittedly among the masters. Byron pronounced his prose "perfect," and later critics are not inclined to dissent from this judgment. As a man he commands universal admiration and respect.

THE BATTLE OF BLENHEIM.

The Battle of Blenheim was written in 1798. The complicated question of the Spanish succession in 1700 brought about a war in which England was involved. John Churchill, the great Duke of Marlborough, was made commander-in-chief of the English and Dutch forces, who were fighting against the French claimant to the throne of Spain. Marlborough, assisted by Prince Eugene of Savoy, won a celebrated victory over the French and Bavarians at Blenheim, August 13, 1704.

WHITE.

360. JOSEPH BLANCO WHITE (1775-1841) was born in Spain and took orders as a Romish priest. Doubts of Catholicism led him to escape to England in 1810, where he settled at Oxford and joined the English Church. He edited at London a Spanish paper and wrote for the magazines. Most of his literary work dealt with religious problems and was of only temporary value; but he is justly remembered for his sonnet *To Night*. This sonnet was dedicated to Coleridge, who considered it "the best in the English language"; Leigh Hunt says of it: "In point of *thought* the sonnet stands supreme, perhaps above all in any language."

SCOTT.

360. WALTER SCOTT was born at Edinburgh in 1771, and died at Abbotsford, the old-world house which he built by the Tweed, in 1832. If Wordsworth was born into one of the loveliest districts of the British Isles, Scott (who came within a year of being the same age) was born into the most romantic. In that historic Border-country—wasted by old-time forays and once fought over by the knighthood of two gallant nations—almost every landscape, beautiful as it may be in itself, is invested with an added charm of wonder and poetry by the associations of a chivalric past. Not only was Scott born in this natural home of Romanticism; he belonged by descent to the days of Border warfare, and the blood of some of those stubborn fighters ran in his veins. Scott came into the world at a time when men's minds had already begun to turn to the lately-despised Middle Ages with a new curiosity and delight, for already that side of the protest against eighteenth-century materialism which has been called "The Renaissance of Wonder" had begun. Inheritance, natural disposition, early surroundings, and the pressure of his age, all combined to give Scott that leading place in this Second Renaissance which he soon took and retained. He responded to the impulse which came to him from the rising Romanticism of Germany, and his first published poem was a translation of Bürger's ballad of *Lenore*, 1796. But his best inspiration came from his own land. He contributed two original ballads, dealing with Scottish themes, to a collection of pieces brought out by M. G. ("Monk") Lewis, entitled *Tales of Wonder* (1800). The loving minuteness of his researches into the past is shown by his *Minstrelsy of the Scottish Border* (1802–3), a collection of old ballads which exercised an influence hardly inferior to that of Percy's *Reliques*. The *Lay of the Last Minstrel* (1805), his first long original poem, was the natural successor of these early labors. It was received with enthusiasm, and with its publication Scott entered upon a long period of popularity phenomenal in the annals of authorship. From this time until the appearance of Byron's *Childe Harold* in 1812, Scott surpassed his greatest poetical contemporaries in popular favor. Having conquered the world by his verse, he next conquered it a second time by his prose, and by his publication of *Waverley* in 1814 began a series of triumphs in a new field. Whether in prose or verse, he was the Magician who, more than any other, threw open to all men the newly recovered regions of wonder and delight. Others among his contemporaries or immediate successors may have had a finer or rarer poetic gift, but in the "Renaissance of Wonder" none could approach him in influence on his own and succeeding times. Byron was his follower in romantic poetry, Dumas in romantic prose. When the extent and variety of his work is fairly taken into account we are impressed by a creative energy that for richness, ease, and power is almost unmatched in modern literature.

HAROLD'S SONG TO ROSABELLE.

This poem originally appeared in the *Minstrelsy of the Scottish Border* (1802), and was afterwards incorporated into the *Lay of the Last Minstrel.*

BALLAD. ALICE BRAND.

362. Scott tells us that this poem is founded on a Danish ballad which occurs in the *Kæmpe Viser*, a collection of songs first published in 1591.

CANTO XII.—2. **Mavis, Merle** = thrush, and blackbird.— 8. **Wold.** Although this word originally meant wood or forest, it somehow acquired the directly opposite meaning, of a field or open country. It is used here in this second sense.

363.—14. **Glaive** = sword.—17. **Pall** = a covering, mantle. —25. **Vair** = a kind of fur.

364. CANTO XIII.—37. **Elfin King.** In his comments on this poem Scott quotes from Dr. Graham's *Scenery of the Perthshire Highlands.* Graham says that the Highland elves were not absolutely malevolent, but rather envious of mankind. "They are believed to inhabit certain round grassy eminences, where they celebrate their nocturnal festivities . . ." Mortals were sometimes admitted to their secret abodes, and if they partook of their fare forfeited any return to human society. (See Scott's *Demonology and Witchcraft*, Letter IV.)—38. **Won'd** = dwelt.—48. **Christen'd man.** The idea that an evil spirit could be dispelled by the sign of the cross was universally held, and although the elves were not necessarily in league with the powers of darkness, they also were thought to dread the Christian sign.

365. CANTO XV.—92. **It was between**, etc. The popular belief that witches, fairies, ghosts, and the like had an especial power in the middle hours of the night is frequently referred to in literature (see *Ham.* I. 1. 156). In his *Witchcraft and*

Demonology, Scott says that the elves kidnapped adults as well as children, but only when the former were "engaged in some unlawful action, or in the act of giving way to some headlong and sinful passion."

366.—111. Dunfermline. See n. on *Sir Patrick Spens*, l. 1.

EDMUND'S SONG.

Palgrave remarks that "this poem exemplifies the peculiar skill with which Scott employs proper names—a rarely misleading sign of true poetical genius." Greta woods are on the Greta River in Yorkshire; the estate of Rokeby was situated at the junction of this river with the Tees.

A WEARY LOT IS THINE.

368. Scott says that the closing lines of this song are "taken from the fragment of an old Scottish ballad," of which he could only recall two verses. The last six lines reproduce with only a trifling modification, the third verse of the original ballad, which ran as follows:

> " He turned him round and right about,
>   All on the Irish shore ;
> He gave his bridle-reins a shake,
>   With, Adieu for evermore,
>   My dear!
>   Adieu for evermore!"

In his skilful use of chance suggestions from old songs and ballads Scott resembles Shakespeare and Burns, and some of his happiest lyrics have been composed in this fashion. (See Beers' *English Romanticism in the 18th Century*, 277.)

SONG, THE CAVALIER.

370. The events related in *Rokeby* are supposed to have taken place immediately after the battle of Marston Moor in 1644, when the struggle between Cavalier and Puritan was the great issue of the time. This song has therefore an especial appropriateness.

JOCK OF HAZELDEAN.

373. This is another instance of Scott's successful use of the early minstrelsy. The first stanza is ancient, the original ballad being "Jock o' Hazel Green."

MADGE WILDFIRE'S SONG.

374. This is one of the pathetic snatches of song which Scott represents the unhappy Madge Wildfire as singing on her deathbed (*Heart of Midlothian*, Ch. XXXIX). Its melancholy suggestiveness is greatly heightened by the circumstances with which Scott associates it. As he says : "It was remarkable that there could always be traced in her songs [Madge Wildfire's] something appropriate, though perhaps only obliquely or collaterally, to her present situation." Prof. Beers remarks that this song "is a fine example of the ballad manner of story-telling by implication." (*History of Eng. Romanticism*, 277.)

BORDER BALLAD.

375.—11. **Hirsel** = a flock of sheep or a herd of cattle.

COUNTY GUY.

376. Sung by the "maid of the little turret, of the vail, and of the lute" in the fifth chapter of *Quentin Durward*. Scott says that the air was exactly such ' as we are accustomed to suppose flowed from the lips of high-born dames of chivalry, when knights and troubadours listened and languished."

CAMPBELL.

376. THOMAS CAMPBELL was born in Glasgow in 1777. As a youth of twenty he was known to the literary circle of Edinburgh,—Walter Scott, Francis Jeffrey, Lord Brougham, and others,—but his career is chiefly associated with London, where he settled in 1803. He died at Boulogne in 1844, and was buried in Westminster Abbey. Campbell's first published poem, *The Pleasures of Hope* (1799), won immediate and general admiration. By this single effort he made a high place for himself among the poets of his time ; and it may be said of him, almost more truly than of Byron, that he "awoke to find himself famous." The poem has genuine merits, but it belongs to a school of poetry now out of favor, and it has lost popularity in common with Akenside's *Pleasures of the Imagination*, Rogers' *Pleasures of Memory*, and other poems of the same character. Campbell wrote several other long poems, but his place in our literature now rests admittedly on his martial lyrics. Mr. Saintsbury has recently pronounced his "three splendid war-songs [*Hohenlinden, Ye Mariners of England*, and *The Battle of the Baltic*] the equals, if not the superiors, of anything of the kind in English, and therefore in any language," and has declared that they "set him in a position from which he is never likely to be ousted." Campbell, he concludes, stands "the best singer of war in a race and language which are those of the best singers and not the worst fighters in the history of the world,—in the race of Nelson and the language of Shakespeare. Not easily shall a man win higher praise than this." (*Hist. 19th Centy. Lit.*, p. 94.)

YE MARINERS OF ENGLAND: A NAVAL ODE.

This ode was written in 1800, when England, arrayed singly against France and the greater part of Europe, had greatly strengthened her position by her fleet. Her navy was supreme ; and on the maintenance of that supremacy at this critical time England's safety depended. Within the last five years England had won important victories over the French and Spanish, most of which were achieved by Nelson's genius and daring, even when he was not the chief in command. (For Nelson, see also n. to *The Battle of the Baltic, post.*) England's greatness has continued to depend upon her navy—a fact which has been recognized by Tennyson in *The Fleet*, a poem similar in spirit to this of Campbell's. Still more recent is Kipling's tribute to English naval power in his *Seven Seas*.

377.—15. **Blake.** Robert Blake (1599–1657) was one of England's greatest admirals. He is particularly noted for his victories over the Dutch, whose strength on the sea in his time threatened England's power. Blake was sent out against the famous Van Tromp in 1652, and in an engagement May 19th forced the latter to retreat. He was also successful in routing two more of their great commanders—De Ruyter and De Witte. Blake's last and most brilliant victory was won over a Spanish fleet off Santa Cruz in 1657.

HOHENLINDEN.

378. During a tour on the Continent, 1800–1, Campbell was near Hohenlinden at the time of the battle fought there between the victorious French under Moreau (one of Napoleon's generals) and the allied Bavarians and Austrians under Archduke John. Campbell visited the scene of the battle and wrote his famous poem in 1802.

THE BATTLE OF THE BALTIC.

379. This poem was written in 1809. The Battle of the Baltic (or of Copenhagen, as it is sometimes called) was fought on April 2, 1801. At this time Russia, Sweden, and Denmark, instigated by France, had formed a confederacy against England. It was to break up this alliance that England fitted out an expedition for the Baltic, making Sir Hyde Parker commander-in-chief. Nelson was, however, put second in command and selected to lead the van, and Campbell is right in naming him as the hero of the victory. Parker, who was unable to reach Nelson at the time of the fiercest action, thinking him too hard pressed, gave a signal for recall, but Nelson refused to see the signal and, bravely encouraging his men to fight on, gained the battle in spite of heavy loss. (See Southey's *Life of Nelson*, Ch. VII.)

381.—63. Elsinore, which is about twenty miles from Copenhagen, was considered next to the capital the most flourishing of Danish towns. It is situated at the narrowest part of the Sound, and, being well fortified, commands the entrance to it. On the promontory adjoining Elsinore stood Cronanburgh Castle, a famous palace defended by a fortress and formidable batteries. This castle has an especial interest for the student, as it was here that the scene of *Hamlet* was laid.—**66. With the gallant good Riou.** Southey says, in his *Life of Nelson:* "There was not in our whole navy a man who had a higher and more chivalrous sense of duty than Riou." Nelson put him in a position of great trust, giving him command over several ships. He was killed, fighting on board the Amazon.

MOORE.

383. THOMAS MOORE was born at Dublin in 1779, and died at Sloperton, England, in 1852, after a life of great popularity. After graduating from Trinity College he went to London in 1799. A translation of *Anacreon*, dedicated to the Prince of Wales, first brought him into notice, and he steadily rose in popular favor. In 1817 he wrote his long Eastern poem *Lalla Rookh*, which met with instant success. His *Irish Melodies*, which appeared in parts (1807–34), is a collection of songs, many of which hold an enduring place in our literature. Although a great part of his work is but little read to-day, his contemporaries held him in high esteem. Shelley says that he is proud to acknowledge his inferiority to him, and Byron was a close friend and admirer. Moore's *Life of Byron* is still accepted as one of the most trustworthy records of that poet.

THE HARP THAT ONCE THROUGH TARA'S HALLS.

384. Tara's Halls. The palace of the ancient kings of Ireland, which is said to have stood on the Hill of Tara in County Meath, Ireland.

BYRON.

385. GEORGE GORDON, LORD BYRON (1788–1824), although distinctively not the greatest, was the most prominent and widely influential English poet of his time. His first work, *Hours of Idleness*, a weak and juvenile production, appeared in 1807, but his tremendous vogue dates from the publication of the first two cantos of *Childe Harold* in 1812. From this time Byron kept the centre of the stage. He transferred Scott's narrative manner to other subjects and scenes, and although he differed from his master in essential particulars, he is properly regarded as Scott's successor in the history of English Romanticism. Scott himself made way for Byron, declaring good-naturedly that he had been beaten out of the field of poetry by the rising favorite. In 1816 Byron left England for the Continent, fleeing from domestic troubles and the tumult of rumor, scandal, curiosity, and condemnation which his affairs had excited. He joined the Shelleys in Switzerland, and later established himself in Italy. The third and fourth cantos of *Childe Harold* (1816–18) mirror much of his life at this time; they show us the Swiss Lakes, Venice, and Rome, but we see them always through the medium of Byron's personality. The brief remainder of his life was spent abroad. Poem followed poem in quick succession; among the rest his unfinished satire of *Don Juan*, the touches of a genuine feeling discernible amidst the froth and effervescence of its wit and cynicism, and his remarkable dramatic poem of *Cain*. He died at thirty-seven, just after he had thrown his energies into the cause of Greek independence. The large space that Byron filled in his own age, his influence on those of his own generation and on their immediate successors, is beyond question. He was the poet of historic Europe; the poet of society in revolt against authority; the poet of a much-admired melancholy, which, however reckless and defiant, did not forget to be interesting and picturesque. When Byron lived there were probably more great poets in England than at any time since the days of Elizabeth. Yet though Scott, Wordsworth, Coleridge, Southey, Moore, Campbell, Shelley, and Keats were among his competitors, the popular verdict of his day gave Byron the first place. This verdict posterity has not confirmed. There was something meteoric in Byron's amazing force, rush, and brilliancy, in the way he burst into the poetic firmament and took possession. But if the stars pale in the path of a meteor, it passes, and they remain. Byron has not passed, but his light has waned, while that of

Scott, Wordsworth, Coleridge, Keats, and Shelley shines with a steady or increasing radiance. (See *Int. Eng. Lit.* 359.)

STANZAS FOR MUSIC.

These verses were prompted by the news of the death of the Duke of Dorset, a former schoolfellow of Byron's. As a boy Byron was (in his own words) "passionately attached" to his friend. At one time Byron says this event "would have broken my heart." It was the recollection of what he "once felt, and ought to have felt now, but could not," that found expression in this poem. In another place Byron speaks of these verses as "the *truest*, though the most melancholy, I ever wrote." (*Letters*, Mch. 1816.) The mood which inspired the poem is thus found similar to that which went to the making of Gray's *Eton College* ode. (See L. Stephen's remarks on this mood in this and other poems, in *Hours in a Library*, 3d Series, 194 *et seq.*)

SHE WALKS IN BEAUTY.

386. "These stanzas were written by Lord Byron on returning from a ballroom where he had seen Mrs. (now Lady) Wilmot Horton, the wife of his relation, the present Governor of Ceylon. On this occasion Mrs. Wilmot Horton had appeared in mourning with numerous spangles on her dress." (Moore's Ed. of Byron's *Poems*.)

SONNET ON CHILLON.

387. This sonnet, together with *The Prisoner of Chillon*, to which it is an introduction, was written at a "small inn" in the village of Ouchy, near Lausanne, in June, 1816. The sonnet expresses Byron's devotion to liberty, which—while it may have been confused with a mere impatience of restraint, and a general attitude of rebellion—has nevertheless been called his "one pure passion." *Bonnivard* is the "prisoner of Chillon," the chief figure in Byron's poem. He was a man of republican views and of high character. He was imprisoned in the castle of Chillon about 1530, and remained there for six years.

CHILDE HAROLD.

388. *Childe Harold* records the meditations and impressions of a man of romantic, susceptible, and melancholy nature, brought face to face with the picturesqueness, beauty, passing life, and venerable associations of Europe. The poem is without plot. Childe Harold, satiated with the pleasures of a dissolute youth, flies self-exiled from his native land to visit "scorching climes beyond the sea." Harold's travels (his "pilgrimage" in romantic language) afford sufficient excuse for a series of brilliant descriptions of scenes and places through which he is supposed to pass. Always as a majestic background to this Europe of the present, stands the Europe of the past. The poem is thus descriptive or meditative rather than narrative ; the descriptions are the result of Byron's own travels, the meditations probably represent substantially what Byron thought and felt under the surroundings he describes,— with due allowance for such additions and omissions as may have been necessary for the poetic effect.

The first canto takes us into Portugal and Spain ; the second, into Albania and Greece ; the third, into Belgium and Switzerland ; the fourth, into Italy.

The title and the earlier portions of the poem show that Byron began it with the intention of making it distinctly "Romantic" and Mediæval in character. Harold is called *Childe* (the heir, that is, of a noble house), a title made familiar by old ballads like *Childe Waters* and *Childe Roland ;* the poem itself is called a "Romaunt"; it is written in the Spenserian stanza, the verse of the greatest of English romantic poems ; and it is not free from archaic words and phrases (*uncouth, wight, sooth, whilom,* and the like) which were a sign-manual of the revival of romance. While, by intention at least, it thus belongs to the Romantic school, these slight and somewhat forced attempts at Mediævalism were soon abandoned and the poem is, on the whole, distinctly modern.

CANTO III.—19. **In my youth's summer,** etc. The first two cantos of *Childe Harold* had appeared in 1812, or about four years previously.—23–27. **In that Tale,** etc. This passage in its "nice derangement" of metaphors is a good example of Byron's carelessness and confusion of style.

389.—100–126. **But soon he knew himself,** etc. How far the public were correct in assuming that Byron's melancholy heroes were really the poet himself thinly disguised, is a question which has been much discussed. Whatever view we may take, there can be little doubt that these stanzas express a mood eminently characteristic of Byron's poetry and, we may reasonably conclude, highly characteristic of Byron himself. For, on the whole, Byron's poetry (with due allowance for certain exaggerations and omissions) is self-revealing rather than objective.

390.—131. **Then came his fit again.** Adapted from *Mac.* III. 4. 21 : "Then comes my fit again : I had else been perfect," etc.—158. **Pride of place.** A term in falconry, applied to certain hawks which soar to a place high in the air and from there swoop down upon their prey. (See *Mac.* II. 4. 12.)

391.—181–9. This stanza refers to the ball given by the Duchess of Richmond, at Brussels, on the night before the battle of Waterloo. The boom of cannon rang through the city, and the festivities were broken up by a rush to arms. (For account of this ball see Lever's *Charles O'Malley*, Ch. LI.) —200. **Brunswick's fated chieftain.** Duke Frederick William of Brunswick, the head of the black Brunswickers (so called from their uniforms, in mourning for their losses at Auerstadt), who lost his life fighting at Quatre Bras. He was the son of Karl William Ferdinand of Brunswick, who died of a wound received at the battle of Jena.

392–3.—226–234. "**Cameron's gathering**," i.e., the "*pibroch*" (or air played on the bagpipes) to marshal the clan of Cameron. At the battle of Waterloo the 92d or Gordon Highlanders were commanded by Colonel Cameron, a descendant of the famous Highland Camerons of Lochiel. Two of his best-known ancestors, Sir Evan Cameron, and his son Donald (l. 9), called "the gentle Lochiel," fought against England, the first against William III., the second in the Jacobite Rebellion of '45; hence Byron speaks of the Saxon foes of Albyn (or Scotland) as having dreaded the Cameron's pibroch. Donald is the *Lochiel* of Campbell's familiar poem. Scott thus refers to Colonel Cameron in his poem *The Field of Waterloo* :

> "Saw'st gallant Miller's failing eye
> Still bent where Albion's banners fly,
> And Cameron, in the shock of steel,
> Die like the offspring of Lochiel."   (XXI. 12.)

235. **Ardennes.** "The wood of Soignies is supposed to be a remnant of the 'forest of Ardennes,' famous in Boiardo's *Orlando*, and immortal in Shakespeare's 'As You Like It.' It is also celebrated in Tacitus as being the spot of successful defence by the Germans against the Roman encroachments. I have ventured to adopt the name connected with nobler associations than those of mere slaughter." (Byron.)—757. **Clear placid Leman!**, etc. Byron and Shelley were in Switzerland together during the summer of 1816. The stanzas here given, marked by an unwonted tranquillity and elevation, record some of Byron's impressions of this time. It was under these influences that Shelley wrote the *Hymn to Mont Blanc*.

395.—808. **Cytherea.** A name for Venus, from her fabled rising from the ocean near the island of Cythera, off the southern peninsula of Greece.

396.—820. **The sky is changed,** etc. Byron tells us that he actually witnessed the storm here described, at midnight 13th of June, 1816. "I have seen," he says, "among the Acrocerannian mountains of Chimari several more terrible, but none more beautiful."—838. **Now where the swift Rhone**, etc. See, for a far more beautiful use of the same illustration, the famous passage in Coleridge's *Christabel* (conclusion to Pt. I) beginning, "Alas, they had been friends in youth." Curiously enough, these parallel passages appeared in the same year (1816), but as the first part of *Christabel* had been written as early as 1797, Coleridge's priority is sufficiently obvious. Moreover, Byron met Coleridge at Rogers' in 1811, and heard *Christabel*. Byron appears to have been impressed, for he made use of it in an abandoned opening to his *Siege of Corinth*, and in 1815 advised its publication.

398. CANTO IV.—**707. The Scipio's tomb**, one of the most ancient and interesting of the Roman tombs, was discovered in 1780. The entrance to it was by a cross-road leading from the *Appian Way* to the *Via Latina*. The sarcophagus, which was removed to the Vatican, bore the name L. Scipio Barbatus. "The vault itself has been emptied of the slabs and inscriptions, and the copies fixed in the spot where they were found may be thought ill to supply the place of the originals." (See Hobhouse, *Hist. Illustrations of Fourth Canto of Childe Harold.*)

399.—**728. Eureka** = I have found it. (Gr. εὕρηκα = I have found) The familiar exclamation of Archimedes when he suddenly hit upon a method by which he could find the amount of gold in Hiero's crown.—**734. Tully** = Cicero.— 1603–1629. These lines suggest the following passage from Lucretius:

> "So when wild tempests over ocean sweep
> Leaders, and legions, and the pomp of war;
> Their fleets a plaything in the hands of storms,
> How come the proud commanders then with prayers
> And votive gifts, imploring peace from gods!
> In vain: since not the less for prayers they oft
> In whirlwinds seized are borne to shades of death," etc.
> (*De Rerum Naturæ*, Bk. V. 1221. Good's trans.)

The same spirit appears in some of the poems of Leopardi, For an interesting analysis of the conclusion of *Childe Harold*, in which Byron's whole position is severely criticised, see "Byron's Address to the Ocean" (*Blackwood's Magazine*, vol. lxiv. 499.)

DON JUAN.

403. *Don Juan* represents the somewhat ostentatious flippancy, the vain regrets, the weary disillusion of Byron's later years. Here, more than in any other of his poems, Byron is seen in revolt; railing indeed against the shams and conventions of Vanity Fair, but involving in his wholesale onslaught much that is the very basis of the social order. *Don Juan* is the longest of Byron's poems. It appeared, a few cantos at a time, between 1819 and 1824. Its ease, power, and rapid movement, its strange medley of heterogeneous elements, cannot really be appreciated through selections, though the passages given in the text have been chosen with the idea of illustrating (as far as possible within brief limits) the mixed character and quick transitions of the poem.

CANTO III.—721. **Milton's**, etc. See "Milton" in Johnson's *Lives of the Poets.*—731. **Titus' youth and Cæsar's earliest acts.** Titus was in his youth notoriously profligate, and Cæsar (Julius) was also reported corrupt in his private life.—733. **Cromwell's pranks.** See note to Gray's *Elegy*, l. 59.

404.—738. **Pantisocracy** = the equal rule of all. Southey and Coleridge, when young men, planned to found a Utopian community on the banks of the Susquehanna. It was to be governed on improved methods, and they called it a Pantisocracy. (See *Int. Eng. Lit.* 325.)—739. **Wordsworth unexcised, unhired**, etc. As a young man Wordsworth was an ardent advocate of Liberty, Equality, and Fraternity and had the enthusiasm of a high-minded and generous youth who longed to reform the world. In later life this was tempered and he became more conservative, which laid him open to criticism, for he accepted the post, under government, of distributor of stamps for Westmorland and part of Cumberland. Browning in an early poem, *The Lost Leader*, refers to Wordsworth when he says :

> " Just for a handful of silver he left us,
> Just for a riband to stick in his coat."

But Browning's later judgment rather repents of it, and he says in a letter referring to the "silver and bits of riband": "These never influenced the change of politics in the great poet, whose defection, nevertheless, accompanied as it was by a regular face-about of his special party, was to my juvenile apprehension, and even mature consideration, an event to deplore."—740. **Pedlar poems.** An allusion to an early poem of Wordsworth's on *Peter Bell*, a pedlar, which provoked much ridicule.—744. **Espoused two partners.** Southey and Coleridge married sisters, the Misses Fricker of Bath.—746. **Botany Bay.** The well-known penal colony in New South Wales.—756. **Joanna Southcote's Shiloh.** Joanna Southcote was a curious specimen of an exalted visionary. She was born in Devonshire about 1750. She believed that she had the gift of prophecy, and she published predictions both in prose and verse in which many intelligent persons believed. She announced that she would give birth on October 19, 1814, to a second *Shiloh*, or Prince of Peace, and extensive preparations were made for his reception, but instead she fell into a trance, and died in the same year, supposedly from dropsy.

405.—807. **Ave Maria** = Hail Mary, from the opening of the Roman Catholic prayer to the Virgin. Church-bells are rung at dawn and sunset to remind the devout to say this prayer.—835. **Ravenna's immemorial wood.** The celebrated pine forest called *La Pineta*, the most venerable forest in Italy.—837. **Cæsarean fortress stood.** Ravenna was considered one of the most impregnable towns in Italy, and became in the later days of the empire the chief residence of the Roman emperors. Here Odoacer entrenched himself when Theodoric the Ostrogoth invaded Italy, and was only overcome after a three years' siege, 489–492.—838. **Ever-green forest**, etc. The ancient forest of *La Pineta* (The Pine) stretches along the shores of the Adriatic for twenty-five miles; Ravenna is on its inland border. There is a tradition that Dante loved to meditate here (*Purg.* XXXVIII. 20). Boccaccio chose this forest for the scene of a ghastly story, *Nostalgia degli Onesti*, which is the eighth novel in his *Decameron*. In this story the mounted spectre of a knight pursues with dogs the ghostly form of a woman who in life repelled his love with scorn. Dryden availed himself of the legend in his poem of *Theodore and Honoria*.

406.—857. **Soft hour !**, etc. See n. on Gray's *Elegy*, 1.

SHELLEY.

406. PERCY BYSSHE SHELLEY was born near Horsham, Surrey, in 1792. He was by nature a radical and an enthusiast: his father, Timothy (afterwards Sir Timothy) Shelley, was an embodiment of the conservative and commonplace elements of English society. This and other unfortunate circumstances probably aggravated Shelley's inherent tendency to wage indiscriminate war against the existing order of things, and his life was one of struggle and of protest. *Queen Mab* (1813) was followed in 1816 by the characteristic poem of *Alastor*, which showed a marked advance in power. A large amount of work was crowded into the six years which lay between *Alastor* and Shelley's tragic death in 1822. His lyrical drama, *Prometheus Unbound*, perhaps the finest of his long poems, appeared in 1820, and many of his best lyrics were composed during the latter half of his brief poetic career.

LYRICS.

Two essential elements in Shelley's poetry are its remoteness from the world of fact and its lyrical quality. Even in most of his longer poems it is the atmosphere peculiar to his filmy and prismatic world, and the spring of the lyrical movement, which especially attract us. That atmosphere, that lyrical movement, impetuous and rapid, gliding or fluent, is at least equally present in his shorter lyrics. And, in addition, we have in these shorter poems a proportion and a perfection, a power which comes from concentration, to which a longer work can hardly attain. Shelley is consequently represented far more adequately by his short lyrical pieces than are those poets who, beside their lyrical gifts, have a dramatic or narrative power which Shelley did not, to any degree, possess. In such wonderful creations as the *Ode to the West Wind*, *Night*, *The Skylark*, and *The Cloud*, we feel the throb of those emotions which were a part of the poet and an animating principle in his more extended work. A fellowship with the free, elemental forces of nature, and a half-primitive feeling for them as personal living things ; a restless desire for the impossible— " the desire of the moth for the star "; a recurrent tone of personal sadness and despondency, as of one hurt on the thorns of life ; a note of hopefulness for the future of the world, and a desire to share in bringing in that happier future for which he longs,—these moods and emotions we have no difficulty in recognizing as controlling elements in Shelley's lyrical work.

ADONAIS.

416. *Adonais*, a poem which challenges comparison with the greatest elegies of the world, was written in 1821—probably in the latter part of May. It is a lament for John Keats, who had died at Rome on the twenty-third of the preceding February. Shelley had a sincere and increasing, although not an unreserved, admiration for Keats's genius ; and while he was not blind to the youthful shortcomings of *Endymion*, he regarded *Hyperion* as " second to nothing that was ever produced by a writer of the same years." (Shelley's *Preface* to *Adonais*.) A born champion of those whom he considered victims of cruelty or persecution, Shelley was profoundly moved by the opinion (since discredited, but then generally entertained) that Keats' untimely death was the result of a brutal criticism of *Endymion* which had appeared in the *Quarterly Review*. Regret that a poet " capable of the greatest things " should have been thus early " hooted from the stage of life," and a passionate indignation against those who had (as he thought) perpetrated such a wrong,—these two feelings, rather than any keen sense of a personal loss, are the motive impulses back of the poem. In fact while the feeling between the two poets was kindly, especially on Shelley's side, they were hardly more than acquaintances, and the bond between them was not personal affection, but a common devotion to their art. Accordingly in *Adonais*, even more than in *Lycidas*, the note of individual grief is conspicuously absent. The mourners for Adonais are insubstantial personifications, *Poetry*, *Dreams*, *Persuasions*, *Splendors*, *Glooms*, and *Glimmering Incarnations*, and the cry of human suffering seems far off. The very occasion of their grief, the dead poet himself, remains almost as vague and impersonal as the majestic but shadowy abstractions which surround him. To say this is not to disparage the poem, but to suggest its indescribably elusive and phantasmal beauty ; it is simply to indicate that the lament is for Keats the poet, not for Keats the man, and that its true theme is the loss that Poetry, not Shelley himself, has sustained. From this the poem rises toward the close into the lofty and difficult region of philosophical speculation on life, death, and the hereafter. In spite of Shelley's own fear that the poem was "too metaphysical," some of the noblest stanzas occur in this latter and more purely speculative part. Shelley's general idea appears to be that there is back of the world of man and nature an *Anima Mundi*, the single Absolute Energy, the sustaining Power, the source of all beauty, goodness, and love. This Power reveals itself through life and nature, so far as the obscurity and imperfection of the media will permit. Man in this earthly life is really dead ; being partially separated from this Power, when he dies (at least if he have an affiliation with the Divine) that Power which produced him "withdraws his being" into its own. (Cf. *Asia* in Shelley's *Prometheus Unbound*, the *Lady* of the Garden in *The Sensitive Plant*, etc.)

Adonais is classical in form and is obviously modelled on two Greek elegies, that of Bion on *Adonis*, and of Moschus on *Bion ;* it also suggests comparison with *Lycidas*. It should be read in conjunction with these poems. (See Lang's *Theocritus, Bion, and Moschus, rendered into English Prose*.) *Adonais* was first published at Pisa in small quarto in June, 1821; it has been reprinted in fac-simile by the Shelley Society.

The reasons which led Shelley to choose this name *Adonais* have not been satisfactorily explained. The name is apparently not Greek, but its close resemblance to *Adonis*, the youth beloved by Aphrodite and slain by the boar, cannot fail to impress us. It has not escaped the critics that the untimely death of Adonis is the subject of that elegy of Bion's on which Shelley's is modelled, and Rossetti suggests that Shelley wished in this way to indirectly suggest his indebtedness to his Greek master. Dr. Furnivall suggests that *Adonais* is "Shelley's variant of *Adonias*, the women's yearly mourning for Adonis." The fact that this festival symbolized the dying and reviving of nature (see stanza XVIII, etc., and cf. Theocritus, Idyll XV) gives a faint probability to this conjecture. Perhaps Shelley may have had Keats' association with the nightingale in mind (see stanza XVII and Keats' *Ode to a Nightingale*) and given to the dead singer of the bird "not born for death" a name suggested by the Greek $\dot{\alpha}\eta\delta\acute{o}\nu\iota o\varsigma =$ of a nightingale. The necessities of the verse may account for the modification.

1. **I weep for Adonais**, etc. Cf. opening of Bion's *Elegy for Adonis*.—5. **Obscure compeers.** The other hours are obscure because no one of them stands out from the rest as distinguished by the death of Adonais.—12. **Urania**, literally the heavenly one ($o\dot{v}\rho\hat{a}\nu\iota a$), was the muse of Astronomy, but this seems to be no sufficient reason for Shelley's making her the "mighty mother" of the dead poet. Hales reminds us that Milton, using the word in its literal sense, makes *Urania* the goddess of "the loftiest poetry," and bids her "descend from Heaven." (See *Par. Lost*, VII. ll. 1–15, and also Tennyson's *In Mem*. XXXVII.) Rossetti thinks that *Aphrodite Urania*, and not the Muse, is intended. He says: "She is the daughter of Heaven (*Uranus*) and Light; her influence is heavenly; she is heavenly or spiritual love, as distinct from earthly or carnal love. . . . What Aphrodite Cypris does in the *Adonis* [of Bion], that Urania does in the *Adonais*." In either case we may conclude that by *Urania* Shelley meant that higher or heavenly Power back of the world, and the parent of all that is most elevated and beautiful. (Cf. stanzas XLIII and LIV, and the *Lady* of the Garden in *The Sensitive Plant*.)—18. **Bulk of death.** The impression produced by "bulk" here can be felt better than closely analyzed. "Bulk" here carries with it the idea of weight, as an inert, lifeless mass.

417.—35. **Sprite** = spirit.—36. **The third**, etc. Rossetti thinks that Shelley was thinking here of *epic* poets only, and that the two other poets besides Milton here placed among the "sons of Light" are Homer and Dante. He quotes a passage from Shelley's *Defence of Poetry* in which Homer is spoken of as the first, Dante as the second, and Milton as the third epic poet of the world.—39. **Happier they**, etc. This passage, usually spoken of as "obscure," may possibly be thus explained: The minor poets celebrated perhaps for some slight lyrics, although they aspired less high than the great epic masters just alluded to are in one respect more fortunate.

Lofty aspirations often lead to failure and unhappiness, so far as this world goes: the happiness of Milton and Dante was in a posthumous fame which they could not "*know*" except by anticipation, while a lesser poet, more in accord with the world, could "*know*" the happiness of life directly. Moreover, not all those who aspire highly win even posthumous honor: they may give up this world and get nothing. Still a third class are those who are now "treading the thorny road" which leads to fame.—47. **Nursling of thy widowhood.** Rossetti takes this to mean that Keats "was born out of time—born in an unpoetical and unappreciative age. Is it not rather intended to suggest the intense devotion of Urania, who mourned for him as a mother for the child who was "the nursling of her widowhood"?

418.—55. **That high Capital.** Rome, where Keats died in 1821. He was buried in the Protestant cemetery there, thus having literally in that Eternal City "a grave among the eternal."—69. **The eternal Hunger.** Probably "Invisible Corruption," just pictured as "at the door" waiting "to trace" (i.e., point out, indicate) his (Keats') extreme (or last) journey to the tomb, which is her dim dwelling. By "the eternal Hunger" Shelley doubtless means more than the forces which bring the body to decay; he probably means the mysterious and everlasting Antagonist of the durability of things.—75. **Who were his flocks.** While Shelley has followed accepted models in making his elegy pastoral in character, the pastoral element is barely suggested. As in stanza xxx the poets who assemble to mourn for Keats are spoken of as "mountain shepherds," so here Keats is represented as the *Shepherd* of his flock of thoughts. "He being dead," says Rossetti, "they cannot assume new forms of beauty in any future poems, and cannot be thus diffused from mind to mind, but they remain mourning round their deceased herdsman, or master."

420.—107. **Clips** = encircles, or encompasses. (Cf. "Yon fair sea that *clips* thy shores." Tennyson.)—109. **And others came,** etc. The Beings here introduced, the emotions which the dead poet had loved and to which he had given a more definite form by moulding them into thought (XIV), are surrounded with a vague and mysterious suggestiveness that makes this one of the most distinctively beautiful passages in the poem. Cf. the much more concrete and definite personifications in Spenser or Collins, where, although the outline is sharper, there is a loss in delicacy and suggestiveness.

422.—149. **Her mighty youth.** The allusion to the *eagle* nourishing his mighty youth would seem to be a reminder of the familiar passage in Milton's *Areopagitica:* "Methinks I see her as an *eagle* mewing her *mighty youth,* and kindling her undazzled eyes at the full mid-day beam," etc.—151, 152. **The curse of Cain light on his head**, etc., i.e., on the head of the critic whose review of *Endymion* in the *Quarterly* was erroneously supposed by Shelley to have caused Keats' death. By "the curse of Cain" is probably meant merely the penalty or retribution that should fall on a murderer (cf. Rossetti's *Adonais*), not the specific curse of Genesis iv. 11, 12.—154. **Winter is come and gone**, etc. Cf. the passage in the *Elegy* of Moschus beginning "Ah me! when the mallows wither in the garden"; Tennyson's *In Mem.* CXV.; and Arnold's *Thyrsis*, stanza VIII.

423.—177. **Nought we know dies**, etc. If matter is imperishable, never absolutely destroyed, but only changed from one form to another, if even the body, the sheath, or scabbard of the soul does not perish, but, touched by the recreative principle in things, exhales itself in flowers, shall the soul die like a sword (the higher thing) consumed before its sheath, meant but to screen and protect it? Shelley does not really answer this question here, but implies that the soul goes out like an extinguished spark.—187. **As long as skies are blue.** Cf. *Macb.* Act V. 5. 519.

426.—238. **Unpastured dragon** = the savage critic, ravening for prey. *Unpastured* = unfed, hungry (Lat. *impastus*).—250. **The Pythian of the age**, i.e., Byron, who slew the wolves, ravens, and vultures of the critical *Reviews* by his counter-attack in *English Bards and Scotch Reviewers*. He is here likened to Apollo Pythius, or Apollo the Python-slayer.—256. **And the immortal stars**, etc. Keats' genius, which has, like the sun, eclipsed the stars for a time, now takes its place among them in the heaven of poetry.

427.—262. After Urania, the lofty mother of Keats, has finished her lament, the "mountain shepherds," Keats' brother-poets, their "magic mantles" or "singing robes" rent, as a sign of mourning, assemble about his bier. First the poet of *Childe Harold's Pilgrimage*, who, generally identified with the "Pilgrim's" hero, is here spoken of as "the Pilgrim of Eternity," i.e., the Pilgrim who is placed by the greatness of his work above the mutations of time and change. (In *Childe Harold*, Canto IV. CLXXV, Byron speaks of "having won my pilgrim shrine"; see also his *Letter* to Hobhouse introductory to this canto.) Next Thomas Moore, who is described as the "sweetest lyrist" of Ierne, or Ireland. Rossetti suggests that by the "saddest wrong" of Ireland Shelley may mean the fate of Emmet and the suppression of the Insurrection of 1803. He cites the songs "O breathe not his name," "When he who adores thee," and "She is far from the land."—271. **Came one frail form.** In this and the following stanza Shelley describes himself. The passage is one of the most pathetic and remarkable self-delineations in English poetry; it suggests comparison with Cowper's reference to his sufferings in the passage "I was a stricken deer," etc. (*The Task*, Bk. III. l. 108, p. 249, *supra*).

429.—307. **What softer voice.** The last mourner is Leigh Hunt, the early friend of Keats in London, and the head of the so-called "Cockney-school" of poetry with which Keats at first was connected.

430.—343. **Peace, peace! he is not dead.** We here reach the second natural division of the elegy. The first half has been occupied with the expression of grief for Keats, and of indignation at the reviewers; the second part is chiefly occupied with general reflections suggested by the fact of death. As the predominant note of the first part is mourning, that of the second is hope. This arrangement is not peculiar to *Adonais*, but is to be found in most of the great elegies. Cf. *Lycidas*, l. 165; *Thyrsis*, f om " 'Tis done; and see back'd by the sunset," etc.; and the similar transition in the latter part of *In Mem.* Contrast the basis of hope in these various poems. —344. **The dream of life, etc.** The idea that the state which we call life is really death occurs several times in Shelley. Cf.:

> "Death is the veil which those who live call life:
> They sleep and it is lifted."
> > *Prometheus Unbound*, A. III. Sc. 3.

> "Lift not the painted veil which those who live
> Call life," etc.—*Sonnet* (1817).

Also E. A. Poe's *For Annie.*

432.—392. **When lofty thought, etc.** In proof of his assertion that Keats is not dead, the poet goes on to mention the ways in which his spirit still lives: in becoming a part of the life of nature; in being absorbed into the life of that Power which moves back of the physical or material, sustaining it, compelling its denser mass to assume new forms, and revealing its own beauty and love and goodness through matter, so far as it can torture the crude mass to express it and assume its likeness (see stanza LIV). Shelley then passes to the immortality of earthly fame: great souls are like stars, which death may blot for a time (cf. stanza v, "others more sublime"), but cannot extinguish; then, to the immortality enjoyed by those who live, after their death, by their influence on others. This view, more familiar since Shelley's time, is the one expressed in George Eliot's *Choir Invisible*, q. v.—397. **The inheritors, etc.** The thought of the preceding stanza is now illustrated by particular examples. Keats having been untimely cut off, he is received into the company of that group among the great dead whose promise of renown had, like his, been unfulfilled. Chatterton was not eighteen when he died, Sidney but thirty-two, and Lucan about twenty-seven. Lucan left his *Pharsalia* unfinished. He died because of his share in a conspiracy against Nero. Shelley probably speaks of him as "by his death approved" because he showed great courage at the last, and died repeating some lines from the *Pharsalia* on the death of a wounded soldier.

433.—415-423. **Who mourns for Adonais?** I suggest the following paraphrase of this stanza, probably the most difficult in the poem : Let him who, after all the sources of hope and consolation just advanced, still mourns for Adonais, "come forth" out of his narrow view and learn to know aright his own state and that of Keats—or of those we call the living and those we think of as dead. Let him clasp the earth, hung pendant in the abyss of space, and from it, as from a centre, project himself in thought through the infinite. Then let him shrink back into the petty limits of our day and night (the night which we are told (stanza XL) he has outsoared) into the cramping and sorrowful limits of the temporal world. Having once gained this eternal view, and seen the contrast, instead of mourning for Adonais he will rather have to keep his heart light lest "it" (i.e., his heart) make him sink after hope, kindled by hope into a bright flame, has led or enticed him to the verge of the infinite.—424. **Or go to Rome.** In interpreting all this latter portion of the poem we must keep hold of the poet's sequence of thought. The consolation laid down in the preceding stanza (XLVII) is based upon that amplified in stanzas XXXIX, XLIII ; so the present stanza similarly corresponds to that in stanzas XLIV, XLV, XLVI. If the contrast between the eternal sphere (to which Keats belongs) and the temporal (of which you are a part) does not move you, go to Rome, where the poet is buried, and reflect that the city's glory comes, not from conquerors, but from the "kings of thought," and that Keats being one of these gives glory to his resting-place rather than himself borrows it from his surroundings.

435.—455. **Too surely shalt thou find,** etc. Here another source of comfort is suggested; the misery of life is contrasted with the "shelter" of the tomb.—460. **The One remains,** etc. The contrast is between the permanence of the single, Absolute Existence, and the mutability of the many. The undivided white radiance of eternity—one light, but capable of being split up into all the colors of the spectrum—is but stained by the many-colored glass of life which, spread over us like a dome, shuts us out from the heaven. All earthly beauty being partial and transitory, one must die to really find the full and lasting beauty which is its source and into which it is re-absorbed.

KEATS.

440. JOHN KEATS was born in London in 1795; he died of consumption in Rome (where he had gone in the hope of prolonging his life) in 1821. Seven years younger than Byron, three years younger than Shelley, Keats' little day of work was even briefer than that granted to either of his illustrious contemporaries. The last of this great triumvirate to come, he was the first to depart. Keats is said to have written his first poem in 1813, or early in 1814, when he was about eighteen years old; his earliest book of verse, a faulty but promising production, appeared in 1817. *Endymion*, which made him a shining mark for the critics, followed in the next year, and a volume containing *Lamia, Hyperion, The Eve of St. Agnes*, and other poems, was published in 1820. It is on the poems of this last-named collection that Keats' title to be among the great poets after his death chiefly rests; yet these poems were the work of about a year and a half. Yet short as was his life, astonishingly short as was the period during which his genius was fairly in flower, Keats not only produced some poems that have taken their place beside the most consummate examples of shorter English verse, he had in him so large a fund of original force that he did more than either Byron or Shelley to guide and influence the poetry of the Victorian Age. An avowed worshipper of beauty, Keats found it in two great regions of æsthetic delight—Greek mythology and Mediæval Romance. These two worlds of beauty he luxuriates in with a fresh abandonment to sensation, depicting them at his best, with the supreme distinction of phrase. In either world, as the poet of the *Grecian Urn* and *Hyperion*, or as the poet of *La Belle Dame sans Merci* and *The Eve of St. Agnes*, we cannot but be sensible of the vital relation which Keats holds to the poets and poetry of the succeeding time. On the spiritual, moral, or philosophic side, the poetry of Tennyson has nothing in common with that of Keats. But on the purely artistic side, on the side of form and technique, it has long been recognized that Tennyson was Keats' descendant and lawful heir. Keats colored and moulded Tennyson's style, as neither Wordsworth, Coleridge, Byron, nor Shelley was able to do, and to influence Tennyson was to influence nearly all the poetry of Tennyson's time. (See *Int. Eng. Lit.* p. 378.)

THE EVE OF ST. AGNES.

This poem was included in the collection of 1820, and consequently belongs to Keats' latest and best period. Rossetti places it above all the poems of Keats not purely lyrical, with the one exception of *La Belle Dame sans Merci*. Regarded simply as a narrative, the poem shows but little skill ; yet the incidents, although often rather loosely connected, are so chosen as to afford abundant opportunity for gorgeous, highly-wrought descriptions and sharp, effective contrasts. Back of it all there is a sense of richness, warmth, and color ; over it all a languid atmosphere, heavy with sweet, dreamy odors. Keats found the suggestion for such story as there is, in the old superstitions and practices in regard to the Eve of St. Agnes, the night of January 20th. It was supposed that by observing certain ceremonies a maiden might see in her dreams the form of her future husband. Fasting, and lying on the back with the hands placed under the head, are among these ceremonies (stanza VI). See Brand's *Popular Antiquities.*—5. **Beadsman.** Literally a *prayer* (or praying) man (from M. E. *bede* = a prayer), particularly one who prays for another.

441.—37. **Argent** = silver, but here silvery-bright, shining. Cf. Keats' use of it in *Endymion*, III. 185 :

> " Pardon me, airy planet, that I prize
> One thought beyond thine *argent* luxuries ! "

38. **Tiara** = a rich head-dress. Originally a head-covering of the Persian kings ; in later days worn by the Popes, surmounted by the cross and richly ornamented.—39. **Haunting faerily**, etc. Cf. *L'Allegro*, ll. 125-130.

442.—67. **Timbrel** = tambourine.

443.—70. **Amort** (= French *à la mort*) dead, lifeless, uninterested. Cf. *Tam. of the Shrew*, IV. 3. 36 : "What, sweeting, all amort?"—71. **Lambs unshorn.** An allusion to certain old customs in the Roman Catholic Church. See *Translation of Naogeorgus*, after Brand :

> " Then commes in place St. Agnes' Day, which here in Germanie
> Is not so much esteemde nor kept with such solemnitie :
> But in the Popish Court it standes in passing hie degree,
> As spring and head of wondrous gaine, and great commoditie.
> For in St. Agnes' Church upon this day while masse they sing,
> Two lambes as white as snowe the nonnes do yearely use to bring ;
> And when the Agnus chaunted is upon the aulter hie
> (For in this thing there hidden is a solemne mysterie)
> They offer them. The servants of the pope when this is done
> Do put them into pasture good till shearing time be come.
> Then other wooll they mingle with these holy fleeces twain,
> Whereof, being ssonne and drest, are made the pals of passing gaine."

89. Foul. Apparently used here in the sense of "hostile" or "unfavorable."—**90. Beldame** = an aged crone (M. E. *bel* = grand, as *grand*-mother, etc.)

444.—117. **St. Agnes wool.** See note l. 71.

445.—133. **Brook.** Forman notes the "strange misuse of *brook* for the sake of rhyme." "Perhaps," he adds, "the sentiment of *baulk* was in Keats's mind, as that is clearly the meaning of the passage ; and *brook* was probably written in a kind of absence of mind."

446.—155. **Churchyard thing,** meaning that she is near to the time when she shall be laid in the churchyard. One foot in the grave.

447.—171. **Merlin paid his Demon.** Forman thus explains this passage : Merlin was the child of a devil ; consequently his monstrous debt was his existence, which he owed to a Demon, and which he paid back when he died or passed away under the spells of Vivian. "As to the words 'never on such a night,' etc., it is presumable that they refer to the tempest which, according to tradition, passed over the woods of Broceliande the night after the magician was spell-bound." —173. **Cates,** = delicacies, is really synonymous with *dainties.* 188.—**Amain.** The sense is, of course, violently or mightily pleased. The word is not quite correctly used, but Keats is apt to take liberties with his archaisms. See note on *Lycidas,* l. 111.

448.—212. **Stains** = colors. — 218. **Gules.** An heraldic term for *red.*

449.—241. **Swart Paynims** = dark pagans. Leigh Hunt says : "Clasped like a missal in a land of *pagans:* that is to say, where Christian prayer-books must not be seen, and are, therefore, doubly cherished for the danger."

450.—255. **Half-anguished,** i.e., tortured with the tumult of his emotions ; with a pleasure so intense that it becomes half pain.—257. **Morphian amulet!,** a charm capable of producing sleep.—264. **From forth the closet,** etc. Is it hypercritical to suggest that this incident, while it affords an excellent opportunity for Keats' peculiar richness of description, is in itself inconsistent and absurd ? In fact, after these elaborate preparations almost the first idea of the lovers after Madeline realizes the situation, is to seek safety in flight, for, as we are told, "the morning is at hand."— 268. **Argosy,** a vessel carrying rich merchandise, supposed to be so called from the town Ragusa, a port on the east coast of the Adriatic noted for its commerce.

ODES.

455. Keats' *Odes*, as Mr. Colvin remarks, are "quite free from the declamatory and rhetorical elements which we are accustomed to associate" with this poetic form. (See the remarks on the *Odes* of Dryden and Collins, *supra*.) But, remembering Wordsworth, his further assertion that "they constitute a class apart in English literature" seems somewhat extreme. The year 1819 is memorable in Keats' poetic development for his success in this species of composition, for in it *Psyche, The Grecian Urn, Melancholy, The Nightingale, Indolence,* and *To Autumn* (in short, all his greatest odes) were composed. All these, with the exception of the *Indolence,* appeared in the collection of 1820. In the *Ode to a Nightingale* the eternal spirit of gladness as typified or embodied in the bird's song, untrammelled by death and time, is contrasted with the sorrowful and transitory life of man. The *Grecian Urn* suggests the permanence and actual superiority of beauty, as realized in art, over life; of the ideal over the real. Sweet as are the "heard melodies," those "unheard" are sweeter still. Realization and disappointment go together. At the close, reverting to the thought of the *Ode to a Nightingale,* the shortness of human life is contrasted with the permanence of this creation of art, which shall preach to other generations the doctrine (the first article of Keats' creed) that Truth is but another name for Beauty. The *Ode to Autumn,* although less known than either of the two just mentioned, has a simplicity, truth, directness, and subtle beauty which entitle it to a very high place. It is as purely descriptive as Collins' *Ode to Evening,* and it has a wholesomeness, a fine grasp of fact, and a precision of phrase which Keats but too seldom attains.

LA BELLE DAME SANS MERCI.

461. This is Keats' greatest triumph in Romantic poetry, and has aroused the enthusiasm of the best critics. "The title is taken from that of a poem by Alain Chartier—the secretary and court poet of Charles VI. and Charles VII. of France—of which an English translation used to be attributed to Chaucer, and is included in the early editions of his works. This title had caught Keats' fancy, and in the *Eve of St. Agnes* he makes Lorenzo waken Madeline by playing" an ancient song of Provence, "called *La Belle Dame Sans Merci.*" "The syllables continuing to haunt him, he wrote in the course of the spring or summer (1819) a poem of his own on the theme, which has no more to do with that of Chartier than Chartier has really to do with Provence." (Colvin's *Keats*, *E. L. M.*, Series, p. 163.)

SONNETS.

463. It is usual to place Keats with the greatest English sonnet-writers of recent times, — with Wordsworth, Mrs. Browning, and Rossetti. His relative place among these masters need not be discussed here; it is enough to say that while few would deny Wordsworth's supremacy as a sonnetteer among the poets of this group, few would deny that Keats has fairly won a place among the six best masters of the sonnet since Milton.

ON FIRST LOOKING INTO CHAPMAN'S HOMER.

Chapman's translation of Homer, like the *Faerie Queene* and the Elgin Marbles, was one of the early quickeners of Keats' genius. His friend C. Cowden Clarke tells how he introduced Keats to the book in 1815. Clarke adds that on the morning after they had first looked into the book together, he found on his breakfast-table a letter enclosing Keats' sonnet. They had sat up late, but the sonnet had been produced in the brief interval. (*Recollections of Writers.*) It is hardly necessary to add that Balboa and not Cortez discovered the Pacific, or to say that the slip does not appreciably affect the value of the poem.

SONNET, JUNE 1816.

464. Mr. Buxton Forman says: "In a transcript in the handwriting of George Keats this sonnet is subscribed as 'Written in the Fields — June 1816.' . . . He reminds us that the opening line is apparently an unconscious reproduction of *Par. Lost*, IX. 445—'As one who long in populous city pent.'" The sonnet was published in the volume of 1817.

ON THE GRASSHOPPER AND CRICKET.

C. Cowden Clarke enlightens us as to the origin of this sonnet. On one occasion when Leigh Hunt, Clarke, and Keats were together, the conversation turned upon the grasshopper, and Hunt proposed to Keats that each should write a sonnet on the subject then and there. Keats "won as to time," but it may be fairly questioned whether Hunt's sonnet (see p. 465) is not the better of the two.

LAST SONNET.

465. This sonnet was written about the end of September or beginning of October 1820. Lord Houghton tells us that after Keats had embarked for Italy he "landed once more in England on the Dorsetshire coast, after a weary fortnight spent in beating about the Channel." The day was beautiful, and it was under the reviving influence of the scene that this sonnet was composed.

HUNT.

JAMES HENRY LEIGH HUNT, commonly known as Leigh Hunt, was born at Southgate in 1784, and died at Putney in 1859. He went to Italy in 1821, by the invitation of Shelley, to help him and Byron in establishing a paper to be called *The Liberal*. Hunt's residence in Italy had a marked effect upon his style, which shows in consequence a greater warmth and richness of coloring. On his return to England about 1825, he became the head of the so called "Cockney School" of poetry, and had many admirers and followers. His influence on Keats, and especially on that poet's earlier work, is obvious, although the pupil soon surpassed his master. Indeed, Hunt, although a fluent writer, essayist, and poet, is more remarkable for his influence upon his contemporaries than for his own productions.

TO THE GRASSHOPPER AND THE CRICKET.

See note to Keats' poem on the same subject, *supra*.

LANDOR.

466. WALTER SAVAGE LANDOR (1775–1864) was born at Ipsley Court, Warwick, and died at Florence, Italy, in his ninetieth year. He published a volume of *Poems* in 1795, the first parts of his best known work, *Imaginary Conversations*, in 1824, and *Epigrammes* in both Latin and English. His style, which was classical rather than romantic, was greatly appreciated by such men as De Quincey and Southey, but his lack of warmth, and his remoteness from the interests of his own time, were not calculated to make him popular. The mass of Landor's writings is very great, and his place in literature distinguished and assured; yet while many acknowledge his merits, comparatively few read his works. Nevertheless some of his highly finished short poems, like *Rose Aylmer*, are known to every lover of English verse.

PROCTER.

468. BRYAN WALLER PROCTER was born in London, 1787, and died 1874. At Harrow he had as schoolmates Sir Robert Peel and Byron. He went to London to study law, and he began to write in 1819 under the name of *Barry Cornwall;* his first work was *Dramatic Scenes and Other Poems.* A tragedy which he wrote in 1821, *Mirandola*, was performed with some measure of success at Covent Garden. Several more books of verse appeared; memoirs of Kean and Charles Lamb, stories and other literary productions. His *English Songs* (1832) contains his best-known work. As a man he was much beloved, and had among his friends Wordsworth, Coleridge, and Keats of the earlier time, and Tennyson, Browning, Carlyle, and Dickens towards the close of his long life.

HARTLEY COLERIDGE.

469. HARTLEY COLERIDGE, son of Samuel Taylor Coleridge, was born at Clevedon, Somersetshire, in 1796, and died in 1849. He is buried at Grasmere near the grave of Wordsworth. He was a contributor to *Blackwood's Magazine*, and published *Biographia Borealis or Lives of Distinguished Northmen* in 1832. His prose is of good quality, original and interesting. He published a volume of *Poems* in 1833. As a poet he belongs to the school of Wordsworth, and is probably at his best in his sonnets, which have a rare charm of expression.

LAMB.

470. CHARLES LAMB, one of the most charming of English prose-writers, was born in London in 1775. At the age of seven he entered Christ's Hospital, known from the peculiar dress of the pupils as the "Blue Coat School." Here he began his long friendship with Samuel Taylor Coleridge. Leaving school in 1789, he obtained a clerkship in the India House, a position which assured him a modest competence, and (what was even more important) some leisure hours to devote to literature. His best work is in his prose. His *Essays of Elia* (1822–1824), which belong to the same class as those of Addison and Steele, have a delicacy, wit and pathos, a gentle and playful humor, which give them an indescribable charm. His deepest sympathies were with the past, and his *Specimens of Dramatic Poets Who Wrote about the Time of Shakespeare* (1808) was an important contribution to that renewed fondness for Elizabethan literature which was characteristic of his time. While he had an essentially poetic nature, depth, insight, sincerity, and a loving memory of early association, Lamb but infrequently used verse as a medium of expression. (See *Int. Eng. Lit.* 356 *et seq.*)

HOOD.

471. THOMAS HOOD was born in London in 1798, and died there in 1845. In 1821 he became a contributor to the *London Magazine*, but his poems, of a refined and rather melancholy character, were but little noticed. In 1825, in collaboration with his brother-in-law Reynolds, he put forth an anonymous volume of humorous verse, *Odes and Addresses to Great People*, which won instant recognition. Coleridge attributed it to Lamb, believing him to be the only man capable of its composition. This determined Hood's manner. *Whims and Oddities* followed in 1826, to which he added comic pictures of his own drawing. While Hood is chiefly thought of as a light and witty versifier, his nature has another and a nobler side. The depth, earnestness, and insight into suffering shown by such poems as *The Song of the Shirt*, *The Death-Bed*, and *Eugene Aram* make them a lofty and lasting contribution to our literature.

VICTORIAN VERSE

MACAULAY.

477. THOMAS BABINGTON MACAULAY (1800–1859) was born at Rothley Temple, Leicester, and died at Holly Lodge, Campden Hill, Kensington. He was buried in the Poet's Corner, Westminster Abbey. He was a most insatiable reader and a brilliant and versatile writer. History, biography, essays, all flowed from his untiring pen. A trip to Italy inspired a book of poems, *Lays of Ancient Rome*, 1842,—ringing, martial verse, of a healthy robust order. This book with a few other battle-pieces shows his power to grasp and retain the purely picturesque side of historic character and incident, and complete his contribution to our poetry. (See *Int. Eng. Lit.* 407 *et seq.*)

THE BATTLE OF IVRY.

Ivry, a village in France where the battle was fought, March 14, 1590, between Henry of Navarre, the champion of Protestantism, and the forces of the Roman Catholic "League" (see Motley's *United Netherlands*, Vol. III. Ch. XXIII).—6. **Rochelle.** A fortified seaport town of France, a stronghold of the Huguenots.

478.—15. **Appenzel's stout infantry.** Appenzel is a double Canton in Switzerland, one half of which is stanchly Protestant, while the other half is Roman Catholic. The people use a peculiar dialect and wear a distinctive dress. In this passage the Roman Catholics are obviously meant.—**Egmont's Flemish spears.** Count Philip of Egmont, a foremost man in the Spanish army, who commanded a body of Flemish troopers. —16. **Lorraine,** etc. Henry of Lorraine, Duke of Guise, spy and agent of Philip II. of Spain.—**Mayenne,** Duke of Mayenne, lieutenant-general for the League.—17. **Truncheon,** a commander's staff.—19. **Coligni,** i.e., Gaspard de Coligni, the great commander who had espoused the cause of the Huguenots and who was murdered on the Eve of St. Bartholomew by the

Roman Catholics. The remembrance of that horrible massacre always inspired the opposite party to renewed action.—31. **Oriflamme**. The banner of France, a red flag on a golden staff (*or* = gold, *flamme* = a flag).

479.—35. **Guelders**. A Dutch province half Protestant and half Roman Catholic.—**Almayne** = Allemagne = Germany, used sometimes in the broad sense of the land on the Continent within which the Germanic nations are dominant, hence Austria, Switzerland, the Netherlands, etc.—42. **D'Aumale**. Charles de Lorraine, duke D'Aumale, an ardent partisan of the League.

480.—**Lord of Rosny**. Maximilian de Bethune Sully, Marquis and Duke of Rosney. He fought with the squadron which met Egmont's first onset, and received seven wounds.—55. **Cornet**. The standard of a troop of cavalry.—64. **Philip, send, for charity, thy Mexican pistoles.** An allusion to the moneys received from the Spanish conquest of Mexico. A pistole was a common name in Italy, Spain, and elsewhere for coins of differing values.

TENNYSON.

481. ALFRED TENNYSON, in whose verse the deepest life of Victorian England has found its most comprehensive, artistic, and perhaps most enduring expression, was born at the village of Somersby, Lincolnshire, in 1809. He belonged to a family distinguished by physical vigor and a poetic temperament. Tennyson was "the fourth of twelve children, ... most of them more or less true poets, and of whom all except two have lived to 70 and upwards." Tennyson entered Cambridge in 1828; here he became intimate with Arthur H. Hallam, whose early death was the occasion of *In Memoriam*. A book of juvenile verse, written in conjunction with his brother Charles, entitled *Poems by Two Brothers*, appeared in 1826. In 1829 he gained the University prize by his poem of *Timbuctoo*, and in 1830 he published his first independent venture, *Poems Chiefly Lyrical*. A similar collection appeared in 1833, and then, after an interval of silent growth, the collected poems of 1842, which placed him beyond all question among the greatest English poets of his time. In 1850 he published *In Memoriam*, probably the most thoughtful and original of his poems, and succeeded Wordsworth in the Laureateship. During the latter half of his life Tennyson's strength was largely given to the *Idylls of the King*, a poem (or series of poems) on the Arthurian legend, and to his dramas, the most important of which deal with English historical themes. The first ins'alment of the *Idylls* appeared in 1859, while *Balin and Balan*, the last of the twelve Idylls which comprise the completed work, was not published until 1885. Tennyson's work as a dramatist dates from *Queen Mary*, 1875. Tennyson, like Browning, worked to the end of a long life. He died at his home in Farringford, Isle of Wight, in 1892.

LOCKSLEY HALL.

Lockslay Hall first appeared in the volume of poems published in 1842. Tennyson says of it: "The whole poem represents young life, its good side, its deficiencies, and its yearnings" He tells us further that "'Locksley Hall' is an imaginary place (tho' the coast is Lincolnshire), and the hero is imaginary." (*Alfred Lord Tennyson: a Memoir, by His Son,* I. 195.) But the poem represents not merely young life in general, but a young man at a time when the youth of England was stirred by the marvels of invention and of scientific discovery. More than forty years after the publication of this poem Tennyson wrote a sequel, *Locksley Hall Sixty Year After*—a poem which represents not merely the changed attitude of the hero toward science and democracy, but the changed feeling of the time. The two poems are, as Hallam Tennyson says, "descriptive of the tone of the age at two distant periods of his [Tennyson's] life," and should be carefully compared. (See Hallam Tennyson's *Memoir* of his father, II. 329.)

483.—35-41. **Many a morning,** etc. These lines are a good example of the natural background forming a setting in accord with man's mood or feeling. We have seen how love first came in the beauty and life of springtime, but the moorland which the lovers delighted in together becomes "dreary," and the shore "barren," after one of them has proved faithless. It may be that this changed aspect of nature is due to what Ruskin has named "the pathetic fallacy" (*Modern Painters,* Pt. IV. Ch. XII), that is, that man is apt to color his surroundings with the tone of his own feelings; or Tennyson may have chosen to select a season when nature is dreariest for the disappointed hero's return. In either case he has heightened the effect.

485.—59-63. **Cursed be,** etc. Tennyson's general attitude was conservative, but on two points he held very positive and radical views. He was impressed with the dangers of the modern money-getting spirit, and he protested in many poems against allowing a worship of wealth and social position to prevent an otherwise desirable marriage (see *Aylmer's Field* and *Maud*). In *The Miller's Daughter*, on the other hand, he shows us love, triumphant over social differences, resulting in a happy married life.

486.—76. **That a sorrow's crown of sorrows**, etc. When we compare the original (*Inf.* V. 121):

> " . . . *Nessun maggior dolore,*
> *Che ricordarsi del tempo felice*
> *Nella miseria;* "

(There is no greater pain than to recall a happy time in wretchedness), we cannot but notice that Dante's lines gain by their simplicity, a strength which Tennyson's lose by their ornateness. Indeed simplicity is not one of the distinctive merits of Tennyson's style. (See *Int. Eng. Lit.* 473.)

487.—100–107. **Every door is barr'd with gold**, etc. Tennyson felt very strongly, especially in his later years, that England was becoming more and more a slave to wealth. It was not only the door of marriage that was "barr'd with gold," but other doors as well, and even the honor of the nation could be sullied by a love of greed. Note how this danger is pointed out in *To the Queen* (an epilogue to *The Idylls of the King*, and cf. also *Maud*).

488.—117–127. **Men, my brothers**, etc. The system of railroad transportation in England dates from about 1830. The electric telegraph was patented in 1837. The increased application of those two great forces, steam and electricity, meant an inevitable change in the social conditions of England. (See *Int. Eng. Lit.* 402.)—121. **Argosies.** Cf. note on Keats' *Eve of St. Agnes*, 268.

489.—127–131. **Till the war-drum**, etc. Tennyson believed to the last that universal peace could only be attained through war. (Cf. *Epilogue to The Charge of the Heavy Brigade at Balaclava*, and a more direct parallel of this passage in *Locksley Hall Sixty Years After* (ll. 166–175). See, also, H. Tennyson's *Memoir*, I. 400.)—135, 136. **Slowly comes a hungry people,** etc. This is but one of many passages in which Tennyson expresses distrust of the power of the rising democracy. Cf. in *The Palace of Art:*

> " The people here, a beast of burden slow,
> Toil'd onward, prick'd with goads and stings;
> Here play'd a tiger, rolling to and fro
> The heads and crowns of kings."

Cf., also, the allusion to the French Revolution in *Locksley Hall Sixty Years After:*

> " France had shown a light to all men, preach'd a gospel, all men's good;
> Celtic Demos rose a Demon, shriek'd and slaked the light with blood."

489-90.—137-143. **Yet I doubt not thro' the ages**, etc. We find this idea of Evolution, as a law working in nature, for good and with a purpose, expressed again and again throughout Tennyson's work. Take, for example, the following passage from *In Memoriam*, LIV:

> " Oh yet we trust that somehow good
>   Will be the final goal of ill," etc.

Cf. also, sections LV. and LVI. of that poem. The unimportance of the individual in comparison with the working out of this cosmic process, suggested in l. 142, and "the individual withers," etc., recurs more fully in *In Mem.*, LV.

> " Are God and Nature then at strife,
>   That Nature lends such evil dreams ?
>   *So careful of the type she seems,*
>   *So careless of the single life.*"

491.—157-184. **Or to burst all links of habit**, etc. The following picture of a life of pure physical enjoyment and freedom from a civilized man's responsibilities strongly suggests *The Lotus-Eaters*. In that poem the wanderers yield to the same temptation here presented, to lead a life of dreamful ease in the exquisite tropical land before them ; here the hero turns away from the lower life, and his cry is "Forward ! forward !"

> " Better fifty years of Europe than a cycle of Cathay."

Tennyson also suggests the natural reaction of an over-civilization toward a primitive life in his stanzas beginning :

> " You ask me, why, tho' ill at ease."

492.—182. **Let the great world spin for ever down the ringing grooves of change.** Tennyson tells us : " When I went by the first train from Liverpool to Manchester (1830), I thought that the wheels ran in a groove. It was black night and there was such a vast crowd round the train at the station that we could not see the wheels. Then I made this line." (*Memoirs,* I. 195.)

ULYSSES.

493. This poem, published in 1842, is a contrast-study to *The Lotus-Eaters*. There we see Ulysses and his comrades yielding to the enchantments of a land that offered a life of perfect rest and peace. Here the desire is all for action. We learn through Hallam Tennyson (*Memoirs,* I. 196) that *Ulysses* was written soon after Arthur Hallam's death, and that it gave Tennyson's "feeling about the need of going forward, and braving the struggle of life perhaps more simply than anything in 'In Memoriam.'" (See, also, appendix of above, I. 505.) The immediate source of Tennyson's *Ulysses* is a passage in Dante's *Inf.* (XXVI. 90).—10. **The rainy Hyades.** Cf. *Pluvias-que Hyadas geminosque Triones* (*Æneid* I. 744; also III. 516).

494.—22-25. **How dull it is to pause,** etc. Contrast the spirit of these lines with those in *The Lotus-Eaters* (57-70), beginning, "Why are we weigh'd upon with heaviness," etc. (Cf. also *Troilus* and *Cressida*, III. 3. 150.)

MORTE D'ARTHUR.

495. This poem first appeared in the collection of 1842. It was afterwards incorporated into the *Idylls of the King*, where it forms the main part of *The Passing of Arthur*. In this later form some preliminary matter and a brief conclusion have been added and the *Introduction* and *Epilogue* of the earlier version omitted, but the poem itself remains almost un-changed. The *Morte D'Arthur* is distinguished from the other poems in which Tennyson approached the great central theme of his later verse, by the nature of its style or form. By mere measurement a short poem, it is in manner and by the fiction of the poet a fragment of a long one. Unlike its companion-studies, *The Lady of Shalott* and the rest, its mode of treat-ment is *epical*, and in it the large epic handling of the Arthurian story in the *Idylls* is thus first distinctly fore-shadowed. Tennyson adopted the same plan in his presenta-tion of the *Morte D'Arthur* that he afterwards followed in *The Princess;* in both instances he gave his old-world story a modern setting. The world of the present—its every-day dress and pressing interests—is thrust upon us in a prologue and after piece, and contrasted by implication with the world of the past. The introductory lines to the *Morte D'Arthur* also ex-plain the fragmentary character of the poem and call attention to its real nature. We learn that it is part of an epic on King Arthur, which consisted of the conventional twelve books, and that in style these books (according to their supposed author) were "faint Homeric echoes nothing-worth." The discussion as to the wisdom of thus going back to the past for subjects and, by imitating the great master of the epic, seeking to "re-model models," cannot but suggest to us that the same debate may have gone on within the mind of Tennyson himself. Edward Fitzgerald, Tennyson's life-long friend, has informed us that the *Introduction* and *Epilogue* were an after-thought. They did not exist, he says, when Tennyson read the poem to

him in manuscript in 1835.—7. **How all the old honor,** etc
An instance of what has been said of Tennyson's custom of
introducing modern problems and placing them in juxtapo-
sition with the past. In modern England the honor has gone
from Christmas, and the parson, "hawking" at recent science,
laments its results in a "general decay of faith." In the England of the past, to which the poet then abruptly introduces
us, Arthur, a Christian champion of the great ages of faith,
declares that men who know God and pray not are on a level
with "sheep and goats" (298–306). Finally, it is hinted in the
Epilogue that Arthur, the great type of the old ideals, shall
come again "like a modern gentleman." Then the sleeper
wakes to hear in very truth

> "The clear church-bells ring in the Christmas morn."

50. **Read, mouthing out,** etc. This seems to be an accurate
description of Tennyson's manner in reading his own works
aloud. Edward Fitzgerald, with this passage in mind, describes him as "mouthing out his hollow oes and aes . . . with
a broad North-country vowel. . . . His voice, very deep and
deep-chested—like the sound of a far sea or of a pine wood."
Bayard Taylor writes: "His reading is a strange monotonous
chant, with unexpected falling inflexions. . . . It is very im-
pressive."

497.—1. **So all day long the noise of battle roll'd.** Tradition tells us that King Arthur was mortally wounded in a
battle he fought against his nephew Mordred in 542. Slaughter
Bridge, which is still pointed out as the place in Cornwall
where this fight took place, is about a mile north of Camel-
ford, on the river Camel, and three miles from Arthur's castle
at Tintagel.—6. **The bold Sir Bedivere.** For Bedivere cf. *The
Coming of Arthur,* 173–176.

498.—27. **Thou therefore take my brand Excalibur,** etc.
The idea of a hero accomplishing wonderful deeds by the help
of a magic weapon is a favorite one in romance. In the legends
of Charlemagne, we have the account of Orlando, or Roland,
winning from a Saracen the famous sword Durindana, which
had once belonged to Hector of Troy and was of such strength
and temper that no armor was proof against it. The early
English hero Beowulf finds "the victory-blessed weapon . . .
the hand-work of giants," a sword too great for any ordinary
man to wield, and with it kills Grendel's mother (*Beowulf*,
XXIV. 1557). In the *Nibelungenlied* the possession of the
famous sword Gram or Nothung, with which Siegfried slays
the dragon, holds an important place in the story.—29. **In
those old days,** etc. See *The Coming of Arthur,* 283.—36. **But
now delay not,** etc. We cannot but notice how closely Tenny-

son has followed Malory in his description of what follows, in some places even preserving the wording of his original. Cf. the account beginning : "Therefore, said Arthur unto Sir Bedivere, take thou Excalibur, my good sword, and go with it to yonder waterside, and when thou comest there I charge thee throw my sword in that water, and come again and tell me what thou there seest. My lord, said Bedivere, your commandment shall be done, and lightly bring you word again." (*Le Morte d'Arthur*, Bk. XXI. Ch. V.) The word *lightly* is used here and by Tennyson in the sense of quickly.

499.—60. **This way and that dividing the swift mind.** A reminiscence of Verg. *Æneid*. IV. 285 : *Atque animum huc celerem, nunc dividit illuc.*—80. **Lief** = beloved. This use is not found except in poetry (cf. "My liefest liege," *II. Hen. VI.* III. 1.)

501.—128. **And flashing round and round,** etc. The metrical structure of this line has been justly admired. It is to be noted that the last foot (*in an arch*) is an anapæst, not an iambus, and that the effect of this is to accelerate the *tempo* and run the movement of the verse over to culminate in the abrupt monosyllable "shot" at the beginning of the next line. The repetition "and round and round" subtly impresses us with the feeling of a gathering momentum, a feeling heightened by the gradually accelerating movement of the latter part of the line, until with the word "shot" we reach the climax, as the sword leaves Bedivere's hand.

502.—186. **Dry clash'd his harness,** etc. This passage is a good example of Tennyson's skilful employment of sound effects. The lines which describe the armed knight struggling over the rocks, fairly bristle with harsh consonants ; the movement, moreover, continually accented by the sharp, rough monosyllables ("bare," "black," "juts," "crag," etc.) is what musicians would term *staccato*. But as we turn abruptly from the clatter of steel on stone to the lake shining in moonlight, the verse glides upon *l*'s and is melodious with soft vowel-sounds. A somewhat similar effect is found *supra* in ll. 101–2. (Cf. *The Princess*, III. 343.)

503.—220. **Mix'd with the knightly growth,** etc. When he chooses, Tennyson is as complete a master of periphrasis (the art, as Lowell dubbed it, of calling "everything something else") as any disciple of Pope. This helps to give his poetry that ornateness, that "curious elaborateness" that have been dwelt on by Walter Bagehot and Matthew Arnold. So in *Enoch Arden* the sailor's fish, in baskets of a very ancient and fish-like smell, appear as

> . . . "Enoch's ocean spoil
> In ocean-smelling osier."

505.—259. **To the island-valley of Avilion.** In Celtic legend the island of *Avilion,* or *Avalon,* was thought to be an earthly paradise for great heroes, in the western seas. This enchanted land is often mentioned in the poetry of the Middle Ages, and the early Romances of Arthur tell us that he was borne away to Avalon to be healed of his wounds. Glastonbury was at one time called Avalon, and in Henry II.'s reign a tomb, which was supposed to be Arthur's, was discovered there. Malory, after telling how the king went to the vale of Avilion and mentioning the uncertainty in regard to his death, speaks of the belief some hold that he was buried at Glastonbury.—278 **Perhaps some modern touches here and there.** This accurately describes Tennyson's method of dealing with classical or mediæval themes. While preserving the ancient setting, it was his custom to infuse into it a spiritual meaning which was essentially modern.

506.—300–354. **With all good things,** etc. Cf. Tennyson's idea of the coming of a fuller Christianity in *In Memoriam,* CVI.

SIR GALAHAD.

506. The Arthurian Legend appealed to Tennyson at an early period, and he has given us a number of short poems, *The Lady of Shalott* (1832), *Sir Launcelot and Queen Guinevere* (1842), and *Sir Galahad* (1842), which may be regarded as preliminary studies to his epic treatment of the whole theme in *The Idylls of the King.*

Sir Galahad and *St. Agnes,* while not avowedly companion-poems, are in a real sense complementary studies of the mediæval ideal. In the one, those ideals are presented to us in a masculine and militant, in the other, in a feminine and purely devotional form. As Tanish remarks: "Galahad's rapture is altogether that of the mystic. He is almost a St. Agnes, exchanging only the rapture of passivity for the transport of exultant effort." (*A Study of Tennyson's Works,* p. 75.)

507.—42. **Three angels bear the Holy Grail.** Tennyson has given us a fuller account of Sir Galahad's quest in his Idyll of *The Holy Grail.* Inasmuch as the promise was made only to the pure in heart to see God (*St. Matt.* v. 8), so the vision of the Holy Grail was only possible to those who possessed great purity.

508.—51. **The cock crows ere the Christmas morn.** Cf. *Ham.* I. 1. 158:

> "Some say that ever 'gainst that season comes
> Wherein our Saviour's birth is celebrated,
> The bird of dawning singeth all night long."

BREAK, BREAK, BREAK.

509. These verses (pub. 1842), which seem as if they must have been written within sight and sound of the sea, were in reality composed "in a Lincolnshire lane at 5 o'clock in the morning, between blossoming hedges." (*Memoirs*, I. 190.)

It was not until 1850 that Tennyson published *In Memoriam*, which was inspired by the loss of his friend Arthur Hallam, who died in 1833. But this short poem of *Break, Break, Break*, is an exquisite expression of Tennyson's own grief, and we find in it two lines almost parallel to some he wrote just after Hallam's death. Hallam Tennyson says : "On the evening of one of these sad winter days my father had already noted down in his scrap-book some fragmentary lines, which proved to be the germ of ' In Memoriam ' :

> ' Where is the voice I loved ? ah, where
> Is that dear hand that I would press ? ' etc." (*Memoirs*, I. 107.)

TEARS, IDLE TEARS.

509. This is one of the six songs which appeared in the third edition of *The Princess*, published in 1850. They were introduced, Hallam Tennyson tells us, ' to express more clearly the meaning of ' the medley.' "

These songs

> " The women sang
> Between the rougher voices of the men
> Like linnets in the pauses of the wind."

Tennyson said that " The passion of the past, the abiding in the transient, was expressed in 'Tears, Idle Tears,' which was written in the yellowing autumn-tide at Tintern Abbey, full for me of its bygone memories. Few know that it is a blank-verse lyric." (*Memoirs*, I. 253.)

INTRODUCTION TO "IN MEMORIAM."

511. This opening poem, in which Tennyson has concentrated much of the essence of *In Memoriam*, was written in 1849, after that work was complete. The whole was published in 1850.

1. **Strong Son of God**, etc. Mr. Churton Collins suggests the following parallel from Herbert's *Love:*

> " Immortal Love, author of this great frame,
> Sprung from that beautie which can never fade;
> How hath man parcel'd out thy glorious name,
> And thrown it on that dust which thou hast made."

15. **Our wills are ours**, etc. Mr. Collins says : " The best commentary on this, is the whole of the third canto of Dante's
Paradiso." (Cf. also *In Mem*. CXXXI, and the poem entitled
Will.)—17. **Our little systems**, etc. Mr. Collins also cites Herbert's *Whit-sunday :* " Lord, though we change, thou art the
same."

511, 512.—21-28. **We have but faith**, etc. Cf. *Heb*. xi. 1:
" Now faith is the substance of things hoped for, the evidence
of things not seen."

512.—25. **Let knowledge grow**, etc. Cf. *In Mem*. CXIV;
Locksley Hall, 141; and Cowper's *Task*, Bk. VI. 88.

SELECTIONS FROM "MAUD."

Maud, which has been appropriately classified as "a mono-
dramatic lyric," appeared in 1855, following *In Memoriam*
and *The Princess*. It is daringly modern ; attacking the mania
for money-getting, the adulteration of food and drugs, and
kindred abuses which are seldom allowed to invade literature.
It has been harshly criticised and is undeniably unequal, but
it contains passages which must be placed among the highest
achievements of Tennyson's genius. If Tennyson has ever
equalled, he has certainly never surpassed, the two great
spousal-songs, " I have led her home" and "Come into the
Garden, Maud," in any poem of similar range and intention.
In intensity of emotion, freedom and flow of lyric movement,
and delicate beauty of fancy and imagination, these love songs
are among the poetic glories of the Victorian Era.

CROSSING THE BAR.

515. Hallam Tennyson writes : " ' Crossing the Bar' was
written in my father's eighty-first year, on a day in October
when we came from Aldworth to Farringford. Before reaching Farringford he had the Moaning of the Bar in his mind,
and after dinner he showed me this poem written out. I said,
' That is the crown of your life's work.' He answered, ' It
came in a moment.' He explained the ' Pilot' as ' That
Divine and Unseen who is always guiding us.' A few days
before my father's death he said to me: ' Mind you put
"Crossing the Bar" at the end of my poems.' " (*Memoirs*,
II. 367.)

BROWNING.

516. ROBERT BROWNING had the keenest and subtlest
intellect, the deepest and broadest human sympathy, of any
English poet of his generation. He stands apart from his

poetic contemporaries by the originality of his methods and by the unconventionality and power of his style. He was born in Camberwell (a suburban district of London, on the Surrey side of the Thames) in 1812. His father, a clerk in the Bank of England, was, in his son's words, "a scholar and knew Greek." As a boy Browning came under the spell of Keats and Shelley, the influence of the latter on his early style being especially marked. *Pauline*, his first published poem, appeared in 1833. Later in the same year he visited Italy, which exercised so important an influence on his thought and work that he once called it his "University." Within the next five or six years he produced a play and two long poems, one of them dramatic in form. In 1841 he began to publish poems in a series, to which he gave the mystifying name of *Bells and Pomegranates*. The poems in this series were issued in shilling numbers, and many of Browning's best works first appeared in this form. In 1846 Browning married Elizabeth Barrett (see p. 539), and the two poets settled in Italy. Browning's poetic activity extends over nearly sixty years, and the number of his poems makes any enumeration of them here impossible. Among many notable works *Men and Women* (1855), *Dramatis Personæ* (1864), and his monumental masterpiece, *The Ring and the Book* (1868–69), demand especial mention. After the death of his wife in 1861, Browning lived for a time in England ; but he returned to Italy, and died there at Asolo in 1889. Whatever place he may ultimately hold among English poets, Browning, "ever," as he says, "a fighter," has been one of the most wholesome and inspiring forces in the literature of our time. When other "kings of thought" have doubted, wavered, or retreated, his voice has been a trumpet-call rallying a dispirited, bewildered, and sophisticated generation.

MY LAST DUCHESS.

This poem is a conspicuous example of Browning's mastery of the dramatic monologue ; a poetic form of which he is commonly thought to have been the inventor, and which, at least, he brought to an artistic perfection never before attained. These fifty-six lines, alive with suggestion, and revealing in a perfectly unforced and natural conversation the depths of two characters and the history of two lives, are sufficient in themselves to prove Browning a consummate artist of a strong and original type. The poem first appeared in *Dramatic Lyrics*, the third number of *Bells and Pomegranates*, in 1842. It was there entitled *Italy*, and was the first of two companion poems,— *Italy and France*. The *Duke*, like the *Bishop* who ordered his tomb at St. Praxed's Church, is a characteristic product of the Italy of the Renaissance. He exemplifies Browning's favorite doctrine that we are not saved by taste, and that a fine æsthetic appreciation is by no means incompatible with a small, ignoble, and worldly nature.—6. **Frà Pandolf** is an imaginary artist, as is *Claus of Innsbruck* (56).

517.—45. **This grew ; I gave commands.** Prof. Corson. holds that this "certainly must not be understood to mean' commands for her death, as it is understood by the writer of the articles in 'The St. Paul's Magazine' for December, 1870 and January, 1871." See, however, preface to Corson's *Introduction to Browning*, ed. 1899.

HOME THOUGHTS FROM ABROAD.

518. These verses appeared in *Dramatic Lyrics*, the seventh number of *Bells and Pomegranates*, 1845. It was the first of a group of three poems, *Here's to Nelson's Memory* and *Nobly Cape St. Vincent* being the other two. The famous description of the thrush's song has a beauty that comes from an absolute truth to fact. Cf. Lowell's hardly less famous passage on the song of the bobolink in *An Indian-Summer Reverie*.

THE GUARDIAN ANGEL.

519. This poem was written in 1847, the first summer the Brownings passed in Italy. It was published in *Men and Women*, 1855. *L'Angelo Custode*, the picture which inspired the poem, is in the Church of St. Augustine at Fano, a town on the Adriatic. It was painted by Guercino and "represented an angel standing with outstretched wings by a little child. The child is half kneeling on a kind of pedestal, while the angel joins its hands in prayer ; its gaze is directed upwards towards the sky, from which cherubs are looking down." The poem was addressed to Alfred Domett (Waring). I have omitted the last three verses, which are on a less exalted level and seem to add little to the poem. They explain the circumstances under which the verses were composed, and close with a regret at Domett's absence in Australia.

ANDREA DEL SARTO.

521. This is one of the most satisfying and finished of Browning's dramatic monologues ; it is as perfect a work of art as *My Last Duchess*, but more complex and on a larger scale. We naturally associate it with *Fra Lippo Lippi, Old Pictures in Florence, The Bishop Orders His Tomb at St. Praxed's*

Church, and other poems which show both Browning's views of the true function of art in relation to life, and the profound effect that Italy and Italian art had upon his genius. In his portrayal of the characters of Andrea and his wife Lucrezia, Browning has followed the life by Giorgio Vasari, who himself was Andrea's pupil. Browning had also in mind a portrait of Andrea del Sarto and his wife supposed to be painted by himself and now in the Pitti Palace, Florence. John Kenyon asked Browning for a copy of this picture, which he was unable to give. As a substitute he put the spirit of the picture, as he understood it, into the sister-art of verse. Andrea, called " del sarto,"—or, as we would say, the tailor's son,—was born at Florence in 1487. After working at gold-smithing, wood-carving, and drawing, and studying under several painters, he executed some frescoes for the Church of the Annunciation at Florence, with such accuracy and skill that he gained the name of *pittore senza errore*—the faultless painter. At twenty-three he is said to have had no superior in Central Italy in technique. In 1512 he married Lucrezia, "a beautiful widow." "But," says Vasari, "he destroyed his own peace, as well as estranged his friends, by this act, seeing that he soon became jealous, and found that he had fallen into the hands of an artful woman, who made him do as she pleased in all things." In 1518 he went to Paris without Lucrezia, at the invitation of Francis I. This is the period of adulation and substantial rewards that he looks back upon in the poem as his long festal year, when he could "sometimes leave the ground." But Lucrezia wrote urging his return. The king granted him a brief leave of absence, and commissioned him to buy certain works of art in Italy. Andrea, beguiled by his wife, used the money which Francis had entrusted to him, to build a house for himself at Florence. His career in France being thus miserably interrupted, he remained in Florence, where he died of the plague in 1531. (See analysis of the poem in "Study List," *Int. Eng. Lit.* 502.)

15. **Fiesole.** A small town on a hill-top about three miles to the west of Florence. Possibly the convent to which Andrea alludes is that of San Domenico, which was situated between Florence and Fiesole. Browning apparently makes Andrea build his house on the outskirts of Florence immediately facing the Convent of San Domenico, with Fiesole in the distant background. If this was the convent intended, the pathos of the poem is heightened by the contrast between Fra Angelico, the heavenly-minded painter with whose early life it is associated, and Andrea, the painter incomparably superior to him in technical skill, but weighed down with a mind that cannot rise above earthly things.

522.—49. **Love, we are in God's hand**, etc. This is not piety, but Andrea's characteristic way of evading responsibility. Later he attributes his comparative failure to his wife (125), and then, suddenly shifting to the other view, declares that after all "incentives come from the soul's self."

523.—78. **Less is more.** Vasari says of Andrea: "Had this master possessed a somewhat bolder and more elevated mind, had he been as much distinguished for higher qualifications as he was for genius and depth of judgment in the art he practised, he would beyond all doubt have been without an equal."—93. **Morello.** A mountain to the north of Florence.

524.—105. **The Urbinate** = Raphael, who was so called from his birthplace, Urbino.

525.—130. **Agnolo** = Michael Angelo or Michelangelo Buonarroti, whose name is sometimes given, it is said, more correctly as Michelagniolo.

526.—166. **Had you not grown restless**, etc. In the first edition of his *Lives of the Painters*, Vasari dwells at some length upon the complaining letter which Andrea's wife wrote him from Florence. Her "bitter complaints" dressed up "with sweet words" ordered Andrea (as Vasari says) "to resume his chain." The passage, like others relating to Lucrezia, was omitted from the subsequent editions.—178. **The Roman's** = Raphael, who left Florence to settle in Rome about 1508.— 189. **Friend, there's a certain**, etc. In Bocchi's *Bellezze di Firenze*, Michael Angelo is reported to have spoken thus of Andrea to Raphael: "There is a bit of a mannikin at Florence who, had he chanced to be employed in great undertakings as you have happened to be, would compel you to look well about you."

527.—210. **The cue-owls**, etc. A name applied to the Scops-owl (*Scops Giu*). Common on the shore of the Mediterranean and a summer visitant to Britain. (*Murray's Dict.*) "To my ear its cry is a clear metallic ringing *ki-ou*, whence the Italian names *Chiù, Ciù.*" (Howard Saunders, *Manual of British Birds*, p. 298.) See *Aurora Leigh*, Bk. VIII. 36.—240. **Scudi**, pl. of *scudo*, a silver coin of the Italian States, about the value of the American dollar.

528.—250. **My father and my mother died of want**, etc. Vasari says on this point: "He (Andrea) abandoned his own poor father and mother, . . . and adopted the father and sisters of his wife in their stead; insomuch that all who knew the facts mourned over him, and he soon began to be as much avoided as he had previously been sought after."

529.—263. **Leonard** Leonardo da Vinci (1452-1519). While on earth this great painter, sculptor, architect, and engineer came more than once into direct competition with Michael

Angelo, who is said to have regarded his older rival with jealous dislike.

PROSPICE.

This fighter's challenge to Death is distinctively English and distinctively religious. The abrupt masculine vigor of its verse, the unflinching courage with which it looks squarely in the eyes of the "Arch-Fear," these things are in keeping with the spirit of the Anglo-Saxon, from its earliest literary records until now. But it is no less true that the speaker is sustained by a confidence in the issue of the inevitable struggle, to which his earliest forefathers were strangers. The spirit of the Christian is united to the spirit of the Viking. It is not only emphatically English, but equally characteristic of Browning, himself a good example of sterling Anglo-Saxon manhood. The same unconquerable spirit is shown at the last in the "Epilogue" in *Asolando*. *Prospice* was written in the autumn of 1861; Browning had lost his wife earlier in that year, and the poem is evidently born out of the depth of his own experience. It was published in *Dramatis Personæ*, in 1864. The passage from Dante that Browning wrote in his wife's *Testament* might be taken as an expression of the essence of this poem : "Thus I believe, thus I affirm, thus I am certain it is, that from this life I shall pass to another better, there, where that lady lives of whom my soul was enamoured."

Prospice = look forward (imp. of *prospicio*).

RABBI BEN EZRA.

530. This poem was first published in *Dramatis Personæ*, 1864. Alive in every line with courage and quickening power, it is charged with the vital spirit that animates Browning and his work. The poet has expressed the ideals which dominate it in many ways and in many poems, but it would be difficult to name another poem in which he has summed up his philosophy of life in a form at once so brief, so clear, so beautiful, and so comprehensive. It is above all a poem to live by, and it contains the essence of Browning's creed. The poem is dramatic, but only in a secondary and formal way. The personality of Rabbi Ben Ezra is consequently of minor importance, since he is but a mouthpiece for Browning himself. Nevertheless the Jewish teacher who is supposed to be imparting to youth the ultimate wisdom of age is not an imaginary person, but a man whose views, so far as we can judge, were really similar to those the poet has put into his mouth. *Rabbi Ben Ezra*, whose real name is said to have been *Abraham ben Meir ben Ezra*, and who is variously spoken of as

Abenezra, Iben Ezra, Abenare, and *Evenare,* was one of the most distinguished Jewish scholars and Old Testament commentators of the Middle Ages. He was born at Toledo, during the latter part of the eleventh century, and is said to have died at Rome, about 1168. A hard student throughout his life, he lost none of his vigor or ambition through age, as he began a *Commentary* on the Pentateuch at sixty-four, and afterward entirely rewrote it. His view of life was lofty; to him the only reality was spirit, and he regarded material things as of very minor and temporary importance. (For fuller account, see "Rabbi ben Ezra" in Cooke's *Browning Guide Book.*)

7. Not that, amassing flowers, etc. The construction is, I do not remonstrate that youth, amassing flowers, sighed, etc., nor that it yearned, etc.

531.—31. Then welcome each rebuff, etc. This idea is a fundamental one with Browning, and is often reiterated in his poems. Cf. *Saul:*

> "By the pain-throb, triumphantly winning intensified bliss,
> And the next world's reward and repose, by the struggle in this."

In *Rephan*, the passage beginning:

> "Oh gain were it to see above," etc.

And in *Cleon:*

> "That, stung by straitness of our life, made strait
> On purpose to make sweet the life at large," etc.

532.—40. What I aspired to be, etc. Cf. *Saul:*

> "'Tis not what man Does which exalts him, but what man Would do!"

46. To man, propose this test. This thought is strikingly close to the real Aben Ezra's philosophy as summarized by Dr. Friedländer: "The Soul, only a stranger and prisoner in the body, filled with a burning desire to return home to its heavenly abode, certainly demands our principal attention."— **57. I, who saw power,** etc. This idea that Love as well as Power is to be discerned as a motive force in the universe, more than once alluded to by Browning, is made the main theme of "Reverie" in *Asolando.* The central idea of this poem is found in the following stanza:

> "I have faith such end shall be:
> From the first, Power was—I knew.
> Life has made clear to me
> That, strive but for closer view,
> Love were as plain to see."

533.—84. Indue—in the original sense of *to put on, to clothe* (Lat. *induere*).

535.—121. **Be there**, etc. Let there be, finally, the true station assigned to each. Was I who arraigned the world right, or they who disdained my soul?

536.—142. **All instincts immature.** The idea that a man's aspirations as well as his actual accomplishment must be taken into account in the absolute judgement of his life is also expressed in Lowell's poem *Longing.* Cf. further, on the insufficiency of the world's judgment, *Lycidas:*

> " Alas! what boots it with uncessant care," etc.

151. **Ay**, note that **Potter's wheel**, etc. Cf. *Is.* lxiv. 8, and *Jer.* xviii. 2–6. Rolfe cites the *Rubáiyát of Omar Khayyam,* LXXXIII–XC. See, also, Longfellow's *Keramos.*—156. **Since life fleets**, etc. This maxim of the Epicurean philosophy has found frequent and beautiful expression in verse. Cf. Horace, *Odes,* I. II. 8 : '' *Carpe diem, quam minimum credula postero.*'' Herrick *To the Virgins, To Make Much of Time,* etc.

537.—157. **All that is at all.** Cf. *Abt. Vogler,* IX. 5. :

> " There shall never be one lost good," etc.

538.—190. **My times be in Thy hand !** See *Psalms* xxiv. 15: '' My times are in thy hand.''

E. B. BROWNING.

539. ELIZABETH BARRETT BROWNING (1809–1861) was born at Carlton Hall, Durham, England. Owing to ill health she led a secluded life, devoting her time to reading and study in many languages and to the writing of poems. Among her earliest efforts is a spirited translation of Æschylus' *Prometheus Bound* (1833). In 1846 she met and married Robert Browning, the poet. Her love for him inspired her to write *Sonnets from the Portuguese,* which are among the most impassioned and beautiful love poems, and are almost unique as the presentation of love from the woman's point of view. She wrote many poems and sonnets ; *Aurora Leigh,* the best known of her long works, is a poem of considerable beauty and interest, but of unequal literary merit. In 1848 her *Casa Guidi Windows* appeared, showing her deep sympathy with her adopted country, Italy, which was then in a transition state. She died at Florence on the 29th of June 1861, in the Casa Guidi, where a tablet now records the esteem in which the city of Florence held her.

KINGSLEY.

544. CHARLES KINGSLEY, clergyman, novelist, poet, and social reformer, was born June 19, 1819, at Holm Vicarage, Dartmouth, Devon. He took his degree at Magdalene College, Cambridge, in 1842, and soon after became curate and then rector of Eversley, Hampshire, which was his home for the remaining thirty-three years of his life. For a time he was Professor of Modern History at the University of Cambridge; he held a canonry at Chester, which was exchanged in 1873 for a canonry at Westminster. He died at Eversley, January 23, 1875. Kingsley, a man of aggressive energy, intense enthusiasms, varied interests, and lofty ideals, was one of the most stimulating and wholesome influences of his time. He worked in his parish; he threw himself into the cause of the poor of England, and became their champion in tracts, novels, and poems. His collected works fill twenty-eight volumes, including sermons, criticisms, historical lectures, books on geology and on education. His work as an author began with poetry (*The Saint's Tragedy*, 1848), but the diversified activities and duties of a busy life were hardly compatible with the serious pursuit of so exacting an art. When this is considered, Kingsley's place as a poet is seen to be surprisingly high. He was a true song writer, and *The Three Fishers, The Sands of Dee*, and some of his other lyrics and shorter poems, are likely to be loved and known long after many lengthy and elaborate productions of more ambitious poets have been forgotten.

CLOUGH.

548. ARTHUR HUGH CLOUGH was born at Liverpool in 1819. He was an earnest child fond of reading and the old Greek stories. In 1829 he was sent to Rugby and came under Dr. Arnold's influence. He gained the Balliol scholarship and went to Oxford in 1836. This was a turning-point in Clough's career. Oxford was at that time agitated by the Tractarian movement and Clough was thus brought in to the storm-centre of theological controversy. In 1842 he was elected fellow of Oriel, and in the following year was also appointed tutor of his college. During 1843 his first volume of verse appeared entitled *Ambarvalia*. He felt that teaching was his natural vocation, and yet, being bound by his position to silence on the subject of his mental struggle over the religions questions then pending, his honesty led him to resign his post of tutor in 1848. In that year he wrote his first and perhaps his best long poem, the *Bothie of Tober-na-Vuolich,* and also *Amours de Voyage.* He received an invitation to take the Headship of University Hall, London, an unsectarian institution, and he entered upon his duties there in 1849. In 1850 he took a short trip to Venice and wrote *Dipsychus,* a long poem bearing the impress of this Venetian visit. He resigned his post at University Hall in 1852 and made a visit to America, where he remained for about a year. During this time he composed his *Songs of Absence,* wrote for the magazines, and began a translation of *Plutarch's Lives* for an American publisher. In 1853 he returned to England, and in 1860 was obliged by failing health to leave England again for foreign travel. During this trip he composed his poem *Mari Magno,* a series of tales told by a party of friends on a sea-voyage, and dealing with the social problems of love and marriage. Not gaining in health, he went to Italy, but was stricken with fever and died at Florence in 1861, in his forty-third year. Matthew Arnold, Clough's warm friend, wrote the beautiful elegy, *Thyrsis,* to his memory.

ARNOLD.

551. MATTHEW ARNOLD (1822–1888) was born at Laleham, a town not far from London in the valley of the Thames. His father, Thomas Arnold, was one of the greatest of English teachers, and Matthew, who was educated at the great public schools of Winchester and Rugby, and at Balliol College, Oxford, had every help which the academic training of his day could afford. He won a scholarship at Balliol in 1840, gained the Newdigate prize by a poem on *Cromwell* in 1844, and was elected fellow of Oriel in 1845. He was made Lay Inspector of Schools in 1851, and labored indefatigably in this onerous and exacting position until 1885. From 1857 to 1867 he was Professor of Poetry at Oxford. The earlier half of Arnold's literary career was devoted almost entirely to poetry; the latter almost as exclusively to prose. His first book of verse, *The Strayed Reveller and Other Poems,* appeared in 1849, while his essay *On Translating Homer,* which marks his advent as a critic, was not published until 1861. It was not until 1853, when he published a book of collected *Poems* under his full name (formerly he had only given the initial M.), that Arnold became known as a poet outside a limited circle. In prose, Arnold stands at the head of the literary criticism of his time: in poetry, if his greatest contemporaries excel him in range, emotion, or power, his place is nevertheless an honorable one, and his work possesses within narrow limits an excellence distinctively its own. That excellence lies chiefly in a certain exactness of phrase; a marked refinement of tone; in a lofty but austerely intellectual temper, and above all in a classic beauty which we associate with severity and restraint. Arnold was avowedly a pupil of Wordsworth in poetry; but while he shared in his master's love of Nature, his poetry has not the serenity nor religious hope that animate his predecessor. Yet Arnold's verse possesses unmistakably the quality of distinction: it represents a classic purity of outline in an age when Romantic poetry had carried to great lengths the color and warmth of a lavishly decorative art.

THE GRANDE CHARTREUSE.

The Grande Chartreuse is a famous Carthusian monastery, founded by Bruno in 1084. Bruno, tired of the world, longed for a life of seclusion and religious contemplation. He consulted with Hugo, bishop of Grenoble, who suggested the wilds near Chartreuse, a little town in the mountains of the department of Isère, France, from which the monks took the name of their retreat. The large buildings with high roofs, and turrets surmounted by the cross, loom up in this almost inaccessible spot. The poem gives a good description of the narrow mule-track leading past the tiny villages, and the Dead Guier (*Guiers Mort*, a tributary of the river Rhone).

    552.—37. **Where no organ's peal.** This does not harmonize with stanza 34, "The organ carries to our ear." The writer of the article on "Carthusian" in *Enc. Brit.* says that "on feast-days they eat twice, and *sing* all the offices of the Church," but I cannot find which statement of Arnold's in regard to the use of the organ is correct.—49. **The library.** In the early days of the order this library had a most valuable collection of books and manuscripts.

    553.—62. **Each its own pilgrim-host.** There are four separate halls for the reception of visiting monks from France, Italy, Germany, and Burgundy.—85. **Wandering between two worlds.** This stanza clearly shows Matthew Arnold's unsettled state of mind, his intellectual side warring with his religious nature, and his inability to hold fast to either. (See *Int. Eng. Lit.* 435, etc.)

    554.—99. **Sciolists** = pretenders to scientific knowledge. —115. **Achilles ponders in his tent.** Achilles, angered at Agamemnon, who has taken a captive maiden, Briseis, from him, retires to his tent and refuses to take any further interest in the battle. (See the opening of Homer's *Iliad*.)

    555.—139. **Shelley.** Shelley was drowned while sailing on the "Spezzian bay."—146. **Obermann** = Étienne Pivart de Senancour, born at Paris in 1770 and destined for the priesthood. He was an insatiable reader, and his study of Helvetius, Malebranche, and the eighteenth-century philosophers entirely destroyed his faith. He escaped from France and his destined profession, went to Geneva, married, lost his fortune, and turned to his pen for support. He wrote *Obermann*, his most famous book, in 1804. Matthew Arnold shows his great admiration for Senancour in his two poems, *In Memory of the Author of Obermann* and *Obermann once more*.

ROSSETTI.

565. GABRIEL CHARLES DANTE ROSSETTI, or DANTE GABRIEL ROSSETTI as he is more generally known, was born in London in 1828. He was the son of an Italian exile,—a poet, Dante-scholar, and man of letters,—who, forced to leave Italy for political reasons, had settled in London as a teacher of Italian. Much that the father thus exemplified, entered by inheritance and early surroundings into the character of his more distinguished son, and found expression in his art. From childhood Dante Rossetti's ambition was to be a painter, and at fifteen he left school and began the study of art. Through these studies he became acquainted with the young painters John Everett Millais and William Holman Hunt, and with them he started the so-called Pre-Raphaelite Brotherhood. The artistic reforms which the Brotherhood hoped to effect included poetry as well as painting, and Rossetti—who loved and excelled in both arts—expressed these ideas in both. On the side of literature, the bent of Rossetti's taste is shown by the publication in 1861 of his translations from the early Italian poets, afterwards published as *Dante and his Circle*. His original work in poetry began early, but his first book of poems (many of them written years before) was not published until 1870. Another volume, containing some of his best ballads and the remarkable sonnet-sequence *The House of Life*, appeared in 1881. He died in the spring of the following year. Rossetti is as distinctly an exponent of the Romantic as Arnold is of the Classic spirit. Like Keats he surrounds mediæval subjects with a glow of warmth and color; like Keats, too, he is a pictorial poet. But he reaches the Middle Ages through Italy, and the atmosphere of early Italian religion, poetry, and art, is almost inseparable from his work.

THE BLESSED DAMOZEL.

Rossetti wrote this poem in the nineteenth year of his age, or in the early half of 1847. His brother, Mr. W. M. Rossetti, is quite right in saying that it "ranks as highly remarkable among the works of juvenile writers," especially when its "total unlikeness to any other poem then extant is taken into account." Mr. Hall Caine is the authority for the statement that the *Blessed Damozel* grew out of Rossetti's youthful love for Poe's *Raven*. "I saw," Rossetti said to Mr. Caine, "that Poe had done the utmost it was possible to do with the grief of the lover on earth, so I determined to reverse the conditions, and give utterance to the groaning of the loved one in heaven." The poem was published in the second number of *The Germ*, in February 1850 ; it next appeared in *The Oxford and Cambridge Magazine*, 1856, and finally in the *Poems* of 1870. In each case, Rossetti made some changes. Mr. Joseph Knight, after remarking that the poem "seems to have no literary prototype," adds : "Such inspiration as is traceable to any source whatever belongs assumably to the pictures of those early Italian painters whom Rossetti had lovingly studied, and to domestic influences to which he yielded." (Life of "Rossetti" in *Great Writers*.)

1. Blessed. Specifically, one of the blessed in paradise. Cf. *Ancient Mariner* :

> "I thought that I had died in sleep
> And was a *blessed* ghost."

See also *Par. Lost*, III. 136.—**3. Her eyes were deeper**, etc. It is instructive to note the poet's changes in these two lines. In the first version they stood :

> "Her grave blue eyes were deeper much
> Than a deep water, even."

This was changed to :

> "Her eyes knew more of rest and shade
> Than waters stilled at even."

13. Herseemed = it seemed to her. The word appears to have been coined by Rossetti, as I can find no authority for its use.

566.—**19. To one.** In these parenthetical verses, we are suddenly transported to earth, and hear the bereft lover speak. —**25. It was the rampart**, etc. Mr. Knight cites this description as "marvellously daring and original."—**49. From the fixed place**, etc. This is one of the most strikingly imaginative conceptions in the poem, and one of the most admired. The idea was apparently suggested by the Ptolomaic cosmology, which has an assured place in the imagination of readers of poetry, through Dante and Milton. According to the Ptolomæan ideas, the earth, the centre of the universe, was encompassed by a series of hollow crystalline spheres ; the tenth sphere or *primum mobile* was supposed to impart its motion to the others, while the fixed heaven, or Empyrean, lay outside of them all. The "music of the spheres" was supposed to have been produced by the vibration arising from the rubbing of the one against the other. This music seems to be alluded to at the end of the stanza.

568.—86. That living mystic tree. The poet may possibly have been led to this conception by the Tree of Life (*Gen*. ii. 9), or by the tree Yggdrasil of the Scandinavian mythology, which bound together heaven, earth, and hell. In the latter case it may have been intended to symbolize the mystic union of spiritual existence, every leaf or part of which is said to respond in praise to the breath of the Divine Spirit. In Rossetti's picture founded on this poem, "a glimpse is caught (above the figure of the Blessed Damozel) of the groves of paradise, wherein, beneath the shade of the spreading branches of a vast tree, the newly-met lovers embrace and rejoice with each other, on separation over and union made perfect at last." (See Shairp's description of this picture in his *Dante Gabriel Rossetti*, 251.)

THE SEA LIMITS.

576. This poem appeared in the volume of 1870. The sound within the shell, alluded to in the last stanza, is a favorite illustration with the poets: see the instances given in Stedman's *Nature and Elements of Poetry*, 255.

WILLIAM MORRIS.

573. WILLIAM MORRIS, one of the most perfect representatives of the æsthetic and archaic sympathies which have so largely affected the English art of the last half-century, was born at Walthamstow, near London, in 1834. At Oxford, where he was educated, he formed a lasting friendship with Edward Burne-Jones, the painter. After successively attempting and abandoning painting and architecture, his artist-nature found in poetry a medium apparently more suited to his powers, and his first book, *Guenevere and Other Poems*, appeared in 1858, the year in which Tennyson published the first of his *Idylls of the King*. Unlike Tennyson, however, Morris, in his treatment of mediæval or old-world themes, sought pure delight, as a respite from present problems, in a fair world of the past. The ugliness of modern life jarred on his beauty-loving nature, and in 1863, with Rossetti, Ford Maddox Brown, and Edward Burne-Jones, he founded in London an establishment for household decoration. Morris steadfastly continued in the work of infusing a greater beauty into English life until the last, and his firm became a powerful agency for the spread of Pre-Raphaelite ideas. In spite of this and other interests he found time to produce an astonishing quantity of literary work. Among this we may mention *The Earthly Paradise*, a series of twenty-four tales, which appeared between 1868 and 1870; his translations of the *Æneid* and the *Odyssey;* his version of Icelandic Sagas; his own sagas and mediæval romances, which may be described as prose-poems; and various works illustrating or expounding his socialistic theories. It was a life of enormous labor, easily and buoyantly done. He died October 3, 1896.

RUDYARD KIPLING.

576. RUDYARD KIPLING was born in Bombay, India, in 1865. His first book of verse, *Departmental Ditties*, was published in 1886, *Barrack-Room Ballads* in 1891, and his *Seven Seas* in 1896.

RECESSIONAL.

This poem was written in 1897, in celebration of the sixtieth anniversary of Queen Victoria's reign. It appeared in the London *Times* in a place of honor immediately beneath a letter from the Queen. The *Times* remarked, in commenting editorially upon the poem : "At this moment of imperial exaltation, Mr. Kipling does well to remind his countrymen that we have something more to do than to build battle-ships and multiply guns." Perhaps no English single poem since Tennyson's *Crossing the Bar* has won such an instantaneous and wide-spread recognition.

INDEX OF TITLES

	PAGE
Achitophel (Selection)................................*Dryden.*	143
Adonais...................................*Shelley.*	416
Agincourt.................................*Drayton.*	83
Ah! Sunflower.............................*Blake.*	271
Ah, what avails the sceptered race........*Landor.*	466
Alexander's Feast.........................*Dryden.*	147
Andrea Del Sarto.......................*R. Browning.*	521
Apelles' Song.............................*Lyly.*	56
Apology, An (*Earthly Paradise*)..............*Morris.*	573
Ariel's Song (*The Tempest*).................*Shakespeare.*	76
Argument to Hesperides....................*Herrick.*	107
Armour of Innocence, The..................*Campion.*	60
As slow our ship...........................*Moore.*	383
Author's Resolution in a Sonnet, The..........*Wither.*	99
Ballad, Alice Brand (*Lady of the Lake*)..........*Scott.*	362
Ballade of Charitie.......................*Chatterton.*	242
Banks of Doon, The........................*Burns.*	290
Bard, The.................................*Gray.*	222
Battle of Blenheim, The...................*Southey.*	356
Battle of Ivry............................*Macaulay.*	477
Battle of the Baltic......................*Campbell.*	379
Better Answer, A..........................*Prior.*	155
Blessed Damozel, The......................*Rossetti.*	565
Bonnie George Campbell	18
Border Ballad (*The Monastery*).................*Scott.*	375
Break, Break, Break......................*Tennyson.*	509
Bridge of Sighs, The......................*Hood.*	472
Bruce's Address to his Army at Bannockburn....*Burns.*	289
Bugle Song (*The Princess*).................*Tennyson.*	516
Castaway, The.............................*Cowper.*	262
Character of a Happy Life, The............*Wotton.*	66
Cheerfulness Taught by Reason.......*E. B. Browning.*	541
Chevy Chase...............................	1
Childe Harold's Pilgrimage (Selections)........*Byron.*	388
Clear and Cool (*Water Babies*)...............*Kingsley.*	547

PAGE

Cloud, The.................................*Shelley.* 413
Collar, The..................................*Herbert.* 96
Composed upon the Bridge near Calais. ...*Wordsworth.* 330
Composed upon Westminster Bridge.......*Wordsworth.* 329
Content......................................*Greene.* 56
Corinna's Going A-Maying...................*Herrick.* 107
Cotter's Saturday Night, The................*Burns.* 272
Crossing the Bar............................*Tennyson.* 515
County Guy (*Quentin Durward*)..............*Scott.* 376
Courtier, The (*Mother Hubberd's Tale*).........*Spenser.* 53

Day of Days, The............................*Morris.* 575
Death Bed, The ....*Hood.* 471
Departed Friends............................*Vaughan.* 98
Deserted Village, The......................*Goldsmith.* 227
Dirge (*Cymbeline*)..........................*Shakespeare.* 75
Dirge in *Cymbeline*.........................*Collins.* 213
Dirge, A (*Contention of Ajax and Ulysses*).......*Shirley.* 103
Disdain Returned............................*Carew.* 104
Don Juan (Selections)........................*Byron.* 403
Dover Beach................................*Arnold.* 560
Drawing Near the Light......................*Morris.* 576

Edmund's Song (*Rokeby*)....................*Scott.* 366
Elegy to the Memory of an Unfortunate Lady.....*Pope.* 184
Elegy upon the Death of Lady Markham, An...*Donne.* 88
Elegy written in a Country Churchyard.........*Gray.* 217
Elixir, The ....*Herbert.* 95
Epic, The (Introduction to *Morte d'Arthur*)..*Tennyson.* 495
Epilogue from Asolando..................*R. Browning.* 538
Epistle to Dr. Arbuthnot......................*Pope.* 188
Eve of St. Agnes, The.........................*Keats.* 440
Expostulation and Reply..................*Wordsworth.* 298

Faerie Queene, The..........................*Spenser.* 21
Fortunati Nimium...........................*Campion.* 61

Garden, The.................................*Marvell.* 134
Geist's Grave................................*Arnold.* 558
Good, Great Man, The.......................*Coleridge.* 353
Good Morrow.............................*T. Heywood.* 59
Grasshopper, The ....*Cowley.* 102
Guardian Angel, The.....................*R. Browning.* 519

Hag, The....................................*Herrick.* 112
Hark, Hark, the Lark........................*Shakespeare.* 75

PAGE

Harold's Song to Rosabelle (*Rokeby*)............*Scott.* 360
Harp that once through Tara's Halls, The.......*Moore.* 384
Helen of Kirconnel................................ 19
Hohenlinden.....................................*Campbell.* 378
Home Thoughts, from Abroad............*R. Browning.* 518
Hunting Song....................................*Scott.* 372
Hymn to God the Father, A..................*Donne.* 93

Il Penseroso.....................................*Milton.* 119
In Memoriam (Selection)....................*Tennyson.* 511
Introduction to Last Fruit Off an Old Tree.....*Landor.* 468
Introduction (*Songs of Innocence*)...............*Blake.* 265
Is there for Honest Poverty...................*Burns.* 291
I wandered lonely as a cloud.............*Wordsworth.* 324

Jock of Hazeldean ....*Scott.* 373

La Belle Dame Sans Merci...................*Keats.* 461
L'Allegro.......................................*Milton.* 115
Lamb, The......................................*Blake.* 266
Lament, A.....................................*Shelley.* 439
Last Sonnet, written 1820....................*Keats.* 465
Lines composed a few miles above Tintern Abbey.
                                            Wordsworth. 293
Lines written in Kensington Gardens.........*Arnold.* 562
Locksley Hall................................*Tennyson.* 481
London, 1802................................*Wordsworth.* 328
Lycidas...*Milton.* 126

Mac-Flecknoe...................................*Dryden.* 137
Madge Wildfire's Song (*Heart of Midlothian*)......*Scott.* 374
Mariners of England, Ye....................*Campbell.* 376
Maud (Selections)............................*Tennyson.* 512
Michael ....*Wordsworth.* 302
Mild is the parting year and sweet ....*Landor.* 466
Minstrel's Roundelay.......................*Chatterton.* 240
Morte d'Arthur.............................*Tennyson.* 497
Musical Instrument, A ....*E. B. Browning.* 539
My days among the dead are past............*Southey.* 358
My heart leaps up.........................*Wordsworth.* 317
My Last Duchess............................*R. Browning.* 516

Night...*Blake.* 267
Nymph's Reply to the Passionate Shepherd, The.*Raleigh.* 67

Ode, On a Distant Prospect of Eton College......*Gray.* 214
Ode, On a Grecian Urn.........................*Keats.* 459

PAGE

Ode, On the Intimations of Immortality.... *Wordsworth.* 318
Ode, The Spacious Firmament............. *Addison.* 156
Ode, To a Nightingale................... *Keats.* 455
Ode, To Duty........................ *Wordsworth.* 326
Ode, To Evening...................... *Collins.* 207
Ode, To the West Wind............... *Shelley.* 406
Ode written in the beginning of the year 1746... *Collins.* 213
O mistress mine, where are you roaming?.. *Shakespeare.* 74
On a Girdle....................... *Waller.* 113
On a Lap-dog....................... *Gay.* 159
On Another's Sorrow................. *Blake.* 269
On First Looking into Chapman's Homer....... *Keats.* 463
On the Foregoing Divine Poems............. *Waller.* 114
On the Grasshopper and Cricket......... *Keats.* 464
On the Life of Man................. *Beaumont.* 65
On the Loss of the Royal George............. *Cowper.* 261
On the Receipt of My Mother's Picture........ *Cowper.* 257
On the Tombs in Westminster Abbey....... *Beaumont.* 65
Orsames' Song....................... *Suckling.* 104
O Sweet Content................... *Dekker.* 58
O wert thou in the cauld blast............. *Burns.* 293

Painter who Pleased Nobody and Everybody, The. *Gay.* 157
Passionate Shepherd to His Love, The. .... *Marlowe.* 57
Passions, The, an Ode for Music............. *Collins.* 209
Petition to Time, A.................. *Procter.* 468
Prospect, The.................. *E. B. Browning.* 541
Prospice....................... *R. Browning.* 529
Pulley, The....................... *Herbert.* 94

Qua cursum ventus................. *Clough.* 548

Rabbi Ben Ezra.................. *R. Browning.* 530
Rape of the Lock, The................. *Pope.* 160
Recessional.................... *Kipling.* 576
Red, Red Rose, A................. *Burns.* 291
Retreate, The.................. *Vaughan.* 97
Rime of the Ancient Mariner, The.... .... *Coleridge.* 331
Rule Britannia.................. *Thomson.* 206

Sands of Dee, The (*Alton Locke*)............. *Kingsley.* 546
Say not the struggle naught availeth........... *Clough.* 549
Sea Dirge, A (*The Tempest*)............. *Shakespeare.* 76
Sea Limits, The................. *Rossetti.* 570
Seasons, The... .... *Thomson.* 195
Self Dependence.................. *Arnold.* 563

PAGE

Shakspeare.........................*Arnold.* 564
She dwelt among the untrodden ways...... *Wordsworth.* 302
She walks in beauty......................... *Byron.* 386
She was a phantom of delight............. *Wordsworth.* 325
Sibylla Palmifera......................*Rossetti.* 371
Silvia....................................*Shakespeare.* 73
Simplex Munditiis.........................*Jonson.* 70
Sir Galahad.........................*Tennyson.* 506
Sir Patrick Spens.......................... 11
Solitary Reaper, The.................. *Wordsworth.* 317
Song, Allan-A-Dale (*Rokeby*)....................*Scott.* 369
Song, A weary lot is thine.................*Scott.* 368
Song for St. Cecilia's Day, 22d November, 1687. *Dryden.* 145
Song from The Saint's Tragedy, The.........*Kingsley.* 544
Song, Go, lovely Rose.........................*Waller.* 113
Song, Men of England......................*Campbell.* 381
Song of the Priest of Pan..............*J. Fletcher.* 63
Song (*Pippa Passes*) ....*R. Browning.* 518
Song, Sabrina Fair (*Comus*).....................*Milton.* 125
Song, She is not fair............. *Hartley Coleridge.* 469
Song, Sweet Echo (*Comus*) ....*Milton.* 124
Song, Sweetest Love, etc....................*Donne.* 91
Song, The Cavalier..............................*Scott.* 370
Song, To Cynthia.........................*Jonson.* 72
Song, To Pan .... *J. Fletcher.* 64
Song, To the Evening Star.................*Campbell.* 382
Sonnet, A Superscription....................*Rossetti.* 573
Sonnet, Cyriack Skinner.......................*Milton.* 133
Sonnet XXXIII, Full many a glorious, etc..*Shakespeare.* 81
Sonnet VI, Go from me, etc..........*E. B. Browning.* 543
Sonnet XLIII, How do I love thee, etc..*E. B. Browning.* 544
Sonnet XXXV, If I leave all for thee, etc.

E. B. Browning. 543
Sonnet LXIII, Inclusiveness... ....*Rossetti.* 572
Sonnet I, I thought once how, etc.....*E. B. Browning.* 542
Sonnet, June 1816. To one who has been, etc....*Keats.* 464
Sonnet CXVI, Let me not, etc...........*Shakespeare.* 82
Sonnet LX, Like as the waves, etc.......*Shakespeare.* 81
Sonnet XL, Mark when she smiles, etc........*Spenser.* 54
Sonnet, On Chillon.........................*Byron.* 387
Sonnet X, On Death..... ....*Donne.* 83
Sonnet LXXV, One day I wrote, etc....*Spenser.* 54
Sonnet, On His Blindness....................*Milton.* 132
Sonnet, On his having arrived at the Age of twenty-
three................................. ..*Milton.* 131
Sonnet, On Sleep......................*Drummond.* 79

PAGE

Sonnet, On the Late Massacre in Piedmont......*Milton.* 132
Sonnet XIX, Silent Noon......................*Rossetti.* 571
Sonnet LXI, Since there's no help, etc........*Drayton.* 79
Sonnet LXXIII, That time of year, etc....*Shakespeare.* 82
Sonnet LI, To Delia...........................*Daniel.* 78
Sonnet, To Night ....*Blanco White.* 360
Sonnet XXIX, When in disgrace, etc......*Shakespeare.* 80
Sonnet XXX, When to the sessions, etc...*Shakespeare.* 80
Sonnet XXXI, With how sad steps...........*Sidney.* 77
Stanzas for Music..............................*Byron.* 385
Stanzas from the Grande Chartreuse...........*Arnold.* 551
Stream of Life, The...........................*Clough.* 550

Tables Turned, The ....*Wordsworth.* 299
Take, oh, take those lips away...........*Shakespeare.* 74
Tam O'Shanter ....*Burns.* 282
Task, The (Selections)......................*Cowper.* 245
Tears, Idle Tears (*The Princess*)............*Tennyson.* 509
Three Fishers, The.........................*Kingsley.* 545
Three Years She Grew.....................*Wordsworth.* 300
Tiger, The....................................*Blake.* 270
Time..*Shelley.* 437
To a Child of Quality Five Years Old, MDCCIV..*Prior.* 154
To Althea from Prison.......................*Lovelace.* 106
To a Mountain Daisy ....*Burns.* 280
To a Mouse....................................*Burns.* 279
To a Skylark................................*Shelley.* 409
To Autumn.....................................*Keats.* 460
To Daffodils................................*Herrick.* 111
To Hester ....*Lamb.* 470
To Lesbia...................................*Campion.* 59
To Lucasta on Going to the Wars.............*Lovelace.* 105
To ——. Music when soft voices die, etc.......*Shelley.* 437
To Night....................................*Shelley.* 437
To ——. One word, etc.......................*Shelley.* 439
To Primroses Filled with Morning Dew.......*Herrick.* 110
To Robert Browning ....*Landor.* 468
To the Divine Image...........................*Blake.* 268
To the Evening Star ....*Blake.* 265
To the Memory of Shakspeare.................*Jonson.* 68
To the Grasshopper and the Cricket............*Hunt.* 465
To the Muses..................................*Blake.* 264
To the Virgins, to make much of Time........*Herrick.* 111
Triumph of Charis...........................*Jonson.* 71
Twa Sisters o' Binnorie, The.............................. 14

PAGE

Ulysses...*Tennyson.* 493
Under Mr. Milton's Picture...................*Dryden.* 153
Under the Greenwood Tree (*As You Like It*).
                                Shakespeare. 73
Universal Prayer.............................*Pope.* 187

Valediction Forbidding Mourning, A...........*Donne.* 90
Vertue.......................................*Herbert.* 93
Vote, A......................................*Cowley.* 101

Waly, Waly, love be bonny..................... 13
When I have borne in memory............*Wordsworth.* 329
With whom is no variableness.................*Clough.* 549
Work...
Work without Hope.........................*Coleridge.* 355
World is too much with us, The ....*Wordsworth.* 330
Written in London, September 1802.......*Wordsworth.* 328

Yes, I write verses...........................*Landor.* 467
Youth and Age..............................*Coleridge.* 354

The Temple School Shakespeare

This series, entirely distinct from the well-known "Temple Shakespeare," is published in co-operation with Messrs. J. M. Dent & Co. of London. It is intended especially for school use, and the editing has been done with this in view. The distinctive features include a large-type text, the last word as to text; introductions that introduce; notes that are to the point, not in the air; thorough glossaries; illustrations which both inform and stimulate. Price, 35 cents a volume.

THE TEMPEST
Edited by OLIPHANT SMEATON, M. A.

MACBETH
Edited by GEORGE SMITH, M. A.

JULIUS CAESAR
Edited by F. ARMITAGE MORLEY, M. A.

AS YOU LIKE IT
Edited by FLORA MASSON.

HAMLET
Edited by OLIPHANT SMEATON, M. A.

RICHARD II.
Edited by W. KEITH LEASK, M. A.

THE MERCHANT OF VENICE
Edited by R. M'WILLIAM, M. A.

A MIDSUMMER NIGHT'S DREAM
Edited by Rev. W. H. FLECKER, M. A.

HENRY V.
Edited by W. H. HUDSON.

COMMENTS

JAMES B. SMILEY, *Lincoln High School, Cleveland:* "The books as a whole are excellent and surpass every other school edition that I have seen. A pupil will be fortunate who can study his Shakespeare with such a book in his hand."

R. H. BOWLES, *Phillips-Exeter Academy:* "The introductions are unusually good, the illustrations interesting, the page clear and open—in short, everything about the books is more than ordinarily well done."

MARGARET P. SHERWOOD, *Wellesley College:* "The books seem to me admirably edited for the use of students, and the illustrated glossary is certainly a very effective and original feature."

C. B. BRADLEY, *University of California:* "I am much pleased with the wise selection of the illustrative material, and with the general excellence of the workmanship throughout."

JEANNETTE A. MARKS, *Mount Holyoke College:* "I like particularly the idea of stimulating the students' visualizing powers by the use of illustrations. It is, I suppose, the next best thing to actual stage settings."

Henry Holt and Company   NEW YORK   CHICAGO

iii '04

PANCOAST'S INTRODUCTION TO AMERICAN LITERATURE

By HENRY S. PANCOAST, author of "An Introduction to English Literature."

With study lists, chronological tables, thirteen portraits, and full index. xii + 393 pp. 16mo. $1.00.

The primary aim is to help the reader to approach certain typical works in the right spirit, and to understand and enjoy them. He is led to observe the origin and history of the literature and the forces which have helped to shape and develop it; he is taught to regard literature as a part of national history, and to relate it to contemporaneous events and social conditions. He is made to take up the works suggested for study in their chronological sequence, and to note their relations to each other and to their time.

In the sketches of the few leading writers selected for comparatively extended treatment the effort is to avoid dry biographical details, and to present each author as a distinct living person. In the critical portion the object is rather to stimulate appreciation and lead the student to judge for himself than to force opinions on him in a purely dogmatic spirit.

The Nation: "Quite the best brief manual of its subject that we know. . . . National traits are well brought out without neglecting organic connections with the mother country. Forces and movements are as well handled as personalities, the influence of writers hardly less than their individuality."

The Dial: "We find in the volume now before us the same well-chosen diction, sobriety of judgment, and sense of perspective that characterized its predecessor. We should say that no better book had yet been produced for use in our secondary schools."

J. M. Hart, Professor in Cornell University: "Seems to me to accomplish exactly what it attempts; it introduces the reader carefully and systematically to the subject. The several chapters are well proportioned, and the tone of the entire work is one of kindly and enlightened sympathy."

A. G. Newcomer, Professor in Leland Stanford University: "He succeeds in saying the just and needful thing without being tempted beyond, and students of the work can hardly fail to obtain the right profit from our literature and the right attitude toward it."

H. Humphrey Neill, Professor in Amherst College: "Having used Mr. Pancoast's book on English Literature for three years with my class, I know about what to expect from the present volume, and am sure it will fill the place demanded in the teaching of American Literature which his other book so well fills in the teaching of English Literature."

Edwin M. Hopkins, Professor in the University of Kansas: "It seems to me fully entitled to take rank with his English Literature as a text-book, and I shall at once place it on my list recommended for high-school work."

HENRY HOLT & CO., 29 W. 23d St., New York
378 Wabash Ave., Chicago

FOURTH EDITION, with a new chapter by H. E. KREHBIEL,
covering Richard Strauss, Cornelius, Goldmark, Kienzl, Humperdinck, Smetana, Dvorak, Charpentier, Elgar, etc.

LAVIGNAC'S
Music and Musicians

Translated by WILLIAM MARCHANT.

With additional chapters by HENRY E. KREHBIEL on
MUSIC IN AMERICA and THE PRESENT STATE OF THE ART OF MUSIC.

With 94 Illustrations and 510 examples in Musical Notation. 518 pp., 12mo,
$1.75 net. By mail, $1.91.

¶ A brilliant, sympathetic and authoritative work covering musical sound, the voice, musical instruments, construction æsthetics and the history of music. A veritable musical cyclopedia, with some thousand topics in the index.

HENRY HOLT & COMPANY,
NEW YORK. (vj', '03). *CHICAGO.*

Date Due

APR 3 '51			
FEB 29 '56			
MAY 22 '65			
MAR 13 '70			
JAN 20 '73			